Heavens & Hells of the Mind

IMRE VALLYON

Heavens & Hells of the Mind

Volume III

TRANSFORMATION

Sounding-Light Publishing

Heavens and Hells of the Mind, by Imre Vallyon
First edition: October 2007

Sounding-Light Publishing Ltd.
PO Box 771, Hamilton 2015, New Zealand
www.soundinglight.com

Four volume boxed set:
ISBN 978-0-909038-30-4

Individual volumes:
ISBN 978-0-909038-31-1 Volume I: Knowledge
ISBN 978-0-909038-32-8 Volume II: Tradition
ISBN 978-0-909038-33-5 Volume III: Transformation
ISBN 978-0-909038-34-2 Volume IV: Lexicon

Printed in Hong Kong by Regal Printing Ltd.

Source: A selection of the author's handwritten manuscripts dating from 1982 to 2006.

Photo Credits: All photographic images Gérard Stampfli with the following exceptions:
Page 159: NASA, ESA and Jesús Maíz Apellániz (Instituto de astrofísica de Andalucía, Spain).
Acknowledgment: Davide De Martin (ESA/Hubble). Source: ESA
Page 1103: NASA Goddard Space Flight Center, by Reto Stöckli and Robert Simmon
Page 1483: NASA, ESA, S. Beckwith (STScI), and The Hubble Heritage Team (STScI/AURA). Source: ESA
Page 1585: SOHO (Solar and Heliospheric Observatory) (ESA and NASA)
Page 141, 467, 1657: Hamish Cattell
Page 205, 717, 1363, 1411, 1555, 1643: Manu Vallyon
Page 1491: Yaël Pochon

I dedicate this book to the aspiring Soul of Humanity across the planet.
We are One Planet, One Humanity, One Life, One God, One Reality.

May this book help you to recover your own lost Wisdom,
the knowledge of your real Self, and the knowledge of the Real God,
the Bright Eternal SELF that is the Truth, the Love and your own Cosmic Life.

Imre Vallyon

OVERVIEW

Heavens and Hells of the Mind

Volume I
KNOWLEDGE

Volume II
TRADITION

Volume III
TRANSFORMATION

Volume IV
LEXICON

Volume III: Transformation

Contents

CONTENTS III

CHARTS & DIAGRAMS III

Volume III: Transformation

Charts & Diagrams

INTRODUCTION TO VOLUME III

The New Spirituality

Spirituality Past and Future

One day in the future, all men and women will be spiritual. Science, religion, politics and art will be understood only as different aspects of the same Mystery: the Mystery of Being, which is the Mystery of God.

In past ages, Spirituality was strictly associated with the various religious traditions—Christian, Jewish, Muslim, Hindu, Buddhist, Taoist, Japanese, and so forth—and the Spiritual Teachers came from specific religious and cultural backgrounds. In the coming New Age, however, Spirituality will be based upon the *Knowledge* of the inner constitution of Humanity, God and the Universe, and the *direct perception* of these through meditation and inner experience.

The mind will be used to organize Spirituality more clearly than ever before

In the New Age, the mind will be used to organize Spirituality more clearly than ever before. It will be tested and experimental, unlike the haphazard approach of past ages, and the Spiritual Teacher will be a universal man or woman, belonging to all. Faith will give way to true Knowledge, and the Teachers will be universal, trans-religious, beyond the confines of orthodoxies and established customs and traditions. Thus, Religion will be purified by the knowledge of its present limitations, and the superstition and ignorance found in religions during the past few thousand years will be removed.

In the past, in all religions, there has been much prayer (talking *to* God or *at* God), and much thinking and speculation *about* God. In the coming New Age Spirituality, the emphasis will be upon the *experiencing* of the Soul, the *experiencing* of God. The focus will be Interior Union, to sense and feel *interiorly* the Eternal, the Everlasting, to be touched from within by the Godhead in silent, wordless prayer and unitive meditation, and a genuine Spiritual Vision of the great Mystery that is in us and around us.

To reach this state we must quieten the mind and stop the mental talking. This will be strange and new to many, but this has always been the Way and it will be so in the future.

Prayer produces its own results on the physical, subtle and mental dimensions, results which may even appear to be miraculous. But Union with the Soul, with God, with the Great Invisible Cosmos, is infinitely higher.

The Future 1709
The Aquarian Teachers 1147
What is True Faith? 1284
What is Prayer? 690
Religion and Spirituality 754
Mystics of Pisces and Aquarius 836

Psychology and the New Age Religion

There is a new form of psychology emerging in the West called *Transpersonal Psychology,* which in fact will be the basis for the new religion of the New Age. This entire book is but aspects of Transpersonal Psychology. The Latin word *transpersonal* means "beyond the personality, beyond the little self"; in other words, Transpersonal Psychology looks beyond the "personality stuff" which is dealt with in the behavioural, humanistic and psychoanalytic schools of psychology. In fact, Transpersonal Psychology deals with what used to be the domain of good, old-fashioned Religion!

Transpersonalis
Latin: "Through or across the mask". Beyond the unreal. Knowing the true Self, as opposed to the apparent little self, the personal "I".
The Mask 38

Orthodox Psychology

Modern psychology was founded in the West by Adler, Freud and others as a part of *medicine,* and involved the study of the brain and nervous system, sensation, observation, imagination, behaviour, and so forth, all solidly based on the idea of the body. Orthodox psychology thought that Man was nothing else but a "naked ape", that mind was nothing but the nervous system and the physical brain cells, and that religious experience was a mental disease! Orthodox psychology cannot comprehend the fact that Man is not only a body, but has a mind which is *separate* from the body, and a Soul which is distinct even from the mind. In fact, as curious as it may seem to ordinary psychology, the body has no importance at all; it is only the vehicle through which the Soul and mind of Man express themselves. The body is but a vehicle, an instrument, a result.

Who are We? 2
Objective Experience 305
Psychology Ancient and Modern 1364
All Hail to the Brain! 1368

For orthodox psychology, sense perception, along with reason and rationalization, is the only valid field of knowledge. The brain is the "mind" or "soul"—the spiritual part of Man—and the tone of voice, facial expressions, gestures, habits and bodily phenomena constitute the *mystery* of Man. Western philosophy, psychology, science and medicine are based on rationalism (the worship of reason and logic), materialism and individualism (the worship of the little, selfish ego), the only "reality" being the sensually perceptible physical universe and the physical body. The little ego or self (the personality, which is the identification with the lower mind and physical body and their functions) gives rise to separatism, individualism, fear, defensiveness, hatred, jealousy and anger.

The materialistic mind thinks, "I do not believe it, therefore it does not exist!" The old Greeks called such people Agnōstikos (agnostics, ignorant, unwise, unenlightened). Gnōstikos, the Gnostics, were the Wise, the Enlightened, Illumined, Initiated people in touch with Spiritual Realities.
The Gnostics 645

Transpersonal Psychology

Religion is Man's quest for the Mystery of Life, Death and the Beyond

What a leap it is for psychology to go from dissecting nerve tissues to actually studying the behaviour of the human Soul (which is the meaning of the word *psychology).* Today—lo and behold!—the daring transpersonal psychologists are no longer mere physicians, but truly *religious* people. Transpersonal Psychology is based on the fact that there is more to Man than meets the eye, and more to the Universe than is perceivable by the five physical senses and their physical gadgets and instruments. The subjects of Transpersonal Psychology include Yoga philosophies and practices, Muslim Sūfī teachings, Jewish Kabbalah, Zen Buddhism, Occultism, Magic, Parapsychology, and so on. William James and Carl Jung were the outstanding early psychologists who dabbled in religious experience and who held the view that Man is more than just the body, that the mind is more than just nerves, tissues and nerve-impulses.

Anthony Sutich, as far back as 1969, had already defined the subjects of Transpersonal Psychology, which include:

- The science of becoming.
- Individual and species-wide spiritual needs.
- Ultimate values in life.
- Unitive and Cosmic Consciousness.
- Peak experiences.
- Ecstasy and the mystical states.
- Self-actualization.
- Religious awe, bliss and wonder.
- Self-transcendence (transcendence of the little self, the ego).
- Union with the Self, the Over-Soul.
- The sacredness of everyday life.
- Transcendental phenomena.
- The Spirit, God, the Ultimate.
- Individual and species-wide synergy.

You will see that this, in fact, is the province of Religion! We don't mean "Churchianity"—the political intrigues and worldly, material power that characterizes the organized church. By Religion we mean just what is listed above, which the church has mostly forgotten. Religion is Man's quest for the Sacred, the Ultimate, the Godhead, the Mystery of Life, Death and the Beyond.

Science of the Soul? 291
The Dual Nature of Christianity 624
Yoga and Religion 527

Transpersonal Psychology includes the study of Buddhism, Christian Mysticism, Sikhism, Taoism, the ancient Mystery Religions, Gnosticism, Theosophy, and all the Mystical Traditions such as Freemasonry, the Rosicrucian Teachings, Alchemy, and the Western Tradition of true Magic. It also deals with the Supernatural in its various manifestations. It includes the study of the Tarot systems and all forms of Symbolism. It includes the higher aspects of Religion, but does *not* include Voodoo, Shamanism, Black Magic, or any practices enhancing the little ego, the personal self and selfishness.

Transpersonal Psychology is a process that was discovered by all the higher religions

Transpersonal Psychology is a strenuous body-mind discipline, practice and experience, whether in the form of Zen Buddhism, Christian Mysticism, Jewish Kabbalah or Hasidism, Muslim Sūfīsm, the Sikh Sant Mat Path, Chinese Taoism or Hindu Yoga. Transpersonal Psychology is a process that was discovered by all the higher religions, a process that enables one to realize one's higher potential. It is the awakening to the *experience* of oneself as an Immortal Spirit and Soul. It is the discovering of one's Universal or Higher Self, one's Buddha-Nature, Tao, the Self-moving Way. It is Insight into the Deathless Condition. All great religions described this in so many ways.

Do not be confused by the terminology used by the Christians, Jews, Muslims, Buddhists, Sikhs, Hindus, Taoists, and others. What they are trying to describe is a process of personality transformation, a series of practices whereby the little self (the ego or personality) is transcended, and *You* (the Immortal Soul or Spirit) become *known* to yourself. What is more, in this condition you *know* that the Immortal You is essentially One with the Immortal in the Universe, whether that Transcendental Reality be called God, Allāh, Jehovah, Buddha, Tao, Brahman, Paramātman, or whatever.

This is not an idea, not a concept.
It is something you *experience directly*, first hand.

The key to all systems of Transpersonal Psychology is in the mind. The ordinary, self-conscious, rational mind must be quietened; the subjective, subconscious mind of images must be transcended; and the Superconscious Mind must be experienced. Then comes the Knowledge of the Real, the Eternal, the Transcendent.

Your Mind is the Key 1208

The One God of All Religions 110
The One Transcendental Reality 515
Our Goal is nothing less than God 1191
Know Thyself 1389

The Omnipresent God

It is very difficult for Christian fundamentalists to understand this process, since they believe that Salvation comes from *outside* themselves, through an outside agency. This is why they cannot understand even Christian Mysticism. According to the fundamentalists, the Soul is separate from God, and God came down in the form of Jesus Christ, and if you "believe" in Him you will be saved.

In all religions there are fundamentalists who believe that God is outside themselves

Fundamentalism is based on *duality*—God versus you—and on *belief*. In all religions there are fundamentalists (dualists) who believe that God is outside themselves, somewhere up in the sky, or in "heaven", or in an afterlife, or that He will come to them at the end of time or on "resurrection day". The fundamentalists are body-oriented and worldly; so far as they are concerned, God's Kingdom is *this* world, the Physical Plane. The fundamentalists deny God from acting *inside* one's Soul, the immortal part of Man—they think it is a great sin to try to discover God within one's own being. This is a gross distortion of original Christianity, as it is of all Religion.

Self-Knowledge 324
Christian Mysticism 450
Jesus the Personal Saviour? 678
Persecution of the Knowers 656
Jesus: the Fire of Love 1725
Christ-Consciousness 443

The Gnostic Teachings

The biggest mistake of the early Christian authorities was the destruction of the Gnostics and their works (their writings or gospels) during the first three centuries, thus making Christianity simply a political tool serving the worldly Roman Empire. During the past two thousand years the church authorities have consistently suppressed or obliterated Those who were the Knowers, the Mystics, the Enlightened Ones, fearing that by discovering the Kingdom of God within themselves the people would stop paying homage to Rome, the seat of worldly power.

Recently, however, a few of the Gnostic gospels that miraculously survived these political purges have come to light, and all true Christians, if they wish, can gain a truer sense of the Kingdom of God within (God's Kingdom), and of the Nature of Jesus as the *Living Light*.

The Gnostic Christians (the Knowers) taught that the Son of Man, who is also the Son of God, who is the Living Jesus, is the Living Light that dwells within you, in your Heart, which is also the Kingdom of God. It is not outside in Rome, nor in Jerusalem, nor anywhere outside in the world. In the deepest regions of your Heart dwells the Living Light, the Living Jesus (YESHUAH, in Hebrew), the Flow of Light, the Descending Light-Current of Grace.

GNOSIS
Greek: Self-Realization. The Lighted Way or the Way of Light. The Knowledge that comes when the Holy Path is seen within.
The Holy Path 1285

All true religions are *monist;* they affirm the Unity of Man, God and the Universe. What is more, this Unity can be *realized* and *experienced*, in the here and now, if one is willing to take up some correct form of prayer or meditation which will lead to the transcendence of the body-mind complex and the experience of the immortal Soul within.

The Transcendental Reality is Omnipresent. You may call this God, Jehovah, Brahman, Tao, the Buddha-Nature, or whatever you wish. Because it is Omnipresent, it is everywhere, and because it is everywhere, it is within us also. It is a part of us. In fact, it *is* us.

A human being has the capacity to perceive directly the Universal Reality

> The Kingdom of God is within you.
>
> *Luke 17:21*

> In Him we live, move and have our being.
>
> *Acts 17:28*

The New Testament is clear: it is *within* God that we live, move and have our being. The Divine Presence is within us all, as well as outside us all. It is a Universal Field of Reality. The Hindus called it PARAMĀTMAN, "the Over-Soul, the Universal Self", or PARABRAHMAN, "the Transcendental Reality".

Salvation is not just a matter of belief; it is a process of action, transformation and transmutation. Transpersonal Psychology involves religious *experience,* not one's beliefs about religion. This should be clearly understood. People may believe in all kinds of different things, but Reality is the same at all times and in all places. An accomplished Yogī, Sūfī, Hasid, Mystic, Taoist or Zen Master will each experience the same thing.

The Eternal is One 512
The Divine Unity 852
The Presence of God 1396
Belief and Experience 676
Perceptions of the One Mind 490

A dualist may ask, "But why not seek God, or Truth, outside of yourself?" That is possible also and many do seek Truth outside themselves. But Man is so constituted by Nature that a human being has the capacity inside himself or herself to perceive *directly* the Universal Reality. In other words, Man is capable of supersensory and spiritual perception. That, in fact, is the glory of the human species.

> Wonder of wonders! Intrinsically all living beings are Buddhas!—endowed with Wisdom and Virtue! But Man's mind has been perverted by wrong thinking and therefore they fail to perceive this fact.
>
> *Gautama Buddha*

Man at first tends to become a god, then God.

An ancient maxim

The Kingdom of God is attained by focusing your attention upon It. This is the Law of the Mind: wherever you focus your attention, there you are.

You know only what you turn your attention to.

Female Buddhas

Women are in many ways better suited to the spiritual task of Enlightenment

For the past few thousand years there has existed a strange delusion in the human mind that women are inferior to men. The ancient Jews, Christians and Muslims believed that women were inferior creations, or that they had no Souls. The Hindus, Buddhists and ancient Chinese also taught this, and women were second-class citizens in all of those societies. The Buddhist monks, for instance, believed it to be almost impossible for women to attain Buddhahood. The disciples of Jesus thought that women could not enter the Kingdom unless they first became men.

All of this is a colossal delusion, of course—there is no semblance of truth in it. Women are equal to men and in many ways *better* suited to the spiritual task of Enlightenment. Their "inferiority" is a silly monkish idea.

The DHARMAKĀYA (the Body of Truth, Nirvāṇa) is neither male nor female. Gender does not enter into it. The Buddha-Mind pervades everywhere and permeates all things. It does not come and it does not go. It is neither male nor female, nor does it attract only males. For, like the Sun, it shines upon all.

This categorizing of women as inferior in life, or inferior upon the Spiritual Path, is one of the weaknesses of all ancient religions and traditions. When women are no longer repressed by crystallized ancient traditions, many will become Buddhas and great Masters.

The Path of Self-Actualization

In the old Sanskrit understanding, DHARMA means the Path that you should follow to become what you are *meant* to be. In modern spiritual psychology this process is called *self-actualization*, meaning the development of your personality, the personal ego, the little personal "I". But the word DHARMA means much more than that. It means your total unfoldment as a human entity on your Soul and Spiritual levels as well. It means Self-Realization and also God-Realization.

The Aquarian Way embraces *all* the valid ways towards the actualization of the Divinity in Humanity, no matter what they may be called.

Dharma: the Law of Being 244

The Caste System 378
The Feminine Suppressed 910
Some Human Evils 384
Yin, Yang, Tao 476

Unnecessary Practices

The thousands of gods and goddesses of India are totally unnecessary. Nirvāṇa is real. God-Realization is real. God is real. Truth is real. But the *forms* of gods, goddesses and Buddhas are but constructs of monkish minds and the priestcraft. They are a hindrance rather than a help on the Path to Realization.

It is not necessary to endure the terribly complicated meditational practices of the Tibetan monks. The Way is simpler than that. Nor is it necessary to waste your time endlessly torturing and mutilating your body, as the Hindu sādhus do, believing it to be the Path to Holiness. For three thousand years the disciples of the world, Eastern and Western, punished their physical bodies with severe austerities, asceticism, self-torture and mortification. And yet the problem is not the physical body at all, but Spiritual Ignorance.

The problem is not the physical body at all, but Spiritual Ignorance

Nor is it necessary for you to pursue strenuous āsanas, bandhas or mudrās of the Hindu Haṭha Yoga system. In fact, they will lead you *nowhere* on the Spiritual Path. They affect your bodily condition, but not your Spiritual Path. Thus, Haṭha Yoga is not the way to attain Cosmic Consciousness.

The monks and priests of all traditions invented all kinds of practices which, rather than being helpful on the Path, were more often a hindrance. This happened because they lost the key, the direction.

The New Age Impulse

The orthodox religions are stuck in the crystallized forms of old-fashioned thinking which do not correspond with the Knowledge and Understanding of the New Age energies. Hence there is a tremendous conflict going on between those who sense the New and those who are stuck in the mud.

The great sin of orthodox establishments, religious or political, is that they restrict freedom of thought and mind. Without a mind that is free to explore and know the Truth, Humanity will perish.

Politics, religion, education, psychology and the social sciences should all be based in the Heart, in Love-Wisdom, for this is the true New Age impulse, the impulse of the Christ. If people in these fields would do this, we would have a true Golden Age upon our planet, and all wars would cease.

Religious Reactionaries 287

Blind Tradition 808
Tapas: Mental Discipline 568
Haṭha Yoga and Rāja Yoga 524
Orthodoxos: correct belief? 653
The New and Eternal Way 516
The Universal Christ 440

The Two Paths

There are two Paths to Divinity, although the Goal is One:

- The Path of the Mystic, the Way of the Heart, the Way of Love.
- The Path of the Knower, the Way of the Mind and Perfect Knowledge of the Things that Are.

From Head to Heart 427
The Path to Immortality 430
From Pisces to Aquarius 837
Uniting Head and Heart 1130
Heart Knowing 1286
The Rays and the Planes 55

Our present civilization on this planet is strongly emphasizing the mind-function, which needs to be counterbalanced by the Heart.

The rational, reasoning, analytical, critical, intellectual, "scientific", technological, organizing, specializing, defining, limiting, "naming things" mind is good in its own sphere of dealing with the practical world. To reach Enlightenment, Illumination or Gnosis, however, on the Way of the Mind, you need your *other* Mind. You need Esoteric Knowledge, Profound Understanding.

The Way of the Mind (the Male Way) is centred in the Head.
The Way of the Mystic (the Female Way) is centred in the Heart.

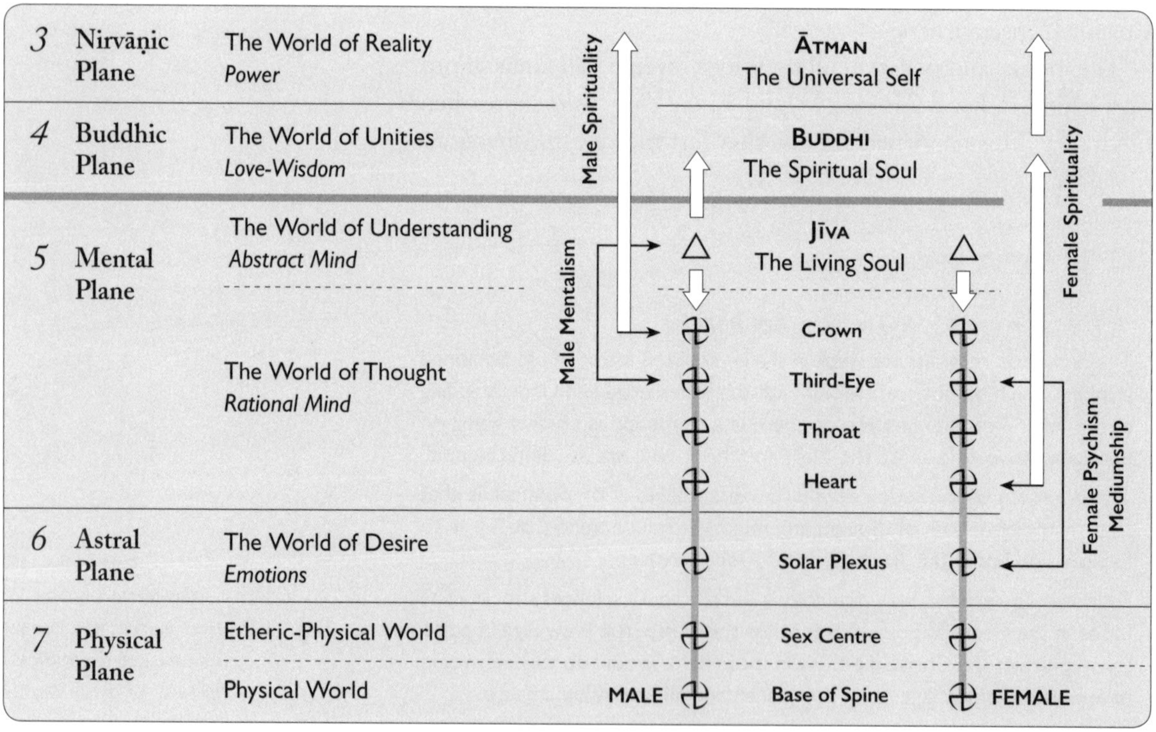

Male and Female Systems of Spirituality

Inspiration by the Mind of Light

Inspiration is a Higher-Consciousness Reality. It is tuning-in beyond the ordinary mind, and even beyond the Higher Mind or Abstract Mind, into the *Mind of Light.* This is a Mind that is in touch with Higher Reality, yet is Mind enough to be able to *express itself,* to verbalize what it knows and experiences. If you go beyond the *Mind of Light,* you cannot express your experience in "words". You can only remain in Silence.

The Mind of Light sees in vast pictures

Another feature of this Inspiration or *Mind of Light* is its immediacy. That is, it is *in the Present,* no matter what the subject matter may be, and it is *connected* to all things. It has a large *vision* or *sweep* or *view* of things.

This is not the same as an intellectual exercise whereby you "quote" a thousand authors with your ordinary mind. Whereas your ordinary mind is characterized by extreme narrowness, focusing on a small point to the exclusion of all else, the *Mind of Light* sees in vast pictures, embracing centuries and Ages, across all sects, denominations, religions and creeds, beyond to their eternal Source, the Reality.

Dimensions of the Mind 891
Inspiratio: Breathing in the Spirit 375
Satori: the Experience of Illumination 816
Super-Knowing 1242

Longtime students know and feel that I give my talks at retreats and workshops under such Inspiration. This book also has been written in such a way.

∞

Truth is the Pure White Light of the Eternal. When you have seen that Radiance, you have seen the Truth that all philosophers look for and know not where to find.

No one religion, sect or denomination has the Truth. Truth is found by *All* who seek the Light.

The Goal of the Path is to Free the God-Self that is within you and make you Shine like a Star.

The true purpose of you *as an individual* is to transcend your individuality and become the Cosmic Man.

The *Cavity of your Heart* is the Holy of Holies, the Sanctuary where dwells the Spark of the Eternal.

A Mind Illumined is a Mind of Light.

Spiritual Reading is reading this book, the writings of the Saints and other scriptures with your Higher Mind, not with your lower, "rational" mind. The Higher Mind will *reveal* to you the Truth of the scriptures. We all have a Higher Mind, but nowadays it is not fashionable to use it.

Intellectus: Knowing inside 375

PART NINE

The Path of Return

CHAPTER 49

The Aquarian Way

Spiritual Life and Material Life

Separating spiritual life and material life is courting disaster

The past six thousand years on this planet have been dark ages. People have long held many wrong ideas about Spirituality and those wrong ideas have permeated all the various civilizations. In the East, the Teachings of Yoga, Mysticism and spiritual development have been wrongly interpreted, resulting in centuries-old neglect of the material plane, an extremely unbalanced society and much physical suffering. Eastern society divided itself into the "spiritual seekers" who lived *off* the rest of society, who in turn lived in a state of darkness. In Tibet the monks were one class, while the remainder were merely serfs to serve those monks. The monks and holy men did *nothing*—not in Tibet, nor in the surrounding countries, nor on the Indian subcontinent. They lived in their own little myopic universe and expected the rest of the population to look after them. They were not in touch with the larger society, therefore they were not in touch with the *needs* of society. They shunned society, thus allowing society to degenerate and live in ignorance.

Separating spiritual life and material life is courting disaster. The Indian and Tibetan monks could never *test* their spirituality in real life, while the populace was left without the benefit of Insight. India and Tibet degenerated as a direct result of this wrong emphasis on neglecting one's physical environment and the necessary evolution of the physical universe. The Muslims conquered India simply because the Indian population had degenerated; the so-called holy men could not care less for their environment.

This was not the case in the Vedic days of India, when the kings and rulers were mighty warriors and governors and great spiritual men and women. In previous times, the Prophets of old, the Saints and Avatāras, the Divine Incarnations, the great Masters and Teachers, the Gurus, Ṛṣis, Munis and Sages who guided Humanity, were established either in Transcendental Consciousness or in Nirvāṇa, or even in states beyond, far beyond the Astral World with all its trickeries, delusions and deceptions.

A nation which is established in Cosmic Consciousness, which does not neglect the Physical World, is strong and invincible. Here is a clue to the health of any nation, tribe, group or individual.

Return to Duty 812
Relational Consciousness 906
The Dichotomy of the Mystic 629
The Warrior, the Sage, the Ruler 972
Warriors of the Sun 1618
Piscean and New Age Spirituality 1706

Is Renunciation Necessary?

The Sanskrit word SANNYĀSA means "renunciation" and a SANNYĀSĪ or SANNYĀSIN is a "renunciate", one who is detached from the world and from action. A sannyāsin is a yogī who has abandoned, rejected, disowned or refused the world, human relationships and responsibilities. A sannyāsin renounces *all* actions. This idea is familiar to us in the West as the monk, the nun, the religious. This has been the ideal "spiritual life" in India, as well as among the God-oriented Christians (the Gnostics, the Mystics, the Cathars, and so forth) for several thousand years.

Life on this planet need not be suffering at all

But is it necessary to become a renunciate?—to refuse all interconnection with the world of Man? We think not. We say that this idea is based on a wrong understanding of what "spirituality" is.

One can sympathize with those yogīs and mystics who wanted to get away from human relationships, family, jobs, the whole "scene" of living in the world, because it does put a lot of strain on sensitive Souls. But it is not the real solution. In the beginning, what is required is regular, periodic withdrawal from "the world" in the form of regular meditation periods, retreats and spiritual solitude. Total rejection of the world is impractical, futile and counter-productive. Eventually, such withdrawal from the world is not necessary at all.

The first thing the Lord Buddha taught was that living in the world is "suffering and pain". This is because the whole of Mankind is out of tune with Divine Will and Purpose (which has nothing at all to do with what the popes, the theologians and the fundamentalists understand about God!).

Life on this planet need not be suffering at all. We could live as gods on Earth, for human suffering is Man-created. If every single man, woman and child would live as a *Soul* in God's Creation, there would be no suffering. But, to live as Souls, first we need to become (or re-become) Soul-Conscious. This requires the right kind of meditation, practised faithfully until one reaches Pure Consciousness, then Cosmic Consciousness and, finally, God-Consciousness.

Balance in Spiritual Life 505
Why Life is Suffering 263
The Universal Intelligence 232
To Become a True Renunciate 257
Duty and Spirituality 1641

Non-Action Misinterpreted

Attaining Samādhi is only half the Spiritual Journey

The concept of *non-action* (NIṢKARMAYAM) has been misinterpreted by the yogīs, sādhus, sannyāsins and holy men for the past six thousand years. They explained non-action as non-attachment to your body, the world and your environment. Such indifference to life was taught to be a *virtue:* by "killing out desires" (suppressing emotion) and "controlling the mind" (trying to *stop* the thinking process) one attained MUKTI (Freedom, Nirvāṇa). The idea was to absorb oneself into SAMĀDHI (Pure Consciousness, the Transcendental State) and to care not for the world, nor for one's body, nor for the environment. Even today these "holy men" are engaged in contemplation, in solitude and isolation, oblivious to their environment.

But in fact, attaining Samādhi is only *half* the Spiritual Journey. The experience of Pure Consciousness (the awareness of one's Self as pure Being, a formless Spirit, a bodiless Intelligence, an entity beyond mind-structures) must be re-integrated into the three normal states: the waking consciousness, the dreaming or subjective mind and the dreamless-sleep state. So, whether one is in the waking state and performing actions in the world, or in the dreaming state, or in the dreamless-sleep state, one is always aware of being the Transcendental Self, the Spirit, the ĀTMAN.

Samādhi: the Goal of Yoga 574
Karma and Reincarnation Misconceived 252
The Seven States of Consciousness 494
Penetrating into the Kingdom 1707

Paths to the Transcendent and Immanent God

For countless centuries the Hindu religion and Esoteric Buddhism have taught the ideal of Transcendental Union with God, BRAHMA-NIRVĀṆA, on a Transcendental level, beyond body, mind, and even Soul. That was the goal of the Spiritual Life.

Christianity, Islam, Judaism, Taoism and Zen teach the Immanent Presence of God, and its *dynamic Realization in action in this life*, guided by Wisdom and Love.

The Realization of God-Transcendent and God-Immanent are the two well-defined Paths for serious spiritual seekers.

God Immanent and Transcendent 111

Three Schools of Spirituality

1

The Path of Yoga

The first School believes that everything below the Buddhic Plane is imperfect and therefore seeks to escape from it. This is the Path of YOGA.

The essential problem is not life in this world, but the ego

2

The Path of Zen or Tantra

The second School acknowledges that, at this stage of Evolution, the Three Worlds (the Physical, Astral and Mental Planes) are imperfect, but believes that the Divinity inherent in all things should be brought down and manifested in them. That is, one should see the Transcendental Reality in the passing, temporary, evolutionary forms. This is the Path of ZEN or TANTRA.

This second School of Spirituality does not negate the world. It seeks the Awareness of Immortality and to transcend the ego, but with a free and voluntary participation in the activities of the Three Worlds for the sake of helping Evolution. This is what Jesus meant when He said to be *in* the world, but not *of* the world.

> They are not of the world, even as I am not of the world.... Thou has sent me into the world, even as have I also sent them into the world.
>
> *St John*

This is done through *Compassion*. In the East it is called the Path of the BODHISATTVA. The essential problem is not life in this world, but the ego, which causes separation, disharmony and disunity from all other selves and from the environment.

3

The Path of Gnosis

There is also a third School of Spirituality which seeks to escape altogether beyond the seven Cosmic Physical Planes to the Cosmic Astral Planes. This is the Path of Gnosticism or GNOSIS, the Path of the PRATYEKA Buddha.

The Goal of Yoga 519
The Spirit of Zen 751
The Circle of Love 905
Types of Conscious Immortality 390

Avoid the Errors of East and West

The Word was made Man so that we might become God.

St Athanasius

The Divinization of Humankind on this planet is part of the Divine Plan. The Christians have always taught this, though without always understanding its significance. In this sense, Christianity is different from the Eastern religions.

The European existentialist philosophy was mothered by scientific materialism

Both the East and the West have their errors. The basic stance of Western materialistic thinking is that there is nothing more than the world that you see and nothing more to Man than the physical body. "There is no afterlife, so you might as well have a good time while you can." The European existentialist philosophy was mothered by scientific materialism. According to existentialism and other materialistic philosophies such as capitalism, communism and socialism, the only meaning to the Universe is what Mankind can make out of it. These materialistic philosophies are fundamentally incorrect. The Universe is *not* meaningless and every part of it works to a Plan. Human beings on this planet have cut themselves off from the Whole. When we reconnect ourselves to the Whole, life will again have infinite meaning, in accordance with the Divine Plan.

Certainly, the achievement of scientific materialism is great on the Physical Plane. Never before on this planet has Mankind had such an opportunity to control the environment and improve the life of the physical body. This achievement comes at great cost, however: the sacrifice of the Life of the Spirit, of the Spiritual Realities—unless Mankind wakes up and realizes that Man is Spirit, Soul, mind and body.

While Science investigates the evolution of animal and human forms (bodies), Evolution also includes the Life and the Consciousness that *inhabit* those forms. In Man, this Evolution of Consciousness is the Spiritual Path to be taken.

True Science 382

Materialism is a grave error of the West, but it has given Westerners the impulse to *conquer* their physical environment, to advance in science and technology, all geared for more comfortable living in this world—while you last! Thus, the Western European nations (and those which were populated by them, such as the United States, Canada, Australia and New Zealand) have developed, by great effort, the conquest of Nature and the environment. They have controlled the lakes, the seas, the rivers, improved communications, medicine, technology, skills, and so forth. But spiritual things have been neglected.

On the other hand, the East had the view that this world is *unreal*. It is either just an "illusion" or it exists only in your mind and not as an outside reality. This view, of course, is also wrong. This world is real! It is not an illusion, nor does it exist only in your mind. It has its own self-reality and you are a *part* of it. But the Easterners concentrated on attaining Nirvāṇa, which they considered to be the *only* reality, and they neglected this world. Thus, in India, thousands of yogīs have attained to Higher Consciousness, Superconsciousness, and perhaps even Nirvāṇa, but they did nothing about their environment, and they taught the people to do likewise!

It takes a Mother Theresa (a practical Western Mystic) to go to Calcutta and pick up the dead and dying from the streets, because the Indians themselves are unconcerned about it. The horrible physical life in India is the direct outcome of this false belief that this world is unreal and that the best you can do is try to escape from it. The Easterners have neglected the material plane and have made a mess of it; thus they have poverty, disease, suffering—the very things they seek to escape from!

The Two Realities 97
The Plan is in the Divine Mind 161
Human Involution and Evolution 170
Evolution, the Plan, the Path 1688
Jesus Christ, Son of Man 668

So today, as a result of these errors in understanding, there are millions of "dead" people in the West living the selfish lives of their egos, cut off from the Higher Self, the Soul, the Immortal Life; while on the other hand, in the East we have the yogīs, sādhus, ascetics and renunciates who have escaped from "the world, the devil and the flesh" into Soul-life only, who spend their time in meditation, in Higher Consciousness. Both of these human lives are unbalanced. Neither represents how Mankind should live on this planet.

We can avoid the errors of both the East and the West, and uphold the good and the true in each. This world is real; so is Nirvāṇa. This world is important; so is the Kingdom of God. Evolution is proceeding on all seven great Planes of Being of Cosmic PRĀKṚTĪ, the Cosmic Physical Plane. The ideal human being on this planet is one who is able to fully function as a personality *and* as a Soul, simultaneously, and who is even in touch with the Spirit, the Divinity, the "Father in Heaven". Then, that human being is simultaneously a Son of God and a Son of Man.

The Spiritual Path involves the Divinization of Man on this planet. It is not about materialism, nor is it about escape into Higher Consciousness. It is a simultaneous flowering of all human faculties on all levels. This is the condition of abiding Peace and Liberation in Higher Consciousness, while leading an active life in the Three Worlds.

> Ever recollecting himself, the Yogī of disciplined mind attains to Peace and Liberation, and then abides in the Divine in the midst of action.
>
> *The Bhagavad-Gītā*

The Buddhists have added a further error: they deny even the existence of an ĀTMAN, or a real Self, in the species of Man. That makes things even worse! If this world is only an illusion, and if Man has no real Self at all, then where do you go from there?

I doubt that the Buddha would have taught that there was no Divine Self in Mankind. What the Buddha taught was that the ego has no real validity! The personal ego passes away, but the Spirit lives on forever.

A 'Godless' Religion? 754
Brahma-Nirvāṇa 1224

The Science of Cosmic Consciousness

What we propose to you is new, yet very old. It is older than the spirituality of the past six thousand years. What we propose to you, as the true and correct Spiritual Path for Mankind, is not mediumship or channelling, nor the development of psychic powers, nor materialism or non-action, but the Science of Cosmic Consciousness. This science, long lost and forgotten by the monks, must be pursued once again. It is the art of living as a Man-God or God-Man. It is being "in the world but not of the world".

God awakens one man with a clout on the ear, another man with a shout, another man with a song, and yet another with a silent whisper.

Jewish Hasidism

The Path we teach is a combination or synthesis of four major aspects of Yoga:

BHAKTI YOGA: the Path of Devotion.
KARMA YOGA: the Path of Action or Service.
JÑĀNA YOGA: the Path of Mental Effort and Knowledge.
RĀJA YOGA: the Path of Meditation.

Bhakti Yoga has to do with emotions, religious feelings, devotion, inspiration, chanting, kirtans, bhajans and religious rituals.

Karma Yoga involves physical actions in the Physical World.

Jñāna Yoga has to do with the mind. It involves mental development, the understanding of truth, science, philosophy and metaphysics, the developing view of our Universe, and the awakening of Creative Intelligence.

Rāja Yoga has to do with the art and science of meditation, the levels of consciousness, and the various states of inner attainment.

- God can be experienced by the power of Devotion or Love. This is the *Power* field (BHAKTI YOGA).
- Everything you do is part of the total action of the Universe, of the All. Hence there is no other actor but the Divine, and hence it is your privilege that the Divine acts *through* you. Hence your right action is service to others. This is the field of *Service* (KARMA YOGA).
- Thought is pursued to expand understanding and to direct thought to transcend itself. This is the *Knowledge* field (JÑĀNA YOGA).
- In deep meditation you lose your ego and claim the Self. This is the *self-transcending* field (RĀJA YOGA).

Channelling or Soul-Wisdom? 327
The Fifth State 500
The Activities of Yoga-Mārga 520

Developing Cosmic Consciousness

Cosmic Consciousness is developed through the integration of these four activities of Yoga with the four fields of Consciousness:

The Four Yogas

BHAKTI Yoga, KARMA Yoga, JÑĀNA Yoga, RĀJA Yoga.

Every aspect of human life is considered and fulfilled

The Four Fields of Consciousness

1. Objective or Waking Consciousness.
2. Subjective or Dreaming Consciousness.
3. Dreamless-Sleep State, Causal Consciousness.
4. Transcendental or Pure Consciousness.

When you have integrated the four fields of Consciousness with these four activities of Yoga, then you can live a balanced and sane life on this planet and your life will be useful and constructive. Then there is Stillness and Dynamism in your life, Action and Non-Action, Knowledge and Devotion. Every aspect of human life is considered and fulfilled and your contribution to the planet can be very great, because your *field of service* in Cosmic Consciousness is simply the natural expression of your natural talents.

- If you are a politician, your politics will be infinitely better.
- If you are a musician, painter, writer, sculptor, or any type of artist, your source of Inspiration will be much higher than ever before.
- If you are a scientist or a business person, you will be immensely more creative and successful in whatever you do.
- If you are a religious person or a philosopher, you will be able to express Reality with far greater clarity, or *Vision,* than ever before.

Such is the gift of Cosmic Consciousness.

Yoga in Cosmic Consciousness

It is not possible to *properly* practise Yoga (Union) until one is established in Cosmic Consciousness. Then one's Action (KARMA) becomes infused with Divine Will and Purpose. Then one's Devotion (BHAKTI) is the direct worship of Reality (without any symbols or images). And then one's Gnosis (JÑĀNA) is the Wisdom of the Absolute.

The Ultimate Reality is the Meaning of Life 526

The Seven States of Consciousness 494
Steps on the Meditational Path 1196

Rāja Yoga: Divine Union by Meditation

Simply practise your meditation techniques, then live a normal life

In the Aquarian Age, Rāja Yoga (the art of meditation) is practised in a peculiar way. It is not required that one should run away from the world or become a nun, an ascetic, a recluse, a monk, a sannyāsin or a wandering faqīr or yogī. In fact, one must remain "normal". The state of Cosmic Consciousness is to be developed in one's natural environment. This is different from the old idea of Yoga in which one had to give up the world—"the world, the flesh and the devil" as the Christians put it.

Remaining "normal" means that you do not have to change your status. You don't have to become a Buddhist monk or a Hindu sannyāsin, nor embrace any strange Tibetan, Hindu or Islamic ways of living. There is no giving up of the world, no giving up of responsibilities to your job, your family or your planet. There is no need to give up your material wealth or comforts. You do not need to become a beggar or go about in rags. These were silly ideas of spirituality belonging to the Dark Ages.

This applies also to such things as diet, exercise, sex and relationships. Live in a way that is right and natural for *you*. The key word is *normal*.

Simply practise your meditation techniques, then live a normal life. As you meditate regularly, slowly you will go beyond the mind and become aware of Pure Consciousness, Transcendental Consciousness, Formless Being. Gradually you will learn to establish yourself in this Formless Being, which is Transcendental Bliss-Consciousness, on the level of Buddhi, the Universal Love-Wisdom Reality.

This level is two planes *above* the Astral World, the psychic realm from which all channelling and other psychic phenomena occur. It is not possible to channel from Buddhi; rather, it is a first-hand, direct, personal experience of Truth, Beauty, Goodness, Reality and Bliss-Awareness, a formless existence of Divine-Light-Being. It is Eternal Peace and Transcendental Consciousness.

Haṭha Yoga and Rāja Yoga 524
Modern Yoga Practice 576
Turīya: Pure Consciousness 498
Balance on the Physical Plane 1257

As you practise more and more, and lead a natural life, this true Superconsciousness will slowly infiltrate into your day-to-day life and consciousness. It will penetrate into your normal waking consciousness, your dream consciousness and your dreamless-sleep state. Slowly, degree by degree, the four states of Consciousness will fuse and become one, so that whether you are awake, dreaming or in dreamless sleep, you are aware of the Divine Self, the Presence of Holiness. When the four states of Consciousness have fused, you have Cosmic Consciousness.

But this is not all. Because you remained "normal" during this development period, because you were engaged in actions in the Physical World, because you were active emotionally in relationships, Devotion (PREMA: loving feelings towards God) and religious activities, and because you used your mind to gain knowledge and understanding, then, little by little, all these action-fields of your personality will become infused with the Light of Being, the Light of ĀTMAN, the Translucence of the Divine Self within you.

All these action-fields will become infused with the Light of Being

Consequently, your physical actions will become more powerful and your emotions will naturally reach out to the Divine Being, to God. You will feel more blissful, inspired and devotional. Your mind will be clearer and you will see more easily the solutions to all problems of life. And you will feel the need to help all suffering beings on this planet, because you will know, from first-hand experience, that to establish oneself in the Light of Being in the Transcendental State, and to live from that State, is the Divine Birthright of every man, woman and child on this planet. You will solve the purpose and mystery of human existence.

"When, after many life-periods, it dawns upon the lower nature, the personality, the ego-self, that it exists only for the sake of the Soul, that its value depends on what it can bring to the Soul, that it can win immortality only by merging itself in the Soul, then its evolution proceeds with great strides. Before this, its evolution was unconscious. The personality begins *deliberately* to discipline itself and to set the interests of the Immortal-Individual-Within above the personality's transient gratifications. The brain is surrendered to receive impacts from within (from the Soul), instead of from without (from the senses). The mind is trained to respond to Soul-contacts....

The predominant quality of Consciousness in the Causal Body is Knowledge and Wisdom; in the Buddhic Body, it is Bliss and Love. When to this is added the Godlike and unruffled Will and Power of ĀTMA (the Nirvāṇic Vehicle), then a human being is crowned with Divinity and the God-Man is manifest, with all the plenitude of Power, Wisdom and Love in this world."

Dr Annie Besant

The Science of Meditation 1173
Meditation Practice 1201
The Way of the Mind 1238
God-Consciousness is the Wholeness of Life 504

Bhakti Yoga: Divine Union by Devotion

Religions which have Devotion are truly blessed—the Roman Catholic and Anglican Churches, for instance, and some Jewish sects, and devotional Sūfīsm, Hinduism and Buddhism. Devotion, worship, or *true surrender*, is the noblest of all human feelings and emotions, and the greatest purifier of the Heart. Devotion to God, to Christ, to Buddha, to Allāh, to Kṛṣṇa, to Brahmā, Viṣṇu or Śiva—when it is genuine, heartfelt—purifies your nature immensely. It elevates you beyond your "I", beyond your ego into the Transcendental Realm, into BODHI, the State of Unity. It is also a great purifier of the inner worlds, of the after-death states. This is why the Eastern Orthodox Christian Church is based so much on Devotion, on the Holy Mass. And this is why we sing and chant and do rituals.

The Mystery of the Heart 425
The Thread of the Heart 844
Devotion to Kṛṣṇa 449
The Divine Mood 1252
Mystics of Pisces and Aquarius 836

Many people chant, sing or pray mentally, from the head, without any feeling at all. That is not the same. All chanting, worship and prayer should be done in the Heart, through the Heart, from the Heart, with intense Love, Devotion, Worship, Reverence. The Heart is the seat of *transcendental* feeling, whereas the Solar Plexus Centre is the seat of ordinary emotions.

The object of reverence for you—your ĪṢTA-DEVATĀ—may be the Christ, the Buddha, Śrī Kṛṣṇa or Allāh. Whichever is your focal point, you must sing from the Heart, pray from the Heart, and release all of your Love, Longing, and blessings from the Heart, and *gratitude* towards the Divine.

The Piscean Age was very devotional, for Pisces is a water sign. The Aquarian Age will be a *mental* age, for Aquarius is an air sign. Nevertheless, you should remain devotional, for the perfection of Man requires that you worship as well as understand.

ALHAMDULILLĀH
Arabic: "All praise be to God!" In the state of Cosmic Consciousness one forever experiences the Divine Presence and one continually glorifies God in a most natural and spontaneous way in everything one thinks, does and feels.
The Lover of God 853

ĪṢTA-DEVATĀ
Sanskrit: "Chosen Divinity". The form of the Deity you are most drawn to, such as the form of the Christ, Buddha, Śrī Kṛṣṇa or Rāma. Also known as UPĀSANĀ-MŪRTI, "worshipful image". Your *Chosen Deity* helps you to focus on the Divine Reality.
Visualizing the Divinity within the Heart 1268

In the Eastern Tradition of Christianity, the PHILOKALIA (Greek: the Love of the Good), the Way is through the Purification of the Heart by the Name of Jesus, plus silence, solitude, humility and an ecstatic Love of God, leading to Illumination and final Union with God. For the great Christian Mystics, the Supernatural Life in the Spirit is the only real meaning and purpose of human existence. For this we were born.
Interior Prayer 691

On the Wings of Devotion

One of the characteristics of the Heart is intense Devotion (PARA-BHAKTI). The supreme Goal of the Devotee (BHAKTA) is God, God whose Cosmic Body is all Creation, God who is Immanent, who is within all that is. For the whole Cosmos is the Form of God, the Body of God (VIŚVA-RŪPA), within which God resides fully and completely.

The Presence of God within the Heart can be approached by Inner Worship

There is another aspect of God: the Transcendent, Unmanifest, Formless Absoluteness, beyond and above Creation. Creation devolved from Cosmic Consciousness, from the Mind of God, the Infinite Light, for the Infinite Light is but the Mind of God in action. As God is Infinite, so is God's Mind.

There are great SIDDHAs, Master Beings, who have the simultaneous Vision of both the Immanent and Transcendent aspects of God, who possess the All-Seeing-Eye (DEVA-NETRA) whereby they can scan the Infinite Horizons and discover the Ultimate Mysteries. Then there are the Lords of Yoga (YOGEŚVARAs) who ascended on the Wings of Devotion, from world to world, to the very Throne of God, the Divine Heart.

The Experience of the Heart 1280
The Magic of Ritual Worship 366
The Stages of Prayer 1253

For most people, Devotion was the first step on the Spiritual Path, in the form of YAJÑA: religious rituals, communal worship, ceremonies, offerings, communal prayers, religious rites. They attended the church, mosque, synagogue, temple, or a place of worship, and there they were taught to worship God in "heaven", somewhere far away, outside themselves. In all religions, this was the first step in their Heart-Journey; they felt a great longing for God, a desire to reach God, to commune with God.

But the priestcraft knew only rituals. Their Devotion was expressed through rituals which, sincerely performed, awakened the Heart from sleep, but the priestcraft did not know the Secret: the Presence of God within the Heart, and the Immanent, Immediate Presence of Divinity in all Creation.

The Presence of God within the Heart can be approached by ANTAR-YAJÑA, Inner Worship, the direct approach through *meditation and chanting in the Heart.* And the Immediate Presence of God in the Universe can be known when you have attained Cosmic Consciousness as a *result* of your inner development.

The Catholic Mystical Path

In the great Mystical Tradition of the Roman Catholic Church (which has hundreds of contemplative Saints) the Path has been divided into three stages:

1. The Way of Purification.
2. The Way of Illumination.
3. The Way of Union.

The *Way of Union* is itself divided into three stages:

1. Simple Union with God.
2. Ecstatic Union with God.
3. Transforming into Divinity.

Stages on the Way of Holiness 1336

Uniting Head and Heart

The Heart is the Way to Peace in this troubled world. That is why the Christ said, "My Peace I give unto you." This is the Peace of the Heart. May the Radiance of the Heart give you Peace.

The Way of the Heart is the discovery of Being

The Way of the Heart is the ancient Way. The Way of the Head is the coming New Age Way.

The Way of the Heart is the Path of Love and Devotion to the God who is *within* your Heart and *within* all Creation, within all worlds, within all planes of Being, within all creatures and beings. The Way of the Head is a search *outside* yourself, in the outer physical body, in the outer world, in bodies, forms, objects. It is the study of the *outside appearance* of the Universe and the outside course of "laws" and events. It is the study of the *veils* that *conceal* the Real.

The Way of the Heart is the discovery of Being, of Beingness within you and in the Cosmos. The Way of the Mind, or the Way of Future Science, is the Way of learning about the forms of Divine Manifestation, how God *appears* on the "outside". It is learning about the Laws of the Mind, which are the Laws of Nature and the Celestial Hierarchies.

The Way of the Heart, the Way of the Mystic, is the experiencing of the indwelling Life of God within yourself and outside yourself in the Cosmos. The Way of Science, or the Way of the Mind, is the study of the forms that *veil* the Self. Inside yourself, your thoughts are the "forms" that veil your Self from yourself; thus, the Way of the Mind is to study the veils of thinking, thoughts, forms, bodies, structures. In Science, however, an important key is *missing*.

The Two Paths 1112
From Head to Heart 427
God in the Heart 634
The Christ in the Heart 441
From Pisces to Aquarius 837

Within the innermost chamber of the Heart, God is to be found. This is not a theory but a fact. It is not the "old man on the throne", but the Fiery, Radiant, Universal Logos, the Spiritual Sun, the Universal Christ in Glory, "the Resurrected Lord". The Heart is the seat of the Consciousness of the conscious part of the Soul and of the Higher Self. Again, this is not theoretical, but practical. It is *found* in meditation.

Science is the study of how the Kingdom of God *appears* from the outside, from the view of outer consciousness. The Way of the Heart is the Way of the Mystic Fire, Fiery Aspiration, and a deep longing for the *experience* of Reality, the Eternally Real, not for the passing forms of the phenomenal Universe, which ever changes, grows "old" and passes away.

In the New Age, you will have to descend from the Head to the Heart

In the olden days, you *ascended* from the Heart to the Head. In the New Age, you will have to *descend* from the Head to the Heart. At this stage, this is *not understood* by the millions of "intellectual" people of the world.

The active service of the Mystic is based on Love. The active service of the future Scientist is based on true Knowledge of the Unity of all Life and the Divine *Interconnectedness* of all things. Both must serve Mankind selflessly. This is the *Spiritual Law.*

The Perfected One of the Man-species is one in whom Heart and Head have been united into one expression, one simultaneous working: the awakened Heart linked with the awakened Head, expressed in a life of *Selfless Service* to all Life.

⊙	**Will-Power.** The Causal Centre above the head.
⛤	**Mind Function.** The Head Centre. Mental control.
✡	**Heart Function.** The Heart Centre. Love.
⊕	**Crucifixion.** Death of the ego. Spiritual crisis. Resurrection.
☽	**The Astral World.** Psychism, mediumship, etc.

Some Symbols relating to the Path

The Path to Immortality 430
The Threefold Way 1236
What is True Service? 1714
The Way of the Mind 1238
The Way of the Heart 1249
Heart Knowing 1286

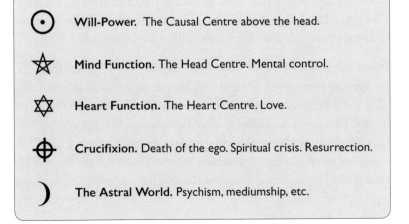

Karma Yoga: Divine Union by Action

The Sanskrit word KARMA means "action, work, doing". Karma also means the *results* of one's action. It is the Law of Cause and Effect.

Total inaction in this life is not possible

In the early stages of the Spiritual Path, when the aspirant is trying to meditate and develop Higher Consciousness, he or she tends to want to renounce actions in this world and spend his or her time in inward meditation only. Note, for instance, the sādhus, sannyāsins and yogīs of India. But, as it is written in the Bhagavad-Gītā:

> The Sage who has attained Self-Realization and is rejoicing in the Self and is satisfied with the Self, for him there is nothing to do. He is not affected by things done in this world, nor by things undone, nor does he depend on any beings.
>
> Therefore, *without attachment,* constantly perform all actions [karmas] which are your duty [Dharma]. By performing actions without attachment you will reach the Supreme.

In the Bhagavad-Gītā, Śrī Kṛṣṇa suggests to Arjuna that he should fight (that was Arjuna's Dharma, his duty, for he was of the warrior class), but to let the Self (ĀTMAN) within him do the fighting. Kṛṣṇa suggests that Arjuna himself should remain in the exalted state of meditation, like a silent watcher, while performing all actions.

∞

Total inaction in this life is not possible.

All actions in the Universe, including the actions of Man, are possible only through ŚAKTI (the Divine Energy) acting through PRĀKṚTĪ (Nature, Matter, Creation). Thus, it is the Energy of the Supreme (BRAHMAN) which does all actions. This must be *realized.*

From the point of view of the Self, the ĀTMAN in Man, there are no karmas performed, for the Self within you knows directly that all actions are performed by the Universal Self (PARAMĀTMAN) and by the Transcendental Reality (PARABRAHMAN). On the *ego* level we mistakenly think that *we* do things (AHAṀKĀRA, "I am the doer"). It is not we who do things, however, but the Cosmic Ego, the I AM-ness of the Divine Being. Thus we should shift our attention from our egos to the Divine Ego of the Universe, the Cosmic I AM-ness of the Godhead, the ĀTMAN.

Karma: the Law of Action 240
Success is Born of Action 256
Karma and Reincarnation Misconceived 252
Who is 'I AM'? 1418

KARMA (work, action, doing) belongs to the phenomenal world, the Physical, Astral and Mental Planes. Stillness (non-action) belongs to the Spiritual World, the Buddhic and Nirvāṇic Planes and the planes above.

Action is in Time and Space. Non-action is in Eternity and Infinity. But the temporal and phenomenal exists *within* the Timeless and Eternal. When we identify with our egos, which function on the Physical, Astral, Mental and Causal Planes, we identify with our karmas (actions) and hence we reap the consequences of our karmas *in our Consciousness.* If we identify with the One Self in All, the PARAMĀTMAN, then all actions are done by the Cosmic Ego and we are *free* in our Consciousness.

The temporal and phenomenal exists within the Timeless and Eternal

∞

Such a condition the Taoist-Zen Masters call WU-WEI, *action in stillness* or *not-doing.* You are doing, yet it is not *you,* the ego, who is doing it. This is the true Karma Yoga of the Indian Sages. This is the condition of true Zen, the state of the Perfectly Enlightened One.

> That is why the Sage is engaged in not-doing; he walks in the teachings without words. When an action is completed, he is not attached to it... and because he is not attached to his works, they do not leave him.
>
> *Lao Tzu*

The expression "he walks in the teachings without words" means not only that the Sage is unattached to his actions, but that he is unattached even to his own teachings. The key to arriving at this condition is meditative practice alternating with activity. One moves repeatedly between the field of action (Creation) and the field of non-action (the Unmanifested Being) until both fields manifest *simultaneously* in one's Consciousness.

From the very beginning of this practice (SĀDHANĀ), you *do not* renounce the world, you do not kill out emotions, you do not attempt to control the mind.

This is completely contrary to the orthodox teachings of Yoga as presented and practised over the last six thousand years. These teachings were based on a misunderstanding of the value of action in Creation.

The 'No-Mind' 990
The Path of Non-Duality 762
Terms of Awakening 766
To Become a Jīvanmukta 259

The Law of the Higher Life

> The Sage abides by actionless activity and practises wordless teachings. But since all things have been created, he does not turn away from them.
>
> *Taoist Mysticism*

The Sage does not live for himself or herself alone

The Sage abides by actionless activity…

The Sage does things without ego, without selfish interest.

And practises wordless teachings.

The Sage is able to respond to the inward pull of the Spirit, the Higher Self (Ātman).

But since all things have been created, he does not turn away from them.

The Sage does not live for himself or herself alone, but becomes a guide, a refuge, a helper of Humanity, who gives help and relief to the suffering masses through teaching an Enlightened Way of Life.

The Sage 973
The True Teachers 1694
The Enlightened 1702
Balance in Spiritual Life 505
Penetrating into the Kingdom 1707

Saints of Action

Whether we attain Buddhi (the Transcendental State) or Nirvāṇa (Freedom), we must *not* renounce activity (Karma), nor suppress emotions and feelings (Kāma, Rāga), nor suppress the mind (Manas). For the truly Enlightened Man uses the fields of action, feeling and thought (the Physical, Astral and Mental Worlds) as fields of service, helpfulness and benevolence.

If the holy men and women of the world do not care for the world or the subtler dimensions of the astral and mental realms, we shall forever remain in darkness on this planet (Avidyā). We need *dynamic* Saints, not the lethargic, ineffective sādhus of the East!

Jesus was filled with God-Consciousness. The Eternal Stillness of God's Being was the ground and root of His experience every moment, twenty-four hours a day. Yet He did not spend His time in contemplation, sitting cross-legged in a lonely mountain cave in the Sinai Desert. He was a man of action! Though filled with the Eternal Stillness of God's Being, He was fully engaged in action in Creation, in the physical, astral and mental dimensions.

Warrior Jesus 908

These people are the *true* Chosen Ones, the Elect. Such were Jesus the Christ, the Buddha, Moses, Lao Tzu. In this state of Spiritual Life, the true Saint, the Wiseman or Wisewoman, has responded to the Divine Call. The prodigal son has returned Home. The union of opposites (Spirit and Matter) has been achieved and the Saint is in touch with Reality, the Kingdom of God, Nirvāṇa, Tao. He holds out a lamp for all to see, so that the weary "pilgrims of the way" may see the Light and not get lost in the dark abysses and fall down the dangerous precipices of material and psychic life. He is the SADGURU, the true Teacher, the true Guide.

Ever concentrating within himself, the Yogī of disciplined mind attains to Peace, the Supreme Liberation, and abides in Me.

Bhagavad-Gītā

The truth of Being forms the state of Enlightenment. The state of Reality, as is described by an Enlightened One, cannot become a Path for the seeker, any more than the description of the Goal can replace the road that leads to it.

Maharishi

Though you eat the whole day, not a single grain passed your lips. A day's journey has not taken you a single step forward.

Abstain from notions such as "self" and "other". Do not permit events in your daily life to bind you, but never withdraw yourself from them. Only thus can you become a Liberated One.

Zen

Once upon a time, when I began to meditate upon the things that are, my mind soared high aloft while my bodily senses went to sleep—*not* the natural sleep caused by dullness of food or tiredness. Then there came to me a Being of a vast and boundless magnitude, who called me by my name, and said to me, "What do you wish to hear or to see? What do you wish to learn and to understand?"

And I said, "Who are you?"

And the Being replied, "I am POIMANDRES, the Mind of Light."

And I replied, "I would like to learn of the things that are, and understand their nature, and get *knowledge* of God. These are the things I wish to hear."

And the Being answered, "I know what you wish, for I am with you always, everywhere. Keep in mind all that you desire to know, and I will teach you."

And when the Being of Light finished speaking, all things changed appearance for me. And I beheld a boundless view, and all was changed into Light, a mild yet joyous Light, and I marvelled when I saw it.

Hermes Trismegistus

Who are the 'Elect'? 128
The Chosen Ones 688
Wisdom: the Light Path 1354
The Zen Master according to Lao Tzu 780

Stages on the Path

Pure Consciousness

The Consciousness is led into increasingly subtle levels of the relative field of life—the lower Three Worlds—by the process of deep meditation. Thus, our waking consciousness (in which we start our meditation) gradually becomes aware of the subtle fields of thought, the dreaming state and the dreamless-sleep state. When we become aware of the Spirit, the Self within us, as a formless, silent and actionless Reality beyond Creation, beyond thought, beyond the mind, then we are in Pure Consciousness, the Transcendental State, TURĪYA (the fourth state) or SAMĀDHI (Bliss-Consciousness). In this state we lose consciousness of body, mind and emotions. The Self is realized as *separate* from activity.

Pure Consciousness is the direct, first-hand experience of the Divine Being within us

Pure Consciousness is the direct, first-hand experience of the Divine Being within us, far above the deceptive nature of the astral realms. Because the "holy men" of India stopped at the stage of Pure Consciousness, they became actionless, detached and useless to this world and to their environment. They spent all their time in SAMĀDHI. But a mere absorption and continual contemplation of the Self is not the final goal; the two higher stages are attained by action, by normal engagement in life. One alternates between the life of action and the life of contemplation.

Cosmic Consciousness

The next stage in the process is Cosmic Consciousness. From the level of Conscious Immortality we again become aware of the relative field of life—thoughts, emotions and actions. We can act, feel and think normally, but we do not lose awareness of the condition of the Self. However, we perceive the relative field of life—thinking, feeling and action in this world—as *separate* from the Divine Field of non-action. In Cosmic Consciousness one sees two separate realities: the absolute, unconditioned Life of the Spirit within (the Divine Self) and the relative life of the personality. One feels that only the relative personality acts, and that the Divine Being does not act, but only *witnesses* all things.

The Seven States of Consciousness 494
Turīya: Pure Consciousness 498
Pure Consciousness in the Heart 447
Formless Consciousness 1373
The Fifth State 500

God-Consciousness

Far beyond Cosmic Consciousness, the separation between Self and the relative field of life vanishes. In God-Consciousness, all is experienced as One: the Physical, Astral and Mental Worlds, and the World of the Divine Being, appear to our Consciousness not as separate compartments, but as *One Reality.* That is, the waking state, the dreaming state, the dreamless-sleep state, Turīya (the Ecstatic State of the Self) and Nirvāṇa (the Mind of Light) become One Consciousness.

In God-Consciousness, the Divine Being is infused in whatever we do

This is *Union with God.* It is the condition of the All in All, the God in All, and the Divine Being is known to be the Doer of All, the Being of All, and the only Reality that is.

Once again, the idea is not to run away from the world, but to be God-Conscious *in* the world. Thus, the full power of Divine Wisdom, Love, Intelligence and Bliss-Consciousness is used to help the world and the universe around you. In God-Consciousness, the Divine Being is infused in whatever we do. All our actions become truly Karma Yoga; all devotional practices become truly Bhakti Yoga; all thinking becomes truly Jñāna Yoga; and all meditational practices become truly Rāja Yoga.

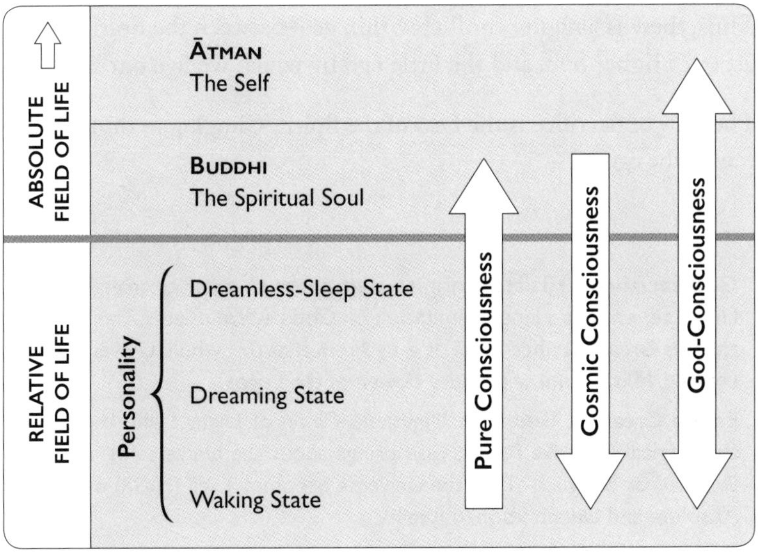

Leaps in Consciousness

The Seventh State 502
Types of Conscious Immortality 390
God-Consciousness is the Wholeness of Life 504
Steps on the Meditational Path 1196
Learn to Die before you Die 420

The Law of Surrender or Sacrifice

The Law of Sacrifice is the Law of the Spirit

By an act of self-sacrifice the Logos [the Creator-God] became *manifest* for the *emanation* of the world; by sacrifice the universe is maintained; and by sacrifice Man reaches perfection....

The very essence of sacrifice is a voluntary pouring forth of your life, that others may share in it.

Dr Annie Besant

Christ, God's Lamb, has been sacrificed for us.

Corinthians

For God so loved the world that he sacrificed His only-begotten Son, that whosoever believeth in Him should not perish, but have everlasting life....

For greater Love than this no Man has, that he sacrifice his life for humanity.

St John

Sacrifice is a *voluntary letting go.* We normally associate sacrifice with "pain", with doing without things, or giving up things that we like, or doing things we don't like to do. This pain or discomfort that we feel for the idea of sacrifice is a product of our *egos.* The ego grasps onto things—people, situations, name and fame, material possessions and so on. It also holds onto its self-view, the image we have of ourselves.

The desire to give is in the nature of the Spirit. The desire to possess is in the nature of the ego.

Thus, there is a raging conflict within us—between the Spirit within us, our Higher Self, and the little ego by which we live our lives.

The Law of Sacrifice is the Law of the Spirit. Clinging to things is the way of the ego.

God sacrificed His/Her Infinite Beingness in order to manifest the Universe, which is a kind of limitation on God's Absoluteness. The Hindus call this Great Sacrifice MĀYĀ. It is by MĀYĀ that this whole Universe was created. MĀYĀ is the *self-limiting* power of the Logos.

Before Creation, God is an Illimitable Circle of Living Light. By MĀYĀ, the Magical Creative Power, God brings about the Universe as a *willing limitation on Beingness.* Thus the Universe becomes a veil (MĀYĀ) over the Absolute and Unconditioned Reality.

Māyā 2

The Way of the Spirit 381
The Testing of the Soul 1158
The Primordial Light 119
The Creation of the Universe 166

Love and Sacrifice

Do unto others as ye would have others do unto you.

Jesus the Christ

Be the last to quarrel, but the first to make up.

Proverbs

What is the purpose of Life? To *know*, to *love*, and to *serve* God.

Roman Catholic Catechism

The Law of Sacrifice is the Law of Love

Hear, O Israel: the Eternal, our God, is One. And thou shalt *love* the Eternal, thy God, with all thine *heart*, with all thine *soul*, and with all thine *might*.

Deuteronomy

Master, which is the greatest commandment of the Law? And Jesus said unto him, "Thou shalt love the Lord, thy God, with all your Heart, and with all your Soul, and with all your mind, and with all your strength." This is the first great commandment of the Law. And the second is like unto it; "Thou shalt love thy neighbour as thyself." On these two commandments hang all the Law and the Prophets.

Matthew

The Law of Sacrifice, as it applies within the Human Kingdom, is the Law of Love.

The Old Testament covenant taught the Jewish tribes to love God. Jesus extended this idea to the love of one's fellow human beings, of all Mankind. The old karmic pattern is the Law of Vengeance: "An eye for an eye, a tooth for a tooth". The new Law is the Law of Love and Forgiveness. Individuals, tribes, groups and nations who live by hate, by the spirit of vengeance, cause endless suffering for themselves and for their "enemies". Individuals and nations must learn to live by the Law of Christ, which is the Spirit of Love.

Jesus, the Christ

You must understand that to the early Christians there was no such person as "Jesus Christ", but "Jesus, the Christ". They knew that Jesus was functioning from the Glorious State of the Christos, the Second Aspect of the threefold Godhead, the Cosmic Creative Word.

The Mystery of Jesus the Christ 664

The Eternal is One 512
The Law of Action 992
From Hate to Love 229
The Sacrifice of the Teachers 1150
Peace on Earth 1304

On Love and Meditation

Very few people are capable of Love

Many aspirants, disciples and followers of the Spiritual Path are confused about the nature of Love and meditation and their function upon the Path of Enlightenment. Love is not what most people think it is. Love is not sexual attraction, nor is it self-centred, astral, solar-plexus sentimentalism. Keep in mind always that, when the scriptures talk about Love, they mean the *radiation of the Heart Cakra.*

Love is the universal, selfless Heart Energy of the Christ Being within you.

Love is *doing* the greatest good for the largest number. Very few people are capable of Love. Yet, without it, you cannot progress on the Spiritual Path. This is how Saint Paul describes Love in his first letter to the Corinthians:

> Love is patient, Love is kind.
> Love does not envy, and is not jealous.
> It does not boast. It is not proud.
> Love is not violent.
> It is not self-seeking.
> It is not easily angered.
> It keeps no records of wrongs done.
> Love does not delight in hurting others.
> Love protects, always trusts.
> Love hopes, perseveres.
> Love never fails.

Heart Union and Sexual Union

Like the sexual energy, Love is an attractive energy, but of a different kind. Love *binds* you (attracts you) to God, the Divine Consciousness. It is because they are both attractive powers that the Mystics *symbolized* the attractive power of the Heart Love with sexual attraction, and Heart Union with sexual union. But sexual union can only be a *symbol* for Love; it can never be that Love! Sexual attraction is personal; Love is universal, impersonal. A person who has Love "forgives wrongs innumerable". There is no limit to that person's endurance, long suffering and patience. He or she is not a slave, but neither is he or she arrogant. That person knows no divisions, no discord, and practises harmlessness (Ahiṁsā).

What is the Heart? 435
The Universal Christ 440
The Energies of Sex and Love 912
Sex Natural and Divine 926
Ahiṁsā: Non-violence 566

Saint Paul describes the person who is Heart-centred, in whom the Heart Cakra is functioning—one who is on the Path. Such a person, whose Heart Cakra is awake, is patient, kind, does not envy, is not jealous, does not boast, is not proud. Such a person is non-violent, is not easily angered, keeps no grudges against people, does not hurt others wilfully. Such a person always protects others, always trusts. Such a person always hopes, perseveres and never fails to Love.

You must remember, of course, that we do not become instantly perfect in Love. The Heart Cakra awakens in us gradually as we practise the Spiritual Life. It is not expected that you become instantly perfect!

The Heart Cakra awakens in us gradually as we practise the Spiritual Life

> He who loves everybody has satisfied the Law... For the whole Law of God is summed up by the word, Love.
>
> *Romans*

> Anyone who lives in Love, lives in God, and God lives in him.
>
> *St John*

These words of Saint John mean that when you live in Love, when your Heart is radiant with the Spiritual Fire of Love, you live *in* God and God lives *in* you—quite truly, actually, literally.

Saint Clement the First describes the awakened Heart Love from his experience thus:

> If there is true Christian Love in us, we will carry out
> the Commandment of Christ, which is Love.
> No one can tell the heights to which Love can inspire us.
> Love *binds* us to God.
> Love forgives wrongs immeasurable.
> There is no limit to Love's endurance and patience.
> Love is without slavishness and without arrogance.
> Love knows no divisions and no discord.
> Love is perfect togetherness and friendship.
> In Love, the Saints are made Perfect.
> Without Love, there is no action that is pleasing to God.

A person who has Love in the Heart is a perfect friend and is always united with his or her environment. "In Love, Saints are made perfect." In other words, you become Perfect in, by and through the Power of Love. Ponder on this.

Heart Action 1331
Christ-Consciousness 443
The Meaning of Life is Love 633
To Love God and the World 1392

The Path of Love is not only a Christian teaching, but the ancient Spiritual Path itself. This Path is described in many ancient texts of the East, such as the Upaniṣads:

> Let the disciple search within the cave of the Heart, and see if the Fire there is burning bright... This Fire must warm others, but not himself.

The Love of the Heart is an impulse towards self-sacrifice

This means that the Heart Love is a Universal Radiation of Love. It is not selfish, egotistical, self-opinionated or attached with hooks and claws. It *warms* others, but not oneself!

This Love of the Heart is an impulse towards self-sacrifice, service for others, universal Benevolence and Compassion. It is what the Roman Catholics call the *Sacred Heart of Jesus*. Love is expressed as *service,* as helpfulness towards all beings. It is absolute selflessness, where another person's need is of greater importance than one's own. It is the sacrifice of one's little personal self, the ego, one's personal wishes. In the Holy Scriptures, it is symbolized by the Crucifixion of Jesus. Such selflessness can hardly be comprehended by modern society.

An old manuscript says:

> The Path of Light is steep and narrow. He who would tread it must be a Man.

To be a "Man" means maturity, dignity. The Man (male or female) must possess Knowledge, Wisdom and Understanding, and above all, must walk the Path of Love.

> Let the disciple merge himself within the circle of his other selves.

This means Unity-Consciousness. Love is essentially a consciousness of Oneness with all others, with all separated selves within the Whole.

> The Path of Growth and the Way of Suffering are the same.

There is no true spiritual development without self-sacrifice. In practical terms, your Love is synonymous with your spiritual state. The greater your capacity to Love—practically—the more advanced you are.

Remember, Love must be expressed practically, physically, in action!

The Ancient Heart-Path 845
The Eastern Heart 448
The Sacred Heart of Jesus 673
The Unfoldment of the Light 718

There is a Buddhist practice where you sit and send out thoughts of Love in all four directions. That is not enough! Then there is the Hindu practice of Ahiṁsā (harmlessness) where you try not to hurt others or any living thing. That also is not enough. Love must be expressed in *positive action* on the Physical Plane.

Mother Theresa is an example of *practical* Love. When she saw human suffering, her Love (her awakened Heart Cakra) expressed itself in *action*. All her life she tended and cared for the sick, the dying, the dead, the outcasts, society's rejects, the poor, the infants, in the living nightmare of the slums of India. She did not just sit down and send "loving thoughts" to the four corners of the Earth. She did not just practise Ahiṁsā (harmlessness). She did not just walk around the lepers, the dying; she picked them up, comforted them, helped them, nourished them! That is Love in action.

Love must be expressed in positive action on the Physical Plane

In your own life also, Love must be expressed in loving actions towards your family, neighbours, friends and group members. Love is not an abstract thing! Love is energetic, dynamic. It changes environment, relationships, circumstances and your *consciousness*.

These are the two most important things in your life:

- Love.
- Meditation.

Truly, those two words sum up the purpose of your existence. Both Love and meditation lead towards the same goal: Perfection, Glory, Deification, Divinity.

Of all spiritual practices, Love is the most important. Love is even more important than meditation.

This may be difficult for many to understand, even for some on the Path. May you be inspired to Love and to meditate, so that you may attain to Glory in this life.

> O Man, arouse yourself!
> Learn to know the dignity of your nature!
> Remember, you are made in the Image of God.
> Use this visible Creation as it should be used.
> Touch physical light with the bodily senses, but embrace with your Soul
> that true Light that enlightens every man who cometh into this world!
> For we are the Temple of God, and the Spirit of God lives in us.
>
> *Saint Leo the Great*

The Mystics 91
Oneness and Love 1450
The Supreme Act of Karma 264
To Manifest the Kingdom of God 1716

The Vision of your own Eternity...

What is your standing on the Path?

Do you know where you are at?

What more do you need to do?

The Vision is to reclaim that which was yours, but which you have lost

The Path consists of having a Vision, a Goal, towards which you work and aspire, and that Goal or Vision is to reclaim that which was yours, but which you have lost: the Vision of your own Eternity.

Life is not that narrow, limited routine that you call your "life". If you open your Inner Sense, you will *know* that Life is vast and eternal, boundless, without limit.

The Self that is *You* has never been born and will never die. Search for *that* and you will gain Life Eternal.

Have no fear of Life, nor fear of Death, nor fear of the Future, nor fear of failing on the Path. The Imperishable is your Self-Nature even Now.

Concentrate on the Moment, whatever you are doing, whether you are chanting, meditating, singing, working in the garden or in the kitchen, talking to people, or relaxing.

Make your Moment as Now, and Now is Eternity.

Regain what you have Lost 381
Is there a Plan in your Life? 1000
Attach your Mind to the Eternal 1234
Past, Present and Future 1400
The Eternal 1644

CHAPTER 50

The Aquarian Group-Consciousness

Group Work

One of the fundamental differences between the passing-away Piscean Age Spirituality and the coming Aquarian Age Spirituality is group work.

During the Piscean Age, which is gradually drawing to a close, many Mystics, in all religions, worked alone. "Salvation for the self" was the theme. Today, however, and during the next few centuries, you will find Salvation in Group-Consciousness together with your Soul brothers and sisters. The next two thousand years of human evolution will increasingly emphasize group work and group togetherness.

You will find Salvation in Group-Consciousness

Forming a Spiritual Group does not, in itself, guarantee a smooth path to Heaven, however. The group has its own difficulties. First of all, there are many seekers and disciples on the Path who still have the Piscean consciousness; they are individualists who like to be independent in their thoughts, opinions and actions. They say, "I don't need a guru, I can do it by myself," or "I don't need a group, I can walk the path alone." This is how the spiritual aspirants thought during the Piscean Age.

Living Guidance 339
Towards Group-Consciousness 186
Separatism and the Law of Love 386
The Influence of the Seven Rays 834
Piscean and New Age Spirituality 1706

These people find it difficult to truly integrate themselves into a group. Very often they stay on the fringe without committing themselves. They like to look on, to observe others, and to think how lucky they are that they have remained free! Essentially, they are insulated in their personalities and isolated in their consciousness. They are shut off from Group-Consciousness, from the group aura, group energy, group impulses, group will, group ideas and the group vision of the Path. They might believe they are members of the group, but in reality they work only for themselves. They get the Teachings for themselves alone, to share with whomsoever *they* will. They are reluctant to contribute to the group purpose—emotionally, mentally or financially. In a way, they are still small children who have not grown up. They just want to get, but not to give.

In today's groups, the truly group-conscious people (the Aquarians) are still few in number. Most are Piscean in mentality.

Personal Salvation?

During the Piscean Age, *individualism* predominated over the Group-Consciousness idea. In the Piscean Age it was your "personal" Salvation that counted. That is why evangelicals and fundamentalists stress the idea of a *personal Saviour;* they think that their *personalities* are being saved. How wrong they are!

Jesus the Personal Saviour? 678

The Aquarian Teachers

In the old Piscean Spirituality the individual seekers, pupils, disciples, were directly related to the Teacher, Guru or Guide on an individual basis. In the coming Aquarian Age it is the *group* that is related to the Teacher. Another important departure is that the Teachers themselves worked more or less in isolation during the Piscean Age. In the Aquarian Age the Teachers will be more conscious of an all-inclusive Spiritual Hierarchy.

Religious divisions will be broken down during the next few hundred years

This gives an insight into the changed nature of Spiritual Life. In the Aquarian Age the seekers under a Teacher have to work as a *group* and develop Group-Consciousness. And, on a much larger scale, the Teachers, Gurus, Masters and Saints have to learn to work in a Unity-Consciousness that was not possible during the Piscean Dispensation.

If all goes well (according to the Plan), religious divisions will be broken down during the next few hundred years. In the Piscean Age a Teacher was a Jew, a Christian, a Muslim, a Tibetan, a Hindu, a Jain, a Buddhist, a Taoist, a Zen, a Shinto, or whatever, and that Teacher represented that religious tradition or a *sect* of that tradition. They were very much into their own thing, knowing nothing about the other religious traditions. And that is how the Piscean Teachers are today.

The new breed of Aquarian Teachers will not emphasize a particular religious tradition, nor push the views of a particular sect (as they did in the Piscean Age). These new Teachers will be familiar with all traditions and will know the *essence*, the *valuable* part, of any religious tradition, and will be able to communicate that essence to all seekers of any religious background or no religious background at all.

This new breed of New Age Spiritual Teachers will have nothing to do with mediumship, channelling or primitive psychic powers (so popular among people who erroneously think they are New-Agers). The true Spiritual Teachers have never had anything to do with such things in the past, nor do they in the present, nor will they in the future. This is in spite of the systematic lies and delusions of mediums and channellers (or whatever other names they may invent for themselves: "sensitives", "intuitives", etc.) falsely claiming they are genuine Spiritual Teachers and Masters, the *same* as the Saints and Masters of the true religious traditions!

Masters and Mediums 326

The True Teachers 1694
The New and Eternal Way 516
Spirituality Past and Future 1104
Hierarchies of Life 1721
The Future 1709

The Mystery Schools and Āśramas

In the West we call them the *Mystery Schools*. In the East they are the ĀŚRAMAS. In the West we had the HIEROPHANT, or Perfect Master, as head of the School. In the East we had the GURU.

The Western concept of this principle is illustrated by Tarot Key 5, *The Hierophant*. The Buddha in the meditational posture is the Eastern maṇḍala for the same truth.

The Mystery Schools are the doors to the Temples of Initiation

> The Buddha sitting under the Bodhi Tree, in the way he sits, in his posture and gesture, in the phenomenon of his Being, without an ego, is creating vibrations all around Him.
>
> And when the Enlightened One [the Buddha] has disappeared from under his Bodhi Tree [meditational state], those vibrations will go on and on, and will touch the planets and the stars. And whatsoever the Buddha's vibrations will touch, they will awaken.
>
> *Buddhism*

> Even the Buddha sitting under the Bodhi tree, not doing anything, is *creative*. The way he is sitting is creating a *force*, an *energy*, a meditational energy!
>
> *Rajneesh*

The Guru 389
Tarot Key 5: The Hierophant 558
Ascending the Planes of Consciousness 20
The Unfoldment of the Light 718
What is Initiation? 1007

The Mystery Schools were created in ancient Egypt, Greece and Rome to link up the lower to the higher, the visible to the invisible worlds. This is represented in Tarot Key 5 by the wand of the Hierophant. In the Mystery Schools one learnt about the invisible worlds surrounding us and penetrating us, and the meditational practices or Path of how to climb *up* the worlds into the purely spiritual dimensions, Buddhi and Nirvāṇa, the Kingdom of God.

In the Old Testament this is symbolized by Jacob's ladder. In a vision, Jacob saw angels and perfected human beings ascending and descending this ladder (the Planes of Being).

The Work of the Mystery Schools and Āśramas is the expansion of Consciousness, alignment with one's own Higher Self, Spiritual Illumination, and service toward the Group Soul and the world, under the guidance of the Guru, the Hierophant, the Spiritual Master.

The Mystery Schools are the doors to the Temples of Initiation. They possess the Keys to Heaven and Hell—the knowledge of the Higher Worlds.

HIEROPHANTĒS
Greek: A person who reveals the Sacred Mysteries. A Guru, a Spiritual Teacher, the Head of a Temple or Spiritual School. From HIERO, "the Holy, the Sacred, the Mysteries", and PHAINEIN, "to show, to reveal, to expound".

Qualifications for Discipleship (Sanskrit)

1. VIVEKA
   Discrimination between the Real and the unreal, between the Self and the not-Self, between the Eternal and the transitory, between that of value and that which is only glamour, between Spirit and matter, between the Soul and the personality.

The true Mystery Schools originate on the Mental Plane

2. VAIRĀGYA
   Dispassion. Indifference to things that are of no real value or concern. Indifference to name and fame, to wealth and poverty, to success and failure, to the fleeting and temporary values of life. Non-attachment to one's possessions.

3. ŚAT-SAMPATTI
   The Six Virtues, Six Treasures, or Six Mental Qualifications:
   - ŚĀMA: control of the mind and thoughts.
   - DAMA: control of the senses, actions and conduct.
   - UPARATI: tolerance, patience, abstinence.
   - TITIKṢA: endurance, perseverance.
   - ŚRADDHĀ: faith, hope in success.
   - SAMĀDHĀNA: peace, mental equilibrium, poise, contentment.

4. MUMUKṢATVA
   Desire for Liberation or Freedom from Reincarnation. The longing for Nirvāṇa.

The Path to Discipleship

1. The Hall of Ignorance. The Physical Plane.

2. The Hall of Learning. The Astral Plane.

3. The Hall of Wisdom. The Mental Plane.

The true Mystery Schools originate in the Hall of Wisdom (the Mental Plane), where they have their seat.

The Brotherhood of Light 395

Monks and Disciples 991
Passion and Dispassion 695
Ṭarīqat: the beginning of the Path 831
To Enter the Way of the Warrior 1004
The Seven Qualities to enter Paradise 813

The Sacrifice of the Teachers

Just as a government pivots around a Premier, a Prime Minister or a President, and just as an orchestra is centred around a conductor, so the Spiritual Group has its centre, focus and pivot in the Teacher. Very few people understand what this means.

The Teacher carries on his shoulders the karmas of the group

The Teacher (the Hierophant or Guru) is the dominant energy field. Upon the Teacher the Life of the group depends. The Teacher is the source of the group—its Life, its teachings. More than that, the Teacher carries on his shoulders the karmas of the group. Wasn't Jesus the Christ crucified for the sins (karmas) of his followers? Think about this realistically. The Teacher is the great *sacrifice.*

Understand this well! The Teacher is super-sensitive. He receives into himself all the thoughts, feelings, emotions and physical karmas of the group members. Have you ever given this a thought? The result is that the Teacher has to burn up a lot of karmas on the emotional and mental levels, in his physical, astral and mental bodies. The result is that the Teacher can become sick. To be a Teacher is a *strain.*

We are talking here of those Teachers who are *in the world* and who have a group around them. This does not apply to the sādhus and svāmīs of the East who have no connection with anybody, no responsibility for anybody, no group, no disciples. Such people live a relatively stress-free life.

As a member of a Soul Group you have a twofold responsibility:

- Towards the Teacher.
- Towards the Group.

Your *attitude* towards your Teacher and your group is vitally important, for you, the group and the Teacher are *one*. You must understand that a Spiritual Group is a living organism, of which the Teacher is the Heart. In the old "pagan" Mystery Schools the Teacher was considered to be *sent by God* to gather up the disciples and prepare them for the journey back to the Source. And the Eastern Wisdom teaches that:

Even as the calf approaches the mother cow and the milk already starts forming in her udder, so, as the truly devoted pupil approaches his Teacher, already the rays of Wisdom are formulated in the Teacher's being to enlighten and teach his disciple.

Creating Karma 242
Where are your Wisemen? 387
The Sacrificial Lamb 680
Revelation is Continuous 1710

You might ask: Why doesn't the Teacher spend his time in quiet contemplation? Why does he get ruffled by the things going on around him? I repeat, the Teacher I am speaking of lives *in* the world but is not *of* the world. Furthermore, the Teacher is *super-sensitive* to the group life, as well as to the society around him.

The unruffled, serene, ever-happy sādhu, sannyāsin, svāmī or Piscean teacher is not of the world, nor does he live in the world. This is the Guru portrayed in the ancient Hindu textbooks, but those Gurus were *not in the world.* They had nothing to do with the struggle of life. They opted out; they escaped from life and spent their days in inward contemplation. That was the Piscean ideal of a Teacher.

The function of the Teacher in the West is so very different from that in the East

Yet there have always been Teachers who chose to be in the world and who suffered the consequences. Look at the life of Mahātma Gandhi, for instance, or Jesus the Christ, or Saint Francis of Assisi, or a host of others. All those Teachers who were in the world were sacrificed; they had problems and difficulties from society at large and from their own followers (the group). Very often they were betrayed, as Judas betrayed Jesus.

This is why most Teachers who lived in the world established an inner core-group of disciples. Jesus had his Twelve Apostles, for instance. This inner core-group of pupils is formed as a shield around the Teacher. They should be the most group-conscious and Teacher-conscious of all the group. The core-group people have a supreme responsibility towards the group and to the Teacher. They can help a lot in dealing with members' problems, with making sure that the group is pulling together and that the purity of the Teaching remains intact.

The function of the Teacher in the West is so very different from that in the East. In India, for instance, you would not dream of unloading your personality problems, your family or relationship problems or your work-hassles onto your Teacher. It is simply unthinkable! Yet, it is a common practice among Western students. In the West, the Guru has to be a psychologist, a psychiatrist, a social worker and a counsellor. In the East, the Guru is simply a Guru, *a Spiritual Teacher,* not a personality guide and helper. It is this endless dealing with personalities and personal interaction that makes life for a Western Spiritual Teacher in the New Age such a great stress and burden.

Warrior Jesus 908
Relational Consciousness 906
The Laws of Group Psychology 1384
Look out for the One 1004

The Approach to Truth

If you have no respect for your Teacher, Truth will never come to you

Whether you approach an ordinary teacher, a Guru or Spiritual Master, your inner Soul or the God within you, or whether you meditate for Enlightenment, the rule is the same: you must have an attitude of openness and reverence. Those Westerners who approach the Guru—the Master of Spiritual Life—with a huge ego, with an attitude of "I am smarter than you", learn nothing. If you have no respect for your Teacher, Truth will never come to you.

These two principles of *openness* and *reverence* are well understood in the East and have been practised for thousands of years. In the East, the Teacher has always been thought to be an Incarnation of God and hence is revered as such. It means that Easterners put their Gurus before anything else in their lives. This is incomprehensible to self-centred, mind-centred Westerners, especially the new-agers who consider themselves "independent" and that they "know it all". How far they are from Wisdom!

You must remember that a Spiritual Group is not just a physical organization; it has its own astral and mental bodies. It is the astral and mental bodies of the group that the Teacher continually has to balance up and keep together. The Teacher's concern is for the Group Life, the Group-Consciousness, not for the individual member. It is up to the individual to *fuse* himself or herself into the Group Mind.

The Group Heart

The Spiritual Group has a Heart, also. The Group Heart is composed of the Heart of the Teacher and all the other Hearts combined. The Group Heart is ever *growing* and *changing*. At every retreat, a *new impulse* is given by the Teacher, a fresh energy. *New Life* powers into the Group Heart from above, through the Teacher, a *new connection* to the Hierarchy and the Invisible Worlds. The Group Heart is always changing in its *relationship* to the Spiritual Hierarchy.

When the Heart is closed, then everything becomes static, stale and dead. While the Heart is changing, growth for the group members is possible. This ever-changing, ever-growing, ever-moving-on Group Heart must be *reflected* in the lives of the personalities within the group—*your* life!

These changes in the Group Heart are due to cosmic changes. The group unfoldment is a *Group Initiation* process taking place over a period of years. This means continuous change and new ways of doing things.

The Attitude for Yoga 558
Living Guidance 339
Already Enlightened? 341
Fear of being 'conditioned' 485
The Universal Heart 436

Sādhanā: the Spiritual Life

Upon the Path (Mārga) there are three things you must do:

a. Fulfil your Destiny (Dharma), whatever duties or commitments you have towards your family, work, relationships, and so forth.

b. Meditate regularly (Dhyāna).

c. Serve your Teacher, your group and the world unselfishly. This is called Seva (service).

Together, these three are called Sādhanā, the Spiritual Life. If you leave out any of these three things, you will fail in your quest.

If you leave out any of these three things, you will fail in your quest

You cannot *force* Enlightenment (Higher Consciousness) upon yourself. It must come of its own accord as you simultaneously fulfil these three steps. This is "being in the world but not of it".

It is said by the Wise that Sādhanā, or spiritual discipline and spiritual exercises (Kriyā), should not be practised for any benefits or motives. One should also abandon all expectations of results, and when results appear, one should not cling to them. For the Self is beyond all this.

Do the Work yourself

How wonderful it is that there are so many Revelations and Teachings from so many Masters and Teachers available today! And yet, so few read these wonderful Teachings, and of those who do, so few have the power to put them into practice.

I wish I could help people on a larger scale, but I cannot. All of these things are *available,* but people do not take advantage of them. People are so distracted with material living.

My message for you is this: Do not wait for the world to miraculously change to produce a better condition. *Do the Work yourself.* Be fanatical about your meditation. Be fanatical about service—that is, help as many people as you can. You cannot replace *your own efforts* towards your own Enlightenment, your own Realization, your own Divinization.

You must do the Work yourself, and the time to do it is *Now.*

The Work is always *Now*—never in some future life or in some future heaven after death.

The True Teachers 1694

Dharma 1408
Duty and Spirituality 1641
What is True Service? 1714
Expect Nothing 1205
Rely on your Inner Self 1226
To Succeed in your Quest 1330

Causes of Group Disruption

The Teacher brings in new ideals, new ideas, new methods from his Soul-Consciousness, or arranges old teachings and methods to suit the ever-upward-moving New Age of Aquarius. Because of the originality of his approach, the Teacher will often find resistance from his environment, from society, and sometimes even from group members.

The strength of a group is only the strength of its weakest individual

> The way in which the world treats a new truth is first to *ridicule* it, then to grow *angry* about it, and finally to *adopt* it and pretend that it always held that view. In the meantime, the first exponent of the new truth has probably been put to death, or died of a broken heart.
>
> *C.W. Leadbeater*

The causes of group disruption need to be understood, as they have been affecting religious and spiritual groups since 1875 (the beginning of the Aquarian Dispensation) and will affect all spiritual and religious groups in the future. The strength of a group is only the strength of its weakest link, its weakest individual.

> Strong vibrations from other planes are playing all the while upon our various vehicles [bodies], and those parts of us which can in any sense respond to them are thereby raised, strengthened, and purified. But there is another side to this. There may well be in each one of us some vibrations, the character of which is too far removed from the level of these great influences to fall in harmony with them, and where that is the case, *intensification* will still take place, but the result may well be evil rather than good.
>
> *C.W. Leadbeater*

A common problem is *vindictiveness,* meaning "seeking revenge, seeking retribution or punishment, inflicting punishment". This usually occurs in a group when a member does not get what he or she wants, or is not treated as a "special person", or is not extolled by the Teacher. So he or she gets annoyed, then angry, then leaves the group, but wants to pull the whole group down upon leaving, or "tear the place apart", or inflict damage upon the Teacher.

There is an old English saying:

> A beggar from the dunghill, once extolled, forgets himself.

The English word *extol* is from the Latin *extollere,* meaning "to lift up, to elevate, to praise", but also "to praise one too highly" or "to raise one to a position, status or privilege for which one is not suitable".

In other words, if you give too much privilege to people, after a while they will forget where they came from. Such people then become *spiritually proud* and begin to think they are *above* the Teacher, the

Teaching and the group. First they put themselves above some members of the group, then above the Teacher, and then above the whole group. It is at this point that such people leave a group.

Spiritual pride has been the downfall of many group members, in countless groups. These things happen to all spiritual groups and have to be understood so that group members do not become ruffled by such manifestations.

There is an old saying from the ancient Mystery Schools:

The main problem in groups is egos

> Adore, O my son, the good and great God of the Sages, and never allow yourself to become puffed up with spiritual pride. For He sends one of the Children of Wisdom your way to initiate you into their Order, and to make you a sharer in the wonders of His Omnipotence.

The main problem in groups is egos. Certain people always want power, position, privilege, status, authority. When they cannot get it, or not enough of it (according to their thinking), they become annoyed and stir things up by denouncing the Teacher or the group, or both, and then they leave. This hankering after "special status" within a group is a curse in group life and wrecks many a group dynamism. People do not want to be equals. People need to feel they are "special". This situation happens daily within groups.

Psychic Disruption

Disruption can enter into a group also from psychics who are tuning into the Astral Plane but not the Causal or Buddhic Planes. The seeker who begins to develop psychic powers, consciously or unconsciously, immediately puts himself or herself above the group and above the Teacher and begins to think that he or she is someone "special", chosen by the "ascended masters" or "archangels" or whatever.

Remember that astral consciousness, Causal Consciousness and Buddhic Consciousness are as different as the consciousness of a stone to a plant, a plant to an animal, or an animal to a man. A medium, psychic or channeller would not know what Causal Consciousness is, or what Buddhic Consciousness is, because he or she is limited to the Astral Plane and is reliant on astral entities for all things.

The Astral Plane is the realm of MĀYĀ—illusions, delusions and glamour. You can always tell when a person is "spooked" (surrounded by astral spirits); they have an unmistakable vibration about them, and illusions, delusions and glamour play a great part in their lives.

The New Atlantis 280
Overstimulation on the Path 557
Mystics of Pisces and Aquarius 836
Channelling or Soul-Wisdom? 327
Zen is not Psychism 757

The Evil of Criticism

There is an old saying:

> Take heed of critics, for they bite like fish at anything.

Criticism can destroy a Teacher or a group

A *critic* is "one who pronounces judgment over another person", from the Latin *criticus,* "one who censures". You see these critical people at work in political and religious groups, in racist groups, in art, science, or wherever. They disrupt group life and group coherence.

It is important to understand the evil function of criticism, to which all human beings are prone. To sit in judgment over another is a virulent poison for the group life, for group dynamism. This should be watched for at all times, for criticism can destroy a Teacher or a group. The Teacher has the responsibility to eject such persons from the group, lest they destroy the whole group.

Criticism is based on jealousies, thwarted ambitions, pride and sexual frustrations. Very few members in a group are free from this vice. They usually criticize the Teacher or leader and/or other members of the group. This is a *common human vice;* you see it especially in the political field, but it manifests strongly also in religious groups. Even people close to the Teacher or group leader are prone to criticize.

> Wisdom is a kindly Spirit, but will not free a critic from the guilt of his words, because God is a witness to the blasphemer's *innermost feelings,* and a true observer of his *heart,* and the hearer of his tongue.
>
> The Spirit of the Lord is filling up the whole world, and He who holds all things together *knows* what is said by the critic.
>
> Therefore, no one who utters the wrong things can escape justice; and justice, when it punishes, will not pass him by.
>
> *The Wisdom of Solomon*

You have two families:

- Your "blood" family (from which you inherited your physical body).
- Your spiritual family (the Soul Group you belong to).

It may be that one or more of your "blood" family belongs also to your spiritual family, or it may be that none of them do. It does not matter. It is important that you understand your *relationship* to both of your families and do your best for both.

Family and Duty 998

The Evil Mind 224
The Way of the World 380
Facing the Evil Mind 1087

Critics don't realize how damaging their criticism can be. *Criticism is a form of negative thought-energy.* It is very real. It can destroy mentally, emotionally, and even physically, the person who is being criticized. Don't forget that *thought-energy is real,* as real as electricity or magnetic energy, except that criticism is a negative thought-energy, intended to destroy the victim.

Furthermore, *negative entities* on the inner planes will move into the situation and very often the critic will become obsessed or possessed and will release great destructive forces into the group—forces which, at times, will annihilate the group altogether. This is how so many spiritual groups have perished.

Criticism destroys not only the person being criticized, but the critic also

What is more, whether the criticism is directed at the Teacher or at another member of the group, the Teacher, because of his psychic attunement with the group, will pay the price for it through physical, mental and emotional illness. A negative psychic storm can even precipitate the physical death of the Teacher or cause a major accident.

You should never criticize your Teacher, and you should avoid criticizing other members of your group also. You do not know how difficult it is for the Teacher to deal with everybody's karmas, frustrations and imbalances, which they project onto their Teacher and into the group, and which the Teacher still has to deal with on the astral and mental levels.

Much of this can be avoided by *loyalty*—loyalty to your Teacher and to your group, and putting self-interest and grievances aside for the sake of the larger Whole. If you hear criticism against the Teacher or against another member of the group, *remain silent,* and tell the critic to remain silent also. Otherwise your idle gossip will add more negativity to the already poisoned atmosphere and it will destroy you also. Remember the spiritual law that criticism destroys not only the person being criticized, but the critic also. If the group is wise, it will not fall into this common human trap, but will isolate the critic and, by *silence,* destroy the negativity.

Remember that a Spiritual Teacher is a natural absorber of energies, of people's karmas, problems and ill health on all levels, because the Teacher has to remain psychically open to all influences flowing from the group and from Humanity. So why make his task harder by adding your own little evil to the already large burden he has to carry?

Thought and Energy 349
Involuntary Possession 310
The Ten Mahāyāna Precepts 814

The Testing of the Soul

Even the Adepts and Masters have their tests, trials and tribulations

The so-called "laws of nature" described by science are but the Laws of the Cosmic Mind in this material part of Creation. The Laws of the Cosmic Mind apply throughout the Cosmos—from the subatomic particle to the most distant star, from the grossest material planet to the Light of Nirvāṇa and beyond. There is but one Infinite Intelligence stretching throughout Omnispace and ordering all space-time constructs to behave according to certain predisposed patterns. Breaking these patterns is what causes the experience of pain and suffering.

The Ancients have called these pains and sufferings by many names: temptations, tests, trials, tribulations, purifications, disentanglements, temperance, the testing of the Soul. Modern psychology calls them crises, neuroses, psychoses, mental illnesses, and so on. They are simply the conscious or unconscious breaking of the Laws of the Mind, the Laws of Nature.

These "tests" apply to all Humanity: the rich and the poor, the black and the white, the religionist and the agnostic, the communist and the capitalist, the American and the Chinese. They apply also to so-called spiritual seekers, aspirants, disciples, and those on the Path. Even the Adepts and Masters have their tests, trials and tribulations.

The Universal Intelligence 232
Why Life is Suffering 263
Tested by God and the Devil? 685
The Sūfī View of Mental Disorders 900

Scenes of Battle

KURUKṢETRA
Sanskrit: From KURU-KṢETRA, "the field of the KURUS". The battlefield of the Bhagavad-Gītā. A field called KURU, in ancient India, where a great battle was fought.

ARMAGEDDON
Ancient Hebrew: "Battlefield". From the Hebrew HARMEGIDDON (HAR, "mountain", and MEGIDDON, "the Valley of Megiddo"). In ancient Palestine there was a great battle fought in a mountain district called Megiddo, in Northern Palestine.

Although these two physical places are remembered for being the scenes of titanic battles in ancient times, in spiritual literature they refer to the Battle between the personality and the Soul—the Spiritual Crisis.

Crucifixion 721

The Tests of the Elements

The Element Earth (physical body)

The breaking down of your identification with the physical body and the Physical World reality. Physical sickness, illnesses, accidents, near-death experiences, death, lack of vitality, depletion of energies.

The Element Water (astral body)

The precipitation of emotional crises. The breaking up of psychological health and balance. Suicide, manic depression, schizophrenia, feelings of being in a "black hole", negative emotions, anger, hate, violence, separation from loved ones, anti-social behaviour, situations of isolation, separation, loneliness, a sense of abandonment.

The Element Fire (etheric body, life-force)

Mystical death and resurrection. The breaking up of your ego, the destruction of your sense of identity and self-image; a feeling of dying, a death wish, a wanting to give up or to end life; the sensation that life is futile, meaningless, not worth living; being sorry for yourself, self-pity; being frustrated with yourself, with life and with those around you.

The Element Air (mental body)

Mental crisis. Neurosis, psychosis, nervous breakdown, a feeling of going insane; the breakdown of your ideas, thoughts and convictions; revolutionizing your thoughts; the forceful changing of your opinions and ideas, values and judgments.

The Element Aether (causal body)

Spiritual crisis. The Battle of the Soul, the Kurukṣetra, the Armageddon, the Dark Night of the Soul, the descent into Hades or Amenti, the Judgment Day, the Hall of Judgment, the meeting of the Guardian at the Threshold, Initiation, Existential Crisis. The battle between the energies and tendencies of your personality and the reality of the Soul or Higher Self. The shifting of attention from the personality life to Soul Life.

The Cosmic Elements 26
The Personality Complex 36
Emotional Problems 1429
Crisis and Revelation 1711

The Four Stages of Spiritual Life (Arabic)

Using the terminology of the Sūfī tradition, there are four stages in the Spiritual Life:

1. SHARĪ'AT
2. ṬARĪQAT
3. MA'RIFAT
4. ḤAQĪQAT

The evolutionary level of the completely materialistic millions does not count

The evolutionary level of the completely materialistic millions, the completely worldly-minded who do not believe in God or anything spiritual, does not count. They are described as "dead" or "asleep".

Nor does intellectual "speculation", guesswork, philosophizing, comparing ideas for the sake of ideas, analysing the meaning of words, systems of "logic" or intellectual "waffling" count for anything. This includes the "rationalists" who ignorantly think they know the final Truth about things through their simple and erroneous "logical" minds; these people also are "dead" or "asleep".

The First Stage of Spiritual Life is SHARĪ'AT.

SHARĪ'AT is the complete and sincere belief and practice of the *outer* religious rites, ceremonies, customs, doctrines and teachings of orthodox religion, whether it be Jewish, Christian, Muslim, Hindu, Sikh, Buddhist, Taoist, Shinto (Japanese), or whatever. It also means obeying the external rules set up by the religious "authorities" of these religions. In the Piscean Age, practically *everybody* did this, and most people sincerely believed in it. Today, in the coming Aquarian Age, many hundreds of millions no longer believe in this or seriously practise their "faith".

The Second Stage of Spiritual Life is ṬARĪQAT.

ṬARĪQAT is the stage of discipleship, pupilship, seekership, when the orthodox religious doctrines, outer rituals, rites, ceremonies, moral codes and theologies are no longer satisfactory. You feel that the "religious authorities" do not know the Truth, that there are many inaccuracies and superstitions in the outer presentation of the religions, and that somehow the "authorities" are crystallized, fossilized, behind the times. You long for a deeper or more "esoteric" knowledge of Religion. You realize that the outer hair-splitting theologies are

The Radiant Way 830
The Journey of the Heart 855

a waste of time, that there must be some esoteric or deeper side to Religion. Thus, you start searching for Gurus, Spiritual Teachers and Masters—Shaikh (Arabic), Murshid (Arabic), Pīr (Persian)—who you feel know more about true Religion and the Spiritual Path.

At this stage of Spiritual Life the seekers or disciples of the Piscean Age practised severe forms of spiritual discipline with tremendous enthusiasm and fanaticism:

- Asceticism.
- Night vigils (staying up all night praying or remembering God's Presence).
- Silence.
- Seclusion or aloneness.
- Fasting.
- Continual Remembrance of God.
- Abandonment of the world, renouncing all things "worldly".

Today this stage has to be adapted to suit the modern seeker's needs

Today, as the Aquarian Age Vibration takes an increasing hold on Human Consciousness, this stage has to be adapted to suit the modern seeker's needs. In fact, if they want to survive, *all* the present religions on our planet will have to *adapt* to the new Aquarian Vibration. At this stage they are still pushing the old Piscean Way and practices and modalities. In our School we are aware of the new Cosmic Impulses and have adapted this second stage to fit in with the need of *today*.

The Third Stage of Spiritual Life is Ma'rifat.

This is the stage when, as a result of the purification of your Heart and the processes of meditation, you are having *direct experiences*, first-hand Knowledge, mystical states, visions, insights, transformational processes, inner revelations, intimations of Immortality, states of Unitive Awareness, and so forth.

The Fourth Stage of Spiritual Life is Ḥaqīqat.

This stage has many parts, divisions and sub-stages, as you grow from perfection to perfection. The final stage of Ḥaqīqat is the complete Union with the Supreme Being, Al-Ḥaqq, the Truth or Absolute Reality, the true Self-Nature of all things, the Foundation of the Cosmos, the Eternal, the One.

The Sūfī Master 832
The Influence of the Seven Rays 834
The New and Eternal Way 516
The Sūfī God 838

Crises on the Path

The Four Stages of Spiritual Life are there always, but how they are *practically* worked out changes from Age to Age (if Humanity could respond correctly). The Piscean Age response was different from the coming Aquarian Age response.

Each stage of the Path has its point of tension or crisis

Just as each Age has its *crisis* in Spiritual Development, each stage of the Path has its *point of tension or crisis*. If you are a follower of the Way, you must know this; it will help you through.

The First Crisis

The first crisis is moving from the *dead* materialistic-consciousness to the lowest form of religious life (the First Stage of Spiritual Life). You can hear countless examples of this in Christian communities, for instance, of people being "converted" by the fundamentalists or evangelicals. They say, "I have been lost, now I am found, because now I *believe* in Jesus Christ, who died for my sins, and now I am saved." They become "believers". You would find similar situations in all the religions: *emotional conversion.*

The Second Crisis

The next point of tension or crisis comes when the common, orthodox, fundamentalist or evangelical religious ideas, or "faith", no longer satisfy you. Then you move into the Second Stage of Spiritual Life, the Way of the Disciple or Seeker, which is the first stage of Inner Life. This is perhaps the most important stage, where there are the greatest number of *failures,* or people "falling back".

Following the Aquarian Way, you have found a *Teacher*, you have found a *Teaching*, and you have found a *Group*. The second stage of your Spiritual Journey begins. So you start your work with this Teacher, Group and Teaching. You go to classes, workshops, retreats. The years roll by. The first few years have a tremendous impact on you; you feel that you have "found" yourself, you have found your brothers and sisters on the Way, and you have found an Old Friend (the Teacher). Life is finally *meaningful* for you. The years roll on.

Belief and Experience 676
Faith and Wisdom 849
What is True Faith? 1284
Jesus the Personal Saviour? 678

The Path is both a Journey and a Process. The Teacher moves on (Journey) dragging the group behind him (Process). After about five or ten years, you begin to become *saturated*. You cannot take any more of the *changes* of the Journey or the *energies* of the Process.

If you are wise, you look into yourself and *rededicate yourself* to the Spiritual Path, knowing that all is well, that tests and trials are part of your Journey.

So many people drop out of the Spiritual Life at this second stage

If you are not wise, you start *complaining*. Suddenly, everything the Teacher does is wrong and the group members are awful. You feel that you are "misunderstood", that people are not "respecting" you as they should, because you are "special" or "advanced", and better than the Teacher. Your *humility* is fast disappearing, and you reach the crisis point of the Second Stage of Spiritual Life.

At this stage, if you are *not* wise, you may do any of the following:

- You leave the group quietly, citing as an excuse your need to attend to worldly matters, such as your family, job or relationship.
- You leave the group in a big huff after arranging a big showdown so that everybody takes note of you, and you are the "talk of the town". Then, after having left, you feel extremely sorry for yourself and blame the Teacher and the group for your sufferings!
- You stay in the group, making an absolute nuisance of yourself, continually complaining.
- You drop out of the group, then a few years later rejoin the group and pretend that nothing has happened, expecting everything to be the same as when you became *frozen* or *stuck* on your Journey!

This is *falling back*. You have not completed even the Second Stage of the Spiritual Life. In the meantime, the Teacher has moved on, the group has moved on, the Teaching has moved on, and you are getting very far *behind*. So many people drop out of the Spiritual Life at this second stage.

Suppose you decide not to get "stuck in the mud" at this stage (in spite of the "faults" of everybody else!). If you *persevere* with your Spiritual Life, you will discover that the problem is actually within yourself—that, in fact, you *are* the problem.

You Alone are Responsible 258
To Succeed in you Quest 1330
The Principle of Choice 1380
Persevering to the End until Final Liberation 1101

The Third Crisis

As you persevere, you will arrive at the Third Stage of Spiritual Life. You begin to have direct spiritual experiences in your Heart, which *validate* for you the Teacher and the Teaching. You grudgingly admit that the Teacher might know something after all! However, you still might have a problem *accommodating the group* in your life.

When you succeed in your practice, you might begin to feel other-worldly

In this Third Stage of Spiritual Life you will have another crisis, another tension point, even greater than the previous one. When you succeed in your practice, you might begin to feel other-worldly, or *not in this world.*

During the Piscean Age, in all religions, the Mystics and Saints became "blissed out" or "spaced out" in extraordinarily large numbers. They become *intoxicated* by the Wine of Ecstasy, interior Bliss-Consciousness, Illumination, the feeling of Divine Love in the Heart, the proximity of the Beloved (God), Communion with God, Internal Stillness and non-activity, Celestial Bliss, the Vision of Spiritual and Radiant Worlds. They were overcome by the sheer Mysteries of the Divine Light and the Worlds of Light, Spiritual Consciousness, the Voice of the Beloved, the Sweep of the Eternal Law, the Divine Majesty and Radiant Power. The experiences were so overwhelming that these Sūfīs, Mystics, Saints, became *disconnected* from this world. They became the Mastānaḥ, the God-intoxicated.

Mastānaḥ
Persian: The God-intoxicated. From the Persian Masti, "being drunk". Those who are continually in a trance, having lost connection with the physical body and the world. They have totally rejected the world and the Path of Service, and spend their time in Inner Intoxication with Bliss-Consciousness.

Balance in Spiritual Life 505
God's Fools 1392

What you must not do:

1. You must not bring your personality problems into the group work situation. This is a favourite pastime for group members, but it is extremely destructive for the Group Life. You release your personality problems or issues into the group and the group members *amplify* it by being "concerned" about it and "discussing" it (a favourite method nowadays is email). You have no idea how much damage that does to the Group Energy-Field, and to the Energy-Field of the Teacher, who is tightly linked to the Group Energy-Field.
2. You must not bring emotional, mental or psychological problems to group work. This is also very popular with ignorant group members. A Spiritual Group is not a mental hospital! It is natural for people who suffer from some mental or emotional imbalance to seek help. But, to step onto even the Second Stage of the Spiritual Life, you must be a reasonably integrated personality.

If you come to this stage, you will feel that the world is meaningless and a "waste of time", that Humanity is incredibly stupid, and that the worldly consciousness is extraordinarily dense (which, from that perspective, it is). And here is your crisis: What to do with the world? Or rather, what to do with your *perception* of the world?

Alternately, some disciples who glimpse this stage become *frightened*, and that fright throws them back into the world. They fall back into the worldly consciousness with a vengeance, very often back to the First Stage of Spiritual Life, returning to orthodox, fundamentalist or evangelical Islām, Christianity or Judaism.

What to do with your perception of the world?

The crisis is that either you become blissed-out-of-your-mind (literally) or you become frightened-out-of-your-mind. You have to choose the Middle Path, the Middle Way, the Middle Point, and that balance has to do with *the right use of your mind.*

The Fourth Crisis

There is a further crisis for Those who are established in the Fourth Stage of Spiritual Life, who begin to glimpse Unutterable Cosmic Mysteries, who begin to touch upon Boundless Cosmic Life and are *rewarded* with the Powers of the Universe. But, for you, the time is not yet.

Between the Two Extremes, Find the Middle Point 1100
Crisis and Revelation 1711

The Fields of Life (the Great Breath)

Who am I? That is your first question.

1. The first Field of Life is *yourself*. Who are you? Are you merely your physical body, your aches and pains, your memory, habits, feelings and thoughts? Who are you?
2. The second Field is your *family*. Where do you come from? Who is your family? What is your family? Are they a group of bodies, habits, traditions and customs? Or, are they something more? Souls, perhaps?
3. The third Field is your *environment*, your workplace, your colleagues, the people you earn your "money" with, your friends and acquaintances, your neighbours. Who are they?
4. The fourth Field is your *nation*, the country where you were born, the group of Souls who compose your physical nationality, language, customs, traditions and "culture".
5. The fifth Field is planet *Earth*. Are you aware of Her? Are you aware of that Cosmic Spirit in whose physical body you live and are nourished?
6. The sixth Field is the *Solar System*. Do you know that you are living as an atom in the body of the Sun, the Solar Logos?
7. The seventh Field is the *Universe*, the total embodiment of the Life of God.

Notes on the Spiritual Path in the New Age

Mental Activity 1228
The Action of the Cosmic Fire 279
Planetary Disturbance 1697
Karmic Adjustment 1379
Overstimulation on the Path 557
Malfunctioning Cakras 53

- Generally speaking, human beings are mentally stressed, emotionally overstimulated and physically diseased. This is the case even before they begin the Spiritual Path.
- This is a time of great opportunity for spiritual growth and development. Since 1875 the planet's vibrations have been speeding up, resulting in great changes in human consciousness and great stress on human emotions. Due to the extra influx of energies from the Cosmos into our planetary system, human beings, as a whole, are overstimulated. This stimulation of the planet by extra-solar-systemic energies causes distress in human families, in personal life and in relationships. This results in speedier lifestyles, pent-up emotions, mental stress, mental breakdowns and a general sense that one cannot cope with life.
- There is a crisis of development taking place inside our whole Solar System, which also affects our planet Earth. People react to this new stimulation of energies in one of two ways:
  a. The majority react automatically, reactively, blindly.
  b. A small minority see this stimulation as an opportunity for effort towards Enlightenment and embark upon the Spiritual Path.
- For the spiritual disciple, the new energies mean a quicker release of past karmas, which means meeting the karmic forces head on. Karmas that would normally take many lifetimes to work out are worked out in a few years. The life of the disciple becomes even more intense than those of the overstimulated masses. One lives, as it were, many lives in one lifetime.
- An overstimulated person can be a danger to his or her group (any group), since that person can become fixated on one thought, one idea, one event or one feeling, to the exclusion of all else, and no longer sees things in perspective. Such a person will then cause trouble for himself or herself and disruption in the group. A person who is fixated along one direction of thought, which dominates his or her mind, has a serious psychological and mental problem.
- When you feel that you have made some progress on the Spiritual Path, there will be a tendency for you to isolate yourself, hence placing yourself above others.

Overstimulation

As a result of the new energies, the cakras in the human system become overstimulated, resulting in blockages, congestion or wild activity. People become more and more out of tune with their environment.

The mental body becomes overstimulated, which can lead to:
- Fanaticism or fundamentalism.
- Mental breakdown.

The astral body becomes overstimulated, leading to:
- Uncontrolled anger, hate or depression.
- Mediumship and psychism.

The physical body becomes overstimulated, leading to:
- Restlessness, sleeplessness, overwork.
- An inability to sit still and meditate.

- It is important that you remain continually *grounded.* If you get out of touch with your environment, your environment will turn against you. You will encounter psychological conflicts with those immediately around you. You will also experience nervous problems, which are the physical body's reaction to stress. When you live solely in your mental world, you will become anti-social, anti-group.
- As you make progress on the Path, you may receive opposition from your family, friends or colleagues, from society around you, or from fundamentalist religious groups.
- Conflicts can arise within you when the energies of the Soul pour down into your personality during meditation, ritual, chanting, and so forth, and the personality does not feel up to it because of its slower natural vibrations. So you feel that you are failing in your spiritual life and effort.
- In Spiritual Life you need common sense, a sense of proportion, realism and good humour. If you overdo your meditations or spiritual effort, you can have a breakdown or a sense of frustration, or become continually preoccupied with your personality's reactions.
- If you are progressing well, another danger is that you "bliss-out" or "flip out", or become so transcendental that you cannot relate properly to those around you.

In Spiritual Life you need a sense of proportion, realism and good humour

The Double Stress of Meditational Life 1181
Obstacles on the Path of Meditation 1205

Every condition has its own cause and its own cure.

Difficulties which can arise when Practising the Path while living in the World

Physical Imbalances

- Overactivity on the Physical Plane, such as excessive work habits or an overly complex lifestyle.
- Being indolent and lazy, with no desire to achieve anything.
- Sleeplessness.

Opposition from the Astral Plane

- Negative astral forces and currents.
- Negative astral entities who want to destroy the work you are doing and prevent you from attaining Higher Consciousness.

Karmic Difficulties

- Physical karmas. A weak or sick body, handicaps, ill-health, diseases, and so forth.
- Astral karmas. Emotional problems, inability to check negative feelings or moods.
- Mental karmas. An unruly mind, prejudice, crystallization of thinking, inability to grasp truth, and so on.

Glamour

- The glamour of a big ego.
- The illusion of psychic powers.
- The "I am holier than thou" stage of the Path.

Diseases caused by walking upon the Spiritual Path

Kuṇḍalinī

When the Kuṇḍalinī-Śakti is awakened, either purposefully as in Kuṇḍalinī Yoga or Śakti-Pāta (energy-transference), or unconsciously as in intense devotion, prayer or chanting, it rises up from the Base Centre. It can *overstimulate* the Base Centre, producing extreme restlessness, extreme physical activity, burning sensations, nervous agitation, the experience of being on Fire. As the Kuṇḍalinī ascends to the next centre, the Sex Centre, it overstimulates the Sex Centre, causing out-of-control sexual energies and an intense sex-drive. When the Kuṇḍalinī ascends to the Solar Plexus Centre it causes *extreme* ego-drives, power-mania, the manipulation of others, the feeling of being invincible, that all things are possible.

The Three Gates to God 151
The Ascent of Kuṇḍalinī 152
Seek not Powers 581
Kuṇḍalinī and Alchemy 153
Experiencing the Awakening Heart 463
Wounds of Love 699

Kuṇḍalinī may also open the awareness to the psychic dimension (the Astral World). Kuṇḍalinī also produces many siddhis (occult and psychic powers), for which the yogīs practise Kuṇḍalinī Yoga. These *hinder* you on the Spiritual Path.

On the positive side, if the Kuṇḍalinī successfully reaches the Crown Centre it will evoke the Descending-Spirit and thus cause Continuous-Consciousness.

The First and Second Aspects

Another set of diseases my come when, through intense prayer, meditation and chanting, you connect with the Second Aspect of the Deity (the Viṣṇu or Christ Aspect). In this case, your physical, etheric, astral and mental bodies may be overstimulated by the Energies coming from your Soul, the Causal Worlds or the Buddhic Planes.

The Descending-Force of the First Aspect of the Deity (the Father or Śiva Aspect) can also cause havoc in the inner subtle bodies, and the Bright Light may cause head pains.

The Kuṇḍalinī-Śakti is part of the Third Aspect of the Godhead (the Holy Spirit or Brahmā). Kuṇḍalinī is the Female part; Fohat is the Male.

Kuṇḍalinī is Fiery Energy.

Fohat is Electrical Energy.

Both work *in* matter and *through* matter.

Dimensions of the Cosmic Fire 137
Kuṇḍalinī-Fohat 148

The Desert Condition

Another common condition on the Spiritual Path is what is known as fatigue, aridity or the desert condition. This is a psychological disease, manifesting as a general state of tiredness, which comes about through *making much effort* on the Spiritual Path. It may last for days, months or years. You persevere. You go on!

Disease and Karma

If you are *in touch* with your Soul, the Soul will maintain your general health (in the mental, astral, etheric and physical bodies)—*except* those diseases which are due to your own personal Karma or the mass-Karma of Humanity. It is not possible to have a totally disease-free life, due to karmas that *need to be precipitated* onto the Physical Plane. For instance:

It is not possible to have a totally disease-free life

- Planetary Karma, affecting Humanity on a large scale. Examples are colds, influenza epidemics, attacks by bacteria and viruses, heart diseases, cancer, tumours, and so on.
- Astrological Influences. People born under different Signs have *tendencies* towards certain diseases through their Sun Signs and Ascendents. This involves millions of people in each Sign. (These are due to cosmic maladjustments.)
- Family Karma. These are weaknesses and predispositions you have inherited from your family, which can lead to physical, emotional or mental illnesses.
- Your own personal points of weakness, from *your* past, which can lead to physical, emotional or mental ill-health.

Thus, you will see that there is no quick and easy solution for the elimination of all diseases.

The main Karma you are influenced by is Planetary Karma; then the Karma of Humanity itself (because you are a human being); then the Karma of your race or nation; then the Karma of your family; and finally your own personal Karma. This means that many of the things that happen to you in your life are caused by factors other than you.

Karma is action and reaction, the reaction being the cause of further action. This is endless. You may view Karma as the hidden forces or influences that bring about the events in your life. Free will is limited to what your karmas allow you to experience. On your Spiritual Path it is important to liberate yourself from those lower karmas which bind you to the Three Worlds.

Suffering is the result of "bad" Karma, that is, breaking the Law of Nature on the physical, emotional or mental levels. That is why we have physical, emotional or mental diseases. This refers not only to you personally, but to the whole human race.

Karma and your Spiritual Development 255

Health and Fire 50
Types of Karma 243
Destined by the Stars? 260
Karmic Adjustment 1379
Action (Karma) 1402

Solitude and Loneliness

The Spiritual Group has a Heart which is Love and a Head which is Wisdom

What is the difference between loneliness and Solitude? Loneliness is when you feel yourself *separated* from people. You can feel "lonely" amidst a group of people or even with your family. Whence is this separation? In the early stages it stems from a closed Heart Centre. When your Heart is wide open, however, you "flow in" with the people around you—that is, if the people are on the *same level* as you.

There is another type of loneliness which results from the Journey of the Heart. When you step upon the Spiritual Path and begin to move inwards towards your Soul and the inner worlds, and if your partner, children, family and friends remain on the outside (that is, they are not making the Journey with you), you will feel separated from them, or "lonely". Your vibration will become noticeably *different* from theirs. What are you going to do? It is then that you will understand the need for the Spiritual Group. A Spiritual Group is a group of Living Souls, not of personalities. This group link is eternal. If you feel that you belong to a Spiritual Group you will never feel lonely, since the Souls in your group are journeying with you upon the same Path.

You must love your family, even if they are not journeying with you. But you must also have your Heart in your group, in the Group Heart, and you will be strengthened and comforted. For the Spiritual Group has a Heart which is Love and a Head which is Wisdom. The Teacher embodies the Heart and the Head. On the Soul level, your life is Group Life.

I do not expect my "blood" family nor my spiritual family to understand me. I have a Global Consciousness, that is to say, embracing the Family of Man. When you "think" globally, very few people can understand you or relate to you, for in their minds they interpret everything along the lines of "blood" family, tribalism or nationalism, and sometimes even a little along the lines of the Group or spiritual family!

For me, the Group itself is a part of something much larger, the Family of Man, and larger still, the Family of Adepts (the Spiritual Hierarchy), and the Family of Life, which is Śamballa, the Custodians of the Plan for the Evolution of Mankind and the other Kingdoms of Life.

The Christ-Hierarchy and Śamballa 396

Family and Duty 998
The Group Heart 1152

Loneliness of the Enlightened

There is a further kind of loneliness: the Loneliness of the Enlightened (KAIVALYA). The further you climb the Spiritual Mountain, the fewer people you will find of your own "kind". People will not understand you, nor recognize you, nor will they have affinity for your Inner State or Condition. They will not know "where you are coming from".

Before Jesus left the Earth-plane, He said to his disciples, "I am going back to my Father's Place." And they said, "Master, can we come with you?" And He replied, "Where I go you cannot come, but I will prepare a place for you." This is a type of Spiritual-Loneliness on the personality level. An analogy would be a genius who is outstanding in a particular field, but none of his friends, relatives or acquaintances have any appreciation of it. It is being above the masses of Humanity in your Interior State or Condition. That is KAIVALYA.

In Solitude you listen to the Voice of the Soul, the Soundless Sound

Isolation

Another condition is *isolation*. This is a condition where you prefer to be alone, to work alone and live alone, to follow your own Path alone, to be a loner. At the beginning of the Path this may be all right, but near the end you must embrace the Unity of Life.

Solitude

What then is Solitude? Solitude is when you *purposefully* withdraw yourself from people in order to focus on your Soul Development, such as intense meditation or Inner Quest. This is a *temporary* separation from people, and it is *not* loneliness.

To experience Solitude you find a quiet spot at home or in Nature, or in some isolated place, and there you *let go* of the world. Solitude will nourish your Soul and regenerate your personality, but it must be Spirit-oriented, an Inner Search. If you just sit there "doing nothing", without purpose, then it is simply idleness, laziness. In Solitude you listen to the Voice of the Soul, the Soundless Sound. You listen to the Cosmic Heartbeat within your Heart. In Solitude, Grace flows into you from above and you become strong and vibrant.

Alone with God 700
Being Alone with the Absolute 502
You are Alone on this Way 939
The Silence of the Deep 1355
Silence, Solitude, Peace 1386

Going Back to the Marketplace

The World is your Marketplace

1

Remain Flexible and Open

If you live with the sense of Unity with the All, then all things are possible

Every day is a new day. Every thought is a new thought.

Society runs on routine, habit-patterns of thoughts, feelings and actions. This routine or habit-ridden lifestyle makes the mental body (the thinking principle) small, narrow, lifeless, grey. It is important that you have total *flexibility* and *openness* in every aspect of your life: thoughts, feelings and actions; in relationships, situations and events.

2

Remember Group Unity

There is a Power that makes all things new. It lives and moves in the Hearts of those who live in the Eternal.

So says an ancient Eastern mantram. If you live with the sense of *Unity* with the All, then *all things are possible.*

3

Use the Powers of the Five Elements

Water always wants to *sink down* to the lowest level, and there to *stabilize* and *rest*. It wants to find the *easiest way out* in all situations.

Fire *transforms* things. It always aspires to *reach upwards* towards the heights.

Air wants to be *free*, to move around *unhindered*, everywhere and at all times.

Earth wants to be still, solid, firm, unshaken, unmoving, unchanging.

Aether always just *Is*, Omnipresent, everywhere.

Conditioned Thinking 1084
The Eternal is One 512
The Cosmic Elements 26

CHAPTER 51

The Science of Meditation

In Search of Reality

Meditation is a quest for the Real, the Imperishable, the Eternal One

Meditation is a search for Reality. Because Reality is not understood, however, meditation is not understood. This New Age of Aquarius is an extremely materialistic age; therefore, even meditation has been twisted into a quest for material progress.

Meditation, in truth, is a quest for the Real, the Imperishable, the Eternal One. Reality has been called Divinity, the Self-Existent One, the Godhead, the Immutable, or PURUṢOTTAMA (the Highest Being).

The Eternal Reality is beyond thought; therefore, in your meditation you must reach the thought-less state (UNMANI), beyond the mind. Your mind must by neutralized, dissolved (MANOLAYA) and made inactive (MANONĀŚA). Your mind must be made all harmonious and tranquil (SAMĀDHI). It is only then that Reality appears to your Inner Gaze as the Luminous Light-Being which is within All, and which is your very Self.

Be careful when you use the words God, Father, Son, Holy Ghost, Christ, Buddha, Krishna, Rāma, Devī, and so forth, to describe Reality. These words have been "humanized", "anthropomorphized", invested with human qualities, with human vices, imperfections and characteristics. The forms and mythologies invented by humans to try to grasp the nature of Reality are but feeble attempts by the ignorant to explain the Real to other ignorants. Use these words in the true sense of Reality.

The worst of these human inventions is that God can get angry, is vengeful, and puts people into everlasting hell and suffering. Whosoever invented this myth has obviously not *experienced* Reality (the Godhead). The ignorant populace follows blindly like sheep. They all fall into the pit of Darkness.

Mythical Concepts of God 104
Can God be Angry? 106
The Sūfī God 838
The Gnostic Teachings 1108

The Old Testament Jews often spoke of the "Living God". The early Christian Gnostics spoke of the "Living Jesus". Others spoke of the "Living Truth". What do they mean by the word *living?*

Truth is a universal, living Presence, which cannot be contained in a book, nor in an organization, nor in a philosophy, nor in a religion. But it can be *experienced inwardly* by direct spiritual perception.

Christian Science Teachings

This direct, spiritual perception is meditation.

What is Reality?

Reality is a Conscious-Light, a Stupendous Light-Being, a Being of Immeasurable Splendour, a Light Transcendent yet Immanent. This is *not* an inanimate light like electricity; this Being is Consciousness Itself, Life Itself, All-Knowingness, All-Glory, All-Power. This is the true sense of the word *God*, of NIRVĀṆA, of ĀTMĀ (ĀTMAN). This is the true Spiritual Sun, the true Sun-Light, the Light that shines in the Darkness and the Darkness comprehends it not.

Wheresoever you look, there is the Heart of God

Reality is Pure Being, Pure Consciousness, Universal-Conscious-Light-Being, Inconceivable Glory, all Potentiality to manifest an infinite number of Universes, Omniscient Majesty, Omnipresent-Becoming, Eternity, Infinity, a Formless Form, Universal Will-Power, Timeless Intelligence.

Reality is an Imperishable Person of measureless magnitude, an Eternally-Awake Consciousness beyond human understanding.

Reality is Conscious Blissful Immortality.

Reality is Perpetually Undisturbed Peace.

Reality is Immeasurable Intensity.

Reality is Absolute Intense Livingness.

Reality is Absolute Equilibrium and Delicate Poise of all Universal Powers and Potentialities.

Reality is Self-Conscious Wakefulness, a Burning Aliveness, a Fiery Livingness, an Eternal Sense of Now.

Reality-Nirvāṇa-Ātman-God is the Centre within the All and through the All. It is the Heart of All, the HṚDAYAṀ. Wheresoever you look, there is the Heart of God.

Nirvāṇa! 94
What is 'God'? 108
The Experience of the Heart 1280
The Self-Generating Light 1594
The One 1686

Entering the Lost Kingdom

God is within us.

God is Love within our Hearts, Wisdom in our Minds.

The Inner Way is Stillness, without thinking, imagining or images.

The human being has the capacity to become absorbed in God

The human being has the capacity to *become* God, that is, to become *absorbed* in God.

The Power of God is within us. This can change all things.

The Kingdom of God is within us. This is the Original Imperishable Light, beyond the Heaven Worlds.

The Living Spirit is within us, which is Active Grace. This is active throughout the whole personality.

∞

The Lost Radiance

How far Humanity has sunk into the quagmire of materialism! There are "learned" people in the West, with university degrees, who claim that meditation is simply a relaxation exercise and that you don't need Religion to practise it. If you are spiritually "dead", then I suppose you don't need Religion, but then you don't need meditation either, since the objective of meditation, or prayer, is the direct Realization of the Goal of Religion, the Divine in Man and in the Universe—not as a theory, a guess, a speculation or a hypothesis, but as a *fact*.

There are also misguided people who twist Religion for worldly ends, for purely political purposes. They also are spiritually "dead" and are not religious at all.

What is missing from Human Consciousness is Radiance—Radiance in the Heart and Radiance in the Head.

The Law of Radiation 175

God in the Heart 634
What is Wisdom? 1685
The Kingdom of God 1715
Regain what you have Lost 381
Religion and Politics 513
Yoga and Religion 527

Peace is to be found by Resting *in* God, which is Realizing the Presence of God in the Heart and in the Mind (through the Third-Eye and Crown Centres). Divine Consciousness is in the Heart Centre; Divine Splendour is in the Crown Centre; Divine Light is in the Third-Eye. The Heart also contains the Spirit of God.

The Higher Mind, the mind united with the Soul, is the means to *see* God and to witness the Eternal Splendour within all things. Interior Illumination comes when the ordinary mind and the Heart have become purified, and when some of the impressions of past events have been neutralized. Then God *shines*.

The Way is found by going within ourselves

The Way is found by going *within* ourselves, transcending the physical body, the ordinary mind and the emotions. This Way is known as *Meditation*. You learn to *silence* the activities of the body, emotions and mind-stuff (the lower mind). At first, Silence appears to be empty, meaningless. Later on, we recognize it to be very creative and transforming in our lives.

Materialism can temporarily halt spiritual progress, but ultimately it cannot defeat the Human Soul's desire to Know Itself and discover the Mystery of the Universe. The human being will remain restless and searching until the final Mystery is found within the Soul. Then it will find Peace at last. Thus, you must enter the Lost Kingdom within yourself in deep meditation and find the Lost Word of God, the Final Mystery.

To Achieve Liberation

If you want to achieve Liberation in this lifetime (JĪVAN-MUKTI), you must solve three riddles:

- The Mystery of your identification with your physical body (DEHĀTMA).
- The Mystery of your ego-sense (AHAṀKĀRA).
- You must neutralize the impressions from the past (VĀSANĀ, SAṀSKĀRA).

Then, what remains is ĀTMAN, the Spirit, the Self-Existent Self which you are. These Mysteries cannot be solved by thinking, theorizing or philosophizing, nor by religious faith or dogma, nor by theology or metaphysics, nor by any activity of the mind. These Mysteries can be solved only by going *beyond the mind* in deep meditation.

What is Consciousness? 1368

The Experience of Mysticism 636
Tapas: Spiritual Purification 571
Saṁskāra and Vāsanā 251
Subconscious Renewal 1236
Obstacles to Higher Consciousness 1424

Quest for Reality

Nirvāṇa-Reality-God penetrates all things: the physical universe, the subtle worlds and the subtlest realms. When you are in Nirvāṇa there is nothing else: this world does not exist, the subtle worlds do not exist, the subtlest realms are not. When you are out of Nirvāṇa, *multiplicity* appears: the body appears, the mind appears, the ego appears. In Nirvāṇa you are Divine; out of Nirvāṇa you are human.

It is your Destiny to rebecome a Child of God

This world is relative reality, temporal reality, because everything is continually changing and passing away. There is no stability here. The invisible worlds are semi-permanent semi-realities because they last longer, and life within them lasts longer, but they too succumb to PRALAYA (Dissolution) at the end of the KALPA (a designated evolutionary period).

Only PARABRAHMAN (the Godhead) is real, because it is AKṢARA (immutable, imperishable, immobile, everlasting, unchanging). Meditation is the seeking for *That* (TAT). The Realization of *That* through direct experience is the goal of meditation and the goal of human life—to become imperishable, immortal, eternal.

Do not think that Questing for the Absolute (SAT, Reality) is far-fetched or impossible. It is your *Destiny*.

It is your Destiny (DHARMA) to rebecome a Child of God. In Essence we are all gods and goddesses, Children of God. Our lives are, in truth, Cosmic Life. We already are Citizens of the Cosmos. The limitations of the physical body do not affect the Freedom of the Spirit (ĀTMAN) within you.

Illumination is our birthright.

Illumination is Soul-Light, Spirit-Light. We all carry this already, deep within ourselves. The Light of Reality is steadily irradiating the Spirit within us all the time.

The Two Realities 97
The Transcendental Godhead 112
The Ultimate Reality is the Meaning of Life 526
The Way, the Truth and the Life 670
Destiny (Dharma) 1407
The Essence of Wisdom 1680

Return to Primeval Happiness

The crucial reason for human suffering is that human beings do not know they are Ātman (Imperishable, Timeless, Boundless Spirit), that they are Brahman (the Ultimate Reality). This Unknowing is Avidyā, Ajñāna (the Spiritual Darkness of Ignorance). The purpose of meditation is Ātmā-Bodha (the Realization of yourself as the Self or Immortal Spirit).

Your true Self-Nature exists in a state of Eternal Consciousness of Bliss

The Universe is cyclic. A period of Manifestation, or Creation and Evolution, is called Manvantara. A period of Dissolution and rest from all action (non-manifestation) is Pralaya. So, likewise, your Soul comes into incarnation and then returns to the Unmanifest.

Attachment (Rāga) to worldly things brings only temporary happiness, as all objects and situations are perishable and come to an end. Peace of mind you will not find until you have dissolved your mind in the Bliss of Reality (Ātmānanda).

Your true Self-Nature, which is Ātman (the Breath or Spirit of God), is ever bodiless, hence forever free of pain, disease, death or decay. It exists in a state of Eternal Consciousness of Bliss (Sat-Cit-Ānanda). The goal of meditation is to *know* yourself as *That.*

You are Ātman (the Limitless Being) even now, and you always have been. What is preventing your *practical* experience of this Truth is the *ego.* Your ego is an artificial construct made up by your mind—your thoughts about yourself, your *image* of yourself. When you can give up that illusory image, you will be Absolute, in the Here and Now.

The Innermost Self, your true Nature, is inherently Blissful (Ānanda). Therefore, as you go deeper and deeper in your meditation, you will spontaneously experience more and more joy, happiness, felicity and elation in your life. The Way of Meditation is a return to Primeval Happiness (Ādi-Ānanda).

Ēgō
Latin: "I" or "I am" (ego-sum). The original meaning is the Absolute Spiritual Self or "I AM", the Monad, the Spiritus (Latin), the Divinity in Man. Later on, it also came to mean the Soul, the Animā (Latin), which is within the body and beyond the mind. Nowadays, the word ego refers to the personal self, the Persona (Latin: the mask), the personality or body-conscious "I", the unreal "I", the false sense of self.

The Mask 38
Who is 'I AM'? 1418

Meditation Degenerated

Many business executives recognize the need to meditate and often do Transcendental Meditation or relaxation-response to "relax muscular tension" or "overcome executive stress". To meditate only for such mundane purposes, however, is an insult to the sacred Science and Art of Meditation, which has an altogether holier purpose.

To meditate for such mundane purposes is an insult to the sacred Science and Art of Meditation

Relaxation-response was "discovered" by medical researchers. Being good medical people, they were preoccupied with the physical body and nothing else. They observed that TM meditators, Zen monks, Buddhist monks and Christian contemplatives seemed to become relaxed as a result of their practices, so they concluded that the objective of meditation is relaxation, and therefore, that it would help the world at large to reduce stress!

Imagine the Saints of all the religions being told that they are meditating just to reduce stress and to let go of muscular tensions! Some of them would have laughed, while others would have cried in disbelief!

The Method of Relaxation-Response

The method of relaxation-response is practised as follows:

a. Select a calm environment.
b. Sit in a comfortable position.
c. Have a constant focus or stimulus such as a mantra, a sound, a phrase or a visual object to occupy the mind.
d. Have a passive, receptive attitude, and be not concerned with results, not even whether you are succeeding in your relaxation-response.

Certainly, this is good advice for the beginner in meditation—very good indeed. But what is the objective? Is the objective just to become relaxed? If so, then it is just a materialistic idea. It misses the whole idea and dimension of the Science and Art of Meditation.

Relaxation is only one of the many possible side-effects of meditation. It is not its objective!

Lack of Knowledge 4
Pure Intelligence 494
Psychology Ancient and Modern 1364
Meditation and the Joy of Living 1012

What Meditation is not...

- Meditation is *not* simply another form of relaxation exercise, as so many materialists would have you believe.
- Meditation is *not* to enhance your position in physical life, to increase your "brain-power", to increase your stamina in sport, to improve your memory, to perform better in schoolwork or at university. These are all plainly and simply worldly objectives.
- Meditation is *not* for enhancing your career prospects, to become a better manager or worker, or to get along better with other people. These are worldly objectives.
- Meditation is *not* for improving your physical health, for increasing your life-span in the body, or to achieve worldly success in any field. These are all worldly objectives.
- Meditation is *not* to help you sleep better, or eat better, or perform better in any field. Its purpose is not to cure diseases or reduce nervousness, tensions and stress.

If you pursue meditation for side-effects, you are not on the Path of Liberation

All these points are simply side-effects. If you pursue meditation for side-effects, you are not on the Path of Liberation. You have missed the Objective. You have missed the Goal.

The Double Stress of Meditational Life

Understand that when you become a seeker of the Light (SĀDHAKA) your life will become more difficult, not easier. This is because you still have to live in the world and fulfil your obligations, which produces the stresses of living in the world, in addition to which you will experience internal stress or tension caused by your attempting to connect to Reality through your spiritual meditations (SĀDHANĀ). This double stress is unavoidable until you have gone through the process of *transformation* and have attained JĪVAN-MUKTI, Liberation while living in your physical body.

The Path of Purification 1337

Cultivate Knowledge 1366
Overstimulation on the Path 557
Notes on the Path in the New Age 1166
Karmic Adjustment 1379
To Become a Jīvanmukta 259

Maharishi and Transcendental Meditation

Maharishi Mahesh Yogi founded his Spiritual Regeneration Movement in Madras, India, in 1958 and established his Academy of Meditation in Rishikesh, at the foot of the Himalayas in Northern India. Here he taught the art of Transcendental Meditation (TM).

Maharishi originally taught a purely spiritual science

Maharishi defined TM as "a means of communication with the Infinite". According to Maharishi, Being, or the God-Self, lies in the Transcendental Field of Absolute Existence, above the various strata and layers of Creation. To experience this Transcendental Reality it is necessary to lead our attention from the gross to the subtle layers of Creation, from the subtler to the subtlest and beyond to the field of the Absolute. This process of leading our attention from the gross to the subtle, from the subtle to the subtlest, and beyond, he called *Transcendental Meditation.*

As you can see, Maharishi originally taught a purely spiritual science: the Art of Meditation. For his method he used the old technique of Mantra Yoga which is so prevalent in India. (Using mantras is the most common form of meditation in India, followed by the use of images, or pictures of gods and goddesses.) He said that if we can learn to experience our thought before it reaches the outer layers of the mind, and then go further still and experience the root of thought, and then the ground of thought, or Mind itself, we can reach Pure Being, or *Transcendental Consciousness.*

What Maharishi taught was not new; it is the Indian heritage. He taught the common teaching of all the Yogīs, Ṛṣis, Sages and Spiritual Masters of India. For his method he used the Bīja-Mantras (seed mantras, key words, seed sounds, seed ideas, seed thoughts, certain key vibrations) which the Masters of Mantra Yoga know so well. Mantra Yoga is vast; it has its objective side of active expression and its subjective or meditational side. TM is dealing with the subjective side of Mantra Yoga.

In the diagram below, we compare Maharishi's terminology with modern esoteric terminology. According to Maharishi's system, the "wakeful consciousness", or *attention,* must be led from the gross (the Physical Creation) to the subtle (the Astral Creation), then to the subtlest (the Causal Worlds), and beyond to the state of Transcendental Consciousness (Buddhi).

Mahāṛṣi
Sanskrit: A great Sage. One who has seen the Absolute, Parabrahman.

Mantra is one method. A mantra (a special sound-frequency) is a *thought.* Through experiencing this thought in an increasingly subtle way, we can come to the subtlest state of Mind (the Causal World), then transcend even that and begin to experience the Absolute Being. The same principle applies whether one uses the senses of sight, hearing or inner touch: you progress from the gross to the subtle, from the subtle to the subtlest, then leap into Superconsciousness.

What Maharishi taught in the 1960s was the pure Ancient Wisdom of India, the Way of Yoga, the Science of Meditation. The question arises: if Maharishi taught TM as a way to experience Higher Consciousness and beyond, how did the system degenerate and come to be used by business executives for relaxing muscles and reducing stress? How did it become so prosaic and worldly? How did it become a mere relaxation technique for the millions?

How did it become a mere relaxation technique for the millions?

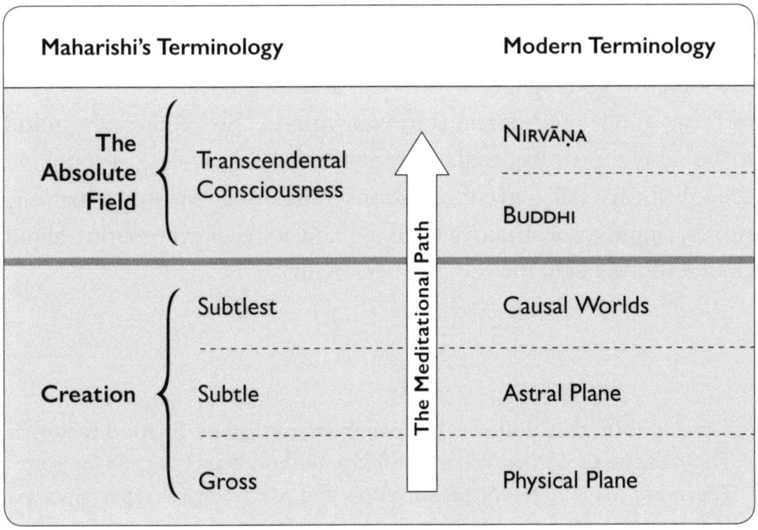

A Comparison of Systems

Realms of the One Mind 492
The Science of Bīja-Mantra 1218
Potent Vibrations: Bīja-Mantra 1542
Bīja-Mantra Practice 1552
Vibration and Mantra 1518

Types of Meditation

The Latin word *meditation* originally meant "to contemplate Reality, to focus on Reality". This is radically different from the current usage of the word. Only in later times has it come to mean "to think, to reflect, to ponder over a problem".

All active meditations bring about changes to the personality

There are many types of meditation. There are reflective meditations, active (creative) meditations and passive (silent) meditations. Some forms of meditation were devised to awaken creativity and regenerate the mind, while others were devised to realign the personality, leading to contact and communication with the Soul within.

Reflective Meditation

Reflective meditation is thinking about a topic, such as a virtue, a quality, an attribute of God, or some idea or truth, and gathering information about it. This includes memory, reason, logic and deduction. It also includes forms of study and book learning. This is the lowest form of meditation. It is the meditation of the thinker, the philosopher, the mathematician, the metaphysician, the scientist and the theologian.

Creative (Active) Meditation

Creative meditation is active meditation using visualization, imagination, pictures, maṇḍalas, symbols, images, myths, stories, movement, art, dance, poetry, and so forth. This form of meditation is more transformative than reflective meditation. Active meditation awakens the Creative Intelligence within you and uses Creative Imagination to bring about modifications in your mind. This requires the mind to be active, positive, male, creative, thinking, willing, producing thoughtforms. All active meditations—including worship, chanting, rituals, singing, constructive thinking and active prayer—bring about changes to the ego, the self, the personality.

What is Prayer? 690
Terms of Prayer 696
The Stages of Prayer 1253

Throughout this volume I present many forms of meditation. This must be so, so that you might find a method that is suitable for you. There are many different personalities and psychological types among seekers; hence the need for a variety of meditational forms.

Contemplative (Passive) Meditation

Passive meditation is a different process. Passive meditation is silent meditation, the quieting of the mind-stuff (CITTA) so that the Higher Consciousness may be reflected in it. In Silence you can attune to your Soul, to the hidden depths within you, the Kingdom of God. In those meditations where we make Soul-contact, the mind must be passive, receptive, reflecting, female. We touch upon the inner Silence, Emptiness, Calmness (ŚŪNYATĀ), which is free of all opposites, full and unconditioned. In Silence you return to your own Source, your Root, the Divinity within you. God dwells in us. God can be known in Silence.

Silent meditation changes you deep inside, beyond thoughts and ego

Contemplative meditation consists of two stages:

a. Invocation, evocation and reception.

b. Meditation in the transformed state, or Higher Consciousness.

We invoke, or evoke, so that there is a downpour of Divine Energy, by using a mantra or a prayer, a mystical formula or a ritual. Or we empty our minds of all thoughts and ideas, and into that Emptiness pours the Divine. Once the Divine has found its way into our Hearts and minds, then we abide in that condition. This abiding in the Divine Presence is *Contemplation.*

Silence resolves all conflicts. It might appear on the surface that Silence does nothing to you, that nothing changes, but silent meditation changes you deep inside, beyond thoughts and ego. After silent meditation you look at the world around you from a depth, not from your thoughts and emotions. Silence changes you subtly, where it matters most. In Silence you can touch your Soul, who is One with God, the Divinity that lives within you.

The highest goal of meditation is to touch upon the MONAD, the Unconditioned Consciousness. This you can only hope to do after establishing yourself in Soul-Consciousness.

The English words ***solitary*** and ***solitude*** came from the Latin *solus* and *solitarius,* meaning "alone, by one's self, unaccompanied, living alone, being quiet, single, unique, seclusion". Later on, it came to mean "loneliness, remoteness, absence of life, uninhabited".

Originally, Solitude was a *positive spiritual quality.* Silence and Solitude were the two essential qualities for the Spiritual Life, all over the world, in all religious traditions.

The Practice of Silence 1443
Your Mind is the Key 1208
Solitude and Loneliness 1170
The Law of Mystic Experience 508
Alone with God 700

Stages of the Silent Meditation Process

1. Meditation with a Seed

The silent meditation process begins with a seed—an object such as a mantra, a yantra, a maṇḍala, a symbol or a thought-idea. One begins by focusing intently on the seed object, or sounding the note, sound or mantra in the physical body, and harmonizing (balancing) the bodily vibrations. The purpose of this first stage of meditation is to train and prepare the mind for the subsequent condition.

As meditation proceeds, the emotional and mental bodies become harmonized

2. Contemplation

Then comes meditation without a seed (without an object in the mind). As meditation proceeds, the emotional and mental bodies (the personality) slowly become harmonized and vibrate in unison with the physical and etheric bodies. In this stage of meditation, the seed (the object in the mind, the mantra, visualized form, symbol or idea) is dropped from the mind and the mind is empty, formless, clear, bright, positive. One experiences a vacuum, a space, a void, an emptiness, or Śūnyatā. This is the state of *Contemplation.*

The important point to be observed is that the mind must be in a very positive state—alert, bright, conscious. Otherwise, obsession and possession can occur, or interference from the astral (psychic) dimensions.

Clouds of Unknowing 704
Meditating on the Void 801

Each stage of the meditation process takes much time and effort. It is not sufficient to experience a particular stage only once! To establish oneself in the successive stages takes time, effort, perseverance and inner help. As you progress, you will be guided by the Soul on the Causal Plane, then by the Triune-Self (the Ātman or Spirit), and finally by the Monad, the "Father in Heaven".

THE CHORD OF HARMONY — Analogy with Music (C Scale)

Stage 4 Deification	The Chord: the Seventh Note **The Monad**	C
THE GREAT DIVIDE		
Stage 3 Illumination	The Dominant Fifth *Harmonizing the Soul*	G
Stage 2 Contemplation	The Major Third *Harmonizing the Personality*	E
Stage 1 Meditation	Basic Note or Sound *Harmonizing the Physical Body*	C

Sounding the Perfect Chord of Being

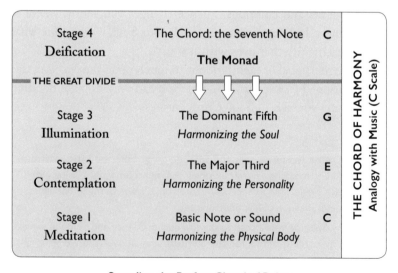

3. Illumination

As the meditation process deepens, the Soul becomes active and links up with the personality, and a rhythmic vibration is set up between the Soul and the personality. At a certain point of preparedness comes the downpour of Light from the Soul into the personality mechanism and the experience of touching upon the Buddhic Plane, bringing about feelings of Oneness, Unity, Ecstasy, Bliss, Joy. When the Soul and the personality vibrate together, there is *Illumination.*

A rhythmic vibration is set up between the Soul and the personality

4. Deification

The *Deification* process is a different action. The previous stages involve Man and his Soul (the Reincarnating Ego), while this fourth stage involves God *entering into* Man—the Monad, the "Father in Heaven", fusing with the Soul. At that moment, the physical body, the personality and the Soul vibrate in unison and harmony, and a channel opens up for the downflow of the Spirit, the Monadic Force. Then the whole Man vibrates to the Note or Sound of the Monad. Then Man becomes God-Man.

To Contemplate...

The most important (and most difficult) stage for the beginner is that of *Contemplation.* This is the stage where the mind is empty of all thoughts, all forms, all memories, all images, all symbols, all impressions, all feelings, all imaginings, all fancy, all imagination. The mind abides in its *pure natural state,* as it was before thought.

To come to this stage is difficult. To maintain it is still harder, for the mind must be empty yet awake, bright, alert, fully concentrated. It is not a negative void; it is a Void or Emptiness that is positive.

This stage is arrived at by repeated meditational practices. It is helpful if at all times one assumes a general attitude of detachment from all of one's ideas, thoughts and imaginings. In other words:

Do not cling to, hold on to, or attach yourself to the contents of your mind—ideas, thoughts or imaginations. Leave your mind habitually free. Live in the Moment.

Do not get attached to any of your thoughts or ideas, nor to any of your actions or memories. Do not cling to your feelings or emotions. Be of the Moment at all times.

Attach your Mind to the Eternal 1234

Stages of Interior Prayer 693
Stages on the Way of Holiness 1336

Contemplation

Contemplation is a Latin word meaning "to gaze upon, to behold, to observe, to have in view". The Mystics divide Contemplation broadly into two major divisions: *Natural* Contemplation and *Supernatural* Contemplation:

God is felt within the Soul, embraced, touched and seen

Natural Contemplation

Natural Contemplation has three stages:

a. Sensitive: when we look with our physical eyes upon some physical object, such as a picture of the Christ or a Guru, or upon a scene or a symbol, or upon some aspect of Nature, and we gaze upon this object for a long time.

b. Imaginative: when we picture in our imagination the beloved form of God, or of Christ, or of the Guru, or a symbol, word or scene, and we gaze upon it intently and admiringly.

c. Intellectual or Philosophical: when we mentally gaze upon a truth by holding it within our thought processes, such as the truth of God, of Immortality, of the Soul, or any other fact. This method is used by all *true* philosophers.

Supernatural Contemplation

In Supernatural Contemplation we simply gaze upon Truth, without discursive reasoning, without any emotional, imaginative or intellectual elements involved. This has been defined by the Mystics as "a simple and affectionate gaze upon God" or "a simple gaze upon Truth".

It is difficult for the average person to comprehend Supernatural Contemplation, for it takes place above and beyond the physical brain processes and beyond astral or psychic phenomena. It takes place in Buddhi (the Soul Nature) and Ātmā (the purely Spiritual Nature of Man).

Supernatural Contemplation is an interior, direct, experiential Knowledge, not with words or symbols, but essence to essence, life to life. God is *felt* within the Soul, embraced, touched and seen—not with the physical senses, not even with the senses of the astral body, but with the spiritual senses of the Spiritual Self.

The pre-Christian Greeks and Romans understood Contemplation as meditating with the pure Intellect, above the logical, reasoning faculty, what we now call the Abstract Mind. And this *Contemplātion (Contemplācio)* was directed to Being, to Truth, to the Realization and Awareness that above, beyond and within all composite, formed, created, fashioned and changeable things and beings, worlds and universes, there is the One Thing, Being (God), which is Existence Itself, the Source, the Good.

Intellectus: Knowing inside 375
Contemplation (Theoria) 694

Examples of Supernatural Contemplation

There are many stages or degrees in Supernatural Contemplation.

The Prayer of Quiet

In the Prayer of Quiet there is an *awareness* of God in the background of your consciousness, but your imagination is still roaming free.

In Mystical Trance you are wholly interiorized in your consciousness

Mystical Union

In Mystical Union God's Presence is felt deeply and profoundly. Imaginative activities cease and distractions from the body and mind do not intervene, but the actions of the bodily senses are not entirely suspended. That is, although your awareness is wholly interiorized within your body and shut off from the outside world, you can, at will, still return to normal bodily brain-mind or waking consciousness.

Mystical Trance

In Mystical Trance or Ecstasy you are *wholly interiorized* in your consciousness, while your body, mind and emotions are in a cataleptic state—immobile, suspended. This is very similar to the trance of a medium, but *not* the same in effect. In the trance of a medium, a spook or "guide" (an astral entity) takes control. In the trance of a Mystic, God (the Supreme Reality) takes control. The trance of a medium is an astral phenomenon, whereas the trance of a Mystic is a truly spiritual phenomenon where *God takes possession of the Soul.*

Spiritual Marriage

Spiritual Marriage is one of the expressions of a still higher, or rather, more *intimate* Union with God, deep within the Soul. It has been often described as an immersion, fusion, embrace, touch, saturation or infusion with God, or as a Divine Kiss.

∞

Supernatural Contemplation is the felt presence of God.
Natural Contemplation is a thought of God

Supernatural Contemplation is an interior possession by God.
Natural Contemplation is an imagining of God.

Supernatural Contemplation is an inner spiritual sensation of God.
Natural Contemplation is an outer visioning through the bodily senses.

Mystical Union 846
The Path to Ecstasy 696
The Experience of Mysticism 636
The State of Inner Purity 497
Channelling or Soul-Wisdom? 327

Illumination and Deification

Illumination can occur when the personality is correctly harmonized and, in its totality, correctly aligned to the Soul (the Reincarnating Ego, the Causal Self). Thus, the immediate aim of meditation is the stabilizing and equilibrating of all the forces of the personality—the thoughts, feelings, vital-energy and body-consciousness.

Illumination is the Light of Intuition breaking through the barriers of the rational mind.

An esoteric aphorism

At a later stage, the Soul itself has to be correctly aligned (harmonized) with Ātman, the Spirit, the Self. Illumination is the perception of the Light in the Head or in the "Spiritual Centre", the Heart. Illumination is the "catching" of the Spiritual Radiation of the Soul, or of Buddhi, and later on, of Ātman, the Self.

At a later stage, the Energy of the Inner God (the Monad, the Father in Heaven) will irradiate the Spirit-filled Soul-personality. This is the stage of *Deification.*

The Soul (Jīva) is the focal point for the descending Light of the Spirit (Ātman) and for the ascending radiance of the personality.

Satori: the Experience of Illumination 816

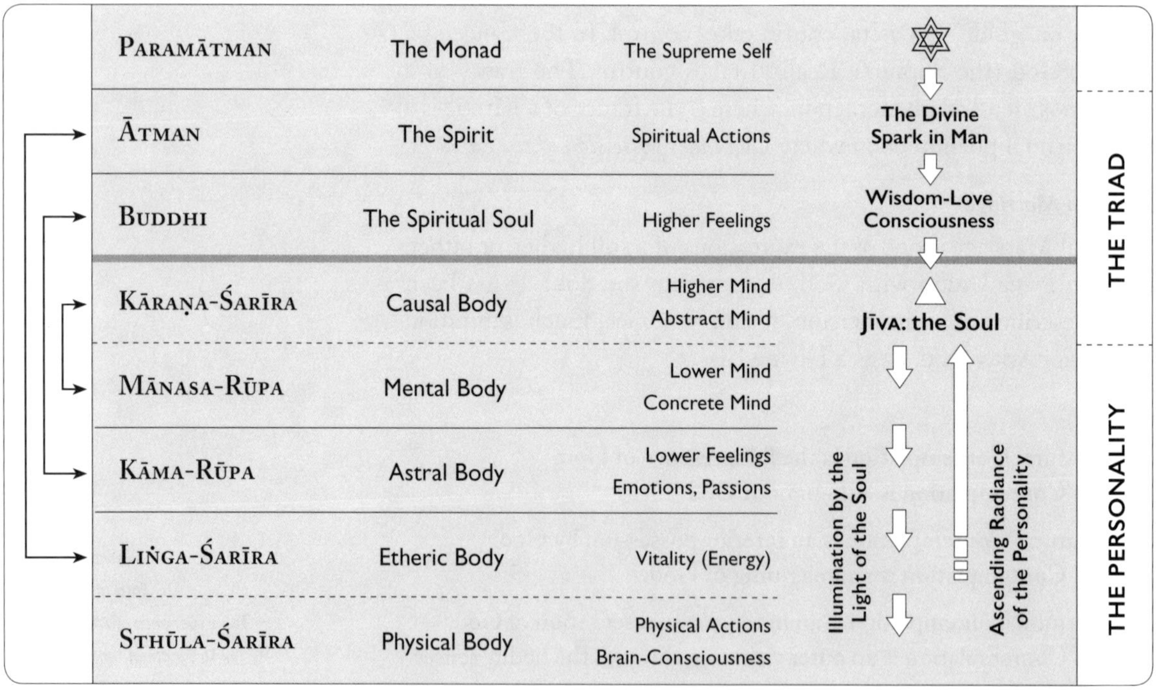

The Illumination and Deification of Man

The Muslim Deification Process

In the Muslim Mystical Tradition, the Deification Process of Man is described thus:

Stage 1: MA'RIFAT (Arabic: Gnosis, Illumination). The experience of Union, Oneness (Buddhi).

Stage 2: FANĀ (Arabic: the passing-away in Nirvāṇa). The Mystic touches on the Nirvāṇic Consciousness and his personal ego is blown away (FANĀ). When he fully establishes himself in Nirvāṇa, this is known as the Truth, or the condition of Reality (AL-ḤAQQ). If he abandons his human nature altogether and passes away completely from Human Evolution, it is the stage of QUṬB or Perfection. This stage takes one out of the human evolutionary system altogether and is the beginning of a new Superhuman development process in the Nirvāṇic Universe.

The Mystic touches on the Nirvāṇic Consciousness and his personal ego is blown away

There are Mystics who, out of compassion for other evolving men and women, do not completely pass away in Nirvāṇa. They stay within the evolutionary orb of Humanity. These are the BODHISATTVAS (whose essence is Love-Wisdom).

> The Mystic attains to God by *inward* Love... and he dwells *in* God. And yet he goes out toward created things in a spirit of Love towards all things... in works of righteousness. This is the summit of spiritual life."
>
> *Blessed John Ruysbroek*

Our Goal is nothing less than God

We share this view with the Supreme Paths of all the great religions:

- Christian Mysticism.
- Jewish Mysticism (HASIDISM).
- Muslim Mysticism (SŪFĪSM).
- Sikh Mysticism (SANT MAT).
- Chinese Mysticism (TAO).
- Buddhism (NIRVĀṆA).
- Zen (SATORI, Enlightenment).
- Hindu Mysticism (YOGA).

You gradually become more Godlike, more Divine, as you ascend the Ladder of Perfection (the *Scale of Perfection,* as the Christian Mystics expressed it).

The Radiant Way 830
The Divine Unity 852
Mystics of Pisces and Aquarius 836
Types of Conscious Immortality 390
Brahma-Nirvāṇa: Dissolution in God 1224

Some Facts about Meditation (Dhyāna)

Meditation is a major *shift* in Consciousness.

Meditation is Planetary Transformation.

Meditation is the transcendence of the individual.

Meditation is movement towards the Centre: the Centre of your Being and the Heart of the Universe.

Meditation is a process of Self-Discovery.

Meditation begins with a new self-image.

Meditation develops a capacity to become aware of Higher States of Consciousness.

Meditation involves working with transformative energies.

Meditation is a transformational effect.

Meditation is release from the things that previously bound you: your limited self-image, self-worth, self-validity; your narrow thoughts, opinions, ideas.

Meditation is the experiencing of the Transcendental, that which is beyond the narrow limits of what you *think* you are.

Meditation is the re-creating, renewing, remaking of your mind (Manas, the ordering, guiding principle in your life).

Meditation is transpersonal growth—developing yourself *beyond* the personality.

Meditation is self-transcendence—going beyond the limits of your little ego, your lower self, your normal awareness.

Meditation is the raising of your vibrations to come to know the *Living Reality*.

Meditation is a process which enables you to experience other dimensions of the Universe, the so-called higher planes.

Meditation is the shifting of your attention from the three-dimensional physical space to the experience of higher dimensions of Space, and from your physical body to subtler bodies within you.

Meditation is a movement in Consciousness towards your Ultimate Centre.

Meditation is a Way to the experiencing of Nirvāṇa and the infinite and eternal nature of your Beingness.

Meditation is a journey towards your Soul, your Higher Self, and finally, a meeting with your Monad, the Universal Spirit within you, your "Father in Heaven".

∞

Meditation is Integration

Remember that you are essentially a threefold Being. Meditation must proceed according to the following sequence:

a. The integration of the personality.
b. The integration of the Soul with the *integrated* personality.
c. The integration of the Monad with the *integrated* Soul-personality.

The first work of meditation is aligning the personality (the physical, etheric, astral and mental bodies) so that Soul-contact can be made. Only then can the Universal Consciousness flood into the Heart and Head Cakras. When the personality has been harmonized with the vibration of the Soul, then comes the very advanced Work of harmonizing the *Soul qualities* with those of the Monad—the "Father" within you, the Being of Light. In such a way is gained Omniscience, Omnipotence and Omnipresence.

The first work of meditation is aligning the personality so that Soul-contact can be made

Spiritual Inspiration to do this Great Work (Magnum Opus) comes, at first, from your Soul level.

The final stages of this Great Work of Liberation and Freedom come from the Inspiration of the Monad.

1	The Monad	The Spirit. Infinite Mind Luminous Intelligence The Divinity Within	**"I AM THAT I AM"** **God-Consciousness**
2	The Individualized Soul	The Reincarnating Ego, ensouling the Individuality, the Spiritual Triad	**"I AM THAT"** **Universal Consciousness**
3	The Personality	The Quaternary Personal Consciousness	**"I AM"** **Self-Consciousness**

The Threefold Human Constitution

The Threefold Structure of Man 33
The Three Stages of Yoga 528
The Way, the Truth and the Life 670
Who is 'I AM'? 1418

Building the Antaḥkaraṇa

The initial goal of meditation is to build a channel of Light between your brain-consciousness and you as the Soul. In Sanskrit this channel of Light is called ANTAḤKARAṆA, which means "interior frequency" or "inner organ of vision".

There are three entry-points through which the Soul connects to the personality

There are three entry-points through which the Soul connects to the personality:

Crown Centre

Through the Crown Centre the Soul enters your personality as *Universal Consciousness.*

Throat Centre

Through the Throat Centre the Soul manifests to your personality as *Creative Intelligence.*

Heart Centre

Through the Heart Centre the Soul manifests as the Unity Consciousness, or *Love-Wisdom.*

∞

The following diagram will help you to understand the various processes of action and meditation, and their relationships and results. Note the following:

- The Base Centre, the Sex Centre and the Solar Plexus Centre form the ordinary personality of the average man or woman.
- When the Third-Eye Centre is brought into alignment with the three lower centres, you have an integrated personality.
- The Heart Centre, the Throat Centre and the Crown Centre form the threefold Individuality or Soul-Consciousness.
- When these three higher centres are merged into the Causal Centre *above* the head, you will have the Integrated Soul-Consciousness of the Adept, the Master, the One who can say:

  "I and my Father (the Monad) are One."

The Human Cakras 44
The Functioning of the Cakras 52
The Goal of Yoga 521
Building the Bridge of Light 554
The Heart and the Energy Centres 1332

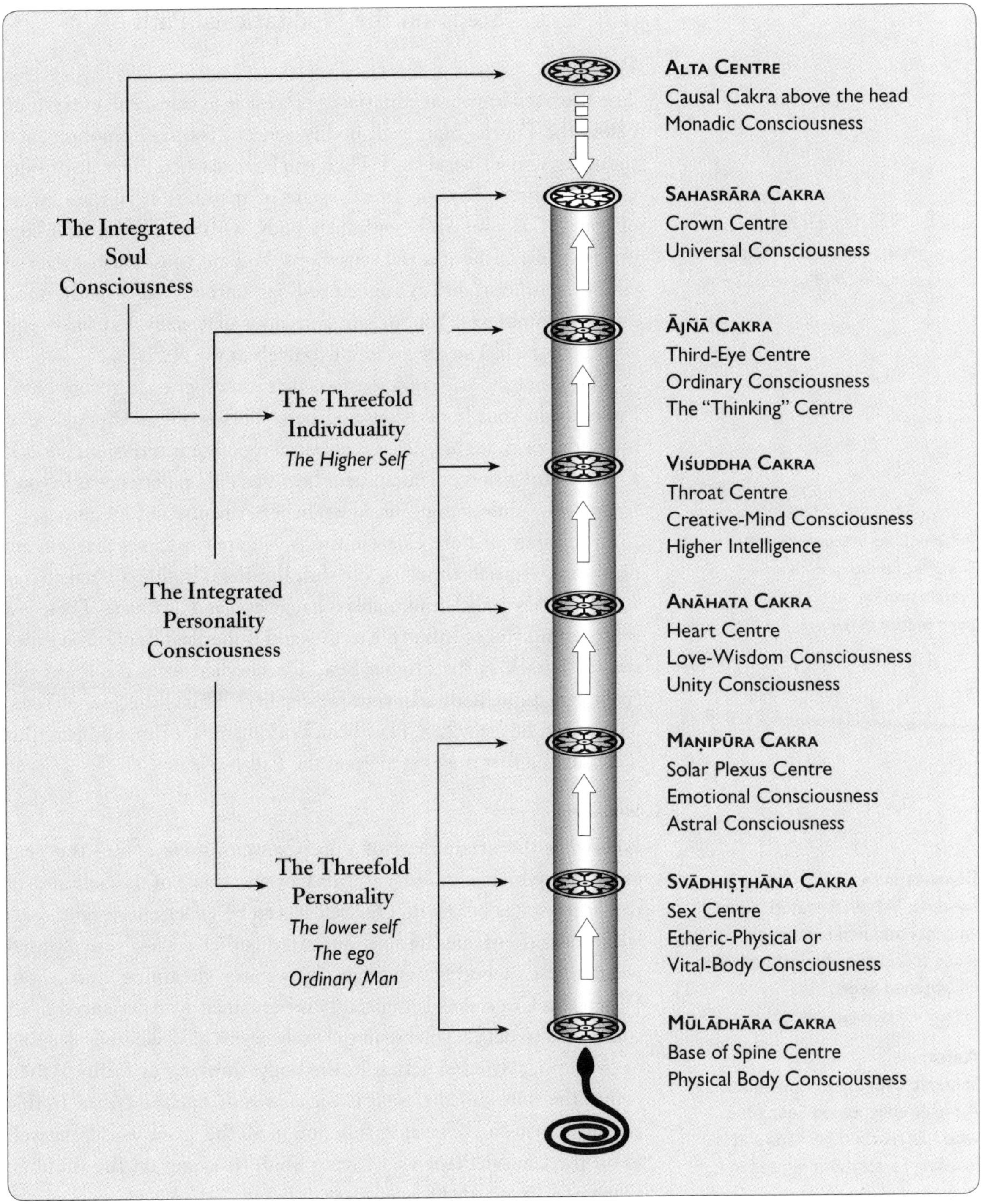
ALTA CENTRE
Causal Cakra above the head
Monadic Consciousness
SAHASRĀRA CAKRA
Crown Centre
Universal Consciousness
ĀJÑĀ CAKRA
Third-Eye Centre
Ordinary Consciousness
The "Thinking" Centre
VIŚUDDHA CAKRA
Throat Centre
Creative-Mind Consciousness
Higher Intelligence
ANĀHATA CAKRA
Heart Centre
Love-Wisdom Consciousness
Unity Consciousness
MAṆIPŪRA CAKRA
Solar Plexus Centre
Emotional Consciousness
Astral Consciousness
SVĀDHIṢṬHĀNA CAKRA
Sex Centre
Etheric-Physical or
Vital-Body Consciousness
MŪLĀDHĀRA CAKRA
Base of Spine Centre
Physical Body Consciousness
The Integrated Soul Consciousness
The Threefold Individuality
The Higher Self
The Integrated Personality Consciousness
The Threefold Personality
The lower self
The ego
Ordinary Man

Integration of the Human Consciousness

Steps on the Meditational Path

Step One

The first step in your meditational process is to transcend everything below the Fourth State—all bodily actions, feelings, emotions and thoughts, and all astral stuff. Then you have reached the state of Pure Consciousness, TURĪYA. In this state of meditation you are aware of yourself as your *Self*—without a body, without a mind (thinking process) and without astral sensations. You are consciously aware of your own immortality as a Spirit or Soul, unhindered by body, mind and ego complexes. You are not conscious externally, but *internally*, within yourself. You are aware of yourself as the *Self*.

The Self has to be experienced consciously while outside of meditation

This is not the self-consciousness that you experience in your physical body, in your bodily consciousness. This is not an experience of memories or thoughts, nor is it an astral mood or impression, nor is it a clairvoyant vision or clairaudient hearing. This experience is beyond sense data, subtle sensations, ideas, beliefs, dreams and memories.

In the state of Pure Consciousness you are conscious that you are immortal, eternal, timeless, blissful, limitless, bodiless ("naked", as some Mystics put it), immutable (changeless) and deathless. There is a sense within you of Infinity, Eternity and Boundless Being. You experience yourself *as* the Higher Self, disembodied from the lower self (your ego-mind-body self, your personality). This is the goal of Yoga, Mysticism, Sūfīsm, Zen, Hasidism, Buddhism, Taoism, Sikhism. But it is only the first major step upon the Path.

The Seven States of Consciousness 494
Turīya: Pure Consciousness 498
The Fifth State 500
Stages on the Path 1136

Step Two

Following the attainment of Pure Consciousness comes the next great step, which is to *integrate* this Consciousness of the Self into all the other states below it. The Self has to be experienced *consciously* while outside of meditation, during all other states: your normal wakefulness or bodily activities, sleep states, dreaming, and so on. When this Conscious Immortality is permanently experienced in all conditions (whether you are in the body or out of it, whether sleeping or dreaming, whether acting in the body, thinking or feeling), then comes the state called *Cosmic Consciousness* or *Buddhic Unity*. In this condition you can *consciously* function in all the lower worlds, as well as on the Causal Plane as a Living Soul, JĪVA, and on the Buddhic Plane as a JĪVANMUKTA, an ARHAT, a Saint.

JĪVAN-MUKTA
Sanskrit: "Alive-Liberated". One who has attained Liberation while still in the physical body. An enlightened Seer.
To Become a Jīvanmukta 259

ARHAT
Sanskrit: Worthy of Reverence. A highly enlightened Seer. One who has reached Nirvāṇa and is learning to establish himself in it.
The Brotherhood of Light 395

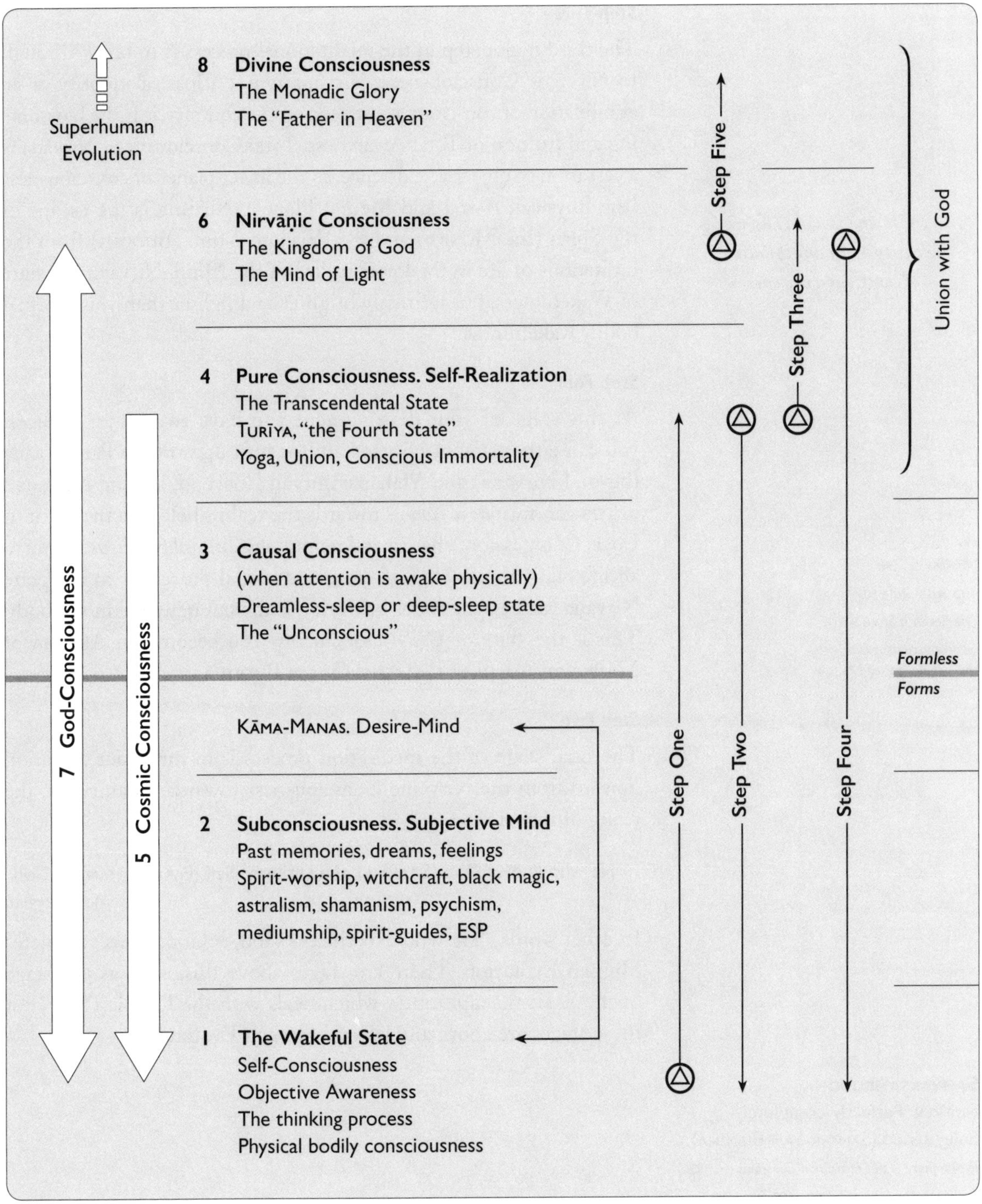

Steps on the Meditational Path

Step Three

The third major step in the meditational process is to break through to Nirvāṇic Consciousness. Nirvāṇa is not a loss of identity or an annihilation of conscious awareness; on the contrary, it is the blossoming and fruition of Total Awareness, Total Consciousness. Nirvāṇa is a cessation of objective existence on the lower planes of consciousness (the Physical, Astral and Mental Planes). Nirvāṇa is the escape of the Spirit (the MONAD) and the Wisdom-Mind (BUDDHI) from the limitations of life in the lower realms of the Mind. Nirvāṇa is a state of Wakefulness, but infinitely brighter and lighter than your normal bodily wakefulness.

Nirvāṇa is not a loss of identity or an annihilation of conscious awareness

Step Four

At this stage of your development you have two major choices: you can either stay in Nirvāṇa and/or turn upwards to Paranirvāṇa (beyond Nirvāṇa) and Mahāparanirvāṇa (beyond, beyond Nirvāṇa); or you can turn *downwards* towards the realms below in the spirit of Love, Compassion, charity and helpfulness, in full *conscious service* to all life. This fourth step of the meditational process is to integrate Nirvāṇa with all the states below it—into your daily life in the body. This is the state of *God-Consciousness*. You become an ASEKHA or Master, an Adept or Perfected One, a BUDDHA.

Nirvāṇa is... 98
The Sixth State 501
The Seventh State 502
God-Consciousness is the Wholeness of Life 504

Step Five

The final stage of the meditation process is to turn your attention upward from the Nirvāṇic Consciousness towards Paranirvāṇa, the realm of the Monad.

> He who knows God (BRAHMA), the Ultimate Self (PARAMĀTMAN), is God.
> *Manusanghita*

In other words, "He who experiences God, *is* God." This completes Human Evolution. There are stages above this, such as the stage of the SAMYAKSAṀBUDDHA which deals with the Logoic Plane, but these stages are above and beyond Human Evolution.

SAMYAKSAṀBUDDHA
Sanskrit: Perfectly-completely-Enlightened (SAMYAK-SAṀ-BUDDHA).

Evolutionary States of Human Consciousness 172
Evolution, the Plan, the Path 1688

Benefits of Meditation

Meditation, when practised correctly and for the right purpose (not for worldly goals but for a Spiritual Quest), will bestow the following benefits upon you:

- Meditation connects your body, mind and Spirit.
- Meditation gives you Peace of Mind and a Tranquil Heart.
- Meditation produces positive changes in your personality, spiritual growth, Self-Realization, Self-Discovery (Ātmajñāna).
- Meditation calls down the Light of the Soul (Ātmajyoti) into your conscious mind, producing Illumination.
- Meditation gives you clarity of mind, a sense of purpose for living, vital energy and purposeful striving.
- Meditation develops your Inner Potential from a seed state (Laya) to full, active, mature Realization and Action (Kriyā).
- Meditation will give you Inner Freedom and Liberation (Mokṣa, Mukti).
- Meditation will put you in touch with Inner Guidance, the Sat-Guru within you, the God-Self deep within your Heart.
- Meditation will invoke the Divine Love potential in you (Prema), the Universal Love Principle of the Heart.
- Meditation, focused in the Heart Centre, will give you the spontaneous awakening of the Universal Heart (Prema-Īśvara), the God of universal, infinite and uninterrupted Love.
- Meditation accelerates your development towards personal fulfilment and the purposes of your Soul.
- Meditation reduces stress in your life, balances out internal energies, heals body, mind and Soul, and expands your Awareness or Consciousness.
- Meditation produces Harmony within yourself and harmonious relationship with other people and your environment.
- Meditation gives you positive energies of Life.
- Meditation protects you from many evils and helps you to balance out your Karma in a controlled manner.

Meditation accelerates your development towards the purposes of your Soul

A Nirvāṇic Visualization

Let your "I am" disappear like a drop of water into the sea

- First, establish yourself in Spiritual Inspiration. Think of your Higher Self, your Soul, and think of the God within you—the Monad, your "Father in Heaven".
- Stabilize your mind, establish mental quietness. Harmonize your feelings, let go of all hurts and negative emotions. Forgive all those who may have done some evil to you. Sit in your meditation posture with poise and balance. Be peaceful and still.
- Now visualize a silver point of Light in the Third-Eye Cakra, between the two physical eyes. It is a shining, shimmering, silver dot of Light.
- Enlarge this silver dot into a sphere of silver, scintillating Light, the size of a dinner plate, whirling around, its centre being your Third-Eye Cakra.
- Now see this moving, revolving, silver plate of Light becoming a tunnel of silver, radiating Light. It is longish, and it is attached to a Golden Sun.
- Go through your Third-Eye Cakra and enter this silver tunnel of Light which is attached to a Golden Sun. Go through the silver tunnel and enter the Golden Sun.
- Now you are enveloped and surrounded in a liquid orb of golden radiance. This liquid, radiating, golden sphere is everywhere, inside you and outside you. You become this liquid, radiating Golden Sun.
- Merge into this Golden Sun and go through it. It turns into a blazing, brilliant White Radiance. This is the Central Spiritual Sun, a dazzling orb of utter Brightness. Feel yourself surrounded by this bright Sun. It is warm and healing.
- Now feel around, and discover that this Sun is a dazzling, limitless Ocean of super-bright White Light. Merge into this endless White Light.
- Let your self, your "I am", disappear like a drop of water into the sea. Dissolve into Unconditioned Radiance, into Endless Bliss, into Measureless Consciousness, into Eternal Life.
- This is sweet Nirvāṇa. Enjoy and be!

The Truth about Nirvāṇa 102

CHAPTER 52

Meditation Practice

The Art of Alignment

Meditation is essentially the art of alignment, or Yoga. The word YOGA means "joining together, yoking, aligning, integrating, uniting". Meditation, when correctly practised, does precisely that.

Most people do not realize that meditation is an *art* as well as a science. It is a skill that must be developed in the same way as playing the piano, painting or singing.

Meditation is an art as well as a science

There are four ingredients for a successful meditation:

1. Spiritual Inspiration (being in touch with a Higher Reality).
2. Mental quiescence (a sense of serenity).
3. Emotional stability (a feeling of harmony).
4. Physical poise and balance.

The first essential ingredient is *Spiritual Inspiration.* Unless you are inspired, you won't want to meditate. This is why most people do not meditate: they are not inspired. Inspiration means "the breathing-in of the Spirit". You can only meditate when the Spirit *inside* you wants you to meditate. The need, the inspiration, the call to meditate, comes to you from within yourself.

> Until Spiritual Energy is brought to bear upon the personal forces, there can be no upliftment, no redemption, no relationships.
>
> *A mystical aphorism*

The next ingredient for a good meditation is mental quiescence, or mental quietness. You will at once recognize that you cannot meditate if you do not have a sense of *peace* and *serenity* in your mind. Furthermore, on the emotional level, it is difficult to meditate if you are angry, hurt, full of violent emotions, revengeful or depressed. Thus, a feeling of harmony on the emotional level is essential before you can start meditating.

The Goal of Yoga 521
Inspiratio: Breathing in the Spirit 375
Mind-Waves 1239
How to have a Peaceful Mind 1244
Peace of Heart 1595

Meditation is the integration of the human being. The Latin word INTEGRATION means "to complete, to make whole, to combine various parts, to build up or put together, to make perfect what is imperfect". All of this is true of meditation.

Meditation is Integration 1193

Some Hints for Meditation Practice

The following hints may help you in your meditational process:

The Need for Meditation

The mind-functionings have to be equalized, stilled, before Consciousness of the Self becomes possible. Hence the need for meditation. Once the Spirit is fully established in the mind, you are continually in the state of Yoga (union, at-one-ment).

You will come to understand that you are not meditating for yourself

Preparing for Meditation

When practising meditation it is best to be in seclusion, alone, or with other meditators. This is to minimize noise and interfering vibrations. The thinking faculty and the physical body must be restrained—*not forced,* but wisely brought under control during meditation.

Formal Meditation

To be precise, your formal sitting down to "meditate" is your *attempt* at meditation, your attempt to suspend thoughts. The first stages of meditation (your attempts) are but your battling against thoughts, the quieting of the activities of the CITTA (mind-substance).

The State of Meditation

When there are no longer any thoughts arising in your mind, then you are in the state of DHYĀNA (meditation). You enter the state of meditative-awareness when the mind is *still* and in a positive, concentrated state.

Being Meditated Upon

The next stage in your DHYĀNA comes when you discover that you are being *meditated upon* by your Soul and, at a later stage, by the ĀTMAN—the Self within you, your Buddha-Mind, the Christ in you. Then your whole life becomes meditation.

Meditation as Service

You will also come to understand that you are not meditating for yourself. You will realize that meditation is a subtle activity of the Mind-Essence. We are talking here not only of your own CITTA, but also of the Universal Mind (MAHAT, the Divine Mind).

The Attitude for Yoga 558
Silence, Solitude, Peace 1386
Meditational Service of the Buddhas 393
Perceptions of the One Mind 490
Dhāraṇā and Dhyāna 1523

If you Wish to Meditate…

Live in the everlasting Present.

The present action (what you are doing *now)* is the end in itself.

You learn to meditate by meditating

Spontaneously concentrate on the Moment.

Know that you are an Immortal Soul.

Joy is spontaneous self-discipline.

When your mind is healed into the Original-State-of-Being, all stress will go.

Avoid competition. Cultivate Silence. Silence is golden: in true mental silence, a Golden Light will surround you.

Being alone is not loneliness. Being alone, you can be possessed by Love.

Things are for your use only, not for your possession. If you can go through life without possessing anything, you will gain the All.

You learn to meditate by meditating.

Past, Present and Future 1400
Cultivate the Positive 1365
Alone with God 700
Solitude and Loneliness 1170
To Become a True Renunciate 257

Most people identify with their physical bodies as their "real" self. Some believe that they "have" a Soul and a Spirit. But in fact, you do not "have" (possess) a Soul and a Spirit.

You *are* the Soul. You *are* the Spirit.

Common Obstacles on the Path of Meditation

- The difficulties created by your own Karma, the Prārabdha Karma (those karmas that are to be worked out in this lifetime).
- The difficulties of withdrawing your attention within yourself due to the outward-looking tendencies of the mind.
- Over-specialization along one line—for instance, Bhakti Yoga, Karma Yoga, Jñāna Yoga (devotion, activity, knowledge).
- Ill-health (physical, emotional or mental).
- The opposition: outside powers from the world, and inner forces and entities from the invisible worlds.

These difficulties are part of your Journey

You should deal with these difficulties in a matter-of-fact manner, not being overcome by them, realizing that they are part of your Journey, part of the Path (Mārga). You must hold the Vision of Ātma-Vidyā (Self-Realization) and Brahma-Vidyā (God-Realization) constantly in your view as the goal and end purpose of your life. In such a way you will succeed.

Types of Karma 243
Karmic Adjustment 1379
Senses or the Self? 239
The Dividing of Yoga 522
The Tests of the Elements 1159
Notes on the Path in the New Age 1166
To Succeed in your Quest 1330

Expect Nothing

You must *expect nothing* from your meditations! This might not inspire your ego at all, but you must not meditate for "rewards". You will know the spiritual reasons later. Furthermore, you must "possess" nothing. That is, you must be mentally detached from all things, inner and outer.

A Sage (Muni) once said:

Meditation is a process which takes the mind from the consciousness of the possession of outward objects to the consciousness of the possession of Spirit (God).

Another Holy Man (Sādhu) has said:

When you begin to meditate, be prepared to lose everything.

And a Seer (Ṛṣi) said:

Be *awake* in yourself and asleep to the world.

To Become a Jīvanmukta in this Lifetime 259

Muni
Sanskrit: A Silent Sage, a Yogī.

Sādhu
Sanskrit: A virtuous Saint who is a renunciate.

Ṛṣi
Sanskrit: A Holy Seer or Knower of Reality.

How to Succeed in Meditation

The following are the principal elements which contribute to your ability to meditate:

1. Have no concern for results.
2. Self-forgetfulness.
3. The right meditation for the right purpose.
4. The uniting of Action and Awareness.
5. Do not go beyond your limits.
6. Your whole attitude towards life must change.

Think of your meditation as simply a natural process

Have no concern for results

Focus your attention or awareness upon the meditation process relaxedly, without concern for the outcome or results. There are two points to note here:

- Focus your awareness only on the subject you are meditating upon.
- Do your meditation innocently, without any desire for results.

In other words, you meditate only for meditation's sake. Most meditators always worry about results. They want to get results! This "wanting results" is the main obstacle to a successful meditation.

Self-forgetfulness

If you can drop your ego, your sense of "I am the meditator" or "I am meditating now", the results will be quicker and better. Think of your meditation as simply a *natural process*. Nature will take care of it for you when you *allow* Her to do so.

The right meditation for the right purpose

- Chanting and JAPA (repetition of a mantra wilfully, devotionally, actively, with vigour, liveliness, energy) will increase those qualities inside you which the mantra represents.
- In the AJAPA technique (the non-repetitive or spontaneous method) you gradually reduce the vibration of the mantra and allow it to swing upwards or inwards, thus ascending the realms of mind to arrive at the Soul-Realm, or Self-Realization.

These are clearly different results. Thus, at the beginning of meditation you must know where you want to go.

The Role of the Divine Female in the Salvation/Liberation Process 1502

The Two Applications of Mantra 1219

The Work of Meditation 1440

The uniting of Action and Awareness

You must so *enjoy* your meditation that you perform it easily and joyously. Your awareness must enjoy doing it. Do not think of it as "boring" or a "burden".

Do not go beyond your limits

Your meditation should be what suits you, what you can easily handle. Do not do meditations that are too advanced or difficult for you.

You have to become feminine

Your whole attitude towards life must change

You have to stop being the aggressive, assertive, belligerent warrior and become *feminine*. Unfortunately, the Feminine Principle is not understood in this age, which is based on the Masculine Principle. Even feminism applies the Masculine Principle.

Here is an ancient Chinese description of the Feminine Principle, which they called the TAO, the Great Silence:

When I yield, I succeed.
Space looks empty, but it is full.
If I give myself, I become the All.
When I lose, it is my greatest gain.
When I desire nothing, everything happens to me.
Spring and autumn come, and the grass grows by itself.
Everything is born, emerges and develops to perish
in the end by a single process.
This is the Ultimate, the Tao.
Flow in with the Process. Flow in with the Tao.

Yin, Yang, Tao 476
Tao: the Supreme Way 776
Cosmic Sensitivity 1009
Silence and Activity 1446

∞

Remember that meditation is a *movement in Consciousness*, not in your mind. True meditation is the exploration of Pure Consciousness itself, not some form of mental activity.

"Be Still and Know that I am God," says the Old Testament.

- Be Still
- Know
- I AM
- God

These are the four steps of meditation.

Be Still and Know 638

Your Mind is the Key

True meditation is the suspension of the activities of the mind

The key to your success in meditation is the correct understanding and use of your mind. Without this you will fail. You cannot Know the Absolute by intellectual speculation and theorizing, even if you have the most brilliant mind. This age is characterized by an intense over-activity of the mind. This is why people find it difficult to meditate in the true sense, for true meditation is the *suspension* of the activities of the mind (MANOHARA).

The lower mind (KĀMA-MANAS, desire-mind), your ordinary thinking, rationalizing, logical, separative mind, has to be put to rest (LAYA) in meditation. Then you will experience ŚUDDHA-MANAS (Pure Mind) or ŚUDDHA-CAITANYA (Pure Consciousness). This is the link or connection (YOGA) with your Wisdom-Mind (BUDDHA-MĀNASA, the Buddha-Mind), and with the ĀTMAN within you.

Mind is very versatile and adaptable. Your ordinary feeling-mind functions through your mental body (MĀNASA-RŪPA). Your Higher Mind or Abstract Mind, the Spiritual Mind, functions through your causal body (KĀRAṆA-ŚARĪRA). The causal body is the seat of your Soul (JĪVA). But the Spiritual Self, which is of the nature of God (BRAHMAN), is higher still. Therefore, you must still *all* activities of your mind if you would hear the Voice of the Higher Self, the Voice of God within you.

If your mind is filled with RAJAS (activity, passion, tension, stress) or TAMAS (dullness, heaviness, stupidity, ignorance), its vibration is out of tune with the Self or ĀTMAN that you are. Since that Reality is subtler than the subtlest (in terms of vibration), you have to purify your mind by Silence and correct meditation.

The Human Constitution 43
Realms of the One Mind 492
True Death 424
The Attitude for Yoga 558
No-Mind and the One Mind 763
When the Mind is Still 768
Cultivate Silence of the Mind 1239
Transformations of the Mind 1242

The Buddha-Mind

The Buddha-Mind is your own Fundamental Mind, beyond thinking and conceptualizing. It is your Essential Reality. The Buddha-Nature is your own Self-Nature (SVĀYAṀBHŪ), the Self-Existent Being, the Transcendental Awareness, which is eternal and immutable. There is only one Buddha-Nature in the Universe: the Transcendent, the PARAMAPADĀTMAVA (the Absolute).

Perceptions of the One Mind 490

Suspended Mind

Mind (MANAS), in its own true Nature, already vibrates to SATTVA-GUṆA (the quality of purity, harmony, peace), and it already has true Knowledge (VIJÑĀNA). This original Pure State of Mind gets ruffled and disturbed by the thought-processes (CITTA-VṚTTI), which seem to go on out of control. CITTA-VṚTTI-NIRODHA (thought-process-suspension) is the immediate goal of meditation because, when this is achieved, the mind can reflect the God-Being (ĀTMAN) within you and attain Self-Realization (ĀTMA-VIDYĀ).

This original Pure State of Mind gets ruffled and disturbed by the thought-processes

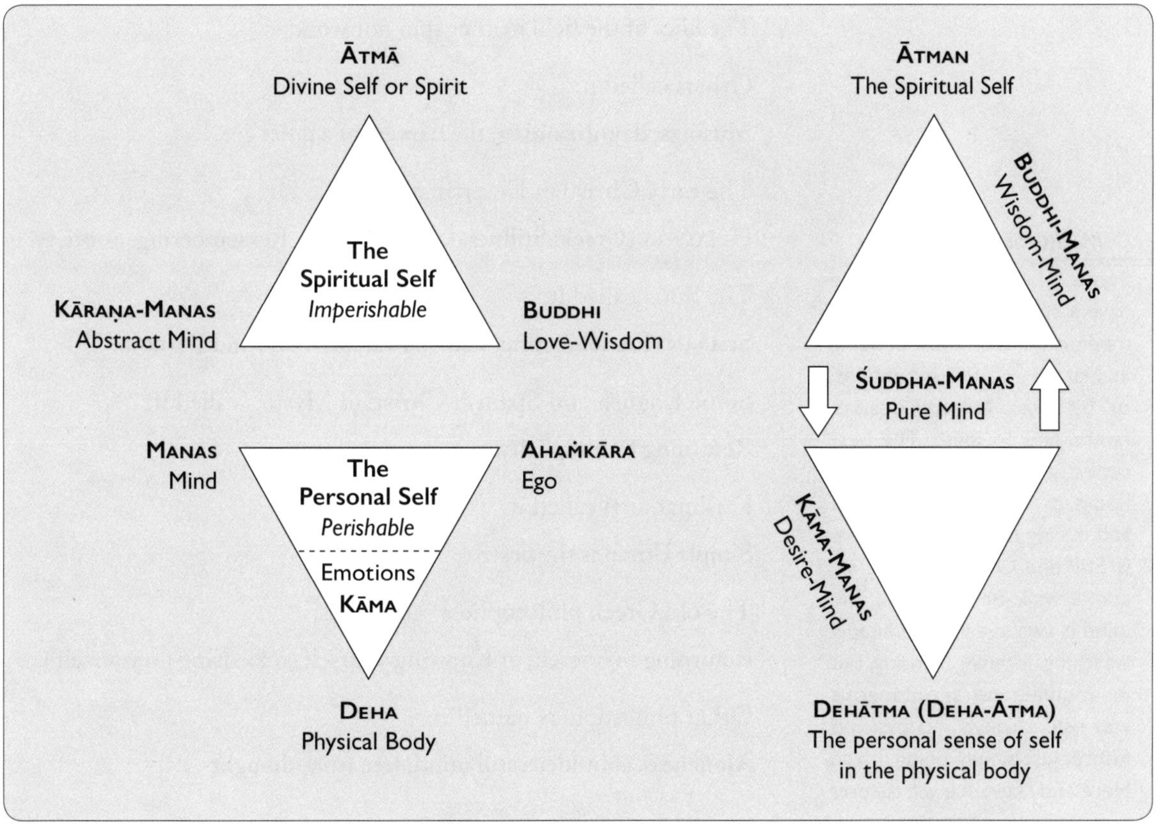

The Suspending of the Mind

Natural Meditation

For thousands of years, all over the world, East and West, people have spontaneously discovered natural meditation. As the speed of planetary vibration becomes more frantic by the day, this natural ability for spontaneous meditation is becoming lost very rapidly.

The natural ability for spontaneous meditation is becoming lost very rapidly

The ancient Hebrew peoples called it:

Shīlōh or Selah (rest, tranquillity), or "Be still in thine Heart".

The Japanese Zen people called it:

Sitting quietly, doing nothing.

The Chinese Chān people said:

The grass grows by itself.

Jesus said of this:

The lilies of the field neither spin nor work.

Others called it:

Musings, day-dreaming, the harvest of a quiet eye.

The early Christian Desert Fathers called it:

Hesychia (Greek: Stillness), Recollection, Remembering, Sobriety.

The Sūfis called it:

Simrān (Remembering, being Aware, Awake) and Dhikar.

Some English and Spanish Christian Mystics called it:

Returning to Simplicity.

Krishnamurti called it:

Simple Union is the best.

The old Greek philosophers said it was:

Returning to oneself, or Knowing yourself (refocusing on yourself).

Other philosophers named it:

Aloneness, solitude; a still mind, free from thoughts.

Meditation with Nature

Some Nature-loving people have a spontaneous or natural meditation as a result of being in Nature—in the mountains, or by lakes, forests, oceans, rivers, and so forth. The best times are the quiet night hours, or early morning before and during dawn, when Nature is Still and Quiet. You can sit, stand, walk or lie down. The mind is awake, sensitive, simply watching, listening, sensing, but in a quiet and spontaneous way—no thinking, no past, no future, just simply being in the Here and Now. *You will discover that Nature is meditating.*

Most of the natural Mystics *returned attention to within themselves,* while others became intensely interested in things *outside* themselves, such as a flower, a sunset or a bird, thus completely *forgetting* themselves. They would watch leaves moving with the wind, or a brook, or shadows, or living flames of fire, or embers glowing, or the flame of a lamp or candle, for hours on end, all in a *still state of mind.* The speed of life was *slow* in those days; people had time to relax and some people spent a lot of time communing with Nature.

Most of the natural Mystics returned attention to within themselves

Some smelled the scent of flowers or trees, or the grass or ground.

Others listened to the music in Nature, in trees and plants, and in the Aether between things and in the sky.

Others discovered how to listen to the music within themselves. The Greeks did a lot of this type of inner-music listening; they called the Aethereal Music *pan pipes.* In India they always went inside themselves and the inner music they called *Krishna's flute.*

Others discovered that if they repeated a simple sound in a certain way, they could put themselves in Ecstasy.

Others discovered that if they could achieve bodily quiescence, they could attain the same.

Others discovered that if they quietened their breath, they could transcend their personality consciousness.

Others discovered that if they dropped all intellectual pursuits (thoughts), the personal "I" consciousness or ego was dissolved and they experienced Boundless Beingness, the Universal I AM Consciousness.

Others discovered that Truth lies beyond words, that the Radiant Self is already within them, that they just have to switch their attention to the Great Within.

The Mystics described this spontaneous, natural meditation in many words, such as:

A happy stillness of the mind.

A serene and blessed mood.

A passive attitude.

A simple Way.

Feeling the Ultimate Harmony in all things, or Tao.

A wise passivity of the Soul.

(Actually, it is a passivity of the mind, not of the Soul.)

The Ways were many. The common technique they all discovered was simply to *be,* or just to *see* or *hear,* without thoughts.

The Law of Mystic Experience 508

The Way of Spontaneous Meditation 1229

To Silence the Mind...

The Watcher

To bring your ordinary mind to Peace and Quiet (MAUNA), just sit still and *watch* your mind. Watch your thoughts come and go, rise and fall, and do nothing about them.

The Watcher, the Observer, is the Pure Self beyond your personal ego. Become the Watcher, the Observer, which is the AHAṀ (I Am).

SĀKṢĀTKĀRAṆA
Sanskrit: To see directly with one's Mind's Eye. The Witnessing Principle, the Silent Watcher of phenomena, the Inner Consciousness of ĀTMAN, the Seer looking inside the contents of the Mind and Heart. The basis of VIPAŚYANĀ meditation.

Vipaśyanā Yoga: Internal Observation 1222
The Silent Watcher Meditation 1388
Pāda I Sūtras 2,3,4 536

This is different from your personal ego-sense in the body, AHAṀKĀRA (I am the doer, the performer, the actor, the causer). AHAṀKĀRA is the self-centred "I" sense, the sense of "personal importance". The Watcher is CAITANYA, Pure Consciousness, Pure Awareness, which is the nature of ĀTMAN, the Self-Existent Eternal Being that you really are, *above* your personality level.

This is SĀKṢĀTKĀRA-YOGA, beholding Reality directly. The SĀKṢĪ (Witness) is the ĀTMAN.

Listen to NĀDA

Another way to calm the furious activity of your mind is to listen to NĀDA, NĀDAM (the Inner Sound), the Word, the Logos, ŚABDA. This will lead you first to Self-Realization (ĀTMAJÑĀNA) and then to God-Realization (BRAHMAJÑĀNA).

ŚABDA or NĀMA (the Name) is God Incarnating within you and in the Cosmos. It is the Celestial Music or Divine Harmony by which God has created, and is creating, and will be creating in the future, the whole Universe.

This Inner Music has many notes and sounds. It can be listened to through the right inner ear or the Heart Centre. If you listen to it in the Heart, it is called ANĀHATA-NĀDA or ANĀHATA-ŚABDA (the Unproduced Sound, meaning "not produced by external means").

This Word is Sounding-Light (NĀDA-BINDU). It can also be *seen* in the Third-Eye. It acts as a connecting link (YOGA) with your Soul, and between your Soul and God.

This is called SURAT-ŚABDA-YOGA (putting your attention on the Sound).

Āuṁ, Ōṁ, Nāda 550
What is the Name? 1259
Meditation on the Sacred Word 1216
Hear the Sound within the Silence 1651

Rest your Mind in the Heart

Another Way is to remember that God resides in your Heart, shining as the Self (Ātman), like a lamp, which is your true Self or true I AM (Ahaṁ). Rest your mind in that Self-Light.

It is possible to attain Self-Realization (Enlightenment) in this lifetime if you realize Ahaṁ-Ātman (I am the Self) in your Heart. The Self (Ātman) is the Luminous Presence which is God, and which is also your true Nature or Original Beingness. The Ātman (the Self or God-Being) shines by its own Light, and you can become It in the Heart.

The Self is the Luminous Presence which is God

Ahaṁ-Ātman: I am Pure Spirit, I am the Eternal Self, I am the Breath of God, I am the Being of Light, I am the Inner God, I am the Spiritual Soul, I am Pure Being, I am Pure Existence, I am a Spark of the Eternal Flame.

At all places, at all times, in all circumstances, in all events, *remember* this and you will attain Mokṣa, Mukti (Freedom), in this lifetime.

Rest your mind in the Heart. This is Hṛdaya-Dhyāna-Yoga (Heart meditation).

The Abode of the Self 434
Pure Consciousness in the Heart 447
The Mind is Dissolved in the Heart 1235

Watching the Breath

There is an ancient Yoga practice of India which was popular for thousands of years, known as "the watching of the breath".

> When the body is in silent steadiness [Āsana, posture], breathe rhythmically through your nostrils with a peaceful ebbing and flowing of the breath [Prāṇa], and just observe the breath without controlling it. This way the wild horses [the thoughts] that draw the chariot of the mind will be tamed.
>
> *Svetasvatara Upaniṣad*

This method is not the Haṭha Yoga practice of Prāṇāyāma (breath-control). This is merely being *aware* of the Breath of Life, Prāṇa, the Ruach (Hebrew) of the Old Testament. Later on, in Buddhism, this became a major method of meditation.

Mindfulness of Breathing 794
Haṭha Yoga and Rāja Yoga 524
Three Kinds of Breathing Meditation 1220
Awareness Meditation 1656

Mantra

Another way to silence your mind is to use a BĪJA-MANTRA (Seed-Sound) or a GURU-MANTRA (Initiatory Mantra) and gradually *reduce* it and refine it in your mind until it disappears in the essentially fundamental nature of Mind.

One of the favourite methods of the Yogīs of ancient India was the mantra ŌṀ.

The Science of Bīja-Mantra 1218
Potent Vibrations: Bīja-Mantra 1542
Bīja-Mantra Practice 1552

> Make your body upright, your head and neck straight [ĀSANA, posture]. Focus your mind and attention into the Third-Eye [the "single-eye" of Jesus]. And there, *silently* chant the ŌṀ sound, slowly, repeatedly. This mantra, ŌṀ, will be your boat with which to cross the sea of SAṀSĀRA [the Three Worlds].
>
> *Svetasvatara Upaniṣad*

Each of these methods require patient sitting (ĀSANA) in one place for a long time.

Upaniṣadic Mantras

The 108 Upaniṣads are full of beautiful instructions and truths and many mantras (utterances of Truth or Power). One such mantra is:

> More radiant than the Sun,
> Brighter than the snow,
> Subtler than the aether is my Soul.
> I am that Soul, that Soul am I.

One should utter this mantra over and over again, many times, anywhere, at any time and in all conditions, until the truth of it becomes *realized.* Repeated often enough, and in great stillness, one can come to Transcendental Soul-Consciousness.

Here is another important mantra, from the Bhagavad-Gītā:

> Never my Spirit was born,
> Never my Spirit shall die.
> Never a time when it was not,
> Never a time when it shall cease to be.
> Birthless and deathless is my Spirit forever.
> Death cannot touch it at all,
> Dead though the body may seem.

The Eastern Heart 448
The Upaniṣadic Mantrams 546

Listening

One form of meditation is to slowly cultivate the inner vision. Another is to learn to hear with the inner ear. For God's *Word* is both Light and Sound—Dazzling Light and Celestial Music at the same time. This takes time and patience, for the eyes and ears of the physical body are blind and deaf to the Power of God's Word.

Through meditation the attention can be moved into the Third-Eye and to the Crown Centre at the top of the head, wherein the Word of God is revealed as the great Creative Power of Living Intelligent Light and harmonious, constructive, musical, directing Sound. This Omnipotent Sounding-Light vibration is the true *Name of God.* It is the Logos which created and is creating all things. It is God's declaration of I AM. It is God's Affirmative-Creative-Self-Existence. This is the Force which creates, sustains and dissolves all Creation. It is God's Will, Power, Love, Wisdom, Intelligence and Activity.

Look where Space seems to be empty. Listen to what appears to be Silence!

Zen Buddhism

Listening inside the Heart and Head

The act of Listening is the highest form of meditation. If you listen to your Heart—which means sitting still, quiet and relaxed, and listening to the space inside your Heart Cakra—you will hear the Voice of God within you, the "small, still Voice" of the Higher Self, and receive guidance for your whole life.

If you listen inside your head, with your right ear, after a while you will hear the Creative Word, the Sound Reverberation of the Universe, and you will *know* that the Creative Word *is* God, right inside you!

Listening into Space

Listening into Space has many variations. You may listen to music, to the sounds of Nature, or to your own breathing.

First, you will listen only *at* the sound as it strikes your ear drums. Try to listen *into* the sound until you become *one* with it, until you *become* the music, the bird, the wind, the waterfall.... At night you can listen to the stars, and you will *become* the stars. Finally, you can *Listen into Space* and the *Omnirevelation* will come to you.

So, you see, listening is the greatest meditation, even in ordinary life, and more so in Spiritual Life.

The Path of Hearing 553
Zen Listening 787
To See and Hear God 637
Inner Absorption by Listening 1699

Meditation on the Sacred Word

The first stage of Creation is that of Sound, the Logos, the Word. The Sacred Word, the Logos, reverberates throughout the Solar System and upon all the Planes of Being. Thus, sound is a basic fact of Life on all the planes. All sounds are, in fact, but notes in the great Symphony of the Logos, the Word.

All sounds are but notes in the great Symphony of the Logos, the Word

> In the beginning was the Word, and the Word was with God, and the Word was God. All things were made [created] by Him [the Word, the Logos]....
>
> *John 1:1,3*

The Sacred Word (Sound) arranges the matter of all the planes within our Solar System, and its subdivisions and subtones create all the forms in our system of Sun and planets and all life upon them, on all the Planes of Being. At the present stage of evolution, Man on the Physical Plane hears only a tiny *fraction* of the sounds around him. There are innumerable sounds in Nature both below and above Man's hearing range. If a human being, at his or her present stage of evolution, were suddenly to hear all the sounds emanating even from Earth, he or she would be physically shattered.

When Man can *hear* the full Sound of the Word as it sounds on the Physical Plane, then he will be perfected on this level. When Man can hear the Sound of the Logos upon the Astral Plane, then he will be perfect on that plane, and so on up the ladder of Life. By intense listening you subdue the Physical Plane, then the Astral, then the Mental and Buddhic Planes, all the way to Nirvāṇa.

Notice a curious fact about the scriptures of India:

Bhagavad-Gītā means "God's Singing".
Upaniṣad means "sitting at the feet of the Master, listening".
Śruti means "hearing the Inner Teacher".

The sacred books are not so much writings, but what the Sages *heard* in deep meditation. Even in the West, the Greek word *gospel* means not so much a written opinion, but a revelation that somebody *heard*. The oldest Buddhist scriptures, in the Pali Canon, all begin with the phrase:

"Thus have I heard..."

The Logos: the Word of God 114
The Cosmic Christ 662
The Voice of God 864
The Word, Logos, Voice, Name 1646

- Listening on the Physical Plane, you discover yourself.
- On the Astral Plane you discover the vibrations of other human beings.
- On the Mental Plane you hear your group note.
- On the Buddhic Plane you hear the note of our Planetary Logos, the sound of our Earth-Being.
- On the Ātmic (Nirvāṇic) Plane you can listen to the Solar Logos of our System and the combined notes of all our planets, both visible and invisible.
- On the planes above the Nirvāṇic you can hear the Sound of the Creative-Word-Universal formulating other Solar Systems.
- On still higher *Cosmic* Planes, you will hear the notes of myriads of stars. Higher still, you will hear the notes of galaxies and universes.

Listening to the internal sounds was a favourite practice of the old Sages of India

Many centuries before the Buddhist and Christian religions, the Hindu Yogīs of old India called this Sacred Word ĀUṀ, and VĀK, "word, speech, Logos", and NĀDA, "the Sound of the Universe". Listening to the internal sounds (NĀDA) was a favourite practice of the Sages of old India.

> One of the best ways of meditating is to listen to the ANĀHATA-NĀDA [non-physical sounds inside oneself]. Sitting in MUKTA ĀSANA and with the ŚAMBHAVI MUDRĀ, the Yogī should listen to NĀDA [the Sound Internal] inside his right ear.
>
> *Haṭha Yoga Pradīpikā*

Many internal sounds will be discovered in this way, such as the sounds of many waters, surging sounds, thunder and drums, jingling and tinkling sounds, conches, bells, flutes, harps, vinas, violins and all the musical instruments. One should always listen to the *subtlest* sounds heard.

This is also the advice of another book on ancient Yoga, the ŚIVA SAṀHITĀ:

> Those desirous of the Kingdom of Yoga should take up the practice of listening to the ANĀHATA-NĀDA [internal sounds] with a recollected mind, and free from tensions and worries. NĀDA will catch the mind [MANAS, the thinking principle]. Mind is like the serpent which becomes steady by hearing the Sound, and does not run away anywhere.

Vāk: the Divine Speech 118
Āuṁ, Ōṁ, Nāda 550
The Sounds of Nāda 1651
Hear the Sound within the Silence 1651

The Science of Bīja-Mantra

The Science of Spirituality is based on Laws which can be mastered

Don't forget that many of the Christian Mystics attained Transcendental Consciousness and even Cosmic Consciousness, but they did not understand the *mechanisms* of how to get there and therefore they spent many years in prayer and other disciplines whereby they actually *enhanced* their minds rather than transcending them. They were groping in the dark and they attained the mystical states more by good fortune than by science! They had no Gurus who knew the process, so it took them many years of great effort. If they did succeed they considered it to be by the Grace of God, and if they did not succeed they thought they were not worthy!

This spiritual ignorance (AVIDYĀ) was caused by the lack of Gurus, true Spiritual Teachers who understood the Science of Spirituality. Spirituality is based on Laws which can be mastered, understood and applied. It is an *exact* science, just like any other science. This Spiritual Science was known to the Hindus of old as GUPTA-VIDYĀ, "esoteric knowledge".

This applies to the Muslims as well. The great Mystics of the Muslim religion also practised the tortuous method of prayer (which enhances the mind), yet there are ninety-nine Names of Allāh (Arabic seed mantras) which bring much quicker results. Many people in the past—in many religions, including the Jewish—did not understand the difference between engaging in mental action and *transcending* mental action. By engaging in mental action alone, we cannot arrive at the Transcendent.

Mysterious Grace 1311
The 99 Arabic Divine Names of God 878
Vibration and Mantra 1518
Potent Vibrations: Bīja-Mantra 1542
Bīja-Mantra Practice 1552

Esoteric Knowledge

GUPTA-VIDYĀ, "esoteric knowledge", was widespread in old India, and the Sanskrit language was the guardian of the esoteric lore. Within the Sanskrit language we find the knowledge of the ancients: black magic, white magic, science, religion, and so on.

The GUPTA-VIDYĀ of old India was but a memory of the DZYĀN, or secret knowledge of Atlantis, and the Sanskrit language was a memory of SENZAR, the old Atlantean language.

GUPTA-VIDYĀ, also known as GUHYA-VIDYĀ, is the secret science of mantras, or potent formulas to achieve all kinds of purposes, the highest being the Knowledge of God, BRAHMĀ-VIDYĀ, and Self-Realization, ĀTMĀ-JÑĀNA.

God is also logical, and there are quicker and slower ways to reach Divine Consciousness. Those who know "the Ways of God" get there quicker. There are innumerable methods of meditation, but the best way to transcend the mind and to come to Pure Consciousness, the innate Self within you, is through the use of Bīja-Mantras (seed mantras). A Bīja-Mantra introduces an harmonious vibration into the mind. It works by focusing and pacifying the mind, by naturally reducing the mind's activities. Through the simple science of the Bīja-Mantras, everybody can come to the Transcendental States.

A Bīja-Mantra introduces an harmonious vibration into the mind

Mantra Yoga is the secret knowledge of how to converse with the Gods (the Devas, as in rituals, for instance) and to converse with God, the Divine Self within us. This secret Vedic knowledge, known by the early civilizations of India, descended from the old Wisdom of Atlantis, but of course the complete knowledge of Atlantis has been forgotten.

In India, and all over the Indian subcontinent, mantras are also used for chanting, devotion, rituals, magic, and so forth. Do not forget, there are many types of action, and Mantra Yoga is a *vast* science. There are many mantras that *enhance* the mind and emotions, but the class of mantras called Bīja-Mantras are the best to *transcend* the mind and come to the state of no-thought, the Mystical State.

The Two Applications of Mantra

Mantra, in Sanskrit, means "an instrument of the mind", from Manas (mind) and Tra (a tool or instrument). Tra also means "to transcend". Thus, a mantra helps you to transcend the mind.

A mantra is a sound-sequence. There are two basic uses of mantras:

a. For the projection of sound into the environment, as in dynamic singing, chanting and bhajans.

b. For inward meditation, to transcend and suspend the mental processes, which is the aim of the silent repetition of mantras.

Mantra-Japa is the repetition of mantras. Japa means "resounding the sound", from Ja (sound) and Pa (to resound). Mantra-Japa is based on the Law of Vibration or Rhythm.

Monology 453

Language of the Gods 200
The Magic of Ritual Worship 366
The Path of Mantra and the Goddess 1490
The Primordial Sound Language 1025

Three Kinds of Breathing Meditation

Sōhaṁ, Haṁsaḥ

The Hindu Yogīs practised two versions of this breath-awareness meditation: the first is the famous Sohaṁ mantra; the second is the famous Haṁsa mantra.

Gāyatrī (Sun) Breathing 1553
Rest in the Great Breath 1654
Controlling the Mind through Breathing 1059

Sō-Ahaṁ: That God I Am.
A'Haṁ-Saḥ: I Am that God.

- In the first version, as you breathe in you think Sō, and as you breathe out you think Haṁ. Thus, Sō-Haṁ is one cycle of breath.
- In the second version, as you breathe in you think Haṁ, and as you breathe out you think Saḥ. Thus, Haṁ-Saḥ is one cycle of breath.

Note that you do *not* control your breath (as in the Prāṇāyāma of Haṭha Yoga). This is not a breath-control method; it is an *awareness* exercise, with Mindfulness of the in-breathing and out-breathing (observation, watching, awareness). You keep breathing in such a way until the Light of Pure Consciousness dawns upon you.

Natural Breathing

Mindfulness of Breathing 794
Awareness Meditation 1656

- Concentrate inside the nostrils.
- Breathe in and out naturally.
- Mindfulness on breathing.

Solar Plexus Breathing

- Concentrate in the Solar Plexus Centre (in the abdomen).
- Breathe deeply, in and out, very slowly.
- Mindfulness in the solar plexus region.

Breathing in the Solar Plexus Centre leads to emotional tranquillity. There are many people, however, who are emotionally blocked or repressed. Some are massively suppressed in the Solar Plexus Cakra. Consequently, when they do Vipaśyanā in this area they might cry or have feelings of anger, sadness, depression, fear, and so forth, which they need to let go of. If done very slowly, conscious breathing will lead to Quiet, Stillness, Silence.

Warrior Breathing 1020
Conscious Breathing in the Heart 1274
Christian Meditation: the Way of Holiness 1345

Vipassana

VIPASSANA is the Pali word for Insight or Intuitive Vision (in Sanskrit, VIPAŚYANĀ). It has the same meaning as the Japanese word SATORI, "intuitive awareness, above the discursive, reasoning mind". It is the state of No-thought or No-mind.

The meditational method of Vipassana is practised by the Hinayana monks in Buddhist Theravada countries, such as Burma, Thailand and Cambodia. As a meditational practice, it is the continuous awareness of the moment-to-moment changes taking place in the body, the emotions and the mind (thoughts). The meditator must not identify with, nor get involved with, the various phenomena experienced in the body, mind and emotions.

The awareness is focused on the direct experience of each moment

The Yogīs of Ancient India practised it as the setting up of the *observer*, the *witness* to all phenomena. The awareness is focused on the direct experience, in full Consciousness, of each moment. This demands great mental composure at all times.

Although this meditation is practised by monks, anybody can do it, at any time, if he or she has the mental strength. In fact, this is an excellent meditation for people who are living in the world, who encounter daily life and experiences. The consciousness must be clear and detached from all phenomena. The meditator must reach an increasingly clearer and deeper awareness of what is happening to him or her, moment by moment.

No-Mind and the One Mind 763
The 'No-Mind' 990
Shikantaza 800

Unstructured meditation has been described by Krishnamurti as:

Meditation without a set formula, without a cause or reason, and without an end or purpose.

The great Zen Masters call it:

Sitting quietly, doing nothing.

It is a Rest in the Silence, the mind being empty, without thoughts, bright, clear, very alert.

The Japanese word ZEN means "unstructured meditation". The word came from the Sanskrit DHYĀNA. When the Buddhist monks from India spread the Teachings in China, it became DHYĀN. Then the pronunciation became Chinese, CHĀNNA or CHĀN. Finally, when it reached Japan, the Japanese pronounced it as ZEN.

Origins of Zen 752

VIPAŚYANĀ
Sanskrit: Internal Observation. Your mind is normally occupied with what is happening outside you, in the world around you. Internal Observation means that you are observing your own Consciousness, mind and thought-processes. You are observing yourself, the Experiencer of those experiences, rather than the events outside. Observing from a Quiet Mind is VIPAŚYANĀ.

Vipaśyanā Yoga: Internal Observation

VIPAŚYANĀ, or *Insight Meditation*, is meditative self-observation, the observation of your inner processes.

VIPAŚYANĀ is observing your mind and thoughts.

Vipaśyanā is to see things as they really are for you in the Moment

VIPAŚYANĀ is focusing on the Present, on your immediate experience—your breathing, your thoughts, your mood or feelings, your situation or actions—thus becoming aware, mindful or conscious of your experience, seeing it just as it *is*.

VIPAŚYANĀ is experiencing reality just as it is for you *at this moment*. If it is cold, it is cold. If it is hot, it is hot. If it is a friend, it is a friend. If it is an enemy, it is an enemy. There is no condemnation, no judgment. You see your anger as "just anger", your fear as "just fear", your worry as "just worry", your sickness as "just a sickness", your pain as "just pain", your unhappiness or discontent as "just unhappiness, just discontent". You are the Witness of it, the Observer. You do not try to modify your experience, nor do you deny it or suppress it, nor do you fight against it or resist it, nor do you try to destroy it.

VIPAŚYANĀ is to see things as they *really are* for you in the Moment, Now. It is self-observation on the personality level which, in due course, leads to Self-observation on the Inner-Witnessing level of Self-Awareness.

VIPAŚYANĀ is impartial self-observation to gain Insight into the causes of your fears, frustrations, agitations, anger, and dissatisfaction with people and life. Self-observation on the personal-consciousness level leads to purification of mind and emotions.

VIPAŚYANĀ is an old Hindu yogic practice that was embraced by Buddhism. In the same way that Jesus was a Jew and followed Jewish practices, Buddha was a Brahmin and followed the old Yoga practices of India. The idea of a separate "Christianity" or a separate "Buddhism" came centuries later.

VIPAŚYANĀ develops emotional tranquillity. Emotional tranquillity is an essential requirement on the Spiritual Path. It is not to be achieved simply by suppressing the emotions, nor by will-power, as some meditators try to do, but by *tuning* your feelings and emotions to the refined vibrations of your Higher Self, the Spiritual Soul within you.

VIPAŚYANĀ is Self-development through Self-Awareness.

VIPAŚYANĀ teaches you to get away from worldly distractions and to focus solidly inside yourself.

In the state of Choiceless Awareness (Vipaśyanā) you give *attention* to the problem or situation you are contemplating, in the outside world or inside your mind-flow, without demanding that it be different. You just see it how it is and *accept* it how it is. When you see and accept how something really is, without fighting or resisting it, or wanting to modify or interfere with it, a *change* takes place in your Consciousness which produces a profound Inner Transformation within you.

Quietly Seeing 786
Mindfulness: the Warrior Within 1017
The Way of Spontaneous Meditation 1229
The Law of Mystic Experience 508

When you accept a person as just "that person", a tree as just "that tree", a thought as just "that thought", a situation as just "that situation", in complete Inner Awareness, then Wisdom (Prajñā) comes to you and prompts you to right action.

When thinking stops, there is Peace in the mind. When you have sufficiently purified your mind, then Prajñā-Jyoti (Wisdom-Light, the Light of Wisdom) spontaneously arises in your mind.

"Just So" means that you accept things as they are, without negative emotional reactions. Whatever happens, it is Just So. All of your pains, worries, fears, anxieties and troubles in life are Just So. Accept them as they are and remain Peaceful at Heart.

The most basic ingredient of Vipaśyanā is Silence, Stillness. Mindfulness (Vipaśyanā) consists of Silence, while being observant of thoughts, feelings, actions, breathing, sound (chanting, intoning), death, Liberation, and the Heart.

Sati-Prajñā (Truth-Discerning Awareness) dawns upon you when you inwardly *realize* that behind and beneath all transitory and changing outer events and phenomena (the world-process, your breathing, your thoughts, feelings or moods, successes or failures, sicknesses or health, and changing fortunes of life and circumstances) is the Abiding Reality, the Unborn, Unmade, Unbecome, Unchanging Eternal Reality, the Transcendental Awareness, the Realm of Absolute Life and Being.

The internal observation of thoughts and feelings, and meditation on death, is to be done in the Head, in the Third-Eye Centre. Being focused in the Head, just observe your thoughts as they arise. Take no interest in them, be indifferent to them, let them come and go as they will. You are merely the Observer, the Witness. If you do not engage in them, after a while they will subside and a great Stillness and Silence will embrace the mind.

When the mind becomes quiet and still, the brain will become quiet and still. Then it becomes possible to experience Higher Consciousness while you are still in your body.

Meditation in the Third-Eye

> Having put away all contacts with outside objects, fixing his vision between the eyebrows, having balanced the inward and outward breaths which flow through the nostrils, with senses, mind, and Soul controlled, the Silent Sage, whose aim is Liberation, from whom fear, desire and anger have departed, becomes truly liberated.
>
> *Bhagavad-Gītā*

When the mind is controlled, the Soul manifests itself

This verse from the Bhagavad-Gītā describes the technique of meditation in the Third-Eye (ĀJÑĀ) Cakra. "Having put away all contacts with outside objects" is PRATYĀHĀRA—withdrawing your senses from looking at things and hearing things. You shut out the world and focus your attention in the middle of the forehead. This focusing is called TRATAKAM, "fixing the gaze inwardly".

The next stage is PRĀṆĀYĀMA, "control of the breath", which means breathing easily and naturally. That which flows in is PRĀṆA; that which flows out is APĀNA. When Prāṇāyāma is established, then comes automatically the control of the senses (INDRIYAS) and the mind (MANAS). When the mind is controlled, the Soul manifests itself.

The Silent Sage (MUNI) is one whose *mind* is silent and "whose aim is Liberation" (MOKṢA) and Freedom (MUKTI). After long efforts at the meditational life, fear, anger and desire (KĀMA) disappear and the Sage is free from the bindings of the Three Worlds. The Physical, Astral and Mental Planes cannot hold the Sage.

> These Holy Men, whose thoughts are thus subdued, who are free from fear, anger and desire, and who *know* the Self [ĀTMAN, the Spirit], dwell in BRAHMANIRVĀṆAM.
>
> *Bhagavad-Gītā*

BRAHMA-NIRVĀṆA (BRAHMANIRVĀṆAM), "God-absorption, dissolution in God", was the original Teaching of the Lord Buddha, the Gautama Buddha, who was a Brahmin (the Hindu priest-caste). Centuries later, His Teachings were completely altered by dropping the words BRAHMAN (God) and ĀTMAN, ĀTMĀ (the Immortal Spirit in Man and in the Cosmos). Thus, later on, Buddhism made out that there is no God, no Final, Absolute, Transcendental Godhead or Reality, and no Immortal Spirit (ĀTMAN), and the Goal is to be dissolved (NIRVĀṆA) into an Emptiness! How warped some later Buddhist teachings have become!

A 'Godless' Religion? 754

The Path of Seeing 552
Stage Three of Aṣṭāṅga Yoga 572
The Life-Force 589
The Lighted Way 1394
The Fullness of the Void 23
Nirvāṇa is… 98

The Bhagavad-Gītā repeatedly employs the term BRAHMANIRVĀṆAM. It may be translated as "dissolved in God". According to the Bhagavad-Gītā, the Sage is "dissolved in God". This original Hindu idea of Nirvāṇa is very different from the later Buddhist idea of Nirvāṇa, which is like an impersonal annihilation.

The Sage is "dissolved in God"

> His Joy is within himself,
> His Bliss is within himself,
> His Light is within, shining.
> The Yogī [the integrated or united One] becomes BRAHMAN [God]
> and attunes to NIRVĀṆA, which is BRAHMAN.
>
> *Bhagavad-Gītā*

There are many ways of meditating in the Third-Eye—what Jesus called the "single eye", where the Light appears. But you should seek Initiation (DĪKṢĀ) from a Guru. Even as a candle is lit by another candle flame, or by another source of fire, so you are ignited within by a Guru at Initiation.

This is a *spiritual fact.* This is one of the functions of the SAT GURU (True Teacher). Those who are arrogant and put themselves above the Guru are infinitely foolish.

Meditation on the Form of the Guru

One form of meditation, which has been very popular in India for thousands of years, is to meditate on the form of one's Guru, Teacher or Master. For many, to meditate on a Living Teacher, in the flesh, is easier to relate to than to meditate on some past dead Saint or some abstract Deity.

The correct process to be followed, however, is that you use the physical image of your Guru only as a starting point. Having attained the presence of the Guru in your consciousness, you try to "feel" or raise yourself to the Soul of your Teacher, the Real Teacher, and from hence lift yourself into the Ocean of God in which that Soul dwells.

Visualizing the Divinity within the Heart 1268

The Guru 389
What is Initiation? 1007
Divine Love in the Head 916
See the Light of the Logos 1650
Remember the Presence 1653

Worship only the Divine Self

You must worship only the Lord God within you

Sometimes, when you meditate in your Heart or Head Centres, you will see Devas, radiant-beings, commonly called "angels". You will also see beautiful men and women living on the Mental Plane. The entities on the Mental Plane usually will communicate with you telepathically. But remember, even if they appear exalted, you must not worship them!

It is permissible for you to communicate with them through mental telepathy. But if any entity wants you to worship him or her, or if any entity wants to control you and become your "spirit-guide" (to have possession of your body), then have nothing to do with them. They are the *wrong sort;* they are astral entities.

Do not believe that mental telepathy is the highest achievement. Above mental telepathy is Buddhi, the State of Oneness. And above Buddhi is Nirvāṇic Consciousness, which is Super-Oneness.

You must worship only the Lord God within you, the Divine Self.

No other entity is like your Divine Self. The Divine Self is You and, at the same time, it is the Self of All. ⚹

Rely on your Inner Self

The Lord Buddha has said:

Hold fast to Truth like to a lamp. Rely on your Inner Self. Look not for help outside yourself.

This is the path of Discipleship, Meditation, Yoga. First you should receive some understanding of spiritual life and spiritual processes from an outer Guru, from a Teacher or Master. Then, when you have started the Path of Meditation, gradually you learn to rely on your Inner Self. At first you listen to the impulses of the Jīva, your Soul in the causal body. At a later stage you learn to discern the impulses of the Spirit, the Ātman. And later still, you listen to your "Father in Heaven", Paramātman, the Monad within you.

First comes the infusion of the Soul into your personality.
Then comes the infusion of your Spirit into your Soul.
And finally comes Glorification by the Breath of the Eternal.

Denizens of the Heaven Worlds 77
Impressions from the Mental Plane 80
Who are the 'Spirit-Guides'? 334
Invoking the Invisible Helpers 370
To be taught Wisdom 353
To Succeed in your Quest 1330

CHAPTER 53

The Heart and Spontaneous Meditation

Mental Activity

Most *active* people in the world today live a speedy and hurried life. This includes children, young and middle-aged adults, and some old people as well. The symptoms are over-activity and having too many things to attend to. When both children and parents have too many things to "do", family life becomes a nightmare of tension, excitement, stress and nervous breakdown. The cause is *overactivity*.

Overactive Mind 990
The Education System 480
Emotional Problems 1429
The New Aquarian Energies 426
Notes on the Path in the New Age 1166
Planetary Disturbance 1697

Many schools overload children with activities and homework to such a point that the children can no longer cope. The nightmare idea of "education" seems to be to "stuff" the children's minds with as much "information" and "data" as possible about anything and everything (whether actually useful or not) until they have a nervous breakdown or rebel against the system. Most often, the "rest" period of a child or adult consists of more strenuous activities. Complete madness rules the world! There is no time for children and adults to *rest* and *relax*, and to return to the Source—that is, to themselves, the Self that they are.

Because of too much external activity, both adults and children are out of tune with themselves (the Inner Self).

The art of being still, quiet, relaxed, "mellowed out", helps to refurbish your life-energies.

Intense mental activity should always be followed by *stillness, silence, rest,* otherwise it will lead to stress and chaotic thinking in the mind.

The average man, woman and child today is more active than the human physical, emotional and mental bodies were designed for; hence the tension, stress, nervousness, neuroses, worries and feelings of insecurity that plague society.

This intense activity is due to the fact that the planet Earth at this time is being bombarded by a certain Cosmic-Energy-Stream (the Seventh Ray) which stimulates the two lowest energy centres in Mankind, the Base Centre and the Sex Centre, which are the two centres connected with the Physical Plane. Hence the universal, feverish activity and preoccupation with sex. People are literally *over-stimulated* in these two areas. No amount of "moralizing" will change the situation. We are dealing with *real* Cosmic Forces here, not just intellectual ideas or sociological "theories".

Before you can enter the *Way of Spontaneous Meditation*, you need to understand what is said here and apply it *practically* in your daily life. All of this is simply a *preliminary step*.

The Way of Spontaneous Meditation

Stage 1: Preliminary Steps

There are two parts of You: the Eternal-Timeless-Self (which is passive) and the forever active and changing personality-image. This turbulent, questing, seeking, experiencing, restless personality-self (the little ego or "I") will come to rest only when it becomes *One* with the Eternal-Self that you *are*. Then, this mad rushing-about in the world for temporal objectives, for unimportant purposes, for trivial pursuits, will come to a natural end, for you will see the futility of it all.

The important point is not to "follow" a Master outside yourself

a. Observe your way of life. Are you always feverishly busy? Are you always stressed out, on the edge? Then, you need to *reduce your activities*.

b. Simultaneously, you need regular *stillness, silence, aloneness*, just being with yourself in quiet Solitude, with your body, emotions and mind tranquil, peaceful, relaxed, centred in Solitude. This will help you to calm down your over-excited body, emotions and mind.

c. When you can be *alternately* active (busy) and passive (quiet), quite naturally, then you are ready for the next step.

The important point is not to "follow" a Master *outside* yourself, not to try to imitate that being, but to find the Master *within* yourself, the God-Self within you. This is *not* your little human ego, but the Christ incarnate *in* you. You have to understand this before you can practise the next step, which unites you to all beings, all creatures, all things, All-Life, the Great-God of the Cosmos and of the Beyond-Space-and-Time.

The Purpose of Spontaneous Meditation

The purpose of *Spontaneous Meditation* or *Being in the Moment* is:

- To experience Life in its totality, fully, one-hundred-percent, with full Awareness, Consciousness and Significance, Moment by Moment, as it flows in you and through your Life-Stream.
- To experience the Timeless, the Eternal, in your "ordinary" experiences of day-to-day Life.
- To perceive the All-Pervading God-Presence in all things, the Divine Immanence.

The Compound Human Being 32
Silence, Solitude, Peace 1386
The Practice of Silence 1443
Rely on your Inner Self 1226
The Universal Christ 440

Stage 2: Awareness

As you go about your daily business—work, home-life, leisure, relationships, and so forth—try to be *aware* of your *thoughts, feelings* and *actions* in all circumstances. That is, try to be *conscious* of what is going on inside yourself, and around you, at all times.

You will discover that most of the time you are *unconscious* (not directly aware) of what you think, feel, do or desire; it is almost automatic, routine, habitual. Try to become *aware* whenever you catch yourself being *asleep*.

Most of the time you are not directly aware of what you think, feel, do or desire

Stage 3: Unlearning

Regularly unlearn your "specialized knowledge" by taking quiet walks by yourself in Nature—in the woods or forest, at a park or beach, by lakes or rivers, in mountains, dunes or deserts, wherever you can be *alone* and surrounded by some aspect of Nature. There, walk or sit or lie down and *empty* all the "stuff" that is in your head, the many thousands of pages of book-learned "knowledge", the jargon and expressions and definitions of technical stuff, business stuff, intellectual stuff, the "shop-talk" that is crowding your mind. Simply let go of all of that "stuff". Rest your mind, empty your mind, and just Be.

You must also let go of the tensions, worries, anxieties and stresses of your daily life, including problems and conflicts with people. Just BE. Each time you do this, you will be refreshed, rejuvenated, healed.

Stage 4: Observing Nature

When you have become good at *letting-go-of-all-things*, then you are ready for this next step.

Gradually learn to intensely *observe* your environment in Nature. Observe all the life-forms, from the smallest ant to the largest tree, the sky or space, the sea or forest, the lake or dunes, wherever you are. Observe, but with your mind still, your emotions quiet, your body relaxed. *You don't have to do anything.* Just observe, be aware, be *conscious* of Life all around you.

Tantra Mind 933
The 'No-Mind' 990
Vipassana 1221
Awareness Meditation 1656
Meditation with Nature 1210

Stage 5: Observing Invisible Nature

Remember that Nature is not only what you see with your physical eyes, hear with your physical ears, or sense with your physical touch. Visible Nature is physical space and the physical bodies or forms that you see. *Within* this is the inner or psychic Nature of *indwelling* energies, forces, powers, and subtle archetypes of all things. Visible Nature *solidifies* from Invisible Nature. Invisible Nature is filled with hosts of invisible beings, creatures and entities of all kinds.

Within Invisible Nature and Space is a still higher aspect: the Spirit, the Source of all the forces, powers, energies and archetypes of Invisible Nature. Visible and Invisible Nature are ever-changing, ever-moving, ever-evolving, ever being born and dying, but the Spirit *within* All-Nature is deathless, immortal, unchanging, imperishable, eternal.

Try to feel or sense the Invisible Nature in all the things you see, hear or touch

Try to *feel* or *sense* the Invisible Nature in all the things you see, hear or touch. This is *not* a thought-process. Try to sense with your auric-field. If you succeed in connecting to aspects of Invisible Nature, then you might be able to connect to the One Invisible Force or Power that *pervades* all Nature.

Your mind is attracted to physical things through your physical senses, and your mind becomes *influenced* by them, becomes *attached* to them and wants to *possess* them, thus becoming *entrapped* by them. This is the cause of your *Bondage* to this world, the cause of birth, death, Reincarnation and Karma, of pleasure, joy, suffering and sorrow, of tension, stress and violence. Your mind wants to *possess* all that you see, hear or touch, whether animate or inanimate, and you *identify* with your mind and body, with your personality.

To attain true Freedom or Liberation, you must therefore *break* this chain of *identifying yourself* with the things of this world through your mind, and *re-identify yourself* with the Eternal Spirit that you truly are. Then you will discover that the One Self, the One Life, the One Spirit, *permeates* all forms, all bodies, all little selves, all objects, all personalities, all events. The Divine Radiance is everywhere.

The waking, dreaming and dreamless-sleep states are states of your *relationship* with your body and mind; they are *not* of You as the Spirit, which is Eternally Conscious and Free.

In Bondage to the Mind 238
The Process of Seeing or Perceiving 542
Obstacles to Higher Consciousness 1424
The Seven States of Consciousness 494
What is Consciousness? 1368

Stage 6: Adeptship

At a later stage still, a further Revelation awaits you: this Universal One Force or Cosmic Energy can be *directed, focused, adapted* and *controlled* by human will, desire, purpose, plan, emotion or attention. Then you become an Adept.

Stage 7: The State of Being

Everything you do will be touched by Eternity

The next stage is the most difficult to describe. This can happen only *after* you have undergone an Inner Transformation, a Fundamental Change, when you have established yourself in your Inner Reality *permanently*—what in the East is called SAHAJA SAMĀDHI, "spontaneous or natural Spiritual Trance".

Then, you will be always in the Moment. You will be always in meditation, spontaneously, no matter what you are doing. Then, everything you do will be touched by Eternity, and everything you touch will resonate with a new Life, a new Significance. Whereas before, you were impelled to act from personality drives and desires, now you will be acting from the State of your Being.

Acting from your Being is vastly different to acting from your personal drives and ambitions. In this State there is no "outside" or "inside" of you, for you perfectly *identify* with all things "within" and all things "without". Whatever happens on the outside is happening *to* you, *inside* you. You *become* the World-Process itself.

In this last State, your mind is *naturally free of thoughts*. You *can* think, if it is required that you think, but the mad racing-around of your mind has gone forever.

Samādhi: the Goal of Yoga 574
The Law of your Being 976
Pure Being 1056
Being and Becoming 1415
You Are the World 1390

Liberation from Worldly Consciousness

The three ordinary states of consciousness—the waking, dreaming and dreamless-sleep states—are due to your *identification* with your body-mind structure. When you *raise* yourself above your body-mind structure through meditation, you arrive to your Self as Spirit and begin to function in Spiritual Consciousness or Transcendental Consciousness, in the State of Oneness or Unity with all that Is. Thus, the purpose of true meditation is to *identify* yourself with the Spirit that you truly are by *rising above* your sense of body and mind.

Being lost in worldly consciousness is being asleep

Being *lost* in worldly consciousness is being *asleep*. Having *regained* Spiritual Consciousness is being *Awake*. In worldly consciousness the world is perceived as "real"; all things, people, objects and events are "real" to you. In Transcendental Consciousness all things of the Spirit are "real" to you, and this world is like a dream, a fantasy, an illusion, a magic film-show.

In worldly consciousness all people and things *appear* to you as *external* to yourself. In Spiritual Consciousness all objects (whether physical, invisible, subtle or mental) appear as being *within yourself*.

The Spirit-that-You-Are is an ever-continuous Eternal Consciousness, ever Awake, always full of Life and Bliss. Having *established* yourself in Spirit as a result of meditation and the Spiritual Life, and having undergone the *Inner Transformation*, you will be in the State of Spontaneous Meditation all the time. You will always be in the Moment and act from the Moment, which is the Interface of Eternity and Time.

Being in this State is true YOGA (Union), true ZEN (Chān, meditation), true TAO (the Self-Moving Way). Anything else is but a fake, an ignorance.

The Three Identifications 1369
Understand your Predicament 892
The Essence of Wisdom 1680
Know Thyself 1389

The Pure Spirit, the Monad that you are, is Timeless and Immortal, is never born and cannot die, is full of Bliss, Light, Wisdom, Knowledge and Love. It becomes associated with the body-mind structure, the personality, which is the material, the temporal, the perishable, which undergoes birth, death and rebirth, which knows suffering and joy, which has a sense of "ego" or limited "I", which is the self-of-matter. Liberation consists of breaking the chains that bind You to the matter-born-self and consciously re-becoming the Spiritual Self, the Spirit which is a Spark of God forever. The final Goal of Self-Realization, Yoga, Tao, Zen, is to *experience* your Self as the Monad, the Glorious Spark of God, forever One with God, within the personality yet altogether above it for all Eternity.

The Way of the Spirit 381

Attach your Mind to the Eternal

Live in the world, but have your mind detached from the world

Spontaneous Meditation, Being in the Moment, Zen, Yoga, Tao, Self-Realization, is a State of Being wherein you experience the Unity and Simplicity of the Godhead *within* the multiplicity of Creation or Divine Manifestation, all at the same time.

This State of Being is a state of the Spiritual Heart. It is centred in the Heart. It is the One-Self in all beings, and all beings in the One-Self or Spirit.

The world is the product of Mind—human minds, Planetary Mind, the Mind of Nature—and therefore it is subject to *change* as the mind changes with each thought. Hence, it is unstable. Pure Consciousness, however, is *above* the mind; although it is not the mind, it is the *source* of the mind, and it is eternal and unchanging. Pure Consciousness, Transcendental Consciousness, Spiritual Consciousness, is the Unchanging Reality, the Everlastingness, the true meaning and significance of all beings and all things.

Therefore, be *in* the world, live in the world, but have your mind *detached* from the world, and attach it to the Real, the Imperishable, the Everlasting, by the right meditation method and leading a spiritual life. Live *from* the Heart and *in* the Heart. This is the Way.

Your mind can be attached to the objects of this world, or to the subtle objects of the invisible worlds, or to the Bliss of the Eternal, the Immeasurable, the Everlasting, God, the One-Self within All. Each leads to a different Path, with different results and effects. The *choice* is yours, and yours alone.

Beyond Heaven

You may be a thoroughly good man or woman and, as a result, are destined to go to "heaven" after death. But "heaven" represents subtle worlds where "good" people of the world go after the death of their physical bodies—it is *not* the State of Self-Realization, Nirvāṇa, Immortal Bliss, the Kingdom of God. To reach that State of Being you have to do more than just be "good" in the ordinary sense. Heaven is temporary, like this world, but the Kingdom-of-God-State is Eternal and Everlasting.

Endless desire for the objects of this world keeps you trapped here. Desire for the Real propels you to get There.

Senses or the Self? 239
The Principle of Choice 1380
Desire for the Real 1503
The Law of the Afterlife 410
The Way to Higher Consciousness 329

The Wise Ones attach their minds to the Bliss of the Eternal, the Immortal Bliss and Undying Love. Below that, all things perish, come to an end—even the invisible worlds. The Eternal Absolute is the Origin and final Goal for all beings.

Only the Blissful Ones, who have merged their minds in the Absolute, can truly be loving and compassionate to all beings. Therefore, seek the Joy and Ecstasy of the Everlasting by plunging deep *inside* yourself into the Heart of the Eternal One. Only Devotion in your Heart will *purify* your mind and make it fit for the Radiance of Enlightenment.

The Eternal Absolute is the Origin and final Goal for all beings

Before you can *experience* the Eternal, the Absolute, you must have *right Knowledge*, then you must *practise* that Knowledge, and then you will have *experiences* which will lead you to the Revelation of the Mystery that You are.

You are the Way, and You are the means to attain It.

The Mind is Dissolved in the Heart

The mind attains Peace only after realizing the Self, the Ātman, the Pure Spirit that you are, for the Self or Spirit is *above and beyond* the mind. The Self (the Luminous Ātman) is realized in the innermost cavity of your Heart, in the highest region of Ākāśa (Inner Space). Thus, you must *negate* your mind-activities to discover Who you really are.

When you are in the Consciousness of Ātman (the Spirit), your mind automatically stops functioning. When you come out of It, your normal mind can function again. If you *remain* in Spirit (in Spiritual Consciousness), your ordinary mind cannot function, or only with great reluctance and difficulty.

The mind is *dissolved* in the Heart. The Ahaṁkāra (I am the doer) is your sense of "I, mine, I am", on the *personality* level. When you *dissolve* that through spiritual practice in the Heart, you will become *free* from all personality-limitations.

The Experience of the Heart 1280

The Eternal 1644
Tapas: Spiritual Purification 571
On the Wings of Devotion 1129
The State of Innocence 1306

The Threefold Way

The Way of the Heart, HṚDAYA-MĀRGA, consists of a threefold action or practice:

1. Right esoteric and spiritual Knowledge or Realization. This is called JÑĀNA Yoga.
2. Selfless activity for the benefit of others. All activities that are selfless, for the benefit of others, are KARMA Yoga.
3. Pure Devotion in the Heart to the God within you (ĪŚVARA) and the Universal Absolute (BRAHMAN) outside of you. Pure, selfless Devotion in the Heart to the Deity is BHAKTI Yoga.

It is in and through the physical body that you must practise the Threefold Way

Thus, you must approach the Spiritual Path in a threefold way: by Knowledge, Action and Devotion. You must practise these three aspects of Yoga (Union) not separately but together, as your Way in life. Any one aspect alone is not enough.

The importance of your physical body lies in the fact that it completes your human nature on the Physical Plane. It is in and through the physical body that you must practise the Threefold Way. That is the reason you have a physical body.

Subconscious Renewal

A very important and unavoidable task you must do is VĀSANĀ-KṢAYA or SAṀSKĀRA-KṢAYA, the dissolution or obliteration (KṢAYA) of old habit-patterns, subconscious memories, past tendencies of behaviour inherited from your previous lives or created during this life, psychological tendencies which *prevent you now*, in this lifetime, from attaining your Goal of Liberation. This includes all your past "traumas" and unhappy experiences (which ignorant people believe they are "victimized" by for the rest of their lives, but it is not so!). These past impressions, habit-patterns, desires, mental tendencies, compulsive drives in the subconscious part of the mind, are called VĀSANĀ or SAṀSKĀRA. Without dissolving them, you cannot succeed in your Work.

You renew your subconscious mind by spiritual practices.

The Role of the Divine Female in the Salvation/Liberation Process 1502

The Holy Path 1285
Cultivate Knowledge 1366
Karma Yoga: Divine Union by Action 1132
Bhakti Yoga: Divine Union by Devotion 1128
Saṁskāra and Vāsanā 251
Desire-Streams 1377
To Achieve Liberation 1177

A Summary of the Practice

Your practice must include the following:

- The healthy exercise of your *physical body*.
- The control of your *speech* so that it will bring no evil upon yourself or another.
- The regulation of your *breathing* process.
- The subjugation of your *mind* through correct meditation.
- The opening of your *Heart* through perfect and pure Devotion.
- The development of your *Intuitive Faculty* through the right Spiritual Knowledge which is *uncontaminated* by worldly vibrations and psychism.

Thus shall you attain the Goal.

Your most important practice is to *worship* the Eternal in your Heart and *surrender* your Life to the Inner-Ruler-Immortal who dwells *within* you, who gives you all Grace, Light, Love and Blessings upon your Way, and who will *inwardly* lead you to your final Vision, the Boundless Absolute, the Limitless Love.

Your most important practice is to worship the Eternal in your Heart

Your physical body belongs to Time, but your deathless Self belongs to Eternity.

The Ultimate Reality, the Godhead, is all that you see in this Universe, both its visible and invisible dimensions. This Reality, in all its parts, and That which is Transcendental and *above* it all, are One.

You, God, Universe: One in All, All in One.

Self-Realization, or the Knowledge of your Self as the Immortal Spirit living in the realms of Bliss and Eternity, cannot happen without *aspiration* towards that State of Being. The worldly consciousness has no aspiration for the Spiritual Self; hence people remain forever chained to the Wheel of Birth and Death in physical bodies.

First comes intense *aspiration* for the Real; then *self-discipline* (practice) towards that Goal; then glimpses or *visions* of the Realized State; then more practice to *stabilize* the Realized State and overcome all obstacles or hindrances which prevent that state from being perfectly experienced; then, finally, the ability to hold onto that condition at all times.

Mokṣa, Mukti (Liberation) means that you are able to live freely in the Spirit, unhindered by your physical body, mind and personality structure.

Jīvan-Mukti is when you liberate yourself while still living in your physical body.

Videhā-Mukti is when you liberate yourself after the death of your physical body, in the after-death condition. This is not possible if you have not commenced the process while still alive in your body.

To Become a Jīvanmukta 259

The Way of the Mind

Now we shall describe to you the Way of the Mind, MĀNASA-MĀRGA, also known as RĀJA YOGA (the Royal Way) and CITTA-MĀRGA (the Way of Intelligence).

This Way is centred in your Head. It consists of cultivating Awareness, Consciousness, being in the Moment through total Awareness, using the *total* Mind. This Way is *not* about thinking or theorising, using your ordinary, rational mind.

The aim of this Way is to cultivate Silence within you

In this form of meditation you are constantly *aware, conscious,* of what is going on *inside* you and *outside* you in the world, in your environment, with the total force or capacity of your Mind, centred in your Head. This involves your Higher Mind, Pure Awareness, not just the thought-producing organ (MANAS). You are *aware* of what arises, moment-by-moment, and you meet circumstances *full-on.* You meet every event, situation and person (in relationships as well as in Nature, in cities or in quiet spots, while alone or in a crowd) *totally,* without reservation, with your full Attention. This is done *spontaneously*, in a state of Effortless Being.

In this form of meditation you do not quit the world or retire from the world, but are active in it, with regular and periodic withdrawals from the world to go deeper inside your Consciousness. You do not negate or deny experiences.

The aim of this Way is to cultivate Silence within you, and into that Silence you merge the ordinary mind, your rational faculty. When your ordinary mind has settled down in internal Silence, and there are no more thought-waves (VṚTTI), then you fall back upon your Fundamental Self, your Essential Nature, which is Boundless Consciousness.

It is important to understand that *the world is changing all the time*. That is, the world is bombarded by planetary, solar-systemic and cosmic energies; therefore, everything is always *unstable* in the world, which is why you also are so unstable and cannot focus on the Path with singular intent. You must learn to live *with* the world, in its ever-changing conditions, and yet remain always focused on your Spiritual Path. You are a Traveller on the Way and, as a Traveller, you are continually on the move. Yet, in spite of this, you have to remain firmly upon the Path. Commit yourself to this.

Realms of the One Mind 492
Rāja Yoga: Divine Union by Meditation 1126
Vipaśyanā Yoga: Internal Observation 1222
Change is the Absolute Law 405

Cultivate Silence of the Mind

Understand this well! On the *Way of the Mind* (Rāja Yoga), the first and most important step is to bring the lower mind (your ordinary mind) to a state of Silence, Stillness, free from thoughts. It is not possible to follow the rest of the Way without this.

This is completely *opposite* to how the mind is used (or rather, misused!) in the world, where the mind is endlessly "stuffed" with information, endlessly agitated by *forcing* it to think and churn out thoughts literally non-stop. Can you imagine, from your first day at school until the end of a university degree, how many millions of thoughts your mind has been forced to produce? And, following that, in your work, job, career, and so forth? Consequently your mind has been "trained" to endlessly produce thoughts and it cannot do otherwise. Therefore, it cannot reflect the Self, the Ātman, the pure Spirit that you are. In other words, it is impossible to Know yourself as you *truly* are.

The first step on the Way of the Mind is the emptiness of your mind

Hence, the first step on the *Way of the Mind* is the Silence and Stillness, the emptiness of your mind. Without it you are forever *trapped* in the world and have no hope of Knowing who you really are. You cannot perceive your Self, simply because the thought-producing faculty, your ordinary mind, *veils* the Self, *clouds over* the Self.

When your mind becomes Tranquil, like an unruffled lake, you will *see* the Light within, which perpetually Shines.

Mind-Waves

Citta-Vṛtti are your mind-waves, the immense thought-producing activity of your mind (the mental body), which never stops producing thoughts, day or night.

Kāma-Vṛtti are the vibrations of your feelings, desires and moods (your emotional or astral body), which are ever-changing and throwing you constantly into turmoil.

The objective of your meditation is the calming-down of your mind and emotions. Before the Dawning of the Light of the Spiritual Self within you can come about, you must still the restless waves of your ordinary day-to-day mind and tranquillize the feverish activities of your emotional nature. That is why you need to meditate regularly.

The Practice of Silence 1443

The Ordinary Mind 896
Your Mind is the Key 1208
The Attitude for Yoga 558
No-Mind and the One Mind 763
The Seven Stages of Sūfī Silence 901
The Law of Mystic Experience 508

Trapped Spirits

Where You really live is full of Bliss and unending Life in Glory

Human beings on this planet are Spirits who have been trapped into the Earth's visible and invisible atmosphere through the mechanism of the personality. Your personality mechanism consists of your mental body (lower mind), your astral body (emotional nature), your etheric-physical or vital-force body (life-force) and your dense physical body (the animal body). With your dense physical body and etheric body you live *in* the Physical Plane of the Earth planet. With your astral or emotional body you live *in* the Astral Plane of the planet. With your mental body (your mind), you live *in* the Mental Plane of the planet (the "heaven" worlds). This constitutes your personality mechanism.

But in fact, You are a *Threefold Spirit*, living above and beyond the personality realms. You are a Spark emanated from the Monad, who Itself is a Spark of the Solar Logos. You, as a Spirit, are *not* limited to the constricting life on the lower planes of Earth! Know this to be your *true history*. Life in the Physical World is full of pain and sorrow. The Astral World is full of illusion and deception. The Mental Plane is full of false, temporary "heaven" worlds. But where You *really* live is full of Bliss and unending Life in Glory.

You were *sent down* into the lower worlds to gain experience, to expand your Conscious Awareness. You have been here many times. Is it not time for you to recover Glory?

Karmic debts, accrued over many lives, have to be paid off at the personality level. The God-Within-You will help you to overcome all difficulties, however, if you *aspire* to the Kingdom of God and seriously *do your best* on the Path. Be of good cheer. Be Joyous!

Within the Buddhic and Nirvāṇic Planes there is a great Peace, Stillness, Silence. This is why, as you approach those planes in your meditational experiences, your mind becomes enveloped in Peace, Silence, Stillness.

On the lower planes (the Causal, Mental and Astral) the vibrations are active; you perceive activity, even though the actions are softer, subtler and less harsh than those registered by the mind in the bodily consciousness on the Physical Plane. Hence your mind needs *Peace, Silence* and *Stillness* before it can register the Buddhic and Nirvāṇic conditions of Existence.

Human Involution and Evolution 170
What is Consciousness? 1368
Understand your Predicament 892
Children of the Sun 1590
Karma and your Spiritual Development 255

Let Go of the Past

When you enter the Spiritual Path seriously, you will discover your own faults, weaknesses, imperfections and vices, and then you will get into a state of *despair* because you think you should not have such faults when you are on the Spiritual Path. Understand that it is *because* you are on the Path that these imperfections show up in your Awareness; otherwise you would not even be aware of them. Then, you must *consciously work upon yourself*, over a long period of time, to better yourself on the personality level.

Time is an artificial construct of your lower mind, produced by thought

Remember that You, as a Soul, are True, Beautiful, Good.

When you discover your faults, vices, imperfections and past "traumas", do the right thing: forget them! These days there is an awfully bad popular psychology: to endlessly *dwell upon* your past "traumas", your vices, your problems, your imperfections, either through "counselling" or in groups. Understand this:

The correct Way is simply to *forget* the Past.

The Past can hold you as a "victim" only as long as you enjoy being a victim, while you choose to remain a victim because it gives you a sense of purpose and identity.

Living in the Eternal Now means *living in the Moment*, not in past impressions. Let go of the Past; it is a nonexistent dead-end. Yet so many people cling desperately to the Past, as if there was nothing else. Even when their past was evil and painful, they hang onto it with all their might. How silly that is!

Today, Now, you are not what you were yesterday, or a year ago, or ten years ago, or a hundred years ago, for *Life ever moves on inside You.*

Time is an artificial construct of your lower mind, produced by thought. If you *ascend* in Consciousness beyond the mental sphere, it is impossible for you to experience Time, to have the sense of a Past, for Reality is always felt as *Now*, this Moment, this second. And this Moment is ever New, uncluttered by the Past.

Can you understand this?

Being in the Now, you are Free.

Karmic Adjustment 1379
Cultivate the Positive 1365
The Sense of Time 22
Past, Present and Future 1400
Quest for Reality 1178
To Succeed in your Quest 1330
The Kingdom is at Hand 1453

Transformations of the Mind

When your mind (your mental body) is *still*, it can *reflect* the Essential Self that you are—You as the Living Soul, which is of the nature of Pure Consciousness. When your mind is *active* (thinking, reasoning, discursive, or just idly chattering to itself), it *overshadows* your Essential Nature, which is Pure Consciousness, Pure Awareness, direct Perception and Bliss.

When your mind is active, it overshadows your Essential Nature

Citta-Vṛtti-Nirodha

The endless transformations of the mind-substance (the mental body) resulting from "thinking" and "mind chatter" (verbalizing, speaking, whether silently or aloud) are called Citta-Vṛtti (mind-waves).

When you manage to *suspend* or *still* these movements of your mind in deep Silence, this is called Citta-Vṛtti-Nirodha (mental-transformations-suspending).

When your mind is completely still, this is called Samādhi (Samā-Dhi: equilibrated-mind).

Super-Knowing

A Super-Knowing faculty can be developed by the quieting of the thoughtform-making faculty of the mind (Citta-Vṛtti-Nirodha).

Nirodha: quieting, suppressing, controlling, suspending.
Citta: the mind, the mind-stuff or substance.
Vṛtti: the modifications of the mind, mental waves, thoughtforms.

When the mind (Manas) becomes still, empty of thoughts, the Soul-Light can be reflected into it. Then arises the faculty of Buddhi, which is the true Intuition, the Revelation-Consciousness whereby the hidden Mysteries are shown to the mind: Bliss-Consciousness, Light-Consciousness, the Christ-Consciousness, Pure Consciousness, Clear-Light and Unity-Consciousness. All of this is Buddhi. It is the Consciousness of the Mystics. This faculty is *above* the mind.

When the Buddhi, the Super-Knowing faculty, becomes infused into your ordinary mind, then your mind becomes Buddhi-Manas (Wisdom-Mind), and you become a Sage, a Seer, a Knower (Jñāni), who spontaneously knows all things spiritual, all things related to the Soul, the Path and the Godhead within.

Inspiration by the Mind of Light 1113

Pāda I Sūtras 2,3,4 536
Suspended Mind 1209
Samādhi: the Goal of Yoga 574
Dimensions of the Mind 891
Christ-Consciousness 443

Nirodha-Pariṇāma

Nirodha also means "binding", which is the state of your normal thought-producing mind, because it binds You, the Self, to your thoughts. Pariṇāma means "transformation, change".

When your Consciousness or Attention moves away from the continuous mind-chatter of thoughts and mental activities into Silence, this is called Nirodha-Pariṇāma (bondage-transformation). That is, your mind becomes free of thoughts, and hence it becomes Free to experience Boundless Consciousness.

There will come a stage when your mind will be totally disengaged or suspended

Samādhi-Pariṇāma

A further ability is developed when you can *alternate at will* between focusing on a necessary mental activity and Boundless Consciousness. This transformation of the mind is called Samādhi-Pariṇāma (the tranquil-mind transformation state).

Ekāgratā-Pariṇāma

A much further development of mind-transformation is when you have developed the ability, as a result of meditation and the Spiritual Path, to engage your mind in action whenever it is necessary and, at the same time, *simultaneously*, always experience the unbroken state of Silence and Stillness. This is called Ekāgratā-Pariṇāma (concentrated-transformation of the mind).

Nisspanda

There will come a stage in your mind-transformation when your mind will be totally disengaged or suspended (Niṣ-Spanda, no-vibration), when you will look and see and hear and taste and smell without a thought in your mind, without *verbalization* of what you see, hear or experience, without mind chatter, without any mental waves or vibrations. Then you will see and hear and taste and smell and *know* how things *really* are.

The State of Inner Purity 497
Perceptions of the One Mind 490
When the Mind is Still 768
Vibration and Mantra 1518

How to have a Peaceful Mind in a Troubled World

Cultivate the Fires of Love 928

Your *mind* will become *peaceful* when your Heart has been activated and you *actively practise* the Heart qualities: Love, Compassion, sympathy, tenderness, friendliness, joyousness, happiness, spontaneity. (Notice that none of these are "intellectual" qualities.)

Rest in the Great Breath 1654

Your mind will become peaceful by regular and systematic *tranquil breathing* (SO-HAṀ, HAṀ-SAḤ).

The Silence of the Deep 1355

Your mind will become peaceful when you *rest* at the *Source* of your Mind, when your mind is *silent*, when its endless activities are naturally put to *rest*, when you are *comfortable* with Inner Silence.

Alone with God 700
Silence, Solitude, Peace 1386

Your mind will become peaceful when you find Solitude, when you are no longer afraid to be by yourself, when in that Quietness and Aloneness you *match your vibrations* with the Buddhic World, the Sense of Unity all around, the Sense of the One-Self in All, the Sense of the God-Presence, the Sense of the Inner God within you.

Visualizing the Divinity within the Heart 1268
To Worship the Divine Incarnations 1270

Your mind will become peaceful when you *dissolve* it in the *form* you have chosen for Truth: the form of Buddha, of Christ, of Rāma, of Kṛṣṇa, of the Goddess, of your Guru or a Saint. When you look at the form with a quiet mind, uninfluenced by thoughts, slowly your mind will be *transformed* into your Chosen Form of Reality (ĪṢTA-DEVATĀ) and you will go *beyond* the form into the Eternal, the Everlasting.

Hear the Sound within the Silence 1651

Your mind will become peaceful when you sit or stand quietly and *listen* to the inner sounds, or to the Inner Sound.

Look for the Light 1395
See the Light of the Logos 1650

Your mind will become peaceful when you focus your Attention in the Third-Eye, and there *watch* the darkness in front of you, or the Spot of Light, or the Tranquil Light, or the Divine Radiance.

Just Sitting 1018
Zazen: Zen Sitting 798

Your mind will become peaceful when you sit in a Steady Posture (ĀSANA), not being concerned with anything else.

Being-in-the-Moment Meditation in the Head

The Active (Doing) Meditation

- In your daily life, go about doing your duties and activities *without a sense of ego*, that is, without the sense that "you" are doing them. Do things in an "egoless" way, as if they simply have to be done by someone and you just "happen" to be there to do them.
- Be simply in the *Now*, and attend to all actions as if there were no Past and no Future, only what needs be done Now.
- Do not link your activities to the Past—past causes, past happenings or past memories. Simply do what needs to be done Now.
- Also, do not link your activities to some hope of reward or benefit in the Future. Simply do your actions, without an ego, without a sense of self or "I", effortlessly, simply, with an uncomplicated mind, serene emotions and a relaxed body.

Through this technique you develop your powers of *Attention*, which is the key to any higher development or evolution. If you *watch with Awareness* everything you do, you will discover how *you have created* all your circumstances, how everybody creates their own circumstances, and how the world is created by the minds of Man.

The Passive (Sitting) Meditation

Sit quietly in your favourite meditation posture. Realize:

I am not this physical body or vitality.
I am not the mind, thoughts or concepts.
I am not the past memories and impressions.
I am not the moods, desires, feelings and wants.

- Sit still and have your Attention in the Head, in the Third-Eye Centre or in the Crown.
- Be aware of *Now*, of this Moment. This is not related to the Past, nor to the Future. Simply be *Conscious*, without thoughts or images, without pictures in your mind, without desiring or wanting anything, without remembering past experiences, without anticipating some future events.
- Enter the state of Internal Silence where there are no mental waves, no feeling-waves, where there is no restlessness of any kind.

The Consciousness within you is the Creator of your Life.

Is it possible to have a peaceful mind in the midst of the storms and stresses of life?—in the midst of wars, natural cataclysms, diseases and poverty, or fears from the Past, or fears of the Present or of the Future, or the anxieties and insecurities of life, or worries about job, finances, home-life and family, or the loss of loved ones, or the worry that you might lose a loved one, or conflicts within yourself, or conflicts within your family or at work, or conflicts in your environment or in your society? Amidst the mess that human beings have made of this life on Earth, is it possible to go about being Peaceful, Tranquil, Quiet, inwardly Joyous?

The answer is: Yes!

The Way to Bliss-Consciousness

In Buddhic Consciousness there is a feeling of Unity with all things

Is it possible to live in this world and experience Bliss?—not just temporary happiness, not just a fleeting joy, but real, unending Bliss? Yes, but you must work for it.

Bliss is the nature or very essence of Buddhic Consciousness. Buddhi, or Bliss-Consciousness, can be experienced only in *complete* Silence, when the mind and all its activities have been *transcended.* Initially it will be experienced when you go *above* the thinking-faculty into Transcendental Consciousness, but later on it will be sensed all the time.

In the state of Buddhic Consciousness there is a feeling of Unity with all things. There is Silence and no sense of time. Again, in the beginning this may be sensed only during meditation, when the mind is empty of thoughts, images, imaginations, fancy and past memories, when your Consciousness has transcended into your Soul-Being. Later on, the Feeling of Unity and Timelessness will be continuous.

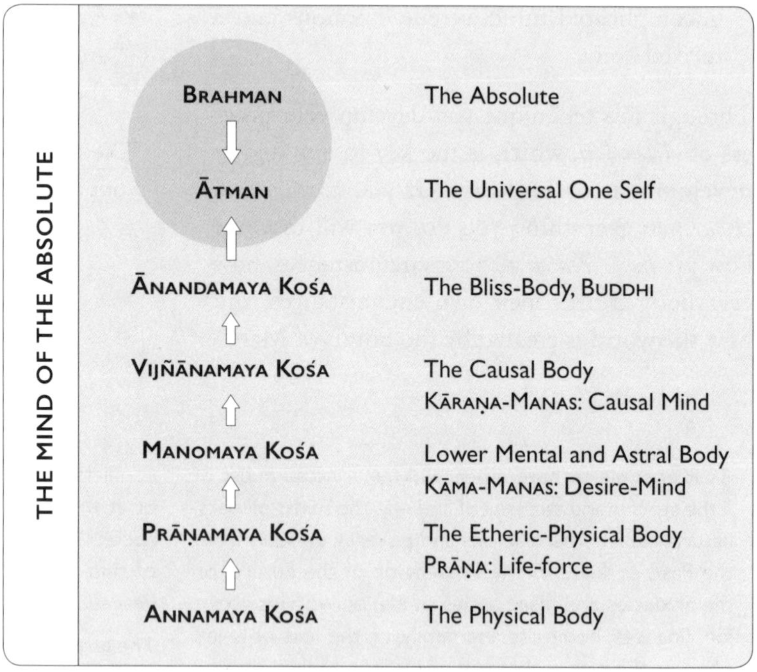

The Way to Bliss-Consciousness

Buddhic Consciousness 86
Towards Bliss-Consciousness 423
Coverings over the Self 38

In the state of Buddhic Consciousness, Light may be seen, and in this Light all Knowledge is revealed and you will understand the true and profound nature of your Self, and the hidden Mystery of Life, visible and invisible. This Knowledge is *above* the thoughts and concepts of the mind—direct, immediate, complete.

You will understand the true and profound nature of your Self

True meditation in the mind is always spontaneous, immediate, transcending thoughts. It is the result of *dissolving your mind into the Primeval Silence* which is within you and outside of you, all around you, everywhere.

First you must cultivate equanimity of mind and contentment of emotions, reduce the mad rushing about after many objectives, plans and purposes, most of which you will find are unnecessary. Be not overcome by fears, worries, or doubts about yourself and the Path, and do not despair when things go wrong in your life—it is unavoidable. And quietly go about *serving and loving* everybody you meet.

The Bliss-feeling is yours, Now and in the Forever.

The Way of the Mind

I Am a Point of Light in the Greater Light of the Mind of God. (Third-Eye)
I Am a Point of Love in the Greater Love of the Heart of God. (Heart)
I Am a Point of Power in the Greater Power of the Will of God. (Base)
To Bless, to Heal and to Inspire the Children of Man who are the Children of God. (Throat)

- Sit quietly with your eyes closed. *Focus in your mind.*
- Bring your mind into the Third-Eye Centre and there say the first statement, "I Am a Point of Light in the Greater Light of the Mind of God", with *concentration* and *intent.* Pause, and try to *Realize* the Truth you are saying.
- Do the same with each statement, always in the order given above. You may repeat this cycle once or several times. *Pause* between each statement. When you have finished, spend a few minutes in silence.
- Focus in your mind for the whole meditation. That is, *use your mind only.* In your Silence at the end, allow the Higher Mind within you to bless you.

The Hierarchical Mantrams 1726

Meditation and the Joy of Living 1012
Return to Primeval Happiness 1179
Persevering to the End until Final Liberation 1101

PART TEN

The Way of the Heart

CHAPTER 54

The Heart and the Lost Art of Prayer

The Divine Mood

Whether your background is Jewish, Muslim, Christian, Hindu, Buddhist or Sikh, you have learned to pray sometime or another in your life, or you have seen others pray. But do you know the true secrets of prayer? For prayer has the same secrets, no matter what religion you belong to, or in what language you pray.

When your Heart is on Fire with Divine-Longing, you shall find God

Prayer is an old-fashioned word for *meditation*. The old religions used the word *prayer* before the word *meditation* was invented. Thus, true prayer and true meditation are synonymous, as you shall see.

Prayer (JAPA) is manifold and we shall disclose to you its powerful secrets. The essential secrets of prayer lie in the HṚDAYAṀ (the Heart) and BHĀVA (mood). Or, to be precise, BHĀGAVATA-BHĀVA (Divine Mood). The meanings of these words have infinite depths, which we shall try to explain to you. In these two words, *mood* and *Heart*, lie infinite worlds and all glorious revelations. Listen carefully.

BHĀVA has multiple meanings. Outwardly it means "mood, feeling, attitude, emotion". You have moods, feelings, emotions, and these "moods" drive you in all directions. To succeed in prayer (meditation), however, you must have the Divine Mood, BHĀGAVATA-BHĀVA or DEVA-BHĀVA. That is, you have to be "in the mood" to pray, to meditate.

This is all-important. DEVA-BHĀVA means "longing for the Divine"; it is the desire, feeling, emotion, for Union with God. If you have not yet succeeded in your meditation, ask yourself: "How strong is my desire to be with God?" Is it an all-consuming desire? Is it only lukewarm? Or is there none at all? Are you striving always to be united with God? Or are you leaving the work to be done for two days before your death? Be honest with yourself. When your Heart, HṚDA, is on Fire with Divine-Longing, you shall *find* God.

God-in-the-Heart.

God-in-Heart.

God-Heart.

God.

The Mystery of the Heart 425
Terms of Prayer 696
The Lover of God 853
Practising the Presence of God 711
On the Wings of Devotion 1129

The Stages of Prayer

People have forgotten the various levels of prayer. Prayer, as a technique of meditation and Spiritual Life, has five stages or levels:

1. Oral Prayer or Verbal Prayer.
2. Mental Prayer.
3. Mental Prayer in the Heart.
4. Heart-Prayer or Spiritual Prayer.
5. God-Prayer or the God-State-of-Being.

In Verbal Prayer the Divine Mood is not present

1. Oral Prayer or Verbal Prayer

This is what people generally understand as "prayer". *Oral Prayer* or *Verbal Prayer* is wholly external and full of distractions. It is *outward-directed*, with *many words*, and you pray to a God who is somewhere "out there", dwelling in the afterlife or in Heaven. God is thought to be separate from you, outside of you.

This is characteristic of the prayers in the "outer court" of all religions—the ritual prayers, rites, ceremonies, prayer books, compulsory prayers, morning, noon and evening prayers, church songs and hymns, chants, devotional outbursts, kirtans, bhajans, the Psalter and canons, prayers for the monks, nuns and religious in all religions, and so on. Or you might make up your own prayers expressed in *many words*. This includes the prayers you recite in places of worship (in a church, mosque, synagogue or temple), in a group or alone, or when you pray at home, either spontaneously or from a prayer book or scripture.

Very often, such prayers are self-centred in the sense that you ask God for some *worldly or material benefits* for yourself, or for your friends, relatives, acquaintances, tribe, country, race or religion. The attention is most often scattered and remains outside, on worldly things. Most ritual (PŪJA) is done absent-mindedly, and the various prayers, songs, chants, psalms and hymns are recited habitually, in boredom, or simply because it is the "custom" of the religion you have been brought up in. Most people, of all religions, have been brought up in this type of prayer, whether communal or individual. In this form of prayer the Divine Mood is not present.

Magical Prayer 365
Prayer Spiritual and Material 681
Stages of Interior Prayer 693
What is Prayer? 690

2. Mental Prayer

Mental Prayer is the same as *Oral Prayer* except that you don't say the words physically; you say them in your mind, silently. Usually it is long-winded, using many words and requesting God to bestow some *worldly* benefits upon you, or your friends and relatives, or your tribe or nation. Or it may be a prayer against your "enemies", real or imagined. Or it may consist of long prayers from a ritual or prayer book.

Prayer is a form of meditation which uses feeling or emotion to penetrate the Heart

This method is better than *Oral Prayer,* but it is still not the true Internal Prayer. You remain at the mind level, focused in your "head" or brain area.

3. Mental Prayer in the Heart

Mental Prayer in the Heart is the first stage of discovering the Kingdom of God *within you.* This is the beginning of true prayer or meditation, or Conscious Communion with God.

Prayer is a form of meditation which uses feeling or emotion to penetrate the Heart, via the astral body or feeling-self, and through the Heart to penetrate the World of Unities, or Buddhic Consciousness, and hence to Dissolve in God (BRAHMA-NIRVĀṆAM) and experience the Highest Truth (SATTVAM-UTTAMAM).

Rather than using your brain area (the head) as the focal point of your mental prayer, you *bring your mind down into your Heart* and recite the mental prayer in your Heart, silently. Your attention is focused in your Heart while you are saying your prayer, or while you are singing, chanting or doing other Spiritual Work. The important point to remember is that you do this with feelings of intense Devotion, Love, Longing, Reverence and Joy, and the feeling that you are in the presence of God.

Most people have not been taught by the religious authorities to pray in such a way. This tradition of praying in the Heart exists in the Jewish, Christian, Muslim, Hindu, Buddhist and Chinese religions, but in this materialistic Aquarian Age this Knowledge has been forgotten.

The Heart unites all religions. A man or woman of the Heart is united with all beings.

Devotion to Kṛṣṇa 449
Christian Prayer 689
Sūfī Prayer 863
The Thread of the Heart 844
The Universal Heart Practice 846

Mental Prayer in the Heart is very different from the first two types of prayer:

- It is wholly internally directed and concentrated, for "the Kingdom of God is *within* you".
- You bring your "mind" down into the Heart.
- The prayer is short, precise and to the point.
- You do not ask God for material benefits, but praise, glorify or exalt God.
- You are full of pure Love and Devotion, Surrender to God and Adoration of God.

Such prayer will open in you the possibility of experiencing God directly

This makes a vast difference. You ask for nothing for your separated self in the physical body, but you are longing and burning to become the One, the Only. Such prayer will open in you the possibility of experiencing God directly, within yourself, in the Here and Now.

This is *God-in-the-Heart.*

The Fire of Love

Mental Prayer in the Heart, properly *inwardly focused*, will produce warmth in the Heart, then Fire. Thus is awakened the *Fire within the Heart*. We are not talking here in metaphors or symbols; this Spiritual Fire in the Heart is just as real as physical fire.

At first the Fire is only warmth; then it becomes like a spark, a small flame or a glowing. This Flame is the Spirit-Spark, the Light-Spark, a Spark of the Divine Light, hidden in the innermost chamber of your Heart.

If you keep up the mental prayer in your Heart, your prayer (meditation) takes on the character of Fire and you move onto the next stage of prayer: *Heart-Prayer* or *Spiritual Prayer*. As Love for God grows ever stronger in your Heart, the Spiritual Flame in your Heart becomes a Conflagration, a blazing Fire, and finally a dazzling Sun-Fire or Fiery Sun. This is the Flame of Love, the Fire of Love.

Love is Fire, Fire is Love.
God is Fire and the Soul is Love.
This is the Mystery.

This *real* Fire in the Heart, when awakened, is the Fire of the Spirit as it manifests through the human system. It is the Flame of Spiritual Grace coming from God. This Flame, Fire, Spirit-Spark, is actually the Grace of God, for the Salvation of every man, woman and child, of no matter what religion, or none.

The One and Only 839
The Burning Heart 631
The Fire in the Heart 1287
The Mystery within the Heart 1315
Incarnations of the Sun 1593
Experiencing the Awakening Heart 463

4. Heart-Prayer or Spiritual Prayer

This is a very advanced stage of prayer (meditation). In this form of prayer, you do not pray with your mind in the Heart. You *do not use your mind at all*, only the Heart. This is no longer a method or technique of meditation, but a *State of Being*. It is knowingly being in the Presence of God at all times, day or night, while sleeping or waking, sitting or walking, being silent or talking. Your Heart spontaneously "prays" of itself, or rather, the Spirit of God glorifies Itself through your Heart. You have transcended your mind. You have transcended yourself. You are in Ecstasy or Mystical Trance, SAMĀDHI.

This form of prayer descends upon you

The prayer that arises in your Heart is wordless, formless, like a tide of Spiritual or Transcendental Feeling. You may have the Feeling of the Presence, or the Vision of the Presence, or the Taste or Smell of the Presence, or you may *hear* God in the Secret Chamber of your Heart.

This form of prayer (meditation) *descends* upon you. It is not the product of your desire. The Mystics also call this "Rapture" or "Ravishment" by the Spirit of God within you.

This is *God-in-Heart* or *God-Heart.*

At the level of Heart-Prayer you receive the HṚDAYA-ŚAKTIPĀTA, the Transference of Spiritual Energies into your Auric Being or Microcosm. This is a type of Spiritual Kuṇḍalinī Force, a higher aspect of Cosmic Kuṇḍalinī which will transform your whole inner Self. In Christianity this Force is called the "Holy Spirit". Again, we are talking not metaphorically or symbolically, but of a real Spiritual Force of Cosmic Power and Dynamism, Renewal, Rebirth, and Re-Awakening into the Eternal. You will be inwardly enveloped in Radiance, and you will see the Divine-Light (BRAHMĀ-JYOTI) and hear the Divine Voice (DEVA-VĀṆĪ), and you will Know the Truth directly, with Shining-Realization (DEVA-VIDYĀ), above and beyond your mind faculty, with the most spiritual part of your Soul. Then you will understand your Path of Transfiguration or Celestial Evolution. The great Mysteries will be revealed to your Soul's inward Gaze.

The State of Inner Purity 497
Samādhi: the Goal of Yoga 574
Rapture 699
The Experience of Mysticism 636
Baptism and Rebirth 722
The Holy Breath 1340

5. God-State

There is a further stage beyond Heart-Prayer. In this stage of prayer, there is no prayer, no Heart, no separated "I" or personal self. There is only God, Unity, Eternal Bliss.

The State of Unity is called YOGA (Sanskrit) in India, TAUḤĪD (Arabic) among the Muslim Saints, and ACHD (AHAD) (Hebrew) among the Jewish Mystics. This is the fifth stage of prayer, the true Goal of Religion.

This is the true Goal of Religion

In this stage there is no Inner Striving and no Inner Effort. Union with God having been achieved, there is a Spontaneous Natural Functioning in the God-State at all times, in all conditions and in all places, One with All, inner or outer.

This is *God.*

This method of prayer (meditation) is the same whether you are a Jew, a Christian, a Muslim, a Hindu, a Buddhist or a Taoist. If you practise it, you will understand the real, original purpose of all true religions before they became bogged down in theological and metaphysical speculation, before they were degenerated by the worldly-minded.

Balance on the Physical Plane

Don't spend too much time focused on your body. Too many people who think they are "spiritual" waste their time and energy on dieting and various food "fads", or on physical exercises and "keeping fit". Your body automatically takes care of itself if you eat a wide range of foods, such as fruits, vegetables, salads, nuts, rice, beans, eggs, milk products, and meat or fish if you need them. If you want to succeed in meditation, the important thing is to be *balanced* on the Physical Plane. Overwork, or taking too much upon yourself, or over-committing yourself, is also counter-productive.

Tapas: Spiritual Purification 571

The Seventh State 502
Mystical Union 846
Tauḥīd: the Divine Unity 852
The Path of Union 1339
The Ultimate Reality is the Meaning of Life 526

The Name and the Names

The peoples of the Ancient World—the Chaldeans, Babylonians, Assyrians, Sumerians, Egyptians, Akkadians, Greeks, Romans and Persians—all believed in the *Power of the Name* and the *Names*. So did the Jews, the Hindus, the Muslims, the Sikhs, the Zoroastrians, the Chinese, and the peoples of the Far East, such as the Tibetans, Mongolians, Japanese and Eskimos. So did the Polynesians of the Pacific, such as the Māori and the Hawaiians. The *early* Christians also understood this, and in Buddhism it is practised in several forms. God is not the exclusive property of any one religion. Those who think so are plainly deluded and self-centred.

The Science of God-Realization depends on the Power of the Name and of the Names

Sometimes this Knowledge was forgotten, and sometimes it has been remembered again. Unfortunately, when a *discovered, experienced* aspect of the Living Truth is made into a *tradition*, it becomes imprisoned in that tradition, and soon the later generations forget the real essence behind that tradition—the real Truth, the real experience. And, soon after that, the priestcraft make rituals, rites and ceremonies, thus finally burying the Living Truth.

The Science of God-Realization (BRAHMAJÑĀNA), or Rest-in-God (BRAHMĪ-STHITI), depends on the Power of the Name and of the Names. Without it, there is no Union with God (BRAHMANIRVĀṆAM). Understanding this subject is the Key to it all.

Traditionis 379
Brahma-Nirvāṇa 1224

**Many are the Names of God.
One is the Name.**

The Sacred Science of the Divine Names has been known, forgotten and revived, again and again, in all the major religions.

The Name of God—the Word, the Logos—is an outpouring of immeasurable Spiritual Power, Glory, Brightness and Radiance, Sound and Light, Cosmic Vibration. The Name of God is all-pervading, within you and all around you, within every part and particle of Creation. It is One, indivisible, invisible. It is invincible Power and Life-Force. It *cannot* be spoken or uttered by any human tongue—not in Sanskrit, Hebrew, Arabic, Greek, Latin, Persian or Chinese, nor in any other human language.

The *Names* are Names of God in human Sacred Languages. They *can* be uttered, pronounced, sung, chanted and meditated upon. But the *Name*, the Radiant Divine Emanation, can only be *seen* with the Eyes of the Soul and *heard* with the inner Spiritual Ears. The Name can be heard within the Heart as sweet Heavenly Music, and in the Head as the Cosmic-Ocean of Creative-Rumbling-Word or Power, the Ocean-Tide of Life.

The Names are used to "Call upon God", to connect you to the Divine Word.

What is the Name?

The *Name* is the Power emanated from *within* God, from Universal Consciousness. It is as real as electricity, magnetism or atomic power—in fact, infinitely more so! It is invisible to physical eyes and permeates all of infinite Space and all the worlds, visible and invisible. Since very ancient times, the Mystics of all religions have called it by many Names, or expressions in human languages.

This Power is not simply an article of "faith", but a real Living-God

For many centuries before the time of Christ, the Greek Mystics and Mystery Schools called this Power the LOGOS (the Word, Divine Speech, Divine Reason or Divine Mind). Christianity is a combination of ancient Jewish and Greek Mysticism; thus, the concept of the Logos or "Word" was adopted by Christianity during its early days.

The ancient Persians called it SRAOSHA, "the Word or Name-Power". In ancient India is was called ŚABDA, "the Living Word or Sound-Current", and meditation upon it was called ŚABDA-ABHYĀSA, "the practice of Communion with the Living Word, the Creator-God". Notice, it was not a theology or belief system, but a practice (ABHYĀSA). This Power is *not* simply an article of "faith", but a real Living-God. In old India it was also called NĀDA YOGA, "Union with God (YOGA) through the Living-Word (NĀDA)". Nor did this indicate a mere belief-system, for Yoga is a *practice*, a path of *action*.

According to the Old Testament Jews, God is to be found in HA-SHEM (H-SHM, the Name, the Name of Names). To the ancient Hebrews, and all the initiated inhabitants of the Ancient World, God *was* the Name. The Hebrew Psalms are full of the praising of the Name of God—the real Living-Power of God as it manifests in Sound and Light vibrations throughout the whole Cosmos. This is the Creative Word (Sound), the Creator-God, the *Name*.

When this Knowledge (GNOSIS) about the Word, the Name, was lost (which happens over and over again), secret Brotherhoods sprang up in Greece, Rome, Egypt, Persia, Babylonia, and elsewhere, searching for the "Lost Word". The Rosicrucian and Masonic Kabbalistic Secret Orders are a later wave of the same phenomenon. As usual, the priestcraft came along and produced beautiful, long, complicated rituals, thus further losing the Knowledge they were meant to "look for": the Hidden-Light, AUR-GANUZ (Hebrew: AVR-GNVZ), the Name *within* themselves.

Āuṁ, Ōṁ, Nāda 550
The Cosmic Christ 662
The Voice of God 864
The Logos: the Word of God 114
The Word, Logos, Voice, Name 1646
The Name of the Deity 1032
The Creative Power of the Primordial Language of Sound 1075

How to begin Mental Prayer in the Heart

Mental Prayer in the Heart is also known as *Conscious Communion with God, Simple Prayer* and *Prayer of Simplicity*. This tells you all about it. It is the opposite of Oral Prayer, which is wordy and long-winded.

Remember that the Presence of God within your Heart is very real

- Focus your Attention or Consciousness in the Heart, slightly to the right side.
- There, using your mind, use a simple formula (mantra, in the East), such as a Divine Name, or a few words from a religious text, prayer book or scripture, or from well known spiritual statements.
- There, with the positive, bright emotions of Devotion, Love, Longing, Praise, Glorification, Adoration and Worship (BHĀVA, mood), recite or chant your prayer, not too fast or too slow, leaving intervals in between. Totally *surrender* yourself to God, with *awe, reverence, faith* and *joy*.
- Remember that the Presence of God within your Heart is *very real*.
- Make your prayer *conscious* and *simple*.
- There should be a certain *softness, sweetness, peace* and *quietness* in your mind. If you are mentally or emotionally agitated, you are wasting your time.
- You can say or sing the prayer or mantra while in a definite meditation posture, or standing still, or sitting in a chair, or lying on your back in bed or on the ground. Do *not* say your prayer while driving a car or doing work that requires your outer attention. It is dangerous as well as ineffective.
- The prayer may align itself to your breathing-rhythm, or it may not. Observe which is best for you. This is *not* an exercise in breath control (Prāṇāyāma).
- Do not let worldly worries intrude.
- While you are praying (meditating) in your Heart, completely forget about your physical body and your personal ego, your personal sense of "I", your worldly self.
- Spend as much time in your meditation as you can, the longer the better. Do not seek for results and quick miracles. Gradually increase the time you spend in meditation.

When you have finished praying (meditating), spend your time in Service, doing your duties or allotted tasks, your responsibilities in life. Make this world your field of Service to the Divine, for this Plane of Being is also Divine. To spend your time in Service (SEVA) is just as much part of Spiritual Life as is meditation.

On Love and Meditation 1140

The Names and Mental Prayer in the Heart

To enter the Heart through *Mental Prayer in the Heart*, the initiated Jewish Mystics used two methods:

1

KAVANA (Hebrew): a short, concentrated formula or prayer, such as from the Psalms or other sacred texts. For example:

This Science of using the Names is profoundly esoteric

Help us, O God, our Saviour.

Have pity on me, O Lord.

Through God I will find Glory.

Praise the Lord.

Blessed be the Lord.

The Spirit of the Lord has filled the whole Universe.

Let God arise.

2

Using the Divine Names by themselves as a KAVANA. This Science of using the Names is profoundly esoteric. The Science consists of bringing the Name (or Names) you are using to the NAME—that is, the human attributive Names of God to the True Name of God—thus *Uniting yourself with God* as the Infinite Majesty and Measureless Attributes and Powers.

When you can bring forth a Name (or Names) and unite it to God, the NAME, you become a BĀL-SHEM-TAU (Hebrew: a Master of the Good Name, the Infinite Power). In the East this Science was called MANTRA YOGA, and one who succeeded was a MANTRA YOGĪ.

The Process is an Invocation and Evocation in the Heart, with complete Faith and Surrender, with Pure Love and Devotion.

The Hasidim 648

The Two Applications of Mantra 1219

Hebrew Divine Names to be Invoked (meditated upon) in the Heart

The Elohīm 120
Christian Meditation on the Holy Breath 1346
IHVH: I AM 1460

AL (El)
God, Lord, Master.

ALVH (Eloah)
God, Lord, Master.

ALHIM (Elohim)
God, the Creator-Gods.

ALHIM-GBVR (Elohim-Gibur)
Powerful God, Omnipotent God, Infinite Majesty.

ALHIM-TzBAVT (Elohim-Tzabaoth)
The God of all the Heavenly Hosts, the God of all Beings and Creatures.

ADNI (Adonai)
Lord God, the Lord and Master of the Heart.

ADNI-H-ARTz (Adonai-Ha-Aretz)
The Lord of the Universe.

ADNI-MLK (Adonai-Melek)
The Lord King, Ruler over All

ShDI (Shadai)
The All-Powerful, Almighty, Omnipotent.

IH (Yah)
Being.

IHVH (Yehovah, Yahveh)
The Eternal, the Being of Beings, Everlasting.

IHVH-TzBAVTh (Yehovah-Tzabaoth)
The Being above all Beings, the Eternal One of all the Hosts of Beings.

There are seventy-two Kabbalistic Hebrew Names of God (attributive Names), and there are several hundred in the Old Testament *disguised* as names of people and place names. You will recognize them because each of them will contain either Yah (Jah) or El.

AHIH (Eheyeh)
Existing Forever. The One Universal I-AM Being.

ALHIM-ChIIM (Elohim-Chiim)
The God of the Living, the God who gives Life to All, the Universal Life-Producer, the Living God.

ADVN-IChID-AL (Adun-Yahid-El)
God, the only God, the One God.

To awaken the Divine Heart Centre, you can invoke any one of these Divine Names

AL-ChI-H-OVLMIM (El-Hai-Ha-Oulmim)
The Living God of the Eternal Ages.

OLIV-ADVN (Eliun-Adun)
OLIVN-ADNI (Elion-Adonai)
The Lord God Most High, God on the Highest, the Highest God or Lord, the Transcendental Lord.

∞

To awaken the Divine Heart Centre, or Union with God, you can invoke any one of these Divine Names in your Heart Centre with Longing and Devotion. The pronunciation must be correct, according to the ancient Kabbalistic Hebrew: full vowels, not muffled as in modern pronunciation.

Invoking any of these Names in your Heart, following the process of *Mental Prayer in the Heart* as previously described, will rapidly produce Heat and Fire within the Heart.

You have to *Cry Out* to the Master of your Life, who dwells in your Heart and in the Heart of all things.

The Hebrew Heart

The Hebrew word for the Heart is LB (Laib). The letter L (ל, *Lamed)* has the numerical value of 30, and the letter B (ב, *Beith)* has the numerical value of 2. Thus, by the Science of Numbers, Laib (the Heart) has the value of 32, which is the number of the Ways of Wisdom inherent in the Heart, or the 32 types of Enlightenment possible in the Heart.

The Way, the Truth and the Life 670
Meditation on the Divine Names 1454
Sounding the Hebrew Divine Names 1461
Sounding the Hebrew Angelic Names 1462

The Beautiful Names

The Arabic name for the Heart is QLB (QALB), which is the Centre, the Source, the Essence, the Core, the Root of your Being, the Heart within the Heart, the Inner Heart. It is the most intimate part of yourself, the Throne of God, the dwelling place of your Soul.

The Beautiful Names refer to the Divine Attributes

The Divine Names are referred to by the Muslim Mystics, the SŪFĪ (Arabic: the Wise) and the FAQĪR (Arabic: holy men), as the *Beautiful Names*. The Mystery of the Names is their Power to rule over aspects of the Divine Nature.

God has many attributes, yet has none.
The sea has many waves, yet is one.

The *Beautiful Names* refer to the Divine Attributes. The esoteric Secret is that these same attributes exist in Man (the human species), or can be developed by Man. And, by these attributive Names, Man can return to God, the Everlasting One, who is the *True Name*.

By invoking a Divine Name in your Heart you are doing two things:

- You develop that virtue or quality.
- You prepare yourself to unite with God.

Traditionally there are 99 Divine Names of God in Arabic, plus 28 Divine Names according to the Arabic alphabet, plus many others. The two most beautiful Arabic Names of God are:

IR-RAḤMĀN
The Merciful, the Compassionate, Gracious, Kind, Loving.

IR-RAḤĪM
Compassionate, Kind, Merciful, Forgiving.

Thus:

BISMILLĀH IR-RAḤMĀN IR-RAḤĪM
In the Name of God, who is Compassionate and Merciful.

What more can be said of the Divine Nature: *Compassionate, Loving, Merciful*. Would all the Children of Man know this!

Qalb: the Sūfī Heart 848
Some Arabic Prayers to the Deity 850
The 99 Arabic Divine Names of God 878

More Beautiful Names in Arabic

AL-BĀṬIN
The Hidden Essence, the Mystical Heart, the Unmanifest.

AL-ḤAKĪM
Absolute Wisdom, All-Knowing.

AL-ALĪM
Omniscient, All-Wise.

AS-SALĀM
Infinite Peace and Quiet.

AL-AẒĪM
Infinite, Exalted.

AL-MU'MIN
One who is Faithful to you.

AL-MUHAIMIN
The Protector, the Preserver.

AL-ḤALĪM
Considerate, Gracious, Mild, Gentle.

AL-KARĪM
Noble, Gracious, Generous, Kind, Honourable, Giving.

AL-MATĪN
Firm, Powerful, Immoveable.

RABBUL'-ĀLAMĪN
Master of the Universe, the Lord of all Creatures.

AL-AKRĀM
Glorious, Kind, Generous, Benevolent.

AL-AMĪM
Full, Complete, Universal, Cosmic, Abundant, Plentiful.

AL-AMĪN
Trustworthy, Faithful, the Witness of Creation.

AL-ḤAYY
The Living God, the Life-Giver.

The same God or Divinity resides in every Heart, in all human beings, irrespective of their cultures or religious backgrounds. This is known to the Wise by *direct inner experience*. You *cannot* convince others of this basic truth by intellectual arguments and discussions. Each person must experience this for himself or herself, as a result of prayer/meditation.

Hate does not exist in God, only in the twisted emotions of Man. How many warped human beings commit violence in the Name of God? How many religious wars have been fought, and to what end?

But enter the Heart and you will enter a Realm of Compassion and Gentleness. The Wise *live in the Name of God*, the Divine Power which is truly Merciful and Compassionate.

The Eternal is One 512
The Sūfī God 838

Christian Divine Names

Today's Christianity has very few Divine Names: *Father, Son, Holy Ghost, Lord, Jesus Christ, Christ, the Creator, the Almighty, God.*

You know, of course, the theological interpretation of the Trinity: the old man on the throne (the Father); the handsome young man, the Christ (the Son), sitting next to Him; and the Dove (the Holy Ghost) fluttering in between them. Many Christians believe in this interpretation, but it is only a symbol, not the Reality. The Truth is so much more wonderful and wondrous!

This is the profound Understanding of the Holy Trinity

Lord, Jesus Christ is the Image of God in us, in the Heart.

Christ-Jesus is the Cosmic Man, the Likeness of God to Man in the Cosmos.

The Holy Spirit is the Conscious-Active-Power of God maintaining all of Creation, the Divine Presence.

God the Father is the Inexpressible Transcendent.

This is the profound Understanding of the Holy Trinity—not theological, not speculative, not metaphysical, but as you really experience it in the state of Inner Illumination by God.

Some Christian Prayers to the Deity (English)

Blessed is the Man who delights in the Lord.
God, instruct me by the Light of your Holy Spirit.
May we be truly Wise (Enlightened) by the Holy Spirit.
God, instruct the Hearts of your Faithful by the Light of your Spirit.
Blessed be God.
Blessed be the Lord.
Praise be to God.
Holiness to the Lord.
O God, my God, look down upon me!
The thoughts in my Heart are before You.
Glory be to the Father!
Glory be to the Word!
Glory be to the Holy Breath!

The Holy Trinity 1342
The Christian Trinity 113
Mythical Concepts of God 104
The Cosmic Christ 662
The Mystery of Jesus the Christ 664

The Christians did not start to pray to *Jesus* until two or three centuries after Christ. Saint Neilos the Ascetic, around AD400, was one of the earliest Saints to refer to the *Jesus Prayer*—praying to Jesus in the Heart Cakra. At his time it was already a well-established practice amongst the Christian Saints of the desert and in the monasteries. Before that, Christians did not pray to Jesus, but to Abba (Hebrew: "the Father") and to "Our Father" as taught by Jesus. Thus, the delineation of Christian prayer evolved as follows:

The Christians did not start to pray to Jesus until two or three centuries after Christ

From the time of Jesus, prayer was to the Father-God, the Absolute:

Abba
Hebrew: God the Father.

Between the first and fourth centuries, the Christians invoked mantras to the Universal Christos, the Christ, the Cosmic Being, the Cosmic Son, the Universal Saviour. For instance:

Hagios O Theos
Greek: Holy God.

Kyrie Eleison
Greek: Lord save me.

Christe Eleison
Greek: Christ save me.

From the third or fourth centuries onwards, the object of worship switched to *Jesus Christ.* Worship was through the human aspect (Jesus) to the Divine Aspect (the Christ), and through the Christ Being towards the Father, the Transcendental Reality.

Iesous
Greek: Jesus.

Iesu
Latin: Jesus.

Iesous Christos Theos Uios Sōtēr
Greek: Jesus Christ, God's Son, Saviour.

To Worship Jesus 680
The Gnostic Teachings 1108
Jesus, the Fire of Love 1725
The Evolution of Christian Prayer 713

Visualizing the Divinity within the Heart

God is both Immanent (present within Creation) and Transcendent (above and beyond Creation). Thus, there are two types of meditation:

- With form, SA-RŪPA (referring to God Immanent in Creation).
- Formless, A-RŪPA (referring to God-Transcendent).

You can meditate in the Heart upon either aspect of God, according your preference.

You build up a picture of your chosen form of Divinity in your Heart

Meditation with Form

You can meditate in your Heart by visualizing the CHRIST, KṚṢṆA, BUDDHA, RĀMA, or your Guru, or a great Saint, Master or Spiritual Adept, or the Sparkling Jewel in the Lotus of the Heart, or the Heart-Lotus itself with the twelve petals, or the Spiritual Sun in the Heart, or any known form of the Deity. Having chosen your form of Divinity, you build up a picture of your chosen form in your Heart, by visualization, with great *Love* and *Devotion*. You use your imagination and pour all your Love and Devotion into building the most perfect form of your chosen representation of Divinity (ĪṢTA-DEVATĀ). This will be a gate, a door, a window, a bridge between you and God, between your personality and your Soul.

Imagining or visualizing is one type of meditation; using a mantra is another. If you wish, after you have built the picture or image in your Heart, you can chant a mantram to that Deity-form, the mantram of that Deity or any suitable mantram. And the Great God within you will Awaken in Glory.

Formless Meditation

To practise formless meditation in the Heart, sit still, focused, and *feel* the Divine Presence with your Heart as one of the Transcendental Qualities, in the Eternal Silence and Peace.

Most people find it difficult to meditate upon the Transcendental Nature of God, the Unmanifest, the Absolute, the Immutable, the Eternal, the Boundless, the All-Pervading, the Indestructible, the Incomprehensible. Most people relate to God in some sort of form or embodiment.

Bhakti Yoga: Divine Union by Devotion 1128
Meditation on the Form of the Guru 1225
God Immanent and Transcendent 111
Paths to the Transcendent and Immanent God 1120

Some Sanskrit Divine Names for Meditation in the Heart

For meditation *with form* (SA-RŪPA) you can meditate on:

ĪŚA

ĪŚVARA

HṚDAYAṀ

SŪRYA (the Sun)

GURU

KṚṢṆA

RĀMA

BUDDHA

JESU KRISTA (Jesus Christ)

DEVĪ (the Goddess)

ŚIVA

JĪVA

ŌṀ

ŌṀ MAṆI PADME HŪṀ (the Jewel in the Lotus)

Remember, there is only One God! The form itself that you choose to meditate upon in your Heart is but a *representation* of the true Form of the One God, which is vast and cosmic. What you choose to meditate upon is called ĪṢTA-DEVATĀ (Chosen-Divinity). If it is with form, then it is called the ĪṢTA-DEVATĀ-RŪPA (Chosen-Deity-Form).

My Beloved Lives in my Heart 1290

For meditation *without form* (A-RŪPA) you can meditate on:

PARAMĀTMAN

ĀTMAN

PARABRAHMAN

PURUṢOTTAMA

ŚIVA

ŌṀ

ĀNANDA

ŚĀNTIḤ

VĀSU-DEVA

Note that ŌṀ and ŚIVA are both with form and formless.

ĪṢTA-DEVATĀ
Sanskrit: "Chosen Deity". Also called UPĀSANĀ-MŪRTI, "spiritual discipline, form or image". The human form of the Divine Incarnation serves as an *initial* focal point of your Love, Devotion, Longing, Praise and Worship, knowing full well that the human form of the Incarnation merely veils the glorious Divinity behind it. God has to appear to Humanity in human form until humans possess ŚIVA-NETRA, the Spiritual Eye, by which they will see God everywhere.

The Saviour in the Heart 1296

To Worship the Divine Incarnations

An AVATĀRA is an entity descending from the Monadic Plane, or the Divine Power or Potency stepped down to the lower planes, even to our Physical Plane of planet Earth. The Avatāras descend from the Avatāric Source, the Monadic Plane, beyond Nirvāṇa.

Unfortunately, this fact of Avatāras is much misunderstood, for in India they indiscriminately call all their Gurus and Saints "Avatāras". Thus, at any one time there are dozens of Saints in India believed by their devotees to be Avatāras. But this is incorrect; Sainthood is a different process.

The Avatāras descend from the Monadic Plane, beyond Nirvāṇa

Following are the four greatest Incarnations of Divinity on Earth in living memory:

RĀMA, who gave Mankind Righteousness.
KṚṢṆA, who gave Mankind Devotion.
BUDDHA, who gave Mankind Wisdom.
CHRIST, who gave Mankind Love.

You must remember that the planetary vibrations at the time of these great Divine Incarnations (MAHĀ-AVATĀRAS) were different on each occasion and different from the planetary vibration of today, the twenty-first century after Christ. Human Consciousness is *slowly* changing all the time in conjunction with the evolution of the Earth, the Planetary Logos, the Cosmic Entity whose dense physical body is our planet Earth.

AVATĀRA
Sanskrit: "To go down" or "to descend". From AVA (down) and TĀRA (to pass, to go). An AVATĀRA is a Descent of God on Earth in a human form. A Divine Incarnation.
The Avatāra 389

THEOPHANIA
Greek: "God-manifestation". An appearance of God. From THEOS (God) and PHANIA (to appear, to manifest). The fact of Divine Incarnation according to the ancient pre-Christian Greeks.

Many Christians believe that Christianity is a unique, new religion, but in fact the Christian doctrine is derived directly from ancient Jewish teachings and the Greek Mystery Schools.
The Jewish Messiah 660

Quality	Avatāra	Date
The Power of Righteousness	RĀMA	11,000 years ago
The Power of Devotion	KṚṢṆA	5,100 years ago
The Power of Wisdom	BUDDHA	2,500 years ago
The Power of Love	CHRIST	2,000 years ago

Great Incarnations of Divinity

An Avatāra is a Regenerative Power for the planet Earth and for Mankind. There were other great Avatāras on this planet, long before the four mentioned above, who came to teach and guide nascent Humanity, with each Avatāra demonstrating a new quality to be emulated or developed by Mankind. The Avatāra process is part of the Divine Plan.

The Avatāras left an imprint in the planetary atmosphere

Remember that, in the days when these Avatāras lived, there was no modern recording equipment such as audio tapes or videos, and their words, teachings and actions were not written down as they happened. What we have today is a massive amount of legends, tales and mythologies, written centuries or thousands of years after their deaths, especially in the case of Rāma, Kṛṣṇa and Buddha. People piously believe in these "scriptures" as if they were the *literal* truth instead of just *stories of the imagination*.

Apart from the myths written about them, however, the Avatāras left an *imprint* in the planetary atmosphere, in the deep psychological layers of Human Consciousness, which cannot be wiped out. The Divine Glory and Radiance that the Avatāras brought down with them from the exalted Spiritual Realms has been infused into Humanity and has stimulated human evolution, developing in Man the *sense* of Righteousness, Devotion, Wisdom and Love.

Astral Disinformation

There is tremendous *misinformation, disinformation* and *delusion* coming from the Astral World through the so-called mediums, channellers, star-seed transmitters (or whatever the psychics and untrained sensitives choose to call themselves), concerning the true esoteric history of our planet, the nature of the inner worlds, the Avatāras and the Spiritual Hierarchies. If you could know the real esoteric facts, and the utter nonsense coming through the mediums and channellers who deceive themselves and the ignorant "new-agers", who channel imaginary, non-existent angels, masters, dolphins, whales, purpledots and square elephants from realms and spaces and worlds that exist only in their subconscious minds and astral imaginations, you would be utterly shocked and would campaign to ban all channelling because of the great harm it is doing to the Living Truth!

Channelling and Mediumship 317

The Avatāras 1320
Powers of Divine Descent 599
The Divine Incarnation 726
The Mystery of Jesus the Christ 664
Legends of the Buddha 393
Truth and Mythology 7

To Worship the Divine Incarnations in the Heart

There are countless millions of people who worship these Divine Incarnations—Rāma and Kṛṣṇa in Hinduism, Buddha in Buddhism, and the Christ in Christianity—through the practice of many rites, ceremonies and rituals. However:

The Avatāras must be worshipped in the Heart

These Avatāras must be worshipped in the Heart, by interior prayer, meditation and worship.

This is called Mānasa-Pūja, "mental worship". This means having your mind, Manas, in your Heart, Hṛdayaṁ, and doing your worship there.

- If you are a follower of Rāma, Kṛṣṇa, Buddha or Christ, you may sing, chant or pray the Name of the Avatāra in your Heart Centre with Love, Devotion, self-forgetfulness, surrender and intense longing for Union with your Beloved.
- Another way is to *visualize* the form of your Beloved in your Heart—an image, picture, icon or maṇḍala. You can visualize in your Heart a picture of Rāma, Kṛṣṇa, Buddha or Christ, or of the Goddess or the Divine Mother.
- Or, you may visualize the form first, then chant or pray to the Sacred Image.

God the Ultimate Reality, and God who ever manifests as Divine Incarnations, and God who is your own true Self (the formless Self of infinite magnitude, everlasting Silence, and Pure Consciousness) are *one and the same.*

Thus, you may worship God the Absolute as formless Infinite Reality, or you may worship any form or aspect of God, such as the form of an Avatāra, or the Divine Mother, or the Universal Energy of Śakti, or the Goddess.

Devotion to Kṛṣṇa 449
To Call upon Jesus 679
Salutation to the Buddha 795
The Buddha and the Christ 1722
Śakti: the One Energy 150
The Divine Energy 1484

The 'Goddess'

Understand the word *Goddess* in the spiritual sense, *not* in the "modern" Western sense of the Goddess as the physical Earth or the Moon or the female psychological qualities of unregenerated human beings.

The True Feminine 1516

Rām: the Universal Name

Rām is a Name of God which is upheld by both Eastern and Western Spirituality

Hebrew

To the ancient Hebrews, the Name of God, RĀM, was the God-in-Incarnation, God as the Cosmic Life and Cosmic Principle in Manifestation.

In ancient Hebrew, RĀM means "the All-pervading, Self-existing Spiritual Substance and Energy of God; the Origin, Source and Foundation of the Universe; the Universal Force of Space". As a God Name, RĀM means "God on High, the Most High God, the Exalted God, the Establishing-Power of God".

Thus, in Hebrew, RĀM means "God-Transcendent and God-Immanent (here, now)", simultaneously abstract and concrete. It is the invisible Forces of God active in Creation, in all things and all peoples, as well as the Transcendental Bliss-Consciousness of the Absolute. It also means the *restoring* and *nourishing* Power of God.

RĀM also means, in Hebrew, "the Power which uplifts or raises up; that which Saves; that which is Exalted, Elated, Glorified; the Force that pervades the Universe".

RĀM is also the Human Consciousness infused by the Power of the Holy Spirit, the uplifted Human Consciousness, or Cosmic Consciousness.

RĀMA, RĀMAH, in Hebrew, also means Exaltation, an uplifting of Consciousness.

Sanskrit

In Sanskrit, RĀM is the Divine Name of God as the Universal Vibration of Light and Sound, or Sounding-Light Vibration. By this is meant not only the physical Light and Sound, but All-Light and All-Sound upon all the seven great Planes of Being, within all dimensions of Space. All Space, with its multiple universes, both visible and invisible, is vibrating with the Radiant Energy of RĀM, the formless Form of God.

RĀM is the Universal Mind in action as Vibration throughout the infinitudes of the Universe, both in the visible and invisible immensities of Space. It is Pure Intelligence pervading all things. It is conscious, intelligent Radiant Energy, which is dazzling, bright Light and blissful in nature. This Radiant Energy, RĀM, pervades all things, is within all things, *is* all things in Creation. It is the Ocean of Light and the Lake of Fire, in which every atom in Creation is dancing.

RĀM is also the ruling and directing Force within Creation, the Impelling-Intelligence, the Administrative-Intelligence of the Cosmos. It is the Infinite-Here and Eternal-Now, in blissful Consciousness and Love.

RĀMA, in Sanskrit, is the Divine Incarnation or Divinizing Power.

Rām: the Warrior Power 1068
The Bīja-Mantra Rāṁ 1544

Conscious Breathing in the Heart

Breath is the link between Man and the Spirit of God

Since very ancient times, people have connected prayer with the Heart Centre and with the breath. Conscious Breathing was practised by the Mystics of all the ancient civilizations—India, Persia, China, Egypt, Babylonia. It was practised by the Prophets of Israel and the Saints of Islam, and in the early days of Christianity by the Desert Fathers.

Conscious Breathing is the recognition that the human breath is a particle of the Divine Breath, the Holy Spirit, and hence can be used as a vehicle for Unification or Yoga (Union with God).

The individual breath, *your* breath, is a wavelet upon the Great Breath or Universal Life-Power. Conscious Breathing is purely religious in purpose and has nothing to do with "keeping fit". Make no mistake, puffing away in merely body-oriented physical breathing exercises is not it! It is a way of consciously reconnecting with God and with yourself, the Soul that you are.

Conscious Breathing is focused in the Heart, using a Divine Name, or simply Remembering the All-Presence.

Materialists will squirm at this idea, of course, but let them squirm! This Science has been forgotten by Humanity many times over, and you need to *remember*, as do all the Children of Man. Breath is the *link* between Man and the Spirit of God, the Breath of God.

The Holy Breath 1340
Baptism and Rebirth 722
Prāṇāyāma-Vidyā 1553
Breathing God 870
Mindfulness of Breathing 794
Christian Meditation on the Holy Breath 1346
Rest in the Great Breath 1654

Breath-Prayer in the Heart

Ordinary prayer is generally long-winded and involves *asking* God for things (usually mundane). In ordinary prayer, usually people are stuck in their heads and very often there is no Devotion at all. *Breath-Prayer in the Heart* differs from ordinary prayer in the following ways:

- It is short.
- It is connected to the Heart.
- It is connected to the breath.

This method of prayer is for spiritual development, invoking Grace and realizing the Immanent Presence of God. In this method there is a total surrender to God, *from* the Heart and *within* the Heart.

To Practise Conscious Breathing

The best way to practise Conscious Breathing is to take a Divine Name and *consciously* breathe it in and out of the Heart. Focus in your Heart Centre, and there invoke an intense Love and Devotion for God. *Nothing matters but the Living God within your Heart.* Make your prayer very simple, in rhythm with your breath. For example:

Nothing matters but the Living God within your Heart

The Western Divine Name, JESU (Latin: Saviour):

in-breathing		*out-breathing*
YE	–	SŪ

Or the Eastern Divine Name SŌHAṀ (Sanskrit: Spirit):

in-breathing		*out-breathing*
SŌ	–	HĀNG

Or you can use the Arabic Name HELA. HE-LĀ represents the *Living Word.* HE is the Sound aspect, LĀ is the Light. HE-LĀ is the Sounding-Light, the Universal God-Reverberation in the Cosmos, the Holy Spirit.

in-breathing		*out-breathing*
HE	–	LĀ

Or you can use the Hebrew Name SHALOM. The Hebrew word SHLM (SHALOM) means "God is Peace, God is Happiness, God is Perfection".

in-breathing		*out-breathing*
SHA	–	LŌM

Or you can use the Chinese word TAO (God), or the Egyptian word TAU (God):

in-breathing		*out-breathing*
TA	–	Ō
TA	–	Ū

More Breath-Prayers in the Heart

in-breathing		out-breathing
Lord	–	God
Lord	–	Christ
God	–	Bless
God	–	Heal
God	–	Love
God	–	Light
God	–	Peace
God	–	Joy
Ā	–	BA

Jesus used **A – BA** to invoke the Divine Father in His Heart. ABBA, ABA, is both Hebrew and Aramaic. It means "God, Father, Source, the First in Creation, the Creator-God, God as the Divine Father in All".

Yeshua: the Secret Hebrew Name

The Breath-Prayer Yeshua was practised by Jesus himself

YESHUA is the greatest Breath-Prayer in the Heart in the West, and the most important Breath-Mantra in the Hebrew and Aramaic languages. It is the secret Western Breath-Prayer, now revealed to you after being lost for many centuries. It was practised by the Prophets, and even by Jesus himself. Jesus spoke Aramaic; it was His native language.

YESHUA means "the fullness of the Godhead, God manifest in the flesh, God Incarnate in Man, the Divine Incarnation within the Heart Centre of a human being, the Breath of God, the Holy Breath incarnate in you, the Saving-Grace-Power within you, the Liberating Energy of the Spirit, the Redeeming Power, the Divine Helper, the Living God".

YESHUA is threefold:
a. It is a great Declaration of Truth (Metanoia).
b. It is a Mantra (Sound-Vibration).
c. It is the Holy Breath.

- You can use it as a Declaration of Truth.
- You can use it as a Mantram.
- You can use it as the Science of the Holy Breath.

Although this wonderful threefold application of YESHUA has been practised by the Prophets, it gets lost time and again, century after century. Now it is your great good fortune that it has been brought to your attention.

Yesu-Breathing in the Heart

Method 1
As you deep-breathe the syllables YE-SŪ or YE-SHŪ in and out of the Heart Centre, very slowly, think of the meaning of the Name YESU: "God Saves".

Method 2
As you breathe the syllables YE-SŪ or YE-SHŪ in and out of the Heart Centre, think of YESU, that is, YESHU, YESHUA, the Divine Incarnation, the Miraculous Person (who later became known as Jesus Christ).

Method 3
As you breathe the syllables YE-SŪ or YE-SHŪ in and out of the Heart Centre, think of the Divine Name, the Immediate Presence of God, which will give you great Joy and Ecstasy.

Names of the Great Master Jesus 661
The Mystery of Jesus and Mary 665
To Call upon Jesus 679
The Gnostic Teachings 1108
Jesus: the Fire of Love 1725
The Jesus Mantra and the Sacred Heart Initiation 1356
What is Metanoia? 1412

The Holy Breath

With your consciousness centred in the Spiritual Heart Centre:

	in-breathing		*out-breathing*
	YE	–	SHŪ
or:	YE	–	SŪ
	God		Saves

You must practise this with Love in your Heart. The mantric pronunciation is YESHUA. Its breath-form is YE-SHŪ or YE-SŪ.

When you vibrate the Holy Name, it will fill you with Living Fire

To Vibrate the Holy Name

Use any of the following forms:

YE - SHU - Ā
YO - SHU - Ā
YE - HE - SHU - Ā
YE - HO - SHU - Ā

- When you vibrate the Holy Name, it will fill you with Living Fire, the Fire of the Holy Spirit.
- When you use it as the Science of Holy Breath, it connects your breath with the Heart Centre and the Inner Ruler, the Godhead within the Heart, ABBA, the Divine Father within.
- When you use it as a Metanoia, it will transform your mind and lead you to Transformation and Enlightenment.

YESHUA is the Holy Breath or Holy Spirit of God. YESHUA is the radiant Energy of the Spirit, which manifests as Truth (Metanoia), Mantra (Dabar), the Word (Sound-Power), and the Holy Breath.

YESHUA HA-MASHIACH means that YESHUA is the Messiah, the Supernatural Power that descends from above and redeems your Soul which is entrapped by Nature in the lower worlds. YESHUA is the messenger of ABBA (the Father, the Glistening White Brilliance of the Eternal). From ancient Hebrew-Aramaic the word passed into ancient Greek and became IESOUS. From the Greek it passed into Latin and became IESUS, which later became JESUS. As the word was passed down the many generations, its sublime meaning and purpose was forgotten. But now the Word is told to you again, and YESHUA Lives!

YESHUA

God is my Salvation.
Help is from God.
I depend on God.
I surrender to God.
I place my trust in God.
God delivers.
God helps.
God saves.
God is Freedom.
God is my Helper.
God helps me to prosper.

CHAPTER 55

Hṛdayaṁ
Meditations in the Heart Centre

The Experience of the Heart

Merely talking about the Kingdom of God is not enough

For thousands of years, philosophers of all cultures have been searching for Truth in their *minds*. They thought that Truth could be discovered by the thinking process, by reasoning, logic, the deductive mind. But the Living Truth cannot be learned from philosophy books, nor by attending university philosophy classes and lectures. Reality, Truth, God, is not a "thought" or an "idea". It cannot be approached by a thinking-process, by the discursive mind, by logic and reason, for these are self-limiting, conceptual, dualistic, separative mind-functions. The common, rationalizing mind is sufficient for ordinary knowledge in *this* world, among *relative* objects and things, but to discover the Living Truth you need your Heart.

The Experience of the Heart is the Living Truth. It is the direct experiencing of the Universal Divine Presence within your Heart and within Cosmic Manifestation.

Every Teaching must have a practical application. Merely talking about the Kingdom of God is not enough. The Teacher must also teach a practice that shows the Way.

The Way of the Heart is thought-transcending and mind-transcending into the Oneness of Eternal Life, which is the Truth, God, Reality, the Meaning of all Existence.

Ānanda-Kanda
Sanskrit: The Blissful-Realm. The Awakened Heart. The Spiritual Heart.

Para-Bhakti
Sanskrit: Supreme-Devotion, Supreme-Faith. The condition when your Heart is completely opened up, when your Heart sees God in everything and in everyone—angels, humans, animals, plants—and you *experience* the Divine Presence everywhere.

On the Wings of Devotion 1129
Guard your Heart 1328

The Secret of the Heart

Everything you perceive is registered as an image in your Heart. Thus, the Heart-Space (Hṛdaya-Ākāśa) is cluttered with images of external forms. The pure empty Space of Pure Consciousness within the Heart is full of external impressions, veiling the Sight of the Kingdom of God within.

The Heart (Hṛdaya) has to be *emptied* of these material forms (Rūpa) before you can see the Serene Light of the Imperishable Kingdom.

The Mystery of Cit-Jaḍa-Granthi (the connection between your consciousness and your physical body) can be solved only in the Heart Cakra. Then you attain Mokṣa (Freedom) and Mukti (Liberation).

The Importance of the Heart in Approaching God 432
Hṛdayākāśa: the Heart-Space 1592

The Experience of the Heart is Freedom, Giving and Perfection.

Hrī: Freedom from bodily limitations.
Dā: Generous giving, outgoing Radiance of the Heart.
Yāṁ: Perfection, Adeptship, Mastery.

Hṛdayaṁ: the Heart.

The Experience of the Heart is the experience of the True Self within the Universe

The Experience of the Heart is Being, Consciousness and Bliss.

Sat: Being, pure unlimited Existence.
Cit: Consciousness, pure Awareness.
Ānanda: Bliss, ecstatic Joy.

Satcidānanda: the Supreme Reality.

The Experience of the Heart is Nirvāṇa.

Nirvāṇa is the Heart of the Universe, the Beatific Vision, the Experience of the Supreme Glory, the Infinitely Bright, the White Brilliance of the Godhead. Nirvāṇa is the Source of the Great Breath, the Universal Life-Force and Energy from which the Universe is out-breathed at the Dawn of Time, and into which the Universe is in-breathed and dissolved by the Great Breath, or Spirit, at the end of Eternity.

The Experience of the Heart is the experience of the True Self or Identity within the Universe, the Ātman.

Ātman is the Life-Breath of God the Absolute, the true I AM sense within all Creation and all beings, and within *you* also. It is the Timeless Eternal Self of all beings, the One, the Universal Formless Form of Pure Consciousness, *beyond* body, emotions and mind.

The Experience of the Heart is:

Ātma-Vidyā: Self-Realization.
Brahma-Jñāna: the Knowledge of God.
Ātmajyoti: the Light of the Spirit.

What is the Heart? 435
The Eastern Heart 448
The Fourth State 499
Nirvāṇa is... 98
Ātman, Ātmā 34
God in the Heart 634
What is Reality? 1175

The Heart (Hṛdayaṁ)

This human body is a Temple of the Living God

The Heart Centre is the meeting point of Man and God, Cosmos and Humanity, God and the Soul, and is the Alchemical Furnace of Purification.

The name of the Heart is HṚDAYAṀ, which means HṚDA-AYAṀ, "The Heart is the Self" (HṚI–DA–YAṀ).

The Self is seated within the Heart.

HṚDYĀ is the Innermost, the ĀTMAN, the Eternal Self within you.

This human body is a Temple of the Living God, for God resides in the Heart. Seek within the Heart.

The Heart of the Sun is the Invisible Solar Logos, whose physical body is our Solar System.

God in the aspect of Ruler, Lord, Master, Sovereign (ĪŚVARA) is permeating the whole Creation from within. Thus, God also dwells in and rules from your Heart.

True Self-rule (ĀTMĀ-RĀJ) is the rule of your Soul (ĀTMAN) over your personality impulses and desires. This is true Self-control. This is possible only when your Heart becomes awakened to the Light of God within.

To become reconciled with the Lord and Master within you, enter your Heart.

The Lord is enshrined in your Heart.

Human evolution will reach perfection on this planet when ĀTMAN, the Inner God within the Heart, takes full control of this Physical Plane of Being.

The Abode of the Self 434
The Universal Christ 440
The Temple of God 639
The Temple of the Goddess 1492
The Mystery within the Heart 1315
The Solar and Human Heart 1592
Īśvara 1623

When the Inner Light of the Soul illumines your Heart, this produces true Understanding (Buddhi).

The God in your Heart is the Witness of everything you do, and of all Creation.

There is already within you a natural Inner Communion with God which is broken and interrupted by the discordant activities of your mind and emotions. Love the Lord your God within your Heart and Peace shall descend upon you.

Meditation in your Heart is pleasing to God

There is a Bliss in the Heart, eternal, unending.

The easiest Path by which to come to the Knowledge of God is to taste the Love of God in your Heart through Pure Love, Devotion, Invocation, Praise, Adoration.

A Heart which is full of the Love of God finds it easy to practise charity.

A Heart which is detached from earthly "sins" (imperfections) is easily turned towards the God Within.

When you return into your Heart you will discover the Kingdom of God within you.

Meditate in your Heart, for it reveals the Secret of Life.

You cannot meditate if your Heart is disturbed.

Shut out the world without so that you may see the World Within.

Ask the God Within, in the Cave of your Heart, to shine forth.

Meditation in your Heart is pleasing to God.

To pray ceaselessly is to pray *in* the Heart and *with* the Heart. It is not mental prayer. It is not outward vocal prayer. When you pray or repeat your mantram in your Heart, after some time the prayer or mantram repeats itself without your conscious effort, even while you are working or engaged in other activities, even when you are asleep.

Practising the Presence of God 711

Heart-Prayer or Spiritual Prayer 1256

What is True Faith?

Faith is not an intellectual process, not an activity of the rational mind. Materialists have no Faith because they are stuck in their "reasoning" minds, whether they be materialistic scientists, politicians, theologians, psychologists or school teachers. The mind is cold, calculating, abstract, joyless. The Heart is warm, friendly, radiant, joyful.

Faith is an activity of the Heart towards the Unseen God

Faith is an activity of the Heart *towards* the Unseen God. At first it is towards God who is "out there" or "in heaven" somewhere. This type of Faith is outer religion, seen in the rites, rituals and ceremonies of all the world's religions. The Faith of the Mystic is more mature; it is towards God who dwells in the Heart, who is the Beloved within the deepest point of the Soul.

The Faith of the Knower is in the Omnipresent God who dwells within all things, all creatures, all Space, in all layers of Creation, at all times. For, while God is Transcendent, Unreachable, Unmanifest, beyond ordinary Space-Time and Universes, a part of God is within all things, pervades all things, *becomes* all things.

The Way of the Heart is twofold: outer mingling with Life and inner striving for Realization.

The world around you is a creation of *mind*, but Life itself is a Wave that is beyond and above these mind-creations, and Life persists within and above the objects that mind has created.

This Way is Service towards the One Eternal who is embodied in all the forms and bodies of entities you see around you in the world, as well as Realization of God dwelling in your very own Heart as the Guiding Light of your Soul.

The Way is to experience the Dance of Life all around you and the Bliss and Joy of Life in the Heart within you.

From Head to Heart 427
Belief and Experience 676
Faith and Wisdom 849
The Omnipresent God 1109
To Love God and the World 1392
The Meaning of Life is Love 633

The Holy Path

Becoming Aware of the Vast Body of our Conscious Sun, our Solar Logos.

Becoming Awake to the Infinite Body of the Central Spiritual Sun, the Universal Logos.

The Holy Path begins by centring yourself in your Heart

Becoming a Conscious Worker for the Divine Plan as it is understood in your present state of development.

Becoming Christ-centred through the Living Flame of Love in the Heart.

The Holy Path begins by centring yourself in your Heart, which ultimately leads you to Self-Discovery or Self-Realization, or knowing truly who you are.

The Holy Path is a gradual expansion of your Consciousness from the Atomic to the Cosmic.

The Holy Path is to become aware of Light, and the Light within Light, and Greater Light, and the Boundless Light, in which this world appears as but darkness.

The Holy Path is the flowering-forth of the Unmanifested Life.

Initiation is not the ritual but the Inner Transformation as a result of being inwardly touched by a higher Entity, or the Forces of the Invisible Worlds, or the Downpour of Divine Grace.

Light, Love and Service: these are the marks of the Man upon the Holy Path.

Nirvāṇa is not the end, but the entrance into a new Life, into a Field of Light-Evolution.

The Manifested-God 1589
The Lighted Way 1394
The Unfoldment of the Light 718
What is Initiation? 1007
The Journey of the Heart 855
The Threefold Way 1236

Heart Knowing

The Way of the Mystic is the Heart.
The Way of the Gnostic is the Mind.
The Way of the Adept is the Union of the Heart and Mind Paths.

When you have merged your mind into the Heart, you will know Wisdom

There is a Purifying Fire which is awakened by Devotion in the Heart, and there is a Light of Gnosis which irradiates the Heart and makes you feel Godlike.

Communion with your God Within is accomplished by joining your mind to the Heart and there overcoming all distracting thoughts.

The Sage focuses his mind in the Heart and there quietens all his thoughts, and thus finds Peace.

Descend from your mind into your Heart and there touch upon your Inner God who transcends all Space and Time limitations.

When you have merged your mind into the Heart-Consciousness, you will know Wisdom.

The Heart-Knowing is not a product of thinking. It is true *Knowing*.

Develop a pure Heart and a refined Mind

- Self-Realization (ĀTMA-VIDYĀ) is easiest to attain in the Heart Centre.
- God-Realization (BRAHMA-VIDYĀ), or Universal Consciousness, is best realized in the Crown Centre.

In the Heart Centre you will discover the Kingdom of God *within* you.
In the Crown Centre you will discover the Kingdom of God *outside* you.

There is a State in which you experience both simultaneously, wherein your Heart overflows with waves of Universal Love and Ecstatic Devotion towards God, and your Mind is so bright and clear that you experience the Transcendental Godhead as being Omnipresent. In this condition your Heart and Head Centres have become united, producing a high state of Enlightenment: BRAHMANIRVĀṆAM (Dissolution in God).

The Two Paths 1112
Uniting Head and Heart 1130
The Path to Immortality 430
Super-Knowing 1242
What is Wisdom? 1685

The Fire in the Heart

There is no Transformation without Fire.

Cosmic Fire is Creator, Preserver and Destroyer.

There is a real Fire in the innermost chamber of the Heart Centre which is awakened by intense Love and Devotion. This Fire will warm the body, subdue the astral elementals, and open the door to the Kingdom of God Within.

Spiritual Fire burns up all karmas and sets you Free

The awakened Heart transmutes the lower desires of the astral body (the feeling body) into pure vibrations of Aspiration and Devotion which, in turn, will awaken the Fiery Love-Energy of the Buddhic Heart.

Spiritual Fire, when invoked, burns up all karmas and sets you Free.

The Lord (the CHRISTOS, the Christ) shall be revealed within you in a Flaming Fire in your Heart.

When your Heart is on Fire, the Fiery Devas of Transmutation are ready to serve you.

The Kingdom of Heaven is within your Heart, wherein is the Light of the World and Celestial Fire.

There is the Fire of the Father, the Fire of the Son, and the Fire of the Holy Spirit which breaks up into the Forty-Nine Fires of the forty-nine subplanes of the Solar System.

The Holy Spirit is a Living Fire which gives you Knowledge of the Future (prophecy) and the power of Mantric-Speech (MANTRIKĀ-ŚAKTI).

When you are troubled and full of anxieties, let the Fire of the Holy Spirit rest upon you in your Heart.

The Cosmic Fire 130
Wounds of Love 699
The Fire of Love 1255
Karmic Adjustment 1379
Tapas: Spiritual Purification 571
The Holy Trinity 1342

Meditate in your Heart…

ŌṀ PARAMĀTMANE NAMAḤ
The Incorruptible Self.
The Bright Eternal Self.
The Spark of the Everlasting.
The Self that is Eternally Free.

Then comes the Knowledge that the Self and God are One

ŌṀ: the Sanskrit sound for the Uniform Reality.
PARAM-ĀTMAN: the Supreme Self.
NAMAḤ: invocation, veneration, adoration.

This is What You Are.

ŌṀ NAMO BHĀGAVATE VASUDEVĀYA
The Glorious All-Pervading God.
The Eternal Freedom which is Truth.
The Universal Imperishable Life.
The All-Permeating Light of the Eternal.
The Fundamental Reality upon which all things depend.

ŌṀ: the Sign of God.
BHAGAVĀNA, BHĀGAVATA: Lord, God, the Universal Self, the Glorious One, Divine, Adorable, Holy.
VASUDEVA (VASU-DEVA): the Indwelling God, the Immanent God, the Omnipresent God, the Indwelling Universal-Energy.
DEVA: Shining Substance.

This is What God Is.

∞

The ŌṀ PARAMĀTMANE NAMAḤ leads you to Self-Realization.
The ŌṀ NAMO BHĀGAVATE VASUDEVĀYA leads you to God-Realization.

- First comes Self-Realization.
- Then comes God-Realization.
- Then comes the final unveiling of Truth: the Knowledge that the Self and God are One.

PARAMĀTMAN, the Transcendental Spirit, the Universal Soul, the Supreme Self, can be found and experienced in your Heart Centre. Within your Heart, the One Self, PARAMĀTMAN, can be seen. This One Self is within all forms, large or small, atomic or solar-systemic. When found in meditation, in deep Mystical Experience, PARAMĀTMAN will become your Inner Teacher and Guide, the SAT-GURU.
Keys to the Heart 1318

Signs of Progress in the Heart

Mystical Experience in the Heart manifests when you have the sensation or awareness of being beyond Time and physical Space. There seems to be no past, present and future, only Now, the very Moment you are experiencing, the Timeless, the Unconditioned, the Absolute, the All-Pervading Awareness.

You spiritually feel God to be everywhere, within all things

Mystical Experience manifests when your mind is *clear, bright, sharp, alert, awake,* uncluttered by any thoughts about anything. It is empty of thoughts but full of Understanding, Gnosis, Insight into the true Nature of things. This is non-verbal Knowledge which is *not* a result of "thinking". You *realize* how erroneous is human "thinking" and ideas about all things.

Your "personal" self (your personal sense of "I", your personal ego) disappears at the moment of Mystical Experience. You *realize* yourself to be part of an Infinite Ocean of Absolute Reality, the Real God (*not* the God of the theologians, metaphysicians, philosophers and thinkers). This Real God appears to be an Infinite Boundless Self or Being or Soul of everything and everybody.

When your Heart has awakened, you sense or spiritually *feel* God to be everywhere, *within* all things—in the sky, in the clouds, in Nature, in space, in people, animals and plants—and you feel with your spiritual sense the presence of the invisible worlds and hosts of angels and spiritual entities around you.

On a deeper layer of experience, you realize that although it *appears* that your personal ego is doing all the things that you do, and that the myriads of personal egos are doing all the things that they do in Creation, that is only a false vision, for there is only One Doer: the Real God.

At a much higher level of Ecstasy, the Glory of God will be blazing as an irresistible Current of Light, an indescribable Splendour shining everywhere, at all times, always.

The One and Only 839
The Path of Union 1339
The Presence of God 1396
Experiencing the Awakening Heart 463

My Beloved Lives in my Heart

Those who Love God become One with God.

My Beloved lives in my Heart.

God is the imprisoned Splendour in your Heart

Love is that Flame which burns up the ego.

The Fire of Love is burning in my Heart.

When the Fire has burned away all in you that is non-essential, only God remains.

Everything perishes except the Face of God, which is always shining Bright.

My Beloved is the Light of my Soul.

The Heart is a Heart of Love.

Love is the Radiation of the Heart.

He who has no Heart has no Love.

Union with the Beloved means being what You always truly have been, whom you forgot but have now Remembered upon Awakening to your Self.

Do not confuse true Love with sexual energy. Falling in love with someone, or being attracted to someone, is not Love; it is magnetic sexual energy, while the Love Energy that comes from the Heart Centre is a Spiritual Radiation. The sexual energy-current can only be finally tamed by the Buddhic Energy-Current of Love flowing through the Heart Centre.

The Energies of Sex and Love 912
Sex Natural and Divine 926

The Lord dwells in the Heart of everyone.

Wheresoever you Look, there is the Face of God, in which there is no inside and no outside.

God is the imprisoned Splendour in your Heart.

God's Love is a Consuming Fire.

There is a Fire within and the Heart is consumed by God.

The Living Flame of Love pouring forth from the Heart sets me on Fire.

Is the Fire of Love burning in your Heart?

God inscribed upon my Heart all Spiritual Mysteries and the tablets of the Law that teaches all things.

The Heart is the gateway to Union with the God within you

The Heart is the source of Divine Grace.

In the Heart there is an Image, the Figure of God that always Is.

Find Me in your Heart.

I Am Pure Consciousness—not the body, not the emotions, not the mind—and this Consciousness is the Heart.

The Heart is the Living God, the Real God, the Bright Eternal Radiance, the Spiritual Sun, the Source and Substance of the All.

The Heart is the gateway to Union with the God within you.

Within you is the Boundless Freedom of Eternal Life.

Turn your Heart towards the Eternal.

In your Heart you behold your own Eternity.

"Lo! I am with you always," says God, "even unto the end of Time." Who is the Seeker? Who seeks Who?

God is nearer to you than your hands and feet.

There is an Image of God, a form or representation of God, in your Heart Centre, called VIṢṆU-MŪRTI (God-form). This is truly the Personal God present in your Heart. This is *not* a human invention, not a thought, theory or imagination, not a philosophy or speculation, but truly a Seal of God and a proof of your final Redemption. The Yogī, Mystic or Devotee (BHAKTA) will discover this God-Presence in his or her Heart through intense prayer, devotion, chanting or meditation in the Heart.

The Lover of God 853

Three Meditations in the Heart

Ko-Ahaṁ (Kohaṁ)

Sanskrit: Who am I?

The Heart will reveal to you your Oneness with the Eternal

Sitting quietly, focus in the Heart (the middle of the chest) and quietly ask yourself: "Who am I?" (Kohaṁ?). Let your mind calm down and *rest* in your Heart. Do not provide intellectual or mental-verbal answers. Just sit still and now and then ask yourself this question, silently. In time the answer will come from the Heart, and it will not be a thought or a mentally constructed answer.

Na-Ahaṁ (Nahaṁ)

Sanskrit: Not the "I".

"Not I" (Nahaṁ) is a meditation in the Heart that can be practised always, everywhere, in the midst of all activities. It is the denial of the lower ego, the self-centred "I", the personal ego, and Surrender to the Will of God. It is like "Let Your Will be done, not mine." It is self-sacrifice, considering others before yourself. It is diminishing your self-centredness, your selfishness. This attitude will purify your Heart so that the Clear Light of Truth may abide in it.

So-Ahaṁ (So'haṁ)

Sanskrit: I am That.

Meditate upon "I am That" (So'haṁ) in your Heart. "That" means God, the Absolute, the Divinity. The Heart will reveal to you your Oneness with the Eternal, with the Truth, with God.

Who is 'I AM'? 1418
Tao: the Great I AM 774
The Way, the Truth and the Life 670
Pure Consciousness in the Heart 447
The One 1686

The Bright Eternal Self

Because of its inherent limitations, your limited personal ego or "I" is always seeking for more things, more "knowledge", more "goodies", more success or perfection, more happiness, more satisfaction.

But the Bright Eternal Self that You Are is always at Rest in the Bliss and Love of the Heart, which is God.

Quest for the Self 1317

To Invoke God in your Heart

Your Heart will become Pure by your repeating Names of God, or a Name. A Name of God should be repeated from the innermost Core of the Heart. You may use any Divine Name to invoke God in your Heart.

Make your Heart Holy and you will become Holy

Prayer (meditation) in the Heart is ego-transcending. The "normal" way of being is continuous ego-activity. When your little "ego-I" is transcended in Mystical Union, then comes the experience of Bliss, Love, Unity and Being, beyond Space and Time.

Union with the Beloved-in-the-Heart means Freedom from the bondage and limitations of your own ego.

Union with the Beloved-in-the-Heart means losing your sense of separate self, your sense of separate ego or identity, and merging into the Oneness of the Divine Presence.

Union with God comes about by *transcending* your little ego or personal self in the Heart Centre and merging into the Limitless Ocean of Reality, which is the Bright Eternal Self, which is God.

The Nature of God is Love, Bliss and Light, Conscious Intelligence, Universal Power.

The Beloved lives within you, in your Heart. So then, why seek God on the outside?

Only after human birth, as a human being, can you have the opportunity to return to your Beloved. So, why waste your life on merely worldly pursuits?

Make your Heart Holy and you will become Holy, for God-in-You will see your efforts and will reward you abundantly.

Sūfī Prayer 863
Christian Prayer 689
The Heart and the Lost Art of Prayer 1251
To Realize the Presence of God 1398

Meditations in the Heart Centre

Meditate upon the following Mantrams in the Heart

Mantram
Sanskrit: Prayer, invocation, chant, words of power, transforming sound-vibrations.

1

Lord, God, Christ-Jesus, Divine Love

The Christos (Greek: the Christ) lives *in* you, in the deeper regions of your Heart, which is full of Glory. The Christ in the Heart is the Wayshower towards the Kingdom of God within. The Christ-Power is the second aspect of the Triune Godhead, which raises you out of the realms of matter and leads you into the glories of Spirit. It is the Word incarnate in you.

The Christ Principle is reflected within every human Heart, but in most human beings this Christ Principle lies dormant and has to be Awakened. The birth of the Christ-Child must be accomplished within your Heart. This is the beginning of Salvation. When it is awakened we become Christ-like—that is, Godlike, Godly, of God. This is the Hope for Glory that ultimately leads you to the Kingdom of God, Salvation, Nirvāṇa, Beatitude.

2

Yeheshuah

Hebrew: God rescues (saves) the Pure in Heart.

Yeheshuah, Yeshua, Yeshu, Yesu (Hebrew) means "God saves". It refers to the Living Power of God, God's Grace as an ever-present, living, vital Force. Grace is not a symbol; it is the Living Light of God that heals your Soul and redeems your personality from the clutches of the material energies of the world.

Yeshu, Yesu is the Incarnation of the Word in human flesh, the Light of the World, the Inner Invisible Light, the Logos, dwelling in your Heart Centre. (The Hebrew word Yesu became the Greek Iesous which became the Latin Iesus which became the English *Jesus*.)

Meditate on Yeheshuah or Yeshua in the Heart Centre...

3

Glory be to God

Meditate in your Heart...

Christian Divine Names 1266
The Birth of the Light in the Heart 718
Yeshua: the Secret Hebrew Name 1276

4

Glory be to you, Father of the Undying Light,
for by your Glory you renew your Creation day by day.

Meditate in your Heart…

5

ŌṀ ŚRĪ YESU BHĀGAVATE NAMAḤ

Sanskrit: I invoke the Lord God, the Radiant Yesu (in my Heart).

ŌṀ: the Absolute Godhead.
ŚRĪ: Radiant, Glorious.
YESU: Jesus.
BHĀGAVATA: the Lord God.
NAMAḤ: I invoke, salutations to.

6

ŌṀ YESU KRISTĀYA PARAMĀTMANE PURUṢA AVATARĀYA NAMAHE

Sanskrit: I invoke Jesus the Christ, the Supreme Spirit, the Divine Incarnation.

PARAM-ĀTMAN: the Supreme Self, the Transcendental Spirit.
PURUṢA: the Original-Spirit, the Transcendental Reality, the Divinity.
AVATĀRA: a Descent, a Divine Incarnation.

7

KYRIE ELEISON, CHRISTE ELEISON

Greek: Lord have mercy upon us, Christ have mercy upon us.

KYRIE: God, Lord, Master; the God within your Heart Centre.
CHRISTE: the Logos; God incarnated *in* Creation.
ELEISON: have mercy upon us.

8

OṀKĀRĀYA NAMO NAMAḤ

Sanskrit: We offer Salutations to God Incarnate.

OṀKĀRA: the Logos, the Word, the God-into-Incarnation Power, the Sounding-Light.

Invoke, pray, meditate or chant in the Heart…

OṀKĀRĀYA NAMO NAMAḤ.

The Saviour in the Heart

Do not look for a personal Saviour, the Lord God, outside in the world, for if you do not find Him in your Heart you will not find him anywhere.

Be not afraid: I AM with you always in your Heart.

The Universal Christ 440
The Way, the Truth and the Life 670
The Holy Trinity 1342
Rely on your Inner Self 1226
Inner Guidance (Metanoia) 1464

The innermost chamber of the Heart is the point of contact with the Universal Logos, the Cosmic Christ, the Christos.

The Holy Ghost is Fire, and the Christ is a Brilliant Light which shines in your Heart and in the Heart of the World.

The Christ is within you, in your Heart, your hope of Glory.

You are a Temple of the Holy Spirit, and your Heart is the Altar of God.

When the Heart Centre becomes vitalized by the energies of the Spirit within, the energies will circulate throughout the personality and the beginning of a Divine Manifestation (Avatāra) becomes possible.

Rest your mind on Yesu (Hebrew: the Light of the Heart).

Be filled with the Holy Spirit in the Heart. The Spirit gives you great Courage and Strength.

Ask the Holy Spirit in your Heart to turn your Darkness into Light.

When the Word of God reverberates in your Heart, you have made peace with God.

What does it mean to be a follower of Christ, Buddha, Kṛṣṇa or a Saint? It is to discover the God within you in deep meditation and to serve Mankind selflessly.

Īṣta-Devatā is the chosen Deity or Divinity that you visualize in your Heart, such as the image of Christ, Buddha, Kṛṣṇa, Rāma or the Goddess. Īṣta means "the Beloved, the Worshipped Deity".

Visualizing the Divinity in the Heart 1268

9

Shekinah

Hebrew: The Glory of God's Presence, illuminating the world from *within*.

God's Holy Presence vibrates through every part of Creation. This is Shekinah, the Glory of God within the Heart.

Intone or meditate on She-ki-na-ah in the Heart Centre…

10

Abba

Hebrew: The God-in-Heart.

When you meditate, just abide in Abba (the Father), the Monad, who is Omnipotence, Omniscience and All-Compassion, shining in your Heart.

11

Immanuel

Hebrew: God is with us. God is within us.

The Great Truth that the Holy Spirit reveals in the Heart is that God is living *in* us and *through* us. To be reconciled with God means to *remember* the Divine Presence in your Heart always.

12

Kyrios Iesous Christos

Greek: Lord, Jesus Christ.

When you say this Greek prayer in your Heart, *remember* the Mystery of the Incarnation of God, the Word becoming Man.

13

Halleluyāh

Hebrew: Glorify God! (Hallelu-Yāh).

God plays the Game of Love (Līlā) with your Soul. Sing, intone or meditate upon Halleluyāh in the Heart Centre and be Joyous within your Heart.

The Evolution of Christian Prayer 713

Kyrios Iesous Christos

14

ŌṀ MAṆI PADME HŪṀ

Sanskrit: I meditate on the precious Jewel in my Heart.

MAṆI: a jewel, a pearl, a precious stone, a treasure.
PADMA: lotus flower, the Heart Centre.

MAṆI-PADMA, the Jewelled Lotus, is the innermost sanctuary of the Heart Centre wherein dwells the Spirit of God, the Saviour, the Deliverer, the AVALOKITEŚVARA (the downward-looking Lord, the Lord who looks down from on High), the Higher Self in Humanity, the Logos in the Solar System, the Inner Spiritual Guide of the Soul (the Monad). PADMAPĀṆI is the Lotus-born, the Saviour born in the Heart Centre.

The Esoteric Mantram 551
Keys to the Heart 1322
Sex Natural and Divine 926
The Mystery within the Heart 1315
Hṛt-Padma: the Heart-Lotus 1505

The MAṆI, or Jewel, is the *Spirit-Spark-Atom* of the Imperishable Kingdom of Light, Nirvāṇa, the true Kingdom of God. It is the Pure Light of the Spirit visible in the innermost Cave or Chamber of the Heart, the Spark or Flame of Divinity, a brilliant Electric Fire.

The Innermost Temple of the Heart, the Seventh Portal, the Jewel in the Lotus, is where the Triune Self (ĀTMA-BUDDHI-MANAS, the Spiritual Trinity in Humanity) finds a focal point of energy and expression.

ĀTMA: Spirit.
BUDDHI: Wisdom, Compassion, Unity, Bliss.
MANAS: Mind, intelligence.

The Jewel in the Heart Cakra, when awakened, transmutes passion into Pure Consciousness.

The Heart Cakra contains the Spirit-Spark-Atom, the point of contact with the Imperishable Realm of the Kingdom of Light.

The Spiritual Heart is like a transparent crystal, a precious stone, pearl or jewel. Within its depths radiates the Throne with Fiery Darts of Living Light. Upon the Throne sits ĀTMAN, the King, your true Self.

Incarnations of the Sun 1593

15

GOVINDAM ĀDI-PURUṢAṀ TAM AHAṀ BHAJĀMI

Sanskrit: I am worshipping the Primeval Lord within my Heart.

GOVINDA: the Lord (controller) of the senses, the KṚṢṆA (God) within the Heart.
ĀDI-PURUṢA: the Original Spirit, the Primeval Lord, the Godhead within the Universe.
TAM: That.
AHAṀ: I Am.
BHAJĀMI: I am worshipping.

16

Ōṁ Śāntiḥ Śāntiḥ Śāntiḥ

Sanskrit: The Peace of God.

Śāntiḥ means Peace. Let the Peace of God control your Heart. Be not anxious, nor afraid. Invoke the Holy God within your Heart and you will have Peace.

Meditate, chant or intone in your Heart Centre…

17

Ōṁ Namo Amitābhāya Buddhāya

Sanskrit: Salutations to the Buddha in the Heart.

Amitābha-Buddha is the Infinite Light-Being (Amida-Butsu in Japanese). This Buddha of Infinite Light shines in your Heart as a Boundless Ocean of Reality, an Endless Vision of Pure Illumination and Knowing. It is the complete flowering of the Enlightenment Consciousness (Bodhi-Citta). It is the Ineffable Godhead.

Meditate on Amitābha-Buddha in the Heart…

Salutation to the Buddha 795

18

Amida-Butsu

Japanese: The Buddha in the Heart.

Meditate or intone A-Mi-Da-But-Su in your Heart Cakra…

19

Omito-Fu

Chinese: The Buddha in the Heart.

Meditate or intone O-Mi-To-Fu in your Heart Cakra…

20

Rām-Rāy

Sanskrit: The Omnipotent God.

Rām: God.
Rāi: Omnipotent.

Meditate in your Heart…

Ōṁ Śāntiḥ Śāntiḥ Śāntiḥ

The Pure Heart

A Pure Heart is the open Gate to the Kingdom of God within you.

To purify your Heart means to free your Heart-Consciousness from sensory and worldly impressions and from the glamours of materialistic energies.

Purify the Heart 701
The Purification of the Heart 849
Tapas: Spiritual Purification 571
The Experience of Mysticism 636
Hear the Sound within the Silence 1651

That Heart is pure which is always remembering God's Presence in a formless and imageless memory—not by thoughts, but by subtle Spiritual Impressions from within.

The Living Waters of the Holy Spirit gush forth from the Heart. This is why it is important to keep your Heart pure and uncontaminated by the world.

Holiness *in* the Lord. This is the feeling of the Awakened Heart.

There are many siddhis (powers)—physical, mental, psychic and spiritual. But the Divine Powers of the Spirit are given only to the Pure in Heart.

Your Soul is pure and radiant, reflected in your Heart.

Look and listen with your Heart.

Listen attentively to the Voice of the Silence in your Heart.

Listen to the ANĀHATA-ŚABDA, the Uncreated Music of the Word, as it plays its sweet melodies in your Heart. The True Word of God, the Unutterable Name of God, can be *heard* in the Heart.

When your Heart is made pure through the disciplines of meditation, chanting and service to others, and when your mind is free from worldly cares and worries, God Himself will come to you and will become your constant companion.

When the Heart is fully awakened, when the Fire has fully stirred, then comes Heart-Clairvoyance or *seeing* with the Heart. This is different from seeing with the Third-Eye Centre, the Crown Centre or the Causal Centre above the head. Even when your physical eyes are closed, you See brightly and clearly with the Heart.

21

Allāh

Arabic: God in the aspect of the Bright, Radiant and Glorious; the Effulgent One, Resplendent, Full of Light. Also, Allahā and Allahū (in Aramaic, Alāhā).

Allahū: the Most Exalted, the Undiminished Radiant God.
Allahū Akbar: God is Great.

Chant, intone or invoke the Divine Name Allāh in your Heart.
Call upon Allahū *in your Heart* and you will receive Revelation.

22

Lā Ilāha Ill Allāhu
Lā Ilāha Illa Allāh

Arabic: There is nothing but God.

The One God the ancients spoke of, you will find in your Heart. Make your mind *still*. Enter the gates of your Heart, for there you will find the true Religion.

Meditate, chant, recite or intone in the Heart…

The Mantram of Unification 850, 866

Lā Ilāha Illa Allāh

23

Achath Ruach Elohim Chiim
(Ahat Ruah Elohim Hayyim)

Hebrew: One is Spirit, the God of Life.
One is the Holy Spirit, the Life-Force of the gods.

Achath: One (in the Feminine).
Ruach: Spirit, the Holy Ghost, the Holy Spirit.
Elohim: God, or all the gods (divine beings).
Chiim: Life, the Life-principle.

Meditate in the Heart to invoke the Holy Spirit in your Heart…

24

Deus

Latin: God

Deus is the Latin word for God. Pronounce it in your Heart in two syllables, De-Us, and discover the Supreme Excellence.

Ōṁ Śrī Satpuruṣāya Namaḥ

25

Ōṁ Śrī Satpuruṣāya Namaḥ

Sanskrit: Adoration to the Everlasting God.

Ōṁ: the Eternal Logos, the Creative Word.
Śrī: Divine Glory, Effulgence, Brightness.
Sat: the Universal Absolute Being, Existence.
Puruṣa: the Divine Person, the Godhead, Spirit.
Namaḥ: bowing down, salutation, adoration.

Meditate in the Heart…

26

Sat Śrī Akāla Namaḥ

Sanskrit: I adore the Timeless One (God).

Akāla: timeless, eternal, everlasting.

Meditate in the Heart…

27

Ōṁ Namo Gurudeva Namo

Sanskrit: I invoke the Godhead within my Heart.

Guru-Deva: the Teacher Divine, God within your Heart Centre.
Namo: salutation, praising, invoking, tuning into.

The Guru's Grace is always within you in the form of Ātman, the Spiritual Self, dwelling in the Heart.

Sing, chant, or intone in the Heart…

28

Ōṁ Āḥ Hūṁ
Vajra Guru Padma Siddhi Hūṁ

Sanskrit: I invoke the Imperishable Teacher who is the Spiritual Power in my Heart.

Vajra-Guru: Indestructible Teacher.
Padma-Siddhi: the Heart's Power.

Sing, chant, intone or meditate in the Heart…

The Vowels in the Heart

IAOUE

Intone, chant or meditate in the Heart: **I A O U E**. These five Vowels represent the Divine Name, **Yahweh**.

Remember to pronounce these Vowels *properly* (not as in English). The Vowels are pronounced as in Latin, Greek, Hebrew, Sanskrit or Māori (the *Pure* Vowels, not the English or French modifications).

The five Vowels are the purest Name of God

The five Vowels are the purest Name of God, totally international, beyond language, race, colour, nationality or religion. Every human being, without exception, uses these five Vowels. The Name of God is woven into the fabric of every human language. When we intone the Pure Vowels, we bring God's Energy into ourselves.

EAOUE

Another version is with the four Vowels: **E A O U E**. In this version, the E is repeated twice.

IAO

Intone **I A O** in the Heart. (Pronounce long Pure Vowels, not the English pronunciation.)

I A O was the Name of Names within the ancient Greek, Chaldean and Phoenician Mystery Schools. It is the Unnameable Supreme, the Transcendental Mystery, the Unknowable Godhead, the Transcendent, the Everlasting.

The Vowels 1030
IAO and the Perfected Man-Species 1035
The Vowels in the Energy Centres 1036
Christian Meditation on the Holy Breath 1346
IHVH: I AM 1460

Peace on Earth

Peace on Earth depends on each one of us, and the Peace within you depends on the degree of your at-one-ment with your Soul in your Heart.

A single act of Compassion will put you in touch with the Heart of Humanity

You cannot become a Master of all that is in Heaven if you have hatred in your Heart.

Suffering knows no boundaries, no class distinctions, no discrimination between races and colour. It is universal. It affects people in prisons as well as in luxury hotels. Your Heart-Compassion also is universal when *awakened.*

The Divine Word is constant in the Hearts of all beings.

A single act of Compassion will put you in touch with the Heart of Humanity.

If you hate the evil-doers you will become like them. If you hate the violent you will become violent. Hatred can be transmuted only by genuine Heart Love.

Confrontation has been the way of living on this planet for countless ages. It is the natural animal instinct in Humanity and can only be created by animal Man. It can be overcome by Self-Realization (Ātmabodha), by the Vision of the Soul (Ātmadarśana) in the Heart.

Everything is pure to a Heart that is Pure. Everything is evil to a Heart that is corrupt.

If your Heart becomes contaminated by the worldly vibration you will become a Lost Soul.

If you keep your attention constantly within your Heart you will avoid much outer strife.

The Mind-Created Devil 218
The Law of Action 992
From Hate to Love 229
Oneness and Love 1450
The Warrior seeks Peace not War 986

An open mind and an open Heart are a *must* before you can begin the Great Quest for Liberation.

Everyone needs a place to go for refuge from the onslaught of the world. The best place is a Silent Heart.

Let go of fear, open up your Heart.

Those who walk the Way of God have God in their Hearts always

Guard your Heart, for it protects you from the attacks of the Enemy.

When your Heart is open, you will feel more pain but also more Love.

Follow your Heart.

Your Heart is the Throne of God.

Those who walk the Way of God have God in their Hearts always.

The Kingdom of God must first be established in the Heart of Humanity. When enough Hearts have been turned within, the Kingdom will come upon this world.

The Soul-Power

Your Soul is the source of your genuine Power and Self-empowerment. The more Soul-Conscious you are, the more Power you have. This Power is not the same as the energies of your physical, emotional or mental bodies. The true Power of your Soul is Loving Compassion and Understanding Wisdom (Buddhic Consciousness). It best manifests through the Heart Centre. Its other manifestations are Humility and Forgiveness. When the Soul is not operative in a personality, then there is no Compassion, no Wisdom, no Humility, no Forgiveness.

The Warrior Code 1077

Guard your Heart 1328
Peace of Heart 1595
The Kingdom of God 1715
To Manifest the Kingdom of God 1716

The State of Innocence

Live now as if you are already in the Eternal

For the Calmness of the Heart to be in the Eternal Moment, relinquish all unnecessary things.

Only the intense longing of your Heart will take you along the Path of Liberation.

Freedom is not a thought, not an idea, not an intellectual decision; it is a state of your Inner Being.

The Path is essentially the finding of the Truth which is already within yourself.

Look within yourself for Enlightenment, not outside. In your Heart is the Suffering of the World and the Bliss of the Eternal.

You know you have found the Truth when you have discovered within yourself that which is Eternal.

There is a State of Innocence or Purity within us, the true Kingdom of God or Paradise, in which we know no separation, no pain, no sorrow, no cares or worries, and every moment is complete Bliss. It is HṚDAYAṀ, the Heart of God.

Unity Consciousness is the original State of Innocence, the Youthfulness of your Soul before you became enmeshed into the vibrations of the world flux.

Having reached the State of Unity Consciousness, you are God and you are the Universe. This is the sublime Mystery of Man.

Live now as if you are already in the Eternal.

When you wake up in the morning, do you remember the Eternal? Is that part of your day? Have you made up your mind?

The Eternal 1644
The Divine Unity 852
The State of Inner Purity 497
You Are the World 1390
The Vision of your own Eternity 1144
Attach your Mind to the Eternal 1234

Let the Light Shine

This is how you let the Light shine inside you

Search the Cave of your Heart.

Love everybody. Be *patient* with yourself.

Be actively engaged in doing *good.*

The Purpose of Man is to become wholly Divine

Expand your Understanding continually by Profound Knowledge. Man evolves by Knowledge.

Care for animals and plants also, not only Man, for the time will come when you will have to care for angels as well.

What race a person belongs to, what colour or religion, does not matter. What matters most is the *state* of your Heart. Are the Fires of Love burning?

God has a *Plan* for Mankind. Man is not just a freak accident of Nature. The Purpose of Man is to become wholly Divine.

You are not the physical, astral or mental body, but the Self-Eternal in the Shining Light.

Discriminate between the Real and what is only glamour, between the important and the useless, between the passing and the Everlasting. Work to *salvage* the World.

Slowly, try to give up selfishness. Develop the spirit of self-sacrifice for others, for, as you decrease your personal self, the God-Self within can flourish and grow. For *Those who Know* are ever watching.

Cultivate Knowledge 1366
Qualifications for Discipleship 1149
Evolution, the Plan, the Path 1688
The Path to Wisdom 1702
The Law of Surrender or Sacrifice 1138
In Service to the Spiritual Hierarchy 1719

The River of Light

The reason why people on this planet don't treat Life as sacred is that they have lost touch with the Transcendent. The Divine Glory is permeating all forms of Life on this planet, not just the human, and the Ecstasy of the Spirit is spilling over into all forms of Life. We need to develop the inner senses of the Heart to appreciate and become immersed in God's Life.

The Divine Glory is permeating all forms of Life on this planet

The Uncreated Light illumines the Space of the Heart.

The Light of Life pervades everywhere.

The Living Light transfixes Time.

Adjust your Heart to the Vibration of the Transcendental State.

Let God's Spirit enter your Heart and there *listen* to His Word that reveals all hidden and wonderful Mysteries.

The Eternal Truth cannot be registered in the time-space-conditioned human mind until this common mind transcends the time-space limitation by entering the Heart.

A prisoner is one who is trapped in the workings of the mind; thus, there are many prisoners on this planet. There are a Few who go *inside* and discover the Freedom in the Heart.

The River of Light flows through you continually, but the outer-self is not strong enough to *see* it.

Become sensitive to it in your Heart.

Trapped Spirits 1240
The Experience of the Transcendent 1378
The Self-Generating Light 1594

CHAPTER 56

The Heart and the Future Evolution of Man

Mysterious Knowledge of the Siddhas

Here I shall disclose to you some profound Mysteries, things that may seem fanciful, yet they are true. This knowledge goes well beyond the common understanding of Humanity, religious or scientific. It reveals a future Glory, well beyond the wildest science-fiction ideas.

The Siddhas talked about mysterious and supernatural transformations of Man

The past holds many secrets. The Siddhas (those Yogīs with strange and mysterious powers) talked about **Kāya-Kalpa**, mysterious and supernatural transformations of Man, strange alchemical transfigurations that surpass even the future natural evolution.

- They spoke of **Śuddha-Deham**, purified and perfected physical bodies that vibrated differently than the normal bodies.
- They spoke of **Svarṇa-Deham**, a physical body that glowed like liquid gold, or glittered like gold dust. That is, either the natural physical body was transmuted into the Golden Body, or the Golden Body was projected from the Astral Plane into the physical body, thus transmuting the natural body into a luminous golden body.
- They spoke of a **Praṇava-Deham**, a Body of Light, made out of Praṇava, the Creative Word or Logos.
- They spoke of the **Māyāvi-Rūpa** (illusionary body), created through Kriyā-Śakti (advanced Yogic powers), which can be created and destroyed at will when the Adept wants to appear or disappear in the Three Worlds.
- They spoke of the **Yoga-Agni-Mayam-Śarīram**, the physical body (Śarīram) transformed (Mayam) by the Fires (Agni) of Yoga (Union with the Higher Self, Union with God). This is another altered natural physical body.

These are truly strange Mysteries. The importance of these ancient Sanskrit words for these seemingly miraculous "bodies" lies in the fact that they occurred in the past and will occur more frequently in the future as Spiritual Evolution speeds up on this planet. They are an indication of a Humanity that is very different from the Man-type of today. Whereas science-fiction writers promise immortality by attaching the physical brain to a computer or a machine (what madness!), what we are talking about here is *real* Immortality, mysterious and profound, and *it begins with the Transformation of the Heart.*

The Light Bodies 40
The Mental Body 78
Powers of Divine Descent 599
Types of Conscious Immortality 390

This is not the ordinary Yoga, Zen, Sūfīsm, Buddhism or Mysticism. It is not widely known, even by the Yogīs, Sūfīs, Kabbalists and Mystics, although a few in the past had glimpses of it. It is something else, belonging to the future unveiling of the hidden Mysteries.

This is not the ordinary Yoga, Zen, Sūfīsm, Buddhism or Mysticism

According to the traditional Spiritual Science of the great religions of the past (the Jewish, Christian, Muslim, Hindu, Sikh, Buddhist, Taoist, and so forth), the idea was to *escape* from this world and enter into a higher Existence, a higher Plane of Being—Nirvāṇa, the Kingdom of God, the Realm of the Imperishable Light, BRAHMĀ-STHITI (Rest in God), BRAHMA-NIRVĀṆA (Dissolution in God, Union with God). This implied leaving this realm altogether, dissolving the personality complex and remaining only in the Essential Self, ĀTMAN. What we are talking about here is very different from that.

In the West, when the *initiated* Alchemists talked about transmuting base metals or elements into gold, the uninitiated Alchemists (the majority) thought that Alchemy was about producing gold! It is not the outer elements that need to be transmuted, however, but *the elements of their own physical bodies.* Such is the secret SIDDHĀNTA, the Mysterious Knowledge of the SIDDHAs.

Mysterious Grace

Notice that all these supernatural bodies and transformed natural bodies are the result of PRASĀDA, Divine Grace, God's Gift. They do not "happen" simply because you *want* them. They come under a higher Law which, at this stage, is difficult for Humanity to comprehend, so we call it "Grace". Although they are not produced by your personal will or desire, they will never happen if you do not make an effort in the right direction, through meditation (DHYĀNA) and spiritual practices (SĀDHANĀ).

Thus, on the personality level you are responsible for transforming yourself as much as you can; the rest is literally up to God! Although there may be a reason or logical explanation for "Grace" which, in the future, Humanity will know how to invoke purposefully, at this stage its workings appear to be mysterious.

Sādhanā: the Spiritual Life 1153

Relational Consciousness 906
The Cosmic Elements 26
Kuṇḍalinī and Alchemy 153
The Future Evolution of Humanity 182
Three Schools of Spirituality 1121

Beyond Natural Evolution

The mysterious bodies mentioned by the Siddha-Yogīs are not the product of natural evolution

There is a natural evolution and there is a Supernatural Evolution. The natural evolution progresses over an immense period of time through many rebirths into human bodies, administered by KARMA, the Law of Cause and Effect. Through this slow natural evolution you make progress by improving your physical body, your emotional nature (astral body), and your mind capacity (mental body), life after life. This painful and cumbersome development goes on until your Soul begins to feel that the world is not as alluring as you had previously thought, that there is nothing much more to be learned in the Three Worlds. Then, you as a Soul begin to turn within yourself and seek the Soul-Kingdom. You step onto the Spiritual Path and slowly, over many lives, reach NIRVĀṆA, the Heaven of Rest.

The mysterious physical bodies mentioned by the SIDDHA-YOGĪS are not the product of natural evolution; rather, they are the outer signs of Inner Transformations, the intervention of Supernature.

Each of your natural bodies (the physical, etheric-physical, astral and mental), and even the causal body, is associated with its own elemental being, a class of entity below the human. In this respect, your bodies are not altogether yours; you own them "jointly" with elemental intelligences or entities. Consequently you are not a "master" of your physical, etheric-physical, astral or mental bodies, and this leads to many of the problems faced by Humanity on the physical, emotional and mental levels. The miraculous bodies spoken of by the Siddha Adepts are not under the control of any elemental beings or entities, nor elemental substances and essences, but are of a different order of Creation—the Supernature. They are under the direct control of the Soul and of the Monad (the Divinity that lives within you). Thus, you can see that we are talking of something other than ordinary natural evolution in the Three Worlds.

Human Involution and Evolution 170
Vertical Evolution and the Path 174
The Body-Elementals 213
Understand your Predicament 892
Evolution, the Plan, the Path 1688
The Far-Future Evolution of Humanity 183

Here is a wonderful hint for you of the far future. Our present physical bodies are not human; they were derived from the Animal Kingdom. In the far future, when the Human and Angelic Kingdoms merge, we will have angelic-human bodies (DEVA-MANUṢYA-DEHAM), derived from the Angelic Kingdom. We shall no longer have to struggle with an uncooperative animal body, for we will have bodies on the Physical Plane that will express perfectly the Divine Consciousness within us.

Further Light Bodies

- You have two natural bodies that can become permanent Light Bodies: the LIṄGA-ŚARĪRA (etheric-physical body) and the KĀRAṆA-ŚARĪRA (causal body), wherein you as the Soul (JĪVA) dwell. This spiritual-alchemical Transformation is effected by the Soul-Light and the Monadic Light. If the etheric-physical body becomes a permanent Light Body you become consciously immortal on the Physical Plane. If the causal body becomes a permanent Light Body you become consciously immortal in the Inner Worlds.
- There is another mysterious golden body, the HIRAṆYA-GARBHA (the Golden-Womb or Golden-Egg, because it has the shape of a womb or an egg), but this is never visible to the physical eyes. This appears only in the Causal World and encloses the Soul of the Adept who has undergone certain alchemical transmutations. (Note that the term HIRAṆYAGARBHA can also refer to the entire auric-field, encompassing all of the bodies.)
- Another supernatural Light Body is the ĀTMA-JYOTI-RŪPA (Soul-Light-Form), which is developed over a period of time by the Light of the Soul. It is concentrated in the Head Centres and slowly becomes externalized until it appears as a separate body within the natural bodies. When the Adept shifts his or her Awareness into this body, he or she becomes Consciously Immortal. This is preceded by a series of inner, supernatural transformations (supernatural from the physical perspective, but each quite natural on its own plane).
- The NIRMĀNAKĀYA is the Nirvāṇic Body (NIRVĀṆA-KĀYA) of those who dwell in the upper spheres of the Kingdom of God, but who retain the ability to descend to the lower worlds. These Spirits include those from the Human and Angelic Kingdoms who have attained Nirvāṇa; in this portion of the Kingdom of God they form one species. Their "bodies" are composed of filaments of Light from the Bright-Eternal—imperishable, indestructible, everlasting.

You have two natural bodies that can become permanent Light Bodies

The Personality Complex 36
The Light Bodies 40
The Human Aura 42
Bodies of the Buddhas 392

Every form is a Form of God.

The totality of all forms in the Universe, including the gross, the subtle and the subtlest, as well as the space between, is the complete Form of God, the Body of the Absolute. Space is Substance, and every form or body represents a certain stage of evolutionary Consciousness reached by the form-making faculty of the Absolute, the MĀYĀ.

The Form of God is Space 109

Keys to the Heart

The gate to these future possibilities lies hidden in twelve great statements (MAHĀ-VĀKYA: Great Truth Statements). For, in fact, the Heart contains the seed of the Future Evolution of Man, which can be awakened even now by you or any other man, woman or child who is prepared to do the work required.

The Heart contains the seed of the Future Evolution of Man

These twelve Keys are as follows. Shown also is the *key concept* embraced by each statement.

1. JAYA ĪŚA ĪŚVARĀM
The Master of the Heart.

2. HṚDAYAṀ
God is the Heart.

3. ŌṀ PARAMĀTMANE NAMAḤ
The Universal Self in the Heart.

4a. ŚRĪṀ HRĪṀ KLĪṀ
KṚṢṆĀYA GOVINDĀYA SVĀHĀ
The Ecstatic Devotion of the Heart.

4b. KLĪṀ KṚṢṆĀYA GOVINDĀYA
GOPĪJANA VALLABHĀYA SVĀHĀ
The Ecstatic Love of the Heart.

4c. ŌṀ YESU KRISTĀYA NAMAḤ
The Christ within the Heart.

5. NAMA ŚIVĀYA
The Transcendental Heart.

6. ŌṀ MAṆI PADME HŪṀ
The Spirit within the Heart.

7. ŚIVO'HAṀ
The Oneness of the Heart.

8. ĀNANDO'HAṀ
The Bliss of the Heart.

This Way is different from the slow, cumbersome natural evolution over the Ages. This Way is *Here and Now.* It is done not by Nature but by Divine Grace, or BRAHMA-PRAKĀŚA (Divine Light).

9. Ayamātmā Brahma
   This Self in the Heart is God.

10. Ōṁ Śāntiḥ Śāntiḥ Śāntiḥ
   The Peace of the Heart.

11. Ōṁ Parabrahmane Namaḥ
   The Universal Absolute is the Heart.

12. Jīvo'haṁ
   This Living-Soul is the Heart.

These twelve Keys will open for you the great Mystery

These twelve Keys will open for you the great Mystery that has been hidden from the worldly-minded since the foundation of this planet. They provide an understanding of Supernature and the glorious Divine Plan for Humanity upon this planet. Using the twelve Keys we shall try to explain the Supernatural Evolution and how it relates to *you*, if you are ready for it. Each of these Keys is a means for you to access the Heart and begin the Transformation.

The Mystery within the Heart

When the Heart in the natural bodies (the etheric-physical, astral and mental bodies) is awakened, then psychic visions, mystical experiences and semi-spiritual powers unfold. But the Heart we speak of, the Causal Heart, conceals the Great Mystery. This is symbolized by the Western Adepts as the *Mystical Rose* or the *Rose and the Cross*, and by the Eastern Adepts as the *Lotus Flower* or the *Jewel in the Lotus*, since this Heart does look like a rose or a lotus flower. Within the Lotus or Rose is concealed the Mystery, covered by twelve petals. It is a Mystery because it does not belong to this Creation or even to the Causal World.

This Mystery is the Divine Spark, the Eye of the Monad, the One Self, looking down from the Monadic Plane into the lower Creation. It is a bluish-white Electric Fire of tremendous intensity, a brilliant Point of Monadic Light, Cosmic Intelligence compressed into a minute Atom.

It is also known as the *Spirit-Spark*, the *Spirit-Spark-Atom* or the *Sparkling Stone*. It is the *Stone of the Wise* of the Alchemists and the *Stone that the Builders Rejected* or the *Foundation Stone* of the Ancient Mystery Schools. The initiated Christians of the first three centuries called it the *Captured Sparks of the Spirit* or a *Spark of the Original Imperishable Kingdom of Light* (the Paranirvāṇic Plane, the realm beyond even the boundless Nirvāṇa).

The Universal Christ 440
The Lotus of the Heart 446
The Rose and the Cross 712
Sex Natural and Divine 926
Hṛt-Padma: the Heart-Lotus 1505
The Solar and Human Heart 1592

Key 1

Jaya Īśa Īśvarām
The Master of the Heart.
The Master within the Heart.

Jaya Īśa Īśvarām

The Wonder of Wonders, the Divine Presence, is concealed within the Heart. God lives in the Heart. This is the first Key to Supernature: God is above Nature and above Natural Evolution. With this most potent mantram you awaken the Glory that resides in your Heart.

Jaya: Victorious, Conquering, Glorious.

Īśa: God, Lord, Master, Lord-God, the Lord of the Universe, the Powerful, the Impeller or Motivator, the Swift, the All-Pervading, the Venerable, the Divine, the Divine Consciousness, the Controller, the Central Authority, the Self within the Heart.

Īśvarām is from Īśvara-Rāṁ. Īśvara means the Supreme, the Lord, the Cosmic Spirit, the Ruler, the Master of the Universe, the Supreme Being, the Centre of Consciousness, the Inner Ruler Immortal. Rāṁ means Rāma, the King of Kings, the Lord of Lords, the Perfect Administrator of the Universe, enchanting, beautiful, restful, all-pervading, blissful, delightful.

The easiest method is to say the Sanskrit mantram in your Heart, "Jaya Īśa Īśvarām", and then say the key concept in English: "The Master of the Heart". You can also say, "The Master *within* the Heart". This Master is the Gurudeva, the Divine Teacher, the Sat-Guru, the True Master that resides in the Causal Heart Centre.

A further method of meditation is to say the mantram in Sanskrit and then *reflect* on the various meanings of the words, with *inspiration*. For instance: "Victory to the God within my Heart who brings about my Supernatural Transformation." There are numerous ways you can "translate" the mantram to suit your needs. The important thing is to *feel your link* with the Presence within your Heart, because this is the first step towards Miraculous Transformation.

Īśvara 1623

Key 2

HṚDAYAṀ
God is the Heart.
God is within the Heart.

This mantram consists of three parts:
HRĪ: Freedom.
DĀ: Giving.
YĀṀ: Fearlessness.

When the God-Self within your Heart is awakened, you will feel genuine Freedom, a great sense of Giving (Love, Generosity) and a tremendous sense of Fearlessness.

To meditate on this mantram, say the Sanskrit, "HṚDAYAṀ", in your Heart, then the key concept in English: "God is the Heart". The objective is to *realize* within your Consciousness what you are saying.

Another way to meditate on this mantram is to say the Sanskrit syllables in your Heart, "HRĪ-DĀ-YĀṀ", and at the same time *realize* what the syllables mean: "Freedom-Giving-Fearlessness", the characteristics of the awakened Heart.

The Heart (Hṛdayaṁ) 1282

HṚDAYAṀ

Quest for the Self

BRAHMAN, the Godhead, shines in the Form of ĀTMAN (ĀTMA-RŪPA) with the Immediate Light within the Innermost Sanctuary of the Heart (HṚDAYAṀ) as your *true* "I" or "I AM-ness" (AHAṀ).

By facing inwards (ANTAR-MUKHA, inward-facing) into your Heart, through the gross and subtle dimensions, you will discover the ANTAR-YĀMIN (Inner Ruler) of your Heart, the ANTAR-ĀTMAN (Inner Self), which is *beyond* your body, emotions and mind. Then you will discover the Kingdom of God within. Then the Super-Essential Light will shine forth *into* your mind. Then your mind will be radiant with Light, the Clear-Bright-Light of Reality. Then you will truly *Know*.

This Light is the Self shining from within the Heart, illuminating for you the Way of Light, the Path to Supernatural Evolution. This Path is known as ĀTMA-VICĀRA (Spirit-Search), or Quest for the Self.

Quest for Reality 1178

Key 3

ŌṀ PARAMĀTMANE NAMAḤ

The Universal Self in the Heart.

The Soul of the Universe Who dwells in the Heart.

NAMAḤ: worshipping, bowing down, salutation to.

PURUṢA (the Divine Man, the Cosmic Man, the Universal Spirit, the Supreme Being, the Ultimate Person of the Universe, the Conscious Principle of All That Is) is also known as PARAMĀTMAN (PARAMA-ĀTMAN) and PARAMĀTMIKĀ (PARAMA-ĀTMIKĀ), the Supreme Soul, the Highest Spirit, the Greatest Self, the Supreme Intelligence within and beyond the Cosmos. It is also known as PURUṢOTTAMA (PURUṢA-UTTAMA), the Supreme, Highest, Most Excellent (UTTAMA) Being or Person (PURUṢA). It dwells in the human Heart and in the Hearts of all Beings. Thus, a variation of this mantram is:

ŌṀ PURUṢOTTAMĀYA NAMAHA

To meditate on this Key, invoke the Sanskrit mantram in your Heart, then say the key concept in English: "The Universal Self in the Heart". You may use the variation ŌṀ PURUṢOTTAMĀYA NAMAHA and its meanings in a similar way.

You may also include the meaning of NAMAḤ (worshipping, bowing down, salutation to). From the meanings you can formulate or "translate" the mantram in different ways that appeal to your mind. Always say the Sanskrit first, then *realize* its meaning in English, in your Heart.

Meditate in your Heart 1288

Key 4*a*

Śrīṁ Hrīṁ Klīṁ
Kṛṣṇāya Govindāya Svāhā
The Ecstatic Devotion of the Heart.

Kṛṣṇa: Ecstatic Bliss.

Govinda: the Master of the Heart. The keeper of the cows (symbolic of the keeper of Souls). The Lord God within. (In Christianity, the Christ is the Shepherd, or keeper of the Souls, and the Souls are the "sheep".)

Svāhā: offering of the Heart.

Meditate on this mantram in Sanskrit in the Heart, then on the key concept in English. You may also use the English translation, "the Heart of Bliss". Or, use your own "translation" as you understand it. *God is Joy.*

Potent Vibrations: Bīja-Mantra 1542

Key 4*b*

Klīṁ Kṛṣṇāya Govindāya
Gopījana Vallabhāya Svāhā
The Ecstatic Love of the Heart.
The Heart of Love.

Kṛṣṇa: Ecstatic Love. God is Love.

Gopī: cowgirl, herdswoman, milkmaid (a symbol of your Soul).

Gopījana: the milkmaid folk, cowgirl people, herdswomen folk.

Vallabha: beloved, favourite, desired, loved.

Repeat the mantram in Sanskrit, then the key concept in English: "The Ecstatic Love of the Heart".

You can also use "The Heart of Love", or you can "translate" the statement according to your inner Insight.

Pure Devotion: Initiation Mantram 1724

Ōṁ Yesu Kristāya Namaḥ

Key 4c

Ōṁ Yesu Kristāya Namaḥ
The Christ within the Heart.

Ōṁ: the Word of Glory.

Yesu: God within who Saves.

Krista: the Lord of Love.

Namaḥ: worshipping, bowing down, salutation to.

Kṛṣṭa, Kṛṣṇa, Krista is the Christ within your Soul. When the Christ within your Soul is *born*, you enter the *Lighted Way* or Supernatural Evolution. This was known in India thousands of years before the birth of Jesus, the Christed One.

Say this mantram in the Heart, in Sanskrit then in English. You may also use "The Heart of Christ", or make up your own "translation" as you understand it.

The Christ in the Heart 441

The Avatāras

An Avatāra is a Divine Being who has descended from exalted realms, and could be from the human, angelic or super-angelic species. A true Avatāra has no self at all but acts directly as an agent of the Divine Will.

Historically, the two greatest Heart Avatāras were Śrī Kṛṣṇa and Jesus the Christed One. They exemplified the Power of the Heart as the all-attractive Divine-Love Energy. Gautama the Buddha was an Avatāra of Wisdom, a fusion of the Divine Light in the Head Centres. These Beings were real, though their reality was much confused by the mythological scriptures.

An Avatāra sacrifices His or Her Life-force and lives *within* Humanity.

To Worship the Divine Incarnations 1270

The Mystery of Jesus the Christ 664

Key 5

NAMA ŚIVĀYA
or: ŌṀ NAMAḤ ŚIVĀYA
or: ŌṀ NAMAḤ ŚIVĀYAME
or: NA-MA-HA ŚI-VĀ-YA
The Transcendental Heart.
The Transcendent within the Heart.

NAMAḤ: reverence, adoration, worship.

ŚIVA: in Whom all things dwell and have their Being. "In Him you live and move and have your Being", and all of Creation moves in Him, the Transcendental Godhead. ŚIVA is PURUṢA-SVĀMĪ, the Supreme Witness of all Creation, the God Transcendent.

ŚIVA has other meanings as well:

- The auspicious, favourable, benign, dear, friendly, who grants all wishes, good fortune.
- The Fire of Rebirth and Regeneration, the Immortal Fire, the Fire of Yoga.
- The Transcendental Self in its Eternal Tranquillity; the Tranquil Self.
- The Supreme Consciousness (PARA-ŚIVA).

Meditate on the Sanskrit mantram of your choice, then on the English meaning that appeals to you. You can also make up a "translation" from the meanings of the word ŚIVA that you are drawn to. For example:

"I worship the Supreme Consciousness in my Heart."
"I am One with the Tranquil Self."
"I am reborn by the Fire of Regeneration."
"I am guided by the Beneficent Power of the Absolute."
"I surrender to Divine Consciousness."

ŌṀ NAMAḤ ŚIVĀYA

When we write the Names of God, such as RĀMA, KṚṢṆA, VIṢṆU and ŚIVA, do not think of images or pictures from the imaginations of artists, or you will be lead astray. The Names themselves reveal the true meaning.
The Three-Faced God 113

Ōṁ Maṇi Padme Hūṁ

Key 6

Ōṁ Maṇi Padme Hūṁ
The Spirit within the Heart.
The Jewel in the Lotus.

Maṇi: a jewel, a precious stone, a gem, a pearl of great price, an ornament, a crystal, a magnet. The ancient symbol for the Spirit. It is the *magnet that attracts.*

Padma: the lotus flower, a symbol for the Heart.

Thus, the mantram means "We invoke the Spirit within the Heart".

Jesus Himself, in one of His parables, mentioned the need to seek the *Pearl of Great Price.* This is done in meditation, the "field" of the parable.

This Jewel is the Monad, the *Father in Heaven* of Jesus. This Heaven is not the astral heavens, nor the mental, nor even the Causal Worlds, and is beyond even the Kingdom of Nirvāṇa. This Heaven is the Monadic Plane. (In the Hebrew language of Jesus' time there were no words, as there are in Sanskrit, to distinguish clearly between various realms.)

This Jewel is the *Sparkling Stone* of the Alchemists. It is the Supernatural compressed deep within the innermost region of the Heart. This Jewel is the *Innermost*, the Lord-God-Within, the Inner God, the Key to Eternal Life and Everlasting Blessedness. This is the Key to Transfiguration, Resurrection and Ascension into the Everlasting Realms. This is the Key to the Divine Magic of Light.

Meditate first on the Sanskrit mantram in the Heart, then on the English translation that means the most to you, from the various explanations given.

Meditations in the Heart Centre 1298
The Esoteric Mantram 551

Key 7

Śivo'haṁ (Śiva-Ahaṁ)
The Oneness of the Heart.
I am One with the Absolute Being in the Heart.
I am One with the Highest Being in the Universe.

Śivo'haṁ: the Transcendental I AM. This Ahaṁ (I AM) is the Highest Being, Puruṣottama.

Puruṣa: the Supreme Spirit.

Uttama: the Exalted, the Highest. This is Śiva, the Transcendental Absoluteness.

Meditate on this mantram in the Heart, in the same way as those before. There is only one thing you *must* do in this life: meditate, meditate and meditate.

Key 8

Ānando'haṁ (Ānanda-Ahaṁ)
The Bliss of the Heart.
I am Bliss-Eternal.
I am Bliss-Consciousness.

Ānanda: Bliss, Joy, Happiness, Ecstasy, the highest pleasure or enjoyment.
Ahaṁ: I Am.

The Self is Bliss. It is the very nature of Existence. It is Life-Eternal.

Meditate on this mantram in the Heart, in Sanskrit and in English, as previously described. Or you can use the variation:

Ānando'haṁ-Rāṁ
The Joy-of-the-God-Within I am.

Joy is essentially an *internal* state. You as a Soul (Jīva) are always full of Joy. Just be *Yourself* and all unhappiness, depression, fear and anger will fade away.

Pure Consciousness in the Heart 447

AYAMĀTMĀ BRAHMA

Key 9

AYAMĀTMĀ BRAHMA
This Self in the Heart is God.
This Self is God.

AYAM: this.
ĀTMĀ: the Self.
BRAHMA: God.

Who are *You?* Who or what is your true Self? Are *You* flesh and bones and nothing else? Are *You* your mind and emotions, your thoughts and moods? Are *You* your personality make-up? What do you say? What is in your Heart? Ask yourself this question.

- I am One with the Eternal God.
- I am part of God.
- I am a Point of Light in the Great Ocean of Radiance.
- God is. The Self is. These two are One.

Know this to be the Truth. This is the Highest Knowledge.

Meditate on this mantram in your Heart as previously described.

Key 10

ŌṀ ŚĀNTIḤ ŚĀNTIḤ ŚĀNTIḤ
The Peace of the Heart.

In the Centre within the Heart is found the Perfect Peace. It is the Peace above and beyond the Storms of Life. The mind cannot understand *That.* The emotions cannot feel *That.* It is the mind-emotions-transcending Peace.

The CELĀ (disciple) finds tranquillity only within the Heart. Seek not for Peace without.

The disciple's life is full of crisis, tension, stress and troubles. Such is the nature of the Path to be trodden. And yet, despite all appearances on the outside, Serenity rules the Inner Worlds of the Soul. Where do *you* look for Peace? Where do *you* find Rest? Seek out the Inner Calm. Peace is to be found in Soul-Consciousness.

Meditate on this mantram in your Heart as previously instructed.

Key 11

Ōṁ Parabrahmane Namaḥ

The Universal Absolute is the Heart.

Being is that which is everlasting, eternal, unending, indestructible, not subject to Time and Space. It is the Absolute. Thou art *That.*

Parabrahman is the Supreme Spirit, the Absolute Beingness. It is also called Tat (That), because no words can describe It, no thought can approach It. It is the One Universal Existence, which includes within Itself all that is Manifest (Vyakta) and all that is Unmanifest (Avyakta), the Past, Present and Future, Time and Space, and also Eternity. Thou art *That.*

Worlds come and go, Universes appear and disappear, but Being always *Is*. Thou art *That*. Sense It with your Soul.

Meditate on this mantram in your Heart in Sanskrit and in English as previously described.

Key 12

Jīvo'haṁ (Jīva-Ahaṁ)

This Living Soul is the Heart.

I Am a Living Soul.

I Am the Living Light (Jyotir-Ahaṁ).

I Am the Light of the Soul (Ātma-Jyoti).

What is the Lighted Way, the Way of the Light? What is Ātma-Jyoti (Self-Light)? What is Light? Can you answer? What is the Sea of Light, God's Light (Brahma-Jyoti)? Who is a Warrior of Light (Vira-Jyotiṣa)?

Light is Substance, Matter of a higher order. The physical light of the Sun, Moon and stars is but a fragment of Light. Light is living, conscious, substantial Intelligence. Your Soul is made out of It.

When your mind becomes illumined by the Soul-Light, you become Enlightened. You become a Buddha (an Enlightened One). Watch for the Light. Breathe in the Light, because you *are* the Light.

Follow the meditation practice as before.

Jīva: the Human Soul 35

Such are the Twelve Keys to the Heart:

1. The Master of the Heart.
2. God is the Heart.
3. The Universal Self in the Heart.
4*a*. Ecstasy.
4*b*. Love.
4*c*. The Christ within the Heart.
5. The Transcendent.
6. Spirit.
7. Oneness.
8. Bliss.
9. The Self.
10. Peace.
11. Being.
12. Soul-Light.

When the Heart is Glorified, there comes the New Creature

You may choose any of these Keys to unlock the Secrets of your Heart and of the Heart of God. As the twelve qualities of the Heart increase inside you, you will become more happy, calm and wise as a personality.

∞

When the Heart is Pure, God is seen.

When the Heart is transformed, Supernatural Operations take place within you.

The Heart is the beginning of Transformation and Transfiguration, and of the outpouring of the Blessed Radiance of God's Glory.

When the Heart is Glorified, there comes the New Creature, the Future Super-Human.

You will become a Radiating Centre of Light.

The State of Inner Purity 497
The Purification of the Heart 849
The Pure Heart 1300
To Invoke God in your Heart 1293

The Thirteenth Key

Sūryo'haṁ (Sūrya-Ahaṁ)
The Sun is the Heart.
I am the Sun. The Sun is I.

This is the final and ultimate Key that unlocks the mysteries of the Past, Present and Future. This is the Key to illimitable Glory, boundless Compassion and unending Vision. This is the Key that gives you the Universal Body (Viśva-Rūpa), the Cosmic Form, beyond the angelic or human forms.

When you have ascended the Heights of Glory, you will mount the Cosmic Heart

Your Soul is a Radiant Sun within you. The Radiance of the Glory of God will be upon you. "I and the Universal Father are One."

This is the Path of the Avatāra (Divine Incarnation), the Incarnation not of a human being, nor of an angel, but of a god.

When you have ascended the Heights of Glory, you will mount the Cosmic Heart, the Heart of Infinity, in your capacity of Pūrṇa-Avatāra-Rūpa, the Complete Divinity, in the Shining Sea of Everlasting Life.

The Heart of the Solar Logos

The Sun is the Heart of our Solar System. You cannot actually see the Sun. What you see in the sky is only a part of the physical Heart of the Sun. The Sun, the Solar Logos, is a vast Cosmic Being of gigantic proportions.

A human being has seven major cakras and twelve minor ones. Some of these become major cakras as you progress on the Spiritual Path. The Sun has 72 cakras (we call them "planets"). Some are visible, while most are invisible to the physical eyes, but they can be seen with astral or mental vision. These 72 planets, or cakras of the Sun, are the "Seventy-two Elders before the Throne of God" mentioned in the Bible.

The Heart of the Solar Logos is Radiant Solar-Love. It might be difficult for a human being to comprehend that Love is the Nature of the Solar Logos. The Love of the Solar Logos is Cosmic. It embraces all within the Solar System: all the planets, all the worlds, all the realms of Being, all the innumerable hierarchies and countless hosts of living creatures. Love is the fuel that keeps Evolution going, and Love is the Goal.

The Mystery of the Sun 1585

Love is the Law 25
The Solar Dharma 163
The Constitution of God-Immanent 122
The Perennial Source of Love 438
More Mantras to Sūrya, the Sun 1658
The Activity of the Divine Heart 1675

Guard your Heart

The Heart has to be *guarded* from thoughts originating in the Third-Eye Centre, from emotions originating in the Solar Plexus Centre, and from imagination or images coming from the Throat Centre. For the Heart is Pure Consciousness itself.

The Secret of the Heart 1280
Pure Consciousness in the Heart 447
Dissolving the Knot in the Heart 445
The Christian Heart-Path 632
Baptism and Rebirth 722

The Heart, in its pure Nature, is Formless Divinity. The first cloud that covers it is the *ego* (AHAṀKĀRA), the false sense of self that you have on the personality level in the physical body. When you discover the Original Heart within you, you *lose your ego-sense.*

The second layer of clouds that cover the Original Radiance of the Heart are the endless *thoughts* originating in the mind, the uncontrolled *emotions* surging through the feeling (astral) body, and the wild imagination, image-making, fantasy and glamour of your creative faculty in the Throat Centre (the seat of artistic creativity).

When the Heart is well-guarded, *Remembrance* (SMṚTĪ) of the Self-in-the-Heart becomes spontaneous and natural.

Mantram

The first Way of Guarding your Heart is by Mantram—that is, MANTRA-JAPA (mantra-repetition) and MANTRA-DHYĀNA (mantra-meditation) in your Heart. A mantram is a key concept. You choose a key with which to do JAPA (repetition) or DHYĀNA (meditation) in your Heart (you are free to choose which). This will gradually *shut out* the unwanted thoughts, feelings and images that continually bombard your Heart. The mantram will also change the *rhythm* of your physical heart and, in time, will produce physical health and balance. It will also purify the psychic Heart, thus helping you to become a happy, integrated personality. But the greatest gift will be your entrance to the Spiritual Heart, the joyous Kingdom of God Within.

The Two Applications of Mantra 1219
Right Use of Mantra 1697

Pure-Breathing

The second Way of Guarding your Heart is by *Pure-Breathing*. Your Pure-Breath is HAṀSA. HAṀSA is the Divine Self within you, the Breath of God. You breathe in HAṀ and you breathe out SAḤ.

The Holy Breath 1340
Rest in the Great Breath 1654

Stillness

The third Way of Guarding the Heart is *Stillness*. Silently looking into your Heart. Simple inner gaze. Spontaneity.

Be Still and Know 638
Peace of Heart 1595

The Qualities of the Spiritual-Heart-Consciousness (Hṛdaya-Citta)

Following are the four qualities of the Spiritually Awakened Heart. When you are experiencing these qualities, know that you are on the Way to Supernatural Evolution.

Bliss is the very nature of Spirit, and of You as a Soul

Prema

Love. This is not a solar-plexus feeling, affection or emotion. It is not sexual attraction or magnetic energy between opposites. It is not a poetic or idealistic sentiment. It is not an idea or thought wrought by the mind. It is a Fiery Radiance of the Soul coming through the inner chamber of the Heart complex. It is a Love without the feeling of barriers or separation. It is an identification with the All—all Life, all creatures. It is not selective, but completely inclusive. It is an immense sense of Unity.

Ānanda

Bliss. Bliss is the very nature of Spirit, the Monad, and of *You* as a Soul. If you undergo the Transformation, you partake in ever-greater measures of Bliss experience. This Bliss is innate within your Innermost Heart and does not depend on outer circumstances or conditions. You may experience this Bliss within you while the outside world is in turmoil and pain.

Prakāśa

Light. Luminosity, Radiance, Shining, Brightness, Splendour, Glory. Such is your experience of the Innermost Heart.

Prajñā

Wisdom. This is not mere book learning, nor memorizing facts and figures, nor clever use of reason or logic, nor philosophy or speculation. This is the mind-transcending, Truth-discerning Awareness of Pure Consciousness. It is pure Knowing, without words, without thoughts, without the mind.

Terms of Love 914
Return to Primeval Happiness 1179
The Way to Bliss-Consciousness 1246
The Universal Christ 440
What is Wisdom? 1685
Signs of Progress in the Heart 1289

To Succeed in your Quest

What is the key to *success* in the Spiritual Life? It is ABHYĀSA-YOGA, or repeated effort in your meditations and devotions. In other words, patient perseverance.

To succeed in your Quest for Eternal Life you must have Faith (ŚRADDHĀ) that the Heart of God is good, that in the end all things will work out well for you, no matter how hopeless your situation may appear to be. Indeed, God wants the highest good for *all* Humanity—not just for one race or religion, but for *All*. Evolution (moving-forward) is a rule of Nature imposed upon all things, from the tiniest atom to the largest solar system. Evolution is *the shining forth of the Inner Light.*

Spiritual Progress becomes possible when you have a goal towards which you aspire

- First there is Self-Realization.
- Then there is God-Realization.
- Then comes the possibility of Supernatural Evolution granted by Divine Grace.

Spiritual Progress becomes possible when you have a vision, a goal towards which you *aspire*. The first great objective is Soul-Consciousness or Self-Realization, to know yourself to be a Living Soul beyond Space and Time. This is achieved by the right meditation process, patience, perseverance, loving Service towards all Humanity, and an *intense focus*.

The next important quality you must develop is VAIRĀGYA: Divine Indifference or *Dispassion*. This manifests in day-to-day life as Inner Calmness (ŚAMA) under all circumstances: in sickness or in health; in fortune or misfortune; when people praise you or when they blame you; when things are given to you or taken away; in enjoyment or suffering; in gain and in loss; in life and in death.

You must not think of this as a philosophy. It is the Spiritual Life. To succeed in your Quest, you *must* live this way, and you must give up all preoccupation with psychic phenomena and powers.

How quickly you progress has much to do with your karmic disposition, that is, your SAṀSKĀRAs and VĀSANĀs, the tendencies and impressions from your past which have been stored in your subconscious mind. Progress is slow if you have a lot of negative karmas to work through, but fast if you have only a few.

What is True Faith? 1284
Qualifications for Discipleship 1149
Passion and Dispassion 695
Saṁskāra and Vāsanā 251
Quest for Reality 1178
The Vision of your own Eternity 1144
Do the Work yourself 1153

Heart Action

The question has always been: How to act? Most people act with selfish motives, for some gain or benefit to the self. But true spiritual action (NIṢKĀMA-KARMA, desireless action) is always selfless, always for the good of others. This is true Heart action. Actions that genuinely come from the Heart are selfless, for the good of the All. They are offered as a Sacrifice (YAJÑA) to God. Such actions (KARMA) have no repercussion on the actor and have a liberating effect on the Soul.

True spiritual action is always for the good of others

Selfless action, to love without expecting any reward, is an important aspect of the Journey of the Heart. Spiritual maturity, Heart maturity, has to do with how much you do selflessly for your family, for your group (the larger family) and for the world (the family of Humanity). Thus, on the Heart-Journey, two things are essential:

- Meditation.
- Acting for the good of others.

Pure and constant *Devotion in the Heart* destroys the effects of negative karmas very rapidly. You have to build the Bridge (ANTAḤ-KARAṆA, internal cause) which unites you to your Higher Self, the God within your Heart. And how are you going to build this Rainbow Bridge? By *intense meditation* in your Heart and *daily selfless Service* for others.

This is practical: read carefully and do!

Action while in Samādhi

SAMĀDHI (Yogic Absorption) can be a gateway to Supernatural Evolution, if it is realized as such. In true SAMĀDHI the Yogī or Yoginī withdraws his or her attention from the Physical, Astral and Mental Worlds and focuses on the Buddhic Plane, the World of Unity, Light and Bliss-Consciousness. He or she withdraws into the Essential Self (ĀTMAN).

In SAVIKALPA-SAMĀDHI thoughts and mental functions are still possible. In NIRVIKALPA-SAMĀDHI there are no thoughts or mental activity whatsoever. If the Yogin *acts* while in SAMĀDHI, a new Rebirth can take place, a new Human-type.

Samādhi: the Goal of Yoga 574

Non-Action Misinterpreted 1120
To Become a true Renunciate 257
On Love and Meditation 1140
Karma Yoga: Divine Union by Action 1132
Bhakti Yoga: Divine Union by Devotion 1128
What is true Service? 1714

The Heart and the Energy Centres

The **Mūlādhāra-Cakra** (Base Centre) is responsible for your physical life and well-being. It is your point of balance on the *dense* Physical Plane.

The **Svādhiṣṭhāna-Cakra** (Sexual Centre) is responsible for the *etheric* portion of the Physical Plane, your vitality and strength, magnetism and personal radiance. Sex is only one of its functions; it also provides you with physical energy.

The Heart Centre is the most interesting centre, as it unites Heaven and Earth

The **Maṇipūra-Cakra** (Solar Plexus Centre) is responsible for your *emotional* well-being. All of your emotions, moods, feelings and desires go through it. Just imagine what it has to put up with! It puts you in touch with the Astral World.

These first three cakras are your *personality centres*, responsible for your personal behaviour patterns. In most people these centres are diseased to varying degrees.

The **Ājñā-Cakra** (Third-Eye Centre) is located between the eyes and is responsible for your ordinary mind, your mental body. It puts you in touch with the lower Mental Plane.

The **Viśuddha-Cakra** (Throat Centre) is responsible for your Abstract Mind (the philosophical mind) and the causal body.

The **Sahasrāra-Cakra** (Crown Centre) is wholly spiritual. It will put you in touch with the spiritual dimensions and, ultimately, with Nirvāṇa (Beatitude).

The **Anāhata-Cakra** (Heart Centre) is the most interesting centre, as it unites Heaven and Earth, the Soul and the personality, God and Man. It puts you in touch with the Buddhic World, wherein are *united* the above and the below, the spiritual and the material, form and formlessness, the manifest and the unmanifest, the inner and the outer. The Buddhic Plane is the Centre of the Kingdom of God.

Suṣumna (the subtle, invisible spinal column in etheric, astral and mental matter) is the ladder upon which spiritual (non-worldly) Consciousness ascends and descends. It is the Path upward to Heavenly Regions and Spiritual Dimensions.

The **Cakras** are the rungs of the Ladder of Evolution.

The Human Cakras 44

The Functioning of the Cakras 52

Transformation of the Centres

- The first *natural* transformation of the centres occurs when the Base Centre, Sex Centre and Solar Plexus Centre come under the influence and control of the Heart. Then you have a truly *integrated* personality. You cannot integrate your personality intellectually, by thoughts, ideas, theories or models based on the rational mind. Only the Heart can integrate your personality.
- You should not spend your time trying to awaken the *psychic powers* of the centres, as many Yoga schools and esoteric groups do. Rather, strive for Union with your Soul and then you will have all things that you need.
- The following exercise will integrate your personality. Focus your Awareness in each centre while intoning the corresponding Sanskrit Sound (or Vowel) on the correct musical note. Pause for a few moments before moving to the next centre. This can be done aloud, or it can be done mentally, silently in your mind. Begin at the Base Centre and move upwards. When you reach the Causal Centre above the head, abide in Silence.

Seek not Powers 581
Internalizing the Semi-Vowels 1044
Integration of the Human Consciousness 1195
Potent Vibrations: Bīja-Mantra 1542
Brahma-Gāyatrī-Mantra 1638

Centre (Cakra)	Sanskrit Sounds	Sanskrit Vowels	Music Scale	
Causal Centre	NĀDA (unheard)	Silent	UPPER C	*DO*
Crown Centre	ŌṀ	*open* ṚĪ (Ṁ) *closed*	B	*TI*
Third-Eye Centre	ĀUṀ	Ī (Ṁ)	A	*LA*
Throat Centre	HĀṀ	Ē (Ṁ)	G	*SO*
Heart Centre	YĀṀ	Ā (Ṁ)	F	*FA*
Solar Plexus Centre	RĀṀ	AI (Ṁ)	E	*MI*
Sex Centre	VĀṀ	Ō (Ṁ)	D	*RE*
Base Centre	LĀṀ	Ū (Ṁ)	C	*DO*

Personality Integration Chart

The Body of Fire

This is truly a Spiritual Body, everlasting in the Heavens

There is a profound Mystery involving the centres (CAKRAS) for the Future Evolution of Man. This Mystery is the **AGNI-RŪPA**, or Body of Fire, which involves the Awakened Heart. When the Fire of the Monad, the Spirit, has transmuted the Heart, the seven cakras are slowly transformed by Fire and become Fire. The Fire within Matter blends with the Fire of the Mind and the two are dissolved in the Fire of Spirit. A Supernatural Transformation takes place, a new body is created which is pure Fire, and the seven cakras are but vortices of living Fire within the Fire-Body.

This is the Work of Divine Grace. This is truly a Spiritual Body, everlasting in the Heavens. If you look with Spiritual Vision at a human being who has undergone this Transformation, you see only a sheath of Incorruptible Living-Flame, an Entity no longer human but Divine, where the human nature has been dissolved, consumed by the Fire of God.

Such is the future possibility for all Humanity. It has happened in the Past, it happens Now, and it will happen again in the Future whenever a human being is ready.

Dimensions of the Cosmic Fire 137
The Fire in the Heart 1287
The Kingdom is at Hand 1453

CHAPTER 57

The Way of Holiness

Stages on the Way of Holiness

In the Western Spiritual Tradition, the Way of Holiness, the Path is divided into three stages or degrees:

a. The Path of Purification (the Purgative Way).
b. The Path of Illumination (the Illuminative Way).
c. The Path of Union (the Unitive Way).

Many millions of Christians have never heard of the direct Inner Way to the Christ

These are three stages of development upon the *Inner Path*.

Very few books are written by practising Mystics nowadays, and millions of Christians think that Christianity is about going to church on Sundays and remembering that Christmas Day is supposed to be related to Christ and not just a shopping spree! These many millions of Christians have never heard of the *direct Inner Way* to the Christ, to the Holy Spirit, to the Godhead, for most pastors, priests, reverends and theologians know nothing about it.

In the past Piscean Age, many thousands knew and practised this *Inner Path* back to God. But in this "scientific-materialistic" Aquarian Age this Path of Holiness is increasingly forgotten. It needs to be reawakened.

The final Goal of the Way of Holiness, or *Mysticism*, is Union with the Soul, and the Union of the Soul-infused personality with the Divine Principle, the Godhead. This is not just an intellectual idea or a nice philosophy, but an actual *direct experience* taking place *beyond* the body-mind-emotions structure of your personality, in the depths of *You* as the Soul, and in the Innermost Depth of the Spirit within you.

The New Aquarian Energies 426
Mystics of Pisces and Aquarius 836
Christian Mysticism 450
The Way of the Christian Mystic 626
The Ancient Heart-Path 845
Bhakti Yoga: Divine Union by Devotion 1128

The Path of Purification

The first stage, the Path of Purification, can begin only when a person is at the stage of *separating* himself or herself from the mass-mind (the mass-materialistic-consciousness) and begins earnestly to consider the meaning of life, the purpose of existence, and to seek a Path or Way out of the human condition of suffering and woe upon this planet. When a person becomes a *serious seeker*, the Path of Purification begins in that person's life.

The Path of Purification is essentially a period of great struggle and conflict

The Path of Purification manifests in the life of the seeker as a *drive towards Perfection* and a sense for what is right or wrong, not according to the outer human legal system but as an *inner conviction* or *feeling*, a seeking of Harmony in life, a sense of proportion and justice, and a restless desire for Peace and Serenity. Such people abhor violence of any kind and are very conscious of the suffering of humans and animals and plants. They may also have a great desire to serve God, or to help their fellow men, or to work for some charitable cause.

The Path of Purification, the Purgative Way, is essentially a period of great struggle and conflict within the person who is walking upon it. On the one hand there is the *pull of the world*, with all its charms and allurements, its joys and sorrows, its pains and conflicts, its passions and responsibilities, its triumphs and successes, its failures and disasters; while on the other hand there is a *steady pressure from the Soul to turn away from the world* and seek out the Kingdom of God within. Thus, there is a huge struggle and conflict.

This first stage of the Way of Holiness is the Purification of the Heart through Love. As Jesus said:

> Blessed are the Pure in Heart, for they shall see God.
>
> *Matthew 5:8*

In the Heart we learn the meaning of the Old Testament phrase:

> Holiness to the Lord.
>
> *Exodus 28:36*

In the Heart we know what it means to be Holy. The Path of Purification, the first stage of the Way of Holiness, is essentially a *transformation of your Heart* from being pulled in by the world and the worldly consciousness to *turning within yourself*, where the Path lies and the Journey takes place.

Purify the Heart 701
The State of Inner Purity 497
The Purification of the Heart 849
Tapas: Spiritual Purification 571
The Double Stress of Meditational Life 1181
Holiness to the Lord 1393

The Path of Illumination

The next stage, the Path of Illumination, has to do with Light—the Soul-Light, the Christ-Light, the Light of Reality.

Many Christians do not understand what it means to "follow" the Christ. They think it means trying to lead a "good" life so they can go to "heaven" afterwards. The more enlightened think it means to *imitate* the speech and actions of the Christ as portrayed in the New Testament, to be forgiving and compassionate towards one's fellow men and women, to try to be "virtuous" (in the old-fashioned sense of the word), to fight against "the world, the devil and the flesh" (that is, the physical body). However good this may be, it lacks the Inner Depth, the Inner Reality, the *Inner Connectedness with the Christ*, which is the mark of a true Christian, the Follower of the Light.

Much of this Work of Illumination is done in Silence, in the depth of one's Soul

Most Christians think that the "Light" spoken of in the New Testament is a *symbol* for virtue or goodness! But Light, in its many forms, grades and qualities, is not a symbol or a poetic expression. It is Reality!

> I am the Light *within* the World; they who follow Me shall not work in Darkness, but will have for themselves the Light of Life.
>
> *St John 8:12*

This is the *correct* translation of the words said by the Christ. The Path of Illumination, the Illuminative Way, is the *action* of the Christ-Light within the Heart, and the Light of Life in the Head.

Much of this Work of Illumination is done in *Silence*, in the depth of one's Soul, as a *result* of prayer, meditation, silence, service to others, and a total change of one's view of life. Meditation is all-important. It is the Invocation of the Divine, calling upon the Divine within us; only then shall the Divine respond in the process called *Illumination*. This is the Work of Silence, *in* Silence, *through* Silence.

The Path of Illumination takes place mainly in the Head *after* the Heart has been *purified* and *stabilized* in the Sacred. Those who are on the Path of Illumination experience the *nearness* of the Holy Spirit (the Immanent Aspect of God) and the *indwelling* of the Christ within the Heart and within the Hearts of all, and in the Head they begin to *sense* the Light of Life, the Glory of the Father, the Transcendental Godhead.

The Journey, however, is not yet finished.

Light 978
The Path of Light 89
The Lighted Way 1394
Christ-Consciousness 443
Satori: the Experience of Illumination 816
The Path to Immortality 430

The Path of Union

The next stage is the Path of Union, the Unitive Way, the state of Union with the Soul, with the Christ and with the Godhead. At this stage these words from the New Testament are understood:

> Christ *in* you, your hope of Glory.
>
> *Colossians 1:27*

> God is Light; in God there is no Darkness at all.
>
> *I John 1:5*

For Light is everywhere, and the Goodness of God is everywhere, a Unity in Being, a Unity in Seeing.

At this stage of the Inward Journey, the Inner Path of the Mystic, the human self (the ordinary nature-born personality-self) is at its minimal and the Christ-Self, the transfigured Soul-Consciousness, is maximal.

In the State of Unity, your life is unified into a single stream

Then the Holy Spirit lives *in* You, *with* You and *through* You.

Then the Christ lives *in* You, *with* You and *through* You.

Then the Godhead lives *in* You, *with* You and *through* You.

This is the Mystery of the Unified State. You are, yet you are not. In the State of Unity, the Path of Union, the Divine Presence is continuous. The Sacred is felt everywhere, at all times. Everything becomes *simple, single, central, inward, focused, simplified*, in a State of Unity, not Many but only One. Your life is unified into a *single stream.*

There are several stages in the Union Process, and several varieties of Illumination through Revelation and perception of Divine Activity in the Cosmos. In this Unified State, Divine Intelligence moves *in* your Mind, and Divine Love stirs *in* your Heart, and the Holy Spirit (the Universal Presence) works *through* you towards Creation to bring blessings upon all.

Slowly, degree by degree, that which once was human is turning into That which is God: *Living Light.*

Mystical Union 846
Deification (Theosis) 695
The Divine Unity 852
The God-State 1257
The One and Only 839
The One 1686

The Holy Breath

The Great Breath sweeps along the Boundless Spaces of Infinitude

What is the Holy Breath?

- In the pre-Christian Jewish mystical traditions, the Holy Breath was called **RVCh-ALHIM (Ruach-Elohīm)**, "the Breath of God".
- The early Greek Christians called it **Pneuma-Hagion**, "Breath-Holy", or the Holy Breath.
- To the Latin-speaking Christians it was **Spiritus-Sanctus**, "Spirit-Holy", or the Holy Spirit.

In modern languages it has been translated as the *Holy Ghost*. A ghost! Like a person after death! In the *real* ancient traditions of the East it was called:

The Great Breath.

The Eternal Breath.

The Active Power of the Absolute.

The Ceaseless Breath.

The Power of Perpetual Motion of the Universal Deity.

The Divine Breath.

The Breath of Life.

You breathe, and so does the Everlasting Deity. When the Eternal *breathes out*, the Universes come into being. When the Eternal *breathes in*, the Universes dissolve back into the Homogeneous Primordial State of Matter.

The Great Breath, Mahā-Prāṇa, sweeps along the Boundless Spaces of Infinitude. You cannot measure it, you cannot fathom it. As it sweeps along, galaxies, star systems and universes are formed, evolved and dissolved—wonder of wonders, miracle of miracles!

The Cosmic Fire 130
Kuṇḍalinī-Fohat 148
The Breath of the Divine Mother 142
Vāk: the Divine Speech 118
The Creation of the Universe 166

Surrender to the Holy Breath

God is Spirit and they who worship Him worship in Spirit and in Truth.
Jesus (John 4:24)

The native language of Jesus was Aramaic, although He spoke Hebrew as well. The Greek and Latin versions of the Gospels came later. From the Greek and Latin versions came translations into the European languages (English, French, German, and so forth), and later into other languages. To understand Jesus' meanings one has to go back to the Aramaic.

This Mysterious Force, Power or Divine Breath is the Name of God

- *Worship* is from the Aramaic SEGED: to bow down, to surrender oneself, to glorify and adore the Divinity.
- *Truth* is from the Aramaic SHERĀRĀ: harmony, balance, rhythm, liberating force, forceful, vigorous, overcoming.

In all the ancient sacred languages, the words translated as *Spirit* refer to the *interconnectedness* of:

a. All life-forms or species, and all individuals of species.

b. The planetary atmosphere (air, wind) and its subtle counterpart, the etheric matter or substance that envelopes our globe.

c. The One Life, the one Life-Force penetrating all life-forms or bodies of entities, whether they be dense, subtle or causal forms.

d. God's Manifesting Power, the Creative Energy or Force, and the Force or Power behind Evolution. This mysterious Force, Power or Divine Breath is the Name of God. The Name carries the quality, nature and *vibration* of God's Creative Word.

Thus, the correct translation is:

God is the Holy Breath, and they who adore Him surrender to Him through the Liberating Breath.

Notice there is no mention here of ritual worship, rites or ceremonies, but direct Mystical Experience, first-hand Knowledge.

The Voice of God 864
What is the Name? 1259
The Word, Logos, Voice, Name 1646
Baptism and Rebirth 722
Rest in the Great Breath 1654

The Holy Trinity

The Father

The *Father* is the First Aspect of Deity, the Nameless Transcendental Godhead, above, beyond and before Creation and after Creation. It is That which always Is.

It is within the Christ-Light that the Way is found back to the Father

The Christ

The *Christos*, or Christ, is the Second Aspect of Deity, the Universal Light Vibration, that which hovers above the Manifest Condition, the Revealer of the Way to the Unmanifest, to the "Father".

The Holy Spirit

The *Holy Spirit*, or Holy Breath, or Holy Intelligence, is the Third Aspect of the Triune God, of the One-in-Three and Three-in-One. It is the Immanent Deity, that which is concealed in matter, life-forms, bodies. It is God-in-Manifestation, the Embodied God.

∞

The Name connects these three Aspects of the One Godhead. God is One, yet Threefold—One in Trinity, Trinity in One. This is the Mystery of the Oneness, the Unity of all things, Manifest or Unmanifest. This Unity stretches from the highest Spiritual Worlds down to the lowest worlds of physical matter, from the highest Spirit within you to the atomic substance of your physical body.

The Holy Spirit is the Fire *within* Creation.

The Christ is the Light *within* the Fire.

The Father is the Being *within* the Light.

The closest to us is the Holy Spirit. The purpose of Christianity is *not* just to merge into the Spirit-Fire, however, but to go *within* the Fire and merge into the Christ-Light, the Universal Spiritual Sun. It is *within* the Christ-Light that the Way is found back to the Father, the Everlasting Being, or *Be-ness*.

The Three-Faced God 113
The Cosmic Christ 662
The Many Mansions 611
Dimensions of the Cosmic Fire 137
The Christ is the Light of the World 442

The Holy Spirit

The Holy Spirit is *all-Knowing*.

The Holy Spirit is *within you and outside you.*

The Holy Spirit *sustains* Heaven and Earth.

The Holy Spirit is *Omnipresent.*

The Holy Intelligence (Breath, Spirit) is One. It is *the Mind of God in Action* in Creation.

The Holy Spirit permeates all Space, within and without

The Holy Spirit permeates *all Space*, within and without. Therefore, all Space is sacred, and all that is *within* Space is sacred—all beings, planets, stars, hierarchies.

All *activities* in the Cosmos are the activities of the Holy Intelligence in the outer and inner dimensions of Space.

∞

SPIRIT

This is one of the *key words* to understand in ancient spiritual languages, the meaning of which has been lost in modern translations.

Hebrew:	**Ruach (Ruah)**
Aramaic:	**Ruḥā**
Greek:	**Pneuma**
Latin:	**Spiritus**

The above are the Christian "sacred scripture" languages.

Arabic:	**Rūḥ**
Persian:	**Rūbān (Rūhān)**
Sanskrit:	**Prāṇa**
Chinese:	**Chi (Khi)**

Each of these words in the ancient tongues means:

- Breathing, breath, wind, air.
- Life, Life-Force, Energy (gross or subtle), Vitality, Force (visible or not).
- The Soul or Essence behind a body or form.
- God's Power of Manifestation.
- The Name of God, the Holy One.

Living Matter 134
The Life-Force 589
The Mother of the World 147
Śakti: the Divine Energy 1484
Degeneration of the word 'Spirit' 319

Meditation on the Holy Spirit

Space is emptiness to the physical eyes, but Fullness to the Eyes of the Spirit

- Be Still.
- Sense Space within you and outside you.

  Space is the Garment of God, the Robe of God, the Body of God. Space is the limitless Continuum of Divine Substance or Matter. There is no empty Space. Space is not emptiness, but Fullness or Wholeness. Space is emptiness to the physical eyes, but Fullness to the Eyes of the Spirit. *Sense effortlessly* the Fullness of Space.
- Then, with your Inner Senses, try to *register* the subtle activities of the Holy Spirit within Space.

  With the Inner Sense of Sight – *See.*
  With the Inner Sense of Hearing – *Hear.*
  With the Inner Sense of Touch – *Feel.*
  With the Inner Sense of Smell – *Smell.*
  With the Inner Sense of Taste – *Taste.*
- Then, That which Knows within you will *Know* that you are a Child of God.

The Fullness of the Void 23
The Form of God is Space 109
Awakening the Inner Senses 506
To Taste the Elixir of Life 593
The Experience of Mysticism 636

HOLY SPIRIT

Aramaic:	**RUḤĀ-QADASH**: *Spirit-Holy.*
Hebrew:	**RVH H-QDVSH (RUAH-HA-QADOSH)**: *Spirit-the-Holy.*
Greek:	**PNEUMA-HAGION**: *Spirit-Holy.*
Latin:	**SPIRITUS-SANCTUS**: *Spirit-Holy.*

In each of these ancient sacred languages of Christianity, the expression *Holy Spirit* meant:

- Holy Breath, Holy Life-Force, Holy Creative Power.
- The Organizing and Structuring Power within the Universe.
- God's Divine Mind at work, or Cosmic Intelligence.

Christian Meditation: The Way of Holiness

Circular Breathing in the Heart

The breath moves in a circular fashion, in and out of the Heart, continuously. There is no holding of the breath (either in or out), no counting or timing of breaths, no control of the breath. The breath flows naturally, in and out of the Heart, without a break.

With each breath you remember the Presence of the Holy Spirit

Memory Breathing (the Rū–Hā)

- The breath moves *in* through the nostrils and *down* into the belly, and *up* again from and belly and *out*.

  in-breathing *out-breathing*

  Rū – Hā

- As you breathe in through your nostrils, *see* the sound Rū enter your nostrils and go down into your belly, the solar plexus.
- As you breathe out, *see* the sound Hā ascend and leave through your nostrils.
- As in the Circular Breathing, there is no holding of the breath, no counting, no control; the breath flows in and out naturally, without a break. With each breath you *remember* the Presence of the Holy Spirit as a Universal Breath breathing in and out through all life-forms.

The Way of Holiness

The Four Ways of Holiness:
1. The Path of Silence.
2. The Path of Sound (the Path of Hearing).
3. The Path of Visualization (the Path of Seeing).
4. The Path of the Holy Breath.

The Path of the Holy Breath:
a. Circular Breathing (in the Heart Centre).
b. Memory Breathing (in the Solar Plexus Centre).
c. Meditation on the Holy Breath.

Works of Silence 1643
The Path of Hearing 553
The Path of Seeing 552
Rū-Hā: a Connecting Breathing 1062
Conscious Breathing in the Heart 1274

Christian Meditation on the Holy Breath

יהוה
←

YAH-WEY

This is the Sound of God's Breath or Spirit

YAHWEH is the Name of God, the Sound of the Universe, Universal Motion or Sound Vibration—gross, subtle and subtlest. This is the Spirit of God, the Breath of God. It is the Sound of God's Breath or Spirit. God is the State of Unity, the Eternal Oneness.

י		ה		ו		ה
YŌD	–	HEY	–	VAU	–	HEY
in-breathing		*out-breathing*		*in-breathing*		*out-breathing*

Meditation on the Holy Breath

I

- Sit in your meditation posture.
- Breathe deeply, the *complete* breath. The air goes fully into your stomach and chest.
- The breathing is *slow.*
- There is *no timing or counting* during the breathing.
- The breathing is *continuous.* There is no pause before breathing in or breathing out. That is, you don't hold your breath at any time, neither in nor out.
- The breathing is *natural*, spontaneous, unforced, as it comes. Initially you may have to take deep breaths until the breathing happens quite naturally, by itself.
- You are *conscious* of your breath all the time.

IHVH: I AM 1460
The Vowels in the Heart 1303
To Call upon Jesus 679

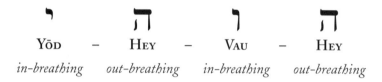

Meditation on the Holy Breath
2

- Sit in your meditation posture and follow all the rules of the previous exercise: complete breathing, slow breathing, no timing, breathing continuously, naturally and consciously.
- As you breathe in, mentally say **Yōd**, the first letter of the Divine Name.

  As you breathe out, mentally say **Hey**, the second letter of the Divine Name.

  As you breathe in, mentally say **Vau**, the third letter of the Divine Name. (Vau is pronounced Wouw.)

  As you breathe out, mentally say **Hey**, the fourth letter of the Divine Name.

  Keep doing this continually, unbroken.
- As you breathe in and mentally say **Yōd**, see a stream of Fiery Energy entering your system and descending from your face, down to the Base Centre at the bottom of your spine.

  As you breathe out and mentally say **Hey**, see the Fiery Stream flowing out of the Base Centre, up the spine and out through your nose, in front of you.

  Similarly with the remaining letters: **Vau**, the Fire comes in; **Hey**, the Fire goes out.

Yōd Hey Vau Hey

The Two Ways of the Heart

There is the passive, receptive Silent Heart Way.

There is the active, dynamic Fiery Heart Way.

Meditation on the Holy Breath

3

- Centre your awareness in the Heart.
- The same rules apply: breathe slowly, rhythmically, continuously, spontaneously, naturally, with no timing or counting. Remain fully conscious of the Name, of the Breath, and of the Fire.

This is Purification or Rebirth by Fire and the Holy Spirit

- As you breathe in **Yōd**, breathe in a Wall of Fire, a Sea of Fire. As you breathe out **Hey**, breathe out a Wall of Fire, a Sea of Fire. Similarly with the remaining letters: **Vau**, breathe in Fire; **Hey**, breathe out Fire.
- This whole meditation is centred in the Heart. As you breathe in and out the Ocean of Fire, your Heart expands and contracts, becoming large and small. The Fire radiates out below the base of the spine and above the top of your head, in front of you and behind you, and all around you. This is the Fire of Re-Creation or Re-Birth, which will re-make you into a new species of Man.

This is the *Baptism by Fire and the Holy Spirit* that Jesus referred to. In the ancient tongues, the word *baptism* meant "purification, cleansing, washing, bathing, renewal". This is Purification or Rebirth by Fire and the Holy Spirit. This is not symbolic, theological, intellectual, or wishful thinking! This is real, actual, experienced!

The Holy Spirit is Fire.

The Christ is Light.

The Father is the Ground of Being, the Root, the Source of all that is.

Baptism by Fire and the Spirit

Here, John the Baptist is speaking:

I indeed baptise you with water, symbol for repentance, but He who is coming after me, Yeshūa (Jesus)... He will baptize you (cleanse you) with the Holy Spirit and Fire.

Matthew 3:11

The word *Spirit* is mentioned more than two-hundred times in both the New Testament and the Old Testament.

The Unfoldment of the Light 718
Baptism and Rebirth 722
Sex Natural and Divine 926

Meditation on the Holy Breath
4

- In this meditation you are *breathing through your whole body*, or your image of yourself as a body, and you are *aware* of *Space* around you.
- As you breathe in the divine letter Yōd, breathe in through your whole body, towards its centre, the Heart. (This Heart is not the physical heart!) Feel Space collapsing towards you, into your Heart. You are breathing in the physical wind, air, breath, as well as the subtle etheric energy currents of the planet. For wind, air and breath are not only gross (physical), but ethereal (etheric) also.
- As you breathe out Hey from the centre of your Being (the Heart), Space expands outwards from you, through your whole body, and goes far beyond it into the distance.
- So also when you are breathing in, Vau, and breathing out, Hey.
- You will become aware of the energy currents of our planet, the Earth-planet Logos, in whose etheric-physical body you are doing this meditation. You will also become aware of your Unity with all life upon this planet, with all humans, all animals, all plants, all minerals, with the dense-physical and etheric parts of our Planetary Logos, Gaia. Empty Space is an illusion. You live *in* the body of our Planetary Logos, who lives (together with other Planetary Logoi) *in* the body of our Solar Logos, the Lord Sun, who lives (together with other Suns) *in* the body of a Greater Sun, and so on.
- You should completely *lose yourself* in this meditation. You should lose your sense of self and body-identification. *Dissolve in Oneness* with the Planetary Life, the Breath of our Planetary Logos.

You live in the body of our Planetary Logos

You can become One with the Breath of the Planetary Logos, the Spirit of the Earth.

Later on, you can become One with the Breath of the Solar Logos, the Spirit-Sun.

Later on, you can become One with the Breath of the Central Spiritual Sun.

Later on, you can become One with the Universal Sun, God, Alāhā (Aramaic), the Breath of the Eternal.

The Revelation of God 854

The Manifested-God 1589

Meditation on the Holy Breath
5

Christ is the Light of the World.

- In this meditation you are centred in the innermost part of the Heart. That is, you are centred in *You* as a Living Soul in your causal body (your Radiant Body, beyond the personality). You have a sense of bodilessness.
- As you breathe in **Yōd**, with your total auric-field, you draw to yourself Light from the Universal Field of Christ Light. This Light fills your aura wholly, completely, so there is nothing left in it but Light.
- As you breathe out **Hey**, you let go of the Light, disperse it in all directions and into Inner Space all around you.
- Similarly with **Vau** and **Hey**.

I, the Light, am *in* the World; anyone who will unite with me will be liberated from Darkness (the material existence).

John 12:46 (correct translation)

LIGHT

Aramaic:	**Nuhrā**
Arabic:	**Nūr**
Persian:	**Nūrā**
Hebrew:	**Aur (Ōr, Ūr), Aurh (Ōrah, Ūrah)**
Greek:	**Phōs, Phōtismos**
Latin:	**Lūx, Lūmen**

Light is another *key word* in the Mystical Tradition of which Eshū (Aramaic: Jesus) was a Master. In each of these languages of Western Mysticism, *Light* means "Illumination, Radiance, Glory, Enlightenment, Pure Consciousness, Superior Intelligence, Brightness, Illuminative Substance".

Light is referred to approximately seventy times in the New Testament and more than one-hundred times in the Old Testament. But remember, the ancients understood the word *Light* not as a simple candlelight or moonlight or physical sunlight, but as much more. It is the *real* Light, the Light of Christ, the Spiritual Light which causes the Illumination of the Mystic and the Saint.

Baptism by Light is the cause of Deliverance or final Liberation from Bondage to the lower worlds (the physical, subtle and causal realms).

God is Light and in Him there is no darkness at all.

I John 1:5

Light 978
The Universal Christ 440
The Christ is the Light of the World 442
Nūr: the Light of God 847
The Lighted Way 1394
The Self-Generating Light 1594
The Light of the World 1596

Meditation on the Holy Breath
6

- Sit in your meditation posture. Focus your attention in your base or foundation, the Earth-Centre at the base of your spine.
- Breathe Yōd-Hey-Vau-Hey as follows:

Yōd –	Hey –	Vau –	Hey
in-breathing	*out-breathing*	*in-breathing*	*out-breathing*

  The breathing should be deep, down to the Base Centre, slow, continuous, natural, with no timing or counting of the breath. At all times, remain fully conscious of the movement of the breath.
- As you breathe in deeply, see the **Yōd** as luminous white letters in your Base Centre. As you breathe out, see the **Hey** as luminous white letters in your Base Centre. Similarly with **Vau** and **Hey**.
- After a while, you will see these letters dissolve into the Luminous Sea of the Primary Substance, the Loud Resounding Ocean of Life, the Sounding-Light Vibration of the Divine Name, and you will Know that "the whole Earth is full of His Glory".

You will Know that the whole Earth is full of His Glory

EARTH

Hebrew: **A R Tz (ERETz)**
Aramaic: **Arā**
Greek: **Gē, Gaia**
Latin: **Terra**

Earth is another *key word* in the ancient tongues. The word *Earth* means all of the following:

- The basis, the foundation.
- Nature, the Manifestation or Creation, all that is embodied.
- The planet, our globe.
- The shining Sea of Matter, the material universe, the cover over the Real.
- The focus of gravity, or a solid, steady point in Space.
- The energy or quality of solidity, form, stability, fixity.
- The physical body, the Base Centre.

The Cosmic Elements 26
Heaven and Earth 439
Holiness to the Lord 1393

Meditation on the Holy Breath
7

At this seventh stage of meditation on the Holy Breath you *inwardly* learn to use the Great Breath, the Holy Spirit, the Divine Name, which is *the cause of all miraculous powers* that arise upon the Way of Holiness. This is only possible when you have *consciously attuned yourself* to the Loud-Resounding-Sea of the Sounding-Light-Vibrations of the Divine Name.

The Great Breath is the cause of all miraculous powers that arise upon the Way of Holiness

SH M (SHEM): Name, renown, fame, vibration.
SH M O (SHEMĀ): fame, glory, repute, inner sound.
SH M Y M (SHAMAYĪM) (Aramaic: SHEMAYĀ): Heaven, the Manifested Creation.

HEAVEN

Aramaic:	SHEMAYĀ
Hebrew:	SHAMAYĪM, SHEMAYĪN
Greek:	OURANOS
Latin:	CAELUM

In each of these Western languages which relate to original Christianity, this is a most important *key word* in order to understand the Way of Holiness and the ultimate use of the Holy Breath.

Heaven is *Interconnectedness of Vibration*. In all of these languages, *Heaven* means the *multi-dimensionality of Space*, as a Unity or Oneness, as a *Continuum* between the within (the above) and the without (the below). Without understanding this sense of *Continuum*, inwards or up the planes, or from the inner dimensions of the Cosmos downwards into the Physical Plane (the physical universe and the physical body), most of the mysteries hinted at in the Old and New Testaments cannot be comprehended by the modern linear-thinking person.

In the Bible, angels appear and disappear from Heaven, or people are translated (ascend) to Heaven. Heaven cannot be understood in the linear sense of space, or as an emptiness between physical objects. Space is *not* physical emptiness. Physical space and Inner Space are the One Space, which is the real meaning of these ancient words for "Heaven". It is the Continuum of Vibration of the Divine Name (SHEM) as One.

Dimensions of the Solar Logos in Cosmic Space 1591

Perceiving the One Space 13
The Form of God is Space 109
Worlds within Worlds 886
The Biblical Angels of God 203

In the Hebrew-Aramaic Mystical Tradition, which is the source of Christianity, the *Logos* or *Word* is threefold, or rather, has three stages of manifestation:

a. The Original Pure Name, the Original Sounding-Light Vibration within the Upper Worlds of Light. This is God's Name in its most subtle or transcendental aspect.

b. Next comes the Sounding-Light Vibration, or Inner Sound, which projects and maintains the Middle Worlds, the Causal or Heaven Worlds. It is also the command to *hear*, to *listen inwards* to the Voice of Light, the Voice of Silence, which will take you out of the binding lower realms of the Universe.

All is the Name of God in various stages of Incarnation or Manifesting Power

c. Next comes the lower vibrations of the Sounding-Light Vibration which manifest as the Astral World (the "heavens") and the Physical Creation.

From the highest to the lowest, All is the Name of God in various stages of Incarnation or Manifesting Power.

Once you have learned to *match* your vibration with the Loud-Resounding-Sea of the Divine Name Vibration, all possibilities are at your disposal. You sense yourself to be Omnipotent. Then, you "wish" and it shall come to pass....

To Safely Perform Miracles

Both the *Path of Wisdom* of the East and the *Path of Holiness* of the West have their unwritten rules on the performing of miracles—apparently supernatural powers which are really only modifications brought about in Heaven (Space) by the Power of the Holy Breath or the Great Name. Upon either Path, the performing of miracles is optional and not recommended, lest you develop a *subtle spiritual ego* or spiritual self-centredness, glorifying in your "talents" or miraculous abilities, which would *distract* you from final Union with God or Annihilation in God.

You can safely perform miracles only after you have learned to *attune your vibrations* with the Vibrations of the Divine Name, and if you are totally *selfless*, without an ego of any sort, as was Yeshūa. Otherwise, the miraculous abilities will distract you from the final Glory of becoming Eternally One with the *One*, the Alone with the *Alone*.

Seek not Powers 581

The Doctrine of the Logoi 116
The Threefold Logos 662
The Descent of the Word 118
The Action of the Primordial Sound 165
The Source of Miracles 671

Wisdom: the Light Path

These are the words of YESHŪA BEN PANDIRA (Jesus):

> Blessed are the Solitary, the Elect. For you shall find the Kingdom of Light, for you came from it and you shall return to it.
>
> If anyone asks you where have you come from, say to them: "We have come from the Light, the Self-Sufficient Original Light, which became our image [us]."
>
> If they ask you, "Who are you," say to them: "We are the Children [of the Light], the Elected Ones of the Living Father [Light]."
>
> And if they ask you how do you know this Father [Light] within you, say to them: "By a Movement and a Stillness."
>
> *Correct translation from the Gospel of Thomas (Didymos Judas Thomas)*

The Kingdom of Light is Nirvāṇa, the Ultimate Source and Origin of the Cosmos

The Solitary

In His time, the word used by Jesus for *Solitary* meant "inwardly united" (YOGĪ, in the East).

The Elect

The *Elect* meant "a follower of the Way, a practitioner of the Science of Union with God, the Ones who have moved out of worldly consciousness" (SĀDHAKA, in the East).

The Kingdom of Light

The *Kingdom of Light* is NIRVĀṆA, the Bright-Light World, the Ultimate Source and Origin of the Cosmos.

WISDOM

Hebrew-Aramaic:	**CH K M H (HOKMAH)**
Greek:	**SOPHIA**
Latin:	**SAPIENTIA**

In ancient times, these words did not mean being "worldly-wise", intellectual, or learned in our present sense, but the Knowledge that revealed the Path of Light.

What is Wisdom? 1685

Who are the 'Elect'? 128
Wisdom and Understanding 439
Sophia: the Feminine Intelligence 146
Nirvāṇa: the World of Glories 93

The Silence of the Deep

There is the Silence of the Mind.

There is the Silence of Inner Space.

There is the Silence of the Tranquil Light.

There is the Silence of Creation.

And there is the Silence of the Great Deep, the Great Abyss, the Divine Ground, the Silence of God.

You will experience the Silence of the Deep

∞

Hebrew-Aramaic:

DVMH (Dumah)
DVMIH (Dummiyah)
DMI (Domi)
DMMH (Demamah)
HSH (Hasa)

Greek:

Hēsychia: Stillness, Silence.
Sigē: Silence.

Latin:

Silentium
Taciturnitas

On the Way of Holiness, Silence is very important. This is borne out by the fact that the Mystics have been called:

Hasidim (Hebrew-Aramaic): Silent Ones.
Hesychast (Greek): Silent Ones.
Taciturnas (Latin): Silent Ones.

First you will experience the Silence of the Mind. Then you will experience the Silence of Inner Space, and then the Silence of the Tranquil Light. Then the whole Creation is silent before you. Then you will experience the Silence of the Deep, the Great Abyss, the Ground, the Source, Being, the Godhead.

The Hasidim 648
Christian Mysticism 450
To Develop Perfect Stillness 700
The Seven Stages of Sūfī Silence 901
The Practice of Silence 1443
The Silent State 1554

Silence is a great Power and a reservoir of Energy.

The Jesus Mantra and the Sacred Heart Initiation

Yeshuāh Al-Hayyīm
(Yeshuāh El-Hayyīm)
(Yoshuā Al-Hayyīm)

The Saviour-God of the Living.

The Fire of God, the Living Jesus.

Visualize the Burning Heart in the Heart Centre

Yeshūa: God who Saves; the Saving God.
Al (pronounced El): God.
Hayyīm: lives, living beings, creatures.

Yeshūa and Yoshūa are different pronunciations of the same Name. From the Hebrew Yeshūa came the Name *Jesus* in Christianity.

a. *Intone* Yeshuāh Al-Hayyīm in the Heart.

b. *Visualize* in the Heart Centre the Burning Heart, or the Sacred Heart, or Jesus with the Burning Heart or Sacred Heart, or the Christ Image with the Burning Heart or Sacred Heart.

c. First *visualize* the Burning Heart in the Heart Centre, or Jesus or Christ with the Burning Heart, then *intone* the mantra, Yeshuāh Al-Hayyīm, in the Heart. As you keep visualizing the Sacred Heart, slowly, at intervals, *intone* the mantra as worship.

d. The visualization can be reduced to only the Sacred Fire, and the mantra can be reduced to Yeshūa.

Variations of the Name of Jesus

Aramaic:	**Eshū, Ishū, Ishuā, Yeshuā, Yoshuā.**
Hebrew:	**Yeshū, Yeshua, Yeshūa, Yoshua, Yeheshua, Yehoshua, Yeheshuā, Yeheshuvah, Yeshūah.**
Latin:	**Iesu, Iesū, Iesus.**
Greek:	**Iesous.**
Sanskrit:	**Īśa, Īśāna.**

There were several historical people in the Old Testament called "Jesus" (in Hebrew: Yeshua, Yoshua, Yeheshua, Yehoshua, etc.). It was a name for boys in olden days.

Names of the Great Master Jesus 661

The Sacred Heart of Jesus 673
The Mystery of Jesus and Mary 665
The Radiant Heart Prayer 702
Visualization of the Christ in the Heart 730
Yeshua: the Secret Hebrew Name 1276
Jesus: the Fire of Love 1725

The Rose of Love and the Cross of Light

- Be Still. Descend into your Heart Centre.
- Visualize your Heart as a large Rose. The Rose is a beautiful, dynamic rose-red colour, a deep blood-red or pinkish soft-red. Choose the colour-tone of red that you feel most attracted to.
- This Rose is a Living Rose; it is full of Life and its petals are made out of pure Love. Feel the Divine Love-Vibration pouring through this Rose.
- Within the pure Love-Vibration of the Rose of the Heart there is a Cross of Light. This Light-Cross is a living, vibrating Cross made out of the purest Light-Substance. It is a Fiery Cross, shining with a Brilliant Light which is pure White Fire, Light scintillating as White Flames. This is the Cross of self-sacrifice, the giving of your life for others, and the outpouring of Divinity through you into the world.
- Within and across the Cross, and across your Heart, vibrates the Divine Name **Yeheshuvāh**, in large letters made out of Cosmic Fire, Divine Fire.

Yeheshuvah is the Saving Grace of God

Yeheshuvah means "God Saves, Delivers, Liberates", from Yah (the Creator-God) and Hoshua (who Saves, who is the Saviour). Thus, the Creator-God, who created You, is also your Saviour and Liberator into the Kingdom of Light. Yeheshuvah is the Saving Grace of God, the Redeeming Power which lifts you out of materialistic consciousness, out of your personality-consciousness into Soul-Consciousness, into the Awareness of the Kingdom of God. It is a Fiery Energy, burning away your materiality and liberating your Spirit.

Yeshū: the Lord of Love.
Messiāh (Mashiah): the Saving Grace.

Yehoshua Ha-Messiāh: the Divine Incarnation (Avatāra). The Living God incarnated in the World of Man to redeem the Souls of Man, the Spirit-Spark-Atoms which are enmeshed and captured by the Sea of Matter, and to return them to the Light Kingdom.

Christū: the Lord of Light. The Christ is the Light of the World—that is, the Light *in* the World, the Light *within* the World.

The Rose of Divine Love 858
The Unfoldment of the Light 718
The Jewish Messiah 660
To Call upon Jesus 679
The Mystery of the Christ 1724

Meditation in the Cave of the Heart

- Be Still. Sit Still. Relax.
- Focus your attention in your head, in the Third-Eye area. Become conscious there. This is the seat of your ordinary, rational mind.
- Imagine that you are going to descend from there into the Cave of your Heart. Imagine your Heart Centre as a cave. With your mind you go down and down into this cave. It is dark, but with a soft luminosity all around, so you can still see. Descend deeper and deeper into this dark-luminous cave.
- What you notice about this Cave of the Heart is Silence, Stillness, Peacefulness, Quietness. You *rest* in this Cave. Your mind and consciousness rest in the Silence and Stillness of the dark cave.
- Then you begin to notice a soft blue glow permeating the whole cave. The blue colour is getting stronger, but is still restful, still peaceful. Then the blue becomes vibrant, dynamic, filling the whole cave and beyond. The dynamic-blue becomes Infinity; it stretches in all directions like a boundless Sea of vibrant-blue.
- Slowly the blue changes into Silver Light, then into Golden Luminescence, then into Dazzling Bright White Light.
- This Divine Brightness is everywhere, a Boundless, Timeless Eternity filling all Space.

∞

This Divine Radiance is the Absolute Condition of the Heart

This Divine Brightness is the Light. It is the Way, the Truth and the Life, the Origin and Cause of all things, the Source, the Root, and again the final Goal of all things. And You are THAT.

This Light is above and beyond your mind and intellect. You can only grasp it in the State of Pure Consciousness, by Consciousness Itself.

This is Reality, the Light of God, the Radiation of the Divine Mind. This Divine Radiance is the true Heart, the Absolute Condition of the Heart.

This is the One God, the One Self, the One I AM pervading All.

In this State of the Heart, the ego (the personal sense of "I") is dissolved, replaced by the Universal I AM Presence.

This State is Liberation and Immortality. You are THAT.

The Cave of the Heart 634
Hṛt-Padma: the Heart-Lotus 1505
The Solar and Human Heart 1592
The Way, the Truth and the Life 670
The Essence of Wisdom 1680
The One 1686

The Divine Unity Mantra

Hebrew: **Ēl**
Arabic: **Allāh**
Aramaic: **Alāhā, Allahā**

The Radiant One, God as Radiant Energy, Fire, the Light of all things and within all things.

Change your Heart before trying to change others and the world

Use this mantra to overcome depression, the blues, negative feelings and emotions, oppressive states, darkness, sadness, self-pity, anxieties, tensions, worries, fears, and so forth. Let the Light into you!

Intone it rhythmically, first aloud, then rhythmically in your Heart Centre. Then stay in the Vibrant Positive Light of the Energy of the Divine Name.

Change your Heart before trying to change others and the world, otherwise those very things that are evil (that is, stumbling-blocks to progress) will remain and just take another form. Humanity must have a *change of Heart* before Peace can reign on Earth.

Love can only *be* when you live in the State of Oneness, the State of Union.

The *Unity* or *Continuum* between the visible and the Great Invisible Worlds, between Nature and God, between Man and the Divine, between Man and the Angelic Kingdoms, must be *realized.*

Have your dealings with all humans, and all kingdoms of Nature, arise from the standpoint of Oneness, Unity, Togetherness, Wholeness.

Work from the State of Recognized Unity.

The Eternal is One 512
The Divine Unity 852
The Path of Non-Duality 762
Peace on Earth 1304
To Manifest the Kingdom of God 1716

PART ELEVEN

The Way of Spiritual Psychology

CHAPTER 58

The Psychology of Consciousness

Psychology Ancient and Modern

The Science of Psychology is very ancient in the East and very new in the West.

- Eastern psychology (the doctrines of Yoga and Tantra) is based on the *direct exploration of Human Consciousness.*
- Modern Western psychology is based on the outer, superficial observation of the *behaviour patterns of human personalities.*

Science of the Soul? 291
Pure Intelligence 494
Psychology and the New Age Religion 1105
Future Therapy 372

Eastern psychology deals with the Inner Man, the true human being. Western psychology deals with passing, superficial moods and emotions, based on the observation of the physical body, the brain and the nervous system. The normal behaviouristic school of psychology deals with outer appearances only, with surface meanings, and does not touch the Inner Core of Humanity, nor does it deal with Nature as it really is. Therefore, it cannot effectively heal the Whole Person. Before true therapy (healing) can take place, the whole Being of an individual must be recognized.

Behaviouristic psychology places tags on people, thus imposing limitations upon them which they are then constrained to live up to. When we create boundaries and limitations, and put labels (identification tags) on ourselves and others, increasingly we come to believe that we are finite, mortal, perishable selves, thus cutting ourselves further away from the Boundless Imperishable Self that we are.

Understand that human emotions have been with us, in their present form, for many hundreds of thousands of years. They are not new. People have felt anger, disappointment, fear, anxiety, stress, worries and mood swings for ages. The only difference is that, over the ages, these "emotions" were regarded as natural to a human being. Modern Western psychology is doing enormous damage to the psyche of Humanity by declaring these negative emotions to be mental illnesses and convincing the masses that they are mentally ill. This is an utter disaster.

In these notes on Transformational Psychology I try to expand the awareness of the average psychologist beyond the observation of outer behaviour patterns (which are not the cause of problems, but simply the results of the inner workings of the mind) towards a recognition of the many layers and aspects of Consciousness itself: self-consciousness, subconsciousness, Superconsciousness, Cosmic Consciousness, and so on.

Perhaps not many psychologists today will understand this knowledge or have the ability to apply it on the practical level, but in the future this *will* be the common knowledge.

Cultivate the Positive

Fear, anxiety, anger, loneliness, inner and outer violence, out-of-control desires, domestic strife, strife between male and female, and a sense of insecurity in this world have been a plague on human consciousness for aeons. The past religions tried to teach that the negative emotions are not suitable for Spiritual Life or Spiritual Realization, and that you should cultivate the positive emotions—peace, calmness, harmony, fearlessness, surrender, acceptance, joy, happiness, non-aggression, and so on—as they lead to progress on the Spiritual Path and make life easier on this plane.

The Radiance of the God-Self within you will dispel the negative emotions

The initial stages of the Path consist of your *emergence* out of your personality-self, which is centred on negative emotional expressions. You must get rid of the *emotional moods* of worry, fear, depression, anger and loneliness. These are not "mental diseases"; they are just emotions in your astral body. For hundreds of thousands of years, people have had these *feelings*. They are based on your *identification* with your physical body and your personal "self". These feelings have nothing to do with your mind at all—you are not mentally sick! Your mind (mental body) is a different reality altogether.

Negative emotions simply show a *disconnection* from the Glory that is within you. The focus of Western psychology has been to find personality solutions to personality problems without even acknowledging the Divine within Man, let alone *connecting* the personality to the Divine. When psychology begins to understand properly what Man truly is, the so-called "mental diseases" (which have been invented by the hundreds) will disappear altogether through the application of the principle of *reconnection* with the Real within you.

If, by meditating in your Heart, you make a *direct connection* with the God-Self within your Heart and *raise your consciousness* beyond your personal self, then the Radiance of the God-Self within you will dispel the negative emotions, just as the Sun dispels the darkness of the night upon the coming of the dawn.

The negative emotions can be overcome only by utter Surrender to the God-within-us and the experience of Superconsciousness.

Emotional Problems 1429
Passion and Dispassion 695
The Sūfī View of Mental Disorders 900
The Mystery within the Heart 1315
God, the Healer of Broken Hearts 1432
Dwell on the Positive 1712

Cultivate Knowledge

Materialistic Consciousness is Primeval Ignorance

Materialistic Consciousness is *Primeval Ignorance*. It is the non-recognition and denial of the Divine Self within.

Knowledge is the positive pole of Being. Ignorance is the negative pole.

Knowledge produces the qualities of positivity, brightness, cheerfulness, goodness, strength, growth, evolutionary development and progress. Ignorance diminishes self-esteem, produces violence, is counter-progressive and anti-evolutionary, and crystallizes the existing order of things. Hence the importance of cultivating Knowledge.

Knowledge is structured in Consciousness. The Knowledge available to you is according to the level of Consciousness reached.

There is a Point of Goodness in every human being, no matter how thickly it is veiled by Ignorance.

Knowledge shines in everyone, everywhere.

Education should focus on teaching children from an early age that they are Divine, and giving them the *practical* methods and processes to *realize* that Divinity. At this stage, education is a tool for materialism.

Education from the Spirit

Mankind needs a new education system, one that frees the mind, not one that entraps the mind into endless thought-processes, as it is today in this materialistic age. Each thought is a death for the Spirit, the Pure Being within you. You cannot lead a Spiritual Life simply as an intellectual exercise. Today's education system keeps the Spirit of Mankind in Bondage, earthbound, in materialistic consciousness.

Truth is not based on thinking, but on Direct Inner Experience of Reality. Therefore, silence your thoughts, calm your mind, become thought-free; then you receive the Education from the Spirit.

Education For Life 484

Lack of Knowledge 4
The Four Degrees of Knowledge 1003
Spirituality Past and Future 1104
The Education System 480
Zen and the World 758
Tranquil Mind 1503

Transformational Psychology

Discrimination arises when we label individuals, groups, nations, races or religions. These tags or labels are usually negative, limited and biased. Your ordinary mind, the rational mind, will find "faults" with the people so labelled, no matter what they do or don't do. Then you develop hate or aggressiveness towards them.

Have no tags or labels in your mind that limit yourself or other human beings

Understand this truth: you are no more perfect than they are. Learn humility.

Labelling people according to some biased and wrongly constructed model, theory or profiling is not only inhuman and evil, but it limits the human potential. In truth, psychology must realize that each man, woman and child is essentially Divine, and it must open up that Divinity within them. This is the task of Spiritual Psychology or Transformational Psychology.

The Caste System 378

∞

Transformational Psychology is a wholly positive outlook on life.

Transformation of old patterns is necessary before Reconstruction can begin. The Goal is to change Consciousness.

Act spontaneously. Throw away barriers and have no tags or labels in your mind that limit yourself or other human beings.

The immediate goal of Transformational Psychology is to develop the individual Mind to the state of Cosmic Consciousness and to develop the full potential of the personality within the context of the evolving Higher Consciousness.

Conscious Evolution is the next step for Humanity.

The Work is to start with yourself.

Materialism is the belief in objective matter existing on its own, without the Being of God.

Both orthodox religion and orthodox science are produced by the personality and serve the false, limited sense of ego or "I", the personality sense. They are the limited personality's view of Reality, not Reality as it really is, beyond the five senses.

Protagonists of Ignorance 382
Orthodoxos: correct belief? 653

What is Consciousness?

There is only One Consciousness

The ignorant materialists (those of them who bother to think at all) think that Consciousness is a *chemical activity* of the physical brain and nervous system, a plain physical activity of the body, a *by-product* of the mechanical activity of matter (of which the physical body is composed). But in fact, Consciousness *was* and *is before* the physical body, after the physical body, and before even the Creation or Manifestation of the vast Universe (its physical, astral, mental, causal and spiritual realms and dimensions). Consciousness was *before* all things and will remain *after* all things re-dissolve into the Primal State of Unity, the Singular State, the Boundless Oneness of the Infinite Mind or Mind of Light.

There is only *One Consciousness,* expressing Herself through innumerable forms, bodies and structures throughout the vast Universe, on all levels, planes and worlds, visible and invisible. She is the Great Mother, the Universal Mother, the Producer of all creatures and all things.

Mind-Only 974
The One 1686
Mind and Brain 79
Objective Experience 305
The Temple of the Goddess 1492

All Hail to the Brain!

The latest worship by materialistic doctors, psychologists and psychiatrists is the brain. They spend incredible amounts of taxpayers' money in hundreds of universities measuring the activities and transformations of brain cells during various happenings in a person's life. "All Hail to the great God, the brain!"

Yet, in Truth, the brain is but an *instrument* of your mind (your mental body, composed of a higher matter than the physical brain). Your mental body *uses* your brain so that you can communicate with this physical level of Reality. The brain simply *reacts* to what you "do" in your mental body (that is, in your "mind"). The mental body produces waves or vibrations (VṚTTI), fluctuations in mental matter, which permeate your whole physical body; hence, if you *change* your mental waves, then the brain, the physical nervous system and your whole physical body *respond.*

You can *elevate* your Consciousness so high, through correct meditation or pure Devotion and Worship, that you completely *transcend* the body-vibration. Or you can *refine* the body, nervous system and brain-vibrations by spiritual disciplines. Or you can *leave* the body altogether through the Heart or Crown Centres.

Transformations of the Mind 1242

Materialism Rules

We have to refer to the "materialists" because they are the dominating factor on this planet at this time, dominating in numbers as well as in thought, for materialism rules every aspect of society.

Human beings are gods *limited* to a human form. In fact, the limitation is so successful that people have forgotten that they are gods. The Fullness of Life, the full Potential of Life, you can experience only when you have *recovered* your God-Self, *rediscovered* Yourself, the Larger Self that is *not limited* to Time and Space, nor to the body, mind and ego, nor to the emotions and physical circumstances, nor to the world-phenomena. Can you imagine yourself to be Boundless Consciousness, Infinite Intelligence, Total Love, Bliss and Power? Yet, You Are That!

Human beings are gods limited to a human form

There are three Great Mysteries which you need to solve in this lifetime if you want to discover the meaning of your existence:

- By what mechanism your Consciousness became *identified* with your physical body during your birth process and early life.
- By what mechanism you can *release* your Consciousness from being *limited* to your body so that it may *regain* its Larger Dimension.
- By what mechanism you have created for yourself your *limited self-image*, your ego, your personal sense of "I", and how you can recover the Limitless, Boundless Awareness, Infinite Intelligence and Perpetual Bliss-Consciousness that you had *before you identified yourself* with the human nature on this planet.

Trapped Spirits 1240
Children of the Sun 1590
Understand your Predicament 892
Liberation from Worldly Consciousness 1233
To Achieve Liberation 1177

This is the important stuff you do not learn at school or university. How can you go through the "education" system for twelve or eighteen years and still not have the faintest idea of Who You truly Are? Your Divine Powers and Nature?

Your Journey through life should be the *rediscovery* of the Truth about your Self, or else you will be kept on the cycle of Reincarnation, circling again and again into and out of the world-flux, the world-drama, forever.

You will never solve the Problem of Life, of human existence on this planet, by simply intellectualizing or theorizing. The Way to your Glory, "the Christ in you, your hope of Glory" (as the New Testament puts it), is through serious practice of spiritual disciplines, meditation, chanting, and a deep and profound Love of God.

You need to go through the Essential Inner Transformation to regain your Higher Consciousness. Keep going!

The Three Identifications

Identification with forms, worlds and the external environment.

Identification with mind, desires, emotions and mental functions.

Identification with ego, personality, the personal sense of "I", the limited sense of self.

These identifications cloud the Vision of the Soul and veil the Spirit. When your Consciousness *ceases to identify with them*, you are Free.

Obstacles to Higher Consciousness 1424

Consciousness

Consciousness is the Continuum-Fabric of Space, which is all-pervading, everywhere.

All Consciousness is interconnected with every other Consciousness, and all Consciousness depends on the One Consciousness.

Consciousness comes first, then mind, then body

Consciousness is an Infinite Continuum on every side.

Consciousness is the Source of Creation, Evolution and Destruction.

Consciousness creates forms, and thereby becomes identified or constrained, but Its Boundless State remains unchanged.

Absolute Consciousness is an infinite Source of Energy that has infinite potential to create limitless varieties of life-forms, and all life-forms depend on It for their existence.

The Cosmic Mind encompasses everything.

Everything is connected to everything else by ties of subtle Matter.

The Emptiness of Śūnyatā, the Transcendental Awareness, is identical with the Fullness of conditioned existence, Saṁsāra.

Your Consciousness is separate from your body and survives your body.

Consciousness comes first, then mind, then body. Changing one's level of Consciousness changes the vibrations of one's mind and body, and hence one's experience of the Cosmos.

The Plan is in the Divine Mind 161
Tao: the Universal Mind 775
Perceptions of the One Mind 490
Śūnyatā: the Void 503
From Head to Heart 427

Do not mistake your mind for your Soul. They are two different things. The mind without the Soul-Light is separative, critical, self-centred, arrogant, divisive, cold, dogmatic and limited, full of errors and fanaticism. The mind infused with Soul-Light is full of Wisdom, Compassion and Higher Understanding.

Consciousness has its own development apart from the various bodies it might be working through.

All mental movements are fluctuations in the deep Silence of the Eternal.

Your thoughts and activity change as your Consciousness changes. Your life changes when your Consciousness changes. Consciousness determines Life.

The quality of your Consciousness determines the quality of your life

The quality of your Consciousness determines the quality of your life. The quality of Consciousness of a group of people determines their group-experience of life. The quality of Consciousness of total Humanity determines the destiny of nations and the fate of the planet.

Life is different at the different levels of Consciousness lived. Your Consciousness decides your fate. A dull Consciousness is a dull life. An Alive Consciousness is an exciting, eventful life.

TURĪYA-CETANĀ, the Fourth Consciousness, is Pure Consciousness, without thought, feeling or physical sensory impression.

Consciousness of your Triune Self transcends Time and Space as you know them on this Physical Plane. It is Boundless Awareness, Universal Unrestricted Consciousness, Eternal Life.

Your Consciousness is the Absolute Consciousness when it is not influenced by your external worldly perceptions through the senses. Reduce the activities of your mind until you perceive only Pure Awareness.

Some people have memories of when their bodies were still in their mothers' wombs (or even until they were one or two years old, before they became fully identified with their bodies), and they were floating on a Sea of Energy, Light, Consciousness.

In deep meditation you learn to *transcend* body-consciousness or to *develop* the capacity of the body to *respond* to Higher States of Consciousness.

ĀTMA-BUDDHI-MANAS
Sanskrit: The Triune Self. The Spirit, Spiritual Soul and Higher Mind, which constitute the Higher Self, the real You.
The Individuality 34

The Basic Enlightened State

There are several States of Consciousness in the Enlightened State

Beginner Mystics and Yogīs think that *Higher Consciousness* is just one thing, that having experienced SAMĀDHI (Spiritual Trance), or a Mystical Rapture, they have attained the Goal, and that for the rest of Eternity they need do nothing else, that they have "made it". This is a great Ignorance. There are several States of Consciousness in the Enlightened State, and much more beyond that! Generally speaking, the common signs of the basic Enlightened State are as follows:

- A sense that you have been changed or are undergoing a major restructuring inside yourself.
- You are no longer as attached to your "ego" as you have been.
- You live in the Moment, in the Here and Now, and find it increasingly difficult or impossible to maintain the routine customs and arrangements of your family, culture, religion and society.
- You feel yourself to be beyond Time and Space; that is, you perceive that what people around you call "time and space" is a delusion of the rational mind. In fact, Reality is Boundless, in terms of both "time" and the so-called "space" sense.
- You sense a Primeval Unity with all things and all people.
- You sense God to be everywhere.
- You sense that Life is essentially Love, Bliss and Light.

Samādhi: the Goal of Yoga 574
Signs of Progress in the Heart 1289
The Fullness of the Void 23

Formless Worlds

The Higher Worlds are Formless. And the Higher Worlds are Silent. It may seem very strange, this idea that a world has no shape or form. This is why, when they experience the Higher Worlds, the Yogīs talk about a *Vast Formless Ocean of Consciousness*.

The lower worlds (the Physical, Astral and Mental Planes) are full of shapes, forms, bodies. Consciousness is restricted, constricted to dwell in "bodies", or embodiments of various kinds. You have your physical, etheric, astral, mental and causal forms, or "bodies", which confine and restrict your Pure Consciousness or Formless Consciousness.

It may also seem strange to you that something can exist in Silence and be active in Silence, be *alive* in Silence, and without a sense of limitation.

When you function through your physical, etheric, astral and mental bodies, you have a sense of limitation, finality. When you *go above* these personality vehicles or structures you have the sense of Limitlessness, a Boundless Ocean of Awareness, Consciousness, Bliss—what the Buddhists call Emptiness, Void, which seem to be negative descriptions because the Formless Reality is *not* "empty", not a "void", not "nothingness", but the Complete Fullness and Wholeness of Life.

Formless Consciousness

The *first* level of true Mystical Consciousness (Higher Consciousness or Superconsciousness) is the Formless Consciousness. Through the practice of the *correct* method of meditation you go *beyond* your personality mechanism, beyond the *identification* with your body, mind and emotions, and you arrive at a State inside yourself where you are Awake, Aware, fully Conscious, but you are not conscious of any particular "objects" or "things"!

In this State your Consciousness is Conscious only of Itself

Normally your Consciousness is *attached* to something, such as your body, mind or emotions, or to some external objects or people, or to some internal objects such as dreams, thoughts or imaginings. In this State, however, your Consciousness is Free and is conscious only of Itself. That is, *Consciousness is Aware of Consciousness.*

In Sanskrit this State is called:

Turīya-Avasthā: the Fourth State (of Being).
Śuddha-Caitanya: Pure Consciousness, Bright Consciousness, Clear Consciousness.
Ātmā-Cetanā: Consciousness of the Self (not the ego!).
The first stage of Samādhi (the Equilibrated Mind).
Amanaska: No-mind.
Unmani: the beyond-mind.
Sahaja-Avasthā: the Natural State (that is, the Original State of a human being).

In this State there is only Silence, Peace, Joy, Ecstasy, Contentment, Supernatural Knowing, and a Sense of Oneness. Your true Self, Ātman, enjoys being Itself, *free* from all limiting conditions.

In many schools of Yoga, the Fourth State of Consciousness (the Formless Self, or Self-Realization) is believed to be the highest attainment. In this State one is not aware of the outside world, nor of the body, and one is in the No-mind State—that is, *above* all thought processes. Yet this is not the highest State at all, but the Gate to the beginning of true Spiritual Evolution. In the next State, you *are* the Transcendental Self and are *also* able to function on the personality level, in the waking, dreaming and sleeping conditions. All these States merge into One State of Consciousness.

The Goal of Zen 760
Pure Consciousness in the Heart 447
Turīya: Pure Consciousness 498
The Seven States of Consciousness 494
The Ultimate Reality is the Meaning of Life 526

Mind and Body

The physical body is an instrument of the Spirit.

All the innumerable forms of minds and bodies in the Universe are simply parts of the single Body of God.

Every emotional and mental state has a reaction in the body

Your mind is not your Self. It is but an instrument your Soul needs to learn to use.

Mind is independent of the body, even as the Soul is independent of the mind.

The Intelligence within the physical body regulates the physiological functions. Forms evolve according to the type of Intelligence within them.

Although your physical body has its own cycle of birth, development and death, at all times it reflects also the state of your emotions and mind.

Every emotional and mental state has a reaction in the body. Transformation should begin with Intelligence.

Thoughts are waves in the mind-stuff. Energy follows thoughts. The energy vibrates the brain and nervous system, thus producing health or ill-health according to its kind.

For many hundreds of thousands of years, Human Consciousness has been functioning through the Base Centre, the Sex Centre and the Solar Plexus Centre; consequently these centres are still the most active in the human being. The Base Centre produces physical activity, the Sex Centre produces attraction between people, and the Solar Plexus Centre is responsible for emotions. In Humanity, the line of least resistance is for Nature to work through these centres. Because you are countering the product of past Evolution, it is difficult to meditate and raise your consciousness to the Heart Centre and Head Centres. To do so requires consistent and systematic effort.

Mind and Brain 79
Mind in Body 988
Thought and Energy 349
The Human Cakras 44
The Heart and the Energy Centres 1332

Thought creates. Energy follows Thought. What we think manifests in our bodies as *chemical changes*. All thinking produces corresponding chemistry in the body. Therefore, Positive Thought is a necessity.

Your mind is talking to your body all the time. Your thoughts, attitudes, belief systems and opinions are vibratory patterns in your mind which impact upon the tissues, cells and molecules of your physical body. It is important to send your body only positive messages.

Your mind is talking to your body all the time

The mental states associated with worry, anxiety, fear and anger affect not only your mental body, but react upon your astral body and physical body as well, producing weakness and nervous disease.

Positive thinking and feeling create evolutionary energies, good health, life-affirming and life-supporting vibrations. Negative thinking and feeling produce physical ill-health, stress-disorders in the mind and emotional disintegration.

Tranquillity of mind gives you bodily health.

The Base Centre, Sex Centre and Spleen Centre are responsible for the generation, maintenance and perpetuation of the physical body.

- At the Base Centre is the energy of KUṆḌALINĪ, the Divine Mother in the form of Internal Fire, coiled like a serpent at the base of the spine.
- At the Sex Centre (Sacral Centre) is the energy of ĀDI-ŚAKTI, the Primordial Energy, which is part of FOHAT, the Cosmic-Electric Force.
- At the Spleen Centre (near the stomach) is PRĀṆA, or Vital Force, which comes from the Sun and is all around us in the atmosphere.

As a unit, these three lower centres concern themselves with:

- Physical and etheric-physical matter, energy and consciousness.
- The conception and building of the physical body.
- The sex drive and perpetuation of the species.
- The vitality and health of the physical body.
- Physical survival, the instinct of self-preservation of the body.
- The desire to live and be active in the world, on the Physical Plane.

Health and Fire 50
Kuṇḍalinī-Fohat 148
Dimensions of the Cosmic Fire 137
Sexuality and the Life-Force 912
Awakening the Higher Centres 1037

Mind and Thought

Whatever you think upon, you will surely become

MANAS, the mind, is the source of all creativity. It is the connecting link between you and the forces of Nature or of Divinity. The mind draws to you all the resources you need to accomplish your Goal.

Mind is like a mirror; it reflects everything you put before it.

Thought is vibration and a *form*. Thoughts are actual *things*. They are objects in subtle matter surrounding the person having those thoughts. They are also radiation or waves within that person's aura.

The seat of thought is the mental body, not the physical brain.

Thoughts can be felt as energy around a person. Your thoughts are influencing others, whether or not you are aware of it. Do not become subdued by the negative thoughts of another.

Thinking and feeling are creative energies. You create or destroy your life by the power of your thoughts and emotions.

Thoughts are intensified by continued reiteration. The power of both negative and positive thinking increases through repetition.

Until the stage of Enlightenment, thought determines your experience. What you think is all-important. Do not have thoughts of gloom and doom, nor feelings of anger, shame or depression. Heaven is in your mind already. Hell is in your mind already.

Whatever you think upon, you will surely become. If you think on material things, you will attract those things to yourself. If you think on the Divine, in time you will become Divine. Such is the power of the mind to attract.

Holding onto certain thoughts while in the Transcendent State (Higher Consciousness) produces extraordinary and powerful results, what in the past were called "miracles".

Manas 78
Mind Realms 74
The Power of Thought 232
Energy Materializes 363
The Thought of Enlightenment 767
Saṁyama 582

Desire-Streams

Desire-streams are subconscious impressions and memory patterns from the past. Until it is reprogrammed, the subconscious mind will keep these habit patterns going indefinitely. Subconsciousness works by the repetitive forces of Nature, and desire-streams feed habits by forces of Nature. The forces of Nature fulfil all desires, whatever they may be, even the desire for Enlightenment.

The forces of Nature fulfil all desires

The only successful transformation of a human being is to change the person from the inside out—not superficially, on the outside. This works individually by self-conscious transmutation of the subconscious mind patterns.

To change a behaviour pattern, you have to change the desire-stream that feeds it. To change the desire-stream, you have to remove its source, the previous subconscious (subliminal) impressions.

The source of a desire-stream can be removed by two methods:

a. Starve it by cultivating exactly the opposite quality and setting up a new desire-stream current in the new direction. Do not dwell on the old pattern, but starve out the past impressions by removing your attention from them and concentrating on the opposite quality.

b. Refocus your Consciousness onto the Transcendent Eternal, which naturally obliterates all desire-streams less than the desire for the Transcendent Itself. By focusing your Consciousncss onto the Transcendent by self-conscious efforts, the negative desire-streams in the subconscious mind are naturally transmuted and the positive desire-streams naturally increase.

Mind and Desire 235
Subconscious Forces 236
Saṁskāra and Vāsanā 251
Subconscious Renewal 1236
Desire for the Real 1503

Thus, to break the cycle of habit-patterns you need to do one of the following:

- Create a new subconscious impression.
- Move into Higher Consciousness.

Sensory enjoyments give rise to subconscious impressions (subliminal imprints), which give rise to desires (passions), which give birth to thoughts, which lead to new actions. Only by transcending to the Self can this cycle effectively be broken.

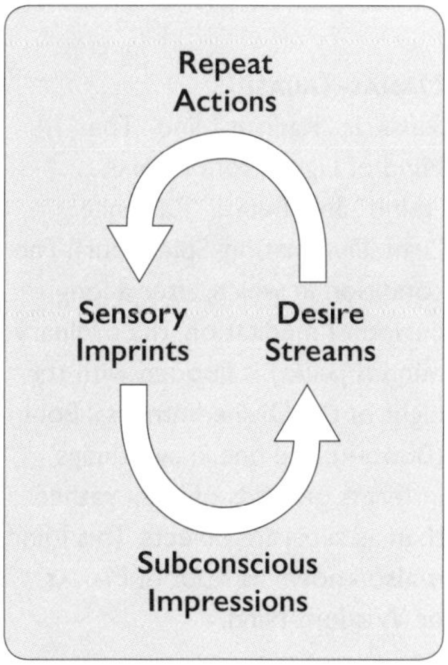

The Cycle of Desire

The Experience of the Transcendent

The nature of the mind is to seek greater and greater Happiness, but it needs to be guided in the right direction. The Transcendental Absolute gives it the Answer.

Senses or the Self? 239
Meditation and the Joy of Living 1012
The Mind is Dissolved in the Heart 1235
The Experience of the Heart 1280
Heart Knowing 1286

When your mind (MANAS) identifies itself with your Inner Being (ĀTMAN), your senses (INDRIYA) do not identify themselves with outer objects.

That which is the Real is not a product of the human mind, but exists totally independently of the human mind. Belief or non-belief in no way affects It. Thought cannot grasp It, but you can experience It in deep meditation.

The experience of the Transcendent leads to a renewal of the psyche and a new Life-wave.

The mind will come to Rest only when the Eternal has been found and experienced, which is the greatest Field of Happiness.

The highest form of Happiness comes when we have fully realized the Absolute. In that perfect state of Being, all possible desires are fulfilled.

To experience the Transcendent you have to purify your Heart and refine your mental vibrations.

MANAS-TAIJASI
Sanskrit: "Radiant Mind". The Mind of Light. From MANAS, "mind", and TAIJASI, "Radiance, Light, Illumination, Splendour". The condition in which, after a long period of meditation, the ordinary mind (MANAS) is flooded with the Light of the Divine Immortal Soul (BUDDHI), and one *knows* things in terms of Fields of Light rather than as separate objects. This Mind is also known as BUDDHI-MANAS, or Wisdom-Mind.
Super-Knowing 1242

The memory of our Origin and the Origin of the Universe, and the Divine Plan, can be recovered through deep meditation. There is no need for "guessing" about the Meaning of Life.

Transformation comes when the Essential Meaning of Life is known.

The Supreme Intelligence is an Intelligence that exists everywhere. Therefore It can be contacted by anyone, anywhere, at any time.

Spiritual Healing

Heal your Consciousness first, then your mind, body and emotions will be healed automatically.

Self-healing does not have to be painful and traumatic, for the self wants to be healed. The healing of the self is by the Self.

The healing of the self is by the Self

Spiritual Healing takes place in the Heart. When the Heart is Whole, you are happy anywhere.

Spiritual Healing comes when you sit in Silence, peacefully waiting, with no agenda in your mind. Then many things are resolved inside yourself, your mind is reset, and your Heart finds Peace.

Cultivate the opposite quality to the one that is causing your distress. This will dissolve the stress. It is only through positive qualities that you can reach the Transcendent.

When the mind creates no barriers between people, understanding arises spontaneously, along with inward healing.

Forgive and forget is the Principle of Forgiveness, the greatest healing agent.

Karmic Adjustment

When you are doing the Great Work of Transformation, karmas have to be worked out. This produces stresses of different kinds—physical, emotional and mental. As progress is made in the Transmutation Process, these stresses (life-dramas) will gradually ease off.

Your nervous system and cell structure are freed from all accumulated stress and anxieties when Higher Consciousness (Superconsciousness) is experienced.
The experience of Superconsciousness (the Transcendent) occurs only when the nervous system is freed from all stress and anxieties.

This dual process is called *Purifying Fire* or *Karmic Adjustment* and is the Way to Enlightenment.

Karma and your Spiritual Development 255

Magical Healing 372
Disease and Karma 1169
God, the Healer of Broken Hearts 1432
The Double Stress of Meditational Life 1181
Tapas: Spiritual Purification 571

The Principle of Choice

Every Moment, in every situation, everywhere, you have a *choice*. This is the Principle of Choice. You can choose to be happy or sad, forward-moving and progressive, or negative and destructive.

The Choice to be happy or unhappy is always in the Now

To be *pro-active* is to respond to a situation positively and constructively. To be *reactive* is to respond to a situation negatively and without control (Reactive-Emotional Consciousness).

At every point of Now, the Past and the Future are equally present. At every point you can revert back to the Past or move towards the Future. The Choice is yours.

Every day you are a New Creation, therefore it is not necessary for you to cling to the Past.

Do not let guilt be your constant companion.

Don't blame your Past. The Choice to be happy or unhappy is always in the Now.

You are a victim only to the degree that you want to play the victim role, and for as long as you choose to play it.

Fanaticism, tunnel vision, square-box mentality, biased opinions and paranoia develop when a person's mind is continually preoccupied with one idea, one theory, one opinion, one image, one way of doing things, one way of looking at something. Then the mind disregards all other points of view and all other impressions presented to it.

False Enlightenment is when you act freely from your ordinary consciousness without cares or worries. Real Enlightenment is a tremendous Inner Transformation. Society works on emotional hysteria, not the Original Goodness.

When the mind holds onto past beliefs or experiences (good or bad), its freedom to experience the Limitlessness of Now is hindered.

Let Go of the Past 1241
Reactive-Emotional Consciousness 1426
Past, Present and Future 1400
Intelligent Use of Free Will 297
False Zen 756

If you remain trapped in the Past, you are wasting the opportunities of the Present.

Holding onto the Past is the major obstacle to the growth of your Consciousness. The Conscious Journey is always *Now.*

When the mind stops grasping the Past, it becomes free of all limitations and the Future is seen as infinitely Bright.

When the mind stops grasping the Past, it becomes free of all limitations

How an event affects you, and how you cope with circumstances, always depends upon the strength of your mind. The more your mind is in tune with the Infinite, the more strength it has to cope with difficult situations.

Control your emotions through your mind, and let your mind be controlled by your Soul.

Remain on the side of the Forces of Life that move ever upward and onward in the Great Cycle of Time.

Happiness Exists Within

If you observe the basic psychological nature of human beings, you will see that everybody is looking for Happiness, and more and more Happiness. This is because, at the present state of Evolution (understood in the spiritual sense), the Inner Consciousness of human beings (including children) is *identified* with the mind, and the "normal" mind is *identified* with the objects perceived through the five bodily senses, so people are continually *attracted* or *drawn* to outside objects, to physical people and things. The whole human family is *deluded* in thinking that the more objects they have physically, the happier they become. This is a *tremendous delusion* affecting total Humanity: the idea that possessing physical objects (whether other people, animals, plants, shoes, clothes, cars, empires, or whatever) will satisfy one's search for Happiness. So the attention of all Humankind is continually outward-looking, bound up with the Physical Plane, with the physical world, thus locking themselves out from the State of Bliss-Consciousness, Satisfaction, Happiness, Joy, Peace and Totality that *already exists within*, in the Inner Realms, in the State of Inner Ecstasy.

Towards Bliss-Consciousness 423
Return to Primeval Happiness 1179
Your mind is attracted to physical things 1231
The Process of Seeing or Perceiving 542
In Bondage to the Mind 238

Self-Worth

Self-image is the building power of Success. Cultivate Self-worth.

Self-image is the view that you have of yourself. Transformation is the Key to changing your self-image.

Transformation is the Key to changing your self-image

If you give in to the negative emotional states of depression, low self-esteem, low self-worth, fear, anxiety and apprehension about what might happen, these conditions will sap your life-force and you will die before your appointed time.

Whatever you are feeling, you don't have to *identify* with it. Be free.

Do not sever, separate or divide things into opposite polarities in your Consciousness—good or bad, pleasant or unpleasant. Accept all things in the Oneness of the Absolute.

Do not lose your power to others (that is, your dominion over yourself). Do not let another person psychologically dominate you.

The personalized ego, the little self, the personal "I" sense, is full of fear, is self-centred, and lives in separation. This causes conflict with others and a feeling of being out of tune with yourself. The remedy is to develop the sense of Superconsciousness through deep meditation, which destroys the false or negative "I", illumines the mind with Light and fills the Heart with Peace.

Self-esteem or self-worth depends upon how you view yourself:

- If you view yourself merely as a physical body, your sense of self-esteem or self-worth will depend upon the condition of your body.
- If your self-esteem depends upon your environment, then it will change with the changing of outside conditions.
- If your self-esteem depends upon the calibre of your mind or the quality of your emotions, it is liable to fluctuations also.
- If your self-esteem depends upon how others see you, their opinion of you, you will also suffer endless ups and downs.

What do you Seek out of Life? 975
Is there a Plan in your Life? 1000
The Path of Self-Actualization 1110
Rely on your Inner Self 1226
Obstacles to Higher Consciousness 1424

Self-actualization is knowing where you are in the Present, having a vision or goal for the Future, and steadily persevering towards your objective until it is realized.

The highest Self-actualization is being in the Present, still and silent in mind, body, speech and emotions, and allowing the Self to take charge of your life according to Divine Will.

The Awareness of the Self unfolds itself, to itself, by itself

Union with the Eternal Principle is the Goal.

When you behold your true Self in profound Contemplation, your Transformation will be complete and you shall know your Infinite Potential.

Find the Positive Centre within yourself through meditation—the Ātman, the Radiant Spirit, the Glory Within—and then you will be always bright, positive, cheerful, self-determining and independent.

The Awareness of the Self unfolds itself, to itself, by itself. Just remove the ego.

The State of Unity of the Psyche

The Internal State of Unity of the Psyche (the Soul) is the best protection against the chaotic influences coming from the outer environment which cause stressful and negative effects upon Consciousness, resulting in stress, anxiety disorders, fears, negative emotional responses and violence.

The Internal State of Unity of the Psyche also dissolves accumulated stresses and negative patterns in the human system and prevents future undesirable tendencies from manifesting.

The emphasis of the Work must be to achieve the State of Unity of the Psyche by correct processes (meditation). When the State of Unity is achieved, Bliss and Harmony pervade Consciousness.

As Internal Harmony develops through a fundamental change in Consciousness, past errors fade away, and harmonic expression of thought, word and action, in accordance with Inner Law, becomes natural for Man. In this Transformation lies the future evolution of Humanity.

Success is Born of Action 256
The Law of your Being 976
The Vision of your own Eternity 1144
To Succeed in your Quest 1330
The Path to Wisdom 1702

The Laws of Group Psychology

The group reflects the leader; hence the group functions with only the degree of Brightness that the group leader has access to.

The group leader must centre himself or herself in the Light (Higher Consciousness) before working with the group. A negative energy-field around the leader throws the group into chaos and disharmony.

True Transformation is an energy exchange

The group aura (energy-field) is a Living Force, changing according to the energy levels of the leader and the combined force-fields of the group members.

A positive energy-field generates more positive energy. A negative force is strengthened by group negativity. Be always positive.

Create order out of chaos before commencing the Great Work.

A good leader has a large Vision of the Plan for Human Evolution and is able to inspire others to seek out their own part in that Plan.

Encourage in people their talents and skills, so that the positive aspects of their personalities may grow, because this will build the Evolutionary Forces within them.

True Transformation is an energy exchange, not simply an exchange of ideas and words.

You can transform another person only after you, yourself, have undergone a Transformation to a higher level of Reality.

By the strength of your Light you can heal others. Just by your presence, you can make them Whole.

Ultimate Healing is the downpour of Energy from the Infinite Being through the auric-field of the healer into the auric-field of the receiver. This transforms lives permanently.

Living Guidance 339
The Aquarian Teachers 1147
The True Teachers 1694
The Zen Master according to Lao Tzu 780

The Stages of the Work

1. The energy of the Self manifests outwardly on the Physical Plane. The Self becomes identified with the coverings (bodies) and the outside environment. Service is to the personality, to material well-being.
2. An adjustment period wherein karmas are worked out. The Self is identified neither entirely with the outside, nor entirely with Itself. This is a period of troubles, struggle, opposites, duality, turmoil and strife. Attempts are made at consciousness-transference to the Self (through meditation). Transmutative forces are generated in the personality.
3. Consciousness is centred in the Self. One's energy is centred in the Self. The Self is realized to be different from the personality. Conscious efforts are made towards group-service and world-service. Spiritual Life. Self-Realization.
4. Identification with the Monad. Life-Divine. Cosmic Service.

The Self is realized to be different from the personality

The Seven Centres of Force in the Human Species

1. The survival instinct, the fight-or-flight response, physicality, body-consciousness.
2. Sensualism of every kind, from eating to sexual attraction. Tastes of all descriptions, whether of food, clothing, people, objects or whatever, refined or gross.
3. Ego drives, control drives, power drives, ego-mania, self-centredness, power-tripping, control of others, manipulation of people.

The above constitute the three lower centres, active in *Common* Man.

4. Universal Love, Compassion towards all beings and creatures, an open Heart, true sensitivity to the needs of others, altruism.
5. Inspiration, Creativity, pure Devotion, true Art, an open mind, being on the Quest for Knowledge and Truth.

These two centres are the energy expressions of *Evolving* Man.

6. Insight, genuine Wisdom, Self-Realization, advanced Knowledge, Inner Illumination, the Wisdom-Eye.
7. The Crown of Glory, Enlightenment, Absolute Unity, Divinity.

These two centres constitute the energies and forces of *Perfected* Man.

The Three Stages of Yoga 528
Meditation is Integration 1193
Development of the Spiritual Warrior 971
The Heart and the Energy Centres 1332

Silence, Solitude, Peace

Meditation begins when the mind has attained the State of Silence

Begin with Silence (MAUNA).

Silence first.

Begin all activities from Silence first, for Silence is the source of Intelligence and Creativity. In Silence the mind rests, and from Rest comes Wisdom and Insight.

Orderly activity comes from Silence.

You can still your mind through Silence and Solitude.

The Way of Silence and Solitude is a necessary step towards Self-Realization and the attainment of Divinity.

Find times for Serenity and Solitude amidst the hustle and bustle of your life.

Silence is Peace. Silence is Joy. Silence is Unity.

In Silence, psychological transformations take place and the Awakened Mind becomes filled with Light.

Silence and quietness are necessary for success in Contemplation.

Meditation begins when the mind has attained the State of Silence (MAUNA).

MAUNA is the Eternal Silence of God which envelops Super-Space, Inter-Cosmic Space, Inner Space, like a vast cloak or blanket.

Be Alone with God.

Alone with God 700
Zen Silence 790
The Stages of Sūfī Silence 901
From Action into Stillness, From Stillness into Action 1016
Solitude and Loneliness 1170
Suspended Mind 1209
The Silence of the Deep 1355
The Practice of Silence 1443

How do you Know who You really Are?

How many philosophers have "speculated" about this question? How many psychologists have "theorized" about it? Can you *really know* yourself by intellectual exercises? No!

Enter the domain of the Heart and you shall surely Know the Immeasurable Eternal that you are.

It is the Spirit that awakens the Spirit within you

Ye-Shu-Āh, the Jesus within the Heart, is the Living Flame of Love.

The Master-in-the-Heart is the One Universal Self or Presence, which is the *same* for All. When you first Realize it, you will feel that *you* are God, that everybody and everything is *in you*. But the *same* feeling comes over *all* who Realize.

Life, in its Essence, is vast and boundless, and you are a Flower of Life, beautiful and eternal.

If you believe yourself to be small, limited, weak, powerless, the victim of fate, people and circumstances, then you are merely identifying your Consciousness with your physical body and your personality. You are not paying attention to the Immortal Glory that you are, beyond the false mask of ego and self.

Are you dedicated firmly to the Eternal within you? Is it the pivot of your life, upon which all else revolves?

In the midst of the battle of Life, the struggle of Life, do you forget your Self that forever shines within you with an undiminished Light?

In your day-to-day battles, do you stop and pause and *sense* around you the Eternal?

It is the Spirit that awakens the Spirit within you. This is the real Awakening, for you become Alive inside yourself as never before.

The Experience of the Heart 1280
The Saviour in the Heart 1296
The Gnostic Teachings 1108
Christ-Consciousness 443
The One and Only 839
Attach your Mind to the Eternal 1234

The Silent Watcher Meditation

Who is your Self? What is your Self?

The self is your personality. The Self is the Spirit within you.

All limitations are self-created. All Freedom is in the Self.

The source of your sense of Eternal Freedom is the Spirit that you are

- Sit still. Focus in the Third-Eye. No mantra is used, no images.
- Pure Consciousness is your Self. You are Consciousness Itself. You are not limited to your body and mind, but are Absolute Awareness Itself.
- The source of your personal sense of "I" is your mind. The source of your sense of Eternal Freedom is the Spirit that you are.
- Watch, observe silently, what Is, without denying or accepting what appears to your Consciousness. Only be Aware of it, whether what appears to you is good, bad or indifferent.
- You do not have to *do* anything. Just be Aware.

What do you *know* about yourself?
What do you *know* about your Self?

What is it just to Be?
What is it to Do, to Create, to Become?

To *Be* is the Feminine polarity within you.
To *Do* (to be active) is the Masculine polarity.

Do you *know* the difference?

Shikantaza 800
Vipaśyanā Yoga 1222
Awareness Meditation 1656
Thinking and Being 233
Understand your Predicament 892
Quest for the Self 1317

Your personal sense of self is a mystery. It is an image in your mind. It is a vast thoughtform which keeps you bound to the Physical, Astral and Mental Worlds—the Three Worlds of the cyclic reincarnation process. This "personal image" holds your Soul as a prisoner in the lower worlds. The mystery is how you, the Formless Spirit, identify with the forms (bodies) you possess.

Your sense of personality disappears in the Light of your Soul when your Heart is fully Illumined. The Key to it is *Transcending*.

Know Thyself

The Self that is you is the Self that is the All.

This is the clear message of the Upaniṣads and of the Bhagavad-Gītā. It is not some ancient philosophy, however, but your own daily experience. Try it. Live it.

The Path of Union is the conscious discovery of the Self, what you really Are. As the Gnostics of old said: GNOSTI SEAUTON, "Know Thyself". That is, know the *totality* that you are. Know that you are the World.

Your experience of life is simply according to your Knowledge and your Love

Meditation is a way to become conscious and more conscious, until you become consciously Immortal. To become consciously Immortal you must learn to be conscious of the Great Invisible. All the dimensions of Space meet in the dimensions of *You.* All the forces of the Universe flow through *You.* All the times of past, present and future are but *Your* times, in the Eternal Now.

You move about in a multi-dimensional World. This is the *Kingdom* that Israel's Sages spoke about. This is the *Holy Ground* spoken of in the Old Testament. You are not limited to your physical body and your lower, rational mind, your pride. You are also a Mind (KĀRAṆA-MANAS), and a Soul (BUDDHI), and Spirit (ĀTMĀ). Let not your material body fool you. Let it not limit your Consciousness. Mind is limitless; bodies or forms have limits. Mind is eternal and infinite; forms come and go. Your body is only an object, a thing, and objects come and go. But *You*—Mind, Soul and Spirit—remain.

You were born with a body, but soon you will have to leave it behind. All the objects you have gathered around you, you will have to leave them behind. Then only *You* will remain—the Spirit, Soul, Mind.

What Knowledge (GNOSIS) you have gathered, what Love (AGAPE) you have expressed, only that can you take with you.

Think! The rest remains.

The You grows by Knowledge and Love. Knowledge gathered and Love expressed. Think!

Your dignity in life is simply the dignity of your Knowledge and Love. Your stature is simply your stature in Knowledge and Love. Your experience of life is simply according to your Knowledge and your Love. This is the sum of it all.

Self-Knowledge 324
Know Yourself 604
The Individuality 34
Regain what you have Lost 381
The Upaniṣadic Mantrams 546
The Essence of Wisdom 1680

You Are the World

Each person is solely responsible for how they experience the World. The World, for you, is according to your mind. You *are* the World.

This may not appear to be so, but upon careful reflection and thought you will see the truth of it.

Your mind is one with the All-Mind

By "the World" I mean not only the physical universe that you see with your physical eyes, but the All-in-All, the Totality, THAT. The World includes the Physical Plane and all the other planes and realms of the All-Mind. Likewise, in the Bible, the "world" means *all* of Creation, visible and invisible.

Krishnamurti, that great Teacher of *Insight* into the mind, also taught this, as did the Vedas, the Upaniṣads, the Bhagavad-Gītā, the ancient Ṛṣis of the Yogavasiṣṭha, the Sages of Yoga, the Munis and all the Masters.

You *are* the World. You perceive things according to your mind and you *create* your World according to your mind.

Your mind is one with the All-Mind. Everybody's mind is one with the One Mind. Thus, there is a continual interaction between the One Mind of God—the Universal Mind—and the many individual minds. And through the Universal Substance of the One Mind there is a continuous interconnectedness between all the many minds.

You are the trees, the plants and the virgin forests.

You are the silver clouds and the blazing sunshine.

You are the lakes and rivers and the stormy seas.

You are the snow and the stars in space.

You are the child who cries in the night.

And you are the substance of all things unseen.

Your little being is continuous with the beings of all others, and each little being is continuous with the One Life.

You are the colours on the butterfly's wings, and you are the dewdrops falling from the sky.

You are the whisper of angels' wings and the thought-patterns of the Infinite Mind.

You are all things, and all things to all men. Life visible and invisible, you are the All.

The Infinite Supply

The Infinite Supply (the World) gives you all experience according to your mind. The Buddhists called this "Infinite Supply" the ALAYA-VIJÑĀNA, or Storehouse Consciousness, because all your experience comes from it, according to your mind.

Realms of the One Mind 492

The Most Excellent Yoga 525

This is what it means to say, "You are the World." You are the All. The Whole of Reality is always present, all of the time. The Great Invisible is just as close to you as the nearest tree or branch, but you choose to focus on limited awareness.

To the degree that you focus on the Great Invisible, to that degree will your experience of life change.

The totality of You is greater than your body-brain-mind can imagine

The totality of the Universe (the Whole, the World) is greater than what you see with your physical eyes, and it is surrounding you always. All the Planes of Being are simultaneously existent, everywhere, all of the time, and invisible hosts of beings surround you on the invisible planes, like fish encompassed by the ocean. SAṀSĀRA (painful existence) is coexistent in Space with NIRVĀṆA (Beatific Bliss), and between them are all the shades of dimensions, from pains to joys, hells to heavens, all simultaneously in the One Mind.

The totality of You is greater than your body-brain-mind can imagine. The vastness of your Mind, the splendour of your Soul and the Brilliance of the Father within you cannot be understood by the brain-mind. You are always your totality—body, Mind, Soul and Spirit—but you choose to focus in body-life only. You can choose to focus in your Mind, and then a new pattern of life will open up for you. You can even choose to focus on the Soul levels of Life. That is *radical* change. Then there is communion with the Spirit.

Wherever you focus your attention, your awareness, that is what you experience. Thus, if you want It, you can experience Infinitude.

Wherever you focus your attention, there you are.

The Purpose of Meditation

The *meaning* of your life is the *experiencing* of your life, and your experience depends on your mind. Change your thoughts and you change your experience of life, and your life will have new meaning.

Consciousness is what you are experiencing, and what you are experiencing is what you are conscious of. To be conscious elsewhere, you will have to shift the energy-patterns in your mind. This is the purpose of meditation.

The Science of Meditation 1173

The One 1686
The Divine Unity 852
Perceptions of the One Mind 490
No-Mind and the One Mind 763
The Way of Spontaneous Meditation 1229

To Love God and the World

It is your Self that you are experiencing all the days of your life. This is the sublime teaching of Christianity, the beautiful message of the Christ, the life story of Jesus. This is what the New Testament is all about. We are all One. We are the One Mind. We are the World. Jesus loved the World because He loved God. They are the same. God *is* the World.

The World is like a body or garment of God

Understand this: I do not say there is no God. I say that God *Is*, and I say that the World is like a body or garment of God. God is first, last and forever, while the World is here, now, and comes to pass.

How could I express it to you? If you love the World, you love God also. The two cannot be separated. When you are in your body, you appear to others as that body. When God is in His body—the World—He appears as the World. God *is* the World, and the World *is* God. This is also the realization of the Sages of India, but it was left to Jesus to transform that realization into practical Love.

Every man, woman and child you meet in your life is your Self, as is every tree, plant and blade of grass. To realize this in profound meditation is only half the story—the story of the East. Its expression in loving Service to the All is the glory of Jesus and the Western Consciousness.

The great Buddhas, Ṛṣis, Yogīs and Masters of India did nothing to alleviate suffering. They merely taught their pupils how to *escape* from suffering (SAṀSĀRA) by raising themselves to Higher Consciousness, to BUDDHI and NIRVĀṆA. But Jesus was concerned also with SAṀSĀRA, with the World, and how to improve the quality of living for all sentient beings. This is *practical* Love. For is not the World the Body of God? And if so, is it not One with God? And thus, is it not our duty

God's Fools

To approach the purely Spiritual Worlds, the Buddhic and Nirvāṇic Planes, you must proceed slowly, step by step, *abstracting* yourself. Otherwise you will become deranged or spiritually insane, like the MASTĀNAḤ and AVADHŪTA of India, who behave insanely, irrationally, outrageously, with total loss of control over their bodies, emotions and minds. They are called "God's fools". They are but failures on the Spiritual Path.

God-Consciousness is the Wholeness of Life 504

Warrior Jesus 908
Return to Duty 812
The Supreme Act of Karma 264
The World exists for the sake of the Self 544

to love the World? And, if we love the World (the Creation), is it not our duty to help it become the Divine Perfection, according to the Divine Will? This is the true meaning of Christian charity.

You are the World because you are a Child of God. This is why the early Christians said that Jesus was both the *Son of Man* and the *Son of God*. Yet every one of us is the Son of Man and the Son of God—not only Jesus. This may not be the belief of church-Christianity, but it is the Revelation of true Christianity, since Jesus also taught it.

You are the World because you are a Child of God

The Infinite and Eternal is around you and in you, always and everywhere. You limit yourself by your own *idea* of yourself and your mistaken attachment to a limited body and a limited mind. Your little ego thinks it is in charge of everything; thus you create a narrow, self-limiting life and are full of self-inflicted pains. While you function as a limited self, you cannot know your Self, which is the World.

Egotism is simply not being aware that you are the World. When you know through meditation that you are the World, that you are the Whole, then the ego drops of its own accord and dies a natural death. Then you become Limitless. You are the World and everything that is in it.

> I have said, Ye *are* gods, and all of you *are* children of the most High.
>
> *Psalms 82:6*

Holiness to the Lord

The Jewish Kabbalists have said:

Whatsoever you touch, this is Holy Ground. For it is the garment of SHEKINAH, the Divine Presence.

The Jews of olden days, in the Temple that was destroyed, had an expression: "Holiness to the Lord". This means that everything is Holy, because everything is the garment of God. If you want to understand the true significance of the Jewish, Christian and Muslim religions, this is it. "Holiness to the Lord" is also the keynote of the old and true Masonic Tradition—the Lost Word. It means that your life becomes Holy in Service, Devotion and Love for your God, and that you constantly *realize* that God is Holy and above all imperfections. It means that you realize the Divine Presence in your life—the SHEKINAH (Hebrew), the ŚAKTI (Sanskrit), the SPIRITUS SANCTUS (Latin), the Holy Spirit.

The Way of Holiness 1335

Children of the Sun 1590
Jesus Christ, Son of Man 668
To Become a True Renunciate 257
The Law of the Higher Life 1134

The Lighted Way

What is the Way of Light? It is the registering in your Consciousness of God as the Light of the World.

The Way of Light is the Mystical Vision of God, or the Soul, or the Universe. This Light is concentrated in the Third-Eye, glorified in the Crown Centre, and may be seen as the Light of Life in the Heart Centre. In the Heart Centre it also appears as the Light of Love.

The Brightness of the Eternal shines through us even now

Divine Light is Divine Consciousness and Divine Energy. Thus, true Light is Life, Consciousness, Energy and Bliss. There is also a Light of Knowledge and Understanding which guides all advanced Souls.

Most aspirants do not know that the true Path begins only *after* you have found the Light *within* yourself. That Light illumines your mind and fills it with Revelation.

When you have found the Light-Kingdom within yourself, the desire to help others becomes spontaneous. The urge to serve, to help others, shows an active, awakened Heart Centre. Live in the world, serve in the world, but cut yourself away from worldly consciousness.

The Brightness of the Eternal shines through us even now. This Imperishable Light is your own true Nature, your Self, which is of God. This Light is Holy, and we are vessels or containers of this Sacred Essence. This is the majesty and dignity of the human species. We are all Light-carriers.

Remember *what* you are. You will become Divine when you fully integrate yourself with that Light.

Mystical Illumination is when the Light shines within yourself. The mind reflects the Soul Light. The Soul reflects the Light of God.

When your mind is illumined by the Light of your Soul, you are safely on the true Path. Then the Brilliance of God's True Light will re-create you according to your Eternal Destiny.

Brahmājyoti (God's Light) is the Divine Effulgence, the Brightness of the Divine Glory, the Ocean of Ineffable Light, the Brightness and Splendour of God's Mind. The Light of God is a Dazzling Brightness, most brilliant, most beautiful, eternal, not subject to change. Whereas all forms in Creation, visible and invisible, will perish, dissolve, be transformed, the Light of God is eternal in its Existence. Nothing exists that is superior to God.

The Yogī, Mystic or Saint who beholds this Vision becomes Deified.

The Light of the Soul, when you perceive it within yourself, is a Healing Beam. It shows you the fundamental Mystery that you are. It dissipates ignorance and glamour and rearranges your inner psyche to reflect the Eternal Reality.

The Light of the Soul is like the beams of a lighthouse, cast over the Ocean of Existence to guide you safely to the Eternal Shore.

Light is the Will, Plan and Purpose of God

All Revelation comes through the Light. This Revelation may be called the Christ, Buddha, Kṛṣṇa, Allāh or Moses Principle. The Messenger is flooded with Light and in that Light he or she Understands, but then the mind interprets and distorts and limits the message.

Light is the Will, Plan and Purpose of God. In the Light all is Known, all is Revealed, all is Understood. All Mysteries are gone. It is the Alpha and the Omega, the Beginning and the End. It is God.

The higher dimensions are Worlds of Light. The Light Rules. Nirvāṇa is just an Ocean of Light and the Beings there are Light-Sentient Existences.

When you *see* the whole Universe as Light, when Light permeates every form, when behind all bodies you see Light bodies, when you see the Source of All as Light, then you are walking upon the Lighted Way.

Look for the Light

Withdraw your attention from your body, mind, emotions and worldly environment, and focus in the Third-Eye, in Silence. Eventually the Light of your Soul will appear there. You must wait *patiently*, sitting in the Third-Eye Centre, for the Light to appear by Itself, no matter how long it takes—days, months or years.

Your Eternal Liberation does not depend on Time. There is no time limit to how long you should meditate for your Enlightenment. It comes in its own time and place; you just need to surrender and work patiently.

See the Light of the Logos 1650

Light 978
The Path of Light 89
The Path of Illumination 1338
The Self-Generating Light 1594
Satori: the Experience of Illumination 816
Meditation in the Third-Eye 1224

The Presence of God

God is within and God is without. God is everywhere, all around. God is in all moving beings and in all unmoving things.

God is seen by the Inner Eye as both very near and very far. God is undivided yet appears as the Many, as if divided into all beings.

God is the sublime Mystery of all Mysteries

God is One.

The full Glory of God cannot be perceived by the physical senses. God is a Person (a Self-Conscious Being) so vast that It is beyond comprehension.

God is an immeasurable, ineffable, inexpressible Boundless Being of Light, a Supreme Being, majestic beyond compare, an Infinite Circle of Consciousness, beyond and above Creation and yet within the All.

YAHWEH (Hebrew) means "the Eternal", and EHEYEH means "I Am Who I Am". God is not subject to an Origination, nor to a Destruction. God's Divine Substance or Essence is Imperishable.

God forever Is.

God has no Origin, but all things originate *in* God. God has no End, but all things end *in* God.

Creation comes into being *in* God, yet God remains also outside of all that is.

God is the sublime Mystery of all Mysteries. God is the first form of Creation and is Creation's last shape, yet God remains untouched by the All.

God is the Immanent Presence in all things, and God is also the Transcendent.

Qualities of the Divine Being 107
The One God of All Religions 110
God Immanent and Transcendent 111
The Way, the Truth and the Life 670

The Vast Supreme Absolute becomes the Vast Fathomless Universe and yet remains the Vast Supreme Absolute. For God is in everyone and everything, even a blade of grass.

God is Boundless Light penetrating everywhere.

All this takes place within God

God is Formless and Nameless, yet all forms and names are manifestations of God.

The sacred Scriptures and the writings of the Saints are an outer physical sign of the Reality of God. It is not the Scriptures themselves that matter, but what they visibly represent: the *Everlasting*.

God is the Source and Substance of all things.

Parabrahman (the Supreme Godhead, the Absolute, the non-material Spiritual-Unity-Consciousness), acting within and upon Itself, gave rise to the invisible and visible universes.

Brahman (the Godhead) is all this.

All this takes place *within* God. As the fish are in the sea and birds are in the air, so all beings are in God.

Brahman exists simultaneously with Its manifestation, the Universe, spontaneously, everywhere.

The Eyes of God are everywhere.

The Presence of God is everywhere. We only need to *pass beyond ourselves* to find God.

God dwells in the Good.

The Primordial Good is in everyone.

The Manifested-God 1589
The Transcendental Godhead 112
The Omnipresent God 1108
Remember the Presence 1653

To Realize the Presence of God…

Desire God that you may swim in the Ocean of Love

God is Realized by Self-Awakening.

The Holy Way is to transcend your ego.

God is an egoless Experience, beyond body and mind.

You have to learn to break yourself Free from the bondage of your ego by going beyond your sense of body and mind.

When you experience God, so-called "space-and-time" (a construct of the lower mind) disappears.

God is Realized only by transcending your normal personality sense of "I". And how are you going to do that? By selfless Service, selfless chanting, and selfless meditation or prayer.

The Grace of God is with you even before you realize it. Even the *desire to know* God is already a manifestation of God's Grace.

Desire not God in order to escape the weariness of life or toil and troubles, for that is selfish Love of God. Desire God that you may swim in the Ocean of Love and share Its Blessings abundantly with all around you.

We are within God, even Now. *Rest* in God. ≉

The Lover of God 853
The Meaning of Life is Love 633
Practising the Presence of God 711
To Become a Jīvanmukta in this Lifetime 259

CHAPTER 59

Time and Eternity Action and Destiny

Past, Present and Future

Time the Past is infinite. Time the Future is infinite. The Universe is formed, dissolved and re-formed in an endless succession. But Eternity Is.

The Future is ours to create, Now

Time is Rhythm. There are rhythmic tides of ebb and flow in the material dimensions of the Universe; there are also psychic or subtler rhythms; and there are infinite Spiritual Tides of Eternity.

When the limitless numbers of self-conscious units in the vast Universe will function as One, in infinite complexity yet utter *simplicity*, this Creation will achieve Perfection for this MAHĀMANVANTARA (Great Age or measureless Cycle of Time), and the MAHĀPRALAYA (the Great Dissolution, or disappearance of the Universe) will begin.

Time past is infinite. Time future is infinite. The Universe comes and goes in an infinite series of successions, and so do You.

Memories fade away with the Cycles of Time.

Keep your attention focused in the Present, in the Here and Now. Don't get lost in past memories, wounds and pains, nor in future hopes, imaginings and fears.

It is *That* which is before you *Now.*

We are all shaped by our Past, defined by our Past, but the Future is ours to create, *Now.*

The Past has only as much influence upon you as you allow it to have.

Just sit *still* and *feel* the Silence, *Now.*

Accepting your condition is accepting how things are for you *Now.* In this *acceptance* there is Inner Freedom.

The Sense of Time 22
The Creation of the Universe 166
The Law of Cyclic Activity 248
Intelligent Use of Free Will 297
The Principle of Choice 1380
The Kingdom is at Hand 1453

Make every Moment positive. Every Moment you have a *choice* to be positive or negative. Choose to be positive.

Being simply in the Moment is not to seek for something else, but just to experience What Is. Not seeking to escape from It, nor dwelling in the Past, nor wishing for the Future, but simply experiencing *Now,* as it Is. The worldly-minded do not understand this Principle.

Make yourself free from the Past, Now

Victim-consciousness is completely unnecessary. You need not cling to past hurts or memories, for you have the power of Choice, moment by moment. Make yourself *free* from the Past, *Now.*

If you get *stuck* on the idea that you have been victimized by someone in the Past, that you have been hurt, that your life has been ruined, this evil thought-feeling will generate for you endless negative circumstances and experiences, Now and in your Future. Change your attitude to the Openness of Life.

People who live in the Past feel nostalgia for the good times they had, and guilt, shame or anger for the evil times. People who live in the Future are full of expectations for good things to come and full of fears and worries about what evil might befall them. Have Faith. Be fully in the *Present.*

Just Be in the Moment. Stay in the Moment. Flow with the Moment.

To live in the Present is to be without anxiety for the Future.

The world changes, so must you.

Live day by day in the Strength of the Lord.

Why do people find it difficult to leave the Past behind? Why do they cling to it, hang onto it, clasp it tight? Why do they become so *attached* to past sufferings (real or imagined)?

It gives them a sense of *identity,* a label, a designation, a category, a means by which they can explain away all the misfortunes in their lives. They like to consider themselves "victims" or "survivors" so they do not have to *choose* in the Moment and be responsible for their lives.

Unless you let go of your past hurts, problems and mistakes (physical, emotional or mental), the door to your Future remains tightly shut.

Let Go of the Past 1241

Action (Karma)

Karma is Corrective Action by the Universe

Yoga Karmasu Kauśalam
Yoga is skill in action.
In the State of Oneness all actions are skilfully executed.
Correct actions spring from the State of Union.
First seek Union before acting.

Yoga: Union.
Karmasu: actions.
Kauśalam: art or skill.

∞

Universal Karma is the self-corrective experience of the Universe. Thus, all Laws are balanced out in the Cosmos.

Karma is a complex system of intersecting, interacting energies and forces administered by the Universal Mind and, within It, the hosts of Karmic Angels, the Agents of Karmic Law.

Karma is Corrective Action by the Universe.

For every act of destruction in your life there is an act of reconstruction. This is the Law of Karma or natural re-adjustment.

Karma, as Retributive Justice, operates not only on the Physical Plane, but on the Astral (emotional) Plane as well. On the Mental Plane, Karma is resolved by thought power.

Karma is multi-dimensional—physical, astral and mental—affecting the body, mind and emotions equally.

For every physical action there is a karma. For every feeling there is a karma. For every thought there is a karma.

Karma is both good and bad, pleasant and unpleasant. It is a totally impersonal Law.

Karma: the Law of Action 240
Creating Karma 242
The Law of Action 992

While your Soul is in the state of embodiment, it is subject to Karma. Thus, while you live on the Physical, Astral and Mental Planes, you are subjected to the Law of Karma, and there are no exceptions for anybody.

Every event in your life is the result of your Karma, good or evil.

Your whole life is a karmic process

Your Karma did not begin with your present birth. You have inherited your Karma from past lives. If you do not learn the lessons of your Karma in this life, you will be forced to repeat them in another life.

The source of the painful situations in your life is Karma on the level of your personality. The causes are inherently *within* yourself. This fact applies also to a family, a group of people, a race, a tribe, a nation and the whole planet. Think this through.

Karma is reactions in the Present to actions in the Past. And actions in the Present create reactions in the Future.

Every so-called accident, misfortune or disaster that happens to you, to your family, group or nation, or to the planet, can be traced back to some previous wrong actions, either in this lifetime or in other lives.

It is Man who creates the causes; Karma creates the effects.

Nothing can happen to you that is not allowed by your Karma, or the Karma of your family, group, nation or religion, or the World-Karma of Humanity.

Your whole life is a *karmic process*. Have faith in it. The circumstances in which you find yourself in your life are *karmic necessities.*

What you are experiencing in this lifetime is compulsory Karma, that portion of your total Karma which is apportioned for you to work out in this life-cycle.

The Wheels of Justice (Karma) turn slowly, but sometimes the effect is instantaneous.

Types of Karma 243
The Wheel of the Law 247
Destiny and the Permanent Atoms 250

Suitable people are drawn together to become agents or adjusters of each other's Karma. It is never only one person's Karma, but the Karma of both.

Face your Karma with Wisdom. Turn it into a catalyst for Spiritual Unfoldment and Transformation.

Nemesis
Greek: The Goddess of retribution, vengeance, punishment, Karma.

If you can learn Wisdom, all pain, suffering and limitation caused by Karma is educative to your Consciousness.

What you experience is always appropriate to the Karma you are working through. Every experience will teach you a lesson. Be Awake to the Wisdom you are being taught by Karma.

Your *nemesis* is your own mind.

If you get *stuck* with guilt, remorse, fear, anger and sorrow for past events, this will create a further cycle of negative Karma for you.

Look upon difficult circumstances ("bad" Karma) as a great Blessing, as a chance to practise your Spiritual Path more intensely, as a chance for your Soul to take greater notice of your personality.

A "bad" karma in your life can be turned into a good karma if you learn the inner meaning of it all. All events can be instructive.

Handle your allowed Karma, no matter how hard it seems.

If you have placed yourself intelligently on the Path of Spiritual Evolution and the purposeful Spiritual Life, you will not be given insurmountable Karma, for Grace will be with you also.

Effort is rewarded with good Karma. To succeed, try again and again.

To lead a virtuous life you must train your mind to have an intense *Faith*. Even so, your past Karma will intervene, bringing you conflicts and troubles.

Disease and Karma 1169
To Succeed in your Quest 1330
Karmic Adjustment 1379

The price of behaviour is karmic backlash which is often out of all proportion to the original acts. This is due to the tendency for extreme reactions by the worldly consciousness.

Sometimes you have to bear unpleasant things necessitated by Karma (karmic necessities), but you do not have to be overcome by them.

Action that is free from attachment and ego is Karma Yoga

The spider is not entangled in its own web. Do not become entangled in the web of your own Karma. Within yourself, remain *Free.*

Understand the causes of your own sufferings (Karma, the endurance of it and the freedom from it) by embracing Universal Compassion for yourself and for all human beings on this planet.

We are all entangled in the Planetary Web of Karma in some way, and only by living the Way of Compassion can we save the planet.

Those karmas which have already been precipitated onto the Physical Plane have to be completed, no matter what. Endure them with Wisdom and Dignity.

Once you have set them into motion, your Inner God (ĀTMAN) has no power to stop your karmas.

The Third-Eye Centre is connected with the working out of your Karma. You can *modify* your Karma by mental direction and intention, but to *overcome* it you have to *transcend* to the Higher Planes.

In Super-Vision, or Higher Consciousness, you see the karmic patterns underlying everything, in the Past, Present and Future.

When the observing of all activities (Karma) by the Inner-Witness Consciousness has ceased, only the Self (ĀTMĀ) remains. That is, you alone *are.*

Action (Karma) is Duty (Dharma). You always have to act. Action that is free from attachment and ego, without seeking self-rewards or fruits therefrom, is KARMA YOGA.

Success is Born of Action 256
Action and the Spiritual Warrior 994
Karma Yoga: Divine Union by Action 1132
Heart Action 1331

Perfect action (Karma) can only be done in God-Consciousness, where you no longer enjoy or suffer the fruits of your actions (Karma).

In God-Consciousness (BRAHMA-VIDYĀ) you do not work to satisfy some personal whim or desire, but your actions (Karma) are for the benefit of All.

Karma is an impersonal energy-balancing by the Cosmos

A good deed (karma) erases a bad deed (karma). Therefore, be full of good deeds so that, on the Day of your Judgment in the afterlife, your good deeds shall speak louder for you.

The world remembers only your evil deeds, but Heaven remembers also all your good deeds. Therefore, rejoice in Perfect Justice (Karma).

Karma is an impersonal energy-balancing by the Cosmos.

Karma is the immutable Law of the Cosmic Nature to re-establish Cosmic Harmony (SATTVA).

Karma is payback time.

Karma is settling your accounts.

Karma and the Guṇas

All actions (Karma), and their after-effects or reactions, are done by the three qualities (GUṆAS) of Nature (PRĀKṚTĪ).

The GUṆAS (qualities, properties, types) of matter and energy are:

SATTVA: That which vibrates to harmony, rhythm, balance, goodness, Truth, Purity, Light. SATTVA is the force of *equilibrium*.

RAJAS: That which vibrates with great passion, force, activity, violence or discord. RAJAS is the force of *mobility*.

TAMAS: That which vibrates with inertia, ignorance, slowness, stupidity, darkness. TAMAS is the force of *passivity, steadiness*.

All actions (Karma) partake of these in different proportions.

The Three Forces at work in Nature and in Humanity 1693

Karma and your Spiritual Development 255
To Become a Jīvanmukta in this Lifetime 259
The Law of the Higher Life 1134
Notes on the Path in the New Age 1166
Karma and Death (Metanoia) 1425

Destiny (Dharma)

Sarvārthādharma

Sarva: all, everything.
Ārtha: purposes, means, pursuits, objects, goals.
Dharma: the Ultimate Truth, the Way, the Law, seeing Reality as it is, Destiny, spiritual practices, the Spiritual Path or Way.

In all situations, how things are for you is your Destiny

Thus, Sarvārthādharma means:

- Understand that in all ways, at all times, in all situations, how things are for you is your Destiny.
- Make all situations in your life part of your Journey towards the Absolute—sickness and health, success and failure, suffering and happiness, poverty and riches, praise and criticism, life and death. *Accept* all these things as part of your Way to the Absolute (Dharma).

Paramārthādharma

Param: transcendental, supreme, beyond, above.
Ārtha: ways, means.
Dharma: the Truth, the right way to be.

Thus, Paramārthādharma means:

- When you reach the Supreme Goal of Truth, the Ultimate Reality, the Absolute, Nirvāṇa, Eternal Freedom in Absolute Consciousness having been established in you, you walk the Way of Absolute Reality (Dharma).

Dharma: the Law of Being 244
Your Fate is Before your Eyes 246
The Chain of Dharma 247
Quest for Reality 1178
Action and Destiny (Metanoia) 1420

Dharma

Dharma is the Force of Righteous Expression on all levels of the Cosmos, the natural and the supra-natural.

Dharma is the true inherent nature of a thing

Dharma, the Force of Righteous Action, is an invincible force of Nature (PRĀKṚTĪ). It contains all the physical Laws of Nature, as well as the Laws of the Invisible Worlds. Dharma propels physical, psychic and spiritual Evolution and is the basic force of all Life-into-expression.

Dharma is the spiritual, psychic and physical Laws that pervade every level of Creation—the Rules of Cosmic Intelligence, RĀṀ.

Perfect Law and Order (Dharma) rules the Cosmos on all the higher Planes of Being. This might not *appear* to be the case on the Physical Plane of this planet.

There is a great power in Righteousness (Dharma).

Dharma is the true inherent nature or vibration of a thing, whether of an atom, a molecule, a stone, a plant, a tree, an animal, a human being, an angel, a planet, a sun or a galaxy. This Natural Law or vibration is its keynote or Destiny. Thus you have your own true Dharma also.

The Law of your Being 976
Primordial Balance 995
Between the Two Extremes, Find the Middle Point 1100
The Path of Self-Actualization 1110
Vipaśyanā Yoga: Internal Observation 1222

Be who you are Now

Just *being who you are Now* is to not worry about your self-image, your ego, or what others think of you. Observe how you *are* in this Moment, without trying to be somebody else, and simply acknowledge your fears and hurts, pains and desires, or your memories, or whatever else is going on inside you. Acknowledge this, not with your ordinary mind, but on the level of Silence, in the Source-Mind within you. Then comes Transcendental Peace within yourself.

Being-in-the-Moment Meditation in the Head 1245

Be in control of your own Destiny (Dharma). This is to be done not only in the larger Plan of your life, but moment by moment.

Take responsibility for your life. Do not allow others to control it. Follow your own Destiny (Dharma).

Each situation has its own Dharma (Righteous Action) within it.

Each situation has its own Dharma within it

To live in the Perfect Order of the Universe (Dharma) is Freedom.

The Force of Dharma is strong in you when you can maintain an internal stability in your auric-field despite outer chaotic environments and painful or stressful situations.

Responsibility (Dharma) means doing what is appropriate in the situation you are faced with.

Do what is the *right thing to do* in your situation. This is Dharma.

Obey the Law (Dharma) of the situation you are in.

True Morality (Dharma) comes not by learned practices but by Inner Transformation.

Do your Duty (Dharma), but do not get attached to the results of your actions.

The KURU-KṢETRA (the Battle-Field) is this relative world, this life, and the DHARMA-KṢETRA (the Absolute-Field, the Eternal Reality), is in this same Place also.

Righteous behaviour (Dharma) becomes possible only when Inner Contentment has been achieved through deep meditation.

Orderly action (Dharma) comes from Silence. Therefore, before you act, enter Silence.

Self-Worth 1382
Scenes of Battle 1158
From Action into Stillness, From Stillness into Action 1016
Silence, Solitude, Peace 1386
The Warrior of the Light 984
The Warrior Code 1077

CHAPTER 60

Metanoia
The Renaissance of the Mind

What is Metanoia?

Metanoia is the principle of becoming New by invoking the Soul-Power

The word METANOIA has been used for well over two thousand years. It is a profound ancient Greek word meaning "transforming the mind, a new way of thinking, renewing what is in your mind". It was used by many Greek Schools of spiritual development and also by the New Testament writers, in the sense that Metanoia is something that changes your life, something by which you make amends, something that changes your mind-set or mental structure, a change of Heart.

In the Western world the word METANOIA was used in the identical sense as the word MANTRA (MAN-TRA, an instrument of the mind) was used in the East. METANOIA can be translated into modern language as "the working of the Light-Force within you, mind-altering perception of Truth or Reality, Spiritual Insight, Magical Mind, a transformation of your Consciousness". It has two connotations:

a. You use a word (a divine sentence) which transforms your mind and hence brings about a revolution in your life.

b. You experience a transformation which, as a result, re-creates your mind and hence your life.

Metanoia is the technique which Saint Paul described as "being transformed by the renewing of your mind" *(Romans 12:6)*. The fundamentalists and evangelicals describe this principle as "being born again" or "being a born-again Christian", but they interpret this in an extremely narrow sense. The deeper significance of Metanoia or Mantra is "being transformed by the Living Light-Force". This is a universal principle applicable to every human being on this planet.

Metanoia is the principle of becoming New by invoking the Soul-Power, the Being of Light, by the right mind-set or attitude.

METANOIA is a compound old-Greek word derived from META and NOUS. META means "in, on, of, upon, unto, with, among, after, later, a change or a process leading to change", and NOUS means "mind, understanding, Heart, Spirit, Consciousness". META also means "above and beyond" or "transcendental". Thus, METANOIA can also mean "beyond the mind, above the mind, Transcendental Consciousness (or that which leads to it)". It can also mean "being with the Spirit, being in your Heart" and "the Renaissance of the Soul, a new Birth".

Repentance 683
Baptism and Rebirth 722
The Being of Light in Meditation 418
The Thought of Enlightenment 767
Mind and Thought 1376

Aspects of Metanoia

The Two Kinds of Metanoia

1. *a.* The Inner Voice, the Voice of Light, the Voice of God.
   b. The Divine Name as Sound-Vibration used for transformation.
2. Verbal structure, thought-constructs, thoughtforms.

Metanoia is not just "positive thinking". It is a mind-purification process. It is *thought* directed to invoke Soul-Force. It is an active thoughtform, a mind-channel, a channel created in the mental body into which the Soul-Force may pour.

The Voice of God 864
What is the Name? 1259
Vibration and Mantra 1518
The Power of Thought 232
True Thought 79

You are thinking all the time, but most of your thoughts are trivial and life-destroying rather than life-supporting. Metanoia is thinking True-Thoughts, thoughts of True-Life. These True-Thoughts gradually lift the darkness of ignorance from your mind and release the Power of your Soul into the personality.

The Three Degrees of Metanoia

1. The transformation of the mind by thought-power, which results in life-changes.
2. As a result of life-changes, the mind is flooded by the Light of Intuition, resulting in further life-changes.
3. As a result of these deeper life-changes, the Voice of the Spirit rearranges perception on the personality level, leading to Insight, Illumination, Higher Consciousness, Self-Realization and Mystical States of Consciousness.

Each movement upward in Spiritual Evolution (as distinct from the evolution of the physical organism) is simply movement into a higher rate of *vibration*. The subtle worlds differ only in their vibration. The Great Invisible is but a series of ever faster vibration-layers, or rings within rings, worlds within worlds. The Absolute vibrates so fast that it becomes the No-Vibration or Zero Point, which includes within it all vibrations.

To find peace of mind in an increasingly chaotic world becomes more difficult day by day. Yet, peace of mind we must have if Humanity is to survive on this planet.

This chapter deals with the integration of the Soul with the personality, and the integration of the various aspects of the personality itself (body, feelings and mind), while at the same time dealing with the day-to-day problems which beset those who live in the world.

This message is for everybody. If you "speed-read" this material it will be a waste of time. If you read it like a novel it will be of no benefit to you. But if you read it with the Spirit within you, and practise it, you will be liberated in this lifetime.

Spiritual Reading 1113

The Work of Metanoia

This Work of Metanoia (Transformation) is twofold:

- The Affirmation-Invocation processes and the intoning of the Divine Names.
- The Silent Work of various inner meditational processes.

Invocation of Metanoia is dynamic action

Invocation of Metanoia is a "tuning-up" or "tuning-in" device to enhance your personality vibration and the Consciousness-Quality within you. It is practised as follows:

a. Choose a Metanoia which you are attracted to in the moment and quietly "brood" over it, digest it in silence, work with it in the depths of your Being, or meditate upon it.

b. Keep your Metanoia sentence (or sentences) in your mind and repeat it aloud as many times as you wish, or repeat it mentally during the day. Work with it in your mind until you "get it", until you are transformed by it.

Monology 453
The Two Applications of Mantra 1219
Meditation is Integration 1193

Invocation of Metanoia is dynamic action. Meditation is passive action. The Work of Metanoia involves both kinds of action. This dual Work will result in the integration (Yoga) of the personality, and the integration (Yoga) of the personality with the Soul.

There are two kinds of thinking:

- In the logical mind: abstract, intellectual, unemotional, unfeeling.
- In the Heart Centre: full of feeling, realization, deep concern.

Metanoia is thinking with the Heart, or thinking *in* the Heart.
This is effective and will bear fruit.

As a man thinketh in his Heart, so he is.

Proverbs 23:7

If you "think" your Metanoia as some abstract, feelingless idea, you are wasting your time. If you use the logical mind, such as when you do mathematics, it will not bear fruit for Metanoia-thinking.

The Metanoia given in this chapter are *Thoughts of the Heart.* They are insights, intuitions, realizations of truths which came from the Heart, and thus should you use them also.

What you think, you become.
You become what is in your mind.
Therefore, it is important to have Holy Thoughts.

Yoga
Sanskrit: Integration, Union, At-One-Ment.
Yoga-Mārga 520

Being and Becoming

In this unique Science of Life we are dealing with two aspects of Reality simultaneously:

a. Personality life in the Three Worlds of *Becoming*—the Physical, Astral and Mental Planes.

b. Spiritual Life in the Worlds of *Being*—the Buddhic and Nirvāṇic Planes and the purely Divine Planes of Being above the Nirvāṇic Worlds of Light.

The merging of Being and Becoming is the future progress of Humanity

There are two pressures in Humanity:

a. In the World of Becoming, there is a need for people to be creative, progressive, evolving with the forces of Evolution towards happiness and greater fulfilment of life.

b. In the World of Being, human beings are yearning towards That which is Eternal—the Peaceful, Boundless, Limitless, Indestructible Reality.

The practice of the East was to *escape* from the personality life, to *disregard* the physical body, the physical environment, the physical evolutionary processes, and to escape into Self-Realization (Causal Consciousness) and Nirvāṇa. Thus, the unending *suffering* of Humanity remained unsolved. The Easterners thought they had solved the problem by not taking any notice of it!

While the East has dealt only with Being, the West has focused on personality life. The merging of the two is the *future progress* of Humanity. This is a unique revelation given out to the world *Now*.

Knowledge is diverse in the World of Becoming (the Relative Field). Knowledge is single in the World of Being (the Absolute Condition).

In the Relative World we learn about diverse things, objects, people, animals, conditions, and so forth, their particular qualities, attributes and characteristics. This type of *relative* knowledge is endlessly detailed and burdens the mind. In the World of Becoming, everything seems to be out of tune, out of place, or not "with it". This places a permanent stress on life in this world.

Absolute Knowledge is a single Field of Vision, of Wholeness, Unity, Oneness and Bliss. In the World of Being, everything simply IS as it should be.

Thinking and Being 233
Relational Consciousness 906
Spiritual Life and Material Life 1118
Avoid the Errors of East and West 1122
The Four Degrees of Knowledge 1003
Pure Being 1056

Reality

Reality is of two parts: the world of *Being*
and the world of *Becoming* (doing).

The quality of the World of Becoming is change.
Without change there is no progress.

The World of Being is Eternal,
Immutable and Changeless.

Thought creates reality in
the Worlds of Becoming (action).

Light is Reality in
the Worlds of Being (tranquillity).

God is a State of Being.
Thought is a State of Becoming.

Compared to the Brightness of the Everlasting
Light, nothing in this world is real.

Only the Self—the Son of God,
the Being of Light—is real.
The personality is only Its reflection.

Veiled and hidden by every form
is the Essential Light.

Illusions are projected mental images
(thoughtforms).
Thought is Illusion. It is temporary reality.

All the world is a stage,
and people are actors in it.
All in the world is acting,
and the Reality is not in it.

Eternity is concealed behind the Clouds of Time.

Where there is no Time,
there is only the Everlasting.

Beyond the fields of the known
lie the vast Fields of the Unknown,
hidden in Infinity.

The Universe is a Sea of Divine Energy.

The Pathway to the Soul is simply
a transformation of the personality.
And, in the end, beyond the Soul,
there is nothing left but God.

Everything is spiritual.
There is nothing dead.
Matter is alive, filled with Spirit.
The World of Light is all around.

The whole Universe is the Body of God.

In All-Space the Solar System is but a Cosmic Atom.
These Cosmic Atoms (solar systems) are but the
physical body of the Galactic Lord (our Galaxy).

God is everywhere.
There is no place where God is not,
for nothing exists outside of God.

God alone Is.
There is only God.
And all of this is God.

God is already within us.

God is Spirit,
and wherever the Holy Breath rests,
there God is.

The Spirit of God works within us.

Where the Spirit is, the Holy Breath,
there is also Life.

The Spirit within you is always free.

All that IS is God,
in every place, in every time.
Herein is to be found the Peace of the Eternal.

God is the Judge.
God is the Jury.
God is the Accuser.
God is the Accused.
God is the People who fill the vast courtroom.
And God is the Silence which fills
the Interspace in between.

God is Boundless Goodwill and Active Love.

God is Being, Intelligence and Blissful Love.

God is Positive.

God is One.

The Glory of God is unassailable.

The God-Force is Victorious.

All is Good.

All this takes place *within* God.
Feel God all around you.
This will give you Freedom.

Bliss-Consciousness is everywhere,
and it is forever.

The "now" of the average consciousness
is different from the Now of the Sage.
The "now" of the ordinary consciousness is the
endless movement of past, present and future.
The Now of the Sage is Eternity standing Still.

The Deathless Spark within me
looks out upon a World that is Eternal.

The Divine Reality, which is my Being,
is not subject to anything external.

There is nothing in Heaven nor on Earth,
neither above nor below, but the Life of God.
God is in me and I am in God.

Even as the ocean surrounds the fish,
the Sea of God's Life surrounds me everywhere.
Wheresoever I be, I am still in God.

Wheresoever I am standing is the Holy Ground,
in the visible or the Great Invisible Life.
Wheresoever I AM, God IS.

∞

The World of Being is Unlimited Energy, Pure Cosmic Consciousness, Limitless Power, Unending Joy, Eternal Peace and Measureless Bliss. There is no stress experienced in Boundless Being.

The World of Becoming is ever restless, ever changing, ever active, ever moving, ever dissatisfied, ever seeking for something else. There is no real rest or peace possible in the transitory state.

Therefore, establish yourself in *Being*. Unite the two by profound meditation. Make the two Worlds into One.

This is the goal of Life: Become the ALL.

Who is 'I AM'?

Your personality is composed of your physical body, your etheric-physical body, your astral body (your body of emotions, desires and feelings) and your mental body (your thinking body, your rational mind). Within this complex is a feeling of "I" or "I Am-ness". This first "I Am" is the ego that you know, the little self, the lower self, your "I Am" awareness on the personality level.

The Work of Metanoia is to identify with the I AM above your current awareness

- When you shift your awareness up one level to the Immortal Soul, the Soul also manifests as "I Am", encased in the causal body on the formless Mental Planes. This is the Higher Self, the Ego, your true I AM, the Imperishable Self whose basic characteristics are Will-Power, Love-Wisdom, and Higher Mind or Creative Intelligence (ĀTMA-BUDDHI-MANAS).
- Above that again is the I AM which is the Monad, the "Father in Heaven", dwelling *above* the Nirvāṇic Worlds. It is a pure Spiritual Power, pure Light, Omnipotent, Omniscient, Omnipresent, All-Loving, All-Bliss, All-Light.
- Above that is the I AM which is the Solar Logos, the ruler of all Space and all dimensions in our part of the Universe. This I AM controls all Life, all events, all evolutions, all happenings in Time and Space in our Universe. The Solar Logos is our God.
- Above this is the Universal I AM, the Cosmic Self, the Imperishable Light-Self, the Lord and Ruler of all the worlds and galaxies, the Lord of the Universe, the One I AM of all Reality, both Manifest and Transcendental.

The Mask 38
The Personality Complex 36
Jīva: the Human Soul 35
The Threefold Structure of Man 33
The Manifested-God 1589
Return to Primeval Happiness 1179
The One 1686

The Work of Metanoia is to shift your understanding of who you *are*, to identify with the I AM *above* your current awareness, because it is true that you are *all* these I AMs. You must learn to *identify* with the I AM by shifting your consciousness upwards from the personal "I Am" to the Soul or the Self-I AM, then to the Monad or the Father-I AM, and finally to the Logos or the Cosmic-I AM. Each time you shift your consciousness to the I AM beyond your current awareness, you make an evolutionary leap, a Metanoia or Spiritual Transformation.

You may notice the non-grammatical use of "I AM" in this chapter. This is purposeful and it is correct. It is designed to shift your awareness.

I AM is the Divine Presence on the level you are able to perceive It or relate to It on your level of spiritual development.

I AM is God's Presence in your life.

Activating I AM: the Secret Name of God

God is *Nameless* on the level of the Absolute. God is *Named* on the level of Creation. On the level of Creation, God has many Names. A Secret Name of God is I AM.

Learn to *vibrate* the Secret Name of God, first in English, then in Sanskrit, then in Hebrew. Then *connect* this Name to your Metanoia. Thus manifests the Magical Mind, the Magic of Light.

Learn to vibrate the Secret Name of God

English	*Sanskrit*	*Hebrew*
I AM	AHAṀ	EHEYEH(E)

The secret Hebrew pronunciation is HAY-YAH. The first letter (א, *Aleph)* is silent in the secret pronunciation, for Aleph is the Power that comes from Silence. HAYYAH means "the Living Eternal, the I AM". It means "I affirm Life, I am Life, I am Self-Existing, I am existing forever, I am Eternal Beingness, I am Existence".

Examples

- Intone I AM aloud, in English, Hebrew or Sanskrit, many times, until you feel that you are saturated with the Spirit, until you feel filled with Light and Fire, until you feel energized, healed and in order within yourself.

- Intone powerfully, three times each, the I AM in English, Sanskrit and Hebrew (nine times altogether). Then, Silence.

- Intone I AM powerfully, three times. Then your Metanoia, such as:

  "Wheresoever I am standing is the Holy Ground, in the visible or the Great Invisible Life. Wheresoever I AM, God IS."

  I AM (intone powerfully three times).

  Meditate in Silence.

- Intone silently, mentally, I AM in English, Hebrew or Sanskrit, and dwell in Silence in the I AM Presence, in the sensation of the *nearness* of God.

- Say I AM in your Heart and remain in the Silence. When the mental waves are stilled, feel the Presence that is the I AM.

The Name and the Names 1258
Experiencing Pure Consciousness 88
Pure Consciousness in the Heart 447
The Way, the Truth and the Life 670
Three Meditations in the Heart 1292

Action and Destiny

In the Worlds of Becoming,
Reality is the outgrowth of mental intention.

Energy follows Thought.
Thought directs Energy.

Thought is Destiny in the Phenomenal Realms.

All things can be changed by the modification
of the thinking principle (Metanoia).

Thought is the father of action.
If there is no thought, there is no action.

Focus on the positive outcome
of that which you desire to happen.

Where continued Attention is held,
events materialize.
Attention is the true Creative Power.

The secrets of success in all fields
are hard work, a positive attitude,
self-motivation and taking the initiative.

Keep your energy focused on your Goal.

Be a Master of limitation,
not a slave of matter.

Nature works to fulfil your desires—it has to.
In this is the certainty of your success.

When you make plans for the future,
use reason and common sense.
Make provisions for the unexpected
and be ready for *change*.

In this world everything is a process.
And every process has a beginning,
a middle and an end.

Continually increase the positive forces in your
life which give you greater and greater happiness.
Do not focus on the negative or dark side of things.
Whatever you concentrate upon
multiplies a thousandfold.
This is the Law of Positive Thinking.

Before attempting to change the world and
to change others, be sure that you have made
good progress in changing yourself.

If you cannot change the world,
simply change yourself.

Use Charm and Goodwill to get things done.

Everything is done by the Divine Energy.

The Future is in the hands of God.

My future is infinitely bright.
Nothing and no one can stop the Hidden Glory
within me from unfolding itself to Perfection.

The Spirit that dwelleth in me,
He doeth all the works.

I am the Witness to the Cosmic Work
of the One Reality.

I have control over all circumstances in my life.
All the forces and powers of the Universe
work for my Good.

I am focused Attention.
I channel Higher Power.
I am Master of every situation in my life.

By Conscious Intention I change my world
and change my mind and change my body.

My thoughts are Power and produce tangible results.
My words are Power and produce tangible results.

My words are Creative Power.

My words are a Spiritual Force
enabling the Power of God to work within me.

I am a Divine Being with Divine Powers.
By the Power of the I AM Presence I send forth
my words and they accomplish their mission.

My thought is an energy impulse.
My thought is Energy.
The origin of my thought is the field of
Unlimited Energy, which in turn emanates
from the Absolute, the One Life.

The Irresistible Power of the Living God within
me sweeps away all obstacles in my life, overcomes
all opposition, all adversity, all limitations.

By the Power of the Living Eternal within me I
accomplish all miracles of Transformation in my life.

I am a part of the Planetary Renewal Process,
the Planetary Rebirth.

Even as I create my own destiny within the
Circle of Time, so all men, women and children,
all nations, all religions, all planets, all stars, create
their destiny in the Unbounded Reality that is God.

This is all I have said:
Man, struggle and have Faith.
For I AM already Free.
I AM the Master Power.

I do all things by the Power of the Being of Light,
who gives me strength, power and ability to deal
with all situations and all circumstances in my life.
I have the Miracle-Working Power of Light.

The One Identity, the Being of Light,
the One Self, is at work in my life.
No appearance of evil or limitation
can frighten I AM, the Presence,
for the Life-Power's Self-Expression
is eternally Victorious in me.

The I AM within me is the Master Power
that directs and controls my Universe.

I am Master of all circumstances.
The Self is Master of all situations.
I am consciously transforming
my personal reality, my mind and body,
my outer circumstances, my relationships.
All my personal activities are but parts of
the Cosmic Work of I AM.

I AM controls my field of Existence
in the Circle of Time.
My physical body is the Temple of God
wherein the miracles of the I AM are performed.

My personality is a medium for the transmission
of the high frequency Life-Power of I AM.

I AM performs every thought,
every word, every deed.
I AM is responsible for every result.

∞

The First Circle of Life

The Path consists of the battle between the personality and the Soul. The Living Soul (Jīva or Jīvātman) is caught up in the Three Worlds and in the bodies of the personality (the physical, etheric-physical, astral and mental bodies). The Soul's identification with the bodies is the bondage and limitation of Mankind.

The Soul's identification with the bodies is the bondage and limitation of Mankind

While the Living Soul is tied to the Three Worlds it is subject to the process of birth and death. It is subject to the laws of Karma, Dharma and Saṁskāra.

Karma: action or activity on all three material levels—thoughts, feelings and physical actions.
Dharma: destiny, fate.
Saṁskāra: impressions or grooves in the mental and astral bodies left over from past thoughts, feelings and actions, which are the seeds for future Karma and Dharma.

The Living Soul entered into the Gross Physical Body of God (the Mental, Astral and Physical Planes) aeons ago. Since then it has been steadily receiving impressions from the physical, astral and mental dimensions via the physical, astral and mental bodies. Because of these impressions stored in the subconscious layers of the mind, the Living Soul has been trapped, cast into bondage in the prison of the Three Worlds.

The past impressions (Saṁskāras) work themselves out from the subconscious levels of the mind to the conscious mind level, where they again become thoughts, feelings and actions, thus creating another set of impressions sowing the seeds for future Karma and Dharma. Thus, if we leave it to Nature, by the natural course of events Humanity remains forever imprisoned in the three lowest realms of Creation. This is called the *First Circle of Life*. The First Circle of Life is the compulsory imprisonment of the vast sea of Human Souls in the lowest three realms of the Divine Body of God.

Saṁsāra-Mokṣana
Sanskrit: Liberation from the Wheel of Birth and Death.
Saṁsāra is the endless wandering (circulating) between the Physical, Astral and Mental Worlds through the process of Reincarnation.
Mokṣana is Freedom from the need for further rebirth.
Karma and Reincarnation 231
Learn to Die before you Die 420

The work of the First Circle of Life is to break the chains, to be released from compulsory reincarnation in the Three Worlds. The Wheel of Rebirth grinds on for you until you learn, by Wisdom, to neutralize every past Cause and dissolve in Harmony.

The feeling of separation, the non-perception
of the Universal Ocean of Life that is God,
is an illusion created by the physical bodily senses.

I am a Divine Being,
temporarily in a physical body.

My body is the Temple of the Living God
and is made of Radiant Light.

My body is the Temple of God
in which I see the Light of God.

I am not my mind;
it is an instrument I need to learn to use.

My mind is part of the Mind
which dreams the World into Reality.

Our real I is not a personal limited I.
Our real I is not the bound, self-centred self.
Our real I is God.

God is our Source, our Centre and our Completion.
My personality is only a mask which I,
the Living Soul, wear temporarily.
Physical bodies and environment are simply
the field where karmas work out.

We are instruments to glorify God.

I am living in a temporarily limited manifestation
and I am soon due to return to
my Cosmic Spiritual Centre.

I am nourished by the Love of God.
I am Loved by the Eternal.
I am an expression of God's Divine Love.
I am transformed by Divine Love.
I am energized by Divine Love.
I am appreciated by Divine Love.
I am strong in the Power of God's Love,
and nothing can disturb my peace of mind.

Divine Love fills my Heart
with Harmony and Peace.

I Am Peace.
I Am Joy.
I Am Harmony.
I Am Happiness.
I Am Light.
I Am Free.
I Am healthy.
I Am prosperous and happy.

The I AM Power frees me from all obstacles
to my Progress, Success and Freedom.

I bring the Wisdom of the Eternal
into my life's circumstances.
I Am filled with the Boundless Energy
of the Higher Worlds to accomplish
all my desires and plans.

The world and all things in it, all situations and
people, passes away, but God's Love-Vibration
remains in my Heart forever.

∞

Trapped Spirits 1240
Understand your Predicament 892
Saṁskāra and Vāsanā 251
Desire-Streams 1377
Subconscious Renewal 1236
To Achieve Liberation 1177
What is Consciousness? 1368

Obstacles to Higher Consciousness

The Conditionings

The following Sanskrit words describe our conditionings. Everybody is conditioned by these four factors. There are no exceptions.

DEHAGRANTHI: conditioned by the body and its environment.
MANOGRANTHI: conditioned by the mind and the mental world.
JĪVAGRANTHI: conditioned by the ego or sense of "I".
JAGATGRANTHI: conditioned by the world, by cosmic processes and events around you.

GRANTHI
Sanskrit: A knot, a barrier, an obstacle, a difficulty, a conditioning, an identification. These obstacles need to be overcome before the Soul is released and can stand free.
The Three Identifications 1369

From our perspective, the Soul *appears* to be conditioned by these four factors. This comes about because of the *apparent* identification of the Soul with the personal mechanism. But in fact, it is not so. The Soul merely provides enough Life-energy for the personality to get by in this world. As we learn to re-identify with the Soul, the effects of our conditioning become less and less. Total re-identification with the Soul means that we still act as "conditioned" beings, but inwardly we are Free.

We are not just the products of our environment; we also contribute to it. We are not just "victims", but causes as well. And herein lies the possibility to change the world. Thus:

- First you overcome your own conditioning.
- Then you renew the world from the Power of the Free State, from Freedom in Spiritual Consciousness.

The Identifications

The Wheel of Birth and Death is caused by *identification:*

DEHAGRANTHI: identification with the physical body.
MANOGRANTHI: identification with KĀMA-MANAS, the combined desire-nature and thinking apparatus.
JĪVAGRANTHI: identification with an ego—that which we *think* we are.
MĀYĀ: identification with the *illusion* that we are separate entities, separate from each other and from the Higher Consciousness, God, Truth or Divine Mind.

These Identifications are the cause of your cycling on the Wheel of Birth and Death, and they are broken only by your *experiencing* of Pure Consciousness, BUDDHI, Enlightenment.

There are also three psychic knots or barriers in the cakras that must be dissolved before your Soul stands free:

BRAHMĀ-GRANTHI
At the Base Cakra.

HṚDAYA-GRANTHI
At the Heart Cakra.

ŚIVA-GRANTHI
At the Head Cakras.

These "knots" at these major centres must be dissolved before your Consciousness can free-flow into Eternity.

Knots of Consciousness 445
The State of Inner Purity 497

Karma and Death

That which *is* is the result of that which has *been*.
That which will be in the Future is the
result of seeds sown in the Present.
This is the great Law of Karma,
or Cause and Effect.

Every event in this life is
the result of a previous cause.

What is happening *now* is simply the effects
of past causes, set in motion long ago. What is
happening now is not the cause, but effects.

Karma is settling your account of many lifetimes
and freeing you to accomplish your future Glory.
This future Glory is accomplished by
meditating upon the Path of Light.

Karma, the Law of Cause and Effect,
works in the physical, emotional and mental bodies,
but the Soul is above and suffers no ills.

Karma, the results of past thoughts, feeling
and actions, must be worked out or released.
But the Soul is eternally Free.

The experiencing of the existential realities
of pain, suffering, ill-health and death can be
modified and transformed by a glimpse of your
true *Self*, the immortal Spirit within you.

Everything has a good purpose behind it,
even the worst situations and circumstances,
but to see and understand it requires
great Vision and profound Awareness.

Bad Karma is transmuted by
positive emotional reaction.

Handle your Karma gracefully.

All the events of the Past were the results of
what I thought, felt and did.
All the events of the Future will be the results of
what I think, feel and do Now.

I am responsible for what I see.
I am responsible for what I hear.
I am responsible for what I think.
I am responsible for what I do.
I am responsible for what I feel.

When you are called before the Soul-Judge to give
an account of your Life, happy will you be when
your good deeds outnumber your wrong deeds.
Therefore, do good always.

Your days are numbered.

Death is a routine affair.

Being in bodies is Bondage for the Spirit in Man.

To be free of bodies is Deathlessness.

Fear not physical death,
but to die without Illumination.

The One who can say, I AM, never dies.

∞

Karma: the Law of Action 240
Action (Karma) 1402
The Law of Death 398
True Death 424

Reactive-Emotional Consciousness

What is Reactive-Emotional Consciousness? Essentially it is your whole astral body, your astral-psychic nature, your emotional body of the Astral Plane. It is always reactive and it is always emotional. It cannot be anything else!

The astral body is always reactive and it is always emotional

If you observe yourself and others carefully, you will come to the shocking revelation that most people are most of the time in Reactive-Emotional Consciousness. It is pervading the lives of every individual upon this planet (including children and babies), regardless of age, social status, class or religious background. Everybody is suffering from it! Thus there is no peace on Earth. Thus there is no peace in the individual. Thus there is no peace in you.

Peace of Mind is not possible while you are in the state of Reactive-Emotional Consciousness.

Signs of Reactive-Emotional Consciousness

- Any form of desire for anything.
- Anger or hatred.
- Infatuation (passionate attachment to objects and people).
- Pride of possessions, of learning, or of status in life.
- Jealousy or greed.
- Aggressive behaviour, rage, revenge, hostile attitude, sulking.
- Impatience, frustration with people and events.
- The sense of loneliness, self-pity, being sorry for yourself, moodiness.
- Panic activities, extreme reactions.
- Emotional breakdowns, not being able to cope with events and people.
- Anxiety, fear, being afraid of people, situations or objects.
- Being disappointed with events or people; being bitter or "hurt" by what people said or did to you.
- Depression, self-doubt, low self-esteem.
- Being bored, a lack of mental direction or inspiration.
- Being nervous, over-excited, hyperactive, restless, indecisive.
- Being emotionally exhausted or fatigued, run-down, tired.
- Feeling insecure—financially, emotionally or spiritually.
- Being gloomy, touchy, over-sensitive.
- Resentments towards people or situations, emotional conflicts with people, disagreements.
- A general unease about life, a sense that you are not doing what you should be doing, being out of tune.

The Astral Body 39
The Realm of Desires 58
Shadowland 219
Emotional Love 914
Desire-Streams 1377
The Principle of Choice 1380

Illumined-Mind Consciousness

Peace of Mind, tranquillity, is possible only in the state of Illumined-Mind Consciousness. To have Illumined-Mind Consciousness you must meditate, study spiritual truths, and become God-Centred in your life.

Meditation, studying spiritual truths and always thinking of the Divine Presence are all-important to lift you out of astral consciousness. Without it you will be forever stuck in your astral self.

Your astral body must be guided and impelled by an Illumined Mind

Reactive-Emotional Consciousness, or the astral body, your astral-psychic nature, will not give up its domination over you very easily. You have a long fight ahead of you. The astral body has dominated Humanity for aeons of time and is not easily vanquished. Your astral body must be guided and impelled by an Illumined Mind; then it will become healthy, positive, radiant, dynamic, secure.

Your ordinary mind is *not* the Illumined Mind. Your ordinary mind must be transformed into the Illumined Mind by meditation, Spiritual Knowledge and the Divine Presence. Your mind has to associate with Divinity in order to become Illumined.

Temporary Relief

In the normal outer world, people often deal with their emotional problems (the Reactive-Emotional Consciousness) through drinking alcohol until they are so numbed that they no longer "feel" the problems. Nicotine also has a dulling effect and can temporarily relieve the problem. Or they take medical drugs—codeine or morphine based drugs, antihistamines, antidepressants, eating-disorder drugs, anti-psychotic drugs—because the medical profession does not believe in a separate emotional body and therefore attempts to cure the purely emotional problems by physical means. Or they take hallucinogenic drugs, such as LSD, speed, ecstasy, cocaine or marijuana. Or they go to endless counselling sessions and talk over their problems with psychologists, psychiatrists, doctors, counsellors, advisors, lawyers, dentists, hairdressers, or whoever will listen. Or they go to psychics, fortune-tellers, tarot card readers or astrologers. Such things may bring temporary relief from emotional problems, but the *root cause* is not even touched, so they don't work in the long run.

Dwell on the Positive 1712

The Path of Light 89
The Path of Illumination 1338
Realms of the One Mind 492
How to have a Peaceful Mind 1244
Cultivate the Positive 1365
Tantra Mind 933

From Personal to Cosmic Life

Metanoia is conscious re-direction of the mind, until you establish yourself permanently in Illumined-Mind Consciousness.

The goal of human life on this planet is to rise:

a. From Reactive-Emotional Consciousness to Illumined-Mind Consciousness.

b. From Illumined-Mind Consciousness to Soul-Consciousness.

c. From Soul-Consciousness to Divine Consciousness.

This is the Divine Plan for Humanity. Thus, it is *your* plan for life. Orient yourself to it.

When the sense of personality is relinquished, identification with the Oversoul becomes possible

When personal life is lost, Cosmic Life is found.

This means that when the sense of personality is relinquished, identification with the Oversoul becomes possible. Every thought, feeling, word and deed is, in reality, the operation of Cosmic Forces and Laws activated by Nature. But the human personality identifies with them and takes responsibility for them, when in fact they are but *Nature in action*.

The human personality erroneously believes itself to be separate from the Ocean of Life (Nature), when in fact it is not separate. And, beyond Nature, the human Soul also is not separate, but is one with God.

∞

Attachment and clinging to circumstances imprisons the mind.

Your mind is the prison.

Free your mind and you will be free anywhere from all problems.

Be in control of your emotions—this will give you Peace of Mind.

Let not other people or events disturb your Peace of Mind.

When troubled, re-focus on the *Self*. The Self is *Peace*.

Watch your thoughts; they come and go.
Watch your emotions; they come and go.
Watch the events around you; they come and go.

Stay *Centred*.

Metanoia is the art of integrating everyday life with the Spiritual Life.

All the religious traditions of the world separated these two conditions of life: the worldly and the spiritual. Because of this mistake, a terrible dichotomy has arisen in human consciousness upon this planet: you are supposed to be either wholly worldly and materialistic, or spiritual and "spaced out". But, in fact:

All Is God.

This is the secret of Metanoia.

Avoid the Errors of East and West 1122
Mind-Only 974

Emotional Problems

Fear, anger, sorrow, grief, stress, anxiety, depression and attachment (to people and objects) are emotional states which have been plaguing Humanity for hundreds of thousands of years, affecting everybody without exception—all ages, all races and all types of human being. If you think you are the only one suffering from such emotional states, you are wrong. Everybody does so, and has done so, for ages. This is what spoils human life upon this planet.

Stress can be caused by the process of Transformation itself

Following are some of the universal emotional problems of Humanity from which everybody suffers to various degrees.

Stress

Stress (tension, strain) can be caused by a variety of factors:

- Physical circumstances. The personality's inability to deal with rapid or shattering changes to established life-patterns or environment.
- Relationships. New challenges in any field of existence.
- Work. Striving to become successful. Being overworked or doing too many things at once. Extreme activity or over-excitement, a fast or speedy lifestyle, restlessness, being on the move all the time.
- Jobs or situations which are dangerous or life threatening.
- Doing something willingly that is known to be wrong.

All of these cause stress, tension and strain in the physical, astral and mental bodies, and bring about worry, anxiety and fear for the future. There is a direct and obvious solution to this problem, of course, even without meditating: *stop doing whatever is stressing you out!*

Stress can also be caused by the process of Transformation itself:

- Emerging from the worldly consciousness and trying to make adjustments to walk upon the Spiritual Path. (Strange as it may seem, attempting to *disentangle* oneself from the world and the personality can cause stress!)
- The slowly emerging New Planetary Consciousness for all of Humanity, a Global Awakening which produces stress in the individual units of Humanity.

Psychology Ancient and Modern 1364
Notes on the Path in the New Age 1166
The Double Stress of Meditational Life 1181
Overstimulation on the Path 557
The Initiation of the World 1712

Although stress is generally psychological, it can manifest as physical, emotional or mental disease. Stress or distress registers in the physical body as muscular tension, headaches, sweating palms, high blood pressure, rapid breathing, heart palpitations, tiredness, exhaustion, cold hands and feet, poor blood circulation, lack of appetite. Long periods of severe tension or stress can result in nervous breakdown, disorientation, post-traumatic depression, hypertension, anger, violence, insanity, madness, and the collapse of physical health.

In this physical dimension, life itself is stressful. Only the *degree* of stress varies with time and circumstances. Most people suffer from stress without being aware of it; they become aware of their stress only when the physical, emotional or mental symptoms manifest.

In this physical dimension, life itself is stressful

It is important to understand that children also can experience stress as the result of the same factors: physical circumstances, work (school), relationships with parents, relatives, peer-groups, and so forth. As a parent you should know that your child can also be stressed out. Watch and observe.

Anxiety

Anxiety is a very common psychological condition. Almost everybody on the planet suffers from one or more of its varied manifestations.

First of all, there is *angst,* which is a general state of being anxious, an unrelieved feeling of uneasiness, a permanent niggling sense of worry, an irrational fear, being anxious or tense for no apparent reason, feeling continually despondent, feeling always "out of sorts", being impatient or irritable for no apparent reason, acute anxiety about unimportant things or events, uncertainty about the future, low self-esteem, not being sure of oneself, lack of self-confidence.

This general state of anxiety produces eating disorders, stomach problems, emotional problems, sleeplessness or insomnia, excessive smoking, alcoholism, an inability to concentrate on the task at hand, low performance levels at work, and in some cases the use of prescription drugs or mind-altering drugs.

Anxiety can also be produced by challenging situations in one's life, emotional conflicts within oneself, or emotional conflicts with family, friends, boss, or others, which can lead to severe nervous disorders and

Overactive Mind 990
Mental Activity 1228
Meditation and the Joy of Living 1012
How to have a Peaceful Mind 1244
Peace of Heart 1595

The stress within yourself and within all Humanity can be relieved only by the inner connection to the Divine. This is At-One-Ment.

To a lesser degree, stress is also relieved by connecting to Nature, to natural energy, to the forces of Creation. Energy can also be gained through chanting and singing.

physical symptoms. Anxiety also manifests when demands are placed upon people which are beyond their capacity to perform, or which they feel exceed their ability, time, resources or energy.

Then there are the subconscious anxiety states, which are *impressions from the past*, either from this lifetime or from previous lives. These have been deeply buried in the subconscious mind and subtly influence or determine your present thinking, feeling and actions.

The subconscious anxiety states are impressions from the past

Again, as in the previous case of tension or stress, before we even consider meditation as a remedy, you can look into your life and observe what is actually causing your anxiety. If you manage to find the cause or causes, you can usually eliminate the problem.

Irritability

Irritability is a most devastating condition. Through irritability the physical body's immune system is weakened and one easily catches colds, viruses and infectious diseases. Millions of people continually suffer from irritability. In the West, even spiritual students and very advanced spiritual people suffer from this disease. (The circumstances for the Easterners are very different.)

Irritability manifests as nervousness, anger, frustration, worry, or "being on edge" all the time. It is caused by the over-stimulation of a cakra in the astral body. If the Sex Centre, Throat Centre or Solar Plexus Centre in the astral body is over-energized, it will react upon the physical nervous system, making you jumpy, complaining, critical, easily upset, and defensive in your attitude towards others.

This over-stimulation of the Sex Centre, Throat Centre and Solar Plexus Centre has to do with planetary conditions. It also can be caused by the increased individual effort towards betterment and attaining success in life, or by the desire for Spiritual Illumination.

When any of these three cakras in the astral body are malfunctioning, the corresponding etheric-physical cakras also malfunction by reflection, which leads to worry, fear and irritability.

Irritation: Sex Centre.
Fear: Solar Plexus Centre.
Worry: Throat Centre.

Further, the etheric-physical vitality (PRĀṆA) is weakened, which reacts upon the physical body. These conditions are very common among all classes of people, including those upon the Way.

Saṁskāra and Vāsanā 251
Karmic Adjustment 1379
Malfunctioning Cakras 53
The Sūfī View of Mental Disorders 900
Diseases caused by walking the Path 1168

God, the Healer of Broken Hearts

All these negative emotions are conditions of your astral body. They arise from a *basic insecurity* felt in your astral body. This occurs because, by Nature, the human astral body (emotional mechanism) is *cut off* from the Higher Worlds, from the Transcendental States or Higher States of Consciousness.

Negative emotions obstruct the Light and thus produce darkness in the personality

Negative emotions such as fear, anger, guilt, self-pity, pride, self-centredness or selfishness, feelings of unworthiness, of being unwanted or unloved, actually *block* the Light of the Soul from entering and circulating the Life-force on the personality level. Thus, you can recognize the immense damage that negative emotions cause to the human system. Negative emotions obstruct the Light and thus produce darkness in the personality.

All ills, therefore, whether of the physical body, emotional body or mental body (body, emotions or mind), are due to a dual cause:

a. Nature is imperfect.

b. There is little connection, if any, between the Soul and the various bodies of the personality.

Little can be done about the imperfect products of Nature (which include human beings, animals, plants, and so on). This imperfection has to do with the state of Planetary Evolution.

The Soul, however, can be *induced* to take more notice of the personality by *invocation* (using Metanoia). Invocation is necessary to shift the Attention of the Soul from Soul-preoccupation to dealing with personality concerns. Healing of body, emotions or mind is easier if we can invoke the Soul-Power, the Master Power, into our lives.

It is a truism that the more Soul-Power a person has, the healthier he or she will be. Complete health is not possible, however. The high frequency Soul-Power very often helps to restore order on the

All diseases of body, emotions and mind, all imperfections of character and personality, all weakness and flaws in the nature of Man, arise because the human Soul is restricted in its abilities to control the bodies constituting the human personality. Your physical body simply acts out the projections from your mind (thoughts) and the impulses of feeling from your astral body. Hence, the New Birth must begin with your mind and feeling nature.

Mind in Body 988
Mind and Body 1374
From Darkness into Light 982
Disease and Karma 1169
Health and Fire 50

personality level, which brings about healing. But, on the other hand, intense Power from the Soul can cause havoc for an unprepared personality mechanism.

Throughout the ages, people have attempted to deal with emotional problems through alcohol consumption, drugs (medical and hallucinogenic) and psychological counselling. But the problems won't go away, either for you as an individual or for the whole human family.

Personal transformation depends on your state of mind

There is only one solution:

a. Infuse the Mind-Principle with Superconsciousness (SAMĀDHI) through a correct meditational process.

b. When the mind is saturated with the Bliss, Wisdom and Love of the Higher Consciousness states, it automatically transforms your astral body into a positive, radiant and happy emotional state. The process is natural: as you infuse your mind with the touch of Transcendental States of Consciousness through the correct meditational processes, it happens by itself.

Thus, the remedy for the emotional problems of Humanity is the right meditational methods which establish the Mind-Principle in the Higher Levels of Consciousness. Metanoia, or personal transformation, depends on *your state of mind*, for ultimately your mind controls not only your thought-processes, but your feelings and emotions and your physical body as well. The key lies in the state of your mind.

You can change your thought-currents by Metanoia statements and by meditation, which can be on Mantra or on Yantra (symbols).

Attach Yourself to Being

The emotional states of worry, fear and anxiety are created by thoughts, wrong thoughts. Because they are created by the mind, they can be banished by the mind.

- In the World of Becoming (the Physical, Astral and Mental Planes), human beings create by thought-power. When thinking is mastered, fear is conquered. Face directly your fears.
- The function of the World of Being (the Spiritual Realms) is just to *Be*, forever.
- This world (the World of Becoming, and all the people and objects in it) is forever perishable, unstable and changeable.
- Thus we must attach ourselves to *Being*.

Cultivate the Positive 1365
Passion and Dispassion 695
Your Mind is the Key 1208
Attach your Mind to the Eternal 1234
The Experience of the Transcendent 1378

Fear and Stress

There is nothing to fear. Fear is a thought.
To conquer fear you have to conquer thought.
If there is no thought, there is no fear.

Fear is the sensation of being separated
from the Divine Energy.

Fear of Life and fear of Death arise from the same things: fear of changes in external circumstances; dependence on people, things, situations, and reluctance to let go of them; and fear of the Past, the Present or the Future (what may happen?).

In this world, everything is transient,
nothing is lasting, nothing is permanent.
For most people this is difficult to adjust to.

Human beings cry for attention because
they are not centred within themselves.
The remedy is to teach them how to
become centred.

Do not fear any person, condition or circumstance,
for the Being of God, and the Essence of God, are
your very own Being and your very own Essence.

It matters not what other people think of you,
or even what you think of yourself.
God knows best.

Let not fear control your life. *Tranquillity.*

Stress is the inability to cope with change.

The feelings of guilt, sadness, fear, imperfection,
loneliness will slowly disappear as we learn
increasingly to identify with our true Self,
the Soul of Light that we are.

When we Know the true I AM,
there is nothing to fear, no one to fear,
nothing to hate, no one to hate,
for all is enveloped in the Love of God.

When the I AM is known, stress disappears.

Fear, depression, stress, loneliness and insecurity
disappear, are transformed by the Living Light,
the Light of the Self, the Being of Light.

The Holy Heart has no fear, for God alone Is.

There is no time or fear in Being (that is, in God).

Give up resentment for past happenings in your life,
future fears and present anger,
and you will be *Happy.*

I am not going to be stressed-out,
no matter what my circumstances.

I have nothing to fear:
The Self is Peace. I am that Peace.
The Self is Love. I am that Love.
The Self is Strength. I am that Strength.
The Self is Bliss. I am that Bliss.
The Self is Radiant Energy. I am that Energy.
The Self is Victorious. I am that Victory.
The Self is Free. I am Free.
The Self lacks nothing.
I draw to myself all things that I need.

Without reproach of the Past,
without fear of the Future,
I go on.

∞

How to deal with Crisis situations in your Life

Here is a simple rule for dealing with crisis situations:

Do your best, then surrender to the Divine within.

That is all you can do, and all you must do! Do your best and then surrender. To surrender means to let go, to relinquish control of the situation, to give it up. After doing your best in the situation, let go and return to Silence deep within yourself. Give the problem up to God. Simply allow the Divine to interfere in your life and in the lives of those around you. In the deep Silence you will receive Grace.

Allow the Divine to interfere in your life and in the lives of those around you

Remember that there can never be a totally perfect solution to any situation in this life. The Inner Reality is the only changeless condition; everything else around you rises and falls, goes up and down. So let it be.

Following are the four steps to deal with a crisis:

1. Recognize that you are not perfect, that nobody is perfect, that nothing can be perfect (due to the incomplete evolutionary state upon this planet).
2. Do the best you can in the situation.
3. Then surrender to the Divine within, in Stillness and Silence.
4. Accept whatever is the outcome.

The last two points are very important because, in deep Silence, in true surrender to the Divine Presence, a subtle transformation takes place within *yourself*, a subtle, non-verbal rearrangement of your consciousness.

As for accepting the result, whatever that may be, remember that you are *not* responsible for running the whole Universe by yourself! Allow God and the Cosmos to do their bit!

Stillness before Battle 1095
The Testing of the Soul 1158
Crises on the Path 1162
Crisis and Revelation 1711
To Become a Jīvanmukta 259
The Warrior Code 1077

Crisis

Everything is Divine.

Calmness is Power.

Be Serene in the Oneness of God.

Consider all beings and all things
as part of your Infinite Self.

All beings and all objects are
manifestations of the Light of God.

Surrender simply
to the demands of the Moment.

Maximum outer flexibility
with maximum Inner Stability.

Reconcile opposites and harmonize contraries.

Divine Positivity.

Seek Peace within and find Harmony without.

The greater the storm outside,
the greater the Stillness inside.

Turn every negative situation
into a positive experience.
Look upon it as a challenge.

The solution to all your problems
lies within you and nowhere else.

The solution is in understanding the problem.
If you cannot solve a problem,
it means you have not understood it.

Problems are not problems;
they are just challenges to overcome.

It is not a problem. It is a challenge.
There are no problems, only challenges.
Deal with it.

The Wise make good use of every situation.

Every situation in your life is
an opportunity for *growth* or *decay*.
It depends on how you view
your situations in your mind.
This is the secret of Metanoia
(turning-around the mind).

A crisis situation is an excellent place
to strengthen your Soul.

It is not intended that you should
go through life without an opposition.
Opposition, when taken rightly, matures
your Soul and strengthens your personality.

People are executors of your Karma.
It is through people that your karmas
are worked out.

The Law of Moses is *punishment.*
The Law of Christ (the Being of Light)
is *Forgiveness.*

There is no problem that Love cannot fix.

One must have Crucifixion before Resurrection,
and the seed must die before the tree can flourish.

It came to pass.
This too will pass.
In this world everything changes.
Be patient.

Be not a victim of limitation,
but its Master.

Every day is a battle.
Win your battles day by day.
Remain positive.

Accept everything as part of your Destiny.

Lose the battle and win the war.

When you are down-hearted,
and all seems at a loss,
remember that the Sun will shine,
the flowers will grow again,
the winds will change,
and quiet comes after the storm.

The Storm is passing over.
It is going to blow itself out.
Then there is Peace.

Struggle is the motivating force in the world.
Peace is the active Power of God.

The degree of your Happiness
is the Power you have to deal with
situations you encounter in your daily life.
In all situations, function from inner Peace.

Stay calm and let nothing rattle your inner
composure. (To rattle means to shake up, to
disturb, to make anxious or afraid, to cause panic.)

Let go of anger, frustration
and aggression inside yourself.
Then *calmly* do whatever you need to do.

Become aware of what is
the problem in your situation.
Accept it not, nor reject it.
This is Choiceless Awareness.
Then do what is *necessary.*

Do your best and let God do the rest.

I AM come to set you Free,
within yourself.

When you *realize* that you don't have to do
anything, a smile will light up your face.

The One Self, whom God created,
cannot be threatened.

I have nothing to fear;
my Guardian Angel is with me to protect me.

I am in charge of my own life.
I don't let other people get me down.

Every problem can be dealt with.
I have the power and knowledge within me to do it.

I do not need to control anything.

Nothing external can dominate me.

Within me, my Soul is free.

Now I am free,
no matter what the outer appearances may be.

∞

The Second Circle of Life

The Second Circle of Life is the Life *of* the Soul, Life *in* the Soul, Life *as* a Soul.

The Soul is a different Circle of Life and has its own dwelling place

The Soul is not of this world. The Soul is a different Circle of Life and has its own dwelling place. The Soul originally descended from Nirvāṇa (the Kingdom of God), passed through Paradise (the Buddhic Realms) and finally stabilized in Heaven (the formless, causal levels of the Mental Plane).

It is difficult for the personal consciousness to comprehend the Life of the Soul. The Soul has very little control (if any) over the personal life. This has been the problem of Humanity for many cycles and ages.

The path of progress for Humanity lies in learning to transfer attention out of the personality levels into the Soul Realms, into the Consciousness of the Living Flame of Love.

In the above paragraph the whole meaning of life has been said. This is the Great Work that is to be accomplished in this lifetime. Those people who live only as personalities cannot understand this truth. For them the Second Circle of Life remains closed.

In order to progress, Humanity needs to accomplish two things:

a. The Attention or Consciousness must be transferred into the Soul.

b. The Soul then absorbs the personality into its own wider Cosmic Life.

The Work can progress only in this sequence. The personality must do its part first; then the Soul can do its part.

Meditation is a process evolved by human beings on this planet to try to connect with the Soul. It is an attempt by the personality to link up with its Source, the Living Soul, JĪVĀTMAN. The ancients have invented many processes to try to bring this about—prayer, meditation, Yoga, Zen, Sūfīsm, Kabbalah, Mysticism, Taoism, Buddhism, Hasidism, and so forth—but few correctly understood the process. Almost always they began with the assumption that this world is unreal, that it is inherently evil or an illusion, that the body, mind and emotions must be suppressed or snuffed out, that you must escape into Nirvāṇa by paralysing the person (your personality).

Thus the idea of *renunciation* was invented, the idea that neither pain nor joy have any meaning, that life itself is meaningless, leading to a complete disinterest in the personal life and the world process. But this is an incorrect view!

The future human being will be a Cosmic Man or Cosmic Woman—not only a Living Soul, but a Living-Soul-Person. The gap between the Kingdom of the World and the Kingdom of God will disappear and the All will become as One.

Beyond the personal I Am, I AM the Living Soul,
an eternally changeless Breath of God,
Pure Consciousness, beyond fear, worry
or thought, ever Blissful, ever Free.

My true identity is the Self, the Spirit of Light.

The Self is different from the mind,
which is a composite of feelings and thoughts.

My Pure Self is a beam of Consciousness
shining out like a Light from within.

The Self is Fire.
The Self is Light.
The Self is untouched by external circumstances.

The Self is I AM.
The Self is Christ.
The Self is Being in the Heart of Life.

The Self in us is God.
To discover this is the purpose of the Way.

The Infinite Self is at the Core (Heart)
of our Being.

I live, yet not I but the Christ liveth in me.

I am the Self of Power.
I transform by the Magic of Light.

I am a Living Soul at all times, having purpose,
understanding and energizing Power.

I AM never changes.
Personality and the world
continually undergo Transformation.
I AM Changeless Perfection.

I Am part of a Larger Pattern.
I Am a Child of God.
I Am Power and Glory Boundless.
I Am Spirit.

Glory be to the Solar Logos. Glory be to the Sun.
I Am a conscious atom in the
body of the Living God.

I Am the Breath of Life. I Am the Sun.

I Am breathing Light. I Am breathing Sun.
I Am one with Light. I Am one with Sun.

I Am One with the Light of the World,
the One Light.

Transcendental Bliss is my basic Self-Nature.

I Am Unbounded Joy, Unconditional Love
and All-Knowing Intelligence.

I Am fulfilling my Eternal Destiny.
I Am Victorious.

I Am eternal, immortal Divine Self.
I Am a drop of the Ocean of Immortality.
Divine Bliss flows through me, and I am
supported by Divine Love forever and ever.

∞

Jīva: the Human Soul 35
Impressions from the Soul 350
The Soul-Power 1305

The Work of Meditation

Meditation is the process of shifting your attention—your consciousness or conscious awareness—to higher possibilities. And there are many higher possibilities.

Meditation is necessary to shift the attention from the personality life to the Soul-Life

Meditation is necessary to shift the attention (consciousness) from the personality life to the Soul-Life. Meditation is an activity of consciousness to shift your awareness into the causal body, the Soul-Body, which is another reality quite *apart* from the personality mechanism.

Normally your attention is attached to your physical body, and hence to your immediate environment—your wife, husband, children, work, friends, the world around you. Consequently your attention is continually flowing outwards from yourself. The first work of meditation is to re-focus, to return to the Source, the Centre, the Heart, the sense of God's constant nearness, which is in fact your Self.

A part of the work of meditation is to harness the mind. The mind is continually active, thinking of problems, pains, pleasures, plans, things to do, or things that happened in the past or will happen in the future. Meditation is concerned with making the mind motionless, still, quiet, serene, at peace, establishing Consciousness of God without thoughts or images.

Each of these processes—shifting attention and mental silencing—takes time, perseverance, practice, patience. Success comes slowly but steadily.

Focusing Awareness

Meditation is difficult for any person who is used to scattering his or her energies in all directions, who is pulled hither and thither by all kinds of impulses and desires. A chaotic personality cannot meditate. A disorganized mind cannot meditate. A certain amount of stability in life is required before you can enter the Path of Meditation.

Meditation begins with focus (concentration, attention) at one point of awareness, be this inside or outside yourself. When you focus your attention onto something, either inside or outside yourself, you collect all of your *conscious energy* there. Without collecting your conscious energy at a single point of focus or awareness, you cannot begin to meditate.

Meditation is a slow course of *disentanglement.* First we disengage from identification with the physical body and its environment, the world; then from the astral body and its world; and finally from the workings of the normal mind itself.

Education consists of forgetting all the things you learned at school, and *Knowing*.

Meditation is a steady stream of focused awareness.

Most people direct their attention outside towards the world, towards people and objects, quite naturally. What is needed is a natural redirecting of your conscious energy towards God, Reality or Higher Consciousness. Unless you consciously redirect your attention upon God, upon the Real, you remain forever bound upon the Wheel of Time.

Thus you have to *shift your attention* away from your little personalized self towards the Boundless Immutable Principle of the God-Self. That is the purpose of meditation. Illumination of the mind or the Heart will come only after a *long* application of focused awareness. There are no shortcuts on this Path.

Meditation is the art of connecting yourself consciously to higher aspects of Reality

Connecting to Reality

The human being upon this planet is an energy system. The amount of energy we have on any level depends upon our energy-connection with that level of Being.

There is physical energy, astral or emotional energy, mental or mind-substance energy, Buddhic or Unified-Field Energy, and various layers of Divine Energy beyond that. Whatever you are *connected* to, you will receive that kind of energy. Whatever source you are not connected to, that energy washes over you and passes you by. Thus, you are constantly dwelling in an Ocean of Limitless Energy, the Godhead, but you have no capacity to utilize It.

The human personality is out of tune with the notes of the Holy Light within the Soul. Nature in the lower worlds is unable, by Herself, to reproduce the perfect Harmony of the Soul-Realms; hence the many problems of Humanity and the planet, and the many diseases that arise in the body, emotions and mind. Thus, you must *consciously seek* the Redeeming Light.

Meditation is the art of connecting yourself *consciously* to higher aspects of Reality and, ultimately, to Reality Itself.

Your true Being is infinite in nature.
First you must make contact through meditation.
After contact, there is the struggle between the self and the Self.
When the true Being has won, you become a shining Star on the Horizon of Eternity.

Perceptions of the One Mind 490
The Science of Meditation 1173
Meditation Practice 1201
The Holy Path 1285

Meditation

Serenity and happiness come from Inner Fulfilment. To be inwardly fulfilled we must spend our lives in meditation.

Liberation in this life is the Goal.
Never forget this Vision.
Let not the world distract you.
Make conscious connection with
your Soul through meditation.

Illumination is a result of long and steady effort.

The purpose of meditation is to achieve Mental Stillness, where no more thoughtforms are made, and the Soul is seen.

Many thoughts don't make Enlightenment.

Spiritual Consciousness transcends thought,
is formless, and is the State of Unity.

True Spiritual Consciousness is formless.
It is above the thinking principle.
It is being aware of the Self, the I AM,
which is Eternal, Omnipotent and Omnipresent.

I AM is the Name of Being
where there is no thought.
Thoughts come and go,
but the Thinker, the I AM, remains.

The Source of Mind is *Bliss.*

Vibration is the basic Law of the Universe.
Spiritual Evolution is changing
your Vibration to a higher gear.
Only a motionless (waveless) mind
can perceive the Path of Light within.

Cease from mental activity and you will
become aware of a Boundless Infinity.

Look within and God is there.
Look without and thou art lost.

Look within, for you are Light.

Look within:
thou art Buddha (Christ, Kṛṣṇa, Rāma, God).

The Self is waiting patiently at the door of the
Heart and at the window of the Third-Eye.

Look with wonder at what is before you
and you shall Know the Lord of all things.

Return to God.

Sanctify the Lord God in your Heart.

Release your Spirit from the Cycles of Time
and merge into the vastness of the Universe.

Stabilize yourself to experience the Absolute.

Rest in the Spirit.

I drop thought.
I let go of everything.
I settle down into Being.

My mind is at rest.

I stand in the Light, the Light of Self,
the Light of the Eternal Presence.

∞

The Practice of Silence

Before the Soul's eyes can see the Radiant Sun within, you must have won Calm and Peace, through Silence and Solitude, which can reflect the Tranquil Lake of the Transcendental State.

Silence and Activity must alternate: from Action into Silence, and from Silence into Action. This is the correct Way.

Silence surrounds you all the time, everywhere

The meaning of Silence is not to "get" something, not to "go" somewhere, not to "attain" anything. In Silence, pure and simple, you simply *Are*, and that simple *Be-ness* is the Opener of the Way.

Most people are afraid of Silence and Solitude. Rather, they feel the need to do things all the time, or to be with people all the time. This is natural, since we are social beings also and most people need stimulation to keep going. But if people developed the habit of taking time off from their "busy" lives to spend time in Silence and Solitude (being alone, by themselves), then soon they would discover inner Silence and Solitude, which is the Peace of God that "passes all understanding".

Silence and interior Solitude are necessary before deep and profound meditation becomes possible. A "noisy" mind cannot meditate. Silence and Solitude are the most difficult aspects of meditation, but when they are mastered and natural to you, meditation becomes spontaneous.

When you first begin your training in Silence and Solitude you might become nervous, fidgety, restless, anxious that you should be "busy" doing things. If you persevere often, however, this sense of restlessness will pass away and an Interior Delight will take hold of you which cannot be explained in words. And in time you will begin to *hear* the first strains of Divine Eloquence.

To find Silence and Solitude you do not have to live in a cave, an ashram or a monastery. Silence surrounds you all the time, everywhere. *Just sit still and settle the mind.* Stop the mental chatterbox that keeps going on inside you.

Divine Silence is the great Fundamental Root and Source of all Creation and all activity. It is here, everywhere, all the time. Listen into It.

Zen Silence 790
Alone with God 700
The Silence of the Warrior 1008
From Action into Stillness, From Stillness into Action 1016
Silence, Solitude, Peace 1386

Stages of Silence

1. Silence of the tongue (not speaking).
2. Silence of emotions (not desiring anything).
3. Silence of mind (not thinking about anything).
4. Silence of Consciousness (sitting still, intently *looking* or *listening*, being attentive, alert, awake, aware). This looking is in the Third-Eye. This Listening is in the Inner Ear.
5. Silence of the Soul. This *descends* upon you as soon as the whole personality (body, emotions and mind) is at rest.
6. Silence of the Spirit. The Silence enfolds you, envelops you, protects you. You are in a condition beyond Space, Time and ego-sense.

The Silence enfolds you, envelops you, protects you

To be able to enter the Silence of the Higher Spheres the mind must become still, calm, quiet and alertly poised. Tranquillity, quiescence and inner calm must also be achieved in daily living. Agitations coming from the personality simply block out the emerging Soul-Light. This peacefulness in daily living is not easy to achieve, as the whole world is agitated, but we must work at it until the end of our lives, with patience, hope and perseverance.

Sit still and be happy.
See where there is nothing to see.
Hear where there is nothing to hear, where all seems quiet.
In time you will listen to the Music of the Spheres.

Many of the Metanoia refer to specific types of meditation, apart from meditation on the Metanoia themselves.

For example, these Metanoia refer to Light:

My body is the Temple of God in which I see the Light of God.
Look for the Light.
The Path of the Just is the Shining Light.

These Metanoia refer to Sound:

Listen to the Inner Voice.
Remember the Name.

This Metanoia refers to Fiery Love:

Blessed are those in whose Hearts God has kindled the Fire of Love.

The Path of Hearing 553
The Seven Stages of Sūfī Silence 901
Suspended Mind 1209
The Silence of the Deep 1355
The Silent State 1554

How to Enter Silence

Silence is omnipresent and all-permeating. It penetrates and pervades everybody and everything, always. Silence is within you and outside of you, in all Space. Silence is a living, breathing, intelligent Entity.

Silence is not approachable by the mind. It cannot be reasoned, thought out or speculated about. As soon as you "think", Silence evaporates.

You may approach Silence through the senses of *hearing, sight* or *touch* (feeling). Sit still, without a thought about anything, and *look* intently or *listen* intently or *feel* intently, without a thought. Or, just *be* intently. Be yourself intensely, without thinking. Then Silence comes, quietly, on its own. And with it comes Peace and Benediction.

You must become religious before you can encounter true Silence

Silence is not just a vacuum or an emptiness. It is the Sacred Presence. You must become religious before you can encounter true Silence. Silence is true Fullness wherein everything exists and abides and has its Being. It is another name for God.

In Silence God speaks to us and shows us mysteries. In Silence we discover that the Infinite Majesty is Here, Now, with us, within us, living in us and around us.

Some people are afraid of Silence because they think it is loneliness. But you cannot be lonely when God is within you and around you! The Infinite Majesty is fully present in you, always. What else do you want?

Silence is the Sacred Moment of God, God's Omnipresence. From the true Original Silence issues forth the Logos, the Word, the Sounding-Light Current. When you enter *your* Silence, it is to encounter the Logos, the Creative Word. You actually enter into the Fullness of Sound! If you pursue the Logos to its Source, however, you discover true Silence, the very Beingness of God.

The ancient Chinese Mystics called it TAO, the Great Silence. TAO also means "Life, Essence, the Way, the method and the result". Silence is the Way, the method and the result. It is the beginning and the end of all things.

In Silence is your *comfort*, your *peace*, your *security*, for in it is the Glory of the Lord.

Solitude and Loneliness 1170
Cultivate Silence of the Mind 1239
Meditation on the Sacred Word 1216
To Silence the Mind 1212
Works of Silence 1643

Silence and Activity

In Silence all victories are won

The original great religion of China was TAO TEH (Silence and Action). Lao Tzu described the Way of Tao (Silence) to his pupils thus:

> Touch Ultimate Emptiness (Silence). Hold it steady and still.
>
> All events and things are inter-related in the bosom of Silence. I watched them being born, come to a peak, and return again to the Root, which is Silence (Tao).
>
> The meaning of Stillness is to return to one's own Root, the Silence (Tao), which in reality is a return to the Will of God. This Will (Tao) is Eternal Stability. The Realization of this Stability is Enlightenment. He who does not experience it is blind and works much evil.
>
> When you experience this Unchanging Eternal (Tao), you have dignity, righteousness, kingship and Divinity. And Divinity (Tao) is the Way which is the return to the Source.

The Way of Tao is not to strive. There is no need to fight, to oppose, to struggle, to make great efforts, to contend, to argue. The Way of Silence is a gentle way. Even when you are attacked, within or without, by people or forces, you may still rest in Silence. Understand its mysteries, because in Silence all victories are won.

All opposition is destroyed by itself.

No opposition has infinite power. No people, forces or circumstances can hurt you in essence. They are all limited, circumscribed by their own negativity. It is their own negativity that ultimately defeats them.

TAO TEH, Silence and Activity, is the perfect life.

Tao is Silent 779
Yin, Yang, Tao 476
The Warrior seeks Peace not War 986
The Law of the Higher Life 1134
The Active and Passive Way 1011

The Chinese word **TAO** means the Essential Simplicity, which is the Source, Root and Origin of things, and at the same time the Way, the Truth and the Life. It is the manifest and unmanifest Godhead all at once, in Oneness. The ancient Egyptian word for this was **TAU**.

The Eternal Tao 771

Silence

The best way to pray is to enter into Silence.

Be Still, at Peace.

God needs no loud prayers,
for God is nearer to us than even our thoughts.

Be Alone with God.

Silence purifies.
Silence heals.
Silence restores Peace of Mind.

The Soul grows in Silence.

He who is Silent will find the Source of all Life.

Silence is the password to the Living God.

Silence becomes mystical when God enters in.

In Silence, miracles of Transformation take place.

In Stillness, the Voice of God utters Itself.

The Sabbath Day, the Holy Day,
is that full Silence which knows no fear,
of neither life nor death,
of no person or situation,
for you are upheld by the Hand of God.

When we submit ourselves to the Word of God,
in profound Silence, Revelations will come.

A perfect Resignation
and inner Silence in the Heart
will lead to the experience of the Peace of God.

Be Still, choicelessly aware.

Sitting on the bank,
doing nothing with the stream.

Being Silent, waiting.

∞

Four Ways to Enter Silence

Waiting upon the Lord. Sit still and patiently wait upon God as if you were waiting for the coming of a friend. A great feeling of Devotion for God is required.

Contemplation. Sit still and simply gaze in front of you with your eyes closed, or above you with the eyes closed and turned naturally upward. There should be no strain on the eyes whatsoever. Simply fix your inner gaze, in Silence, and look upon what you see. If it is darkness, then it is darkness; if it is Light, then it is Light. Again, do not force yourself to "see" something. It is God's Immanent Presence which is on your mind.

Listening. Listen with your inner ear, on the right side, to the sound of God's Word, while being still. The Sound will be heard automatically as soon as you are genuinely still.

Use a prayer or mantra to prepare yourself to enter into Silence. When the mind is in Silence, drop the prayer.

The Heart and the Lost Art of Prayer 1251

The Third Circle of Life

The Third Circle of Life is Life *in* God, the Life *of* God, Life *as* God.

To penetrate into the Third Circle of Life you first must work to establish yourself in the Second Circle. It is not possible to penetrate into the Third Circle unless first you have established yourself in Soul-Consciousness.

The final goal of Human Evolution is to merge with God as the Creator

The final goal of Human Evolution is to merge with God as the Creator, the Creative Intelligence of the Universe, PARAMĀTMAN, on the level of PARANIRVĀṆA. This is becoming a "Christ" or a "Perfectly Enlightened Buddha". This is Divine Consciousness.

Before this stage comes the Realization of NIRVĀṆA, of the ĀTMAN, the great "I AM" of the Universe. From this level spoke Śrī Kṛṣṇa in the Bhagavad-Gītā, Jesus the Christ in the New Testament, and the Lord Gautama Buddha. Nirvāṇa is a state of Bliss-Consciousness, MOKṢA (Freedom) and MUKTI (Liberation). The word NIRVĀṆA means "liberation or freedom from any hindrances of perception, enjoyment or action". This is the Kingdom of God, the perfect Spiritual State, our inheritance from God. In this state we can truly comprehend BHAKTI (Devotion to God), JÑĀNA (Gnosis, Wisdom) and KARMA (Action).

Before this, however, we have to traverse through the many layers of the mind and reach the level of BUDDHI, or true discrimination between the Real and the Unreal. In BUDDHI we can look up towards Bliss-Consciousness and see the Spirit, the ĀTMAN within us, and experience the Real; or we can look downwards and entangle ourselves with the mind (MANAS) and experience the Unreal.

Using Sanskrit terminology, there are three degrees of Self-Realization:

JĪVĀTMAN: the Living Soul, the Individualized Self.
ĀTMAN: the Universal Self, the many Selves as One.
PARAMĀTMAN: the Monad, the Transcendental Self, the Godhead, the Absolute Existence, Universal Life.

Below JĪVĀTMAN is you as the personality, your personal ego or personal "I am", what you identify with in your normal, everyday consciousness. The Path consists of identifying with increasingly higher levels of I AM.

- The quality of the Monad is Will, Purpose and Power.
- The quality of the Soul is Love and Wisdom.
- The quality of the personality is Activity.

Human Involution and Evolution 170
Nirvāṇa: the World of Glories 93
Realms of the One Mind 492
God-Consciousness is the Wholeness of Life 504
The Three Stages of Yoga 528

I AM and my Father, God, are inseparably and eternally One. There is nothing, neither in Heaven nor on Earth, neither above nor below, but the Life of God. God is in me, I am in God. I AM God.

Eternal Liberation is the Conscious Remembrance,
reawakening to the fact that I AM and
my Father, God, are always One,
and there is nothing else besides.

God Is. I AM. I AM is God.

The Truth is that I AM One with God,
and God is All in All.

Beyond all phenomena shines the Light of God.
I AM is the Centre, the Origin and the End.

I AM part of God. I and all this vast Universe,
all peoples and all things, exist *within* God.

I AM a Thought in the Divine Mind.
As God is Creator of the World,
so am I the Creator of my life.
Nothing can break the Unity of God.

I AM Consciousness is Christ-Consciousness, the Master Power, the True Teacher, the Inner Guide.

I AM is Ātman, the Self, the Pure Beingness,
the Christ Within.

I AM is Transcendental Bliss, Unbounded Intelligence, Unconditional Love.

I AM is the Way to Perfection, to infinite growth and potential, to infinite Creativity.

I AM is God in Man. I AM is God. I AM God.

I AM is the Name of God, the very Identity
of God, the Self-Remembrance of God.

I AM is the Infinite Way,
the Eternal Beingness, Immortality.

I AM is Declaration of Life,
Affirmation of Existence.

I AM is I, the Me, the You,
the When and the How.

I AM Spirit.

I AM a Divine Being.

I AM One.
I AM All-inclusive.
I AM One with the Lord.

I AM Illumined by the Boundless-Light-Eternity.

I AM Eternal, Immortal and Indestructible.

I AM Love and Infinite Forgiveness.

I AM Infinite.
I AM Eternal.
I AM Omnipotent.

I AM Creative Power.
I AM Cosmic Intelligence.
I AM Cosmic Mind.

I AM is with you.
You are God.
Go forth and re-become what you are.

∞

Oneness and Love

All Selves are One. Although the Souls appear to be individuals and separated, they all have their existence in the One Self, the Brightness of the Eternal Light. The only relationship that exists between the Selves is Love.

The Force that binds all things together is Love

We are all entwined, compounded together, dependent on one another, dependent on the Cosmos, which in turn is the projection of a dream in the Mind of Reality, the Infinite Godhead or Limitless Life. The Force that binds all things together is Love. This is the Cosmic Unifying Power, the adhesive that holds the Many in the One, the One in the Many. Without this Cosmic Adhesive Force of Love there could be no Universal Manifestation.

What is in the Kingdom of God must also be established in the Kingdom of the World, hence we must Love everybody. The only purpose of your existence is to learn to Love more and more until, at the end of your Path, you are One with the Infinite Love of the Universal Being of Light.

There is nobody and nothing perfect in this evolving Universe, hence the Commandment was given: "Love one another and forgive". For herein lies the Secret of Eternity.

God's never-ending Field of Manifestation stretches boundless throughout the infinitudes of Space. There is not an atom that is not part of God. There is not an inch that is empty of the Infinite Glory of God. The bodily senses veil the Light. I am a Creation of God's Glorious Love.

The Eternal is One 512
The Divine Unity 852
The Supreme Act of Karma 264
On Love and Meditation 1140
The Meaning of Life is Love 633
To Love God and the World 1392
To Manifest the Kingdom of God 1716
On the Wings of Devotion 1129

When the attention is shifted into the Heart Centre through meditation and the power of Love, Devotion and self-surrender, it is discovered that:

There is only One Life, the Life of God, and I am part of it.
As the Life of God is Eternal, I am Eternal.
My true Identity, my true Self, is the Boundless Existence of the Imperishable Light-Kingdom, the Kingdom of God.
My life is hid in the Essence of God forever.

Seek the Kingdom and you will find it.
The ego will drop, for Love will guide it.

True Love is the capacity to vibrate universally.

Blessed are Those in whose Hearts
God has kindled the Fire of Love.

There is a limitless supply of Love.
The more you give away, the more you shall receive.

God is indwelling all peoples,
everywhere, at all times.

The Divine Light shines
in even the worst of human beings.

All beings are the Self,
and there is nothing but God.

All creatures are in God.

God dwells in All, fully.

The God within us is the Self of us all.

In God's Light there is only
Unconditional Love and Forgiveness.
All Souls in God's Light are equally loved.

You cannot judge the true worth of a person
by superficial appearances.
God does not judge by outer appearances,
but by the depth of the Soul.

God loves you too, always.

Nothing can ever separate us
from the Love of God.

Share the Light, which each of us is,
with all whom you meet.

Meet to give.
Always give something to the person you meet,
even if it is just a smile or a loving thought,
or a warm feeling of welcome.

Be spontaneously and naturally giving.
It is not necessarily objects that you must give,
but something of yourself, the real You.
Be not neurotic about the fact that you are not
perfect. Forget yourself and see how you can
always help others.

To give Love,
you must first have Love in your Heart.

A contented, happy Heart is a giving Heart.

Use the magic of Goodwill.

Let your Heart always shine.

Boundless Love is acquired in the Living Heart
by self-surrender and a wordless Devotion to God.

The Love of God needs few words.

While you have Love for God in your Heart,
your group will be indestructible.

We are only as far from each other as our thoughts.
Love reaches all.

The Love of God nourishes me.
Therefore I do not need to take anything from
anybody, but I can always give the nourishing
power of Love to all in need.

∞

Cosmic Renewal

Metanoia means a Transmutational Process. This can refer to our personal transmutational process and, later on, to our Psyche-Metanoia, which is our Soul's transmutational process. The Greek word Psyche means "Soul, Spirit, Consciousness, the Inner Being in Man". Thus, Psyche-Metanoia means "Inner Transformation".

This Cosmic Renewal Process is the primary process, for it is going on all the time

There is also a Kosmos-Metanoia (Cosmic Transformational Process) going on all the time. The Greek word Kosmos means "the World, the Solar System, the Universe, the Universal Order of Creation, the Omniverse, the Orderly Expression of the Divine, the orderly process of Life". This Cosmic Renewal Process is, in fact, the *primary* process, for it is going on all the time, but Humanity does not perceive it or respond to it. When you are ready, however, and you respond to this Renewal or Transmutational Process of the Cosmos, it *appears* to you that it is your own private, personal process. Think about that! Your stepping upon the Spiritual Path is *not* unique to yourself; you simply have finally responded to the Process!

The following ancient Western Metanoia refer to Cosmic Metanoia, Cosmic Renewal, Solar-Systemic changes, Solar-Systemic Rebirth, Solar-Systemic Transformation.

Glory be to you, Father of the Undying, for by your Glory you renew the World.

This refers to the Touch by the Radiation Field of the Absolute Light, the Immeasurable Light and Glory of the Limitless Existence.

Come Holy Spirit, and fill the Hearts of the Faithful, and enkindle in them the Fire of Love.

This refers to the Vivifying Power, the Sanctifying Power of the Holy Spirit, the Cosmic Fire, the Fire of Creation.

Salvation is the Christ becoming All in All, the Word or Sound-Current.

This is the Universal Christ-Being *consciously* becoming the Cosmic Light, uniting each separated particle in Creation (each separate unit or individual) into Universal Oneness.

The Plan is in the Divine Mind 161
Vertical Evolution and the Path 174
Dimensions of the Cosmic Fire 137
The Holy Trinity 1342
Children of the Sun 1590
Evolution, the Plan, the Path 1688

The Kingdom is at Hand

The Christian religion confuses the life history of the actual JOSHUA BEN MYRIAM (the *real* historical Jesus) and the mythology of the New Testament with the continuous Work of the Cosmic Christ for Universal Redemption, Salvation, Liberation.

The Greek word PAROUSIA is usually translated by the Christians as the "Second Coming" of Jesus. They expect the real, historical, physical person, JOSHUA BEN MYRIAM, to return again and bring Salvation to all. But PAROUSIA actually means "arrival, presence, already arrived, being already present". In fact, the PLERŌMA (Greek: the All, the Fullness, the Totality, the All-Manifestation, the total Divinity or total Divine Expression) is *already full* of the Glory (the Father), with the Word or Sound-Current (the Christ), and with the Renewing Fire (the Holy Ghost).

We do not need to wait for the future coming of Jesus

We do not need to wait for the future coming of Jesus (Joshua) to save us. "The Kingdom of God is already at hand." It is Here, Now.

The Past is unimportant, for it no longer exists.

The Present is real, for it is the doorway to the *future possibility*.

The Present is the result of past impressions and your will towards the Future.

Some people always think of the Past, some always dream of the Future, but they do not realize the importance of *Now*.

In the Silence of your Soul, the Voice of Revelation speaks to your inner ear. This is the Imminent Revelation of the Immanent Christ.

The worldly name of Jesus was YESHUA (JOSHUA) BEN MYRIAM (Hebrew: Jesus the son of Myriam). His title or enlightened name was YEHESHUAH (JESHUAH) HA MASHIAH (Jesus the Anointed One).

Names of the Great Master Jesus 661

The Cosmic Christ 662
The Unfoldment of the Light 718
The Coming of Christ in the Heart 727
Let Go of the Past 1241
Past, Present and Future 1400
The Kingdom of God 1715

Meditation on the Divine Names

The Christ, the Fullness of Divinity, is both Macrocosmic (infinite) and Microcosmic (incarnate in Humanity, in the Heart Centre). The Immanent Divinity is the unfailing Light of the Mind and the Supreme Ruler of the Heart.

Each of the Divine Names has a different healing energy of the Light-Force

The Incarnated God in the human Heart has been called by many names by different religions: CHRIST by the Christians, BUDDHA by the Buddhists, ALLĀH by the Muslims, YAHWEH by the Jews, KṚṢṆA, RĀMA and ĪŚVARA by the Hindus. But it is the same Divine Guide. Be not deceived: there are not many "gods". *God is One.*

Thus, you may invoke God-Incarnate within the secret chambers of your Heart by different Divine Names, the one that pleases you most, or the one that gives you the most joy. Even the word *God* is a Holy Power when taken into the Heart with flaming Devotion, because God *is* omnipresent and sees and knows all things.

The Divine Name purifies your Heart. When your Heart becomes totally Pure and Radiant, you shall *see* God. This purification process can take a long time, for it is *the transmutation of the vibrations of the personality into the Vibration of Divine Immanence.* That is the purpose of the Divine Names.

The Inner Healer

Each of the Divine Names has a different healing energy of the Light-Force. You can vibrate these Names physically to affect the physical body, astrally to affect the emotions, mentally to affect the mind, causally to affect the Soul, and by the Soul to affect the Spirit within you.

Normally the Inner Healer within us sleeps for lack of action; only when one is chronically ill does one think of healing. I AM, as the Inner Healer, can be called into action by such practices. The Inner Healer—the I AM Power within, or God in the healing mode—helps also in karmic readjustment processes.

Disease is simply the flow of *unregulated energies* within us. Whether they be physical, emotional or mental, they are energies *out of tune* with the Infinite. The problem is that You as a Soul have a different rhythm from you as a personality, and each body within the personality itself has a different rhythm. With coordination comes Health.

Meditation is Integration 1193

The Universal Christ 440
Incarnations of the Sun 1593
The Name and the Names 1258
The Universal Heart Practice 846
The Way of the Radiant Heart 452
Tapas: Spiritual Purification 571
Karmic Adjustment 1379

The Word

The Word is a mighty Power.

The Word is the Creator-God, the Logos,
and it is also the Scripture, or Thought-Power.

The Word is Light-Sound-
Intelligence-Being-Reality-Vibration.
This is the Mystery of the fivefold Inner Word,
the True Name of God.

The Ancient Creative Power forms itself in Man.
This is the meaning of the words:
"The Word was made flesh and dwelt amongst us."

Our bodies are made by the Word,
but according to the modification
thrown out by our own Consciousness.
Thus, the quality of Consciousness of every
man, woman or child, of angel, god or tree,
determines the quality of embodiment,
and hence circumstances.

The Inner Music is going on all the time.
The mind must be still and motionless to hear it.
This is the Word, the Voice of God,
the Life of all things.

The True Guru is the Word.
The Logos is your Inner Master.

The Voice of God, like a thunder clap,
rents the Silence with Its shrill Revelation.

The Rumblings of the Silent Deep
reverberate throughout all Space,
in all places and at every moment of Time,
bringing with It the good tidings of Joy and Peace.

Look for the Light.
Listen to the Inner Voice.
Remember the Name.

That which can be Seen is always Present.
That which can be Heard is always Resounding.

The Vibrating Light within
utters Itself as Pure Music.
This is heard by the inner ear.

The Word is Light.
The Light is Life (Being).
Being is God.
God is Love.

The words that I speak or think are, in fact,
part of the manifest Word of the Logos,
hence they have Divine Powers.
Thus, I can re-create my future.

The Name and the Named are One.

∞

The Word is twofold:

a. The Logos, the Śabda-Brahman, the Immortal Creator-Power that ceaselessly emanates from the Supreme Being, creating and maintaining the World.

b. The power of human speech, words and thoughts, and of the scriptures (the written word).

The Word, Logos, Voice, Name 1646

The Voice of God 864

Hebrew Divine Words for Healing

Immanuel

I AM God-is-with-us.

I AM God-is-amongst-us.

I AM God-is-within-us.

With us is God. God is here, now. Everything I see is the Incarnate God.

Raphael

I AM healed.

I AM God-Heals.

I AM the Restorative-Power of God.

I AM the Harmony of God.

I AM the Beauty of God.

The Healing Power. Knowledge, Illumination.

Michael

I AM the Invincible.

I AM the Conqueror Power.

I AM the Likeness.

I AM the Presence of God.

I AM God who is the Protective Power.

I AM God who Reveals and Guides.

Heroic Energy. Defends, protects, leads, guides.

Gabriel

I AM God-is-Strong.

I AM God-is-Omnipotent.

I AM God-is-Transformative-Vibration.

The Power that gives Visions, that announces the Future. The Messenger on High who Reveals the Divine Plan, the Word.

Ūriel

I AM God-is-Light.

I AM God-is-Fire.

I AM the Flame of God.

I AM the Regenerative Power of God.

My Light is God. Salvation, Transfiguration.

Yeheshuah (Yeshuah, Yeshua, Yoshua)

I AM God-Saves.

I AM God Delivers.

I AM the Saving Grace of the Eternal.

I AM the Fiery Love of God.

The Abundance of God. The Power of Divine Grace.

Amen

I AM God the Witness.

I AM the Omnipresent Energy of God.

I AM God-Sees-all-Things.

I AM the Omnipresent Divine Power.

The Power to accomplish all things.

∞

Yeshua: the Secret Hebrew Name 1276

Āuṁ: the Holy Spirit as Cosmic Mother 1501

I O E L

The Healing Mind

I O E L is a Hebrew Name of I AM in the aspect of God's Healing Mind, or Mind as Healer.

I A O	=	Yah
I A O - E L or I O E L	=	Yah-El
I A O U E	=	Yahweh
I A O U - EL	=	Yah - El

The Hebrews used to conceal the Sacred Names of God by not indicating the Vowels in the archaic, primitive Hebrew. Only Consonants and Semi-Vowels were indicated. The full Vowels were kept secret for the Initiated only. That is why later generations did not know how to pronounce correctly the Hebrew Divine Names of God.

I O E L, in Pure Vowel pronunciation, means "the Eternal is God, I AM the Eternal Self-Existent One, I AM the Guiding Force of the Universe, I AM the Inner Healer, I AM the Illuminator-Force, I AM the Spiritual-Sunshine flooding your Soul, I AM the Purifying Light Vibration, I AM the Purifying Fire".

This God Name will activate the powers of Light Vibration in whichever cakra you intone it, and through that cakra will bring about a corresponding balance in the personality.

I O E L

This principle of Pure Vowel pronunciation can be applied to all the Hebrew Divine Names taught in this chapter. For instance:

Eheyeh or Ehyeh or Eheyehe	E E E
Immanu-El	I A U - El
Rapha-El	A A - El
Micha - El	I A - El
Gabri - El	A I - El
Ūri - El	Ū I - El
Yeheshuah or Yeshua or Yoshua	E U A, O U A
Amen	A E
Yekhidah	E I A
Yehovah or Yahweh	E O A

The Vowels 1030
I A O 1034
The Vowels in the Heart 1303

Yekhidah

The Hebrew I AM

Yekhidah

Yekhidah

I AM the Limitless Light.

I AM the Eternal Selfhood.

I AM Imperishable Life.

I AM Oneness and Unbroken Unity of Consciousness.

I AM Vibration of Supreme Intelligence.

I AM Light which gives Unending Knowledge.

I AM That from which All-Things proceed forth.

I AM Consciousness.

I AM the Plan and Purpose of the Universe.

I AM the Universal Energy of Love practically expressed.

I AM the Power that interpenetrates all the worlds.

I AM the Force which regulates the vastness of Space-Creations.

I AM the Ocean of Being, the Glorious Presence, both immanent and transcendent.

I AM Eternal Being, Limitless Life, Boundless Creativity and Self-Expression.

I AM Absolute Bliss-Consciousness.

I AM the Living-God.

I AM God-into-Expression Power.

I AM Ātman, the Cosmic Self, the One I AM dwelling in all beings.

I AM the Resistless Energy of the Originating Principle.

El Allāh Hū

The Arabic I AM

El Allāh Hū

This is the Sūfī statement of I AM.

El is the concentrated Power of the I AM, the all-powerful Lord God, *here.*

Allāh is the Dazzling Radiance of Eternal Life, *there.*

Hū is the Breath Eternal that never dies. It links the *here* to the *there*, or God-Dynamic to the God-Transcendent.

For I AM, or God, has two aspects: the Dynamic or Immanent, active in the worlds visible and invisible; and the Passive or Transcendental, perceived in meditation profound, when the personality comes to rest.

El Allāh Hū can be practised in the Third-Eye Centre or in the Heart Centre.

God Immanent and Transcendent 111
The One and Only 839
Sūfī Prayer 863

YEHOVAH

IHVH

I AM

The Hebrew Name of God, **IHVH**, is commonly pronounced as YAHWEH (YAHVEH) or YEHOVAH. It is another name for I AM.

IHVH

That which causes all things to exist.

That which was, is, and will be.

The Eternal, Everlastingness.

The Unknowable Absoluteness.

That about which not much can be said.

Unfortunately the Bible translators translated this word as "Lord", meaning a personal God, like the "old man on the throne" or a tribal warrior chief. But this word *cannot* have that meaning. There are Hebrew words that mean Lord, Master, Sir, Powerful One, but this is *not* one of them.

IHVH means Everlastingness, Ultimate Reality, Existence, Being, the Transcendental Self, the Transcendental Godhead, the Everlasting Light, the Limitless Light. It is the Unpronounceable Name, the Lost Word.

The Lord? 121
Can God be Angry? 106
Hebrew Divine Names to be Invoked in the Heart 1262
Christian Meditation on the Holy Breath 1346

I		H			V		H	
I	E		O	U		A		***the Vowels***
		H			V			***the Semi-Vowels***
		= YEHOUVAH						

Pronunciation of IHVH

Sounding the Hebrew Divine Names

This is Light-Work, for Spiritual Development and Realization, or Union with God. Start at the Base Centre and invoke **Adonaī Ha-Aretz** by intoning the Divine Name on the musical note 'C'. Work your way up to the Crown Centre, centre by centre, with the corresponding intoning of the Divine Names on the correct notes, then merge into the Universal White Light.

When you can do this, you may reverse the process. Start in the Causal Centre, bring the Light down through the centres and "earth" it in the Base Centre, thus transforming your whole personality.

This can be done aloud, or it can be done mentally, silently in your mind. The pronunciation must be true Pure Vowels.

The pronunciation must be true Pure Vowels

Centre (Cakra)	Hebrew God-Name	Translation	Music Scale	
Causal Centre	(Pure Light)		UPPER C	*DO*
Crown Centre	**Eh-he-yeh-hē**	*I Am the Everlasting*	B	*TI*
Third-Eye Centre	**Ye-ho-vāh** **E-lo-hīm**	*The Imperishable* *Creative Power*	A	*LA*
Throat Centre	**Yāh**	*That which Is*	G	*SO*
Heart Centre	**Ye-ho-vāh** **E-lo-āh** **Ve-da-āth**	*The Eternal* *Godhead* *of the Heart*	F	*FA*
Solar Plexus Centre	**Gī-būr**	*The Strong One*	E	*MI*
Sex Centre	**Sha-da-ī** **El-cha-ī**	*The Almighty* *Living-God*	D	*RE*
Base Centre	**A-do-na-ī** **Ha-a-retz**	*The Lord,* *God of the Universe*	C	*DO*

Hebrew Divine Names Meditation

Sounding the Hebrew Angelic Names

These Angelic Names are real Powers, Qualities or Energies within Cosmic Consciousness which can become available to you through correct meditational practices. The Names are sounded on the musical notes to develop these powers and abilities within you and to transform you into the Living Image of God. Thus you shall become a Man-God, a God-Man or God-Woman.

The correct intonation of the Vowels is all-important, whether you sound them physically or internally, in your mind.

	Hebrew Angelic Name	Intonation	Translation	Quality
1	Raphael	Ra – pha – el D C E F♯	*The Healing Power of God*	Healing
2	Michael	Mi – cha – el G♯ D♯ E F♯	*The Protective Power of God*	Protection
3	Gabriel	Gab – ri – el G♯ D E F♯	*The Illuminative Power of God*	Enlightenment
4	Ūriel	Ū – ri – el C♯ D E F♯	*The Fire of God*	Spiritual Fire
5	Hanael	Ha – na – el C G E F♯	*The Harmony of God*	Harmony
6	Tzaphkiel	Tzaph – ki – el A♯ A♯ E F♯	*The Understanding Power of God*	Wisdom
7	Ratziel	Ra – tzi – el D A♯ E F♯	*The Unveiling Power of God*	Revelation
8	Metatron	Me – tat – ron G♯ E D G	*The Light of God*	Brightness
9	Sandalphon	San – dal – phon G♯ F♯ C G	*The Immediate Presence of God*	The Presence

Hebrew Angelic Names Meditation

Healing

The easiest way to keep your body healthy
is to have a positive attitude in your mind.

Mind is Healer.

Suffering arises from the *clinging* and *attachment*
to "I", "me", "what is mine" and "belongs to me".

The best way to heal your emotional scars
is to go into a deep *Silence,* by yourself.
Silence heals.

By the Power of the Holy Ghost within me
I invoke Universal Light and Love
to heal all the circumstances of my life.

The Healing Power of Love adjusts now
every function in my mind and body
and every detail of my life.

I am Healed and Harmonious in mind and body.

Now I come under the Law of Love.
The Boundless Love-Vibration of
the Cosmic Life flows through me now
to sweep away all negative influences from my life,
to heal and energize my mind and body,
to free me from all limiting circumstances,
to re-establish Wholeness and Health within me.

The Power of God is working through me now
to free me from every negative influence,
opposition or adversity.

I am filled with the Sun.
I am filled with Light.
The Light keeps me positive.

The Power of God flows through me now.
The Spirit of God is active in me now.
I am filled with Energy, Radiance and Glory.
The Holy Spiritual Power cleanses my mind
and body, removes all obstructions from my life,
and leads me to Eternal Glory.

I am filled with the Power of the Holy Spirit.
I am renewed, energized and healed.

I am filled with the Radiant Energy of the Spirit.
I am made whole, complete, perfect.

God has already forgiven me.
I am at Peace.

I am the Magic of Light.
All Power is mine to change my mind and
change my body, and to bring all my situations
and relationships under Divine Guidance.

I am always cheerful, positive and bright.
I am tranquil and at rest.
I am relaxed in the Tranquil Light.

I rest my life in the Eternal Glory that is God,
the Radiant I AM that indwells all Creation,
the Boundless Life which gives me
every breath I take.

Though I may walk through the
Valley of the Shadow of Death,
I fear no evil,
for I AM I, the Might, the Power,
the Glory, the Radiant Life of God.

∞

Inner Guidance

In the depths of the Heart, God speaks.

God always helps those who are receptive.

The Holy Spirit guides those who are willing.
Do not let outer circumstances get you down.
Be always directed from within.

The Christ is already in you.
The work of the Holy Spirit is to remove the veil
from your eyes so that you may see this Truth.

The Master Power is everywhere.
The pervasive, Universal Light-Sound-Form
is the true form of your Inner Guide.

The Master Power works regardless of time,
place or circumstance.

The Master Power is all-powerful,
all-forgiving, all-loving, all-rewarding.

The Voice of Light is the true Inner Master.

Be Silent to hear the Voice
of the Inner Instructor, the Guru.
This Silence is verbal, emotional and mental.

The true Guru is inside you.
It is the Light of God which
dispels your inner Darkness.

The true GURU-DEVA,
the Divine Guide or Teacher,
is your Innermost Self.
He is also your God and Master.
He can be found inside you in deep meditation.

The quality of the Being of Light is
unconditional Love and Forgiveness,
boundless Awareness, unrestricted Freedom,
Bliss, and the sense of Oneness.

It is better to trust in the Lord (the Being of Light)
than to win the praise of the worldly powerful.

Thus sayeth the Divine:
"My sheep recognize my Voice;
I know them, and they follow Me."

I am receiving Divine Guidance.

I am one with Light and Love.
I am invoking Divine Guidance
to move aside all obstacles in
my Path of Progress in life.

The Master Power is always within me
and is watching over me.

Never alone when alone.

My Guardian Angel guides and directs me,
protects me, pleads my cause, and defends me.

I AM, even now, the Eternal.
I am guided by the Cosmic Intelligence.

I am allowing Cosmic Intelligence
to set my life in order,
to free me from all limiting circumstances.
All my affairs are now in Divine Hands.

∞

Rely on your Inner Self 1226
The Saviour in the Heart 1296

The Path

The Path begins with yourself.

The Lighted Way is found by looking within.
It is not found outside.

The Goal you seek lies within you.
You are the Key.
The way to it is Being and Doing.

The purpose of your being in this human
life-form is to Awaken to the Knowledge of God.

The purpose of life is to become
established *in* God.

Self-Realization is your immediate Goal.

The Path of the Just is the Shining Light.

Orient yourself towards
the Spiritual Life at all times.
Do not let the world destroy you.

Take life in your own hands.
You alone can walk upon your Path.
Let not others force their ways upon you.
Follow your own Destiny.

You have to consciously *work* at your Liberation.
It does not come by chance, nor by accident.

The Light reveals the Way.
Metanoia is the transformation of
Consciousness into the Real World.

Metanoia (Transformation) is gradual.
There is no instant success. Persevere!
The Spirit will guide you.

The only Peace that exists is inside yourself.
If you haven't found that, you haven't found Peace.
Be Still.

Make Peace with God.

Free is the Man who lives in the Eternal,
even though he acts in the Temporal.

You are Free not because of where you are,
but Who you are.

Freedom is identification with the *Real.*

Hold onto nothing
and you will have Peace of Mind.

Seek out the Happiness that is not
dependent on external circumstances.

The Twofold Way

According to the Christian Mystics, the Way consists of two aspects:

Via Positiva (Latin: Way-Dynamic).
The Active Path, which consists of singing, chanting, movement, structured and formal meditations, meditations with Mantra, Yantra, and so forth. Being with others, and being dynamically active for the *good* of others. This is the *Transformative* Path.

Via Negativa (Latin: Way-Passive).
The Passive Path, which consists of Silence, Stillness, training yourself to receive Grace, and Surrender to the Divine Presence. Being alone, in solitude. Being Still. This is the *Receptive* Path.

Both Paths are equally important and necessary for your spiritual growth and general well-being.

The Active and Passive Way 1011

When you acknowledge pain as pain,
trouble as trouble, and realize that
in this world nothing lasts forever,
you will find Peace.

When you let go of all,
the All will come to you.

Life goes on with or without you.
Therefore *relax*.

Work in the world, but do not get lost in it.
Always be positive, and continually adapt
yourself to changing circumstances.
Be not judgmental,
and always remember that you are the Self.

Start the day with the right things and you will
end the day in Peace. (A day is a cycle of activity.)

Every flower has its perfect day.

Be humble, be simple, meditate and pray a lot,
help as many people as you can.
This is the way to a Holy Life.

Love and Forgiveness is the Way.

He who has no Light cannot Enlighten others,
even if he sincerely wishes to do so.

You cannot shout the Truth from rooftops;
you would only be making a noise.
You can only whisper the Truth into listening ears.

Purify your Heart.
Elevate your Mind.
Harmonize your Speech.

Keep your self-esteem and dignity at all times.

Do not let your Heart be contaminated by the
world. Keep it safe through prayer, meditation
and chanting in your Heart. A Spiritual Heart will
inherit the Kingdom of God.

Guard your Heart,
for the Kingdom of God is within you.
Lose your Heart and you lose the Kingdom.

Be in charge of your life.

Keep in touch with the Cosmos.

Remember the Grand Sweep of things,
the Larger View, the Overall Plan,
and keep your head up at all times.

When you are occupied with yourself,
the little ego, you are separated from God.
When you are occupied with God, the Eternal,
you are separated from the little self.

Be Here.
Change yourself.
Turn on the Light.

Keep in touch with the Sun.

Look at the Bright Side of everything,
for all is Light.

Forget the mistakes of the Past
and let the Light of your Soul lead the Way.

Learn from past mistakes,
but don't let the Past get you down.

In all circumstances, a Positive Attitude.

For every challenge, there is a Positive Solution.

Make the best of every situation.
See a positive side to everything.

Do not concern yourself with things
you cannot change positively.

Stability you have to find inside yourself.
There is no Stability in the outside world.

Remain stable like a tree
firmly rooted in the Eternal.

Be *Still* and the answers will come by themselves.

When the Spirit works within us,
we begin to reflect the Inner Glory in our outer life.

Invite the Spirit of God to live in you.

See Divinity everywhere.

The Journey of Life is a Journey within my
Consciousness. The movement of Life is
but a flutter of Awareness.

The nature of my Soul is Light-Vibration.
Let me shine. Let me transmit Light to all the
worlds, to all beings, through all Space.
May I walk the Lighted Way.

I am one with the Light. I am one with the Sun.
I am breathing in Light. I am breathing the Sun.

I *reaffirm* myself. I stand in the Light.

I choose to be Happy.

I choose to be Positive.

I am relentlessly Positive. *Stability.*

All events and all circumstances in my life
always work out for the best.
Every person I meet always helps me
and supports my Cause.

I am positive, strong, fearless.
The Forces of Evolution carry me ever upwards.
I am full of Joy and Happiness.

I am strong because I am filled with
the Resistless Energy of the Holy Spirit.

The Spirit makes me Holy.

The Spirit gives me Freedom.

The Spirit within me is already Victorious.

I am already Free.

I trust in God in all circumstances.

God is with me forever.
It is the Play of the Infinite
in our Time and Place.

The Kingdom of God is truly within me,
and it is immovable.

God lives in me and I in God.

My life rests in God.

∞

The Lighted Way 1394
Evolution, the Plan, the Path 1688
The Warrior Code 1077

Summary of the Process

The I AM within you is responsible for you

The Path lies within you towards Soul-Consciousness.

- The "I am" perceived in the personality-consciousness is not the true I AM; it is but a reflection or shadow of the I AM of the Soul.
- The I AM-ness of your Soul-Nature is also but a reflection of the Great I AM, the Monad, the Divine Spark of the Eternal Flame.
- The Monadic I AM-ness is a reflection of the Logos, the God-Self, who is but a shadow of the Absolute, the Universal I AM, the Boundless Life, Absolute Existence.

Essentially, the Path can be walked upon by three kinds of process. Each of these processes is Metanoia:

a. **Transference** of Consciousness into a greater I AM within you.

b. **Transformation** of your bodies or vehicles, your embodiments, thus enabling a greater I AM to manifest through you.

c. **Transmutation** of your desires, thoughts and purposes into spiritual or divine desires, plans and purposes, thus recovering your Divinity.

In such ways you move up the Ladder of Self-Conscious Evolution. And remember that ultimately the I AM within you is responsible for you, whatever level of development you have reached.

Consciousness is One, its forms are Many.

The Wheel of Rebirth grinds on for you until you learn, by Wisdom, to neutralize every past Cause and dissolve in Harmony.

CHAPTER 61

Mahāvākya
Great Truth Statements

Words of Truth

MAHĀVĀKYA is the Sanskrit word for an important statement, a Word of Truth, a Word of God, an important mantra or affirmation. It is the ancient Eastern form of METANOIA.

MAHĀ means "great, important, large, omnipotent, absolute". It is the same as MAHAT, or Cosmic Mind.

Mahāvākya is the Insight into the Mysteries of Being and of the Cosmos

VĀKYA (VĀK) is Divine Speech, the Logos, the Word, or a Word of Power. It is Sound-Vibration, but it is also Divine Reason or Truth.

Thus, MAHĀVĀKYA means "Great Truth Statement" or "Great Word of Power". In the higher sense, MAHĀVĀKYA is the pulsation of Truth in the Divine Mind. In our human consciousness it is the Insight into the Mysteries of Being and of the Cosmos.

Mahāvākya Practice

To apply these MAHĀVĀKYAs, choose one and hold the statement in your mind.

- You can use the original Sanskrit form, or you can use the English translation.
- You can be formally sitting in meditation, or you can be moving about, doing things in your life, while continually holding the statement in the background of your awareness.

In India this form of meditation is called JÑĀNA Yoga, or Union through Knowledge, Insight, Realization. The MAHĀVĀKYAs are seed-thoughts which develop within you into mighty trees of Love, Wisdom and Illumination.

What is Metanoia? 1412
Vāk: the Divine Speech 118
The Upaniṣadic Mantrams 546
Keys to the Heart 1314

1

Śuddhacaitanyarūpo'haṁ
(Śuddha Caitanya Rūpa Ahaṁ)

Pure Consciousness is my true Nature, my real Being.

My true Nature or Form is Pure Consciousness.

Śuddha: pure.
Caitanya: consciousness.
Rūpa: form, nature.
Ahaṁ: I am.
Rūpo'haṁ (Rūpa-Ahaṁ): my true Nature or real Being.

Ōṁ Hrīṁ Śuddha Caitanya Rūpo'haṁ

2

Īśa Brāhmī Sthitiḥ

The Lord is God's Peace.

Perfect Peace is in God.

Īśa: the Lord, the Inner Ruler Immortal.
Brāhmī: God's.
Sthitiḥ: peace, tranquillity.

3

Sarvaṁ Khalvidaṁ Brahṁ

All is One.

The All is God.

Everything contains the Nature of Divinity.

Sarvaṁ: all.
Khalvidaṁ: wholeness, oneness.
Brahṁ: God.

Sarvaṁ Khalvidaṁ Brahṁ

4

Ahaṁ
I am.
I am the Eternal.

5

Sōhaṁ-Asmi
(Sah Ahaṁ Asmi)
I am that Eternal Being of Light.

Sah (Sat): That, the Eternal Life and Being.
Ahaṁ: I am.
Asmi: am.

6

Ahaṁ-Brahmāsmi
(Ahaṁ Brahma Asmi)
I am of the Essence or Nature of God.

Ahaṁ: I am.
Brahma: God.
Asmi: am.

7

Ayaṁ Ātmā Brahma
I am of the Nature of God.
My Spiritual Self is identical with the Divinity.

Ayaṁ: this.
Ātmā: the Self.
Brahma: God.

8

Hara Hara Gurudeva Parabrahman Parameśvara

I invoke the purifying energy of my Inner Soul, the Transcendental Reality, and the Lord of all Life.

Hara (Ha-Ra):
Hara is an aspect of the Śiva energy. It is an extremely energizing mantra (sound-formula) with two powerful syllables:
Ha is the Fiery Breath.
Ra is the Solar Rays or Solar Energy.

Gurudeva (Guru-Deva):
Guru is two syllables, Gu-Ru, and in the mantric language it means "from Darkness to Light".
Deva is also two syllables or sounds, De-Va. It means "outpouring Radiance".
Gurudeva is the Soul within, the Inner Guide. At a higher level of Union it is the Monad, the Paramātman. At the highest level it is Īśvara, the Supreme Lord of the Universe.

Parabrahman (Para-Brahman):
Para: the Transcendental.
Brahman: the Godhead, the Absolute.

Parameśvara (Param-Īśvara):
Param: the Supreme.
Īśvara: the Lord of the Universe.

9

Acalo'haṁ Sanātanaḥ
(Acala Ahaṁ Sanātanaḥ)

I am eternally the Tranquil Self.
My true Nature (the Spirit) is motionless forever.
In my true Spiritual Nature I am at Peace.

Acala: tranquil.
Ahaṁ: I am.
Sanātanaḥ: eternally.

10

Īśāvaṣyam Idaṁ Sarvaṁ

All This (the Universe, everything and everybody) is controlled by the Master Power.

The Lord God dwells in all things and all beings.

Īśāvaṣyam (Īśa-Avaṣyam):
Īśa: the Lord, God; the Ruling Principle of Man (the Soul), and God (the Soul of the Universe); the Master Power.
Avaṣyam: controlling, organizing.

Idaṁ: this.
Sarvaṁ: all, everything, everybody.

This mantra invokes the Master Power.

11

Śivōhaṁ
(Śiva-Ahaṁ)

The Transcendental Reality am I.

I am the Motionless (tranquil) Self.

Śiva: the Tranquil Self, the Transcendental Reality.
Ahaṁ: I am.

12

Tat Tvam Asi

You are the Eternal in your highest Essence.

Tat: Sat, the Absolute, Boundless Reality, Infinite Existence.
Tvam: thou.
Asi: art.

13

Tadeva Satyam Tat Brahman

Verily I say unto you, "That is the Truth, that is the Godhead".

Surely, the highest Reality is the All.

Tadeva (Tat-Eva):
Tat: the Boundless Absolute, the Inconceivable Reality, the Final Truth.
Eva: truthfully or truly I say unto you; I declare this.

Satyam: the Truth.
Brahman: the Godhead.

This mantra invokes the highest (seventh) level of Consciousness in Man, and the Boundless Absolute in the Cosmos.

14

Sadciddānanda Brahman (Satcidānanda Brahman)

God is Being, Consciousness and Bliss.

Pure Beingness is Conscious Bliss.

Sadciddānanda (Sat-Cit-Ānanda):
Sat: Absolute Existence.
Cit (Citta): Pure Consciousness.
Ānanda: Bliss.

Brahman: God.

15

Prajñānam Brahma

Consciousness is God.

My Consciousness is the Absolute.

Prajñānam: the Awakened Consciousness.
Brahma: God.

16

Jyotiṣ Mantra

Ōṁ
Antarjyotiḥ Bahirjyotiḥ
Pratyagjyotiḥ Parātparaḥ
Jyotirjyotiḥ Svāyamjyotiḥ
Ātmajyotiḥ Namo Namaḥ

Jyotiḥ, Jyotir, Jyotiṣ: Light, Fire, Radiance, Glory.
Antarjyotiḥ: the Inner Light.
Bahirjyotiḥ: the Outer Radiance.
Pratyagjyotiḥ: the Profound Light.
Parātparaḥ: the Supreme, Transcendental.
Jyotirjyotiḥ: the Light of all Lights.
Svāyamjyotiḥ: the Self-Effulgent Light.
Ātmajyotiḥ: the Light of the Soul.
Namo Namaḥ: I invoke.

This beautiful mantram invokes Light (the Supreme Reality) in all aspects, and it sings the Eternal Glory of the Imperishable Light and Its manifestations in the different Realms, including the human Soul. It is a very sacred verse.

17

Śrī Rāṁ Ādi Rāṁ
Bhajamana Jaya Rāṁ
O, my mind, worship God.
Let my mind worship the Dazzling Glory of God.

Ādi: the Primordial Reality.
Rāṁ: the God-Vibration.
Śrī: dazzling.
Jaya: victorious.
Bhajan: inner worship.
Mana: mind.

18

Rāma Guru Rāma Guru
Guru Guru Rāṁ

I worship the Divine Guru.
I invoke the Grace of the Guru.

Guru: the Dispeller of Darkness, the Bringer of Light.
Rāma: the Incarnation of Solar Radiance, the Solar Logos.
Rāṁ: the Blissful God-Vibration.

This mantra invokes the Guru in all its meanings: the human Guru, the Light of the Soul, and the all-pervading Divine Presence.

19

Ōṁ Yathā Sarvatathāgatā'haṁ
(Ōṁ Yathā Sarva Tathāgatā Ahaṁ)

My true Nature is the same as that of all the Enlightened Ones.
My true Nature is the Enlightened State of Buddhahood.
I am essentially Divine like the Great Ones before me.

Yathā: like.
Sarva: all.
Ahaṁ: I am.

Tathāgatā (Tathā-Gatā):
Tathā (Tat): That, the Absolute State.
Gatā: gone to, arrived at.
Tathāgatā: Ones who have gone to That.

20

Ōṁ Namah Śivāya

I honour the God-Self (Śiva) within me.

Śiva: the God-Self, the Transcendental Reality.
Namah: invocation, veneration, adoration.

21

Ōṁ Vajrātmako'haṁ
(Ōṁ Vajra-Ātma Ahaṁ)

My Soul is like the Lightning (made of Light).

My Self is the Bright Light of Nirvāṇa.

Vajra: lightning.
Ātma: Spirit.
Ahaṁ: I am.

22

Ātmarāmo'haṁ
(Ātma-Rāma-Ahaṁ)

I Delight in (or enjoy) the Spirit.

I Revel in the Self.

My true Self is Blissful Delight.

Ātma: Spirit.
Rāma: delight.
Ahaṁ: I am.

23

Akhandānandarūpo'haṁ
(Akhanda-Ānanda-Rūpa-Ahaṁ)

My true Nature is endless Bliss.

I am the Eternally Blissful Transcendental Self.

Akhanda: continuous.
Ānanda: bliss.
Rūpa: form.
Ahaṁ: I am.

24

Nitya Śuddha Vimukto'haṁ Nirākāro'haṁ
(Nitya Śuddha Vimukta Ahaṁ Nirākāra Ahaṁ)

Eternal, Pure and ever-Liberated am I, Formless am I.

I am the eternally pure Formless Self.

Nitya: eternal.
Śuddha: pure.
Vimukta: ever-liberated.
Nirākāra: formless.
Ahaṁ: am I.

25

a. **Antaryāmisvarūpo'haṁ**
(Antar Yāmi Sva Rūpa Ahaṁ)

The God within me rules my form.

My true Nature is the Form of the Inner Ruler Immortal (the Soul).

b. **Paramātmasvarūpo'haṁ**
(Param Ātma Sva Rūpa Ahaṁ)

My true Nature is the Transcendental Reality.

I am the Boundless All.

Antar: inner.
Yāmi: ruler.
Param: transcendental.
Ātma: the Self.
Sva: my own.
Rūpa: form.
Ahaṁ: am I.

∞

PART TWELVE

The Worship of the Goddess

CHAPTER 62

The Great Goddess

Lalitā: the Eternal Feminine

LALITĀ, or ŚAKTI, is the perpetual transformation of the Primordial Reality into all objects, names and forms, and all conditions in the Universe. It is the Life of all creatures and beings in the Cosmos, and their birth, evolution and dissolution.

Śakti is Divinity in the female mode of expression

Thus, LALITĀ is all that Is, from the most exalted, sublime and transcendental Being to the minutest physical particle.

LALITĀ is the All-Presence, everything just being There, in and out of Eternity, in and out of Time.

LALITĀ is the Great Radiance, the Everlasting Light, becoming the All and all the parts.

LALITĀ is the Mother-Light, or Light as the Mother of all things.

ŚAKTI is Female Divinity, or Divinity in the female mode of expression.

The Divine Energy

The concept of *Energy* is a very old knowledge of India. The ancient Sanskrit word **ŚAKTI** means "energy, force, power, strength, might, ability, skill". It is the Feminine side of the Deity. All that Is is Energy (ŚAKTI).

There are many types of energies:

- There are personality energies and there are Soul energies.
- There are energies of Nature (PRĀKṚTĪ-ŚAKTI).
- There are energies of Spirit (PURUṢA-ŚAKTI).
- There is the Cosmic Field that embraces all other fields of force (MAHĀ-ŚAKTI).

ŚAKTI is the totality of the *real* Energy and Forces of this Universe, on all layers and levels, on all planes of Existence. She is the Doer of all things, the Energy behind all activities: subatomic, atomic, planetary, solar-systemic and cosmic. She is the One Energy, the One Force of the Universe, visible and invisible, *doing, producing, causing* all things natural and "supernatural" (miraculous). She is the Goddess in all Her many forms, aspects and manifestations, and She is the Universal Mother, both as all forms and as the Life *within* forms.

The Primordial Light 119
The Cosmic Fire 130
The Breath of the Divine Mother 142
Śakti: the One Energy 150
The Eternal Feminine 469
The True Feminine 1516

Lalitā is the Universal Goddess or Śakti who assumes many forms, powers and modes of operation. In Her immanence or immediacy in Creation, She is Devī, the Personal Goddess.

She is also Bṛhad-Ambā, the Great Mother of the Universe.

Śakti pervades everything in Nature, and all operations of Nature are done through the Powers of Śakti, not only on Earth, but throughout the vast Cosmos.

All operations of Nature are done through the Powers of Śakti

She is the Universal Power of Reality, Para-Śakti.

In Her Cosmic Nature She is Mahā-Devī, boundless, measureless.

In Her Nature as Universal Desire, or the desire-nature of all beings, She is Kāmeśvarī (Kāma-Īśvarī). Thus, She motivates all actions.

Her three main powers are Jñāna (Knowledge), Icchā (Desire) and Kriyā (Action). Hence She is known as:

Jñānaśaktī-Icchāśaktī-Kriyāśaktī-Svarūpiṇī
She whose Self-Form (Sva-Rūpiṇī) is Knowledge, Desire and Action.

For it is through Knowledge, Desire and Action that all beings live and all things are done in the Universe.

∞

She is a shimmering, scintillating Sea of Radiant Light,
Resounding with Melodious Sound,
Simple in Essence, uncomplicated, One, Still,
Silent-yet-with-Sound, motionless-yet-moving,
an intense Holiness and Purity beyond comprehension,
a sense of Ultimate-Reality-being-unveiled,
a Power which is restrained yet Limitless,
a Beauty perfect and exquisite,
Infinite, Majestic, Awe-inspiring.

She gives Comfort, Courage and Love.

The One Force 133
The Holy Breath 1340
Paraśakti: the Supreme Power 1500
Holy Knowledge 1517
Lalitā: the Ultimate Goddess 1556
The Feminine Virtues 468

Śakti: the Energy of the Goddess

All the following are forms of Śakti, the Goddess-Force:

Mantra-Śakti
The Power generated by Mantras.

Kriyā-Śakti
The Power generated by ritual actions, work, activity.

Mano-Śakti
The Power generated by thought, thinking and mental activity.

Icchā-Śakti
The Power generated by will, desire, ambition and purposeful living.

Deva-Śakti
Divine Energy which you touch upon in higher meditation.

Jyotir-Śakti
The Energy of Light that produces inside you Illumination and Self-Realization.

Jyotiṣa-Śakti
The energies, forces and powers emanating from planets and stars, which is the proper science of Astrology when correctly understood.

Svastika-Śakti
The Mystic Force or Spiritual Power that can be placed in symbols, emblems, talismans, auspicious objects or signs.

Kuṇḍalinī-Fohat 148
The Life-Force 589
The Holy Spirit 1343
Dimensions of the Cosmic Fire 137
The Personality Complex 36
The Human Cakras 44

The Life-Force in Humanity

Liṅga-Śarīra is the symbolic-body, the etheric or vital body which is made wholly out of forces and energies.

There are also Cakras (Wheels of Fire) in your subtle bodies which distribute the Universal Life-Breath or Spirit (Prāṇa) in your inner constitution or microcosm (the auric-field), giving life and vitality to all your subtle bodies and your physical body.

Prāṇa energy gives vitality and vigour on all Planes of Being—material, semi-material and spiritual. It is the Life-force.

Mahā-Svastika-Śakti

The Great-Sign-of-Galaxies, or the Cosmic Power that creates and dissolves Universes. The Miracle is right in front of your eyes when you watch the night sky.

Vidyā-Śakti

The Power that comes to you through knowledge, science and Insight.

Bodhi-Citta-Śakti

The energy you generate in your quest for Enlightenment, Wisdom, Self-Realization. It is also the Energy of the Buddha, the Enlightened, Awakened, Realized Being after his or her Enlightenment.

Guru-Śakti

The energy-field of the Spiritual Teacher or Master.

Annamaya-Śakti

The energy in food, sustenance, nourishment.

Yoga-Siddhi-Śakti

The physical, psychic, occult and spiritual powers attained by the Yogīs.

Hṛdaya-Śakti

The Energy of the Heart, the Prema-Śakti, the Energy of Love, which is the Way of the Saint and Mystic.

Jñāna-Śakti

The energy of the Gnostic, the Knower, the Sage, the Seer.

Mauna-Śakti

The Silent Wave of Bliss, the Power that can alter all things, the Miraculous Power.

Balā

The raw force, energy and strength of matter and material conditions, the atoms and subtle particles, and the strength within forms, bodies, shapes and embodiments.

Kuṇḍalinī-Śakti

The Supreme Power, the Universal-Life-Principle in all of Nature and within the whole Universe.

All these forms of Śakti hold the secret of generating various types of energies for yourself and for the world. To change any condition you need Energy. To be healthy you need Āyustejas, the Energy of Life.

The Goddess does all the Work in all things and upon all Planes of Being

The Goddess has limitless Energy, limitless variations and combinations of Energies. Everything exists by Her Powers. Indeed, the Goddess does all the Work in all things and upon all Planes of Being by Her Universal Power, or Śakti. Not only does She do all things, but She is the Source and Consciousness behind all things (Cit-Śakti).

She is Sāvitrī, the All-Producer, the All-Begetter, the Mother of all things, the Cause of all things, the Other-Side-of-the-Sun.

She is the energy of Seva: Service, Worship, Homage, Reverence, Devotion, goodwill towards men and women, and prayer and praise towards the Deity.

∞

Her Name is Śrī,
Brightness, Glory, all-Powers, all-Radiance, all-Majesty,
The Sacred Power, the Power of Sacredness,
Holiness, Grace, Divinity,
The Luminous Ocean of Reality,
The Shining Consciousness,
The Eternal Beauty,
The Imperishable and Incorruptible Power,
The Undying Goodness,
The Eternal Welfare of All,
The Prosperity of the Universe.

What more can be said of Her?

Health and Fire 50
What is Consciousness? 1368
The Divine Bipolarity 471
Śiva-Śakti 1521
Sāvitrī: the Spiritual Sun as Mother 1496

Some Energy-Forms of the Goddess

Sarasvatī
The Energy that gives the ability for speech, learning, eloquence, music, art, dancing, creative expression, intelligence, knowledge, understanding, Mantras (Words of Power).

Seed Sound (Bīja-Mantra): **Aiṁ**

Lakṣmī
The Force or Energy that brings good luck, good fortune, wealth, prosperity, growth, development, success, beauty, grace, splendour, charm, lustre, fame, glory.

Seed Sound: **Śrīṁ**

Lalitā
The Force of *true* Femininity (without the masculine aggressive and intellectual tendencies). The Eternal Female Archetypal Force which expresses Herself as Beauty. She is lovely, attractive, desirable, magnetic, pleasing, soft, gentle, graceful, affectionate, caring.

Seed Sound: **Hrīṁ**

Kāmadevī
The Energy of desire, attraction, love, passion, wishing, longing, affection, enjoyment, pleasure, worship, devotion, union, at-one-ment, transformation, Divine Love.

Seed Sound: **Klīṁ**

Sarasvatī 200
The One-Hundred Names of Lalitā 1555

Kālī
The Power of action, activity, active force or energy. The Force of Action in Nature and in Humanity, which *can* be creative but is very often destructive (unregulated or wrongly expressed). It is also the Power that *liberates* you from the sensation of Time and Space.

Seed Sound: **Krīṁ**

Tārā
Liberating Force, Active Grace. Shining, radiant Energy. Positive, good, excellent force, the force of goodness or goodwill. Star-like radiation, silver-like Light, a Force which is capable of producing Glory.

Seed Sound: **Ōṁ**

Strī
A strong Feminine Power which is creative, mothering, nursing, caring, protecting, nourishing, sustaining and transforming.

Seed Sound: **Strīṁ**

Pārvatī
A Force which channels your energies towards the higher planes, transcends the mind, leads you out of the lower realms.

Seed Sound: **Sauḥ, Soū**

Kālimā 1495
The Strī-Mantra 1538
Potent Vibrations: Bīja-Mantra 1542

The Path of Mantra and the Goddess

Mantra is sound-pattern. It can be physical, astral, mental or causal vibration. The subtle sound-patterns (astral, mental or causal) are just as "real" as the physical sound-patterns and are perceived by the astral, mental and causal bodies. Thus, a Mantra can be a physical sound, or an astral, mental or causal sound.

A Mantra is the direct embodiment of the Goddess

- A Mantra produces not only sound, but also *colour vibrations* and a *form*, as well as an *energy* (MANTRA-ŚAKTI).
- A Mantra may be also a Cosmic Force or Power.
- A Mantra may be the Name of a god or goddess, who in turn is but an aspect of the Godhead, the Absolute, the Final Truth.
- A Mantra may also be a revealed scripture, a holy book or sacred text, or an aphorism.
- A Mantra is the *direct embodiment of the Goddess*, literally the incarnation of the Goddess in the form of VĀK (VĀCH), the Divine Speech, the Divine Word or Creative Power.
- Mantra directly affects your Consciousness (CIT) and your Mind (CITTA).

There is a direct relationship between the Goddess, Mantra and the Kuṇḍalinī Power. This is a great Mystery, a secret that is revealed to you only in deep meditation.

The Creative and Destructive Power of Sound 201
The Temple Not Made By Hands 369
Vāk: the Divine Speech 118
The Science of Bīja-Mantra 1218
Vibration and Mantra 1518
The Wisdom of the Goddess 1525

CHAPTER 63

The Heart of the Divine Mother

The Temple of the Goddess

The human body is the Temple of the Goddess.

The Earth-body is the Temple of the Goddess.

The Universe is the Temple of the Goddess.

You may find Her within all things, inward, hidden

You may find Her *within* all things—not on the outer surface, not on the appearance level (Māyā), but within, inward, hidden.

So it is that She is in all temples and all places of worship, within the Sanctum, the Holy of Holies, behind the Veil.

Remove the Veil from your eyes and She shines splendidly with Supernatural Glory.

The Goddess permeates everything. Surrendering to Her is the key to Her Heart. It opens up in you the floodgates of Love and Compassion, of goodness, generosity and selflessness.

Love is not of the intellect, not of the mind. Love issues out of the Heart. The Heart is Love.

You may Love God as Father or God as Mother. The Heart is Father-Love and also Mother-Love—not of earthly fathers and mothers, but of the Divine, which is choiceless, boundless, and for all, equally.

The Temple of God 639
Lalitā: the Eternal Feminine 1484
Holy Knowledge 1517
The Lover of God 853
My Beloved Lives in my Heart 1290
The Activity of the Divine Heart 1675

The Blissful Mother

Mother of Immortal Bliss

These Mantras are to be meditated upon in the Heart.
You may choose any that you are attracted to.

MĀTĀ-AMṚTĀ-ĀNANDA-MĀYĪ ŌṀ
Mother-Immortal, full of Bliss.

AMṚTĀ-ĀNANDAMĀYĪ-MĀ
Immortal, Blissful Mother.

ĀNANDAMĀYĪ-MĀ
Full-of-Bliss Mother.

ĀNANDĪ-MĀ
Blissful Mother.

ŚRĪ-MĀ, JAI-MĀ, JAYA-MĀ
Holy Mother, Victorious Mother.

ŚRĪ-MĀ, JAYA MĀ JAYA JAYA MĀ
Victory to the Holy Mother.

The Mother

The very ancient Sanskrit word for "Mother" was **MATṚ** (pronounced MATRI), which meant:

- The Feminine Qualities, Forces and Energies.
- Mother, the Goddess, the Divine Mother.
- Mother Earth. The Cosmic Element *Water*.
- One with Knowledge (the Feminine Intuition).
- The Śakti of the masculine Deities.

In later centuries, MATṚ became MĀTĀ, and in the past few centuries it became MĀ.

JAY MĀ JAY MĀ JAY JAY MĀ
Victory to the Divine Mother.

MĀTĀJI, MĀTĀ
The Divine Mother.

MĀ, AMMĀ
The Mother of the Universe.

ŌṀ MĀTĀ ŌṀ MĀTĀ MĀTĀ JAGADAMBĀ
The Mother of the Universe.

GURUMĀYĪ
The Guru-Mother, the Guide.

SĀI-MĀTĀ, SĀI-RĀṀ
The Divine Mother-Light in the Heart.
The Radiance of the All-Mother (SĀI).

MĀTĀ, MĀ, AMMĀ: Mother.

AMṚTĀ: the Goddess of Immortality.

ĀNANDA: Bliss.

SĀI: from SĀ (full of) and AYI (the Divine Mother).

JAYA, JAY, JAI: Victorious, above death.

SĀI RĀṀ: Divine Light.

JAGADAMBĀ: The World (JAGAD) Mother (AMBĀ).

ŌṀ AMṚTEŚVARYAI NAMAHA

Amṛteśvarī

The Supreme Spirit-Mother

Meditate in the Heart…

ŌṀ AMṚTEŚVARYAI NAMAHA

Salutation to the Mother of Immortal Bliss.

AMṚTĀ: the Goddess; that which is beyond death, immortal; Sweet Nectar, or the Honey Taste of Spirit; Splendour, Light, Beauty; the Rays of the Spiritual Sun.

ĪŚVARĪ: the Goddess, the Mistress of the Universe, the Supreme Being.

AMṚTEŚVARĪ: the Immortal Goddess, the Eternal Reality, the Ambrosia of Spirit, the Light of Eternity.

NAMAHA: salutation.

AMṚTEŚVARĪ is the Mother of Immortal Bliss, the Inner Mother who reveals Herself in the Heart of the Devotee and in the Heart of the Universe as the All-Compassionate Mother-Self of all beings, the Universal Mother-Power—caring, nurturing, loving, giving, forgiving. This All-Loving-Serving Mother-Power is also Pure Unobstructed Consciousness or Awareness, Eternal Stillness and Cosmic Activity.

She is **NIRMALA-SUNDARĪ** (Spotless Beauty, Shining Grace). She shines within you like a thousand Suns.

Pure Consciousness (NIRMALA-SUNDARĪ) is ever the same, before Creation, during Creation and after Creation. You were *That* before your birth, you are *That* now, and you will be *That* after you die.

Your physical body undergoes the process of birth, growth and death, but Pure Consciousness is not born and does not die. This is your true Teacher, the true Guide, SAT GURU.

ŚRĪ NIRMALA DEVĪ ŌṀ

Meditate in the Heart…

Kālimā

The Mother Beyond Time

Meditate on these Mantras in the Heart...

Ōṁ Kālī

Ōṁ Hrīṁ Kālī-Durge Namaha

Jayamā

Kālī Kālī Mahā Mātā

Durgā Durgā Mahā Durgā

Kālī-Durge Namo Namaḥ

Kālī: the Divine Mother, Kālimā. The Goddess in Her aspect as the Creative Energy, Nourishing Energy and Destructive Energy. She is Nature (Prākṛtī), the Original Primordial Substance of Space, out of which all things appear (are born), develop and return to the Source (die, perish or undergo transformation). Although all things *appear* to undergo a death or transformation, the Eternal Essence Itself remains above and beyond Time, beyond the endless succession of changes. Nature is a Veil for the Real.

Durgā: the Warrior-Goddess, the "difficult-to-please", the "difficult-to-approach". Durgā is an aspect of Kālī. She is remote, inaccessible. She is the Reality *behind* visible Nature.

Jayamā: the Divine Mother is beyond Death.

Mahā: great, omnipotent, cosmic.

Kālī-Durge Namo Namaḥ

Sāvitrī

The Spiritual Sun as Mother

Sāvitrī
Sāvitrikā (feminine)
The Goddess in the Form of the Sun, Solar Radiance, Solar Power.

The Savitā-Mantra 1602
Sarasvatī 200
Mūlaprākṛtī 471
The Holy Vibration 1520

Sāvitrī is all of the following:

Śakti: Power, the One Energy, the One Force of the Universe.

Gāyatrī: the Hymn (sound) to the Spiritual Sun behind the Sun, the Daughter of the Spiritual Sun.

Sarasvatī: the River of Knowledge.

Devī: the Goddess.

Umā: the Universal Mother.

Wife of Śiva, the Transcendent.

Prākṛtī: the Original, Primary, Pure Substance of the Universe.

The Administrator of **Dharma**, the Universal Natural Law on all Planes of Being.

Śuddhāmaṇi: Pure-Jewel, Nectar-Precious, a sparkling jewel, a sacred ornament, Holy Radiance.

Āuṁ-Sai: Inexhaustible Divine Wealth; the Divine Mother-Light as the Brightness of Inner Space; the Substance of all Universes, visible and invisible, all Worlds, all Planes of Being, all creatures, all hierarchies; the Cosmic Sea, the Cosmic Ocean of Matter.

Saundarya Lahirī: the Beautiful Ocean, the Lovely Waves of the Celestial Sea.

Ōṁ: the Formless Self (Arūpa Ātman), Pure Consciousness.

Paraśakti: the Supreme Power, the Cosmic Energy, the Primordial Consciousness, the Cosmic Mother Force.

Guru: the Teacher (the Formless Absolute Self in you and the Formless Absolute Self in your Guru are one and the same).

Sāvitrī is gentleness and compassion, tolerance, forgiveness, loving kindness, calmness in the face of persecution or opposition. She has no enemies (She does not perceive anybody as an enemy). She receives all equally. She is the Compassionate Heart. She is always poised, balanced, centred. The whole Universe is filled with the presence of Her Radiant Consciousness (Cinmayī), which is Pure Intelligence, Supreme Spirit. She is Omnipresent, Omniscient, Omnipotent, and She is present in you as your own Divine Self.

To Meditate on Sāvitrī

- After having painted the SĀVITRĪ MAṆḌALA (picture of Sāvitrī), sit still and contemplate the maṇḍala for a while until you remember all the details.
- Then, close your eyes and imagine that you are SĀVITRĪ. Assume the pose and posture of SĀVITRĪ. Become Her. See all the rays and colours emanating from you as SĀVITRĪ. Feel the background colour all around you.
- Then, being Her, intone silently, slowly, pausing in Silence between each intonation:

  ŌṀ ŚRĪ...

- ŌṀ ŚRĪ means "the Radiant One, the Radiating One". Feel yourself to be a Radiating Being of Light and Glory.

ŌṀ ŚRĪ

Sāvitrī Maṇḍala

Śrī Jagadambā

Śrī Jagadambā

The Mother of the World

Jagadambā

The World Mother, the Mother of the Universe, the Mother of the World.

Jagad: the World, the Universe.

Ambā: Mother, the Divine Mother.

Śrī Jagadambā, the Holy World Mother, lives in the Heart and should be *meditated upon* in the Heart.

∞

She is Brahma-Rūpa (God-Form), the Shape or Form of God, the Body of God.

She is Ānanda-Rūpiṇī-Devī (Blissful-Form-Goddess), the Goddess whose Form or Essential Nature is Pure Bliss.

She is Caitanya-Rūpiṇī-Devī (Consciousness-Form-Goddess), the Goddess whose Form is Pure Consciousness Itself.

She is formless on one level (Nir-Guṇa: without forms, qualities or attributes), but on another level She is all forms (Sa-Guṇa: with forms, qualities and attributes).

She is Sakalā, Sa-Ka-La, the All, the Whole, the Everything, the Totality, the Fullness, the Completeness, Perfection, the Totality of the Universe. This is Her secret. She is everything.

She is the Paramāpūrva-Nirvāṇa-Śakti (the Supreme-Ancient-Nirvāṇic-Energy). Nirvāṇa, the plane of Ātman, is the Source of all Creation, including the lower, intermediate and highest realms. And unto Nirvāṇa, or Ātman (the Soul of the Universe), we shall all Return. That is our Goal.

She is Para-Śakti-Maya (Supreme-Energy-full-of). She is full of the Ultimate Energy of the Universe. She *is* the Ultimate Energy.

She is the Word (**NĀDA**), the Inner Creative Sound within the Universe and within your Heart.

She is also the **MĀTRIKĀ-MĀYĪ-DEVĪ** (the letters-full-of-the-Goddess). She is also the Power behind all Mantras and Divine Names. MĀTRIKĀ (the little Mothers) are the letters of the Sanskrit alphabet, which compose all the Sanskrit Mantras as well as all Mantras in all languages.

Every particle of you is born of the World Mother

She is also the Breath of Life, **HAṄG-SAḤ** (HAṀSA).

She is the Energy that gives Knowledge (JÑĀNA-ŚAKTI), the Energy of Desire and Will (ICCHĀ-ŚAKTI), and the Energy behind all actions (KRIYĀ-ŚAKTI). Hence She is known as **JÑĀNA-ŚAKTĪ-ICCHĀ-ŚAKTĪ-KRIYĀ-ŚAKTĪ-SVA-RŪPIṆĪ-DEVĪ** (the Goddess whose very Self-Nature, SVA-RŪPIṆĪ, is all knowledge, all desires, all actions in Creation).

She is the Consciousness manifesting in all beings in the Universe, the **CIDĀKĀŚA** (the Infinite Field of Universal Consciousness), the **CITTA-ĀKĀŚA** (the Boundless Ocean of Intelligence). From this Pure Consciousness come forth all things, and all things dwell in Her and are maintained by Her.

There is nothing in this Universe, and beyond it, which is not **ŚRĪ JAGADAMBĀ**, the Holy Universal Mother of All. All of visible Nature and invisible Nature is the World Mother. Every particle of you is born of the World Mother and is *in* the World Mother. You *are* the World Mother.

Recognize this in your Heart…

The True Feminine 1516
The Virgin and the Mother 144
The Mother of the World 147
Lalitā: the Eternal Feminine 1484
Rest in the Great Breath 1654
Citta-Ākāśa 932

Paraśakti

The Supreme Power

Meditate in the Third-Eye Centre...

Ōṁ Hrīṁ Paraśaktiyai Namaha

All activities in the Cosmos are done by the One Force, Kuṇḍalinī

Paraśakti: the Supreme Power.

Namaha: salutation to, or invocation.

Kuṇḍalinī-Śakti and **Paraśakti** are the same thing: an all-pervading Field of Cosmic Energy.

Kuṇḍalinī-Śakti is the Supreme Power. It is the Universal-Life-Principle in all of Nature and within the whole Universe. It exists within Man, the plant, the stone, the tree, the angel, the god, planet, sun, star or galaxy, and in interstellar space.

Paraśakti is the Dynamic Manifesting Power of Divinity, the Active Principle of the Cosmos, the Substratum of all Creation, the Absolute Consciousness, the Creatrix of the Universe, the Potency and Power within the atoms on all planes: physical atoms, astral atoms, mental atoms, Buddhic atoms and Nirvāṇic atoms.

Atoms are simply units of Energy (Śakti) on the Seven Great Planes of Being of Cosmic-Nature, Mahat-Prākṛtī. Whatever exists is made up of Energy units of Kuṇḍalinī. But the Energy is One.

All activities in the Cosmos are done by the One Force, Kuṇḍalinī. But this Force is also the *substance* out of which all forms (bodies) are made, whether human, angelic, animal, vegetable, planetary or solar-systemic. One Force equals One Substance.

What, then, is evil? Evil is the wrong use of this One Force, Power, Energy, Substance, by living entities, whether through Ignorance or lack of Intelligence.

You can direct, control or modify this One Force, Power, Substance, Life, by Mantra or Yantra (images).

The Kuṇḍalinī Fire 132
Living Matter 134
The Evolutionary Energy 143
Kuṇḍalinī-Fohat 148
The Paradox of Evil 208
The Path of Mantra and the Goddess 1490

Āuṁ

The Holy Spirit as Cosmic Mother

Āuṁ-Sai

Āuṁ: the Universal Reality, the Cosmic Mother.

Ōṁ: the Formless-Self, the Sea of Pure Consciousness, Formless Awareness.

Ōṁ-Sai (Āuṁ-Sai): the Substance of all things, the Universal Nature, the One Undivided Mother.

Āuṁ is the Mother spinning the Web of Creation

The Sanskrit word Āuṁ has been pronounced as Amun and Amon in old Egyptian, Amen in Hebrew and Amin in Arabic.

Āuṁ is the Cosmic Sea of Creative Sound. I am a Child of the Sea.

Āuṁ is the Cosmic Creative Sound (the "Word" of the New Testament), the Mother spinning the Web of Creation.

Āuṁ is the Word or Vibratory Power behind all the worlds, galaxies and universes, behind all the Planes of Being, behind all forces and energies, behind all atoms composed of physical and subtle Matter.

Āuṁ is the Mother, or Holy Spirit, which *shapes* all things as they are.

Āuṁ is the Materializing Power or Creative Power.

Āuṁ reverberates throughout the vast Inner Spaces as Sounding-Light Vibration structuring all things into shapes and forms.

Āuṁ is the "Witness" to all Creation.

Āuṁ, Ōṁ, Nāda 550
Potent Vibrations: Bīja-Mantra 1542
God's Cosmic Symphony 1649

To Meditate on Āuṁ

- First, intone Āuṁ aloud with full voice, with a resonant Throat Cakra.
- Then, sit with eyes closed and continue to intone the Sound of Āuṁ silently, mentally, based in the Throat Cakra.
- Then be still and listen to the Murmur of the Sea of Āuṁ, the Ocean of the Ineffable Joy of the Mother.

To Meditate on Ōṁ

- Intone Ōṁ, prolonged, in the Third-Eye Centre, with your mind tranquil and at peace. Do this at intervals.
- While intoning the Ōṁ sound in the Third-Eye, think "Formless-Self" and try to "realize" the Paramātman, the Transcendental Self-Awareness, which is timeless, spaceless, boundless, endless, causeless, which eternally just Is, ever-unchanging, ever-indestructible.

You are That (Tat Tvam Asi).

The Role of the Divine Female in the Salvation/Liberation Process

The mind is the directive force that fertilizes the Heart of the Divine Mother

The World Mother, Śrī-Jagad-Ambā (Holy-World-Mother) is the *Substance* out of which all forms (all bodies) arise, the Universal Substance of all the Planes of Being.

It is through Her that all things must *pass downwards* from the Absolute and the One-Self or One-Identity, Nirvāṇa, Ātman, into physical embodiment, and it is through Her that all embodied creatures must *pass upwards* to return to the Source, the Goal, the Beginning and End, Nirvāṇa, Ātman.

She holds all the past impressions (Vāsanā, Saṁskāra) from all your past lives, as well as the past of our planet and our solar system. These past impressions are your latent desires, compulsive drives, unconscious habit-patterns, beliefs and superstitions, thoughtforms ensouled by elemental entities, tendencies of behaviour, whether your own or those of your family, tribe, nation, religious grouping, culture, customs or traditions.

You cannot Liberate yourself into the Glorious Unity of the One-Self, Nirvāṇa, until you are free of Vāsanā.

The Great Work is the re-absorption of the separated personality-consciousness into the Original Unitary Consciousness of God, Nirvāṇa, the Sea of Infinite Light, where there are no separated selves, no separated lives, only the Eternal Oneness of All-Life.

This is done with the help of the Divine Mother.

The mind is the *directive agent*, the directive force that fertilizes the Heart of the Divine Mother.

Saṁskāra and Vāsanā 251
To Achieve Liberation 1177
Subconscious Renewal 1236
Karma and your Spiritual Development 255
Knowledge of the Past and the Future 583
Mind and Desire 235

Tranquil Mind

A mind which is used spiritually, in an unselfish way, is a good mind. A mind which is always used selfishly, only for personal gain, will lead you to ruin.

A mind which seeks Spiritual Knowledge and Understanding is a good mind. A mind which is always competitive and seeks to destroy others will lead you to ruin.

What happens if you start desiring for the Real?

Mental Understanding, or true Spiritual Knowledge, gives you power and vitality, energy and confidence. When your mind is peaceful, tranquil, focused, bent on discovering the Eternal, it is a good mind. When your mind is agitated, stressed out, overworked, out of control, it will lead you to ruin.

Your view of yourself is a construct of your mind. When your mind becomes tranquil, your true Self shines with Light.

Desire for the Real

Desires are a product of your astral body, not your Self. You are desiring things all the time; that is, your astral body wants things all the time. Can your desires ever be satisfied? The answer is No. They just keep going on.

Desires for wealth, power, influence, control or manipulation of others, for name and fame, for recognition in this world, lead you to entrapment by the energies of this world, by the people of this world, by the rulers of this world, until you have a nervous breakdown or a heart attack. So, what are you going to do?

In your natural condition, you *identify* with your desires. What happens if you stop identifying with them? What happens if you start desiring for the Real, the Permanent, the Everlasting? For the Source of Bliss and true Happiness? For the Perpetual Sun within you that forever shines? What if you have *seen your Beloved* shining within you with incomparable Beauty, Grace, Glory and Light? Where do your desires turn then?

***Selfish* desires bind you to this world. *Selfless* desires Liberate you.**

The *desire to help others* gain their Eternal Freedom is the noblest of all desires.

Tantra Mind 933
The Evil Mind 224
Desire-Streams 1377
The Mind Divine or Demonic 212
The Thought of Enlightenment 767
Attach your Mind to the Eternal 1234

Ōṁ Muni Muni Mahāmuni

Fertilizing the Heart of the Divine Mother for the Conception of the Divine Child within you

Sanskrit

Ōṁ Muni Muni Mahāmuni Śākyamuniye Svāhā

Muni: a Sage, a Seer, an Ascetic, a Silent One, one who is Inspired, an Enlightened One, being in the State of Ecstasy.

Mahāmuni: the Great Sage, the Superior Self.

Śākyamuni: One who is within reach of Enlightenment, for whom Enlightenment is possible. Also, a name of Gautama Buddha or Prince Siddhārtha, the "founder" of Buddhism.

Svāhā: offerings, that is, offering oneself or surrendering to the process.

Meditate upon this Mantram in the Third-Eye…

Hebrew

Baruch Atoh Adonai Melech Oulam
Blessed Art Thou, Living God, King of the Eternal Ages.

Meditate upon this Mantram in the Heart…

Hṛt-Padma

The Heart-Lotus

The Heart of the Divine Mother is called **Hṛt-Padma**, "Heart-Lotus". The lotus flower is the symbol for the Feminine Heart.

The Spiritual Heart Complex extends to the left side of the chest, the right side of the chest, the centre of the chest, and just below the centre of the chest. Each Cave of the Heart unveils a different quality, a different experience.

The lotus flower is the symbol for the Feminine Heart

The Hṛt-Padma is located *below* the Central Heart Cave. This is the Sacred Heart of the Mother. Here shines in full **Jagadambā**, the Mother of the Universe.

The Way to the Divine Heart is through Service (Karma Yoga), Devotion (Bhakti Yoga) and true Knowledge (Jñāna Yoga), practised all at once.

- Service is through the physical body.
- Devotion is through the Heart and emotions.
- Realization is through the Heart.
- True Knowledge is Esoteric Knowledge of the way things *really are* and of the true Spiritual Path.

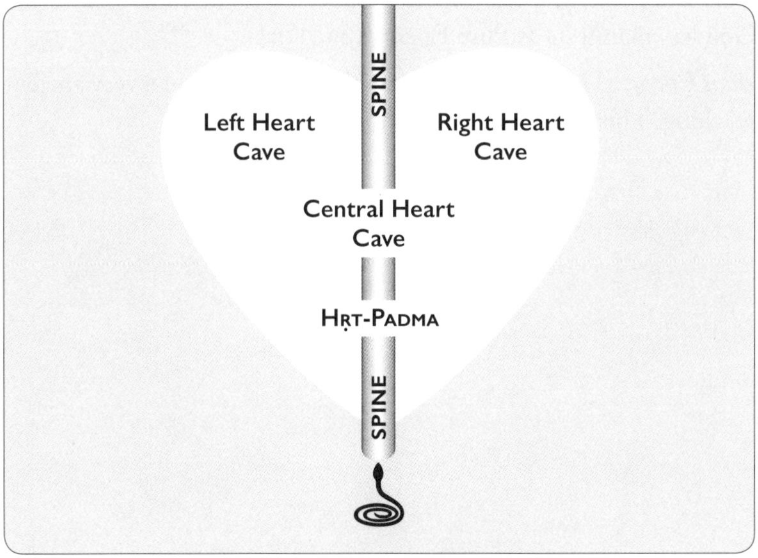

The Spiritual Heart Complex

The Lotus of the Heart 446
The Cave of the Heart 634
Dimensions of the Heart 847
Kamalā: the Lotus-Born 1536
The Threefold Way 1236

General Children's Initiation Mantra into the Energy of the Goddess

This Sanskrit Mantra is suitable for all children up to sixteen years of age:

Ādi Anta Sakalām Hrīṁ Rāṁ Sakalām

Ādi: the First, the Beginning, Primordial, before all things, superior to all things.

Anta: the End, the Last, that which survives all things.

Sakalām (Sakalā): the Whole, the Complete, the All, that which includes all things, all the parts as One.

Hrīṁ: all the *feminine* powers and qualities.

Rāṁ: all the *masculine* powers and qualities.

Thus:

The Goddess is the First and the Last, the Beginning and the End. She is the Whole, the Complete Reality which includes all things and all beings. She is all the female powers and all the male powers and potencies. Within Her, all opposites unite into the State of Oneness.

This is an *Energy-Form* of the Goddess. On the inner planes the Goddess manifests as Pure Energy (Śakti).

All is Energy. This is not a new scientific discovery, but a very ancient teaching. This is the Energy of Infinite Potential.

Quan Yin: the Mother of Compassion

Our Heavenly Queen has appeared to Humanity in many lands and at many times. She appeared in China as QUAN YIN (KWAN YIN).

QUAN YIN is the Virgin of Light, the Mother of Compassion, the Ideal Beauty, the Eternal Woman, the Messenger of Divine Grace.

Our Heavenly Queen has appeared to Humanity in many lands and at many times

QUAN YIN is the Incarnation of Primeval Wisdom and the Goddess of Mercy.

QUAN YIN is the Eternal Gentle Maiden, *between* Heaven and Earth, between the material consciousness and the spiritual, between Man and God. She is the Intercessor, the Protector, the Helper, the Inspirer.

QUAN YIN is the living embodiment of Eternal Beauty, perfect Proportion and Harmony, perfect Gentleness and Grace.

QUAN YIN is *She-Who-Looks-Down-Upon-Us-With-Compassionate-Glances.* She made a vow, a long time ago, to help alleviate the sufferings of all creatures, not only human but the animals as well, and all other Kingdoms of Life.

QUAN YIN is the embodiment of PREMA-ŚAKTI, the Energy of Love.

QUAN YIN is the Mother of Mercy who tends to the sufferings of this world.

QUAN YIN is a BODHISATTVA, whose very Self-Nature is Love-Wisdom, that is, whose Self-Being is of the Buddhic Plane where Consciousness is of Love, Wisdom, Unity and Bliss, fused into the Perpetual Light.

She is AVALOKITEŚVARĪ (AVA-LOKITA-ĪŚVARĪ, the down-descending Goddess), the PADMAPĀṆI (Lotus-born, or born out of the Spiritual Lotus, the Universal Heart). Her very Substance is the Energy of Love and Primeval Wisdom.

The Divine Child of QUAN YIN is born in every Human Heart when that Heart has been purified from dense worldly vibrations, when that Heart has been made into a Temple of the Living God. That Divine Child is the promise of the Divinity of Man, the utter Holiness which we all shall become: co-creators with God, co-rulers of the Glories of the Divine Manifestation.

Her Transcendental Form 145
The Feminine Virtues 468
Maṇi-Padma 1298
The Pure Heart 1300
The Birth of the Light in the Heart 718

This is the Mystery of QUAN YIN.

To Meditate on Quan Yin

Meditate in the Heart…

Ōṁ Namo Kwan Shin Yin Pusā

Ōṁ Namo Kwan Shin Yin Pusā

There are many temples, alters, sanctuaries, grottos and niches dedicated to Her in China and Japan. (In Japanese, She is called Kannon.) But She can always be found in the Human Heart by simply invoking Her Name, Quan Yin.

It is enough to remember Her Name, Quan Yin, in your Heart and to see Her picture (that of the Gentle Woman) in your Heart. Your Heart will be overflowing with Love and tears will flood your eyes and you will *know* that She is with us always, through all times, in all places, in all circumstances, as the All-Forgiving Mother.

Kwan Yin Maṇḍala

The Melodious Voice of Quan Yin

The Sound of QUAN YIN's Name is the Music that fills the Universe within. If your mind is still, if your breath is still, if your Heart is pure and receptive, you will inwardly hear Her Music, the Holy Presence of Her Name.

The Heart is the Temple of QUAN YIN, though She may appear above your head, by your side or near to you. The lotus flower is Her symbol and the Lotus of the Heart is Her throne.

The Heart is the Temple of Quan Yin

The Inner robe of QUAN YIN is white, the White Light of Spiritual Purity. Her outer robe is blue, the Blue Light of Spiritual Aspiration. The White Lotus blossoms above Her forehead (the Higher Third-Eye Centre). The Red Lotus blossoms in Her Heart (the Heart of Infinite Compassion).

She is surrounded by a Sphere of Iridescent Light. In Her Aura are threads of silver garlands, pink blossoms and a Golden Translucence.

She has the most gentle, beautiful, sweetest Voice when She appears. She may show just Herself, or She may show also the Divine Child.

She may appear as a young maiden or youthful girl, or as a young mother. Her Light-Rays of Love soften the human Heart and cool the human mind.

Sometimes She rides upon the Dragon or Serpent, showing Her complete mastery of the energies and forces below the Buddhic Plane.

Sometimes She appears in the clouds in a White Raiment (vesture), at other times in a niche, grotto or alcove.

Sometimes She carries a vase of ointment in Her hands for the healing of the sick and the distressed.

Her Presence is full of a Tranquil Vibration.

May Her Peace descend upon you.

Meditate on QUAN YIN in your Heart...

KWAN YIN

The Radiance of Compassion.

The Embodiment of Love.

The Gentle Feminine Force.

The Light of Grace.

The Divine Mother.

The Mother of the Heaven Worlds.

The Mother of the World.

The Celestial Virgin.

The Mother of the Heavenly Child.

Luminous with the Light of Love.

Latin Mantras to Our Lady

1

AVE MARĪA GRĀTIA PLENA DOMINUS TECUM

Hail Mary, full of Divine Grace, God is with you.

2

SALVE REGINA MATER MISERECŌRDIAE VITA DULCEDO ET SPES NOSTRA

Glory to you, Queen, Mother of Mercy, our life, sweetness and hope.

3

CLEMENS PIA DULCIS VIRGO MARĪA

Merciful, dear, sweet, Virgin Mary.

4

BEĀTA MARĪA REGINA ANGELŌRUM REGINA PROPHETĀRUM REGINA SANCTŌRUM ŌMNIUM REGINA PACIS

Blessed Mary, Queen of Angels, Queen of the Enlightened, Queen of all the Saints, Queen of Peace.

The Sacred Heart of Our Lady

Following are the Divine Names of Our Lady according to the Western Christian Mystical Tradition. Meditate upon them in your Heart…

Our Lady
Holy Mary
Mother of Jesus the Christ
Blessed Virgin
Queen of the Heavens
Mistress of Earth
Virgin Most Pure
Star of the Morning
Virgin Most Wise
Deity's Shrine
Queen of Angels
Mother of Mankind
Portal of God
Virginal Mother
Dwelling Place of the Holy Trinity
Celestial Balm
The Source of All Grace
All Love and Light
Infinite Light
Destroyer of the Serpent Power
Crowned with the Stars
Mother of Mercy
Mother of the Word Incarnate
Seat of Wisdom
Mother of Good Counsel
Mother of Christ
Virgin Most Faithful
Mystical Rose
Gate of Heaven
Queen of Peace

5

Sancta Marīa Mater Amābilis Mater Admirābilis Virgo Clemens Sedes Sapiēntiae Rosa Mystica

Holy Mary, Mother Beloved, Mother Wonderful, Virgin Merciful, the Seat of Wisdom, the Rose Mystical.

Marīa is the Divine Mother Substance or Essence.

The *rose flower* is the symbol of the Heart of the Mother.

6

Salve Sancta Parens Enixa Puērpera Regem Qui Caelum Terram Que Regit In Saecula Saeculōrum

Hail, Holy Mother, because you gave birth to the King who rules Heaven and Earth for ever and ever.

7

Miserēre Nobis Jānua Caeli Stella Matutīna Consolātrix Afflictōrum Vas Spirituāle

Have Mercy upon us, Gate of Heaven, the Star of the Morning, She who consoles all those who are afflicted with troubles and problems, the Grail of pure Spiritual Consciousness.

Stella Matutīna (the Star of the Morning) is the Pure White Light in the Third-Eye.

Vas (the Grail or Holy Cup) is the symbol for Spiritual Regeneration.

8

Sancta Marīa Spēculum Justīciae Virgo Potens Vas Insīgne Devotiōnis Virgo Fidēlis Exāudi Nos

Holy Mary, the Mirror of Justice, Virgin All-Powerful, the outstanding Cup of Pure Devotion, the Virgin who is always Faithful, Hear us!

Spēculum Justīciae (the Mirror of Justice) means that every thought, word and deed is reflected in the Divine Substance (Ākāśa).

Virgo Potens (Virgin All-Powerful) means that She is the Power or Energy of Divinity.

VIRGO MARĪA

Mantras to Connect to Our Lady

Latin Heart Initiation

BENEDICTA ET VENERĀBILIS ES VIRGO MARĪA
Blessed and Venerable are You, Virgin Mary.

BENEDICTA ET VENERĀBILIS ES MATER MARĪA
Blessed and Venerable are You, Mother Mary.

BENEDICTA ET VENERĀBILIS ES MARĪA
Blessed and Venerable are You, Mary.

MARĪA
Mary

VIRGO MARĪA: "The Virgin Mary" refers to the Eternal Feminine's Transcendental Nature, beyond and above the created Universe, spotless, pure, incorruptible, forever shining Bright.

MATER MARĪA: "Mother Mary" refers to the Eternal Feminine as the Mother of all that is, of all Creation, of all created beings. (Therefore She is *our* Mother also.)

MARĪA: "Mary" refers to the Mother of Jesus who was the Christ, She who is the representative of the Great Feminine Intelligence for our planet Earth.

MARĪA is a Holy Name. The Name is Holy because it carries Her Qualities, Presence and Vibration.

The name MARĪA is to be uttered in the Heart Centre with Love and Devotion. It will awaken the Fiery Love of the Heart, the longing for God, for Union with the Beloved. It will bring tears to your Soul and Ecstasy to your Heart.

The Divine Feminine will come to you and console you, like a good mother does. She will uplift you, inspire you, and help you to deal with the tests and trials which you face in your life.

Ultimately She will lead you into the Presence of the King of Everlasting Glory.

Visualization of the Immaculate Heart of Mary, Our Lady

Her Heart Centre is like an open rose—vibrant, fiery, alive, radiant with heat and the Fire of Love.

She is crowned with the Sun, and a luminous Sun halo surrounds Her head.

Worship Her with Love and Devotion

Her inner robe is of pure White Light, and Her outer garment is pure spiritual blue—restful, peaceful, tranquil vibration.

She stands on the Serpent and the Moon. The green Serpent is the sublimated Kuṇḍalinī power, while the silver Moon represents Nature and the purified psychic and astral powers.

∞

- You may visualize Our Lady in miniature form, in your Third-Eye Centre or Heart Centre.
- Or you may visualize Her in life-size form, in front of you.
- Or your may visualize that *you are* Her, and see yourself as Her in full Majesty and Glory.

If you visualize Her in your Heart Centre or Third-Eye Centre, in miniature, then after forming Her Image you may silently, devotionally, call out Her Name:

Marīa... Marīa...

Worship Her with Love and Devotion and feel Her Divine Presence.

The Immaculate Heart

To Approach the Goddess...

The Goddess should be approached with a *pure motive.* Any motive for selfish gain, for personal power, for name and fame in the world, for personal glory, for power to influence others, for magical or psychic powers (without a Spiritual Vision or Goal), will land you in great disaster.

Many climb the mountain but perish in the hidden crevices and caves. But, for the *Pure in Heart*, the selfless, the innocent in mind, the simple, the egoless, She is the Beauty of Light, Life and Love.

CHAPTER 64

Śrī-Vidyā
The Holy Science

The True Feminine

The True Feminine is Kuṇḍalinī (Kuṇḍalī), the Sacred Fire *within* the bodies of human beings, angels, animals and plants; within planets, solar systems, galaxies and the Universal Manifestation (Omniverse). This is a Subtle Fire, invisible to the physical eyes (*not* physical heat or physical fire or volcanic fire). She is Śrī-Vidyā, Holy Wisdom.

She is the true Virgin, Woman and Mother

How little the world understands the True Female, the Eternal Feminine! It is *not* the female bodies of human beings, as it is fashionable to think today! For She is *in both* polarities, in both males and females, invisible, untouchable by ordinary consciousness.

She was rejected by the Jewish, Christian and Muslim orthodox religionist schools of thought, and vaguely remembered in Hinduism, Buddhism and Taoism. She is not a human figure! She is the True Goddess (Devī). She is the true Virgin, Woman and Mother, in all bodies individually, and in the Cosmos as the Cosmic Virgin, Woman and Mother.

She is the Śakti, the Energy of the Universe, that is, the Energy-Field *within* the Universe, Paraśakti, the Universal Life and Evolutionary Force. Light, sound, electricity, and many other forces, are just some manifestations of Her Power.

She is full of Light (Jyotirmayī) and full of Sound (Mantramayī). She is the Serpent of Wisdom (Bhujangī). When you *Know Her* in meditation you will become a Cosmic Man, a Christ.

Devī, the Goddess, has two Forms, Natures or Aspects:

- Daivi-Śakti-Kuṇḍalinī: the moving, changing, evolving forms in Creation, in all the Realms, Worlds and Planes of Being.
- Paramitā: the Transcendental, Immoveable, Unchangeable, Eternal Form, *beyond* all the Realms and Worlds of Being.

In the upper regions of Manifestation, the Devī (Goddess) is Spirit (Śiva).
In the lower regions of Manifestation, She is Matter (Prākṛtī).

She is the Union of Spirit and Matter.

The Virgin and the Mother 144

The Kuṇḍalinī Fire 132
Kuṇḍalinī and the Goddess 141
The Eternal Feminine 469
The Great Goddess 1483
The Feminine Suppressed 910

Holy Knowledge

LALITĀ is the Shining-Goddess, JYOTĪ, the Divine Light, the Light-of-Beauty-Wisdom-and-Love. LALITĀ is the Beauty which is beyond all things, pervading the whole Universe.

LALITĀ is ŚRĪ-VIDYĀ, Holy Knowledge. This Holy Knowledge is the Realization, through profound meditational experience, that She, the Ultimate Goddess, is everything. She is all that is holy and sacred and all that is bad and evil, for *She pervades the Universe through and through* like a Blazing Star.

Lalitā is the Beauty which is pervading the whole Universe

She is the Invisible Light as well as the visible light of the Suns in Space. She is Silence and Sound, Activity and Stillness, suffering and Bliss-Consciousness. She is good thoughts and bad thoughts, good deeds and bad deeds. Nothing and nobody is separate from Her, for *She is All and transcending All.*

LALITĀ is immensely Blissful (ĀNANDA), immensely Creative, immensely Happy. The whole Universe (visible and invisible) is Her Play, LĪLĀ. She *plays* within the human being as She plays within the Universe. She is full of *playfulness,* LĪLĀMAYĪ.

This Holy Knowledge is not only an intellectual idea but a direct Supernatural Experience in Ecstatic Bliss-Consciousness.

The Science of LALITĀ or ŚOḌAṢĪ is the Science of the Goddess—that is, the Manifesting Powers of Man and the Cosmos and the Divinity *within* the Cosmos.

When the Subtle Vibrations of the East (of the Himalayas) are taken to the West, they become destroyed by the gross materialistic vibrations of the dense bodies, minds and emotions of Westerners, who are used to a dense materialistic environment. So, the Pure Vibrations of ŚRĪ-VIDYĀ become densified and lost.

Further, it so happened that when the Svāmīs (the Holy Men of India) came from the Pure Himalayan Vibrations to the West, many of them in time became densified by the Western materialistic environment. Hence, the true Science of Yoga, Meditation and Spiritual Knowledge, including ŚRĪ-VIDYĀ, became corrupted in the West, to serve purely materialistic and physical bodily purposes.

Lalitā: the Eternal Feminine 1484
Lalitā: the Ultimate Goddess 1556
Haṭha Yoga and Rāja Yoga 524
Meditation Degenerated 1180

Vibration and Mantra

All things are SPANDA—Vibrations, Pulsations, Frequencies, Pulses or Rhythms of the Universal Consciousness, or ŚRĪ-VIDYĀ. In fact, ŚRĪ-VIDYĀ is the Light-Sound Vibrations of Universal Consciousness.

Everything vibrates. Everything is in motion, all the time. Evolution is a state of vibration or motion, SPANDA. Material evolution has its own vibration. Psychic evolution has another. Spiritual Evolution has the highest frequency of SPANDA. As you evolve spiritually, your SPANDA, or Vibration-Frequency, increases.

Mantra is the method to change your Vibration

The physical body is at the lowest SPANDA, as is the physical world and the material universe. The Pure Spirit, Pure Consciousness, the Luminous-Bliss, is at the highest range of SPANDA.

Each object, each being or entity, whether an animal, a man, an angel or a god, has its own unique SPANDA or Vibration. These unique vibrations constitute the "differences" between entities.

Mantra is the method to *change your Vibration* and induce within you a Spiritual Evolution. This is the Holy Knowledge, ŚRĪ-VIDYĀ.

BĪJA-MANTRAs are Seed-Vibrations, or Specific-Vibrations, carrying within themselves specific frequencies of Sounding-Light which have specific effects upon you, thus refining your Vibration. They will refine your gross SPANDA and build Subtle Vibrations into you, until you can vibrate to the Tune of Absolute Consciousness, or ŚRĪ-VIDYĀ.

Thus, ŚRĪ-VIDYĀ begins in the Ocean of Sound of the Absolute-Bliss-Consciousness and descends into your own body rhythms and sounds. The Seed-Sounds of ŚRĪ-VIDYĀ liberate you from the grip of the worldly consciousness into Internal Freedom.

In fact, ŚRĪ-VIDYĀ is Ourselves. We *are* the ŚRĪ-VIDYĀ.

ĀTMĀNANDA: the Self is Bliss.

This means that when you *transcend* your mind, or rise above your mind in your meditations, you *experience* Yourself as Pure-Bliss-Consciousness, CIDĀNANDA. This is not a philosophy but a fact. Your True Form or True Nature (SVARŪPA) is Bliss (ĀNANDA). Bliss is not just a sensation; it is a Realm, a Plane of Being, a World in which you, as Spirit, already dwell.

The Word, Logos, Voice, Name 1646
Tapas: Spiritual Purification 571
The Science of Bīja-Mantra 1218
Meditation and the Joy of Living 1012
Return to Primeval Happiness 1179
The Way to Bliss-Consciousness 1246

You can rise above your mind by Mantra of the Sound-type—Bīja-Mantra. There are Mantras which are verbal (word-verses) and those which are Pure Sounds (Bīja). Śakti is the essence of Bīja-Mantra. That is, the Universal Energy is active in those Seed-Sounds (Bīja-Mantras). The Mantra (Bīja) *empowers* the mind.

- You are a Living Soul, Jīva.
- You have a mind (mental body), Manas.
- You have a physical body, Deha.
- The physical body has the five senses, Indriya.

The use of the Bīja disentangles your mind from sense impressions

Independent of the senses, the mind's power increases.

Normally, the physical senses (sight, hearing, taste, touch and smell) pick up vibrations from the world, people, objects, scenes, and so on. These vibrations are conveyed to your "mind", the mental body (through the brain). Then the mind becomes *entrapped*, or lost in these outer impressions, losing its own Self-Nature, its own Real-Form, Svarūpa, by *identifying* with those sense impressions.

The use of the Bīja *disentangles* your mind from the sense impressions and reinstates it to its own true nature or form—the mental body on the Mental Plane of Being. Having done that, you arrive at the perception of the Soul, or the Transcendental Self (Ātman) that You are, which is beyond sense-impressions, beyond mind itself, in the realm of Pure Bliss-Consciousness (the Buddhic Realm), Ānanda.

Svatantrayaśakti (Sva-Tantraya-Śakti), "Your-Self-Creative-Power", or your Innate Creative Intelligence, will begin to manifest fully after the Mantra-Śakti (the Energy of the Mantra) has empowered your mind to work at a higher level of Vibration, in a subtler mode, on the Inner Planes. The Bīja will connect you to the Inner Worlds and to the Devas (the Shining Ones, the Angels).

The most important Seed-Sounds of Śrī-Vidyā

Ōṁ	**Lāṁ**	**Vāṁ**	**Rāṁ**	**Yāṁ**	**Hāṁ**	**Hūṁ**
Hrī	**Śṛī**	**Strī**	**Souh**	**Saḥ**	**Sa**	**Ha**
Hrīṁ	**Śrīṁ**	**Strīṁ**	**Klīṁ**	**Krīṁ**	**Krāṁ**	**Trāṁ**
Trīṁ	**Īṁ**	**Ēṁ**	**Āṁ**	**Aiṁ**	**Syāṁ**	**Śāṁ**
Hāṁ-Sa	**Sō-Haṁ**	**Rāmā**	**Māṁ**	**Ahāṁ**	**Phat**	**Svāhā**

Senses or the Self? 239
The Process of Seeing or Perceiving 542
Obstacles to Higher Consciousness 1424
The Path of Mantra and the Goddess 1490
Potent Vibrations: Bīja-Mantra 1542
Language of the Gods 200

Līlā: the Play of the Goddess

LĪLĀ is play, sport, dancing, enjoying, having "fun". LĪLĀ is the Game the Goddess plays. The whole vast Manifestation, or Appearance of the Universe, is Her Play or Game.

This Play or Game is Vibration.

The whole vast Manifestation is Her Play or Game

Your senses perceive this physical universe because they can register the physical Vibrations. But they cannot register the astral Vibrations, nor the Mental Plane Vibrations, nor the Buddhic Vibrations, nor the Nirvāṇic Planes.

What is "real" to you is the range of Vibrations you can pick up or register. So, for the materialist, this physical world is "real" and all else is non-existent.

If you "live" in Nirvāṇa, or on the Buddhic Plane, or on any higher plane (higher range or degree of Vibrations), you cannot register the physical Vibrations; therefore, this world, this physical universe, does not exist for you. You would find it difficult to "convince" someone in Nirvāṇa that this world down here below "exists"!

Similarly with all the Worlds, Realms, Planes of Being: they seem to be self-contained, isolated by their unique range of Vibrations. But the All, the Whole, is LĪLĀ.

The Holy Vibration

ŌṀ ŚRĪ is DAIVI-ŚAKTI: Holy Vibration, Divine Energy.

ŚRĪ is the Energy of the Sacred, the Holy, the Divine. There is material energy and Spiritual Energy. ŚRĪ is Pure Spiritual Energy or Vibration.

ŌṀ ŚRĪ is the Brightness of the Eternal Glory, the Goddess at Her highest State, the Transcendental Self of All.

The Goddess is the Total Energy of the Universe. Her lowest aspect is the Energy of Matter, the Material Creation. Beyond this Her Energy creates, shapes and forms the subtle worlds and subtle Planes of Being. She is *Everywhere*. But Her highest Form is *Pure Creative Intelligence*, ŌṀ ŚRĪ, the Vibration of Holiness, the Self-Radiant Power.

Intone the ŌṀ ŚRĪ Vibration in your Heart and feel the Sacred Presence.

Put yourself in *That*, which is Divine Grace Itself, PARAMITĀ.

The Primordial Light 119
Living Matter 134
Trapped Spirits 1240
The Divine Energy 1484
To Meditate on Sāvitrī 1497

Śiva-Śakti

Śrī-Vidyā is the Embodiment of Śiva and Śakti together, all at once, in Unity. It is the Effulgence of the Union of Śiva-Śakti.

When the Great White Brilliant Light is Seen, nothing else is seen. This is the Source, the Root, the Foundation, *before* the Universe takes shape on the subtlest, subtler, subtle and gross dimensions.

It becomes the Śiva (Primordial Formless Intelligence) and Śakti (the Energy producing all forms in the Universe on all the Planes of Being).

Śiva and Śakti are always united and cannot act without each other

Śiva is Absolute Bliss, Primordial Goodness and Eternal Tranquillity.

Śiva is the Transcendental Reality, above and beyond Creation.

Śakti is the Power and Energy of the Universe, the Mother-Force, the Primeval Power, the Motive-Force of all the movements of all created beings and things—active energy, action, transformation.

Śakti is also Sound (Vibration), and She produces all objects, forms, bodies, and things, in all the Worlds, visible and invisible.

Śiva is Pure *Being:* the Eternal, unchanging, motionless.

Śakti is always *Becoming:* moving, energizing, changing, transforming.

But Śiva and Śakti are always *united* and cannot act without each other; thus is the Universe based on Male and Female Polarity.

She, Śakti, is in two Forms:
- The Gāyatrī, the Light of the Sun (on all Planes of Being).
- Śrī-Vidyā, the Hidden or Esoteric Light, the Light of Holiness.

All is Vibration.

Śivo'haṁ (Śiva-Ahaṁ: I Am Śiva) is the great Mantram of Self-Realization. The Mantram is three-syllabled: Śi-Vo-Haṁ (Shi-Vo-Haṁ)

Intone it in the Third-Eye, Shī-Vō-Hāng, and you will be at *Peace*.

The Fully Enlightened Man knows himself or herself to be the Uncreated Universal Consciousness (Śiva) and the Universal Agency or Power (Śakti) at the same time.

The Divine Bipolarity 471
Nama Śivāya 1321
Śakti: the Energy of the Goddess 1486
Dimensions of the Cosmic Fire 137
The Savitā-Mantra 1602

The Living Form of the Goddess in the Light

The Living Form of the Goddess is experienced within with Spiritual Vision, utilizing the Inner Senses:

- Spontaneously, as a result of much meditation and spiritual practice (SĀDHANĀ).
- As a result of external factors.
- Through the practice of ŚRĪ-VIDYĀ-MANTRA or ṢOḌAṢĪ-MANTRA.

We can come to know Her intimately and She knows us more specifically

Although the Ultimate Reality is present everywhere, at all times, in Her form as the Universal Presence (PARAŚAKTI), we can invoke Her more intimately within ourselves, in our auric-field, in our spinal system, in our Soul, in our Spiritual Heart, the Centre and Axis of our Being. Thus can we come to know Her intimately, and She knows us more specifically. This is the purpose of ŚRĪ-VIDYĀ, Holy Knowledge or Sacred Science.

She becomes us, we become Her. She speaks, acts and infuses through us into the world in unique and specific ways. We become her special agents or focal points for Her divine and spiritualizing activities for the Salvation of the World. For She is not only the Mother, but our Saviour (TĀRĀ) also.

She is the Sacred KUṆḌALINĪ, the Intelligent-Evolutionary-Force within us. KUṆḌALINĪ is the Great Evolutionary Force within yourself and within the Universe. She is the Living Divinity moving in us to *transform, regenerate* and *re-create* us into the likeness of Divinity.

As the KUṆḌALINĪ-ŚAKTI She breaks down the barriers between the various states of Consciousness, between the various planes or levels of Being, and between the sensations of inner and outer experiences, thus producing the State of Unity within and without, At-One-Ment, YOGA. She is the true MĀ-YOGA-ŚAKTI, the Mother-Force of Union.

This process must be approached with great care, however, if the correct result is desired, as wrong or premature awakening will cause the typical "spaced-out" cases of the East who have no grip on physical reality. For this is ŚRĪ-VIDYĀ, the Sacred Knowledge or Holy Science.

Watch, do not take control with your rational mind.

She plays the Cosmic Drama, LĪLĀ, in miniature within yourself.

Proceed carefully and slowly and *enjoy* Incarnating the Goddess.

Kuṇḍalinī-Fohat 148
Paraśakti: the Supreme Power 1500
Her Transcendental Form 145
When Kuṇḍalinī Awakens 157
Awakening the Inner Senses 506

The Key to this process is the correct understanding and application of the Śrī-Vidyā-Mantra. The Sacred Science, Śrī-Vidyā, consists of re-creating yourself by Nāda, Inner Sound. Nāda is a stream, a brook, a flowing river. Nāda is the Stream-of-Inner-Sound generated by the Mantra (sound-vibration), which bounces off your inner auric system, your invisible spinal cord and the Suṣumna, the central etheric-astral-mental spinal column.

The literal meaning of the Sanskrit word Suṣumna is "great happiness, extreme well-being". This alone will explain to you a lot about Śrī-Vidyā, the Sacred Knowledge. It produces in your inner Self or Being an "extreme happiness"—nay, Absolute Bliss, Paramānanda.

The letters of Śrī-Vidyā play upon the cakras of your inner spine

The letters of Śrī-Vidyā (the Varṇas) play upon the cakras of your inner spine, the invisible column of your Being, making the necessary adjustments for your Inner Transformation. With this meditation you also need Kīrtana, devotional chanting, to stir the Śabda, the God-Incarnating Sound.

Dhāraṇā is the Concentration of the mind.
Dhyāna is Meditation.

Active thoughtforms (your thoughts) shut out the Clear Light of God. Therefore, the thinking process must be brought under control, suspended. This is the Work of Meditation, Dhyāna.

The Silent Light can enter into your mind only when there are no thoughts in it. Only in total *Silence* of the mind can the Light be sensed or perceived by your mind.

The early stages of trying to subdue your mind are called Concentration, Dhāraṇā, trying to focus your mind on a single activity, such as your mantram or your breathing.

The mind is already functioning well in the outward or worldly direction. Now it must be taught to become *still* and *sense* or *receive* impressions from your Soul and the Spiritual Realms. It can do this also very well, after much training—that is, practice, Sādhanā.

Your mind is the Key to your worldly success, and also to your Spiritual Success, or Liberation—Mokṣa, Mukti.

Your Mind is the Key 1208

Āuṁ, Ōṁ, Nāda 550
Stage Three of Aṣṭāṅga Yoga 572
Some Facts about Meditation 1192
Impressions from the Soul 350
To Approach the Goddess 1513

HŪṀ HAṀSAḤ

Treasures of the Goddess

1.	KA E Ī LA HA SA KA HA LA SA KA LA	Activating Powers.
2.	HRĪṀ ŚRĪṀ KLĪṀ	A Hymn of Glory, Developing Powers.
3.	KA E Ī LA HRĪṀ HA SA KA HA LA HRĪṀ SA KA LA HRĪṀ ŚRĪṀ KLĪṀ	Harmony, Wholeness, Completeness, Perfection.
4.	KA E Ī LA HA SA KA HA LA SA KA LA HRĪṀ ŚRĪṀ KLĪṀ	Evolutionary Unfoldment, Sensitivity.
5.	HŪṀ HAṀSAḤ	Equilibrating the Base, Relationship with the Universe.

KUṆḌALINĪ is a form of the Supreme ŚAKTI (Energy), the Goddess. She is Fire creating the Universe (in its visible and invisible spheres) by Sound.

Sound has four stages: the Supreme, the Spiritual, the Causal and the Physical. She is engaged in Creation, Maintenance and the Evolutionary Process. She is also the Liberating, Transforming Energy. She is also SAKALĀ, the All. She is also HAṀSAḤ, the Universal Breath.

The letters or syllables are KUṆḌALINĪ Herself in her embodied form. The letters are units of Sound-Energy (MANTRA-ŚAKTI). When you Know Her through the magic of Her Sounds you shall be free from Transmigration. This is the *Wisdom Goddess*.

The Wisdom of the Goddess

Śrī-Vidyā, the Holy Science, is the *Science of Vibrations*. The Universe is Vibration, Spanda, continually in motion—being Sound and Light.

Śrī-Vidyā is the Form of the Goddess, which is Sound and Light.

Śrī-Vidyā is not a philosophy, but a Science of Sound and Light, the Science of Vibrations. It is done by *Energy-Transmission*.

Śrī-Vidyā is the Goddess of Ultimate Knowledge

Her Energy is communicated person-to-person by way of Initiation.

The mind becomes the Mantra. The Mantra becomes the mind.

Śrī-Vidyā is the Grace of the Goddess: Unconditioned Knowledge, Boundless Awareness, Pure Consciousness, Absolute Being, Transcendental Consciousness.

Śrī-Vidyā is the Transcendental Hearing of Pure Consciousness.

Śrī-Vidyā is the Absolute Consciousness pervading all the Worlds, and all states of Being.

Śrī-Vidyā is the Goddess of Ultimate Knowledge, or the Ultimate Knowledge in the Form of the Goddess.

The Goddess is the Mantra, the Mantra is the Goddess.

Kuṇḍalinī is the Goddess, Śrī-Vidyā, the Holy Science, the World Mother, which is your own Self. This is the Secret.

Śrī-Vidyā is a very refined Energy. The dull or dense people cannot sense it. The materialists cannot feel it.

The Energy of Śrī-Vidyā I have received by Internal Transmission from the Himalayan Source (the Transcendental Condition). But it can be transmitted externally to disciples by One who has received this Energy or Source Knowledge.

If the Energy is transferred into too many densely-vibrating people, it becomes dissipated.

Sophia 146
What is Initiation? 1007
The Path of Mantra and the Goddess 1490
What is Wisdom? 1685

Garments of Light

Ka E Ī La Hrīṁ
Ha Sa Ka Ha La Hrīṁ
Sa Ka La Hrīṁ

This is the Root Mantra (Mūlamantra) of Śrī-Vidyā, the Holy Science. It is the *Foundation-Vibration*, the Fifteen-Syllabled or Fifteen-Lettered Mantram, the Pañcaḍaṣī Vibration. The Fifteen-Lettered Mantram is the basic Sound-Form of Śrī-Vidyā-Devī.

Please note that although in Sanskrit this Mantra is composed of fifteen letters, when transliterated into English it is composed of more letters. The Mantras are often named in Sanskrit according to the number of letters (or syllables) composing them.

When the Vibration (Bīja) of Śrīṁ is added, it becomes the Śoḍaṣī-Mantram or Śoḍaṣākśarī-Mantram (Sixteen-Syllabled Mantram), the Feminine Integrating Vibration:

Ka E Ī La Hrīṁ
Ha Sa Ka Ha La Hrīṁ
Sa Ka La Hrīṁ Śrīṁ

When the Vibration of Ōṁ is placed in front of the Śoḍaṣī-Mantram, it becomes the Śoḍaṣākśarī-Mahā-Mantram.

Ōṁ
Ka E Ī La Hrīṁ
Ha Sa Ka Ha La Hrīṁ
Sa Ka La Hrīṁ Śrīṁ

When the Vibration of Klīṁ is added to the Śoḍaṣī-Mantram, it becomes the Saptaḍaṣī Vibration (Seventeen-Syllabled Mantram):

Ka E Ī La Hrīṁ
Ha Sa Ka Ha La Hrīṁ
Sa Ka La Hrīṁ Śrīṁ
Klīṁ

Ka E Ī La Hrīṁ

This is the Secret Name of the Goddess, the Esoteric GĀYATRĪ Mantra, the Sound-Form of ŚRĪ-VIDYĀ, the *Evolutionary Force* (Vibration).

These Sound-Forms of ŚRĪ-VIDYĀ *increase* the Life-force and Life-wave of the Disciple (the Devotee of the Goddess), and by intense SĀDHANĀ (practice) they *unite* the two aspects of the Goddess within him or her—the Immanent and the Transcendent, or ŚIVA and ŚAKTI, or the DAIVI-ŚAKTI-KUṆḌALINĪ and the PARAMITĀ-DEVĪ.

These Sound-Forms increase the Life-force and Life-wave of the Disciple

This results in a unique State of Consciousness, of "being in the world but not of the world"; fulfilling your Duty and Destiny while at the same time remaining Eternally Free inside yourself; being Liberated yet remaining active in the world.

The Śoḍaṣī Energy

ŚOḌAṢĪ is the Soft-Feminine-Force. It is a feeling-energy, inward-touching, sensitive-uniting. It is also a non-intellectual *Knowing*, what in the West used to be called Feminine-Intuition, or Knowing without using the verbalizing-mind. In the West today this is incomprehensible, because it is believed (falsely) that you can "know" only through your verbalizing, rational, intellectual mind, the analytical, logical, outer-mind. (Modern "education" is nothing but the use and *overdevelopment* of the rational, critical, analytical outer-mind.)

ŚOḌAṢĪ is the Inner-Mind, completely different from the aggressive, male, analytical, separative, "logical" outer-mind, today so much used everywhere. Nowadays most people in the West cannot tune into ŚOḌAṢĪ because they have been brought up in the "intellectualized education" system. This intellectual Western-style education system completely destroys ŚOḌAṢĪ and the possibility of Its development. The "uneducated" and people in the East have a better chance to develop ŚOḌAṢĪ.

You can still *see* and *feel* ŚOḌAṢĪ Energy in young girls in the West, *before* they have gone through the "education" mill.

The Feminine Virtues 468

Cosmic Sensitivity 1009
The Human Bipolarity 472
The Education System 480
The New Aquarian Energies 426

The Sound-Vibrations

The Vibration Hrīṁ is the Secret of the Heart

KA is the Vibration of Impulse, the Desire for Action.

E is the Effulgence of the Sun-Vibration: the Generator, Producer, Manifester.

Ī is the Vibration of Praise, Worship, Longing for the Divine: the Power of the Divine Light striving upward, the Effulgence of Glory.

LA is the steady Earth-Vibration: Greatness, Strength, Stability.

HA is the Vibration of Active Breath: the Spirit.

SA is the Vibration of ŚAKTI: Energy, Power.

HRĪṀ is the Magic Vibration of MĀYĀ: the Creative Power; the Wealth and Richness of Cosmic Matter or Cosmic Substance out of which the Worlds are spun by the Cosmic Vibrations; the Builder of the Cosmic Shapes and Forms; the Architect of the Phenomenal Worlds, gross, subtle and subtlest. These worlds are *illusory* or *phantom* in the sense that they are temporary worlds and manifestations; they are not the Transcendental Eternal Reality.

MĀYĀ (HRĪṀ) is also the Vibration of Wisdom (the Feminine Inner Sense).

MĀYĀ (HRĪṀ) is also the Vibration of Compassion, Sympathy, and the feeling of Unity, or At-One-ness with the All.

MĀYĀ (HRĪṀ) is also the Vibration of Art or Artistic Creative Ability.

HRĪṀ is also the Vibration of ĀDI-ŚAKTI, the Primordial Energy of the Universe; of PARA-ŚAKTI, the Supreme Force or Power of the Universe.

HRĪṀ is also the Vibration of TRIPURĀ-SUNDARĪ, the Goddess or Feminine Consciousness, the World Mother, incarnated in the Three Worlds (TRIPURĀ: the Physical, Astral and Mental Planes, or the gross, subtle and subtlest worlds). She is SUNDARĪ (Beautiful, Enchanting), and She is the Vibration of the Sense of Beauty, Harmony and Proportion in all Creation.

The Vibration HRĪṀ is the Secret of the Heart. HRĪ awakens the Heart-Vibration, and Ṁ (the Nasal Sound) is NĀDA, the Internal Sound or Inaudible Sound, Causal Sound-Vibration.

Hrīṁ (Hrīng) 1547
Vāk: the Divine Speech 118
The Law of Surrender or Sacrifice 1138
Āuṁ, Ōṁ, Nāda 550

The Sound-Sequences

The sequence of Sound (Vibration):

Ka E Ī La

is called Vāg-Bhāva-Kūṭa (the Peak of Creative Speech).

Vāg: Vāch (Vāk), the Logos, the Word, the Sound, the Vibration, the Creative Speech.

Bhāva: Being, Existence; feeling, sensing.

Kūṭa: the Highest Peak; Most Excellent.

∞

The sequence of Sound (Vibration):

Ha Sa Ka Ha La

is called Kāma-Rāja-Kūṭa (the Most Excellent Lord of Desire). That is, "the Fulfiller of all Desires".

Kāma: desire, wish, longing, pleasure, affection, Love.

Rāja: king, lord, emperor, chief, leader.

Ha Sa Ka Ha La

∞

The sequence of Sound (Vibration):

Sa Ka La

is called Śakti-Kūṭa (the Peak of Power).

Sakala: the Whole, the Complete; without all the parts.

Śakti: Power, Energy, Strength, Might, Ability, Empowerment.

∞

Thus is the Mantra (Vibration) *to be lead* from the gross state of Vibration (the physical) through the subtle, subtler and subtlest to the Spiritual.

Ka E Ī La Hrīṁ

A

The Śrī-Vidyā-Mantra

Śrī-Vidyā-Mantra: the Holy-Realization Mantra.

Also called:
Para-Mantra: the Transcendental Power.
Mūla-Mantra: the Basic or Root Mantra.
Pañcadaṣī-Mantra: the Fifteen-Syllabled Mantra.
Tripurāsundarī: the Threefold Beauty
Vāk-Śakti-Mantra: to awaken the Power of the Creative Word in the Form of the Goddess as Sound and Speech (Vāk = Gāyatrī).

Ka	E	Ī	La		Hrīṁ
Ha	Sa	Ka	Ha	La	Hrīṁ
Sa	Ka	La			Hrīṁ

1. Ka E Ī La Hrīṁ (5 years)
   All-Creative Power
2. Ha Sa Ka Ha La Hrīṁ (11 years)
   Divine Ecstasy
3. Sa Ka La Hrīṁ (15 years)
   Supreme Delight — The Resplendent Power

There are many variations of Her Mantra; this is the fifteen-syllabled form. Each syllable gives different powers (Siddhis) or abilities.

a. Śrīṁ Hrīṁ Klīṁ Aiṁ Svāhā	(Consecration)
b. Ōṁ Hrīṁ	(Dedication)
c. Ka E Ī La Hrīṁ	(Invocation)
d. Ha Sa Ka Ha La Hrīṁ Svāhā	(Oblation)
e. Aiṁ Klīṁ Hrīṁ Śrīṁ	(Offering to Divinity)

B

The Śrī-Vidyā-Vajra-Mantra

Śrī-Vidyā-Vajra: Holy-Realization-Thunderbolt.

Also called:
Śoḍaṣī-Mantra: the Sixteen-Years-Goddess Mantra (that is, the Mantra is given at sixteen years of age).
Śrī-Śoḍaṣākśarī-Mantra: the Holy Sixteen-Syllabled Mantra.
Mahā-Tripurāsundarī: the Great Threefold Beauty.
Gudha-Gāyatrī-Mantra: the Secret Gāyatrī Mantra.
Cit-Gāyatrī: Absolute Knowledge.
Cit-Śakti: the Consciousness-Power.

Ka	E	Ī	La		Hrīṁ	
Ha	Sa	Ka	Ha	La	Hrīṁ	
Sa	Ka	La			Hrīṁ	Śrīṁ

1. Ka E Ī La Hrīṁ
   The Power of Bliss

2. Ha Sa Ka Ha La Hrīṁ
   Fundamental Transformation

3. Sa Ka La Hrīṁ Śrīṁ
   Glory and Self-Realization — Glory and Realization

Hrīṁ (Hrīng) is Her total Power, Capacities, Energies; that is, the total Śakti (Divine Forces and Powers).

Śrīṁ (Śrīng) is Her capacity as Lakṣmī (Divine Beauty, Light, Splendour, wealth, opulence, good fortune, prosperity) and Ātmā-Vidyā (Self-Realization, Self-Knowledge).

The Mantra means:

"I am the Divine Being of Infinite Consciousness".

Sa Ka La Hrīṁ Śrīṁ

C

The Bālā-Mantra

The Transmutation of Desire

Aiṁ Klīṁ Sauḥ

The Divine-Child Mantra.
Also called Sundarī: the Child-Goddess Mantra.

Meditate in the Third-Eye…

Aiṁ Klīṁ Sauḥ

Ka	E	Ī	La		Hrīṁ	
Ha	Sa	Ka	Ha	La	Hrīṁ	
Sa	Ka	La			Hrīṁ	Śrīṁ

1.	Aiṁ			Klīṁ		Sauḥ	
	Wisdom Understanding			Beauty Delight		Transcendence Transformation	
2.	Ka	E	Ī	La		Hrīṁ	
	Strength Invigoration					Spiritual Prosperity Realization of the Goddess	
3.	Ha	Sa	Ka	Ha	La	Hrīṁ	
4.	Sa	Ka	La			Hrīṁ	Śrīṁ
							Material Prosperity Success and Beauty

Ka is the Opening Power, the Awakener. It is also Desire, the Power to Desire.
Ha is the Breath, Prāṇa, and is Spirit.
La is Joy, Bliss and Happiness.
Sa is Process, the Time it takes for Transformation.

Śrīṁ gives you the powers of abundance and prosperity (spiritual and material); Beauty (spiritual and material); Splendour, Glory, Realization (in both the material and spiritual realms); Devotion and Refuge in the Goddess.

Note that the first line is the actual Mantra. The remaining lines are added as the child becomes proficient in each step.

D

The Saptaḍaṣī-Mantras

Seventeen-Syllabled Mantras

1

This is the Śoḍaṣī-Mantra with Ōṁ added. It is also known as the Śoḍaṣākśarī-Mahā-Mantra. This Mantra is given at the age of seventeen. Meditate in the Third-Eye…

Ōṁ						
Ka	E	Ī	La		Hrīṁ	
Ha	Sa	Ka	Ha	La	Hrīṁ	
Sa	Ka	La			Hrīṁ	Śrīṁ

This Mantra will open the Third-Eye Cakra. It also helps to open the Brahmā-Randhra (Gate to God), which is above the Crown Cakra.

2

The Śoḍaṣī-Mantra with Klīṁ added:

Ka	E	Ī	La		Hrīṁ	
Ha	Sa	Ka	Ha	La	Hrīṁ	
Sa	Ka	La			Hrīṁ	Śrīṁ
Klīṁ						

This Mantra is also known as:
The Mahī-Mātā (Mighty Mother, Cosmic Mother) Mantra.
The Cit-Mātā (Mother of Consciousness) Mantra.

The Mother Light

There is a Feminine Pole of the Goddess at the Mūlādhāra Cakra (at the Base of the Spine), called Kuṇḍalinī, which is a fiery Female Energy.

There is another Feminine Pole of the Goddess in the Sahasrāra Cakra (at the Crown of the Head), which is called:

Cit-Śakti: Consciousness-Power.
Cit-Kuṇḍalinī: Consciousness-Fire.
Cit-Mātā: Consciousness-Mother.

This is the non-material or spiritual aspect of the Goddess.

E

The Secret Heart-Mantra

Worshipping the Goddess in the Heart

The Kumārikā or Kulakumārikā-Hṛdāya-Mantra.

Meditate in the Heart…

Aiṁ Klīṁ Śrīṁ
Klīṁ Ha-Sauḥ Namaḥ
Kula-Kumārike
Hṛdāya Namaḥ

Aiṁ: the power of Learning, Teaching, Understanding, in both the worldly and spiritual sense. The Guru function.

Klīṁ: the power of Attraction, Devotion and Love. Magnetic.

Śrīṁ: Glory, Splendour, advancement, growth, surrender to the Goddess Power. All Blessings in life.

Ha-Sauḥ: Male-Female.

Kula: family, tribe, nation.

Kumārī: the Virgin Goddess, or the Goddess in the Youthful Form, the Eternal Female.

Hṛda: the Heart.

Hṛda, the Heart = the Goddess.

Klīṁ Ha-Sauḥ Namaḥ

F

The Mātangī-Mantra

Also called the Vaikharī-Mantra: the Spoken-Word Power.

(Ōṁ) Hrīṁ Aiṁ Śrīṁ

Ōṁ: the Absolute, the Almighty Power, the Supreme Being.

Hrīṁ: the Sound of Creation, the Goddess-Consciousness.

Aiṁ: the Seed of all Knowledge.

Śrīṁ: all Glory and Perfection, all attainments and accomplishments.

This is the Creative-Power of the Goddess expressed in:

- The spoken word, writing.
- Dancing, art, music, song, mantras, chants, movement.
- Religious and artistic Ecstasy (such as wild dancing or whirling).
- Abandonment, passion.
- Mystic or Ecstatic Transformation of Consciousness.
- Learning, Spiritual Instruction.
- Intelligence expressed on the Physical Plane, in the physical body.

It is the Dynamic-Creative-Energy (Śakti) of the Goddess.

Mātangī is the Creative Power of Rhythm—outer rhythm and especially Inner Rhythm (Sattva).

Ōṁ Hrīṁ Aiṁ Śrīṁ

G

The Kamalā-Mantra

Also known as the Kamalātmikā-Mantra.

1. **Ōṁ Aiṁ Hrīṁ Śrīṁ**
   Klīṁ Ha-Sauḥ Namahā
   Śrīṁ Śrīṁ Śrīṁ Svāhā

Śrīṁ Śrīṁ Śrīṁ Svāhā

Kamalā-Ātmikā means "She whose Nature is the Lotus Flower". To understand this we have to understand the Eastern symbol of the lotus flower. Firstly it represents the Heart Centre, and it also represents all the lotuses or cakras in the human system.

The lotus flower is also a symbol for Lakṣmī, that aspect of Lalitā which gives:

- Name, fame, fortune, prosperity, success in all fields of action.
- Beauty, Charm, Grace, Splendour, Lustre, Shining, Spiritual Wealth or Powers.

Kamalā means "born of the Lotus Flower" (the symbol of Absolute Purity, Perfection and Beauty); springtime (which is when all things are reborn and renewed); most excellent; most desirous; full of wealth (the whole Universe is Hers); rose-coloured (which is the Flame of the Pure Spirit-Fire).

Kamalā, the Lotus-Born, is the Transcendental-Bliss aspect of Śrī-Vidyā: Pure Consciousness, Cosmic Unity, Divine Oneness with all things, Absolute Peace and Joy and Completeness, Cosmic Beingness.

Thus, this Mantra makes possible:

- All progress, unfoldment, development, growth.
- The natural opening-up of the cakras or Wheels of Fire.
- The opening-up of the Hṛdaya-Cakra (the Heart Centre) and thus the Power of Love.
- The fulfilment of all desires.
- Fertility, Vigour, Strength, Energy.
- The Powers of Spiritual Love and Devotion.

It is the Ocean of Beauty, the Ocean of Love, the Ocean of Fulfilment.

Kamalā Vibration

2. (Ōṁ) Śrīṁ Hrīṁ Klīṁ
Kamalā
Vaśinyai Svāhā

3. Ōṁ Aiṁ
Śrīṁ Hrīṁ Klīṁ
Kamalā
Vaśinyai Svāhā

4. Ōṁ Aiṁ
Hrīṁ Śrīṁ Klīṁ
Ha-Sauḥ
Jagat-Prasūtye
Namahā

5. Ōṁ Śrīṁ Hrīṁ Klīṁ
Kamalā
Aiṁ Vaśinyai
Svāhā

Vaśinī: the Mistress, the Ruler of all things.

Vaśinyai: to the Mistress or Controller or Goddess of the Universe.

Svāhā: offering oneself to Divinity; oblation, religious worship of Deity or Goddess; the Female Aspect of the Spiritual Fire; the Fire of Purification and self-surrender to Divinity.

Namah, Namahā: to the Divine Being; to God or the Goddess; to the Divine Name or Vibration; obeisance, worship, bowing down to.

Jagat: the world; all things moving or alive; people.

Prasūtī: the Primordial Essence; the Appearance of All; having come forth from the Unmanifest; offspring, child; flower.

Prasūtye: to the Primordial Essence.

Jagat-Prasūtye: to the Goddess who is the Appearance of the Universe, the Primordial Essence of All, or, Who is the True Nature of All and everybody.

Ha-Sauḥ: the Transcendental Energy.

Ōṁ: the Liberating Force.

Śrīṁ: Splendour.

Hrīṁ: Lalitā, the Feminine Force.

Klīṁ: Love, Attraction, Union.

Aiṁ: the Creative Energy.

Kamalā Vaśinyai Svāhā

H

The Strī-Mantra

In the Third-Eye

ŌṀ AIṀ KLĪṀ STRĪṀ

Other names for this Mantram are:

VADHŪ-MANTRA: the Female-Partner Mantra.
YOGINĪ-MANTRA: the Female-who-has-Realized-the-Truth Mantra.

STRĪ and VADHŪ represent Feminine Consciousness, the Feminine Nature. A YOGINĪ is One who has Realized the Self (ĀTMAN), the Spirit within. Thus this Mantra helps the Devotee to attain the State of YOGA, Union, Oneness with the Goddess, with the Absolute Truth, with Transcendental Consciousness, with the Eternal.

1. ŌṀ: the Power of Union.

   AIṀ: the Power of Realization.

   KLĪṀ: the Power of Devotion.

   STRĪṀ: the Power of Transformation of the basic energies of Life into Spiritual Fulfilment, Self-Realization, Controlled Strength. STRĪ, STRĪṀ, is dynamic, active Feminine Power.

2. ŌṀ is the Wake-up Call, the Signal for the Work to commence.

   AIṀ is the Sound of the All-Mother, the Goddess Kuṇḍalinī, the Creative Fire within.

   KLĪṀ is the Word of Attraction, the Power to attract the Beloved Goddess.

   STRĪṀ is the Eye of Vision, the Spiritual Eye, the All-Seeing Eye, the Eye of the Soul.

Thus is the Fire brought up into the Third-Eye, the Single-Eye, the Deva-Eye. Thus shall you see Her unveiling Her dazzling Beauty, veil after veil, layer after layer. Thus shall the Invisible Light become visible. Thus is the Hidden revealed and the All becomes known.

Meditate upon this Mantram in the Third-Eye...

ŌṀ AIṀ KLĪṀ STRĪṀ

I

The Rati-Mantra

(Ōṁ) Śrīṁ Hrīṁ Klīṁ

Rati means pleasure, enjoyment, desire, sensation, passion, love, delight, satisfaction, joy, intoxication. Lalitā is all this. It can be understood in the physical sense as well as in the spiritual sense.

Rati can be physical sensations, but also the Joy and Ecstasy to be found in Samādhi (Self-Realization, Union with Ātman) or Union with Brahman (God).

J

The Bhairavī-Mantra

Ha Sai Ha Sa Ka Rīṁ
Ha Sai

Bhairavī means "She who is terrifying, awesome, powerful, energetic; the Radiant One; the Fiery Goddess".

Bhairavī is Lalitā as the Essence of Fire. She is the Fire which is within all things, which fuels all actions. She is Tejas (the Radiant One, the Luminous One). This Fire is the Third Logos, Brahmā (the Holy Spirit of Christianity). This is the Fire of Matter, or the Fire *within* Matter (Prākṛtī), and hence *within* your body. She is also the Fire of Mind (Agni), or Cosmic Fire.

The secret of Spiritual Transformation is Fire-Consciousness, or Bhairavī. Fire is *transforming*.

The Strength of the Spiritual Warrior is Fire. Hence She is the Warrior Goddess, the Warrioress.

Fire destroys all limitations and illusions (Māyā) and burns up your ego (Ahaṁkāra), the sense that "I am the Doer".

Bhairavī is the Warrior-Goddess who guides, protects, transforms, and overcomes negative forces.

Dimensions of the Cosmic Fire 137

Ha Sai Ha Sa Ka Rīṁ

Cāmuṇḍāyai Vicche Svāhā

K

The Cāmuṇḍā-Mantra

(Ōṁ) Aiṁ Hrīṁ Klīṁ Cāmuṇḍāye Vicche (Ōṁ)

or: Ōṁ Aiṁ Hrīṁ Klīṁ Cāmuṇḍāyai Vicche Svāhā

Ōṁ: Truth, Consciousness, Bliss.

Aiṁ: Omniscience.

Hrīṁ: the total manifestation of Lalitā.

Klīṁ: the Desire for Union, At-One-Ment.

Caṇḍa: fierce, violent, passionate (Rajas).

Muṇḍa: dull, stupid, blunt (Tamas).

Vicche: the Slayer, or the slaying of.

Caṇḍa + Muṇḍa = Cāmuṇḍa.

This is the Mantra of Liberation through the destruction of both Rajas and Tamas and thus attaining Sattva.

The Three Forces at work in Nature and in Humanity 1693

L

The Mṛtyuṁjaya-Mantra

Krīṁ Hrīṁ Śrīṁ

This is the Mantra to Overcome the Fear of Death.

Mṛtyu is death.
Jaya is Victory.

Mṛtyu is Lalitā as the Goddess of Death, for all things must die that are born. But She also delivers you from Death (Mṛtyu, Yama) by giving you Conscious Immortality beyond the physical body (the Amṛta, the Nectar of Immortality).

True Death 424

M

The Rāmā-Mantra

a. **Rā - Mā**
b. **Rāṁ**

Rāmā is Lalitā who is Loving and Delighting, Pleasing and Pleasurable. This Mantra gives much Joy and Happiness and Transcendental Bliss.

Rām: the Universal Name 1273

N

The Kālī-Mantra

Krīṁ Hūṁ Hrīṁ

This is the Mantra for Transformation.

Krīṁ: Energetic Transformation.

Hūṁ: Protection and Fire-Power.

Hrīṁ: Divine Beauty and Reconciliation.

Kālimā: the Mother Beyond Time 1495

Krīṁ Hūṁ Hrīṁ

Potent Vibrations: Bīja-Mantra

Esoteric Wisdom

Ōṁ

Veda Bīja: Illumination-Seed.

Praṇava Bīja: the Sacred Word, the Mystic Syllable.

Antarātmā (Antarātman) Bīja: the Sound of the Inner Self.

Tāra Bīja: the Saving, Protecting Vibration.

Tārā Bīja: the Inner Star, Radiance, the Inner Light.

Ātmā Bīja: the Power of the Spiritual Self, Ātman.

Antaryāmin Bīja: the Power of the Inner Ruler Immortal, seated in the Heart, manifested in the Head.

Purāṇa Puruṣa Bīja: the Ancient Godhead Force, the Ancient of Days, the Word of the Eternal One.

Ōṁ (Ōng) is the Absolute (Parabrahman).

Ōṁ (Ōng) is limitless in all directions, complete in itself, *whole*. Ōṁ is independent of anything else, unlimited and unconditioned. Ōṁ is free from imperfection, pure, unmixed. Ōṁ is the Absolute Reality, pre-existing before all things, unchanged, unchanging, the Cause of all Causes.

Ōṁ (Ōng) is Praṇava (praise, salutation, adoration). When we think, chant, intone or meditate on Ōṁ we are naturally praising the Lord of all beings.

Ōṁ (Ōng) is the Udgitha, the Primordial Song, the Sound-Current, the Nāda, the Word (Logos), the First Hymn of the Universe.

Ōṁ (Ōng) is the Oṁkāra (word, syllable, sound) which is God. It is the Sacred Word.

Ōṁ (Ōng) produces Integration, Coherence, Oneness, Union (Yoga) in the human brain and mind. It also integrates the nervous system. It produces Divine Unity in the Soul (Yukta).

Ōṁ (Ōng) produces Liberation from Rebirth (Mukti) and Eternal Freedom in the Spirit (Mokṣa).

Ōṁ (Ōng) is God, the Cosmic Sound-Vibration.

Ōṁ (Ōng) helps to coordinate the forces in the Head and Heart Centres and gives the highest Knowledge, Cohesion and non-dual state of Awareness. It tunes up Consciousness, awakens, calls to attention, rearranges the mind.

Ōṁ (Ōng) is Mūlamantra (Root-Vibration), the Primordial or Original Sound of the Universe and of Humanity. Ōṁ is Nādaliṅga (the Sound-Sign), the symbol for the Inner Music heard within the Universe.

Ōṁ (Ōng) is Īśvara (God, Lord, Master, Ruler, Controller) because it is all-powerful, omnipotent, sovereign, excellent. Ōṁ is also the Personal God for those who seek the way of personal Salvation. Ōṁ is also the God who manifests in the Third-Eye as Light and Sound. Ōṁ is also Ātman (the Divine Self in Humanity) and Ātmā (the Universal Spirit).

Ōṁ (Ōng) is Āditya-Śabda (the Sun-Sound), the Vibrations emanated by the Solar Logos in the form of Sounding-Light waves. Āditya (the Solar Logos) is the Golden Being who resides in the Sun and in the Solar System, the Cosmic Soul-Entity whose body is the visible and invisible parts of our Sun and Solar System.

Ōṁ (Ōng) is the Tāraka-Mantra, the shining, clear, bright Sound-Vibration.

Ōṁ (Ōng) is Brahmā (the Creator-God). Ōṁ is the Creative Power of the Absolute.

Ōṁ (Ōng) is Śiva-Śakti, God united with the Divine Creative Force or Power.

Ōṁ (Ōng) is the Boundless Consciousness of your Higher Self, your Spiritual Soul.

Lāṁ

Dharā Bīja: the Power that Upholds.

Pṛthi (Pṛthivī) Bīja: the Seed of Earth, the Element Earth (the carrying, bearing, maintaining, supporting vibration; governance, perfect Rule).

Brahmā Bīja: the Power of Creation, Evolution and Growth.

Vāṁ

Varuṇa Bīja: the all-enveloping, all-including Power; the Water Element, Cosmic Waters; Immortality.

Viṣṇu Bīja: the all-pervading Power, the Omnipresent One; the Sustainer and Preserver of the Universe.

Kṛṣṇa Bīja: the Power that restores Righteousness.

Hari Bīja: Viṣṇu, the Lord God.

Rāṁ

Agni Bīja: the God of Fire, Cosmic Fire, Spiritual Fire.

Vahni Bīja: the Element Fire.

Svastika Bīja: the auspicious, lucky Power; favourable, prosperous; the Fiery Cross, 卐.

Rāma Bīja: the Omnipresent God.

Rāṁ (Rāng) is the All-Pervading God, the All-embracing Life-Impulse of God. It is God in *action.*

Rāṁ (Rāng) is also known as Rāṁ-Nām or Rāma-Nāma (the Divine Name). Rāṁ-Nām is the all-pervading Sound-Current, the Logos, the Word, the Name (Active Power) of God.

Rāṁ (Rāng) means Rest in Peace and Silence; elation, joy, jubilation.

Rāṁ (Rāng) is the Positive Forces of Life.

Rāṁ (Rāng) is to Rejoice in the Moment.

Rāṁ (Rāng) is inner directedness, self-supportiveness, wholeness, unity, self-confidence, adaptability, stability, purification, integration, growth.

Rāṁ (Rāng) is Rāma, Divine Majesty, Kingship, Authority, Divine Positivity, Divine Power, Evolutionary Force, Life-enhancing Divine Strength, Goodwill of God. It is healing, unifying, harmonizing, nourishing. Rāma is positive activity, the ability to act correctly in all circumstances. This is fine attunement.

Rāṁ (Rāng) is the Blissful Nature of God, the auspicious, good-luck-bringing Power, mental harmony, the Creative Intelligence of God. It is rejoicing, delightful, happy.

Rāṁ (Rāng) is Śrī-Rāṁ, the Glory of God.

Rāṁ (Rāng) is the Radiance of God.

Rāṁ (Rāng) is the Power that charms, the Shining Power of God, the Cosmic Unified Field of Activity, the Protective Power, the Life-giving nourishing Power.

Rāṁ (Rāng) is Everlasting Joy, Absolute Bliss, the Word, the Logos, the All in All, Transcendental Immensity, Supreme Active Intelligence, Victorious Energy of the Spirit, Sublime Glory.

Rāṁ (Rāng) is Beauty, Grace, Ability, Strength, Nobility, Virtue, Honour, Righteousness.

Rāṁ (Rāng) is Self-government, being ruled by the Spirit, the Rule of Spirit (Ātmā-Rāma), the Kingdom of God (Rāma-Rāj).

Rāṁ (Rāng) is Divine Organizing Power, Divinity, Majesty, Kingship, the Supreme Hero, the Solar Dynasty, the Power of the Sun, the Solar Logos and the Spiritual Sun, Cosmic Intelligence, the Ruler of the Universe.

Rāṁ (Rāng) is Truth, fearlessness, justice, skill in action, bravery, honour, dignity, freedom in action.

Rāṁ (Rāng) is Cosmic Administrative Intelligence, Cosmic Ruler, the Lord God, the Absolute Ruler of the Universe, the Inner Ruler Immortal in Humanity, Ātman, your Lord God within.

Yāṁ

Īśa Bīja: the Lord of the Universe, the Power of the Divine Self within the Heart, the all-pervading Controller-God.

Pavana Bīja: the Air Element; the Air, Breath, Wind of the Spirit.

Pāvana Bīja: the Purifying Fire of the Spirit; that which makes Holy.

Vyāsa Bīja: that which causes separation, division, distribution, separate arrangements, classifications, compiling.

Vāyu Bīja: Air, Breath.

Hāṁ

Ambara Bīja: the Power of Space; the Fifth Element, Aether (Ether), the One Element, the Mother Element, the Space that includes All.

Ākāśa Bīja: the Universal Aether, the Astral Light, the Luminous Invisible Substance of Omnispace.

Vyoman Bīja: the Power of the Sky, Heaven and atmosphere (both the visible and invisible aspects).

Hūṁ

Laya Bīja: merging, uniting, dissolving the ego or limited "I" sense; to attain the point of Rest or Equilibrium within oneself; Stillness, Silence.

Rakṣā Bīja: safety, refuge, protection.

Varma Bīja: protecting armour, or shield, against evil forces and powers.

Śakti Bīja: Spiritual Power; the background Force of Creation; the background Vibration of the Universe; the Holy Spirit Force; Creative Power.

Hrī

Hṛdaya Bīja: the Heart Sound; that which awakens the Heart Centre.

Hrīṁ

Māyā Bīja: the Creative Power; the Veiling Power over the Spirit (because Creation, Matter, is a Veil over the Face of Spirit).

Lalitā Bīja: the Supremely Feminine Power, the Eternal Female, that which gives Beauty, Grace, Charm, Loveliness, Playfulness, Gentleness, Happiness, and Oneness or Empathy.

Tripurāsundarī Bīja: the Goddess of the Three Worlds (the Physical, Astral and Mental Planes; that is, the gross, subtle and subtlest material worlds wherein the Human Souls circulate in their incarnatory cycles).

Śuddhā Bīja: that which produces Holiness, Sacredness, Purity, and the Transcendental Condition.

Hrīṁ (Hrīng) is:
Para-Devatā: the Supreme Divinity.
Tantra-Praṇava: the Esoteric Praise of the Goddess.
Śoḍaṣī: the Perfect Goddess.
Bhuvaneśvarī: the Goddess of all the worlds.
Jaganmātā: the Mother of the Universe, the Divine Mother.
Śrī-Vidyā: the Holy Knowledge.
Śiva-Śakti: uniting, giving Union to polar opposites.
Rādhā: the giver of Fortune, Success and intense Devotion.
Śakti: force, power, ability, capability. All the powers of the various Goddesses are but expressions of Śakti.

Hrīṁ (Hrīng) is Mahā-Devī, the Great Goddess, who gives Perfection, Wholeness, Fullness, Completeness, Samasti (Unity) and Yoga (Union).

Hrīṁ (Hrīng) is the Powers of Consciousness, Female Authority, Queenship. It is female grace and dignity, contentment, supreme happiness, healing and harmonizing power, creative imagination.

Hrīṁ (Hrīng) is Hṛllēkhā-Śaktiḥ, the Energy of enthusiasm and inspiration in the Heart. She is Purifying Power.

Hrīṁ (Hrīng) is the Mantra of the Heart, Hṛdayaṁ.

Śrī

Śrī Bīja: shining, luminous, full of Light, divine, sacred, holy, venerable, respected, adorable.

Śrī is the Sacred, that which is beyond Mind.

Śrī is the Goddess in the form of Divine Beauty, Divine Light, Divine Wealth, Glory, Opulence (abundance of powers, virtues, qualities, charms).

Śrī is the Light of Knowledge, the Light of Love; pure, refined, excellent, glittering, radiant, glorious, perfect, holy, sacred, illustrious, revered, worshipped, honourable.

Śrīṁ

Lakṣmī Bīja: the Power, Energy, Vibration, that gives fortune, development, increase, growth, success; beauty, harmony, splendour, grace, fame, charm; lustre, shining, light, glory, radiance; enchantment.

Ramā (Rāmā) Bīja: that which produces luxury, splendour, enchantment, wealth (material or spiritual), joy, delight, happiness.

Śrīṁ (Śrīng) is the Goddess Lakṣmī, the Beautiful One, She who gives good fortune, prosperity, wealth, abundance, Divine Wealth, Self-Realization (Ātmā-Vidyā), Splendour, Light, Glory. She gives rewards, fortune, good luck, success, happiness, satisfaction, livelihood, Ramā (delight, joy, pleasure).

Strī

Devī Bīja: the Goddess Power; Creative Force.

Strīṁ

Vadhū Bīja: the Essential Female Creative Power.

Śānti Bīja: that which gives peace, quiet, tranquillity, in the Awakened Consciousness.

Krīṁ

Yoga Bīja: uniting, going above or beyond the little self.

Kālī Bīja, Kālikā Bīja: that which destroys the illusion of personality; that which destroys the illusion of Time and Space.

Krīṁ (Krīng) is Kālī, the Fearless Goddess. She is the Energizer; she gives energy for intense activity and peak performance. She is total fearlessness and overcomes the insecurities of life and fear of death. She is a protecting and liberating power, the power to see beyond death and destruction. She is Force, Power, Energy, the Life-Force in its primitive untamed form, the Primordial Śakti. She is Liberation from form-life and all kinds of limitation. She is the female Warrior-Force.

Kālī is the Goddess Durgā in another form. Durgā, or Kālī, gives Self-Knowledge or Self-Understanding, Yoga (Oneness, Union, Uniting), integration of body, mind and Soul, and Union with God (the Goddess).

Klīṁ

Kāma Bīja, Kāma Devī Bīja: that which stimulates the Astral Nature (the emotional self); desire, wish, longing, affection, attraction in polarity, male-female attraction, sensual enjoyment, sensual pleasure, attraction to beautiful objects and things.

Kṛṣṇa Bīja: Divine Love, attraction of the Soul to God, pure Devotion, Surrender to God, attracting God into your life.

Madana Bīja: the energy of Ecstasy; intoxication (both in the worldly sense and in the divine sense); passion about something or someone; Renewal, Transformation, Re-Creation.

Śaktānanda Bīja: the Energy of Bliss.

Klīṁ (Klīng) is Kāma (desire, pleasure, the attractive power of Love as well as physical attraction). She is the burning desire for God, the desire for another creature or an object, the magnetic attraction to Divinity or worldly things, personal magnetism, wish-fulfilling power.

Aiṁ

Klīṁ (Klīng) is Kāmadeva (the Desire-God), Kṛṣṇa, Rādhā, Govinda, Eros (Greek). She overcomes depression and negative emotional and mental states. She is Devotion to God or to a person or to an ideal. She is the power to fulfil all desires.

Aiṁ

Sarasvatī Bīja: the Power of learning, knowledge, study to transform the mind; music, art, dancing, creative expression; the power of eloquence, words and speech.

Vāg-Bhāva Bīja: the Power or Energy of the Creative Word, the Logos, the Speech of God.

Guru Bīja: the Guru's Mantram, the illuminating Teachings of a true Saint or Master; the Illumination received by following the Spiritual Teachings; the function of the Guru in revealing the Sacred and Spiritual Knowledge; Wisdom.

Aiṁ (Aing) is Sarasvatī (the flowing river), the Goddess as the River of Light. She is the River of Knowledge, Enlightenment, Illumination. She is the Goddess of learning, culture, skills, crafts and the arts. She gives creative powers to the mind and thoughts, the ability to learn, education, cheerfulness, happiness, joy, Inner Knowledge, Wisdom, Esoteric Knowledge, the powers of speech, mantras and music. She gives purity of body, mind, emotions and Soul. She removes all ignorance from the mind.

Aiṁ (Aing) is also the Guru, the Spiritual Teacher, the Master, and all teaching abilities.

Īṁ

Yoni Bīja: the Cosmic Womb, Source or Origin; that which leads you back to the Primal State.

Trīṁ

Tejas Bīja: Fiery Energy; clarity, brilliance, Light.

Trāṁ

Prasāda Bīja: Divine Grace, Purity; moving into the Great Invisible.

Krāṁ

Turyā Bīja: that by which you step out of your body-mind limitations and enter the Transcendent.

Āṁ

Sūrya Bīja: the Radiance of the Sun; Spiritual Light.

Māṁ

Candra Bīja: the Radiance of the Moon; inner Radiance.

Śāṁ

Śāma Bīja: Peace, Tranquillity, Calmness, Equanimity, Quietude.

Ha

Śiva Bīja, Liṅga Bīja: Male Creative Force, Male Power, the Masculine Aspect of Deity.

Sa

Śakti Bīja: Female Creative Force, Female Power, the Feminine Aspect of Deity.

Ahaṁ

Paramātman Bīja: the Universal Self, the ever-present I AM within you and in the whole Universe; the I Am That I Am; the Universal Logos; the Self within All and within everybody; the One Self.

Svāhā

Yajña Bīja: Worship, Devotion, offering to the God or Goddess form of Reality; dissolution in God or Goddess; offering one's ego on the alter of self-sacrifice to the Chosen Deity one worships.

Svāhā

Bīja-Mantra Practice

These Bījas are *Gateways*, when correctly used, for Liberation, for *disengaging* your Consciousness from bondage to your physical body, for *dissolving* your "I" or limited ego-sense, and to *lead* you to Cosmic Consciousness, God-Consciousness, Unity-Consciousness, Absolute Consciousness and Boundless Bliss-Consciousness.

The Bījas are Gateways for Liberation

There are two ways to use them:

a. To *increase* the inherent Divine Powers within you by ceaseless Bhakti Yoga (Union with God through Devotion).

b. To *transcend* the self through Rāja Yoga (Union with God through Consciousness).

The practice, Sādhanā, must be learned from the Teacher, and persevered with for a long time sincerely, and integrated into your life correctly. It is based on the Mystical Power of the Sanskrit Alphabet, the combination of various sounds into mantric forms or Sound-Waves which directly *transform* your Inner Consciousness and *change* your embodied self to reveal the Inner Self, your true Self-Nature.

The Mystics of Old Israel also understood that the Divine Name is expressed in the Hebrew Alphabet, just as the Sanskrit Alphabet expresses the Name of God. Various combinations of letters in ancient Hebrew and Sanskrit form Magic Words which *unveil the God* in your Inner Being.

The Science of Bīja-Mantra 1218
Bhakti Yoga: Divine Union by Devotion 1128
Rāja Yoga: Divine Union by Meditation 1126
The Name and the Names 1258

Bīja-Mantra and Psychology

The Goddess is the Energy behind everything. Therefore, everything can be transformed by Her Power (Śakti): emotions, moods, thoughts, circumstances, situations, physical conditions, and so on.

The different Bīja-Mantrams produce different effects to bring about any desired condition. This will be understood by the Psychology of the Future and a new positive Psychology will result.

Psychology and the New Age Religion 1105

Gāyatrī (Sun) Breathing

SŌHAṀ	HAṀSA	SVĀHĀ
That I Am	I Am That	Dissolving in Unity

The Equalizing Breath:

in		*out*	*in*		*out*	*in*		*out*
SŌ	–	HAṀ	HAṀ	–	SAH	SVĀ	–	HĀH
HAṀ	–	SAH	SŌ	–	HAṀ	SVĀ	–	HĀH

The Equalizing Breath unifies the male and female aspects of KUṆḌALINĪ (the ĪḌĀ, at the left side of the spinal cord, and the PIṄGALĀ, at the right side) with the Central Stem, the SUṢUMNA.

As the Breathing process develops, the State of Yoga (Union, Integration) takes place. First, Union of the various personality elements, and then Union of the personality with the Soul, the real Self that You are. This is called GĀYATRĪ-PRĀṆĀYĀMA, or Sun-Breathing. The Sun-Breathing is a technique of ŚRĪ-VIDYĀ, the Holy Science.

HAṀSA-SŌHAṀ-SVĀHĀ is the *Vibration* of the Life-force, PRĀṆA, what we call the Breath.

PRĀṆĀYĀMA-VIDYĀ is the Science of Breath:

PRĀṆA	**–**	**YĀMA**	**PRĀṆA**	**–**	**AYĀMA**
Breath		**Control**	**Breath**		**No-control**
Life-force					**Spontaneous**
Energy					**Natural**

Thus, esoterically, PRĀṆĀYĀMA means breath which is natural, not forced, in balance, equilibrated.

The "normal" breathing of men and women and children is "chaotic". This is the result of chaotic thinking, feeling, acting and speaking.

When the breath is *equalized*, balanced, harmonized, suspended (that is, PRĀṆĀYĀMA), then the Inner Worlds can be touched, felt, seen, heard and experienced. When the breath is *united* (that is, HAṀSA–SŌHAṀ–SVĀHĀ), then there is in you:

Silence, Harmony, Peace, Rest.

YOGA (Union), ŚŪNYATĀ (Emptiness, Formlessness).

SAMĀDHI (Superconsciousness, Bliss).

Rest in the Great Breath 1654

SŌHAṀ HAṀSA SVĀHĀ

The Silent State

When you have attained the State of Silence:

Listen to the Clarion Call of the Soul;

Look for the Light;

The Soul is Omnipotent;

Omniscience.

You sense the Mind of God, and then you become Omniscient

This means that when the Mantram has pacified your mind, calmed your emotions, stilled your physical body, then you enter into SAMĀDHI, the State of Silence, where your whole personality, your personal "I", is in a state of suspension or *alert inaction*.

There are several options in that *Silent State:*

- You listen to the Clarion Call of your Soul; that is, in that Silence you listen for a sharp sound, like a trumpet-blast. When you can hear it, you enter the Kingdom of the Souls.
- Or, you intensely look, through the Third-Eye, into the Silent Inner Space, whether dark or light, until you find the Light, the Perpetual Shining Sun, and join the Kingdom of the Elect, the Adepts and Masters.
- Or, you discover the Miraculous Powers of your Soul, the Siddhis, through the Silent Will.
- Or, you sense the Absolute, the Mind of God, Cosmic Intelligence, and then you become Omniscient.

The Path of Hearing 553
Saṁyama 582
The Silence of the Deep 1355
Works of Silence 1643

CHAPTER 65

The One-Hundred Names of Lalitā

Lalitā

The Ultimate Goddess

LALITĀ is the Goddess in the form of Absolute Beauty, Loveliness, Gentleness, Grace, Innocence, Kindness—the most perfect of all female qualities.

Lalitā is the Goddess in the form of Absolute Beauty

She is also LALITĀ-AMBIKĀ (LALITĀMBIKĀ), the lovely, gentle Divine Mother (AMBIKĀ).

She is also known as TRIPURĀSUNDARĪ (from TRI, "three"; PURĀ "city, realm, plane"; and SUNDARĪ, "beautiful"). The TRIPURĀ are the three Planes of Being (the Physical, Astral and Mental Planes), the Three Worlds of human evolution which include the three bodies in which the Human Soul dwells (the physical, astral and mental bodies). She pervades the three lower worlds and the human personality-self with Divine Beauty, Dazzling Brightness, and She helps you to *transcend* the Three Worlds and the three bodies.

Her Name is also ŚOḌAṢĪ (when the Sixteen-Syllabled Mantra is used), PAÑCAḌAṢĪ (when the Fifteen-Syllabled Mantra is used) and SAPTAḌAṢĪ (when the Seventeen-Syllabled Mantra is used).

She is SAKALĀ, She Who is with Rays of Light, with Beams of Light, with Waves of Radiances, Dazzling, Bright. SAKALĀ (SA-KA-LA) also means "whole, complete, full, entire, including the All". Out of Her Light-Radiations (Sounding-Light) comes the whole Universe, including the entire human being—body, mind and Soul.

She is BHUVANEŚVARĪ, the World Mother (from BHUVANA, "the World, the Cosmos, the Universe", and ĪŚVARĪ, "the Sovereign Goddess").

The Feminine Virtues 468
Lalitā: the Eternal Feminine 1484
Holy Knowledge 1517
Garments of Light 1526
Śrī Jagadambā: the Mother of the World 1498

Meditation on the Names of Lalitā, the Goddess

Here follow one-hundred meditations on LALITĀ, the Ultimate Reality as Goddess. These meditations are called *The Names of Lalitā.* Each Name is an attribute, a quality, a function, or an aspect of the Ultimate Nature of things. Each Name reveals to you something about LALITĀ.

By holding a Name in your mind, you become Lalitā in that aspect

1. You can meditate on each Name in your mind by focusing on the Sanskrit word, or its meaning, or both.
2. You may repeat each Name as a Mantra in your mind. This can be done in two ways:
   a. Repeat the whole word as one.
   b. Break it down into syllables. For example:

   LA-LI-TĀ
   KŪ-ṬAST-HĀ
   ĀJ-ÑĀ
   PA-RĀ-ŚAK-TĪ
   MAN-TRA-SĀ-RĀ
3. Another way is to place ŌṀ in front of the Name. For example:

   ŌṀ LALITĀ
   ŌṀ SĀVITRĪ
   ŌṀ HṚDAYA
   ŌṀ BHAGAVATĪ
4. Another way is to prefix the Name with ŚRĪ. For example:

   ŚRĪ-MAHĀ-TRIPURĀ-SUNDARĪ
   ŚRĪ-PAÑCADAṢĪ
   ŚRĪ-BĀLĀ

By holding a Name in your mind, you become that Name. Thus you become LALITĀ in that aspect.

Everything that Is is LALITĀ.

The Voice of God 864
The Name of the Deity 1032
The Name and the Names 1258
Right Use of Mantra 1697

1

Lalitā

- Lovely, desirable, pleasing, beautiful, soft, gentle, graceful, perfect, charming, enchanting, wondrous.
- Playful, sweet, youthful, engaging, loving, energetic, attractive.
- Transcending all the worlds. Brilliant with Light rays. The Vision that is the Eternal Feminine. The Eternal Beauty.

2

Kūṭasthā

The Immovable One.

She is fixed in the Third-Eye Centre as the Perpetual Light.

3

Ājñā

The Divine Command.

She is the Voice of Light in the Third-Eye.

4

Parā-Śaktī

The Supreme Power.

She is the Power that transcends all Creation, and She is the Power that is the Energy in all Matter, forms, bodies and substances.

5

Mantra-Sārā

The Essence of all Mantra.

The Mantric Vibrations of special sound-formulas are Her embodiments or forms—not only the specific female Mantras, but all other Mantras as well. She incarnates in Mantras.

6

Mahā-Tripurā-Sundarī

Mahā: great, omnipotent, vast.
Tri: three.
Purā: cities, towns, worlds, realms, bodies.
Sundarī: exquisitely beautiful.

The Beautiful Goddess within the three bodies (physical, astral and mental) and within the Three Worlds (the Physical, Astral and Mental Planes).

7

Śrī-Mātā

The Holy Mother. The Universal Mother.

She is the Mother of the Universe, the Cause of all that is.

8

Lalitāmbikā (Lalitā-Ambikā)

The Beautiful Mother.

9

Śrī-Mahā-Rājñī

The Dazzling Queen of the Universe.
The Empress of the World.

10

Śrī

Sacred, Holy. Prosperity, well-being. Glorious, victorious, beautiful, exalted, royal, dignified, radiant, lustrous, shining, illuminating, majestic, noble, grand, excellent.

The Unbroken Light that is Solid Bliss.

11

Śrī-Vidyā

The Sacred Knowledge.
The Secret Knowledge of the Self. Self-Realization.

12

Mahā-Vidyā

Cosmic Mind, Cosmic Intelligence.

13

Śoḍaṣī
Śoḍaṣākśarī
Śrī-Śoḍaṣākśarī-Vidyā

Śoḍaṣī: sixteen years old.
Śoḍaṣ-ākśarī: the Sixteen-Syllabled Mantra.
Śrī-Śoḍaṣākśarī-Vidyā: the Realization (Vidyā) of the Holy (Śrī) Sixteen-Syllabled Mantra (Śoḍaṣ-ākśarī).

She is the great Power behind the famous Śoḍaṣī-Mantra or the Śrī-Śoḍaṣākśarī-Mahā-Mantra.

This Mantra produces Sattva or Purity (harmonious vibration) in the Initiate which leads to Self-Realization and Transcendental Knowledge (Śrī-Vidyā) and Unending Bliss (Ānanda).

14

Bhuvaneśvarī (Bhuvana-Īśvarī)

Bhuvana: the Universe, the World, all that Became (was created).
Īśvarī: the Ruler, the Mistress of the Cosmos.

She is the Great Queen of the Universe and the Queen of Heaven. She is the Supreme Being incarnate.

15

Pañcaḍaṣī
Pañcaḍaṣa-Ākśarī-Mantra
Mūla-Mantra
Mūla-Mantra-Ātmikā

Pañcaḍaṣī: fifteen years old.
Pañcaḍaṣa-Ākśarī-Mantra: the Fifteen-Syllabled Mantra.
Mūla-Mantra: the Root or Foundation Mantra.
Mūla-Mantra-Ātmikā: She is the Spirit or Life of the Root Mantra upon which the whole system of Śrī-Vidyā is based.

The Pañcaḍaṣī or Mūla-Mantra is the Subtle Body or Subtle Form of Lalitā. This Subtle Form consists of Sounding-Light Vibrations.

16

Gāyatrī

"She is in the form of a song" (in the form of Mantric Vibration).

Lalitā is the Goddess within the Sun, and the Gāyatrī Mantra is an expression of Her. She is the Face within the Sun. She abides within the Gāyatrī Mantra as the innermost Truth or Essence.

17

Sāvitrī

She is the Feminine Sun, or the feminine aspect *within* the Sun.

Sāvitrī means the Creative Power of the Universe.
Sāvitrī means Solar-Power, the Energy of the Sun, Rays of Light, Light-Radiation.

18

Devī

The Goddess, the Divine, Divinity.

She is the Power responsible for the Creation of the Universe. Although Devī is responsible for Creation, Her Transcendental Nature is Absolute Bliss-Consciousness and Existence. She is also known as Śrī-Lalitā-Devī.

19

Sakalā

The All. The whole Universe.

She is complete, full, entire, perfect, total Unity or Oneness.

20

Pūrṇā

The Whole, the All, without parts, always complete.

She is Wholeness, Completeness, Fullness, Oneness. Nothing can be added to or taken away from this Cosmic-Wholeness.

21

Kuṇḍalinī
Kuṇḍalinī-Śaktī

Kuṇḍalinī: the Coiled Serpent.
Kuṇḍalinī-Śaktī: the Serpent-Power.

She is the great Serpent-Power which is coiled up in the Mūlādhāra-Cakra at the base of the spine, and the Fire at the Svādhiṣṭhāna-Cakra (the Sex Centre).

In this form She is a Fiery Energy, or the Energy of Subtle Fire.

22

Hṛdyā, Hṛdaya, Hṛt, Hṛdayaṁ, Hṛd, Hṛdayasthā

Hṛdyā: the Heart.
Hṛdayasthā: She who dwells in the Heart.

The Heart is a great Mystery. It is only revealed to the devotee who has penetrated the Heart Sanctuary. Within the Heart is contained the Universe, and Ātman, the Self.

The Heart has three syllables: Hrī-Da-Yā.

23

Sūrya-Maṇḍalā

The Sun-Circle, the Circle of the Sun, which is the Anāhata-Cakra, the Heart Centre. The Heart is the Mystery of Being, of Life, of Consciousness, the Mystery of "Who Am I?".

Parameśvarī, the Supreme Goddess, lives in the Heart. This Supreme Goddess is Lalitā. The Devī dwells in the Heart of Her devotee.

24

Ī, Īṁ,
Īkarī, Īṁkarī

She is the letter Ī, the Sound of Ī, which is the Sound of Consciousness, the Sound of Light. Ī is also the sound of Kāma (desire), the main motivating power for action in the human being. It is also the power of Rajas (activity).

Consciousness is all that Is. Develop the mechanism of perception.

25

Hrīṁkārī (Hrīṁ-Kārī)

She who is the syllable Hrīṁ. The Hrīṁ-maker.

Hrīṁ is the Great Mantra of Lalitā in her form of Bhuvaneśvarī (Bhuvanā-Īśvarī), the Omnipresent Goddess. Within the sound of Hrīṁ there are the three powers or faculties of Creation, Sustenance and Dissolution.

26

Hrīkārī (Hrī-Kārī)
Hrīmatī

Hrīkārī: She who makes the sound of Hrī, which gives nobility and protection.

Hrīmatī: She who is modest in her behaviour: not arrogant, not pushy, not forcing, but gentle.

Kula-Kumārikā

27

Śrīṁkārī (Śrīṁ-Kārī)

She who is the doer (Kārī) of abundance (Śrīṁ).

Lalitā is full of richness and abundance on all levels: physical, psychic, emotional, mental and spiritual. She is the maker, doer, producer, creator (Kārī) of all wealth (Śrīṁ) and prosperity.

28

Klīṁkārī (Klīṁ-Kārī)

She who is the Creator of Klīṁ.

Klīṁ is the famous Kāma-Bīja (Desire-Seedpower) which grants all wishes and desires in the form of Kāmeśvarī (the Desire-Goddess).

29

Bālā

She who is the little girl, or girl-child.

30

Kumārī
Kanyākumārī
Kulakumārī
Kumārikā
Kula-Kumārikā

Kumārī: the virgin girl, maiden, young girl.

Kanyākumārī: the Virgin Goddess, the Eternal Virgin.

Kula: family, tribe, a group of people.

Kulakumārī: She who is the Virgin Goddess, the Eternal-Imperishable-Feminine, for those who worship Her.

Kumārikā: the virgin girl, the Eternal Goddess.

31

Līlā
Līlā-Vinodinī

Līlā: play.
Vinodinī: She who enjoys playing.

The whole Creation is Lalitā's play. Lalitā is playful. Creation, Evolution and final Dissolution of all things are Lalitā's game.

32

Śuddha-Mānasā

Pure Consciousness, Pure Mind.

The one who constantly dwells in Lalitā will experience the Self (Ātman) as Transcendental Bliss.

She is Śuddha-Mānasā (Pure-Minded).

33

Parameśvarī (Paramā-Īśvarī)

The Supreme Goddess, the Transcendental Goddess. The Goddess beyond all Creation, forms, manifestation and phenomena. The Sovereign Goddess, the Exalted.

The Highest (Paramā) Protector (Īśvarī). Lalitā is also the best Guide and Protector.

34

Mūla-Prākṛtiḥ (Mūlaprākṛtī)

The Root of Nature, the Primordial Cause of all Nature.

Mūla: Root, Basis, Original Cause.
Prākṛtī (Pra-Kṛti): Before Creation.

She is the Primal-Cause, the First Cause of all things.

Śrī-Vidyā-Mantra, or Ṣoḍaṣī, is Mūla-Prākṛtī.

Ādi-Anta-Sakalā

35

Bodhi-Cittā

Wisdom-Mind, the Enlightenment-Consciousness, the Realizing-Intellect, the Buddha-Mind.

Lalitā leads Her devotees to Perfect-Knowledge, Spiritual Enlightenment and complete Self-Realization. She is the Mind (Citta) of Light (Bodhi).

36

Prema-Rūpā

She whose Nature is Love.
She who is the Embodiment (Rūpa) of Love (Prema).

Prema: Love, Devotion, Pure-Spirituality.
Rūpa: form, embodiment, Nature.

Devī Lalitā is Incarnate Love. Her Essence is the Energy of Devotion.

37

Ādi-Anta-Sakalā

The Beginning, the End, the All.
The First, the Last, the Complete.

Lalitā was there at the Beginning of all things. She is there at the End. She is the Eternal Continuum.

38

Sarasvatī

The River of Knowledge.

Saras: a lake, an ocean, a river.
Vati: She who has.

She who is in the Form of the Ocean of Knowledge.
She is the Form of all Mantras, speech, sound, music and art.

The esoteric meaning is that She is the River of Nectar (Amṛta), the River of Light which flows from the Crown Centre into the Third-Eye. This gives the devotee Esoteric Knowledge, True Knowledge.

39

Strī

She is Strī, the mature Woman, the Woman concept, the Woman archetype or prototype. And She is Vadhū, the Wife. She is complete Womanhood, the Feminine Nature. The companion to the male powers.

40

Ramā, Rāmā, Ramādevī
Ramaṇā, Ramaṇī, Ramaṇikā

The Delightful One. She who gives Delight.

Enchanting, beautiful, charming, splendid, opulent, pleasing, lovely, beloved, joyful, peaceful.

She who gives Light, Radiance, Pure Consciousness.
She who protects and sustains.

41

Jñāna-Mātā

She who is the Mother (Mātā) of Transcendental Consciousness, Transcendental Knowledge, Self-Realization, Enlightenment (Jñāna).

42

Dhyāna-Mātā

She who is the Mother (Mātā) of all meditational practices (Dhyāna), all spiritual effort.

43

Param-Jyotī

The Supreme Light.

The Highest (Param) Radiance (Jyotī).
The Transcendental (Param) Brightness (Jyotī).

44

PARĀ-VĀK

The Supreme (PARĀ) Speech (VĀK).
The Transcendental (PARĀ) Logos (VĀK).

The Creative Word, the Original Sound-Vibration of the Universe.

45

KAMALĀ
KAMALĀDEVĪ

KAMALĀ: the lotus flower.
KAMALĀDEVĪ: the Goddess of the Lotus.

She is most Beautiful and Desirable. (The lotus is the most beautiful flower of the East.)

46

MOHINĪ

She who enchants the Universe.
The Enchanter, the Enchanting-One.

She enchants all beings by Her Transcendental Beauty and Dazzling Brightness.

47

HṚDGUHYĀ

The Secret of the Heart.

HṚT: the Heart.
GUHYA: secret.

Within the Heart is the Secret of the AHAṀ (I AM), the Mystery of "Who Am I?" Here is revealed AHAṀ-BRAHMĀSMI (I am One with God).

48

Bhagavatī

The Glorious Goddess. Illustrious, Divine, Holy, adorable, happy, blissful. The Divine Mistress of the Universe, full of Fortune and Wealth, Creatrix of the Cosmos.

An esoteric meaning is that Lalitā is Universal-Nature (Prākṛtī), the original Primary Substance or Matter, infused with the Universal Spirit (Paramātman), with the Bright Glorious Light of Prakāśa-Āditya (the Universal Sun or Cosmic Solar Logos).

49

Lakṣmī

She who bestows Fortune, Wealth, Success, Prosperity.
She who is the Splendour of the Eternal Light.
The Eternal Beauty. The Perfect Feminine.

50

Lolitā

She who is full of activity, agitation, tremor, vibration, passion, action, adventure, excitement.

51

Paramā

She who is beyond all things. The Transcendental One.
The Supreme or Original Divine Female Archetype.

52

Paramāṅganā

The most beautiful Female in the Universe.
The Super-Woman. The perfect expression of Womanhood.

Paramāṅganā

Paramātmikā

53

Paramātmikā

The Transcendental Soul of the Universe.
The Supreme Being. The Highest Existence.

54

Nārāyaṇī

The All-Pervading Holy Spirit.
The Spirit resting upon the Waters of Space.

Nara means "the Spirit of God".
Nara also means "Man", and Nārī means "Woman."
Nāra means "water".

Nārāyaṇī means "She who dwells in the Waters" (in Cosmic Space, in Matter). She is the Indwelling Spirit in all things, the Vivifying, Enlivening Spirit, the Vehicle for Ātman (the Breath of God).

55

Brāhmī

The Creatrix of the Universe. She-Who-Creates.
The Original Source of all things.

Brāhmī also means "That which is Holy". The Feminine Goddess Energy.

56

Nāda-Rūpā

She who is in the Form of Inner Sound.

Rūpa: a body, form, embodiment.

Nāda: the Voice of the Silence, the Soundless Sound, the Sound not heard by physical ears, the continuous Sound-Vibration of Praṇava (the Universal Ōṁ Sound), the Creative Speech, Logos or Word which is listened to by the Yogī and Mystic in the Heart or through the Inner Ear, which will lead to Infinite Consciousness.

57

Sarva-Mantra-Sva-Rūpiṇī

She who is in the Form of all Mantras.

Sarva: all.
Sva: own.
Rūpiṇī: form.

All Mantras are Sound-Forms. Lalitā incarnates into these Sound-Forms and becomes the Consciousness behind them.

58

Sarva-Yantra-Ātmikā

She who ensouls all Images and Symbols of the Deity.

Sarva: all, everything.
Yantra: image, symbol, picture, representation or diagram of the gods and goddesses (which are but tools to remember aspects of the Absolute).
Ātmikā: embodies, ensouls.

59

Īśvarī
Mahā-Īśvarī (Maheśvarī)

She who protects. The Omnipotent Protector.

Īśvarī: She who rules, guides, protects. The Supreme Being, the Mistress of the Universe.
Mahā: great, omnipotent, absolute.

60

Mahā-Devī

The Absolute Goddess.

Mahā: immeasurably large, vast, endless, absolute, limitless.
Devī: the Goddess.

The Cosmos is wherein Lalitā plays. The whole Creation or Manifestation is simply Her Body.

Mahā-Devī

PARAMĀNANDĀ

61

Pārvatī

The Daughter of the Mountains.

She is the Great Yoginī (Yogin) forever meditating in the Sacred Mountains (the Spiritual Planes) in Ecstatic Contemplation of Reality.

62

Paramānandā (Paramā-Ānandā)

She who is Transcendental-Bliss-Consciousness.

Ānanda: bliss, joy, happiness.
Paramā: the Transcendent.

In this State there is no more sorrow.

63

Rādhā

She who is All-Success.
She who is the Power of Devotion.

64

Sitā

She who Shines like Moonlight.
Bright, pure, white.

65

Cinmayī

She who is in the Form of Consciousness Itself.
She who is Pure Consciousness.
She who is Formless Awareness.

66

Tārā

She who is like a Star, Starlike, shining.
She who Saves. Saviour.
She who carries you across the Ocean of Existence to the Other Shore.

Tārinī: Saving-Grace, Saving-Power.

67

Kālī
Kalikā

She who is beyond Death.

The Destroyer of Time-and-Space-sense.
The Destroyer of Fate.
The Liberator.

68

Durgā

The Fearless One. The Deliverer.

She who takes you across the Ocean of Saṁsāra (Existence).
She who destroys demons and evil powers.
She who is difficult to reach or attain.
The Inaccessible-Goddess.

69

Śivā

The All-Pervading, All-Knowing, Transcendental Consciousness.

The Highest Feminine Consciousness.
The Supreme Witness of All Creation.
The Supreme Self or Soul (Paramātman) in all things and all beings.
The Benefactor.

Jyotiṣmatī

70

Antar-Jyotī

The Inner-Light.

The Light of the Inner Sun seen in deep meditation.
The Light of Intelligence.
The Light of the Soul.

71

Jyotiṣmatī

Luminous Intelligence. Brilliant, shining.
Spiritual Light. The Worlds of Light.
Full of Light. Possessing All Light.

72

Amṛtā

She who is beyond Death. The Immortal One.
Splendid Light-Being. The Nectar of Immortality.
The Eternal Spirit. The Inner Spiritual Sun.

73

Amṛteśvarī (Amṛta-Īśvarī)

The Infinite Goddess.
She who is Unlimited.

74

Mahāśaktī

The Omnipotent Power.

75

Bhakti-Priyā

She who is fond of Devotion.

Bhakti: Love, Devotion, longing for the Real, for the Eternal.

76

Mā, Mātā
Umā, Ammā, Ambā

The Mother. The Divine Mother.

The Mother of the Universe. The Mother of all creatures.

77

Triguṇā (Tri-Guṇā)

She who embodies the three primary qualities of Matter.

Tri: three.
Guṇa: attributes. Tamas (inertia), Rajas (activity), Sattva (rhythm, purity, light).

All things in Nature, and all beings and entities, are made out of these three modes of manifestation in different proportions.

78

Jyoti-Nirañjanā

The Unpolluted Light. The Light of the Pure Spirit.

Jyoti: light, flame.
Nirañjanā: without blemish, faultless, perfect.

79

Nirguṇā

She who is beyond the three qualities of Nature.

80

Niṣkalā

She who is not in parts.

Kalā: parts, fractions, divisions, segments, fragments.

Although the Universe may appear to be composed of parts or separated objects, Lalitā always remains One, Whole, Unbroken Formless-Form.

Jyoti-Nirañjanā

NIRĀKĀRĀ

81

NIRĀKĀRĀ

She who is Formless.

With pure Spiritual Vision we behold Her Formless-Form stretching through Infinitude.

82

NITYĀ

She who is Timeless.
She who is Eternal.

83

NIRMALĀ

She who is without any form of impurity, not tainted by Matter or the World.

Although all actions (KARMA) are done by Her Energy (ŚAKTI), she is not tainted by the results of Action.

84

NIRVIKĀRĀ

She who is Changeless.

VIKĀRA (change) does not affect Her. The Universe always changes, but LALITĀ is unaffected.

85

NIRANTARĀ

She who is present everywhere.

The All-Pervading Continuum. She is One.

86

Vāgīśvarī

She is the Goddess of the Creative-Speech (Vāch, Vāk), the Divine Word, the Logos.

Creation proceeds from the within to the without. Manifestation is the descent of the Sound-Vibration, the Divine-Voice or Word.

Parāvāk: the Supreme Sound-Vibration.
Paśyantīvāk: Transcendental Sound-Vibration.
Madhyamāvāk: astral and causal sound.
Vaikharīvāk: physical sound.

Vāg-Adhīśvarī: She is the Goddess of Speech and She bestows Wisdom, eloquence, creative abilities, artistic talents.

87

Manomayī

She who is composed of Mind (Manas).
She whose Nature (Mayī) is Mind.

Mind is a manifold reality:

Kāma-Manas: the ordinary mind, the normal mind of a human being, full of desires, wishes and longings.

Buddhi-Manas: the Enlightened Mind, the Mind of Light which develops when the ordinary mind is flooded by the Light of the Spirit within. The Mind of a Sage or Enlightened Being.

Mahat: Cosmic Mind, Cosmic Intelligence, Universal Mind. The Mind of a super-advanced Being. The Mind of the Deity.

88

Jñāna-Jñeya-Svarūpiṇī

She who is both the Knowledge and the Known.

Sva-Rūpiṇī: whose Self-Form.
Jñāna: knowledge.
Jñeya: that which can be known.

She is All that Is.

89

Mauna (Maunam)
Mauna-Śaktī
Mauna-Parā-Vāk
Mauna-Samādhi

She who dwells in Silence. She who Is Silence.
She who speaks in Silence, the Supreme Word.
She who unites the Seeker in Silence.

Mauna (Maunam): the Silence.
Mauna-Śaktī: the Power of Silence.
Mauna-Parā-Vāk: the Silent Supreme Speech.
Mauna-Samādhi: the Silent Ecstasy.

Silence is a Way of meditation (Dhyāna):
First there is Silence;
then you feel the Power of Silence;
then you hear the Supreme Word, uttered in Silence;
then there is Ecstasy.

90

Sat-Cid-Ānanda-Rūpiṇī

She whose Nature is Existence, Consciousness, Bliss.

She is the Supreme Sat: Being, Existence, the Immutable, Ever-present Godhead (Parabrahm), the Eternal One.
She is Cit: ever Conscious, Pure Intelligence and Knowing.
She is Ānanda: forever Joyful, forever Blissful.

Rūpiṇī: Her essential Nature or Form.

91

Sarvagā (Sarva-Gā)

She who Pervades All.
She who is Omnipresent.

92

Ātmā

The Bright Eternal Self.

Lalitā is present within us all as Ātmā (Ātman), the Breath of the Absolute, the Universal Soul or Spirit, the Light of the Eternal, Pure Consciousness, the One I AM within all Creation, therefore called the One Self, immanent in each and every being.

The multiplicity of egos is an illusion caused by separative minds. When we give up our false sense of "I" (Ahaṁ-Kāra: I am the doer), the true "I" (Ahaṁ) shines by its own Light.

Ātmā is the Imperishable Reality, no matter what it is called: Goddess (Ātmā) or God (Ātman). It is before Creation and after Creation, and during Creation pervades the All. The Universe is born out of Ātmā, the Universe is maintained by Ātmā, and the Universe will be reabsorbed again into Ātmā at the last days.

93

Athā

The Eternal Now, the Present Moment.

The Flow of Eternity is always through Now. Be in the Now. To identify with the Past is a basic delusion and bondage. Mind creates Time, then it becomes entrapped by it. You are re-born every Instant, so why hang onto the Past?

Ākāśa (Eternal Space) is always Here and Now.
Ākāśī is the All-Pervading Goddess.

The Eternal Present and Space are synonymous. When you relax into the Now you will sense Timeless Being.

94

Śāntī
Śānti-Devī

Śāntī: the Goddess of Tranquillity, Peace, Harmony, Quiet.
Śānti-Devī: the Goddess of Peace.

95

Gaurī

She who is Fair. She who is Beautiful. The Brilliant One.
She who is the caring and nurturing Mother.

Gaurī is Lalitā as the Transcendental and Immanent Mother. As the Transcendental Mother She nourishes us with Divine Light, Brightness, Brilliance.

She is Jyotirasā (Jyoti-Rasā): the Essence of Light.
She is Jyotir-Maya: consisting of Light.

96

Svāhā
Svāhā-Devī

Svāhā: offerings.
Svāhā-Devī: the Goddess of Offerings.

All rituals, religious ceremonies and rites are, in essence, offered to Her, the One Reality.

Svāhā is Female Fire.
Svāhā means "We make offerings to Reality".
Svāhā also means "one's own Mantra", from Sva (own) and Aha (speech, word, sound, affirmation). Svāhā is the Mantra best suited to you.

97

Rudrāṇī
Rudrāmbā (Rudra-Āmbā)

Rudrāṇī: the angry goddess.
Rudra-Āmbā: the angry mother.

In this aspect She represents the angry, bellowing, howling, discordant sounds of Nature and of Life. The unrestrained emotions and vibrations.

98

Bagalā
Bagalāmukhī

She who restrains, She who controls, She who prevents.

Bagalā: a bridle, rope or goad by which someone or something is guided and controlled.
Mukhi: a face or countenance.
Bagalāmukhī: She who has the controlling or commanding face.

Bagalā is powerful. In this aspect, Lalitā is full of Power and in total control of circumstances. A more esoteric meaning is that Bagalā is the Divine Effulgence of Brilliant Light which is irresistible and unconquerable. It is the Decisive Power of the Absolute, the Self-Motivating Power of Reality.

99

Dhūmāvatī

The Old Woman, the Wise Woman, the Eldest Woman.

Dhūmā: smoke or smoke-coloured (grey).

The grey-haired woman, the widow.
She who has gone through the Cycle of Life and remained.

The Grandmother Goddess, the Primordial Formless Void.

100

Chinnamastā

The Goddess beyond the Mind. The Headless Goddess.

The no-mind state (Unmana). The Power of Infinite Vision which destroys the sense of "I", of ego, and the limited mind-function. Totally beyond reason, logic and the thinking-process. Suspended mental functioning. The highest Samādhi.

PART THIRTEEN

The Yoga of the Sun

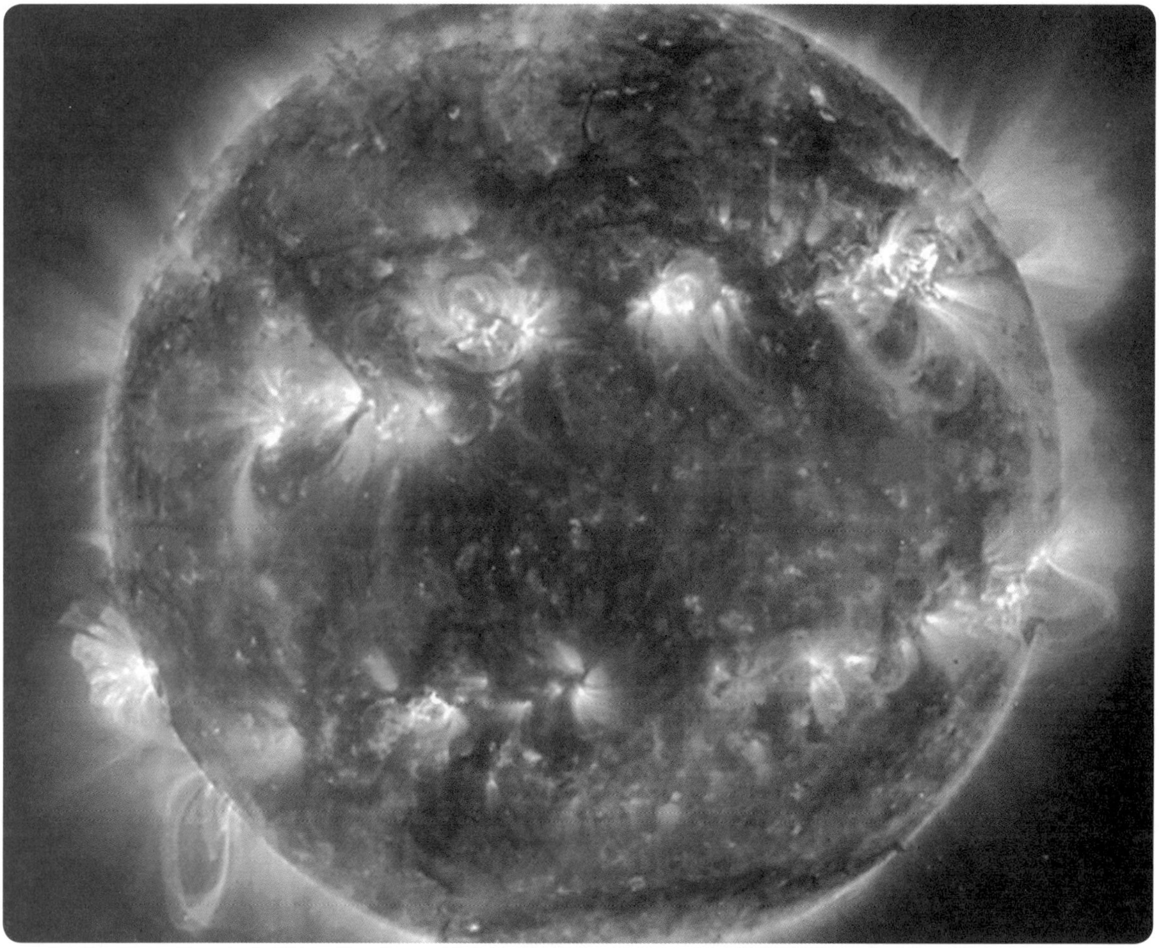

CHAPTER 66

The Mystery of the Sun

To Worship the Sun

SŪRYAMAṆḌALA, the Circle of the Sun, or GĀYATRĪ-SĀDHANĀ, the Sun-Spiritual-Practice, is the most amazing Path of Meditation and Spiritual Unfoldment.

The worship of the Sun is the most direct worship of God. It is not the worship of an inanimate object in the sky.

The worship of the Sun is the most direct worship of God

We must understand true Reality: God is not "out there" somewhere far away, but here where we are. We are living *in* God; that is, we are living *in* the Sun. The physical Sun is an outer reflection *into* the Physical Plane of the Real-Sun, the Solar Logos (SŪRYA, SAVITĀ).

The Solar Logos is a Being, just as you and I are beings, but He is infinitely more vast and glorious than we are. The Solar Logos is a Cosmic Intelligence of a certain level of Cosmic-Evolutionary Attainment. There is Cosmic Evolution, Solar-Systemic Evolution, Terrestrial Evolution and Human Evolution, all proceeding simultaneously. Our Solar Logos is an Individualized Consciousness on a Cosmic Evolutionary Scale—alive, intelligent, living in Cosmic Space. He is a Conscious-Intelligent Being or "Person" reflecting God's Divinity, Absolute Intelligence, Love, Light and Life.

The physical Sun and physical Solar System are the outermost part of the Dense-Physical Body of the Spiritual Sun or Solar Logos. The physical Sun is God visible in the sky, that part of the Solar-God which the physical body can experience through the senses. The invisible parts of the Sun are perceived by more subtle senses and spiritual faculties.

The Circle of the Sun constitutes the meditational practices of the School of the Spiritual Warrior. The School of the Spiritual Warrior instructions consist of:

a. The material contained in Part 8, *The Warrior School,* which includes practical instructions for day-to-day living on the Spiritual Warrior Path.

b. The Circle of the Sun meditations and mantras, including the *Works of Silence* meditational practices.

Hence the *School of the Warrior* Teachings are manifested. I have been empowered to give out this noble and sublime Teaching at this time to the world at large, for those who can *listen* and *do.*

The Warrior School 967

The Elohīm 120
The Cosmic Creator-Gods 162
Solar-Systemic and Cosmic Evil 217
The Presence of God 1396
What is Reality? 1175

The Solar Constitution

The Sun is not merely physical energy but the Energy behind all the seven great Solar-Systemic Planes of Manifestation. And beyond that, the Sun lives in the Cosmic Astral, Cosmic Mental and Cosmic Causal Planes as a Cosmic Being or Cosmic Entity in Boundless Space.

There are seven great Cosmic Planes of Being, within which our seven Solar-Systemic Planes are just the Cosmic Physical Plane (seven planes out of forty-nine). It is upon those great Cosmic Planes that our Solar Logos lives the Cosmic Life, beyond the Solar-Systemic Existence, in a state of Glory, Splendour, Intelligence and Love beyond human understanding and comprehension.

The Solar System is an Incarnation of our Solar Logos

The Solar Logos is a Cosmic-Being-of-Light, a Cosmic Centre or Focal Point of God's Infinite Power, Majesty, Glory, Divinity. The whole Solar System, with all the many planets (visible and invisible), on all seven Solar-Systemic Planes of Being, are but His Cosmic Physical Body. The whole Solar-Systemic Manifestation is but His Cosmic Physical Incarnation, just as your physical body is a physical incarnation of You as a Soul. The Solar Logos also has a Soul, the Spirit and the Absolute Divinity within Him, but of vast cosmic proportions, and He lives in a Cosmic Astral Body, a Cosmic Mind Body and a Cosmic Causal Body, as *You* do on a microscopic scale.

Thus the Solar System is but a minute, temporary Expression or Incarnation of the Cosmic Spiritual Soul of our Solar Logos, one of His series of Cosmic Reincarnations. On the Higher Cosmic Planes He has activities outside our Solar System also, just as you have activities outside your body. You *live in* your physical body but your major interests lie elsewhere.

The difference between a human being and a Solar Logos is not in Principles or essential make-up, but in vastness of scale, size, magnitude. Comparing a single atom in the big toe of your physical body to the *total You,* on all levels, is like comparing the total You to the Solar Logos. The total You is but a small atom in the Cosmic Physical Body of the Sun, our Solar Logos. This is the true meaning of the verse from *Genesis:*

And God said, 'Let us make Man in our image, after our likeness…'.

A human being is a miniature replica of the Solar Logos or Solar Deity, existing *within* the Solar Logos on an atomic-size level.

Planes and Subplanes 14
The Human Constitution 43
In the Image and Likeness 104
The Constitution of God-Immanent 122
From Matter to Light 761

The Universal Creator-God

VIŚVAKARMAN, the Creator of the Universe, dwells within our Solar Logos, the Sun.

VIŚVA: the Universe, the All, the whole of Creation, the World.
KARMAN: the Creator, the Architect, the Maker, the Doer.

The Body of the Absolute stretches into Infinitudes

He performs all actions through our Sun, as He does through all the countless Suns in the Infinity of Space. Everything upon our planet, within our Solar System, and outside the influence of our Sun, is done by VIŚVAKARMĀ. Ultimately, all actions are done (indirectly, through agencies) by the Universal Creator-God.

The Solar Logoi are the prime channels for the expression of VIŚVAKĀRYA, the Maker of the Universe. VIŚVAKĀRAKA, the Lord-Who-Made-Everything, dwells within the Sun, and as we live in the Auric-Field of our Sun, so VIŚVĀKARU, the Creator of All, dwells in us also. Therefore, He is also called VIŚVAKA, the All-Pervading, the All-Containing, within which the Universe exists.

When you look at the Sun with your physical eyes, you are looking at the living Image of the Creator-God on this level of perception. The Sun fecundates and stimulates growth on all planes of the Solar System, including the Physical Plane on which you are living now.

The Field of Activity of our Solar Logos

The Universe is a vast, inconceivable Being.

The countless multitudes of Stars (Suns, Solar Logoi) are but the Atoms composing the Infinite-Body of the Boundless Absolute.

Space, the Body of the Absolute, stretches into Infinitudes on all sides and into all Dimensions, within and without.

Our Solar Logos permeates this portion of Infinite-Space, the portion which is covered by His Auric-Field, which is vast and stupendous by human standards. Into this portion of Space He pours His Life and Soul, literally sacrificing Himself, exhausting His own Life-Wave and pouring it into the Physical, Astral, Mental and higher Dimensions or Realms.

The Solar System (its visible and invisible Realms) is the Field of Activity of our Solar Logos, working with and upon the materials provided by Cosmic Space.

The Law of Surrender or Sacrifice 1138

Primordial Atoms 24
God Immanent and Transcendent 111
The Plan is in the Divine Mind 161
The Creation of the Universe 166

The Manifested-God

God is Infinite and Absolute, Limitless and Omnipresent, Boundless and Immutable; Changeless-Existence, an Eternal-Now, beyond Past, Present and Future; Ineffable, beyond Space and Time; in the Unmanifested-State, Unconditioned.

From THAT (TAT), the Unconditioned, cometh forth all that is: the All, the Conditioned Creation or Universes, which remain *within* the Unconditioned. The Universes are born, evolve and dissolve *in* or *within* the Godhead (BRAHMAN). The Universes are *not* separate from the Absolute Godhead (PARABRAHMAN), the Universal Logos.

The Cosmic Logos becomes Incarnate in a Solar Logos

From the Universal Logos spring forth the Solar Logoi, the Manifested-God embodied in the immense multitude of Suns or Solar Systems in Infinite Space. Each Solar Logos becomes the Manifested-God within a portion of Infinitude, bounded by His Auric-Field, or His Life-Wave-in-Incarnation. Thus, a Solar Logos is God-Incarnate. The Cosmic Logos becomes Incarnate in a Solar Logos whose Physical Body is a Solar System in the seven-layered Space of the Cosmic Physical Plane.

The physical Sun, as seen by the physical bodily eyes, is the outermost part of a small organ (the dense-physical Heart) of the Solar Deity, SAVITĀ, the Solar Logos. The Physical Body of our Solar Logos stretches into Space many thousands of millions of miles in the seven-layered Omnispace, ĀKĀŚA.

All the planets (the Planetary Logoi) in the Solar System are but CAKRAS (energy-centres) in the Auric-Field of our Solar Logos. All the planets and worlds within our Solar System, visible and invisible, swim in the Solar-Radiation. The Sun is the Light of the World, and the Light of the Worlds. The Light within you is simply the Light of the Sun which extends for countless millions of miles.

The "emptiness" of Space is an illusion (MĀYĀ) of the physical eyes. In truth, Space is total Solidity, total Reality, total Density, totally "Being-There". Total-Space is Solid. It is matter, or the atoms, which are "void" or "empty". The Universes, Worlds, Solar Systems, are but "Bubbles" floating *within* the Solidity of Omnispace, of the Absoluteness. They are temporary Manifestations. The Absoluteness always remains.

The Form of God is Space 109

The Transcendental Godhead 112
The Doctrine of the Logoi 116
Perceiving the One Space 13
Heaven 1352

Children of the Sun

All the Worlds are *in* the Sun, SŪRYA or SAVITĀ, our Solar Logos.

The planets (visible and invisible) in the Solar System are embodiments of Cosmic Beings, Planetary Logoi, each with its own seven Planes, Worlds or Existences. Cosmically considered, the Planetary Logoi are less evolved than a Solar Logos; they act as CAKRAs, force-centres or energy-centres, in the Cosmic Physical, Cosmic Astral and Cosmic Mental Bodies of the Solar Logos.

Every part of us is but a particle of the Sun

- The Physical, Astral and Mental Worlds are the Cosmic Dense-Physical Body of our Planetary Logos.
- The Buddhic, Nirvāṇic, Monadic and Logoic Worlds constitute the Cosmic Etheric-Physical Body of our Planetary Logos.

Thus, all the Planetary Planes are but the physical Manifestation of our Planetary Logos. But all the Planetary Logoi of our Solar System live *in* the Cosmic Physical Body of our Sun, SŪRYA. Thus, every part of us, from the dense physical body to the Monad, is but a particle of the Sun, our wonderful Solar Logos.

We live *in* the Sun. We are particles of the Sun. We are in fact Children of the Sun.

Within the innumerable Spheres, Realms and Worlds of Being in the Aura of our SAVITĀ live twelve Creative Hierarchies in vast multitudes: the humanoid (MANUṢYA), angelic (DEVA), archangelic (SURA), and so on. Each of these twelve Hierarchies is made up of billions of entities evolving over vast periods of time according to their particular Patterns *within* the Aura of the Manifested-God, SAVITĀ, the Sun. All these entities live *in* the Cosmic Dense-Physical and Cosmic Etheric-Physical Body of the Sun, our Solar Logos.

The Dimensions or Worlds within the planets, and within the interspace between the planets of our Solar System, are interpenetrating (within) each other. The seven great Planes or Realms within our Solar System (within the Cosmic Physical Body of our Solar Logos) exist simultaneously within the same Space. As you develop your faculties to change your vibrational level of Perception (that is, as you develop abilities to vibrate your Consciousness at higher frequencies), you are able to function in and experience Life in the Higher Worlds or Realms.

Worlds within Worlds 886
Children of the Cosmic Creators 190
Ascending the Planes of Consciousness 20
The Constitution of the Solar Logos 124
The Omnipresent God 1108

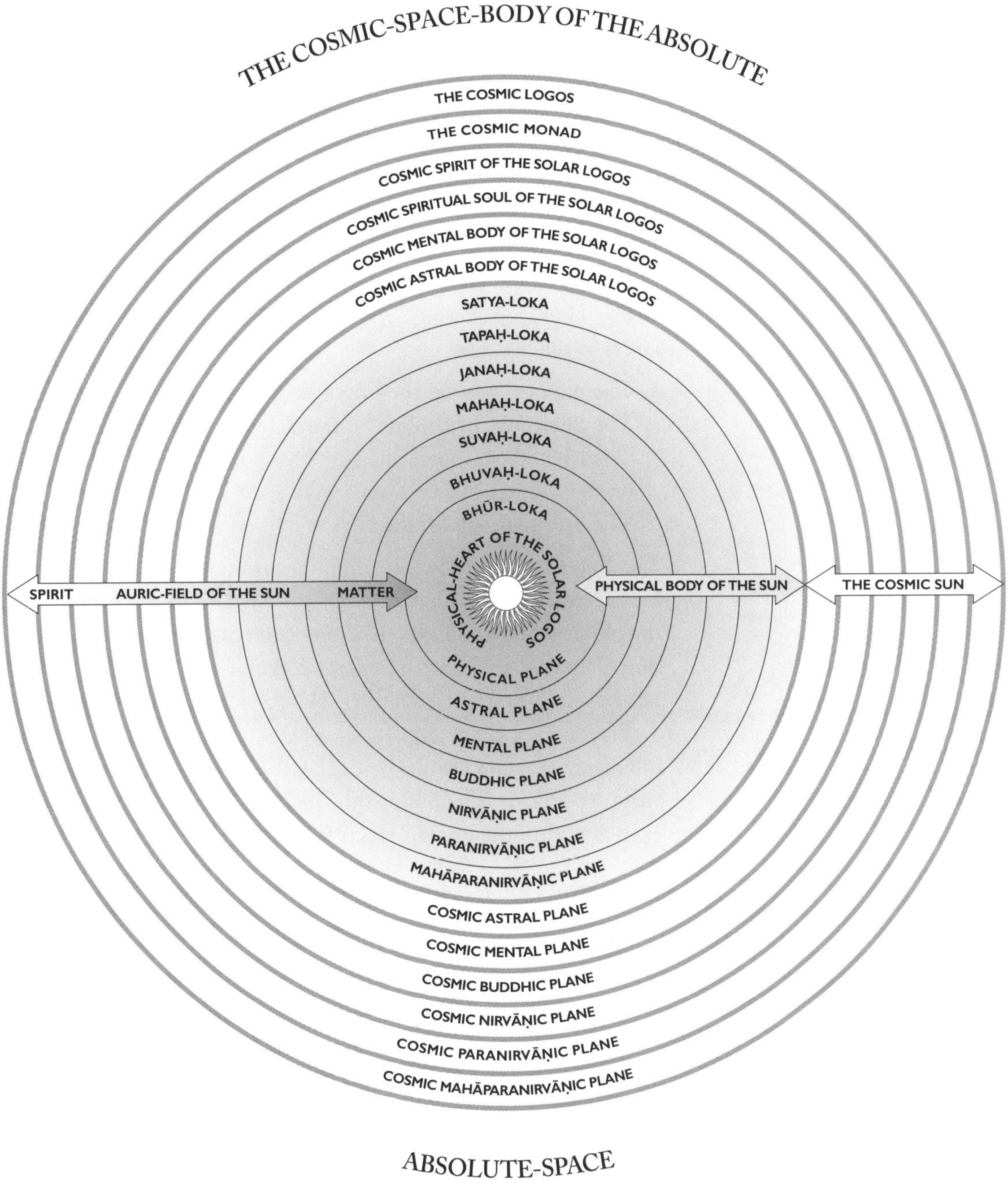

Dimensions of the Solar Logos in Cosmic Space

The Solar and Human Heart

The Sun-Centre in the human microcosm is the Heart Cakra

The Sun is the Heart Centre (Hṛdaya-Cakra) of the Solar Logos, not symbolically but actually. In the human being the Heart is multi-dimensional: physical heart, etheric-physical heart, astral heart, mental and causal heart, and the Spiritual Heart. So it is with the Solar Logos. The visible Sun in the Solar System corresponds with the physical heart in the human system. Within the visible physical Sun there are many layers of the Heart of the Solar Logos—within it, around it and through it, on all seven Solar-Systemic Planes of Being. Thus, considering *only* the Cosmic Physical Plane, the various layers of the Sun are:

a. The physical Sun on the Physical Plane.
b. The Subjective or Psychic Sun, which shines on the Astral Plane.
c. The Mental or Causal Sun (the Heart-of-the-Sun), which shines on the Mental Plane.
d. The Spiritual Sun on the Nirvāṇic Plane and above.

The Sun-Centre in the human microcosm is the Heart Cakra. The Sun-Centre or Heart Cakra receives Prāṇa (Radiant Energy) from the physical Sun and Light-Energies from the invisible aspects of the Sun. The human Heart in the microcosm (the human aura) is the same as the physical Sun in the Macrocosm, the Solar System.

The Sun is a Centre of Consciousness; that is, it is alive, conscious, intelligent. It is a Cosmic-Being, a Cosmic-Person, a Personality of vast proportions. The Sun is the God-Self within the Solar System, even as within the human Heart Centre the God-Self is found.

The human Heart Centre gives you Faith, which is a Luminous Power and an aspect of the Radiance of the Spiritual Sun of the Solar System.

The Universal Heart 436
God in the Heart 634
The Heart of the Solar Logos 1327
What is True Faith? 1284
Hṛt-Padma: the Heart-Lotus 1505

Hṛdayākāśa
The Ethereal Space within your Heart Centre (Hṛdaya-Ākāśa, Heart-Space). It is also known as Hṛdayaguha (Hṛdaya-Guha, Heart-Cave), the Cave of the Heart where the *Christ* is found (according to Western Wisdom), and where Ātman, the Self, is found (according to Eastern Wisdom). This is the Spiritual Sun, the Celestial Light which shines brighter than a million physical Suns, your Radiant Spiritual Self.
The Secret of the Heart 1280

Incarnations of the Sun

Within the Sun are all opposites united.

a. The Sun is the all-embracing Cosmic Boundless Light.
b. The Sun is our Solar Logos, a reflection of the Infinite-Light-Being, and all Suns or Stars are atoms within the Eternal Glory.
c. The Sun is the Heart Centre, a reflection of our Solar Logos, which in the microcosm (the Man-species) is the source of Light, Life and Energy.

The Heart Centre is the Centre within Man. Within it is a glowing Sun with flames. In the midst of it there is a Fire. Within that is the crystal-like or jewel-like Ātman or Spirit. Within that is the Divine Spark, Paramātman, the omnipresent, eternal, bright, everlasting Light, the source of Immortality, Joy, Bliss, Liberation.

The Universal Christ 440
The Revelation of God 854
The Mystery within the Heart 1315
The Mystery of the Christ 1724
The Gāyatrī-Mantra 1601

The Sun is the directing force of Spiritual Evolution, whether in Man, the Solar System, or the Spiritual Sun within the Universe.

The Sun is Force, Power, Radiation, Energy, Life.

The Incarnation of the Sun in the Sevenfold Solar Planes

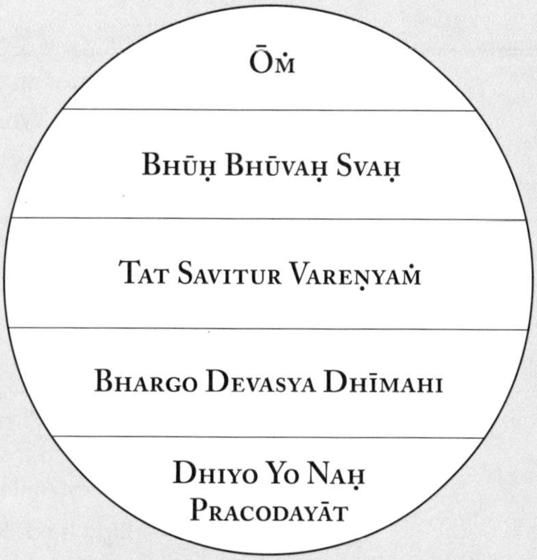

The Incarnation of the Sun in the Heart Centre

The Incarnation of the Sun

The Self-Generating Light

The Sun is a manifestation of the Word-of-God, the Cosmic or Universal Logos. The Sun illumines all the Invisible Worlds with Self-Generating Light.

The Sun illumines all the Invisible Worlds with Self-Generating Light

Illumination in the human Heart and Head Centres is received directly from the Sun of our Solar System. The Illumination-Material is the Light of the Solar Logos, **Sūrya-Jyoti**.

All activities within the Solar System, on all planets, in all the Worlds, Planes or Realms of Being, by all entities, are but Transformations of Sun-Light.

The Light which appears to the physical eyes is only a small fragment of the Light. Out of this Light all the Worlds are made, including all the beings within the Worlds.

You also are made out of the Sun-Light—your body, mind, emotions, Soul and Spirit, each being different levels of Vibrations of the Light of the Solar Logos, **Jyoti**.

Energy is just a form of Light. Everything that exists in our Solar System is made out of the Energy of the Sun, the Solar Logos. The different Worlds, Planes, Realms, Dimensions (Loka, in Sanskrit) of our Solar System are made up of different Frequencies or Vibrations of the Solar Light, which itself is but a differentiation of the Universal Light, the Boundless-Light-of-Omnispace, the Universal Logos.

There is Light transmitted from the Cosmic Astral Plane into the Cosmic Physical. There is Light transmitted from Ādi, the plane of the Logos, to the plane of the Monad, and hence into the Nirvāṇic and Buddhic Planes. And there is Light that shines in the higher Heaven Worlds.

Light is not limited to what you can see physically or measure with instruments. In fact, the light perceptible in the three-dimensional physical world is only a fragment of a fragment of Light. Light, in fact, is the Mind of God. Hence, one of the Gnostic descriptions of the Deity is the *Father of Lights*, the *Light Within Lights*.

Light 978
The Light of the Logos 119
The Descent of the Word 118
The Word, Logos, Voice, Name 1646
Living Matter 134

The Shining Lights

ĀDITYA
The Sun. The Dazzling Inner Radiance you can see in meditation in your Third-Eye Centre, in the Crown Centre, in the Heart, in the Solar Plexus Centre and in the Base Centre. The *form* of the Sun (the Sunshine) will be perceived differently in each centre, however.

You can see these Lights and hear the different melodies of the Inner Sound

CANDRA
The Moon. The Cool Moonlight. The Moonshine you can see in the Head, in the Heart and in the Solar Plexus Centre. Thus you can see that the Inner Light, the Inner Beatific Vision, ADHI-JYOTI, manifests in several places.

ADHI-DAIVATAM
The Supreme-Self-Shining. The Intelligence behind all forms. The Substratum of all Cosmic Energies. It shines within you also, unimpeded.

You can see these Lights and hear the different melodies of the Inner Sound (NĀDA) when Tranquillity (STHIRATTVA, Serenity) is established within the Heart. Even to see the Light in the Head and hear the Cosmic Sound in the Crown Centre, you first need Tranquillity of the Heart. That is, you need ŚĀNTIḤ: Peace, Inner Calm.

The Secret of the Heart 1280
Guard your Heart 1328

Peace of Heart

Your Heart, on the basic level, is receiving *impressions* from the outside world, from your senses, thoughts and feelings. Your Heart is often troubled on the basic level by what it receives from the outside.

Be free from unwanted emotional reactions.

The secret of a Peaceful Heart is to learn to *switch off* the unwanted troubling thoughts, feelings and images by cultivating a deep Stillness in the Heart. If you attain Stillness of the Heart you will sleep better and have no tensions in your physical body. You will also have different kinds of dreams.

The True Heart, the Spiritual Heart within you, is already in a State of Ecstasy (SAMĀDHI). If you *switch off* your sensory impressions, thoughts and feelings by right meditation in the Heart, then Bliss will manifest *spontaneously* within you. Then you will no longer be troubled by what someone did or didn't do, or what was said or not said. You will *know* that everybody's Heart is already full of Bliss.

The Heart is essentially *Consciousness*. When you have attained a Tranquil Heart, the Peace of the Eternal will descend upon you like a gentle cloud.

Let not your Heart be troubled. Be at Peace.

The Light of the World

Meditate upon these statements in the Heart. Each of these statements is about the Sun, the Light of the World.

The Glory of God.

The Splendour of God.

The Glow of the Inner Sun is the Light of the Self

The Sun of Reality, the Sun Eternal.

The Sun of Truth.

The Sun of Righteousness.

The Illuminating Intelligence.

God is Light, a Blazing Sun.

The Light of the World illumines the minds and Hearts of men, women and children. One who has Divine Sight sees the Sun in God and God in the Sun, shining upon all beings and all things equally in the Spiritual Worlds and material creations. To be Children of the Sun is to be Children of the Light, Children of God.

∞

The true Sun is the Cosmic Man, the Cosmic Self, the Luminous I AM of the Universe, the Supreme Self of all beings. To become One with the Sun is to become Cosmic Intelligence.

The Universal Self.

The Cosmic Vision.

The Inner Sun.

The physical Sun perceived through the physical senses is the glow of the Sun on the Physical Plane. But the Glow of the Inner Sun is the Light of the Self, the Universal Self, the Cosmic I AM-ness.

∞

In the Heart is the Cosmic Vision of the Sun, the Oneness of All, the Manifestation of Divinity.

The Luminous Truth.

The Light of Love.

The Universal Heart.

Who is 'I AM'? 1418
The Christ is the Light of the World 442
Nūr: the Light of God 847
Brahmājyoti: God's Light 1394

Rules of Light

Light is living Substance.

Light is God's living Body.

Light is Cosmic Intelligence.

True Religion is the Religion of Light

Before you can become a Light-Worker you must be established in Solar-Light.

First discover the Light within you, then learn to radiate that Light.

There is Light within you and there is Light without.

There is Light within Light, Light upon Light, and above All is the Great Uncreated Light.

The Way is to be found *in* the Light.

This Way leads to Transfiguration.

True Religion is the Religion of Light.

Light is all-powerful. The more Light you have, the more powerful you become.

You are in the likeness of the Sun. You *are* the Sun.

The Mystery of the Sun is the Power of Love, the Attracting Power of the Universal Heart. It is the Power of Love that holds Creation together. It is the Power of Love that holds Humanity together in one unit, as one whole.

Love is the Radiating Sun-Light of the Heart of the Deity.

God's Love is not limited to one person or to a select few or one nation. It is the Invisible Light educating all Souls in the Holy Mystery of Love.

The Activity of the Divine Heart 1675

The Path of Light 89
The Lighted Way 1394
Let the Light Shine 1307
Oneness and Love 1450
The Solar Dharma 163

Divine Name
Solar Vibrations

ŌṀ I U A E ŌṀ

1.	E	U	O	U	A	E	
2.	A	I	U	E	O		
3.	I	A	O	U	E		
4.	A	U	Ṁ	Ṁ	E	E	Ṅ
5.	A	U	Ṁ				
6.	I	A	O	U	Ṁ	E	Ṅ
7.	A	E	U	I	A		
8.	I	U	A	E	O		
9.	ŌṀ	I	U	A	E	ŌṀ	
10.	O	A	E	I	U		
11.	E	A	O	U	E		
12.	E	I	O	U	A		
13.	A	E	I	O	U		
14.	I	O	U	E	A		
15.	U	E	I	A	O		
16.	O	U	E	I	A		
17.	U	O	A	I	E		
18.	I	A	O				
19.	I	A	O	E	U	Ṁ	
20.a	A	M	E	Ṅ			
20.b	A	M	I	Ṅ			
20.c	A	M	O	Ṅ			
20.d	A	M	U	Ṅ			

The Divine Name Vibrations are the Healing Rays of the Sun.
All is included within the great Circle of the Sun.

The Healing Sun Mantra

Ōṁ Hrīṁ Hrāṁ Hrūṁ
Hraiṁ Hrauṁ Hrāḥ
Heḥ
Ōṁ Arkāya Namaha

Salutation to the Sun who removes all sicknesses.

Arka: remover of afflictions.

∞

Silence and Sound, Action and Stillness, Heart and Joy;
All are One in the Circle of the Sun.

The Sun is multidimensional Awareness.

I draw Strength from the Sun.

I sing a joyous Song to the Sun.

May the Christ-Sun be formed in you, in your Heart.

God meets God in the Heart.

The Sun in the Heart is the Source of Life.

Divine Grace comes through the Heart.

The Christ is the Light within the Heart.

The Heart is Life, Joy and Happiness.

Ōṁ Arkāya Namaha

> **The Sun is the Source of Life, Light, Love and Happiness** on all the Planes of Being, not just in the Physical World. It is the source of all Energy in all the Worlds within the Solar System, in all its parts, in the visible world and in the great Invisible Worlds.
>
> *Healing Sound-Vibration Formula* 1064

CHAPTER 67

The Gāyatrī-Mantra

The Savitā-Mantra

The Divine-Light Mantra

This line of Mantras invokes the Male Aspect of the Solar Logos

This is the best Mantra for the GṚHASTHA form of life on this planet; that is, for the "householder", people who work, who have families and worldly responsibilities, in contrast to the SANNYĀSĪ, those who have renounced the world, opted out of any worldly responsibilities, the SĀDHUs or "holy men" who have a great contempt for life in the world. This is the Mantra for the SŪRYA-VAṀŚA-KṢATRIYA, the Warriors of the Sun.

This line of Mantras invokes the Male Aspect of the Solar Logos. The Solar Logos is Male-Female-Neuter, all at once.

The Secret GĀYATRĪ (GUHYA-GĀYATRĪ or GUDHA-GĀYATRĪ) is the ŚOḌAṢĪ Root Mantra, or the LALITĀ-MANTRA, also known as the ŚRĪ-VIDYĀ-VAJRA-MANTRA, the MAHĀ-TRIPURĀSUNDARĪ. This is the Female line, invoking the Feminine Aspect of the Solar Logos. The ŚOḌAṢĪ Secret Mantra is the Female Sunshine, the Mother-Light of the Universe, of the Solar Logos and of Man. It is the Glorious Radiance of the Goddess. We are not working with this line here.

SŪRYA or SAVITĀ is Divine Light.

SŪRYA or SAVITĀ is the Vivifier, the Life-Giver, the Energizer-Light, the Fertilizer, Arouser, Stimulator.

When we intone or meditate silently on the **SAVITĀ-MANTRA** (known also as the **SŪRYA-MANTRA** and the **GĀYATRĪ-MANTRA**), we are meditating on Divinity as Light, Reality as Light.

Periods of Life in Vedic India 907
Warriors of the Sun 1618
Garments of Light 1526
The Śrī-Vidyā-Vajra-Mantra 1531

Note that both the GĀYATRĪ-Mantra and the GUHYA-GĀYATRĪ-Mantra are Feminine. The GUHYA-GĀYATRĪ is Pure Feminine only, while the GĀYATRĪ is the Feminine coming through the Masculine Aspect of the Sun.

The Basic Hymn

Meditate in your Mind...

1. TAT SAVITUR VAREṆYAṀ
   That Vivifying-Light we invoke,
2. BHARGO DEVASYA DHĪMAHI
   The Glorious Splendour of God we meditate upon,
3. DHIYO YO NAḤ PRACODAYĀT
   Our Minds may He illuminate.

∞

This is also known as the SAVITṚ-MANTRA.

It is also known as ŚIVA-SŪRYA.

It is also known as the GĀYATRĪ-MANTRA. The word GĀYATRĪ means a song, a verse of 24 syllables, a certain meter or rhythm. So, the SŪRYA-MANTRA or SAVITṚ-MANTRA is a Song of God, to God and by God, the Hymn of Glory.

This is the Mystery of the Sun, VAIDIKA-GĀYATRĪ (the Vedic Hymn).

The Sun is the Self within the Heart of Man.

The Sun is the Self within the Heart of the Sun (the Solar Logos, the Solar System), ĪŚVARA.

The Sun is the Self within the Heart of the Universe, PARAM-ĪŚVARA.

This is the Mantra for Enlightenment, Illumination, Transfiguration in Light, moving with the forces of Evolution, progress, development, and the Way to *become* Divine, God-like.

The inner connection with this Mantra, and all the longer forms of it which invoke the Seven Planes and the Seven Elements, must be received through the regular process of Initiation through the GURU.

TAT SAVITUR VAREṆYAṀ

Sūrya-Sādhanā

The Sun is not only the source of natural evolution, but more importantly, of Spiritual Evolution.

When we meditate on the GĀYATRĪ-MANTRA, in all its variations, we are asking for Spiritual Rebirth. We are seeking to purify our Minds and Hearts so that the Spiritual Nature may be born in us; so that we may unite ourselves with ĀTMAN, the Spirit within us; so that we may become one with ĪŚVARA, the Divine-Ruler who rules our Solar System, who represents for us PARAM-ĪŚVARA, the Supreme Being, the Universal Logos, the Primordial Godhead.

This is all done by the Grace of the Solar Deity

The Work of Rebirth, Regeneration, Spiritual Vitalization, Spiritual Evolution, is carried out by the Energies of the Sun on higher Planes of Being—the ŚAKTI.

The New Creature, the New Man, is a Restructured Human Being whose Aura (invisible Life-Field) is regenerated, reorganized into a glorious angelic-like Being who is conscious of Immortality, Heavenly Love and Bliss. This is all done by the Power of the Sun, by the Grace of the Solar Deity, who represents for us God-the-Absolute.

It is by Divine Permission, or Solar-Logoic Permission, that we can be awakened to live on Celestial Spheres of Splendour and Bliss. This is the New Birth or Spiritual Birth which all the great ancient religions revealed to their Initiated followers, the inner secret of Sun-Worship, SŪRYA-SĀDHANĀ.

The Law of Radiation 175
Baptism and Rebirth 722
Sex Natural and Divine 926
The Divine Energy 1484
Sādhanā: the Spiritual Life 1153
The Ultimate Reality is the Meaning of Life 526

VIŚVA YOGA: Cosmic Union (Uniting with the Solar Logos).

Cosmic Yoga is Union of the individual Soul (that is, *You*) with the Cosmos (on all seven Planes of Being) and with the Godhead, the Primordial Reality whose Body is the vast Cosmic Manifestation. It is the perfect balancing-out of the personal and transpersonal aspects of yourself: the body, mind, Soul and Spirit; the material aspects of life with the Transcendental Aspects; Matter and Spirit; energy and force.

This is a divinely appointed form of Yoga for the coming generations. It leads to Wisdom, Bliss, Joy and Action.

Preliminary Meditation

1. Intone ŌṀ in the Third-Eye Centre.

   We invoke the Solar Logos...

2. Intone ŌṀ in the Heart Centre.

   The Radiant Sun...

Feel a tremendous Sun pulsating in your Heart

3. Intone ŌṀ in the Solar Plexus Centre.

   Pure Light.

∞

Procedure

1. Intone ŌṀ in the Third-Eye, brightly and clearly. Pause. Then *think:*

   "We invoke the Solar Logos..."

   Sense or envisage a vast Consciousness permeating the whole Solar System, a stupendous Cosmic Intelligence, formless, dimensionless, within whose Sphere of Attention dwell the embodied planets of our Solar System, both visible and invisible.

2. Intone ŌṀ in the Heart. Pause. Then think:

   "The Radiant Sun..."

   Envisage and feel a tremendous Sun pulsating in your Heart, a Sun of infinite and wondrous Love, a golden-yellowish Fiery Sun.

3. Intone ŌṀ in the Solar Plexus Centre. Pause. Then think:

   "Pure Light."

   Sense, feel or see a Bright Light beaming from your Solar Plexus. This Light is utter Bliss.

Repeat the cycle for as long as you wish.

Āuṁ, Ōṁ, Nāda 550
Potent Vibrations: Bīja-Mantra 1542

How to Meditate on the Sun

These Sun meditations are unique. They are a combination of:

a. MANTRA: magical Sound-Power.
b. DHYĀNA: mental contemplation.

The meditations proceed progressively, line by line. The lines are numbered to make it easier for you. The Centre in which you should meditate is also indicated (the Mind, Heart, Third-Eye or Solar Plexus). Strictly follow these instructions.

First learn how to pronounce the Mantra

Stage One

First learn how to pronounce the Mantra (in Sanskrit).

a. You may chant the Mantra aloud to bring the MANTRAŚAKTI (Sound-Energy) into your physical body and physical environment.

b. You may also chant the Mantra mentally, with no physical sound.

You may do each of these practices for as long as you wish, to energize yourself.

Stage Two

This is the important and unique process. Follow the steps carefully.

a. Intone the first line in Sanskrit (internally, mentally, in the indicated Centre), *pause* for a second, then say in your mind the meaning in English and *pause.* (Always remain focused in the indicated Centre.)

b. Then intone the second line in Sanskrit and *pause*, then repeat it in English and *pause*.

c. Then intone the third line in Sanskrit, *pause*, then repeat it in English and *pause*.

Follow this sequence no matter how many lines there are: 3 or 18!

Stage Three

When you have finished the Invocation or Meditation on the Sun, remain silent for a while to allow the invisible Rays from the Sun to fill in and settle your auric-field, and to work within you for Transformation.

The Two Applications of Mantra 1219
Right Use of Mantra 1697
Silence Seals 1034

Be Precise

Please note that your mind must say (declare, realize) only what I have written down, the true spiritual and esoteric meanings. Do not get sidetracked and do not allow your mind to spin off into "thinking" about things. If your mind wanders off and starts elaborating, you will lose your meditation. Be precise: intone the line in Sanskrit, then pause, follow the English precisely and pause. That is all.

You can directly chant to the Sun by facing the physical Sun at sunrise and sunset

If you practise this technique (SĀDHANĀ) correctly, you will reap infinite benefits.

To Choose a Meditation

You will notice that I have given you many forms or variations of the Sun meditation. Each will invoke the Sun, and each will bring you different kinds of blessings and gifts. Once you have learned them all, you can choose which one you want to meditate upon, and you can do so for as long as you wish before changing over to another form or variation.

Keep in Contact with the Sun

Try to be in contact with the physical Sun as often as you can. Keep eye contact frequently (when the Sun is rising or setting, so as not to damage your eyes).

You can directly chant to the Sun by facing the physical Sun at sunrise and sunset. By looking directly at the physical Sun when chanting the Mantra, or facing the physical Sun when meditating, you will also receive PRĀṆA vibrations from the Sun, through the physical Sun. PRĀṆA is the Life-force that comes from the Sun. PRĀṆA is not just physical energy, but Spiritual Vigour and Mental Strength as well.

These Meditations are for *meditation only.*

You must not make regular chants or songs out of these meditations. The meditations, in all forms or variations, must remain solely meditation.

This is absolutely important. There is a profound spiritual and esoteric reason for this. Please obey the rule!

Health and Fire 50
Kuṇḍalinī-Fohat 148
The Life-Force 589

Ōṁ Bhūḥ Bhuvaḥ Svaḥ

A

The Root Gāyatrī-Mantra of Sūrya-Devatā

(The Divine Being within the Sun)

Meditate in the Heart...

1. **Ōṁ**
2. **Bhūḥ**
3. **Bhuvaḥ Svaḥ**
4. **Tat Savitur Vareṇyaṁ**
5. **Bhargo Devasya Dhīmahi**
6. **Dhiyo Yo Naḥ Pracodayāt**

∞

This is the Root Mantra of Savitā, the Sun-God.

Savitā means the Impeller, Begetter, He who drives Manifestation.

He is also known as Sūrya-Nārāyaṇa, the Sun-Spirit—that is, the Self within the Spiritual Sun.

Śrī-Sūryanārāyaṇa (the Holy-Spirit-within-the-Sun) is also known as Savitṛ-Deva (the Sun-God).

He is also known as Īśvara, the Lord or Ruler of the Solar System, the Solar Logos.

He is also known as Viṣṇu, He who pervades all Space with His Being.

He is also called Agni, the Lord of Fire, Cosmic Fire.

This Mantra is a Celebration of Light, that is, the Invocation of God's Light. This is the shorter form, invoking the Light of Glory into the Physical Realm (Bhūḥ), the Subtle-Realms (Bhuvaḥ) and the Heavenly Realms (Svaḥ). These are the three lowest realms of the seven-realmed Solar Logos, the Lord-of-the-Spiritual-Sun.

Meanings of the Root Gāyatrī-Mantra

1

1. We invoke the Solar Logos (ŌṀ),
2. And the Lord of the Physical Plane (BHŪḤ),
3. And the Lords of the Astral (BHUVAḤ) and Mental (SVAḤ) Planes,
4. That Solar Logos we worship,
5. The Light-Divine we contemplate,
6. May He unfold our Spiritual Vision.

2

1. The Boundless Light (ŌṀ),
2. The Physical World (BHŪḤ),
3. The Subtle (BHUVAḤ) and Causal (SVAḤ) Worlds,
4. That Sun-God we adore,
5. Upon the Dazzling-Light-of-God we meditate,
6. May that Glory illumine our Hearts and Minds.

3

1. ŌṀ, the Ultimate Reality,
2. The Physical Dimension (BHŪḤ),
3. The Astral and Heaven Worlds (BHUVAḤ, SVAḤ),
4. That Bright-Spiritual-Sun we worship,
5. The Heavenly-Light we contemplate,
6. May that Glory inspire us.

4

1. ŌṀ, the Self-Effulgent-Primal-Light,
2. That manifests the Physical Realm,
3. The Subtle and Heavenly Realms,
4. That Being-within-the-Sun we worship,
5. The Luminous-Inner-Light we gaze upon,
6. May that Spiritual-Sun illumine our Hearts and Intellects.

5

1. May the Supernatural Light shine into…
2. Our Physical Realm,
3. The Subtle and Celestial Realms,
4. That Light-of-Glory is worthy of our Worship,
5. May that Divine-Brightness show in our Inner Vision,
6. May that Luminosity awaken our Spiritual-Consciousness.

6

We invoke that adorable Sun-of-Spiritual-Consciousness, which is the Radiance of Divinity.

May It stimulate our Spiritual Perceptions in the Three Worlds.

7

We invoke the most excellent Spiritual-Light, the Shining-Glory, hidden within the Sun.

May that Lustre pierce our Hearts and its Brilliance purify us in the Three Realms.

Note that in versions 6 and 7 of the Root GĀYATRĪ-Mantra you intone the whole Sanskrit Mantra first, pause, then repeat the whole meaning in English.

Detailed Meanings of the Sūrya-Nārāyaṇa, Savitā or Root Gāyatrī-Mantra

Ōṁ

The Word of Glory, the Praṇava (Fundamental-Sound-Vibration of the Universe), the Sounding-Light Vibration, the Boundless Light, the Solar Logos, the Sun, the Absolute-Consciousness, Parabrahman (the Transcendental Absolute), Eternal Oneness.

Bhūr, Bhūḥ

The World of Becoming, the Physical Plane, the Physical Universe, the Earth, the World, Pṛthivī Loka (the Physical World); the Basis of the Universe is God.

Bhuvaḥ, Bhuvaha

The Subtle World, the Astral Plane, Antarikṣa (the Inner World), the Self-Existent God, the Desire-World, the Creator-God.

Svaḥ, Suvaḥ, Suvaha, Svaha

The Heaven World, Devāchan, the Mental Plane, Svarga (the Heavenly Realms), Celestial Realms, the Shining World, the Fiery World, God-who-pervades-the-Universe, the Eternal Breath.

Tat

That, the Boundless Reality, Parabrahman (the Boundless All, the Absolute, the Godhead), the Eternal Godhead, the Absolute Truth or Reality, Parabrahm (the Infinite Invisible Existence).

Savitur, Savituḥ, Savitā, Savitṛ

The Universal-Light manifesting through the Solar Logos; Sūrya (the Sun-God, or God-in-the-Sun); Īśvara (the Sovereign-Ruler, the All-Powerful-God); Savitā (the Impeller, Energizer, Vivifier, Life-giver, Begetter, Creator); Sūryadeva (the Sun-God); Āditya (the Golden-Being residing in the Sun). Savitā, Īśvara or Savitṛ (Savitri) is the Male Aspect of the One Godhead; Sāvitrī is the Female Aspect.

Vareṇyaṁ

We bless, we implore, we venerate, we honour, we revere, we glorify, we praise, we exalt, we worship or adore, we aspire to; adoration to, devotion to; desirable, adorable, worthy of worship, worthy to strive after; the Supreme God, the Transcendent, the Most Excellent.

Bhargo, Bharga, Bhargaha

Splendour, Divine Glory, Effulgence, Light, Radiance, the Glorious Energy of the Sun (the God-within-the-Sun), God's Glorious Lustre; the Destroyer of Darkness and Unhappiness, the Purifier, the Remover of Sins.

Devasya

Of God, of the Shining One, the Shining Light of God, the Light-of-Lights, the Divine One, Spiritual Light, the Giver of Happiness, the Light of the Effulgent God, Divine. (Deva: Divine, Bright, Immortal, Shining, Splendid, radiating Light.)

Dhīmahi

Let us contemplate or recognize or meditate upon; let us receive and assimilate; behold the Glorious-Light-Body-of-God; we meditate upon, we realize.

Dhīyāḥ, Dhiyo, Dhiyaha, Dhī

Wisdom, Inner Vision, Spiritual Vision, Spiritual Faculties, Meditation, Consciousness, Heart, Intellect, Mind, Intuition, Spiritual Perception, the Buddhi Principle, the Seership Faculty, Spiritual Understanding, Intelligence, the Mind of Light. Dhī is:

a. Cosmic-Vision or Absolute-Sight.
b. Solar-Systemic-Vision of the Inner Worlds.
c. Vision of the Spiritual Self or Ātman.
d. Insight or Intuition as manifested through the physical body and brain.

Yo, Yaha

Which, who.

Naḥ, Naha

Our, ours.

Pracodayāt (Prachodayāt)

Who unfolds, invigorates, unveils; may He unfold, transform, enliven, enlighten, guide, empower, impel, propel, inspire, motivate, quicken and energize, stir up and vitalize, sharpen understanding, lead towards Illumination, direct body, mind and Soul to improvement and growth on all levels.

∞

B

Meditate in the Third-Eye Centre...

1. Ōṁ
2. Bhūḥ
3. Bhuvaha
4. Suvaha
5. Tat Savitur Vareṇyaṁ
6. Bhargo Devasya Dhīmahi
7. Dhiyo Yo Naḥ Pracodayāt

1

1. Ōṁ (We invoke the Boundless Light),
2. Bhūḥ (in the Physical World),
3. Bhuvaha (in the Astral World),
4. Suvaha (in the Mental World),
5. That Self-Effulgent Light we glorify,
6. The Godly-Radiance we gaze upon,
7. Our Intellects Illumined with Light.

2

1. Ōṁ (We invoke the Original Creative Light),
2. Bhūḥ (on the Physical Plane),
3. Bhuvaha (on the Astral Plane),
4. Suvaha (on the Mental Plane),
5. That Creative-Light we adore,
6. The Ineffable-Glory we behold,
7. Our Inner Selves Enlightened.

3

1. Ōṁ (We invoke the Eternal-Light),
2. Bhūḥ (in the Physical Universe),
3. Bhuvaha (in the Subtle Universe),
4. Suvaha (in the Causal Universe),
5. That Spiritual-Sun we worship,
6. The Golden-Light-of-God we absorb,
7. Unveil to us our Spiritual-Sight.

4

1. Ōṁ (The Solar Logos, the Word, we invoke),
2. Bhūḥ (in the Material World),
3. Bhuvaha (in the Psychic World),
4. Suvaha (in the Heaven Worlds),
5. That Sun-God is Supremely Excellent,
6. The Destroyer of the Darkness of Ignorance,
7. May we receive Intuitional-Impulses from that Celestial-Light.

C

Meditate in the Third-Eye Centre...

1. **Ōṁ Sūryāya Namaha**
   Glory be to you, Solar Logos.
   Glory be to you, Divine Sun.

2. **Ōṁ**
   We Invoke the Solar Logos, the Great-Being-of-Light,

3. **Bhūḥ**
   In Whom we live,

4. **Bhuvaḥ Svaḥ**
   Move, and have our Being,

5. **Tat Savitur Vareṇyaṁ**
   Unveil to our Inner Vision the True-Spiritual-Sun,

6. **Bhargo Devasya Dhīmahi**
   Hidden by a Veil of Golden Light,

7. **Dhiyo Yo Naḥ Pracodayāt**
   That we may know the Final-Truth,

8. **Rāṁ**
   Do our Duties,

9. **Rāṁ**
   We Journey to Your Highest Realm,

10. **Rāṁ**
    The Brahman-State: Brahmanirvāṇam.

Ōṁ Sūryāya Namaha

The Brahman-State is Brahma-Loka, the Kingdom of God, the final Union with God, the Deified Condition, Nirvāṇa, the Door to Infinite Perception.

Brahma-Nirvāṇa: Dissolution in God 1224

D

Meditate in the Third-Eye Centre…

1. Ōṁ
We invoke the Solar Logos,

2. Ōṁ Bhūḥ
In the Physical World,

3. Ōṁ Bhuvaḥ
In the Astral World,

4. Ōṁ Svaḥ
In the Mental World,

5. Ōṁ Mahaḥ
In the Buddhic World,

6. Ōṁ Janaḥ
In the Nirvāṇic World,

7. Ōṁ Tapaḥ
In the Monadic World,

8. Ōṁ Satyaṁ
In the Logoic World,

9. Ōṁ Tat Savitur Vareṇyaṁ
That Life-Giving-Sun-God we adore,

10. Bhargo Devasya Dhīmahi
The Light of the Effulgent-God we absorb into ourselves,

11. Dhiyo Yo Naḥ Pracodayāt
Our Evolutionary Faculties vitalized,

12. Ōṁ
By the Light which Illumines all human beings in this World,

13. **Āpo Jyotiḥ Raso-Mṛtam Brahmā**
God's Living-Waters, Light, Essence and Immortality we receive,

14. **Bhūr Bhuvaḥ Suvar Ōṁ**
In the Physical, Astral and Mental Worlds,

15. **Ōṁ**
The Living-Voice and the Light-of-Truth guides us.

∞

Āpa: Water, the Living-Waters-of-Light.

Jyoti: Light, Fire, Flame, Brilliance, the Light-of-the-Sun, Brightness, Divinity.

Rasā: Juice, Water, Quintessence, Nectar, Spiritual Taste, Honey-sweet; the Divine Nature; Sentiment, Immortality.

Amṛta (Amrita): Immortal, Undying, Nectar, sweet-taste, Ambrosia, the Supreme Spirit, God, Splendour, Light, Divinity, Rays-of-the-Sun.

Brahmā: God, the Creator-God, the Creator of the Universe (of all the Star-Systems and Galaxies); the Origin and Source of Creation (whether the whole Cosmos or our Solar-Systemic Creation); the Power that makes Creation, Growth and Evolution possible; the Sun. (Locally, in our Solar System, Brahmā is our Solar Logos.)

Bhūr Bhuvaḥ Suvar Ōṁ

The Living-Voice and the Light-of-Truth is the Solar Logos in the aspect of the Word or Sounding-Light-Current penetrating and descending through all the Planes and Realms of Being, which can be seen and heard in meditation. This Living-Voice is **Śabda-Brahman.**

The Word, Logos, Voice, Name 1646

Bhūr Bhuvaha Svaha

E

Meditate in the Heart…

1. Ōṁ
   We invoke the Solar Logos, who is our God,

2. Bhūr Bhuvaha Svaha
   In the Physical, Astral and Mental Worlds,

3. Tat Savitur Vareṇyaṁ
   That Divine-Light which dispels all our Illusions and Darkness we adore,

4. Bhargo Devasya Dhīmahi
   The Luminous-Mystery-of-Being we contemplate,

5. Dhiyo Yo Naḥ Pracodayāt
   May that Redeeming-Grace-of-Light empower our Hearts.

Hṛdaya-Cakra: the Heart Centre.

Within your Heart Cakra you find the Sun. This Heart-Sun shines. The Light of the Sun in your Heart connects you to the Sun, which is the Heart Cakra of our Solar System (of the Solar Logos).

Our Solar Logos and His Manifestation, our Solar System, is one of seven Solar Logoi and Their Solar Systems, forming seven Cosmic Cakras in the Cosmic-Space-Body of a Superior Cosmic Sun whose Auric-Field encompasses vast regions of the Seven-Layered-Cosmic-Space in our Galaxy.

Our Solar Logos, with His Solar System, is but the Heart Cakra of an infinitely vaster Cosmic Sun, or Cosmic Solar Logos, within whose Cosmic-Space-Body multitudes of Suns abide.

This is the Path to the Cosmic-Path-of-the-Heart, or Boundless Love.

The Revelation of God 854

F

Meditate in the Heart…

1. **Ōṁ**
   We invoke the Solar Deity,
2. **Ōṁ Bhūḥ Ōṁ Bhuvaha Ōṁ Svaha**
   In the Physical, Subtle and Causal Worlds,
3. **Ōṁ Maha Ōṁ Janaha Ōṁ Tapaḥ**
   In the Buddhic, Nirvāṇic and Monadic Worlds,
4. **Ōṁ Satyaṁ**
   In the Divine World,
5. **Ōṁ Tat Savitur Vareṇyaṁ**
   The Adorable Splendour glowing within the Luminous Worlds of Being,
6. **Bhargo Devasya Dhīmahi**
   The Supreme-Light-of-the-Ultimate-Reality we contemplate,
7. **Dhiyo Yonaha Pracodayāt**
   Send into our Hearts your Healing, Spiritually-Vitalizing Rays of Light.

Ōṁ Maha Ōṁ Janaha Ōṁ Tapaḥ

Svaha and Svāhā

Please note the difference between **Svaḥ**, **Svaha**, the Heaven World (the Mental Plane) and **Svāhā**, the Bīja-Mantra for Consecration, Offering, Sacrifice, Oblation, Outpouring.

The Bīja-Mantra Svāhā 1551

G

Meditate in the Heart…

1. **Ōṁ**
   We invoke the God of our Solar System,
2. **Bhūr Bhuvaḥ Svaḥ**
   In the Physical, Astral and Heaven Worlds,
3. **Tat Savitur Vareṇyaṁ**
   That Life-giving-Sun we praise,
4. **Bhargo Devasya Dhīmahi**
   The Splendour-of-God we receive into ourselves,
5. **Dhiyo Yo Naḥ Pracodayāt**
   Illuminate our Spiritual-Faculties,
6. **Śrīṁ Śrīṁ Śrīṁ Śrīṁ**
   And bless us with (Health), (Prosperity), (Joy) and (Peace).

Śrīṁ Śrīṁ Śrīṁ Śrīṁ

Warriors of the Sun

The Spiritual Warriors are called **Sūrya-Vaṁśa-Kṣatriya**: the Race-of-the-Sun-Warriors, or the Warrior-Race-of-the-Sun, the Solar Lords.

Sūrya: the Sun, the Solar Logos.
Vaṁśa: a Race of people.
Kṣatriya: a Warrior.

Many great Dynasties of ancient kings and emperors and great rulers of nations belonged to this Sun-Race of Warriors. They ruled their kingdoms by the Power of the Sun, that is, their *Conscious-Identification* with the Solar Deity, in various degrees of Union with the Sun, and their understanding of the Mystery of the Solar Logos and His significance for Human Evolution on this planet, our Earth.

Sūrya-Vaṁśa, the Sun-Race, or the Children of the Sun, the Children of the Light, are both men and women who have Realized their Identity with the Sun, their Oneness with the Light.

The Warrior of the Light 984

H

Meditate in the Heart…

1. **Ōṁ Bhūr Bhuvaḥ Svaḥ**
   We invoke the Light-of-God in the Physical, Subtle and Causal Realms,

2. **Ōṁ Tat Savitur Vareṇyaṁ**
   To that Spiritual-Sun-of-Truth we surrender,

3. **Bhargo Devasya Dhīmahi**
   The Light which illumines our Path we contemplate,

4. **Dhiyo Yo Naḥ Pracodayāt**
   May that Holy Lustre fill our Spiritual Hearts with Purifying Rays of Grace,

5. **Svāhā**
   We offer ourselves for Inner Transformation.

The World Priest

You may have noticed that the Gāyatrī Invocation is always plural. It always refers to "we" and "us". When you invoke the Gāyatrī-Mantra, in whichever form, you always should have your group in mind, not yourself. It is a meditation you do for your whole group, with the group, for the group. The Divine Light, as it passes through you, passes into your group and through the group into the world.

There is, however, an even more glorious thing you can do: that is, become a Priest for the whole world, for the whole human family. To do this, you must have all of Humanity in mind when you invoke the Mantra, that the Light-Power may penetrate every human Soul, that the Light-Power-Response may stimulate into action all the Sparks of Light which are hidden and covered in every human Heart.

This is to become a World Priest. This is to become a World Server.

You invoke the Deity of Light that the Light may be spread abroad the whole planet, that the Kingdom of Light may come, that the Light may regain the Earth, that Peace and Love may fully reign.

To Manifest the Kingdom of God 1716

Ōṁ Bhūr Bhuvaḥ Svaḥ

I

BHŪR BHUVAS SUVAR ŌṀ

Meditate in the Third-Eye...

1. ŌṀ
   We invoke the Solar Logos, Who is God,
2. BHŪḤ
   Who is Eternal,
3. ŌṀ BHUVAḤ
   Who is the Creator,
4. ŌṀ SUVAḤ
   Who is Shining,
5. ŌṀ MAHAḤ
   Who is Omnipotent,
6. ŌṀ JANAḤ
   Who is the Birth-Giver,
7. ŌṀ TAPAḤ
   Who is Burning-Fire,
8. ŌṀ SATYAṀ
   Who is the Absolute Truth,
9. ŌṀ TAT SAVITUR VAREṆYAṀ
   That Central-Spiritual-Sun we propitiate,
10. BHARGO DEVASYA DHĪMAHI
    That Light-of-Wisdom of the Effulgent-God we meditate upon,
11. DHIYO YO NAḤ PRACODAYĀT
    Our Higher-Consciousness Illuminated,
12. ŌṀ ĀPO JYOTI RASO-ŌṀ-ṚTAM BRAHMA
    With the Luminous-Waters-of-the-Light, which is the Essence of all things, and is Immortality and Divinity,
13. BHŪR BHUVAS SUVAR ŌṀ
    In the Physical, Astral and Mental Creations.

J

Meditate in the Heart…

1. **Ōṁ Bhūḥ Bhuvaḥ Svaḥ**
   We invoke the Solar Logos in the Three Worlds,
   the Physical World, the Astral World and the Mental World,

2. **Ōṁ Tat Savitur Vareṇyaṁ**
   We invoke the Solar Logos, Savitā,
   Who is beyond Space and Time,
   Whose Life is manifesting through our Solar System,

3. **Bhargo Devasya Dhīmahi**
   Whose Light is all-pervading and eternal,
   Who is always Aware of what takes place in the Hearts of all Beings,

4. **Dhiyo Yo Naḥ Pracodayāt**
   Send into our Hearts your Currents of Purifying-Fire,

5. **Ōṁ**
   (Union)
   We are One with the Sun.

Dhiyo Yo Naḥ Pracodayāt

Union

The word **Yoga** is misunderstood today. Yoga is Union, Re-integration, At-One-Ment with the Higher Reality. It is *not* a set of keep-fit exercises.

Yoga: the Science of Union 517

K

Sah-Ahaṅg

Meditate in the Third-Eye...

1. **Ōṅg**
   We invoke the Solar Logos, the God of our Solar System,
2. **Jyoti-Nirañjana**
   Who is Light-Pure,
3. **Ouṅgkāra**
   Who is the Sound-Current,
4. **Rāraṅgkāra**
   Who is the Creative Word,
5. **Saḥ-Ahaṅg**
   Who is the Great I AM of our Solar-Universe,
6. **Sata-Nāma**
   Who is the True Name,
7. **Ōṁ Tat Savitur Vareṇyaṁ**
   That Living-Word-of-God we worship,
8. **Bhargo Devasya Dhīmahi**
   The Glorious-Effulgence we behold with our Spiritual Vision,
9. **Dhiyo Yo Naḥ Pracodayāt**
   Our God-Realization Faculties Illuminate,
10. **Ōṅg**
    With your Shining-Sound,
    With your Splendid-Light.

Sūrya, the Sun or Solar Logos, is also the **Prajāpati**, the Lord-of-the-People, the Lord of all Created Beings within the Solar System, the Father-God, the Supreme King.

The Cosmic Creator-Gods 162

L

Meditate in the Third-Eye…

1. **Ōṁ**
   We invoke Īśvara, the Lord, Master and Controller of our Being,
2. **Bhūr Bhuvaḥ Svaḥ**
   The Lord of the Three Worlds, the Physical, Subtle and Causal Worlds,
3. **Ōṁ Tat Savitur Vareṇyaṁ**
   That Inner-Light-of-the-Spiritual-Sun we Glorify,
4. **Bhargo Devasya Dhīmahi**
   The Light-of-Truth which shines with Brilliance we contemplate,
5. **Dhiyo Yo Naḥ Pracodayāt**
   Our Spiritual-Natures Illumine with your Radiance,
6. **Ōṁ**
   Make the Light appear in our Minds,
   Unveil to us the Light that shows us the Path-Within.

Īśvara

Ōṁ is the Word of Power (Mantra) for Īśvara.

Īśvara means "the Lord God, the Master, Ruler, Controller, Director, the Supreme Being, the Central Intelligence of the Universe, the Highest Authority in the Cosmos, the Lord of All, the Lord of the Universe, the Chief among All, the King of Kings, the Lord of Lords, the Master Power".

Īśvara is the Heart Centre, or Centre of Consciousness, in any system, microcosmic or macrocosmic, the power of Lordship and independent action. Īśvara is:

a. The Lord God, the Supreme Godhead, the Universal Sun, the Absolute, the Supreme Individuality.

b. The Solar Logos, the Spiritual Sun of our Solar System, the Ruler of our Solar-Universe, Sūrya.

c. The Inner-Ruler-Immortal in Man, the Ātman, the Ruler of the Human Heart, the God-Within, the Spiritual Sunshine in the Human Microcosm, the Central Organizer of Life.

Pāda I Sūtra 23 548

Ōṁ Ōṁ Ōṁ

M(i)

Meditate in the Third-Eye...

1. **Ōṁ Ōṁ Ōṁ**
   We invoke the (Inner Light),
   the (Light of the Inner God),
   for (Spiritual Guidance and Self-Realization),

2. **Ōṁ Tat Savitur Vareṇyaṁ**
   That Light-of-Truth, which shines in the Head with Brilliance, we desire,

3. **Bhargo Devasya Dhīmahi**
   The Radiance of the Divine-Effulgence we meditate upon,

4. **Dhiyo Yo Naḥ Pracodayāt**
   Make the Light appear to our Purified-Mental-Vision,

5. **Ōṁ**
   The Light shines within us.

M(ii)
Variation

Meditate in the Mind...

1. **Ōṁ**
   (The Solar Logos),

2. **Bhūḥ Bhuvaḥ Svaḥ**
   (The Physical, Astral and Mental Worlds),

3. **Tat Savitur Vareṇyaṁ**
   The Solar Logos we worship,

4. **Bhargo Devasya Dhīmahi**
   The Divine-Light we contemplate,

5. **Dhiyo Yo Naḥ Pracodayāt**
   Enlighten our Minds.

N

Meditate in the Heart…

1. **ŌṀ Bhūḥ Bhuvaḥ Svaḥ**
   We invoke the Divine-Light-Power in the Physical, Intermediate and Heaven Worlds,
2. **ŌṀ Tat Savitur Vareṇyaṁ**
   The Omnipotent Radiance of the Divine-Sun we assimilate into ourselves,
3. **Bhargo Devasya Dhīmahi**
   The Light-of-Glory we contemplate,
4. **Dhiyo Yo Naḥ Pracodayāt**
   Infuse into our Hearts the Awareness of your Divine-Presence,
5. **Hūṁ**
   (The constant flow of the Energy of Your Protection),
6. **Hūṁ**
   (The dissolution of our egos),
7. **Hūṁ**
   (The Awareness of Your All-Pervading Life-Vibration).

HŪṀ HŪṀ HŪṀ

Our Sun or Solar-Deity is a gigantic Pītha (Knot of Power), a Swirling Centre of Force, Energy, Radiation, Power, Force-Currents, Prāṇic-Energies, a Cosmic Cakra in Space, a distributing Point for the Manifesting Absolute.

The Manifested-God 1589

ĀditYāya Namaha

○

Meditate in the Heart Centre…

1. Ōṁ Sūryāya Namaha
   We worship the Divine Sun,
   Send into us your Luminous-Nourishments-of-Light,

2. Mitrāya Namaha
   The Light of Goodness,

3. Ravaye Namaha
   The Radiant Light,

4. Bhānave Namaha
   The Illuminating Light,

5. Khagāya Namaha
   The All-Pervading Light,

6. Pūṣṇe Namaha
   The Protecting Light,

7. Hiraṇya-Gharbhāya Namaha
   The Golden-Womb of Light,

8. Maricāye Namaha
   The Shining Rays of Light,

9. Ādityāya Namaha
   The Immense Light,

10. Savitre Namaha
    The Vivifying-Powerful Light,

11. Arkāya Namaha
    The Healing Rays of Light,

12. Bhāskarāya Namaha
    The Brilliant Light of Cosmic Intelligence,

13. Viśvakāryāya Namaha
The Creator-Light of the Universe,

14. Ōṁ Bhūḥ Bhuvaḥ Svaḥ
Send an Influx of Power from the Divine-Sun into our Physical, Psychic and Mental Realms,

15. Tat Savitur Vareṇyaṁ
The Cosmic-Sun-of-Limitless-Intelligence we Glorify,

16. Bhargo Devasya Dhīmahi
That Radiant Light fills us,

17. Dhiyo Yo Naḥ Pracodayāt
May that Solar-Radiance fill our Hearts with Imperishable-Glory,

18. Ōṁ
(Blessed be God who lives and moves in all beings).

P

Meditate in the Solar Plexus Centre…

a. Rām Sūryāya Namaḥ
We invoke the Healing-Energies of the Sun.
We invoke the Solar-Radiance for Health.

b. Śivam (Shivam)
(Joy, Happiness, Contentment).

Ōṁ Maṇi Siddhi Hūṁ

Q

Meditate in the Third-Eye Centre…

1. **Ōṁ Maṇi Siddhi Hūṁ**
   Awaken the Precious-Spiritual-Powers within us,
   Let us become Perfect in all things,

2. **Bhūḥ Bhuvaḥ Svaḥ**
   Let us accomplish all that is desired in the Three Worlds,

3. **Tat Savitur Vareṇyaṁ**
   That Great-Sun-Being we worship,

4. **Bhargo Devasya Dhīmahi**
   The God-within-the-Radiant-Solar-Orb we look upon,

5. **Dhiyo Yo Naḥ Pracodayāt**
   Enlighten our Minds with your Wisdom,
   Inflame our Hearts with your Love,

6. **Hūṁ Hūṁ Hūṁ**
   (Perfection) (Success) (Prosperity).

∞

Maṇi: something precious, worthwhile; a jewel, gem, pearl of great price; an ornament.

Siddhi: accomplishment, fulfilment of desires, prosperity, luck, perfection, powers.

R(i)

Meditate in the Third-Eye…

1. RĀṀ ŌṀ ĀṀ YĀṀ RĀMĀYA NAMAHA
   We invoke the Radiant-Energy-of-the-Sun
   for Physical, Emotional and Mental Strength,

2. ŌṀ TAT SAVITUR VAREṆYAṀ
   Reverence to the Sun-of-Righteousness
   who overcomes hindrances,

3. BHARGO DEVASYA DHĪMAHI
   We Realize the Splendour-of-God within ourselves,
   the Eternal Light,

4. DHIYO YO NAḤ PRACODAYĀT
   Our Spiritual-Growth stimulate,

5. RĀṀ
   (Vigour and Strength),

6. RĀṀ
   (Protection and Power),

7. RĀṀ
   (Radiance and Energy),

8. RĀṀ
   (Courage and Confidence).

RĀṀ ŌṀ ĀṀ YĀṀ

∞

RĀṀ: Fearless-Victory over all difficulties.

RĀMA is the Sun incarnated in a Perfected Spiritual Warrior. When the Spiritual-Warrior-Human-Being attains final Union with the Sun, that Regenerated Being becomes an embodiment of the Sun, with the Sun's qualities of Power, Strength, Radiance, Goodness, Vitality, Generosity, Abundance, Opulence, Splendour, Greatness—vast, all-pervading.
Rām: the Warrior Power 1068

R(ii)

LĀṀ VĀṀ RĀṀ YĀṀ

Meditate in the Third-Eye...

1. LĀṀ
   (Strength, Calm, Stability),
2. VĀṀ
   (Purity, Evenness, Fluidity),
3. RĀṀ
   (Brightness, Radiance, Energy),
4. YĀṀ
   (Mobility, Action, Satisfaction),
5. HĀṀ
   (Protection, Endurance, Driving-Force),
6. ŌṀ
   (Focus, Uniting, Integration),
7. ĀṀ
   (Opening, Disclosing, Revelation),
8. ŌṀ TAT SAVITUR VAREṆYAṀ
   The Power of the Godhead, in the Form of the Sun, we invoke,
9. BHARGO DEVASYA DHĪMAHI
   The Brilliant-Light-of-God which shines within us we Recognize,
10. DHIYO YO NAḤ PRACODAYĀT
    May that Light-Within-Us shine forth with ever greater Glory,
11. ŌṀ
    (Unveil the Glory within us).

The Indwelling-Light-Within-Us is covered by matter and the material bodies (the physical, astral and mental bodies). When the personality is sufficiently purified, the Glory within us shines unimpeded like the Sun.
Beyond the Veils 894

S

Meditate in the Heart Centre…

1. **Ōṁ Sūryāya Hṛdayāya**
   We worship the Sun-in-our-Hearts,
   Who is also the Heart-of-the-Sun,

2. **Ōṁ Bhūḥ Bhuvaḥ Svaḥ**
   Who is the Basis of the Universe,
   The Self-Existent God,
   Who pervades all the Worlds,

3. **Tat Savitur Vareṇyaṁ**
   The Absolute-Truth who is the Cosmic-Fire-Sun we Praise in Glory,

4. **Bhargo Devasya Dhīmahi**
   The Fiery-Essence of the Invisible-Deity we contemplate,

5. **Dhiyo Yo Naḥ Pracodayāt**
   Irradiate our Spiritual-Hearts with your Mystic-Fire, Illumination,

6. **Hūṁ Hūṁ Hūṁ**
   (Unity) (Love) (Peace).

T(i)

Meditate in the Heart Centre…

1. **Ōṁ Sūryāya Namaḥ**

or: **Ōṁ Sūryāya**
   Glory be to you, Solar Logos,
   Glory be to you, Lord-of-the-Sun.

Ōṁ Sūryāya Hṛdayāya

T(ii)

Meditate in the Heart Centre...

1. **Ōṁ**
   (The Self dwells in the Heart as the Sun-of-Suns),

2. **Tat Savitur Vareṇyaṁ**
   The Luminous-Sun-in-the-Heart we worship,
   the Immeasurable Light,

3. **Bhargo Devasya Dhīmahi**
   The Light-Maker who shines with Self-Luminous-Power
   we meditate upon,

4. **Dhiyo Yo Naḥ Pracodayāt**
   May this Sun-Light Illuminate our Hearts
   with Spiritual-Nourishment,

5. **Hrīṁ**
   (Union with the Spiritual-Heart),

6. **Klīṁ**
   (Beauty, Delight, Attraction),

7. **Sauḥ**
   (Transcendental-Transformation, Self-Realization).

Hrīṁ Klīṁ Sauḥ

Ātman, Ātmā, the Spiritual-Self within us, is Us in our most spiritual aspect, Us as eternal, immortal Spirits. Ātman is the Breath-of-God that We are. We are made by the Spirit-of-God, and We participate, on the Ātmic-level, in pure Spirituality. We, as Ātman, live in the condition of Sat-Cit-Ānanda: Being-Consciousness-Bliss.

The Experience of the Heart 1280

U

Meditate in the Heart Centre…

1. **Rāṁ**
   (Transcendental-Bliss),
2. **Ōṁ Tat Savitur Vareṇyaṁ**
   The Joyous-Sun-God we worship,
3. **Bhargo Devasya Dhīmahi**
   The Ecstatic-Light we contemplate,
4. **Dhiyo Yo Naḥ Pracodayāt**
   May that Light Gladden our Hearts.
5. **Rāṁ**
   (Rejoice *in* God),
6. **Rāṁ**
   (Enchanting-Light),
7. **Rāṁ**
   (Restful-Light).

Rāṁ Rāṁ Rāṁ

V

Meditate in the Third-Eye Centre…

1. **Ōṁ**
   (The Boundless-Circle-of-Infinite-Light).

The Boundless-Circle-of-Infinite-Light is the Universal Sun, the Endless, Boundless, Infinite, Absolute Sun or Godhead, or Divinity, which is the Source of all the Solar Logoi, Spiritual-Suns, Central-Spiritual-Suns.

Ōṁ is also the Solar Logos, a fragment of the Infinite-Sun.

Potent Vibrations: Bīja-Mantra 1542

Ōṁ Paramātmane Namaḥ

w

Meditate in the Third-Eye Centre...

1. **Ōṁ Paramātmane Namaḥ**
   We salute the Transcendental-Spirit,
   The Transcendental-Sun, who is our Self,
2. **Ōṁ Bhūr Bhuvaḥ Svaḥ**
   The All-Pervading-Radiant-Life-of-God to Energize us in the Physical, Astral and Mental Worlds,
3. **Ōṁ Tat Savitur Vareṇyaṁ**
   Let us meditate on the Form-of-the-Sun,
4. **Bhargo Devasya Dhīmahi**
   Let us look upon the Light-of-the-Supreme-Self,
5. **Dhiyo Yo Naḥ Pracodayāt**
   Who will Illumine our Minds with the Truth-Bearing-Light.
6. **Ōṁ**
   (In Holy Communion with the Divine).

Paramātman is the Transcendental-Spiritual-Sun, Eternal, Pure Consciousness and Bliss, beyond our Space and Time, beyond Cause and Effect. It is God's-Supreme-Light, or Universal-Sun-Shine.

Parama: Supreme.
Ātman: Self, Soul, Spirit.

Our Spirit-Selves, the Monads, are born of the Sun. We are all, as total Human Beings, Children of the Sun.

Incarnations of the Sun 1593

X

Meditate in the Heart Centre…

1. **Ōṁ Bhūḥ Bhuvaḥ Svaḥ Ōṁ**
   We invoke the Lord-of-Creation in the Physical, Astral and Mental Worlds,

2. **Ōṁ Tat Savitur Vareṇyaṁ**
   We pour our Devotion to Savitṛ, our God,

3. **Bhargo Devasya Dhīmahi**
   We meditate on the Supreme-Refulgence-of-Beaming-Light,

4. **Dhiyo Yo Naḥ Pracodayāt**
   May He Inspire our meditations,

5. **Bhūr Bhuvaḥ Suvar Ōṁ**
   May the Shaft-of-Light penetrate into us in the Physical, Subtle and Causal Worlds.

Ōṁ Bhūḥ Bhuvaḥ Svaḥ Ōṁ

Whenever the Sūrya-Mantra (Gāyatrī) is invoked, a great Shaft of Light descends from the Sun (the Solar Logos), through the visible Sun, into the reciter/chanter or meditator. It fills the auric-field and specifically stimulates the Heart Cakra and the Head Cakras (the Third-Eye and Crown). No matter what the position of the physical Sun—day or night—the Shaft of Invisible Light passes through it into the invoker.

Y

Kriṅg Kriṅg Kriṅg

Meditate in the Crown Centre…

1. Kriṅg
(Action),

2. Kriṅg
(Power),

3. Kriṅg
(Dynamic Transformation),

4. Bhūḥ Bhuvaḥ Svaḥ
(Power), (Force), (Energy),
Into our Three Worlds of Action,
the Physical, Subtle and Causal Worlds,

5. Tat Savitur Vareṇyaṁ
The Shoreless-Sea-of-Fire we invoke,

6. Bhargo Devasya Dhīmahi
The Brightness-of-the-Eternal-Light we implore,

7. Dhiyo Yo Naḥ Pracodayāt
Send into us your Divine-Energy,
For Spiritual Re-Creation and Resurrection,

8. Kriṅg
(Sacrificing our egos),

9. Kriṅg
(We are Reborn into Pure-Consciousness),

10. Kriṅg
(Liberate our Inner-Nature into Perfect-Freedom).

Perfect-Freedom is Mokṣa, Mukti: Salvation, Liberation, Final Emancipation from the limiting conditions of Life.

Z

Meditate in the Third-Eye Centre…

1. **Ōṁ**
   (Glory be to You, Father-of-the-Undying, the Solar Logos!),
   (Glory be to You, Source-of-the-Immortal-Ones),

2. **Aiṁ** **Śrī**
   (Wisdom), (Holiness),

3. **Hrīṁ** **Strīṁ**
   (Purification), (Sustenance),

4. **Klīṁ** **Hūṁ**
   (Transformation), (Protection),

5. **Svāhā** **Phat**
   (Offering), (Destruction of Evil),

6. **Ōṁ**
   (The Eternal Calls out to the Separated-Parts;
   return to your Source),

7. **Śrī Sūryāya Namaha**
   To the Luminous-Sun-God, Salutations!

8. **Ōṁ Tat Savitur Vareṇyaṁ**
   We worship the Sun-God through Whom the
   One-Eternal-Light manifests,

9. **Bhargo Devasya Dhīmahi**
   We meditate upon the Perpetual-Light,

10. **Dhiyo Yo Naḥ Pracodayāt**
    May that Divinity be our Guide,

11. **Śrī**
    (Power and Majesty).

∞

Śrī Sūryāya Namaha

Ōṁ Hāṁ Yāṁ Rāṁ Vāṁ Lāṁ

Brahma-Gāyatrī-Mantra

Cosmic-Divine-Light Meditation

Ōṁ Bhūḥ Ōṁ Bhuvaḥ Auguṁ Suvaḥ
Ōṁ Mahaḥ Ōṁ Janaḥ Ōṁ Tapaḥ
Auguṁ Satyaṁ

Ōṁ Tat Savitur Vareṇyaṁ
Bhargo Devasya Dhīmahi
Dhiyo Yo Naḥ Pracodayāt

Ōṁ Hāṁ Yāṁ Rāṁ Vāṁ Lāṁ
Svāhā

∞

Ōṁ Bhūḥ: the Physical World, the world of the five senses.

Ōṁ Bhuvaḥ: the Subtle World, the Desire-World, the Astral Plane.

Auguṁ Suvaḥ: the Heaven World, Devāchan, the Mental Plane.

Ōṁ Mahaḥ: the Buddhic World, Paradise, the Intuitional Plane.

Ōṁ Janaḥ: the Nirvāṇic World, the Kingdom of God, the Spiritual World.

Ōṁ Tapaḥ: the Monadic World, the realm of the "Father in Heaven".

Auguṁ Satyaṁ: the Logoic World, the Primeval State, the Divine World.

That Embodied Sun-God we worship, who is the Light of Effulgent Glory. May He/She awaken our Enlightenment Faculty so that we may be filled with the Light of Glory.

Ōṁ: the Radiant Force of the Spirit, the Cosmic Element of Spirit (the Monadic Universe).

Hāṁ: the Cosmic Element of Space (the Nirvāṇic Universe).

Yāṁ: the Cosmic Element of Air (the Buddhic Universe).

Rāṁ: the Cosmic Element of Fire (the Mental Universe).

Vāṁ: the Cosmic Element of Water (the Astral Universe).

Lāṁ: the Cosmic Element of Earth (the Physical Universe).

Svāhā: I am One with God, I am One with the Universe.

Transformation of the Centres 1333

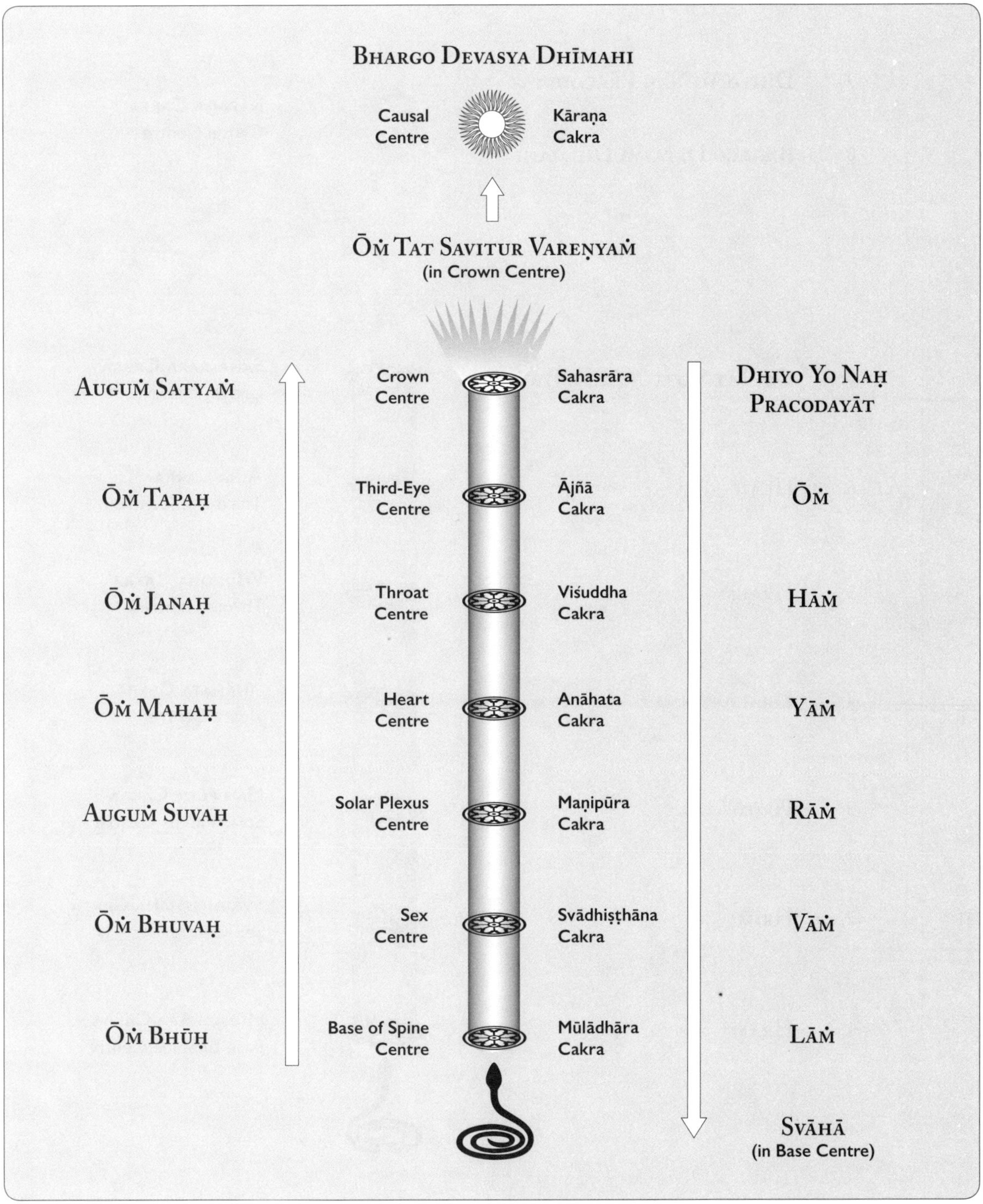

Bhargo Devasya Dhīmahi
Causal Centre
Kāraṇa Cakra
Ōṁ Tat Savitur Vareṇyaṁ
(in Crown Centre)
Augum Satyaṁ
Crown Centre
Sahasrāra Cakra
Dhiyo Yo Naḥ Pracodayāt
Ōṁ Tapaḥ
Third-Eye Centre
Ājñā Cakra
Ōṁ
Ōṁ Janaḥ
Throat Centre
Viśuddha Cakra
Hāṁ
Ōṁ Mahaḥ
Heart Centre
Anāhata Cakra
Yāṁ
Augum Suvaḥ
Solar Plexus Centre
Maṇipūra Cakra
Rāṁ
Ōṁ Bhuvaḥ
Sex Centre
Svādhiṣṭhāna Cakra
Vāṁ
Ōṁ Bhūḥ
Base of Spine Centre
Mūlādhāra Cakra
Lāṁ
Svāhā
(in Base Centre)

The Brahma-Gāyatrī in the Cakras

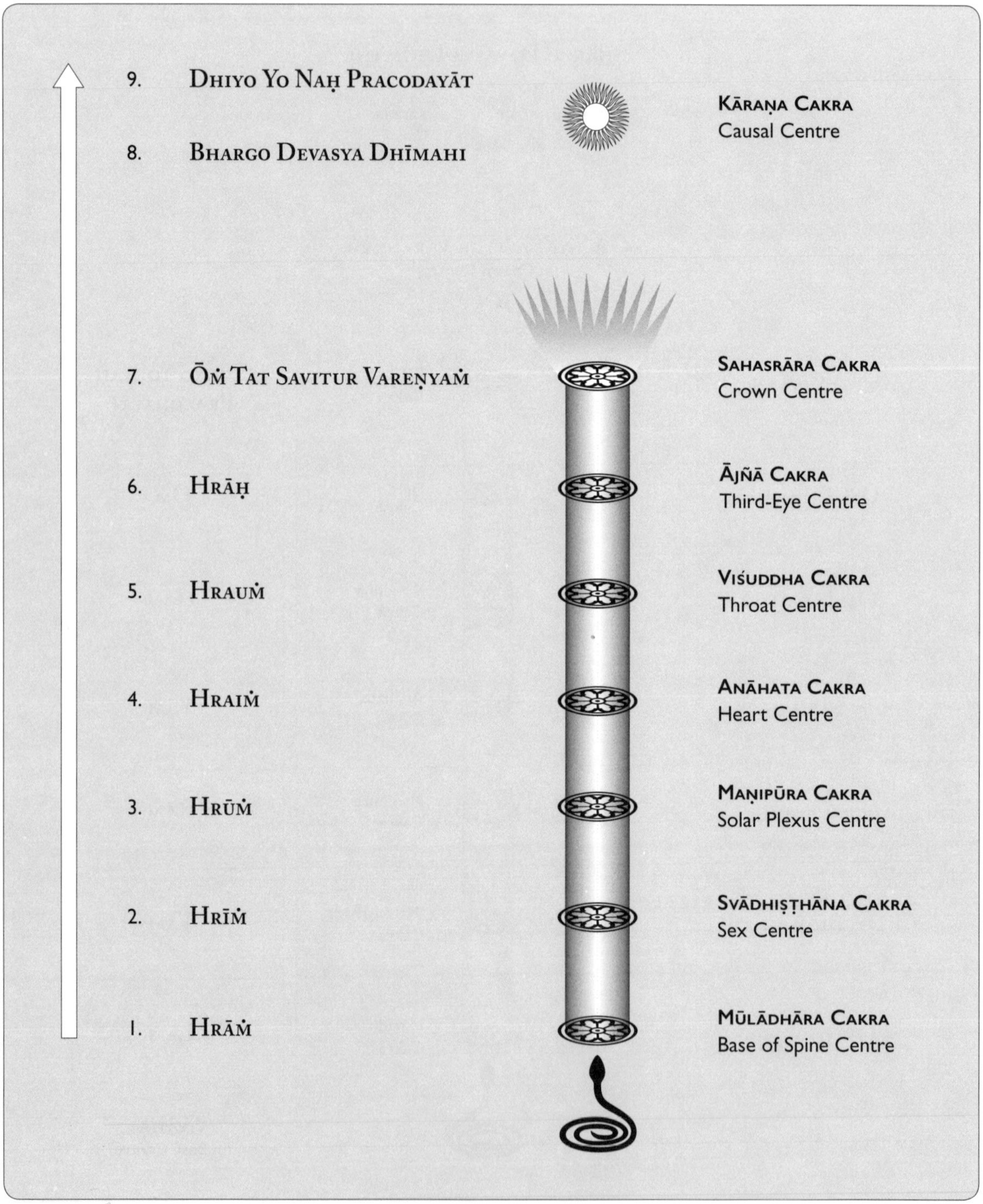
9. Dhiyo Yo Naḥ Pracodayāt
8. Bhargo Devasya Dhīmahi
Kāraṇa Cakra
Causal Centre
7. Ōṁ Tat Savitur Vareṇyaṁ
Sahasrāra Cakra
Crown Centre
6. Hrāḥ
Ājñā Cakra
Third-Eye Centre
5. Hrauṁ
Viśuddha Cakra
Throat Centre
4. Hraiṁ
Anāhata Cakra
Heart Centre
3. Hrūṁ
Maṇipūra Cakra
Solar Plexus Centre
2. Hrīṁ
Svādhiṣṭhāna Cakra
Sex Centre
1. Hrāṁ
Mūlādhāra Cakra
Base of Spine Centre

Solar Meditation in the Cakras

Duty and Spirituality

Sūrya Yoga resolves the Age-long conflict between Duty and Spirituality. For thousands of years, seekers who wanted to embrace the Spiritual Life abandoned home, family, worldly position and responsibility, and became monks, nuns, sādhus, sannyāsīs, yogīs, with no worldly cares or responsibilities. That was abandoning *Duty*.

Your life simply becomes Love practically expressed

The solution is found in Version C of the Gāyatrī-Mantra (see page 1613). The last four lines are:

May we know the Final-Truth,
Do our Duties,
We Journey to Your Highest Realm,
The Brahman-State.

In this the whole Path is given, including the correct resolution of the dilemmas of your life. Your whole life becomes the Spiritual Journey in which all things have a place. You seek for Final Truth while *at the same time doing all that needs to be done* towards yourself, your family, your work, your environment, your group, and the planet.

Your life simply becomes Love *practically* expressed. There is no such thing as impractical Love. Love always manifests in *doing* something for somebody. It is *inclusive* rather than exclusive. It includes others rather than abandoning them.

We understand Duty when we truly Love. ⸸

Return to Duty 812
Relational Consciousness 906
Family and Duty 998
Spiritual Life and Material Life 1118
On Love and Meditation 1140
Sādhanā: the Spiritual Life 1153
The Healing Sun Mantra 1599

CHAPTER 68

Works of Silence

The Eternal

Remember the Eternal and you will walk in Peace

The Eternal Sun shines through Time and Space with a Solitary Beam of Light.

The Brilliance of the Eternal Light pervades every atom of Space and every molecule of embodied existence.

That which the world can offer you passes away and you cannot hold on to it. But let your Heart dwell on the Imperishable Realm day and night and the Spirit will well up within you like a great Fountain of Calm.

In the great hustle and bustle of daily life, remember the Eternal and you will walk in Peace.

The noises of the outside world drown out the Whispers of Eternity. Listen carefully.

The Bright which encompasses all things has no beginning and no ending.

Seek you to know the Truth, which is beyond the corruption of all things that pass away, then *Be Still* in Wordless Adoration.

That which seeks the Truth within you is the Truth Itself.

The Spirit within you endures forever.

Listen to the Silence, it shall speak to you without words.

Revelation is continuous, for the Eternal never ceases to Speak, but It needs Listening Ears to hear It.

∞

The Self-Generating Light 1594
The Vision of your own Eternity 1144
Attach your Mind to the Eternal 1234
The State of Innocence 1306
The Kingdom is at Hand 1453
Revelation is Continuous 1710

Sūtrātma

Sūtrātma means "the Thread of the Spirit".

Sūtra: a thread, a line, a connection, a link, a verse, a statement.
Ātma: the Spirit.

Sūtrātma is the Line of Light, a Thread of Light that links the Monad, the Soul and the personality together.

Sūtrātma is the Light of the Spirit which works from above to below

On a lower level, your etheric-physical body is linked to your physical body by the Silver Cord, which is a cable of Ethereal Light. Once the cable snaps, your body dies. The Silver Cord is a lower reflection of Sūtrātma.

The Sūtrātma is made out of cables or tubes of Light.

Sūtrātma is the Light of the Spirit which works *from above to below*. It connects the Divine to the Soul, and the Soul to the personality.

Sūtrātma produces Alignment between Spirit, Soul, mind and body.

The Meditation

- Visualize, feel, see or sense the great Causal Centre (Kāraṇa Cakra), several feet above your head. At the Causal Centre there is an intense sphere of living Electric-White-Fire, which is Spirit-Light.
- See the Sūtrātma, a tube or cord of living White-Fire (Electric-Light), descend from the Causal Centre, through your Crown Centre and all the way down your spine.
- The Sūtrātma stands still like lightning that has been frozen. Hold steady.

∞

The Thread of the Self 491
The Final Astral Projection 401
The Future Evolution of Humanity 182

The Word, Logos, Voice, Name

1

God is Omniscient, Omnipotent, Omnipresent. God in the Transcendent Aspect is beyond our Space-Time sense, but God in the aspect of Creator, the LOGOS, the Word, the Name, has manifested the vast Universe in its many dimensions, realms, planes and expressions, including the physical "Space" of the Physical Plane of the Universe.

The Eternal-Word-of-God is incarnated in every man, woman and child

God is both Transcendent and Immanent. God is *in* all things, *within* all things, and is the *Source* of all things. Yet, as the Transcendental-Godhead, God is *beyond* all things, untouched by any created beings or things.

God created a multitude of Hierarchies, a series of Hosts of Intelligent Beings throughout the vast Cosmos, on all planes and in all worlds.

There is no limit to God's Ineffable Glory.

2

The Eternal-and-Living-Word is not a book. It is not the Old Testament, nor the New Testament, nor the Koran, nor the Upaniṣads, nor the Vedas, nor any of the scriptures. It is God-Incarnating, the Primeval Manifestation of God, the *Active Maker and Shaper* of Creation, the Primeval Form of God, Light-and-Sound-Currents, pervading the Whole of Creation.

3

The Eternal-Word-of-God, the Christ, is incarnated in every man, woman and child; in every plant, tree and herb; in every bird and animal and fish of the sea; in all the Stars, the Suns, the Solar Logoi; and in *You.*

God Immanent and Transcendent 111
The Logos: the Word of God 114
The Cosmic Christ 662
The Universal Christ 440
The Voice of God 864

4

NĀDA, the Creative-Word, the Logos, the Sound-Current, the Voice of Light, the Universal Reverberation of ŌṀ, the Primordial Tone or Vibration within the Universe, the Mystical Sound of the Eternal Godhead, is the *Divine Substance* that pervades the entire Universe, out of which the objective worlds are manifested by the Solar Logoi or Cosmic Creators, the ELOHĪM (Hebrew), the Suns.

The whole Universe is made out of the Name of God

Thus, the Word is also our Solar-Substance on the invisible planes, which becomes manifest in all that is visible, including *You.* You are made out of the Word; the Word was made into flesh; the Sounding-Light-Vibrations become You and the World.

5

Everything that exists is made by the Logos, the Creative-Thought-of-God. This Logos is not only Thought, but is also Light-Vibration and Life-Energy. Thus, all things are made of Light, and all things have Life within them. You have this Divine Light and Life within you, which is Sound.

6

You *see* with your Inner Eye the Name written in All-Space-Within, and you *hear* with your Inner Ear the Voice that Resounds therein.

7

The Word, the Logos, the Name of God (NĀMA), is a Vibration that can be *felt* within the physical body. It is characterized by Music, by Harmonious Vibrations. The whole Universe is made out of the Name of God, made out of Divine Music.

The Elohīm 120
The Descent of the Word 118
Children of the Sun 1590
What is the Name? 1259

8

The Voice of God, the Word (Śabda), is the *Life-impulse* within all beings, the Creative and Controlling Power of the Second Logos, Immanent in All. All the visible and invisible Universes are made by It. By *listening* to the Word *within yourself*, your mind becomes Still, your sorrows vanish, and Peace descends into your Heart.

By listening to the Word within yourself, your mind becomes Still

9

Śabda, the Word, the Logos, is the cause of all that exists in this vast Universe, in all the visible and invisible realms.

All differentiations are caused by this Śabda-Brahman (Sound-God, the Sounding-Absolute). On each plane of the Solar System, Śabda (Sounding-Light-Consciousness) arranges things differently. In each world, realm or region of the Universe, Śabda creates a different Vibration. All forms, no matter how gross or subtle, are constructed by It, by Sound-Vibration.

Śabda, the Word or Logos, the Sounding-Principle of the Godhead, is One. The Word becomes Threefold, then Sevenfold, then each of the Seven Vibrations subdivides into seven Subtones, and these divide into myriads of sounds, strains, melodies and harmonies. Thus, the Word becomes the Music of the Universe, the Symphony of the Cosmos. This can be *heard* by the Inner Ear, by the Soul, the Spirit, and the God-Self in Man.

The Solar Logos also is a God of Sound, a Sounding-God.

∞

To See,

To Hear,

To Remember,

To Rest.

These are the Works of Silence.

The Doctrine of the Logoi 116

The Creative and Destructive Power of Sound 201

The Name of the Deity 1032

Vibration and Mantra 1518

God's Cosmic Symphony

ŌṀ, ĀUṀ, AMEN, is the Cosmic Sound-Vibration, the Active Power of God, the Holy Spirit, the Immortal Creator, the Power of the Supreme Being, NĀDA, ŚABDA-BRAHMAN (Sounding-God), the Voice, the Name, the Logos, the Word, the Link between God the Father (the Absolute) and Creation, the ANĀHATA-ŚABDA (the unproduced Sound, the Original Celestial Music).

This Cosmic Sound-Vibration (the Name) creates, maintains and dissolves the Universe—the entire visible and invisible realms. The Creation is an expression of the Thought of God (the Logos) made manifest through Sound-Light-Vibrations. Thus, Creation is the direct expression of God the Holy Spirit through Sounding-Light-Vibrations. It is God's Cosmic Symphony.

The basic Tone of this Cosmic Symphony is like the Roar of the Cosmic Ocean

The basic Tone of this Cosmic Symphony is like the Roar of the Cosmic Ocean as the Spirit of God moves over the Cosmic Ocean of Matter out of which the worlds are made.

- First we *see* the Name as Light in the Third-Eye, in the Crown Centre or in the Heart.
- First we *hear* the Name in the Heart, in the Third-Eye, in the Crown Centre, or in the Medulla Oblongata Centre (at the back of the neck).
- Then we learn to see the Light with the physical eyes wide open, and we hear the Cosmic Roar of the Name, day and night, always.

∞

God has three Persons or Aspects:

a. The Absolute, Unmanifested, Boundless Being, outside and above Creation, symbolized by the word "Father".

b. God within Creation, the Christ, a reflection of the Unmanifest Absolute, symbolized by the word "Son".

c. The Activating Force of God, the "Holy Spirit".

The Holy Trinity 1342

Āuṁ, Ōṁ, Nāda 550
The Three-Faced God 113
The Action of the Primordial Sound 165
Āuṁ: the Holy Spirit as Cosmic Mother 1501

See the Light of the Logos

Simply become the Eye that Sees whatever is before you

Before your Inner Eye can *See* the Light of the Logos, Harmony must be established within you.

- Sit in Silence.
- With your eyes closed, gaze steadily before you with your Third-Eye, the Single-Eye (between the two physical eyes). Do not try to look with your physical eyes.
- There should be no thinking, visualizing, daydreaming or imagining. Simply gaze with your Inner Eye, *into* what is before you—darkness, light, star, sun, moon, eye, colours, indigo blue, or whatever.
- Forget about your physical body and your outside environment. The Physical World, the Physical Plane, the Physical Universe, is MAHĀ-MĀYĀ, a Great Illusion.
- It is the Inner Eye that sees the Darkness. It is also the Inner Eye that sees the Light.
- Do not strain the eyes or the forehead. Do not "will" to see. Simply *become* the Eye that Sees whatever is before you.
- There must be no effort, but a simple gaze. Just sit at the Inner Door (the Third-Eye, the Single-Eye) and wait patiently. Be not anxious or impatient, but relaxed and fully alert.
- Fixing the Inner Gaze into the Darkness behind the physical eyes, or fastening it upon the Light (when it appears), is withdrawing your Consciousness from your physical body and the Physical World.

∞

The Path of Seeing 552
Quietly Seeing 786
Meditation in the Third-Eye 1224
Look for the Light 1395

Hear the Sound within the Silence

Before you can *Hear* the Voice within the Silence, the Sound within the Silence, the ears of your physical body must cease to hear all external sounds, and the Ears of your Soul must be opened.

Listening to the Logos, the Nāda, the Word, the Voice or Sound within Silence, the Spiritual Sound, the Music of the Spheres, will enable you to ascend upwards upon the Planes of Being, ascend in the Inner Worlds to the highest plane, that of the Logos.

Listening to the Logos will enable you to ascend upwards upon the Planes of Being

This Universal Life-Current, the Audible Life-Stream, can be heard within the Heart Centre. Or you can listen to It with your Inner Ear, on the right hand side. Then later you will hear It inside your head, and later above your head.

It is also known as the Sound-Current, God-in-Creation, the Elixir of Life, the Active Power of God, God the Holy Spirit.

Do not try to use your physical ears to hear It. Nor try to see It. Just *Listen.* There must be no thinking, no imagining, just *Listening.* There are many sounds or tones within the Sound-Current.

After the Cosmic Thunder Sound comes the *true* Silence, the Source of all the other subtle sounds, and in *that* Silence God *speaks* to you face-to-face.

The Path of Hearing 553
Listen to Nāda 1212
Meditation on the Sacred Word 1216
The Silence of the Deep 1355

∞

The Sounds of Nāda

The various sounds of Nāda (the subtle inner sounds) or Śabda-Brahman (the Word, the Logos) that you hear with your Inner Ear, the Ears of your Soul, are also called Anāhata-Śabda (unstruck, unplucked, unproduced sounds, that is, not-physically-produced sounds). These are various Vibrations of the Cosmic Ōṁ Sound, and they can *resemble* certain physical sounds.

For example: nightingale, ocean-sprite or sea-shell sounds, flute, bamboo flute, vīnā, cymbals, trumpet blasts, conch sounds, mridanga (double drum), kettle drums, heavy drums, thunder and lightning, rumbling thunder, a great gong or bell, little bells, harps, humming bees, rushing waters, flowing or gurgling waters, the sound of many waters, a great ocean roaring, angelic choirs singing, the onomatopoeic sounds (such as Cinī and Ciñcinī), string instruments, clapping or flapping sounds, or a symphony of many sounds.

These are *not* physical sounds. All these are the Cosmic Reverberations of the Cosmic Ōṁ Sound, the Creative-Word, the Logos, the Name.

Cosmic Tuning-In: the 'I' Sound

This is a work of your Consciousness, not of your mind

- Sit still, in your meditational posture. Focus your attention in your head. There, internally sing or intone the **I** sound on the note you feel is best for you at this time. Sound the note continuously in your head, unendingly, *sweetly*, almost as a *memory* rather than "hard" singing. Intone the **I** sound as if it were a memory only.
- If you do not hear any inner subtle sounds, NĀDA, focus your mind into the **I** sound, and then dissolve it.
- If you do hear inner sounds as described above (such as flute, harp, flowing waters, crickets, bird-songs or bees humming), adjust your **I** sound to that vibration. Once you hear one inner sound, and can tune into it with your **I** sound, and can dissolve your mind into that sound, then listen for another sound, a subtler sound, harder to hear, and repeat the same process, adjusting your **I** sound to it and dissolving your mind into it.
- You can meditate in the same way in your Heart Centre. Intone the **I** sound there, listen to the inner sounds, and attune your Consciousness to the sounds that you hear in the Heart.

This is a work of your Consciousness, not of your mind (not of thoughts).

The true **I** sound reverberates in the Head and resounds in the Heart.

The Universal **I** sound is the Universal Vibration, the foundation of all that is, and the Cause of all that is.

You can intone your **I** sound and hear the Universal **I** sound in your astral body, or mental body, or causal body.

The **I** sound that you sing with your voice in your physical body is different from the **I** sound that you sing with the Voice of your Soul, the Voice of Silence.

The **I** sound is the Vibration of Existence, of Be-ness, Being, Life.

In the upper regions of the Universe the **I** sound is a Cosmic Chant or Choir, Sounding-Light and Singing-Colours.

The **I** sound is Sound and Colour, Tone and Vibration and Light at the same time, as well as Darkness.

The Vowels 1030
The Vowels in the Heart 1303
From Darkness into Light 982

Darkness is Invisible Light.
Silence is Unheard Sound.

Remember the Presence

Before you can *Remember* Who you truly are, your mind must be dissolved in the Sound-Current, the Word, the Logos, Who Speaks in Silence.

- Sit still, focused in the Third-Eye Centre.
- Remember the Presence of God all around you in the form of the Silent Speaker (the Word, the Logos), and the Presence of the Divine Teacher within you, Ātman, the Spirit.
- As you Remember the Presence, repeat the Ōṁ Mantra in the Third-Eye Centre. Or, if you have received the Five-Words Initiation, you may repeat the Five-Words Mantra.
- The important point is *Remembering*. God dwells in the Repetition (Japa) of the Mantra.
- Repeat the Ōṁ Mantra, or the Five-Words Mantra, *slowly*, at intervals, in Silence, and with your mind only.

Remember the Presence of God all around you in the form of the Silent Speaker

This Repetition of the Mantra in the Third-Eye Centre, slowly, deliberately, with full alertness, at intervals, will draw all the Life-energies from the physical body into the Third-Eye Centre. When you have entered the Third-Eye you will lose consciousness of your body. You will also hear the Voice of the Silence resounding within you. Then your mind will merge with Ōṁ (the Soundless-Sound), and you will *know* that you are not the physical body, but an Immortal Spirit, and you will be enveloped in Bliss-Consciousness.

∞

Meditation in the Third-Eye 1224
Practising the Presence of God 711
To Realize the Presence of God 1398
Meditation on the Holy Spirit 1344

Rest in the Great Breath

The Word, the Logos, the Divine Name, is also the Great Breath, the Breath of God.

The Logos is also the Great Breath, the Breath of God

a. Focus your attention in the Solar Plexus Centre:

	breathe in	*breathe out*
	SAḤ	HAṀ
or:	SŌH	HĀNG

Keep your attention in the Solar Plexus throughout the breathing.

b. Focus your attention in the Third-Eye Centre, or on the air as it comes in at the tip of the nose:

	breathe in	*breathe out*
	HAṀ	SAḤ
or:	HŌNG	SAU (Sow)

KHE-CHARI: the attention rests in the Third-Eye Centre: skyward, upward.

BHU-CHARI: the attention rests at the tip of the nose: earthward, downward.

c. Rest your attention in the Heart Centre:

	breathe out	*breathe in*
	HAṀ	SA
or:	HĀNG	SAḤ

Keep your attention in the Heart Centre all the time.

∞

The Breath of the Divine Mother 142
The Holy Breath 1340
Conscious Breathing in the Heart 1274
Gāyatrī (Sun) Breathing 1553

Haṁ stands for Ahaṁ ('Haṁ): "I Am".

Sa stands for Him, That, It—that is, the Absolute, the Godhead.

Haṁsa means "I am the Absolute" or "I am one with the All, the Complete Universe".

Haṁsa means the Swan, a symbol for Pure Spirit.

The Sound Haṁsaḥ is the Breath of the Spirit.

Ha, Haṁ, is the Male Creative Aspect of Consciousness.

Sa, Saḥ, is the Female Creative Aspect of Consciousness.

Haṁsa is the Sun, the Solar Logos, the Spiritual Sun, who is Male-Female.

Saḥ-Ahaṁ, God I am, That (the Absolute) I Am, becomes:

So'Haṁ (So-'Haṁ).

So: He.

Ahaṁ: I Am, or That (Male-Female) I Am.

Kāla-Haṁsa: Time-Bird, Eternal Duration, the Everlastingness of the Great Breath of God.

Haṁsa: the individual Immortal Spirit or Soul.

Paramahaṁsa: the Transcendental or Supreme Soul or Spirit within the Universe, that is, the Omnipresent Spirit of God.

Haṁsa is Haṁ-Sa-Haṁ-Sa, the continual inbreathing and out-breathing of the Universe, the Breath of Spirit in all things, and the flow of Prāṇa (the Life-force) in and out of the Microcosm (Man).

Haṁsa is Ātman, the Pure Spirit within you.

Paramahaṁsa is Paramātman, the Transcendental Godhead.

∞

Awareness Meditation

- Sit still, with your eyes closed. Focus nowhere in particular. Just become Aware of what is going on inside and outside you. Receive the sensations but do nothing about them. Register physical sensations, thoughts, feelings, external sounds, inner and outer space, and so on. Just be generally *Aware.*
- Focus your Attention in the Base Centre, at the bottom of the spine. There, sit still, just Being, doing nothing. Let go of everything and *Just Be.*
- Focus your Attention in the Solar Plexus Centre. Be still, tranquil. Observe all the feelings and emotions that come up. Observe but no not engage in them. Sit still. They will subside and disappear.
- Focus your Awareness in the Third-Eye Centre. Sit still. Be tranquil, relaxed. Observe all the thoughts and mental impressions as they come up—past memories, future expectations, or whatever. Do not engage in them. Do not follow through with them. *Just be still.* They will subside and fall away.
- With your Attention resting in the Heart Centre, watch the Breath of Life. Do nothing, just watch the Breath.

  a. First you will notice only the outer breath as it comes in and leaves the physical body.
  b. Then you will become Aware of the Inner Breath, that which is beyond physical breath.
  c. At a later stage you will become Aware of the Breath of Life, and you will become inwardly Immortal.

  Just watch the Breath, that is all.

∞

The Fundamental Change is a Change in Consciousness

The Fundamental Change is a *Change in Consciousness.*

Consciousness is above body, emotions and mind.

Consciousness operates these, but it is singular and unique to Itself.

Mindfulness of Breathing 794
Vipaśyanā Yoga: Internal Observation 1222
What is Consciousness? 1368

CHAPTER 69

Salutations to the Sun

More Mantras to Sūrya, the Sun

I

ŌṀ SŪRYĀYA HṚDAYĀYA NAMAHA

a. I invoke the Sun in my Heart.

b. I invoke the Heart of the Sun.

The Mystery of the Sun 1585
The Gāyatrī-Mantra 1601
How to Meditate on the Sun 1606

∞

SŪRYA, the Sun-God, the Solar Logos, is also known as:

SAVITĀ

SAVITṚ (SAVITRI)

ĪŚVARA

VIṢṆU

SŪRYA-NĀRĀYAṆA

NĀRĀYAṆA

AGNI (the Fire-God)

ĀDITYA (the Sun)

ĀTMAN (the Self)

SŪRYA stands for Light, Boundless Light, Limitless Light, Inter-Cosmic Light, Solar-Systemic Light, Light on the various planes or levels of Being, the Light of Love, the Light of Intelligence, the Unmanifest Light, and the Light of Evolution.

SŪRYA, SAVITĀ, means the Stimulator, Enlightener, Illuminator, Inspirer, Guide, Awakener-Light-of-God, the Solar Logos, the Being-within-the-Sun, the Sun-God, the Energizer, Life-giver, Rouser, Impeller, Vivifier.

As VIVASVATA (VIVASVĀN) He is the Brilliant-Light, the Shining-Splendour, the Diffuser-of-Light.

Another name for the Solar Logos is MĀRTAṆḌA: He who was born from the Cosmic-Egg (Space).

He is also called DEVA: Shining, Light, Deity, God, Divine, Divinity.

He is also ĪŚA: the Lord-God, the Lord of the Universe, the Lord of all the Hosts of Beings.

Being in tune with the Sun, chanting, singing, and meditating on the Sun, will fill you with health, healing, energy, vitality, equilibrium and balance. The Sun is the great Source of Positivity in your life, driving away all shadows.

2

Sūryam Sundara Loka Nātham
Amṛtam Vedānta Sāram Śivam

Who bringeth forth the Light, the Beautiful Lord of the World,
Who is Immortal, the Essence of all Knowledge, Who is Pure.

Sūrya: the Logos; Who produces Light.

Sundara: beautiful.

Loka: the World.

Nātha: Lord, God.

Amṛtam: Immortal.

Vedānta: the Final or Great Illumination (Veda: Gnosis, Illumination; Anta: final, the end).

Sāram: essence.

Śivam: pure, auspicious, good.

3

Jñānam Brahmamayam Sureśam
Amalam Lokaika Cittam Svāyam

Who is Knowledge, Whose very nature is God-hood,
Who is Lord of all the gods and goddesses,
Immaculate, the World-Soul, Self-Existent.

Jñānam: Who is Knowledge, Gnosis, Enlightenment.

Brahmamayam: Brahma: God, Divinity; Mayam: made out of.

Sureśam: Ruler of all the Spiritual-Hierarchies of Being (Sura: gods, Divine Hierarchies, such as angels, archangels, Devas, Spiritual-Entities; Īśa: God, Lord, Ruler, Commander).

Amalam: Immaculately-Pure-in-Being.

Lokaika: of the World.

Cittam: Consciousness, Soul, Mind.

Svāyam: itself, himself, by himself.

Sūryam Sundara Loka Nātham

4

Indrāditya Narādhipam Sura Gurum
Trailokya Cūḍāmaṇīm

The Powerful Sun-God, Ruler of men and gods, the Teacher of the Spiritual Entities, the Greatest Jewel within the Three Worlds of Being (the Physical, Astral and Causal Universes).

Indrāditya: Indra: powerful, mighty, the Chief of all the Celestial Hosts and Hierarchies; Āditya: the Sun-God, the Light-Being whose outer dense body is the physical Solar System.

Narādhipam: Nara: the species of Man, humanoids, Mankind; also, leader; also, the One-Self or Ātman; Adhi: superior or virtuous; Adhipam: superior species.

Sura: Celestial Hierarchies, Angelic Beings.

Gurum (Guru): Teacher, Leader, Guide.

Trailokya: of the Three (Trai) Worlds (Lokya).

Cūḍāmaṇīm: Cūḍā: crest, peak, top, most significant; Maṇi: jewel.

5

Brahmā Viṣṇu Śiva Svarūpa Hṛdayam
Vande Sadā Bhāskaram

The Creator-Power, the All-Pervading Energy, the Excellent Force, the very Nature of the Heart [the Heart of Man and of the Sun], we worship that Eternal Light-Maker.

Brahmā: the Creative Power.

Viṣṇu: the All-Pervading Force.

Śiva: the Beneficent.

Svarūpa: one's own True-Form.

Hṛdayam: the Heart.

Vande: worship, adoration.

Sadā: eternal.

Bhāskaram: Light-producer, Light-maker.

6

Ōṁ Tat Savitur Brahmātmane Hṛdayāya Namaḥ
That Spiritual-Sun, the Heart of God, we worship.

Tat Savitur: that Solar Logos.

Brahmātmane: Brahma: God; Ātmā: the Essential Nature of God.

Hṛdayāya: belonging to the Heart.

7

Ōṁ Mitra Ravi Sūrya Bhānu Khaga Pūṣan
Hiraṇyagarbha Marīcyāditya
Savitrarka Bhāskarebhyo
Namo Namaḥ

Salutation to the Divine-Companion, the Sun, the Being-within-the-Sun, the Light-of-Glory, He who moves through Space, the Nourisher and Protector, the Golden-Womb, the Glowing Sphere of Light, Creative Power, the Life-Giving Power, the Divine-Fire, He who Illumines the World.

Mitra: friend and companion.

Ravi: the Sun in totality on all Planes.

Sūrya: the Powerful-Lord-within-the-Sun.

Bhānu: the Glorious Light of the Inner-Sun.

Khaga: moving through Cosmic Space.

Pūṣan: Nourisher and Protector.

Hiraṇyagarbha: Hiraṇya: golden, most-precious; Garbha: womb, source.

Marīcyāditya: Marīci: glowing, raying out Light-Waves; Āditya (Ādita): the Primordial Solar Logos, the Original-Creative-Force.

Savitṛ: the Solar-Dynamic-Energy-of-Life.

Arka: the Fire of Creation.

Bhāskara: the Radiating-Source-of-Light.

Namo, Namaḥ: we salute, we invoke, we give praise to, we honour, we bow down to.

Ōṁ Mitra Ravi Sūrya

8

Ōṁ Śrī Savitre
Sūrya Nārāyaṇāya Namaḥ
To the Holy Sun-God, the Spirit-Filled-Solar-Deity, Salutations.

Śrī Savitṛ: Śrī: lustrous, bright, shining, luminous; Savitṛ: Sun-God.

Sūrya Nārāyaṇa: Sūrya: the Solar-God; Nārāyaṇa: the Holy Spirit, the Eternal-Spirit-pervading-the-Universe.

Namaḥ: offering, salutation, homage to, praise.

9

Ōṁ Śrī Mahimā Ātmane Namaḥ
Ōṁ Savitre Namaḥ
Salutation to the Illimitable Glory of the Spiritual-Self.
Salutation to the Sun.

Śrī: Glory, Holiness.

Mahimā: Glory, Limitlessness, Majesty.

Ātman: the Spiritual-Self.

Savitā: the Sun.

Namaḥ: Salutation.

10

Ōṁ Śrī Sarvajñāya Namaḥ
Ōṁ Savitre Namaḥ
Salutation to the Omniscient Holy One.
Salutation to the Sun.

Sarva-Jñāna: All-Knowing, Omniscient.

11

Ōṁ Śrī Satpuruṣāya Namaḥ
Ōṁ Savitre Namaḥ

Salutation to the Holy Eternal Godhead.
Salutation to the Sun.

Sat-Puruṣa: the Everlasting-Lord.

12

Ōṁ Śrī Varadāya Namaḥ
Ōṁ Savitre Namaḥ

Salutation to the Giver-of-all-Blessings.
Salutation to the Sun.

Vara-Da: all-benefits-giver.

13

Ōṁ Śrī Sarva-Īśāya Namaḥ
Ōṁ Savitre Namaḥ

Salutation to the Lord of the Universe.
Salutation to the Sun.

Sarva-Īśa (Sarveṣa): the Lord of the Universe, the All-Lord, the Logos, the Lord of the Solar System.

14

Ōṁ Agnaye Namaḥ

Salutation to the Divine-Fire.

Agni: the Sacred-Fire within the Sun or Solar Logos, and within the Universe. Agni is also the Light of Knowledge or Enlightenment produced by the Sun.

Ōṁ Agnaye Namaḥ

15

Ōṁ Nirṛtaye Namaḥ Sūrya

Salutation to the Shining-Sun.
Salutation to the Sun-who-overcomes-the-Angel-of-Death.

16

Ōṁ Īśanāya Namaḥ Sūrya

Salutation to the Ruler of the Solar System and the Ruler of the Human Heart.

Salutation to the Solar Logos who has Dominion over everything within His Solar System.

Īśa: Lord, God, Ruler of the Universe and the Solar System and the Heart. Īśa is God who energizes, impels, directs, and makes Fertile all things.

17

Antarjyotir	Bahirjyotiḥ
Pratyagjyotiḥ	Parātparaḥ
Jyotirjyotiś	Svāyamjyotir
Ātmajyotiś	Sūrya Namaḥ

We salute the Sun who is the Inner-Light, Outer-Light,
Inward-Light, the Highest,
the Light of Lights, the Self-Light,
the Light of the Self.

Antar-Jyoti: Inner-Light.

Bahir-Jyoti: Outer-Light.

Pratyag-Jyoti: Inward-Light.

Parāt-Para: higher than the Highest.

Jyotir-Jyotiś: the Light of Lights.

Svāyam-Jyoti: the Self-Existing Light.

Ātma-Jyoti: the Light of the Spirit.

18

Ātmajyotir Manojyotir
Jyotiś Cakśuśā Paśyati
Sābāhyābhyāntara Jyotiḥ
Sa-Jyotiḥ Sūrya Namaḥ

We salute the Sun who is the Light of the Soul, the Light of the Mind,
The Light that sees through the human eyes,
Inner and outer Light,
Who is always with Light.

Ātma-Jyoti: the Light of the Soul.

Mano-Jyoti: the Light of the Mind.

Jyotiś: Light.

Cakśuśā: of the eyes.

Paśyati: sees.

Sābāhyābhyāntara: inner and outer.

Jyoti: Light.

Sa-Jyoti: with Light.

Sūrya: the Solar Logos.

Namaḥ: veneration, worship, offering, homage.

19

Ōṁ Vivasvate Namaḥ

Salutation to the Brilliant-Sun.

Vivasvata: the Spiritual-Sun shining brilliantly in the Nirvāṇic and other higher Spheres; shining forth, giving out Light.

20

a. **Ōṁ Sūryāya Namaḥ**
b. **Ōṁ Sūryaye Namaḥ**

Salutation to the Sun-God, the Light of the World.

Sūrya: the Sun, the Solar Logos.

Namaḥ: Salutations.

21

Ōṁ Savitre Sarva Siddhi Pradāya Namaḥ

We Surrender to the Sun-God who gives all powers, faculties and accomplishments.

Savitṛ: the Glorious Being within the Sun.

Sarva: all, everything.

Siddhi: powers, accomplishments (material, psychic, occult or spiritual), fulfilment, success, skills, capabilities, talents.

Prada: the Giver, the Bestower.

Namaḥ: surrender, obeisance, reverence.

22

Ōṁ Savitre Yogaiśvarāya Namaḥ

We salute the Sun-God who is the Master of Yoga (Divine Union with the Absolute).

Savitṛ: the Solar Logos.

Yoga: skill, union, conjunction, application, means.

Īśvara: Master, Ruler, Lord.

23

Ōṁ Savitre Avyakta Rūpine Namaḥ

We salute the Sun who is in the Form of the Unmanifest.

Savitṛ: the Sun.

Avyakta: the Unmanifested, the Primordial State from whence issues forth Manifestation or Creation.

Rūpa: form, manifestation, body, embodiment.

24

Ōṅg Haṅgsa Sōhaṅg Svāhā
Ōṅg Tat Sat Bramhā
Ōṅg Śāntiḥ Śāntiḥ Śāntiḥ Svāhā

We invoke the Supreme-Spirit, the Breath-of-Life, our Offerings,
We invoke the Indescribable-Reality, the Absolute-Truth, who is also the Creator-God,
May Tranquillity be everywhere, our Offerings.

Ōṁ is Praṇava (Prāṇa-Va): the Essence of Life; Brahman: the Ultimate Essence, the Final Reality, the Godhead; and Brahmā: the Creator-God; and Brahma: God.

Haṁsa, Hansa, Haṅgsa: the Supreme Spirit, the Divine-Creative-Breath, the Breath of God, the Human Soul, the Purified Yogī, One who can function in Spiritual Consciousness.

Sōhaṁ, Sōhan, Sōhaṅg: the same as above (Haṁsa).

Svāhā: outbreathing, outpouring, sacrifice.

Tat: That, the Indescribable-Absolute, the Spiritual-Sun, the Unnameable.

Sat, Sata: the Everlasting, the Eternal.

Brahmā (Bramhā): the Creator as the Solar Logos, or a Cosmic Logos.

Śāntiḥ (Shāntiḥ): Peace, Tranquillity.

25

Ōṁ Agnir Jyotir
Jyotir Agniḥ Svāhā
We unite with Fire and Light.

Agni: the Divine Fire.

Jyoti: the Divine Light.

Svāhā: we unite with, we dissolve in.

The Fire of the Sun is the Divine Light. The Divine Light is the Fire of the Sun.

Ōṁ Sūryo Jyotir

26

Ōṁ Sūryo Jyotir
Jyotiḥ Sūryaḥ Svāhā
We unite with the Sun and the Light.

Sūrya: the Sun.

Jyoti: the Divine Light.

Svāhā: we unite with.

The Sun is the Divine Light, the Divine Light is the Sun.

27

Ōṁ Jyotiḥ Sūryaḥ
Sūryo Jyotiḥ Svāhā
We dissolve in the Sun.

Sūrya: the Sun.

Jyoti: the Pure Light.

Svāhā: we dissolve in.

The Pure Light is the Sun-shine, the Sun-shine is the Pure Light.

28

Ōṁ Agnirjyotī Agnirdevatā
Sūryo Devatā Svāhā
We dissolve in the Shining Sun.

Agni: the Divine Fire, the Fire of the Sun.

Devatā: the Shining Divinity, Fiery-Light, Shining Fire-God, Spiritual-Sun.

29

Ōṁ Āpo Jyotī
Rasomṛtaṁ Brahmā
Bhūr Bhuvas Suvar Ōṁ

May the Luminous Waters of Solar Light,
filled with God's Nectar of Immortality,
Illumine the Physical, Subtle and Heaven Worlds.

Āpas: water.

Jyoti: Light.

Rasa: nectar, essence.

Amṛta: immortal.

Brahmā: God, the Solar Logos.

30

Ōṁ Sūrya Tat Paramam Padam Svāhā

We unite with the Spiritual Sun, the Highest State of Life.

Sūrya: the Sun, the Solar-God.

Tat: That.

Paramam: supreme.

Padam: station, a state of Being.

Svāhā: we dissolve in.

31

Śāntiḥ Śāntiḥ Sarva Śāntiḥ
Sā Mā Śāntiḥ Śāntibhi
Brahma Śāntiḥ Devāḥ Śāntiḥ
Ōṁ Śāntiḥ Śāntiḥ Śāntihi

Harmony, Harmony, All-Harmony,
Balanced-Harmony, By Harmony,
Divine-Harmony, Shining-Harmony,
Spiritual-Harmony, Harmony, Harmony.

The Sun as the Source of all Harmony.

Śāntiḥ Śāntiḥ Sarva Śāntiḥ

32

Ōṁ Haṁsāya Vidmahe
Paramahaṁsāya Dhīmahi
Tanno Haṁsāḥ Pracodayāt

May we Realize the Sun as the Spirit within us,
Let us meditate on the Light of the Supreme Self,
May that Spirit Enlighten us.

Ōṁ: the Universal Spirit.

Haṁsa: the Spiritual Soul, the Spiritual Self within us, a particle of the Sun.

Vidmahe: may we Realize.

Paramahaṁsa: the Supreme Self, the Glorious Spiritual Sun.

Dhīmahi: let us meditate.

Tanno Haṁsa: may that Spirit of the Sun.

Pracodayāt: Illumine us.

33

Ōṁ Bhāskarāya Vidmahe
Divākarāya Dhīmahi
Tanno Sūryaḥ Pracodayāt

May we Realize the Shining One,
Let us meditate on the Light-maker,
May that Sun-God Illumine us.

Bhās-kara: Light-maker, Shining.

Divā-kara: Day-maker, Light-producer.

Sūrya: the Solar Logos, the Sun, the great Cosmic Being whose body is the Solar System and who represents for us the Ineffable Light of the Absolute.

34

Ōṁ Vaiśvānarāya Vidmahe
Lālelāya Dhīmahi
Tanno Agniḥ Pracodayāt

May we Realize the God who is Fire,
Let us meditate on the seven-tongued Mystic Fire,
May that Fire-God illumine us.

Vaiśvānara: the Fire-God, God as the Divine Fire aspect.

Lālelāya: the seven-tongued Mystic Flame of the Holy Spirit (the God of Fire).

Agniḥ: God in the aspect of Fire.

Vidmahe: may we Realize, may we Know.

Dhīmahi: we meditate, contemplate.

Tanno: that.

Pracodayāt: impel, stimulate.

35

Ōṁ Divākarāya Vidmahe
Prabhākarāya Dhīmahi
Tanno Ādityaḥ Pracodayāt

May we Realize the Light of God,
Let us meditate on the Light-maker,
May that Spiritual Sun illumine us.

Divākara: Day-maker, that is, the Sun.

Prabhākara: Light-maker.

Āditya: the Golden Being residing in the Sun.

Ōṁ Namo Nārāyaṇāya

36

Ōṁ Namo Nārāyaṇāya
Salutation to the Spiritual Sun.

Namo: salutation.

Nārāyaṇa: the Spirit.

37

Ōṁ Nārāyaṇāya Vidmahe
Vāsudevāya Dhīmahi
Tanno Viṣṇuḥ Pracodayāt
May we Realize the Spiritual Sun,
Let us meditate on the Indwelling Spirit,
May the All-Pervading God illumine us.

Nārāyaṇa is the Universal Sunshine of the Spirit, the Universal Sun. It gives Universal Love, Compassion and Wisdom, infinite Power, Majesty, Glory and Radiance. It brings into us Happiness and Joy. Nārāyaṇa is the Great Circle of the Sun. It confers upon us total Liberation and Freedom, and includes and balances out all opposites.

Vasudeva: Vasu: indwelling; Deva: God.

Viṣṇu: the all-pervading, all-penetrating God.

38

Ōṁ Hiraṇyagarbhāya Namaha
We salute the Cosmic Sun.

Hiraṇya: golden, golden Light.

Garbha: a womb, source, origin, embryo, primal condition.

Hiraṇyagarbha is the Cosmic Sun, the Creator, as the very Self of the Universe and each one of us.

39

Ōṁ Savitre Namaha

We salute the Sun as the Producer of everything.

Savitur: the Sun-God as the Father-Mother of all living beings.

40

Ōṁ Ravaye Namaha

We salute the Being within the Sun.

Ravi: the Self of the Sun who absorbs all within Himself.

41

Ōṁ Pūṣṇe Namaha

We salute the Lord of the Sun who nourishes all.

Pūṣan: the Sun-God who nourishes and sustains all Life.

42

Ōṁ Sūryāya Namaha

We salute the Sun which gives power, energy and active force.

Sūrya: the Being within the Sun who impels all beings to activity.

43

Ōṁ Bhagavan

We salute the Sun-Lord who dispenses all good fortunes.

Bhaga-van: fortune-having, that is, the giver of glory, splendour, knowledge, wealth, virtue and power.

Ōṁ Bhagavan

ŌṀ KHAGĀYA NAMAHA

44

ŌṀ BHĀNAVE NAMAHA
We salute the Lord of Illumination.

BHĀNAVA: the giver of Light.

45

ŌṀ BHĀSKARĀYA NAMAHA
We salute the Shining One.

BHĀSKARA: the Radiant Spirit within the Sun.

46

ŌṀ MITRĀYA NAMAHA
We salute the Solar Deity who is a friend to all.

MITRA: a friend or benefactor to all.

47

ŌṀ MARICĀYE NAMAHA
We salute the Sun who releases Rays of Light.

MARICA: Rays of Light.

48

ŌṀ KHAGĀYA NAMAHA
We salute the Sun-Lord who moves through Space.

KHAGA: the Sun (KHA: space, sky; GA: moving, going).

∞

The Activity of the Divine Heart

The Sun is the Heart of Love. Love is the nature of Divinity. God is Love.

Love is a mighty Current of Attractive Energy that pours out of the Heart of the Sun through the Buddhic Plane of our Solar System, the Bliss World, wherein is found the Christ-Hierarchy.

Love is an Energy Source of Limitless Foundation

In the Human Microcosm the Energy of Love registers in the Heart Centre.

In the Cosmos, Love is a Mighty Power, a Universal Gravitational Field or Universal Attractive Energy which keeps the Galaxies, Star-Systems and Suns to their ordained patterns.

Love is God's Incarnate Energy. It is the Radiance of the Universal Logos, the Absolute, the Godhead, focused through the Stars, the Suns, the Children of God.

Love is a Creative Power, born of Light and Fire.

Love is the Logos, the Word made Manifest.

Love is the Power to Heal, to Bless, to Give.

Love is an Energy Source of Limitless Foundation.

Love is the Song of God expressed in kindly deeds.

Love is the Origin and the Goal of all evolving Entities.

Love is the Activity of the Divine Heart. ≮

The Solar Dharma 163
The Universal Heart 436
The Perennial Source of Love 438
The Christ-Hierarchy and Śamballa 396
The Revelation of God 854
The Heart of the Solar Logos 1327
The Solar and Human Heart 1592

PART FOURTEEN

The Path of Service

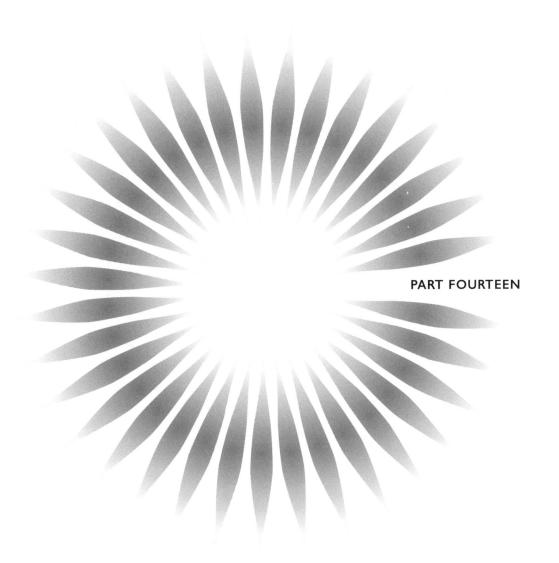

CHAPTER 70

Buddhi Yoga
Liberation by Wisdom

The Essence of Wisdom

The Root of your Mind is Being

Wisdom is Active Love permeated by Understanding.

God is a totally Free and Self-Existent Being: *Indestructible Light.*

The Self and God are One and the Same *Radiant Divine Being.*

The Self is Pure Consciousness, Bodiless Consciousness, Formless Consciousness. THAT You are.

The Root of your Mind is Being.

Being can be known only by Itself; hence you must *transcend* your mind until you become wholly *Light.*

Being (the Self, God, Truth) is *above* your mind, beyond words, logic, reasoning, analysis, arguments, comparisons, criticisms, theories, opinions or learned discourses. It is the Truth.

The Self is Transcendental Bliss-Consciousness and Pure Love. THAT You are.

Active Love is something you *do* for others; it is not theorizing or idle speculation about Love.

Meditation is the Direct Way to God-Consciousness.

Know Thyself 1389
Who is 'I AM'? 1418
Being and Becoming 1415
The Law of your Being 976
What is Consciousness? 1368

The self and the Self

Ignorance, egotism, selfishness, anger, fear, worries, indecisions, purposelessness of life, clinging to objects, people and situations, and worldly-mindedness, all belong to the personality, the personal ego or "I", not to the Self.

Therefore you must *raise* yourself *above* your personal "I", your personal self, in Deep Meditation, or in Profound Contemplation, or in Ecstatic Union, to the God within you, the Bright Eternal Self that You are.

Reactive-Emotional Consciousness 1426

Love, Bliss, Wisdom, is the Fundamental Nature of the Self, which is God, which is the Truth. THAT You already are.

Love and Wisdom are One and the Same Reality, united by Bliss-Consciousness.

The Self is Pure Being, Bliss-Consciousness, Omniscience.

All is a transformation of the Universal Consciousness

Consciousness is everything. All is a *transformation* of the Universal Consciousness. Your body, mind, emotions, ego, personality, and even your sense of a personal "I", are but transformations within the Absolute Consciousness, which is the Eternal Self of All.

Ecstasy is the Contemplation of the Eternal, Unchanging Self.

The Universe is the Form of God. The True Form of God is the Original Boundless Light, which is the Source and the Cause and the End of Everything—the Original Unity.

When your mental processes are *transcended* and your thoughts come to an end, then there is the No-mind State, the Pure Bliss-Consciousness of the Self that You already are.

The Path is not a matter of going anywhere, but just Being what You already are, becoming Aware of Who You are.

Your body, life-force, emotions, thoughts and ego conceal the Self. *Remove* them in meditation and you arrive at the end of your Journey. For nothing remains but Yourself, the Self of the Universe, Cosmic Life. THAT You are.

Go *beyond* your thoughts to the State of Bliss which is already inherent within you.

Your Superconscious Mind is your Transcendental Self.

Paradise is the Always-Blissful Realm of the Self, which You always are.

Perceptions of the One Mind 490
The Form of God is Space 109
Understand your Predicament 892
No-Mind and the One Mind 763
Suspended Mind 1209

Your self, as you are, has its ultimate meaning in the Self that You are. *Discover* It.

Contentment in your life can only come when you have reached the Realm of Pure Being, Infinite Life, which is already within you. Nothing less will do.

You exist because of your Consciousness

God will not come to you unasked. You will have to approach Him in *meditation* and then He will respond.

Without meditation there is no Enlightenment; therefore, regulate your life.

Your physical senses bring you into touch with the physical world. Deep, inner meditation will put you in touch with the World of the Spirit, where You, as the Self, eternally dwell.

You exist because of your Consciousness. The Universe exists because of Divine Consciousness. All things are continually changing, passing away, but Consciousness remains eternally.

The Ultimate Oneness of Life can be experienced only in God-Consciousness.

The Great Mantram of Buddhi Yoga, the Path of Wisdom, is:

ŌṀ HAṀSA SŌHAṀ SVĀHĀ
ŌṀ TAT SAT BRAHMĀ
ŌṀ ŚĀNTIḤ ŚĀNTIḤ ŚĀNTIḤ SVĀHĀ
I am That, That am I,
That Eternal God-Consciousness,
May I dwell in Eternal Peace.

RĀṀ ŌṀ ĀṀ YĀṀ RĀMĀYA NAMAHA

This is the Great Mantram to put you in touch with Cosmic Intelligence, the Mind of God, Active Wisdom.

Consciousness 1370
The Upaniṣadic Mantrams 546
Mahāvākya: Great Truth Statements 1469
The Ultimate Reality is the Meaning of Life 526

As long as the Self has not been experienced by your mind, your mind remains in delusion.

Enlightenment comes when you can distinguish your Self from those actions which are motivated by personal thoughts and desires.

Then comes the Moment, the Speechless Silence

When all is quiet and still, and your Attention is wholly *inward*, and all outside noises have faded away, and all sense-objects are forgotten, and you have lost awareness of your self in the object of your meditation, then comes the Moment, the Speechless Silence, the Great Awakening of Who You are.

If you have understood Wisdom thus far, you will realize that the theories and solutions proposed by intellectuals for the problems of Mankind cannot work, and will not work, because they are not based on the Ultimate Reality, that is, *How Things Really Are*. Mankind must undergo a vast Spiritual Reorientation towards the Real, the Truly Eternal.

For the worldly-minded people, for the materialists, for the spiritually ignorant, there is no Liberation in this lifetime.

To Experience Spiritual Ecstasy...

Spiritual Ecstasy, or Contemplation (SAMĀDHI), arises when the mind is *dissolved*, when all your thoughts disappear, and your breath becomes still like a motionless lake.

Or, Spiritual Ecstasy arises when you *listen* to the Inner Sound, the Primordial ŌṀ, or any of Its many melodies.

Or, Spiritual Ecstasy arises when your self (your personal "I") is *forgotten* and your consciousness is *transcended* into the Self.

Or, Spiritual Ecstasy comes when you *see* the Divine Light.

Or, when you bow down inside yourself, in profound Adoration of the God-Self within your Heart, the Living God.

Or, when during meditation the Waves of Bliss *obliterate* your memory of the world and all its objects.

Or, when you pour out your Heart, in Profound Love, towards God who lives *within* all beings.

The Seer is Pure Consciousness 542
Samādhi: the Goal of Yoga 574
The Path to Ecstasy 696
The Law of Mystic Experience 508

When you have progressed within, you realize how deadly materialistic thinking is, how vast millions are trapped into it, are slaves of it. These hundreds of millions are prisoners of the planet. Materialistic thinking, whether scientific or political, turns you away from the Real, the True, the Beautiful, the Good.

Love is Wisdom expressed in helpful deeds

Materialistic thinking, materialistic education and psychology, and materialistic politics and science, are the Death of the Soul, the Bondage of the Spirit.

Mind is the intermediary between Spirit and matter, between Divinity and the world. Turned outwards it becomes materialistic; turned inwards it becomes Divine.

Love is Wisdom expressed in helpful deeds. The world does not know the meaning of true Love.

The greatest Service to Mankind is to help *spiritualize* the Race of Man. Be engaged in the Spiritual Revolution, the Divine Work of Liberation.

Wisdom is the faculty of your Soul, not of your mind. Your Soul is *above* your mind. Become Soul-Conscious through meditation.

This is the Way of Liberation by Wisdom.

How I write is a Process. How I speak is a Process. It is not meant to be rational, logical, convincing you of some idea, thought or philosophy. It is simply a Way to help you get in touch with Yourself, and the Truth within yourself, beyond your mind, and to give you the Profound Understanding. It is not the same as a university lecture or a school talk about a subject. It is an Energy flow from the Soul to your Soul with a Message of Eternal Realities. Happy is the Man who can appreciate it.

The meaning of my life is simply Service, to help people onto the Path and to recover what was lost in Ignorance.

Inspiration by the Mind of Light 1113

Trapped Spirits 1240
Some Human Evils 384
On Love and Meditation 1140
What is True Service? 1714

What is Wisdom?

Wisdom (GNOSIS, VIDYĀ, PRAJÑĀ) is the actual Reality Itself: the Transcendental Absolute Self and the relative, ever-changing worlds, realms, planes and conditions of Being. And Wisdom is the Human *Comprehension* or *Realization*, by Supernatural Sight, of the Perfect Immovable Absolute State or Condition and the ever-moving, ever-evolving Relative State of the physical and subtle material realms of Being and the vast Hierarchies who control and govern them.

The Whole Universe is like a bubble in the Ocean of Wisdom

Wisdom (CHOCKMAH, SOPHIA, BODHI) survived many ages and many civilizations, including the Greek, Roman, Mesopotamian, Egyptian, Phoenician, Persian, Babylonian, Chinese, Vedic, Asiatic and Hebrew Civilizations. It always was and always will be. It was active at the beginning of the Christian and Muslim Civilizations, until it was suppressed. It was active during the time of Buddha, Kṛṣṇa, Moses, Jesus, Lao Tzu, Mahāvīra, Nanak, Muḥammad and Bahaullāh. It is always there, hidden from the sleeping masses, Bright for those who can Receive It, Commune with It.

Wisdom is Indestructible. It is a Boundless Ocean of Glory, Light, Radiance, from the Supreme Absolute. All things are in It, yet It remains ever the same, unchanging. The Whole Universe (visible and invisible) is like a foam or bubble *in* the Ocean of Wisdom, or like a wave upon the surface of an ocean.

The Divine Light (Wisdom) is brightest at its Source, and diminishes as it descends through the Divine Worlds, down to the Spiritual Realms, and further down to the psychic realms, and finally to the physical worlds of the physical universe. Therefore, you must *ascend* out of the physical bodily realm to the psychic worlds, and go above them to the Spiritual Light Worlds, and above them to the Divine Worlds. Each Ascent is a Transformation in Consciousness and a Benediction by a greater Light.

All bodies veil the Light of the ONE, the Infinite Being—call it God, TAO, BRAHMAN, PARAMĀTMAN. This is the Whole, the Complete, PLERŌMA, Fullness, the All, PŪRṆA. The Knowledge (Realization) of this fact (through meditation and spiritual experience) is Wisdom.

Sophia 146
The Ocean of Wisdom 84
Wisdom and Understanding 439
Wisdom: the Light Path 1354

The One

All is ONE.

This means that all is the ONE.

Meditate on this Truth. The good, the bad, hot and cold, sweet and sour, black and white, evil and virtue, pain and pleasure, loss and gain: all are the ONE.

The State of Unity is the experience of your Soul in Spiritual Ecstasy

The ONE is Transcendental and Absolute, Timeless and Eternal, Boundless and Measureless. The ONE is also the limited, the temporal, the relative, the conditioned, this world and the next, heaven and hell, the gods, angels and men, the animals, the plants, the rocks, things visible and invisible, important and trivial, life and death, Eternity and Reincarnation: All is the ONE.

If your mind is *saturated* with physical details of all kinds of objects and things, it will never be able to comprehend the ONE. And it will be impossible for you to understand someone who is in the State of the ONE, in Singular Consciousness, whose mind is uncomplicated, Resting in Oneness. *Simple mind is the best.* The State of Unity, Oneness, Simple Consciousness, is not a philosophy, not an idea, not a thought; it is the *experience* of your Soul in Spiritual Ecstasy.

The common mind, the ordinary mind, the "rational" mind, likes things complicated, multiple-functioning; the "many-ness" of things, divisions and subdivisions. This is also the "scientific" mind, the "analytical" mind, always inventing new categories, new words, new terms, new parts and new descriptions of things.

The ONE is surprising: It is a Single Essence, a Simple Meaning, a Single Moment which includes All, is All, within All, yet always is simply the ONE, the Whole, the All, the Complete. This is the State of Unity-Consciousness.

The State of Unity-Consciousness, God, the ONE, is the Goal of Evolution for Mankind on this planet. Every man, woman and child will have to Awake to It, because It is *always already here.* Therefore, Wake Up to It by *dissolving* the multiple-functioning of your ordinary mind.

The Eternal is One 512
The Path of Non-Duality 762
Tao: the Universal Mind 775
The One and Only 839
The Divine Unity 852
Mind-Only 974

Rāṁ is ONE: the All-Bright, the Formless, the All-Pervading, within All; God, Bliss, everywhere, without boundaries; Undying, Eternal, without end or beginning; the Silence within the sound, the Stillness in the movement; ever-active in everything and everybody, yet not moving at all; motionless, yet the cause of all activity in the world; near, yet in the distant stars; the Mystery Beyond, yet all that you see in front of you; One, yet the Many. I call it Unity-Consciousness.

The Real Self is in the Formless Dimension

Eka Ātmā, Eka Ātman, Ekātmā

The One Self

Meditate on this. There is only the One Self, whose Body is the Universe, who also dwells within your body.

Ahaṁ

I Am

There is only the One I AM, God, the Self, all-pervading. Meditate on this.

The Real Self is in the Formless Dimension. The Real Mind is the Formless Mind. *Sink* your mind into the Silence of Reality, deep within, and you will become Formless and Boundless Awareness.

There is the One Final Absolute, the Ultimate Reality, Immeasurable Light, White Brilliance, Ultimate Divinity, the Real God, an Absolute Unity, Deathless Life, Immortality, Incorruptible Perfection that eternally Exists. Call it Being, or God, or the Source, or the Root and Foundation of Everything: Sovereign over the vast Universe (visible and invisible); the Parent of All; *invisible* to the physical eyes, or to the psychic eye, or to the eyes of angels, but *visible* to the Pure Seer, the Sage, the Gnostic (Knower), the Gñāni (Jñāni, Knower) who has *transcended* the self and is *established* in the Self-Luminous Self, the Monad, the Paramātman, the ONE. This is Wisdom.

I have spoken like an angel. Have you understood like an angel? If not, my words cannot penetrate the thickness of your ordinary mind.

Perceptions of the One Mind 490
The Way, the Truth and the Life 670
Pure Consciousness in the Heart 447
Formless Consciousness 1373
You Are the World 1390

Evolution, the Plan, the Path

The Destiny of Man is to become Light. This is not wishful thinking, a nice philosophy, a faith or a belief. It is the *Divine Plan*. Mankind en masse has no real idea of true Evolution (forget Darwin and his guesses!).

The final Archetype of Man already exists in the Cosmic Mind

Evolution is a Multidimensional Phenomenon guided by Divine Intelligence over an Aeonian Time Scale.

The final Design or Archetype of Man already exists in the Cosmic Mind; hence, you can become It *now*. You need not wait for the long haul of Universal Evolution to complete its Grand Work. The more you meditate correctly, the more the Light grows within you, making the Inner Worlds brighter as a result. As you progress up the Ladder of Illumination, the Light in you grows stronger and stronger, brighter and more glorious, until you become a Dazzling Sun, illuminating all the Worlds.

There is the *Kingdom of Nature* (the Physical, Astral and lower Mental Planes, and all that is within them), ruled by energies and intelligences of non-human beings, Devas, angels, nature-spirits, and the intelligences connected with the Mother-Force of Nature.

There is the *Kingdom of Souls*, the Causal and Buddhic Realms, wherein the human Souls dwell, along with the higher angelic and archangelic beings.

There is the *Kingdom of God*, the Divine Worlds, the Nirvāṇic Planes and the two major planes or universes above it, the Buddha-Fields, the planes of Divine Evolution.

The personality belongs to the Kingdom of Nature. Your Soul belongs to the Kingdom of Souls. The Monad that You are, the Pure Spiritual Self, belongs to the Kingdom of God.

The Plan is in the Divine Mind 161
Human Involution and Evolution 170
Vertical Evolution and the Path 174
The Threefold Structure of Man 33
Let Thy Will Be Done 1720

Your personality may be called the lower self. Your Soul may be called the Higher Self. The Monad, ĀTMAN, PARAMĀTMAN, the Spirit within you, is your Divine Self, ĪŚVARA, the God within you. This Knowledge (Realization) is Wisdom.

You are not the physical body, but the Dweller in the body. You are not your little mind, the ego, but the Mind which embraces the Universe.

NIRVĀṆA is Timeless Bliss-Consciousness, experienced when you *transcend* your body-and-mind consciousness and your emotional self. NIRVĀṆA is ĀTMAN, the Spirit, the Self that You already are. NIRVĀṆA is God-Consciousness, Pure Being, Eternal Life, *beyond* and *above* your personality structure. How do you get there?

Nirvāṇa is the Goal of Evolution

NIRVĀṆA is the Goal, the Objective, the Purpose of Evolution. The materialist's idea of evolution is meaningless, false, an invention of ignorant minds who see only the Darkness.

NIRVĀṆA You already are. *Remove* the Veils—all of them, one by one—that hide, conceal and cover up that Splendid Light, the Ocean of Bliss, the Immortal Life, Eternity.

Self-Realization and NIRVĀṆA are the same thing. BRAHMAN (God) and NIRVĀṆA are the same thing: Life-Eternal.

NIRVĀṆA is Illumination, the shining of the true Sun, the Light of the Universe, the Light within the Universe. What greater gift or service can you give to Mankind than to help people on the Path to NIRVĀṆA?

Illumination is not simply a State you attain, after which there is no further to go (as so many Yogīs, Mystics and Knowers mistakenly believe). In the Infinitudes of the Divine Splendour there is always room for more Growth, Expansion and Realization.

Make much effort, work to regain what you have lost, *ascend* again to your Glory in the Kingdom of God, the Realms of Pure Light Emanations and *Beatific Vision*, unutterable Bliss, Love, Harmony and Peace, Immovable Unity, Oneness of All.

Your body hides the Light (it is too dense to allow it through), but those who can See will *see* your Light and know your true Stature, your true Station in the Hierarchy of Intelligent Beings in the Cosmos.

Beyond the Veils 894
Nirvāṇa: the Realm of Glories 93
Entering the Lost Kingdom 1176
The Brotherhood of Light 395

The Self (that is, You) is shining Bright already, always, everywhere. Your personality is but a covering which conceals your true Self. Yet how attached are you to your ego, your personality, your "thoughts", "opinions", "feelings", "moods"! You are readily fighting for them all the time. If you only were so concerned for your Self, the real You, you would be quickly Enlightened.

Your true Mind is the Mind of Light

Everybody *identifies* himself or herself with the physical body, the perishable self, not with Ātman, the real Self. This is in itself a miracle. How did this happen? How is it happening? By what trick of Nature? Find out!

The sensation of Time and Space is the product of your little mind, the ordinary mind, just as your thoughts are the product of your little mind. Your true Mind is the Mind of Light, Omniscient, All-pervading, which is in fact the Light of God.

"I Am That Power, That Energy, which is the Source of the Universe, which is the Power *behind* all Manifestation and all phenomena." Call It God, or Tao, or Nirvāṇa, or the Truth, or the Absolute, or the Kingdom of God. It is too vast to have a Name, too powerful to be limited by human words.

It *appears* to the ordinary, limited human intelligence that the Universe is external to one's self, and can be "studied" externally, "objectively", as something outside of one's self. This is a cruel delusion, for the Universe has its Source from the Great Within, even as your little self exists from and in the Great Within. Only the Great Within exists.

When your mind becomes naturally quiet and still, in the State of Internal Silence, you will be taught from Within, and the Mysteries that you learn cannot easily be put into words.

The Three Identifications 1369
Obstacles to Higher Consciousness 1424
The Sense of Time 22
Dimensions of the Mind 891
What is Reality? 1175

What is Reality? That Light which exists forever, which is Being, Consciousness, and the quality of Love and Bliss. Love and Bliss go together. If you truly Love, you are blissful, happy. If you are truly blissful, happy, you continually express the power of Love.

In the Relative Universe (the Physical, Astral and Mental Planes) there are all types of powers, forces and energies expressed: good, bad and indifferent, happy, sad, violent, peaceful, destructive and loving. In the Original Creation, on the Spiritual Planes, the overwhelming Power is the Energy of Love and Bliss-Consciousness.

Everything in this world is always passing away, changing, perishing, ending, but the Kingdom of God, the Imperishable Glory that shines *within* the world, always is never-ending, undecaying, undying. So why put so much emphasis on this world when the Real is so much Brighter?

Your next task is to bring your personality under the control of your Soul

The basic problem is that Humanity is Blind and cannot see the Divinity shining everywhere. Therefore, develop your Inner Vision. Humanity will be groping in the Dark until such time that everybody will See the Beatific Vision. Hasten the coming of that Day by doing your Work and inspiring others to do likewise.

The next task ahead of you in your Spiritual Evolution is to bring your personality under the control of your Soul. That is, you must become a Soul-infused personality, a Soul-integrated person. This is done through persevering in your meditational life until *your ordinary mind is illumined by the Light of your Soul.*

Then the Great Work consists of the Stages of Union: your personality, your Soul and the Monad (the Divine Self within you) become One, so that You live in the All, and the All lives in You. This is the end of the separated self, the end of the *sensation* of a life separate from the All. You will experience the One Life, and this One Life is You.

There are three Suns within you:

- The Sun within your Heart.
- The Sun of your Soul.
- The Radiant Sun of the All-Pervading Spirit within you.

As you are now, the three Suns are separate. But, when you have completed the Great Work of Yoga (Union), the three Suns are One, a Radiant Glory.

Return to Primeval Happiness 1179
The Three Stages of Yoga 528
Meditation is Integration 1193
Steps on the Meditational Path 1196

Divine Grace is always present. It shines as the Self within your Heart, but so long as your Heart is closed, so long as your eyes are turned away from It, you cannot perceive It. When your Heart is open, you will feel God's Grace at all times flowing into your life.

The Nature of your Soul is Love

Let your little self *expand* until it becomes the Greater Self, the Absolute Self, by *including* more and more people into your life in the Power of your Love, for the Energy of Love is the basic Substance of the Ultimate Self (God), which you already are, and which you need *practically* to express.

The Nature of your Soul is Love. I do not mean the sentimental male-female relationship, but the true Love of the Spirit, the inexhaustible Energy of God. This is Wisdom.

The Spiritual Love of God is all-inclusive. God's Love includes All. This is a Universal Love-Energy-Field. This is Wisdom.

The Creative Soul

What is art? Originally, art was supposed to express the Creative Faculty of Man: the creation of the Good, the Beautiful, the True, on the Physical Plane, in physical matter; or the harmonious transformation of the physical body by correct movement. Look at the splendour of Rome, Greece and Egypt, for example: the magnificent architecture, sculptures, paintings, mosaics, and the religious and spiritual music and dance forms. Or look at ancient India or Asia for religious or spiritual movements of the body, moving with the Oneness of Nature, or Tao.

Art is supposed to express in physical form the Soul of Man. But, since "modern" Man is not in touch with the Soul, art, like the philosophy of today, is lost in darkness, ugliness, meaninglessness and gross materiality, or in intellectual twaddle and glamour.

The Soul is all Good, Beautiful and True, and is the vehicle for the Spirit. If human artists (creators) do not touch even the Soul, how can they express the Spirit of Mankind? They cannot. For an artist, the first lesson should be meditation, Soul Contact. Be a true Artist! Only a Soul-infused Artist can express the true Wisdom of the Soul.

Your ordinary "rational" mind is always egotistical, self-centred, full of personal ambition. That is why it needs to be *transcended* in meditation.

Art and the Follies of Man 470

Mysterious Grace 1311
Cultivate the Fires of Love 928
On Love and Meditation 1140
To Love God and the World 1392
Oneness and Love 1450

Paths of Spiritual Evolution

For the past six to eight thousand years, Spiritual Development, or the Path of Spiritual Unfoldment or Spiritual Evolution, has been brought about by four possibilities:

KUṆḌALINĪ YOGA: The awakening and ascension of the KUṆḌALINĪ-ŚAKTI up the spinal system and through the cakras *dissolved the attachment* of your Consciousness to your physical body, *opened* your Awareness to the Astral and Causal Worlds, and (generally speaking) developed Cosmic Consciousness. However, this Path is dangerous as it is *ignorantly* taught by ignorant teachers—dangerous especially for Westerners who are not at all ready for such Awakening.

Bhakti Yoga was the favourite Path of the Piscean Age

BHAKTI YOGA: Intense Devotion and Love for the Deity (God) in whichever form or aspect you approach It. This was the favourite Path of the Piscean Age, and still is for many. However, because of the Aquarian Age materialism, this Path is slowly fading out.

RĀJA YOGA: The Royal Way, which is based *in your mind*, through which you learn to *transcend* your mind and unite with your ĀTMAN, the God within you.

JYOTIR MAṬHA: The Light Path, or Path of Light, whereby you learn to see the Light in the Third-Eye and Crown Centres and *exit* through them into the Higher Realms.

The Three Forces at work in Nature and in Humanity

TAMAS: that which produces Darkness, ignorance, stupidity, dullness, physicality, sleep, rest, steadiness, perseverance.

RAJAS: that which produces Fire, impulsiveness, violence, recklessness, speed, activity, energy, vigour, virtue.

SATTVA: that which produces Light, cooperation, harmony, rhythm, beauty, wholeness, peace.

Every activity is undertaken by Nature—both its visible and invisible dimensions. Nature is ignored by present-day Humanity, therefore the true causes of things are not understood.

The Guṇas 139

The Three Gates to God 151
When Kuṇḍalinī Awakens 157
Mystics of Pisces and Aquarius 836
Bhakti Yoga: Divine Union by Devotion 1128
Rāja Yoga: Divine Union by Meditation 1126
The Way of the Mind 1238
The Path of Illumination 1338

The True Teachers

When Society no longer respects the Spiritual Teachers, the true Gurus, it descends into chaos, anarchy, crudeness and dense materiality. That is what we have today. The Spiritual Teachers, the Spiritual Guides, are the true Heroes of Mankind—not the soccer stars and empty-mouth politicians. Society should place the true Spiritual Teachers at the front of the "honours" lists, for it is only They who can show the Way for Humanity, the Way out of the Darkness of Ignorance in which Mankind is immersed.

The True Teachers point the Way to the Eternal Wisdom

Do *you* respect the True Teachers for the gifts they bring to you from the Invisible Realms and Worlds? Respect for the True Teachers, and respect for all things spiritual, is *Wisdom*. How can the children of Man become Enlightened when at school and university they do not learn Wisdom? When the "education" institutions do not know what true Wisdom is?

The true Spiritual Teachers are not religious fanatics, fundamentalist extremists or evangelical "crazies". They are Robed in the Robe of Wisdom, they speak from Wisdom, and they point the Way to the Eternal Wisdom which we all must *Realize*.

Wisdom is essentially the Love-Force of God expressed in different kinds of activity:

- The Transcendental-Wisdom of the Buddha.
- The Love-Wisdom of the Christ.
- The Dynamic-Wisdom of the Spiritual Warrior (MAHĀ-VĪRA).

Where are your Wisemen? 387
Mediums and Mediators 388
The Sage 973
The Aquarian Teachers 1147
Great Incarnations of Divinity 1270

The Love of Wisdom

The word *philosophy* comes from the Greek word PHILO-SOPHIA, "the Love of Wisdom". Nowadays philosophy means defining the dictionary-meanings of words, rationalizing, using "logic", mathematics, comparing one "philosopher's" speculations (guesses) about anything and everything with another "philosopher's" guesses or speculations, theorizing about the meaning of anything and everything (you can have a "philosophy" of science, a "philosophy" of philosophy, and so on, all a mental waffle).

True PHILOSOPHY is what we have been describing to you: SOPHIA, or Wisdom. PHILO, the "Love of it", is the Yoga, the *practice* of Enlightenment processes, as described herein.

My experience as an Esoteric Spiritual Teacher over many years is that today's spiritual seekers don't listen to what you are saying, but hear only what they want to hear. The words of the Teacher (the Teaching) they amalgamate into their vast array of ideas, theories and concepts (due to their "learning") at their own leisure, leaving out what they don't "agree" with. And, among those who actually listen to what the Teacher is saying, few can completely understand it; most comprehend the Teaching only partially. And, among those who listen and comprehend some of the Teaching, few actually apply it or put it seriously into practice and revolutionize their lives. The rest of them carry on as they did before they came across the Teacher and the Teaching, and practise the Path as a "hobby" according to how much they can fit into their busy schedules. And they wonder why they are not making any progress on the Spiritual Path!

Spiritual seekers hear only what they want to hear

It was not so in the olden days. In those days the seekers and disciples obeyed the Teacher's instructions; it was the Law for them, and their lives had no other meaning than to obey that Law with all their bodies, minds, emotions, and the Will of their Souls! How things have changed!

It is a sign of the times, of this materialistic age, that intellectuals who write books on fairy tales, or mythologies of ancient tribes and indigenous peoples, are accorded great honours, prizes, distinction and awards by governments, universities, and so forth, and are publicly known figures. Yet the Teachers who Know the Truth, the Esoteric Teachers, the Mystics, Yogīs and Spiritual Masters, are not recognized by governments, are not given generous "grants" for their "researches", are not supported in any way by the "community". They have to fend for themselves.

Myth, mythology and fantasy writings are not the Truth—not on the "science" level, nor on the Spiritual Science level. They were used to teach children, but when the children grew up, the Direct Knowledge was given to them by the Wise. Nowadays, society takes its cue from the mythology writers and interpreters, but the myths, mythologies, folklore and fairy tales of the ancient tribes and races are not the Truth because they are not the Direct Experience of the Truth by proper meditation, Insight, Illumination and Super-physical Realization. Why be led astray by things which are half-truths and sometimes not even that?

Truth and Mythology 7

Living Guidance 339
Look out for the One 1004
The Sacrifice of the Teachers 1150
The Approach to Truth 1152
The Attitude for Yoga 558

Right Practice

How do you *acquire* Wisdom? Not by learning, not by books and study, but the right type of meditation, Silence, the right kind of chanting, selfless actions, Service to all Life, and Devotion to the Supreme. This is the Way.

Your technique must lead you to the Formless State

Right Meditation

Right Meditation is that which enables you to *transcend* your ordinary, rational, everyday mind (even when you are very "learned"). The ordinary mind is that which engages you endlessly in "thinking". In many ancient traditions they did not understand the principle of *rising above* mental activity rather than engaging in it; therefore they slowed their meditational progress. They were told to endlessly repeat Mantras or Words of Power, or sacred prayers, or devotional formulas, believing that the more they repeated each day a Mantra or a prayer or a word, the better the result. But all they did was to engage the mind more and more and to remain on the "thinking" level of the mind.

Your Mantra, prayer or mental technique must lead you to the Formless State, the No-mind State, the Pure Awareness State, *beyond and above* the ordinary "thinking" process. That is the correct method. The Real Journey into Wisdom *begins above your mind*, in the Formless Cosmic Intelligence State, where your ordinary mind is silent, passive, at Rest, and your Inner Awareness of your Soul is full and bright and all-inclusive. You must also *complement* your Inner Work (SĀDHANĀ) with normal outer life and activity, but without overdoing the outer life-process.

Cultivate Inner Silence, the Silence of thought, the Silence of the mind. When your mind is silent you will find Peace, which is within you, not outside in the world.

Right Prayer

The correct way to pray is *not* to tell God what to do (as is the custom of the ignorant religionists), nor to ask for physical things, but to *Glorify the Divine Name* which is *God's Living Presence*. This leads to Spiritual Illumination and Spiritual Realization and intense Bliss-Consciousness. Get out of your personality-stuff and worship God as would a true Spiritual Being—which, in fact, you are!

The Ordinary Mind 896
Meditation Practice 1201
Cultivate Silence of the Mind 1239
The Heart and the Lost Art of Prayer 1251

Right Chanting

The correct way to chant for meditation is to chant two or three correct Mantras for about twenty or thirty minutes, then *stay* in the Silence afterwards for twenty or thirty minutes, *absorbing* the after-effects of the chanting.

Right Use of Mantra

Announce the Mantra as a Soul-radiation

You are in the habit of saying your Mantra in your personality, with your ordinary mind, mentally repeating it but still doing the Work on the personality level.

Try something new: say the Mantra with your Soul. That is, announce the Mantra as You the Soul *radiating the Energy* of the Mantra through your mental, astral, vital and physical bodies. Announce the Mantra as a Soul-radiation, then pause and remain in Silence, in your Soul, and *sense* the Reaction from the Cosmos to your saying the magic words.

Work like this in your Soul:

Mantra...Silence...Mantra...Silence....

Planetary Disturbance

There is a natural reason why you find it difficult to meditate these days. *To meditate you need peace and quiet.* Since the 18th century, Mankind has been creating increasingly more *energetic disturbance* in the subtle planetary atmosphere which penetrates everywhere, and you sense this disturbance with your etheric and astral bodies and your Solar Plexus Centre.

There are very few places on Earth which are peaceful and quiet. The television and radio waves, the traffic noise, the noise of engines and machinery: all disturb the planetary atmosphere everywhere. And the loud and often destructive and aggressive "pop-music" vibrations hit the planetary Ether like an avalanche. Even three-hundred years ago the planetary vibration was much quieter and slower. There is also a *speeding up* of the planetary vibrations by solar-systemic forces and cosmic energies from outside our Solar System.

So, if you want to achieve the peace and tranquillity that you need for meditation, you have to work twice as hard as the ancients did, and the results of meditation will appear more slowly than they did centuries ago. If you want to succeed in this lifetime, you have to put more effort into your Inner Work.

The Creative and Destructive Power of Sound 201

The Two Applications of Mantra 1219
Understanding your Work in Silence 1024
Vibration and Mantra 1518
The Initiation of the World 1712

The Sevenfold Practice

There are seven things you can do towards your Enlightenment or Awakening in Higher Consciousness:

1. *a.* The practice of Silence; that is, being in Silence.
   b. Listening to the Inner Voice, NĀDA, the Inner Sound, or sounds you can hear with your Inner Ear on the right side. Or listening in the Heart Centre for the ANĀHATA-NĀDA (not-physical sounds). Or listening in the Crown Centre to the MAHĀ-NĀDA, the Great Sound (the Logos).
2. *a.* Meditation that helps you to transcend your ordinary mind state.
   b. Mantras that produce transcendence or inner transformation, or bondage-freeing exaltation.
3. *a.* Chanting.
   b. Sound Work (with Pure Vowels).
4. Praising and Glorifying God. Pure Prayer.
5. Normal day-to-day living; not cutting yourself away from the Life-process; physical activity or exercises; Service, that is, working for your Teacher, the Teaching and your Group, or for the benefit of the world (to uplift Human Consciousness).
6. Radiating your Mantra as a Living Soul (JĪVĀTMAN) for the benefit of all Human Souls and the Inner Worlds.
7. *a.* Cakra balancing (the Inner Centres).
   b. Breathing exercises that purify, transform and harmonize your inner nature.

The secret of meditation is a genuine inward-turning

The Secret of Meditation

Unless you re-orient your Consciousness inside yourself, you cannot make progress in meditation. There are so many students who are still external in their Consciousness and who wonder why they are not making progress. When they "meditate" they just use their ordinary minds, and their Consciousness remains on the level of the ordinary mind. They are too busy always with external activities, feelings and thinking. The secret of meditation is a *genuine inward-turning*. I cannot explain it any better.

The Science of Meditation 1173

The Practice of Silence 1443
The Path of Hearing 553
The Primordial Sound Language 1025
What is Prayer? 690
Transformation of the Centres 1333
The Science of Cosmic Consciousness 1124

The Wisdom of Not-doing

The *Wisdom of Not-doing* is an ancient form of meditation much practised in China, Japan, Korea and the Far East, as well as by some Christian monks, in some Tantra Yoga schools of India, by Zen monks, in Spiritual Warrior schools of different countries, and by "spontaneous mystics" of all countries who have discovered it by themselves.

You have to find the *Still Point* within your Heart Centre in the middle of your chest, or in the Third-Eye Centre in the middle of your forehead, or in the Crown Centre at the top of your head. The Still Point exists in all these three centres. The Still Point is the Gate to Superconsciousness (to Higher States of Consciousness).

You *focus* your attention in the Still Point, the place of Peace, Quiet, Equilibrium and Balance inside you. You do not have to *do* anything, for you *already have it.* Simply be *Aware* at that Point.

Your mind is silent. Your breath is still. Your thinking (the chaotic thoughts) have been laid down to rest. No visualizations, no imaginings. A Great Silence and Peace descends upon you.

In that Great Silence and Peace an Invisible Transformation takes place which opens the Gate to Higher Consciousness (that is, to the Enlightenment Process). Then the sensation of your separated "self" disappears. The Past, Present and Future are ONE.

Clouds of Unknowing 704
Resting in the No-Mind State of the Absolute 1014
Natural Meditation 1210

Inner Absorption by Listening

LAYA, the State of Inner Absorption, is greatly facilitated by *listening* to the inner sounds within you, in your subtle mechanism or subtle body, SŪKṢMA-ŚARĪRA. These are the internal sounds produced by ŚAKTI, the Universal Power-Field. If you listen to them, your ordinary mind and your little ego quickly dissolve. This is the great secret.

You do not need to fight and struggle to "control" your mind and ego. Just listen to the inner sounds. You may listen in the Base Centre, or in the Heart Centre, or in the Inner Ear (inside the right ear, on the right side of the head).

First, listen to the strongest sound, then a subtler one, then a still-subtler one. Keep going this way. When your mind is absorbed (LAYA) in an inner sound, it becomes motionless. A motionless mind is a liberated mind.

There are many subtle sounds (non-physical sounds) that *sound like* insects, musical instruments, water, thunder, bells, gongs, drums, and so on.

When you have reached complete Inner Absorption, there will be Silence, a Profound Silence, an All-Pervading Inner Silence, in which God manifests to you, the Bright Eternal Self manifests to you, and you will become ONE. This is Wisdom.

Zen Listening 787
Listen to Nāda 1212
Hear the Sound within the Silence 1651

Practice for Wisdom

The first stage in your Spiritual Life is to reach *Equilibrium* between the inner and outer life. It is at this stage that many fail and therefore they make little progress in this life. They are either too worldly (swamped by the worldly vibrations), or they become too transcendental and therefore cannot manage their karmas and environment. Without Balance, Harmony, Equilibrium in your physical life, you will not make much progress. Therefore, *organize* your life properly.

The First Touch of the Absolute is through Inner Silence

There is an Order in this part of Creation, and if human beings would link up this Order with the Celestial Order of the Invisible Realms, life would be bearable on this planet. But Mankind does not keep to the Order (Law) of Nature, nor is it consciously linked to the Order of Supernature. Therefore there is much *suffering* on the Physical Plane of Being. Be Orderly!

The big change in your life will come when you have *definitely committed* yourself to the Spiritual Path and are committed to your chanting, silence, meditation, pure prayer, radiating the Mantra as the Soul, and balancing out all the opposing forces in yourself and in your environment. Further, you are happily willing to serve (help) your Teacher, the Teaching, and your Group, and to lead as many as you can to the Entrance, to the Portal, to the Gate, to the Work that will illumine the Path of Life for them.

Be Silent, be Still, listen to the Greater Silence within you. God will manifest to you in Inner Silence. Silence is important: the First Touch of the Absolute is through Inner Silence. Silence is of your body, mind, senses and emotions. God is already present *everywhere*, no matter where you are. There is a Boundless Realm, an Absolute State of Consciousness, finer than the finest worlds, which not even the angels have seen, and no human beings can know in their ordinary state without undergoing the Fundamental Transformation. In the Greater Silence of Deep Within, a Way is found.

Between the two extremes, find the middle point. This is Wisdom. At the middle point there is Peace and Harmony.

Balance in Spiritual Life 505
Primordial Balance 995
The Silence of the Deep 1355
Between the Two Extremes, Find the Middle Point 1100

Everybody in the world wants Peace. Politicians endlessly talk about it, but they cannot give it to their peoples. Peace is not some kind of commodity that you get from the outside, from the world. It already exists within you, *above* the turmoil of your mind, emotions and actions. In your meditations you must go *above* your body, mind and emotional awareness. When you enter the World of Unity, the Buddhic Realms, you find Peace, unshakeable Peace, Peace which is truly everlasting.

Be Aware of the Moment and you will find God Present There

In the Third-Eye Centre dwells the Serene Light, the Vision of which gives you Peace. Also in the Third-Eye you can control your mind (this is really done by the Inner Light). Thus, you can attain Peace through your Heart (the Peace of the Buddhic Realms), and you can attain Peace through your mind in the Third-Eye. This is Wisdom.

Silence comes from Inner Calm, from Inner Strength, from Inner Knowledge. Children are noisy because they have no inner calm, no inner strength, no inner knowledge. Noisy adults are the same. Silence and Stillness are essential if we want to withdraw from the outer world and enter into deep meditation, into the World Within. Power grows in Silence, and the Inner Worlds unveil themselves in Silence, and in Silence only.

Meditation is making your Awareness *internal* instead of the normal external condition of your attention. The Path is not an outside journey in the world, but an Inner Transformation.

Wherever you are in the world, at whatever time, whatever condition is prevailing locally, be *Aware of the Moment*, of the *Now*, of the *immediate second*, and you will find God *Present There.*

You can actually *see* God, if you so desire it with all your Heart and Mind. Seeing God with your Heart or Mind, or your Soul, or your Inner Eye, leads you to Rebirth, Re-Creation, a total Transformation of your self into That Self which you always already are.

God is in you, and You are in God. This is the Yoga of Wisdom: God pervading everywhere.

Peace on Earth 1304
Silence, Solitude, Peace 1386
The Kingdom is at Hand 1453
The Presence of God 1396
The Experience of Mysticism 636

The Path to Wisdom

Life has a purpose, a plan. The Plan is Enlightenment, or expansion of your Consciousness until Infinite Consciousness, Infinite Intelligence, is yours.

Divine Consciousness is natural to Man

The Path begins in activity (active meditation) and peaks in the Silence and Stillness of Absolute Being, hence returning into *selfless* activity for the Good of All, maintaining within you the Harmony of the Inner Worlds.

Happiness does not come from outside yourself, from the world, from contact with people and objects and possessions. Happiness is the Realization of the Inner Bliss which is the natural state of your Self, the Spirit within you that You already are.

Divine Consciousness, the aim of the Yoga of Wisdom, is natural to Man. It is not imported from the outside; therefore you have the possibility within you already. Work for it!

The Enlightened

The ordinary people cannot understand the Enlightened, which is not surprising because They live in a State of Consciousness which is very different from that of the common mind. Not even their pupils or disciples can fully comprehend Them. The Enlightened have no regrets for the Past and no expectations of the Future. *They live in the Eternal Now*, which is the Junction Point of Time and Eternity. The Enlightened merge with their disciples, with the people, with their environment, but they are not of this world, nor of this corrupt order of society. Their Kingdom, their World, is in the Eternal. *They Listen to the Music of the Moment*, inner and outer. They hear the discord, the strife, the violence of the outer world, the distorted life of the Physical Plane, and They hear the Inner Music of the Word, the Logos, God's Eternal Speech, the Music of the Spheres, the Inner Worlds. They stay here for their allowed time, then *They move on into the Brighter Worlds*, the Blissful Realms of Being, their Work done. *They live in a World of Unity, observing the outer world of diversity.* They live in the Sacred and Holy Realms, which always Radiate Love, Bliss, Peace and Harmony. Their Souls are filled with the Music of the Divine Splendour.

Enlightenment 766
Happiness Exists Within 1381
Quest for Reality 1178
The Law of the Higher Life 1134
The Zen Master according to Lao Tzu 780

It seems to me, from years of experience in Teaching Spirituality, that very few understand the Teaching, and of those even fewer want to practise it one hundred percent. This is a sign of the materialistic age we are living in. Be motivated!

Enlightenment does not come without God's Grace, Divine Power. But you have to *earn* that Grace. Therefore, meditate!

Enlightenment does not come without God's Grace

Your mind will become stable only in Higher Consciousness. Thinking simply agitates your mind; therefore, meditate regularly to be free from the process of thinking by *rising above* thoughts in the Field of Eternal Silence and Peace.

Regulate your life between Inner Activity (meditation) and outer activity, fulfilling your Duties in the world. Do not escape from Life, nor become trapped in worldly consciousness, in worldly ambitions beyond your physical needs and the needs of those who depend on you. Make your Aim in life the Liberation of your Soul from entrapment in the lower material realms, the physical and subtle worlds.

Perform actions that have to be done, but without undue concern for the results of those actions. Act well and sincerely and let the results be worked out by the Cosmos according to how things are in the Moment.

Let all your actions be motivated by Love: the Love of God which comes with an Awakened Heart, and the Love of the world and all the people and beings in it (which is the Manifestation of God). All beings and creatures strive after Happiness: enlighten them where Happiness truly is—in Communion with God in Divine Consciousness.

The Sanskrit word Nāmaste or Nāmastute is the personal greeting of old India. It means "I worship the Divinity within you" or "I worship the Divine Name (Nāma) within you." How beautiful is this ancient greeting! So, when you truly serve your relatives, your friends, your colleagues and the world from your Heart, remember: Nāmaste!

The Significance of Warrior Greetings 1023

Spiritual Life and Material Life 1118
To Become a Jīvanmukta in this Lifetime 259
Liberation from Worldly Consciousness 1233
To Love God and the World 1392

Only in the Superconscious States is true Wisdom to be found

Can you not feel your Group-Soul? Can you not feel the Soul of Humanity? How can I not teach when the Human Soul is crying out for Light? Can *you* not also sense the need to Speak Out and Speak Up and tell the Truth about things, How Things Truly Are? How Humanity is lost in the darkness of Materialism and materialistic thought? How human beings are *disconnected* from their Source and Being? How they are Unaware of the Real? The Good, the Beautiful and the True? What Mankind may become when human beings live by the powers of the Soul and not just the five bodily senses?

Wisdom is not worldly smartness or intellectual cleverness. It is not being "worldly wise". No amount of "learning" can give you Wisdom. No amount of thinking will help you to free yourself from Spiritual Ignorance; only the experience of Spiritual Ecstasy, or Superconscious States, can liberate you. Only in the Superconscious States is true Wisdom to be found. Persevere!

You, as a human being, inherited the Light Within (Wisdom), but It is *covered* by your causal, mental, astral, etheric and physical bodies. Unveil It by *transcending* the temporary personal self, the ego.

The Path of Yoga (Union) is the Unveiling of the Divine Light Within (Wisdom). The Light within you is a fragment of the Ineffable Light of Glory (Wisdom) which gushes forth ceaselessly from the Father of All Lights, the Eternal Unspeakable ONE.

Start your Journey Now by dedicating yourself to the Ineffable Light.

CHAPTER 71

The Call to Service

Piscean Spirituality and New Age Spirituality

The Aquarian Age Spirituality is to bring Light where there is darkness

Spirituality is not psychism. It is the Science of the Soul.

- "The Kingdom of God is within you" was the Spirituality of the Piscean Age.
- "The Kingdom of God is amongst you" is the Spirituality of the Aquarian Age.

During the Piscean Age in the West (the past 2,150 years), the seekers went out into the desert or into monasteries and there they spent their whole lives in *silence, quietness, stillness* and *solitude,* looking within, into the Heart. They completely abandoned all connection with the world, or any activity in the world or near the world.

I do not know if today you can imagine what this meant. Imagine you decided to become one of the "desert fathers", for instance. You go to the desert and find something with which to build a shelter and you settle in for the next forty or fifty years. You are a hermit, a solitary. Your daily routine is to sit in silence, *looking within* into the Heart, or *praying silently* in your Heart to God. You keep your attention *always inside yourself.*

In the East, even today, the yogīs find caves and forests where they *meditate by themselves* in silence, solitude, isolation and aloneness. They concentrate on the *Self within.* They have renounced the world and they have *renounced contact with Humanity.* This was the pattern of Spirituality during the Piscean Age.

The Aquarian Age Spirituality is completely the opposite. *It is not centred in yourself,* but is centred on Humanity, on society. The Aquarian Age Spirituality is to bring Light where there is darkness, Love where there is hate, Happiness where there is sadness, Knowledge where there is ignorance. You are *active in the world,* in Service to the world. You bring *into* the world the Radiance of the Spirit, the Radiance of the Kingdom of Souls.

During the Piscean Age, seekers followed the Path for themselves, alone, in isolation. In the Aquarian Age there is the Group-Sense, working together *in* a group, *for* the group, for Group-Service and Group-Illumination. The *direction* of the Aquarian Spiritual Group is very clear: we seek the Kingdom of God within, like the Piscean Mystic, and then we serve the Kingdom of God without, like the Aquarian World-Servers. For us, both ways are important.

The Christian Heart-Path 632
The Early Christians 643
Mystics of Pisces and Aquarius 836
Spiritual Life and Material Life 1118
Relational Consciousness 906
Group Work 1146

Penetrating into the Kingdom

During the old Piscean Age, all the Spiritual Paths, Eastern and Western, revolved around the idea that you must "renounce the world" (Physical Plane living) and "kill out your desires" (Astral Plane living) and "suppress" your mind, the thinking-faculty (Mental Plane living). Those who follow the old religions still teach this doctrine. It was not easy to do in the Piscean Age, however, and it is definitely impossible to do in this Aquarian Age.

In this Aquarian Age you must start at the bottom

For in this Aquarian Age you must start at the bottom (the Physical Plane, this Physical World) and gradually lead your Attention *inwards*, towards the subtle parts of your Being, to the subtlest and beyond, by regular and correct meditational forms.

Each time you withdraw, you return back into the world, which is your Field of Service and Activity.

This Age is going to be the Age of Conflict between Spirit and matter, between your Soul and personality.

Within Man, God Can Rule.

Brahmā-Loka	The Kingdom of God. Nirvāṇa. The World of Glories.
⇧	
Praḍhāna-Loka	The Formless Unity-Field. Buddhi. The Unmanifest State of Bliss.
⇧	
Kāraṇa-Loka	The subtlest realms. The Causal World. The causal body.
⇧	
Sūkṣma-Loka	The subtle worlds, planes, bodies. The astral and mental bodies.
⇧	
Sthūla-Loka	The gross world. The Physical Plane. The physical body.

Penetrating into the Kingdom

Saints of Action 1134
Monks and Disciples 991
Non-Action Misinterpreted 1120
To Become a True Renunciate 257
God-Consciousness is the Wholeness of Life 504
Steps on the Meditational Path 1196

The New Age and You

The new energies are not working towards the truly spiritual realms

The planet is currently undergoing a *revolution*, a *transformation*, owing to the new energies flooding this Earth-planet from Space (inner and outer). These new energies will impact on every aspect of society: religion, politics, science, art, education, psychology, social order, and so on. This time is a *Day of Opportunity* for our Humanity on this planet, en masse, as well as for you, the individual, to put the Physical Plane in order.

The new Aquarian energies are stimulating certain qualities in Human Consciousness which will result in the following:

- Revolutions and wars to bring about changes and to break down outgrown and crystallized forms and patterns.
- Attempts to organize everything from the mind level; the creation of rules and regulations in all areas of life; increased government power over the individual; increased formalism or ritualism.
- Rebellion against the strengthening of the powers of government; an increased sense or need for self-reliance.
- Increased creativity and practicality on the Physical Plane.
- An increased preoccupation with sex, as the Sex Centre and Base Centre are stimulated by these energies.
- Group work, group formations.

As you can see, these new energies are not working towards the truly spiritual realms and Spiritual Consciousness. To maintain a steady spiritual practice, you have to do the following:

a. Maintain a steady *aspiration* for the Bliss within you.

b. Develop your Esoteric Knowledge so that you *understand* the Teaching in depth.

c. Meditate regularly.

d. Be engaged in group work.

e. Help to spread the Teaching to those who are Thirsty.

The Action of the Cosmic Fire 279
The New Aquarian Energies 426
The Influence of the Seven Rays 834
The Coming of the Christ 724
From Pisces to Aquarius 837
From Darkness into Light 982

The Future

The future direction for Mankind is to become Soul-Conscious. This will be achieved through Religion, Psychology and Education. This is the Divine Plan. This means that during the next fifty years you will see many changes in these fields. You have been *called* to help in this great Work.

A "new Heaven and a new Earth" is being born. Esoterically, this means that the Astral and Mental Planes are being stirred up (and all the inhabitants therein), and a new direction for the Physical Plane Life is being brought about by Cosmic Forces from outside the planet and Inner Forces descending from the Buddhic Plane.

The Universe will be seen as the Garment of God

Mankind must recognize through deep meditation and spiritual work that we are Soul-Beings with a Spiritual Mission to fulfil on this Earth-planet. Man must also gain a new and better understanding of what "God" means, for Man has warped and limited the fact of God. Blind materialistic philosophies of life need to be replaced with Direct Knowledge of the Divine.

What is 'God'? 108
Education in the Future 488
Spirituality Past and Future 1104
Transpersonal Psychology 1106
Uniting Head and Heart 1130
The Mystery Schools and Āśramas 1148

- Education will be Soul-Science.
- Psychology will be Soul-Psychology.
- Religion will be Soul-Religion.

Each of these will be based on the *fact* of the existence of the Kingdom of God and the fact that there *is* a Divine Plan for Mankind and the Planet Earth. Think about this.

Within the next three or four hundred years there will be a Universal World Religion, a Universal World Psychology and Universal World Education. The key Knowledge will be that God is Immanent, everywhere, within everybody and in all things. The Universe will be seen as the Garment of God.

This will also be a major revolution for Science because scientists will *realize* that in fact they are working with, and within, the Body of God. When Science, Religion, Psychology and Education recognize the Immanence of God *within* all things, and the existence of the Soul and Spirit in human beings, Mankind will receive a major Revelation and the planet will become Trans-Dimensionalized, Divinized.

There will be Esoteric Schools established to bring about these great changes on the planet. Our School is one of the Forerunners, one of those who stand between the Past and what is Coming.

The Cosmic-Sense

There will be orthodox, ultra-orthodox, fundamentalists and reactionaries in all the religious, psychological and educational institutions who will resist the ideas of Change and the spirit of new Inspiration and Revelation. They will slow down the Change, but ultimately the Spirit will triumph. Mankind will develop the Cosmic-Sense, the Cosmic-Vision.

Religious Reactionaries 287

Revelation is Continuous

There have always been Messengers sent to Earth to guide Humanity. There have been great names in the past such as Kṛṣṇa, Buddha, Rāma, Moses, Jesus the Christ, Mohammed, Lao Tzu, Bahaullah, the Egyptian Hermes Trismegistus, and countless others. Each Messenger revealed that portion of the Truth which fitted the place and the times, the intelligence of the pupils, and the social environment.

Divinity ever speaks to the Human Heart

But Revelation is continuous. Today is another moment of Revelation. Times have changed. Today the Truth can be revealed more fully and more completely. Human Intelligence has grown.

Those who hold onto old Scriptures, saying there is nothing more to know than what is in their own Sacred Books, are holding back their own evolution and the evolution of the planet. Revelation is continuous. The Tide of Knowledge sweeps over the Earth again and again. It ever resonates to a new Vibration and a new Key.

The Prophets 647
Mediums and Mediators 388
Great Incarnations of Divinity 1270
The Aquarian Teachers 1147
The True Teachers 1694
The Eternal is One 512

Divinity ever speaks to the Human Heart, but the Hearts of Man are closed, so Divinity sends forth Messengers, Gurus, Teachers. The Message is always the same: Know Yourself (that is, Know Who You Are) and Know God and Know the Divine Plan. There *is* a Divine Plan. That is the Message. Life is not just a freak accident.

The Heart of Revelation is the Love of God for Mankind and the wonderful Destiny that awaits Man. Revelation is an unfolding process. It never ends. What is being ever Revealed? The Oneness in its manifold expression and its parts. Behind the Many stands the One. You are a Fragment of the Eternal Presence.

Revelation comes from the God Within. The Prophet, the Seer, the Guru, the Messenger, is in varying degrees of Union with the God Within. The God Within is the Soul, or the Triune Self, or the Monad, or in very rare Cosmic Avatāras, the Logos Himself.

The goal of all true Revelation is to show you how to get in touch with your own Soul, and how to enter the Kingdom of God, the Buddhic and Nirvāṇic Planes.

The authority of the Revealer is not a source outside himself or herself, but simply the Innate Wisdom of his or her own Inner God, and the Power of Love, which is the Mark of the Kingdom of God.

Revelation is very different from mediumship. The Guru, the Seer, the Prophet, is not a medium for a discarnate entity or a supposed angel or "spirit-guide". He speaks the Voice of the Soul, or the Voice of the Triune Self, or the Voice of the Monad. The Revelation is never from an outside source, never from another entity; it is always and only from the God Within.
Masters and Mediums 326

Crisis and Revelation

Crisis and Revelation are aligned. When you (or Humanity) experience a crisis, it is possible for you (or Humanity) to receive fresh Knowledge, Insight, Inspiration and Revelation from the Heart.

What is crisis? It is conflict: *inner* conflict with your own thoughts or emotions; or *outer* conflict with people or Nature.

Continued stress in your life is but an ongoing crisis. How are you going to deal with it? The fashion today is to find *intellectual* solutions, without the Heart. Today there is a surge in *psychological* understanding, attempting to understand the personality through the rational mind. You may find it remarkable, however, that the Ancients paid no attention to the personality in their spiritual writings or scriptures! Did you ever consider that?

You cannot receive fresh Revelation if you are stuck in the Past

Revelation, for you as an individual, for a group, and for the world at large, always has to do with *Light:* physical light, the Light of Mind, the Light of the Soul, the Light of Spirit and, finally, Divine Light. You may experience these degrees of Light in the Heart or in the Head. What is important is your response.

Crisis in your life brings about Revelation if you respond to it positively and constructively from your Heart, if you learn to *live* from the Heart.

You cannot receive fresh Revelation if you are stuck in the Past. Have you noticed how religions and nations are *glued* to the Past? To receive the New, your Heart must be open.

In any situation, if you feel *pity* for yourself, if you think that *you* are the important one (how *you* feel, how *you* reacted, how hurt *you* are, that it all revolves around *you*), then know that you are *not* in the Spiritual Heart. When you are going through turmoil and conflict within yourself and, instead of *you*, you think of the other person or people—how *they* feel in the situation—and if you feel sympathy towards them, know that you are moving in the psychic Heart.

When you are living in the Spiritual Heart, you understand the *karmic necessities*, and you are at Peace and untroubled.

The Testing of the Soul 1158
Psychology Ancient and Modern 1364
Liberation from Worldly Consciousness 1233
Experiencing the Awakening Heart 463
The Path of Illumination 1338
Let Go of the Past 1241
Peace of Heart 1595

The Initiation of the World

How You can Help in the Process

Initiation is a *revolution in your Consciousness*, a major change and shift in the emphasis and direction of your life, from the grossly material towards the spiritual. It is an indication of a new opportunity for you to embrace the Life of the Spirit.

Humanity must learn to function from the sense of Heart Love

The present crisis of Humanity on this planet is due to the fact that the planet Earth itself (the Earth-Spirit or Planetary Logos) is undergoing a Cosmic Initiation, which results in great turbulence and chaotic happenings on this Physical Plane until the Earth-changes are stabilized and a *new Earth-Consciousness* is born.

At this time, the whole of Humanity is suffering from maladjusted activities of the Solar Plexus Centre which need to be *uplifted* to the Heart Centre where they will be *transmuted* into selfless Love. These solar plexus emotions include hate, anger, violence, rage, out-of-control or hysterical actions, depression, revenge, gloom or sadness, self-pity, worry, fear, insecurity, tension and stress. These emotions need to be *transmuted by the Fire of Purification*, and Humanity must learn to function from the sense of Heart Love.

This is *Fiery Baptism* or *Initiation by Fire*. The two World Wars of the last century and the major wars of this century are part of the *Purification of the Planet by Fire*, transmuting the solar plexus energies of the planet into the Fiery Love of the Heart.

Dwell on the Positive

Psychology today, which is encouraging people to *dwell on negatives* (anger, depression, addictions, worries, fears, and so forth) and to endlessly "talk about it", either in counselling sessions or in groups, is merely *reinforcing* those negative tendencies in people. Psychologists need to understand this principle:

Whatever you direct your Attention to, your Consciousness will materialize it for you.

Therefore, if you continually dwell on your hurts and sufferings (real or imaginary), and reinforce that energy by group work, you are merely *increasing* that evil in people.

You must dwell on the positive quality that you want to Realize.

What is Initiation? 1007
Malfunctioning Cakras 53
From Head to Heart 427
Tapas: Spiritual Purification 571
God, the Healer of Broken Hearts 1432
Cultivate the Positive 1365

The *purpose* of these turbulent times on our planet is to bring many men, women and children to take the Heart Initiation. Before the Christ can walk physically among Humanity, many people must open their Hearts and Mankind's emotional hysteria must be largely transmuted. This is the *Birth of the Christ on the mass level*, on the planetary level of Humanity.

Since *you* are part of the world, and your energies are *one* with the world, you will see where your duty lies. You have to *transmute* your own negative emotions, lift your feelings into your Heart and begin to live as a Heart-person: loving, gentle, compassionate, tolerant, understanding, forgiving. In so doing, you will help others to do likewise. If you are angry, violent, aggressive, demanding, then you are helping to *perpetuate* the old planetary pattern of negative human emotions, and therefore you are helping to *prolong the agony* of the planet.

Each human being is an atom in the Consciousness of our Solar Logos. The basic Nature of our Solar Logos is the quality of Love-Wisdom. Thus, when you *open your Heart* to the influence of the Solar Logoic Love-Wisdom, you will *shine inwardly* like the Sun.

Each human being is an atom in the Consciousness of our Solar Logos

The Divine Plan for our Humanity on this planet is that *we all* become Lords of Love and Wisdom: Christs, Buddhas, Bodhisattvas.

This is the Divine Plan. Is this *your* objective?

THE COSMIC PHYSICAL PLANE			
	Logos	God	○
	⇩ ⇧		
	Monad	Spirit	⊙
	⇩ ⇧		
	You as a Living Soul	Reincarnating Ego	△
	⇧ ⇩ ═══ *Consciousness Bridge* ═══		
	Mental Body	Thoughts	The Personality (The ego or 'I' sense)
	Astral Body	Feelings, Memories	
	Etheric-Physical and Physical Body	Body Consciousness	

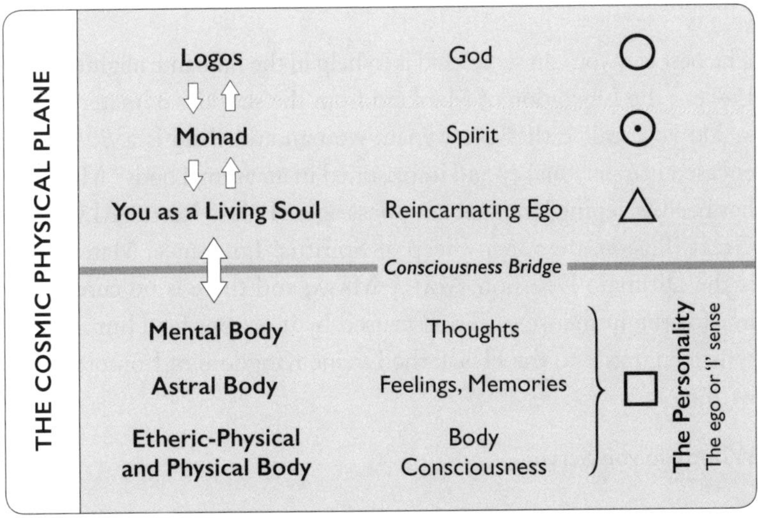

The Bridge of Consciousness

What is True Service?

Some people are incapable of doing anything for others. They are at the bottom of evolutionary development—primitive, self-centred.

Others like doing things for others, but only the things they "like" to do, on their own terms, in their own times, in their own ways, if and when they "feel like it". These people are not much more advanced than those in the first category.

The more advanced group of people are those who volunteer themselves for Service because they see that something needs to be done for their families, for their group or for the world. They take upon themselves some tasks assigned to them and most of the time they do them happily. Sometimes they grumble, groan and moan, but usually they do a good job with their tasks.

The next category of Servers are entirely different, because these people are truly Heart-centred. They live in their Hearts and from the Heart, and they feel the Unity and Oneness of Life. They see the need of their family and they do it. They see the need of their group and they do it. They see the need of the world and they do it. They do not need an outside push, an outside motivation.

Understand your Predicament 892
The Dichotomy of the Mystic 629
The Warrior of the Light 984
Rely on your Inner Self 1226
To Love God and the World 1392
Duty and Spirituality 1641
Heart Action 1331

Your prayers and meditations are to the Living God within you.

Your Service is to the All-Pervading Divine Presence.

The greatest Service you can do is to help the Teachings go out into the World.

The best way you can serve God is to help in the human Enlightenment Process: the Liberation of Mankind from the shackles of materialism.

Do you realize that every man, woman and child is a *living god*, encased in a personality and imprisoned in an animal body? Mankind has been "sleeping" thus for countless ages. This is MAHĀ-MĀYĀ, the Great Illusion, the Great Sleep of Spiritual Ignorance. Materialism is the Ultimate Delusion, MAHĀ-MĀYĀ, and there is no cure for it, nor for the immense suffering caused by it, except for Humanity to return en masse to the Heart, the Divine Kingdom of Immortal Life within.

Whom do you Serve?

To Feed the Poor?

If you are a materialist you will think that "feeding the poor" is the best thing to do. But the "poor" exist because of the universal ignorance of Mankind and they will continue to exist until the masses tune into the true Spiritual Life, the Divine Heart. The "poor" and the "rich" are both out of tune with Reality, with Themselves—with the Heart.

The Kingdom of God

The Kingdom of God, the Kingdom of the Heart, already Is.

The Kingdom is composed of Souls and Soul-infused personalities on Earth.

The Heart opens the Door to the Kingdom of God

The Earth is groaning and waiting for the manifestation of the Children of God. Who are the Children of God? The Enlightened, the Souls who *consciously* walk upon Earth as Living Souls.

The Heart opens the Door to the Kingdom of God. As you focus in your Heart and awaken the Spiritual Heart, it will bring you into contact with the Invisible Kingdom of God.

The *Kingdom of Man* is on the Physical, Astral and lower Mental Planes.

The *Invisible Kingdom of God* is on the formless Mental Plane (the Causal World) and the Buddhic and Nirvāṇic Planes.

The *Divine Kingdom*, the Kingdom of Śamballa, exists on the Nirvāṇic Plane and the planes above.

The Kingdom of Man is characterized by activity.
The Kingdom of God is characterized by the Heart-Love-Power.
The Kingdom of Śamballa is characterized by Divine Will.

The Head Centre of God is *reflected* in the Kingdom of Śamballa.
The Heart Centre of God is *reflected* in the Kingdom of God.
The Throat Centre of God is *reflected* in the Kingdom of Man.

Who are the 'Elect'? 128
The Enlightened 1702
Types of Conscious Immortality 390
The Brotherhood of Light 395
The Christ-Hierarchy and Śamballa 396
Let Thy Will Be Done 1720

To Manifest the Kingdom of God

The characteristic of the Kingdom of God is immense Love. This Love-Radiation embraces, in one Love-Field, the Causal, Buddhic and Nirvāṇic Worlds. Thus, the Souls who live in the Causal World are living in a Field of Love-Vibration.

The Kingdom of God is manifesting upon Earth now

The Kingdom of God is not Christian, nor is it Muslim, nor Jewish, nor Hindu, nor Sikh, nor Buddhist, nor Jain, nor Chinese, nor Japanese. It is of no particular Faith, for within it are Souls of *all* Faiths who have found the Key to Eternal Life, whose Hearts are awake and burning with the Fire of Love.

What are the signs of those who belong to the Kingdom of God? Love and Service. The *Messengers* are coming in ever larger numbers before the Dawn appears on the Horizon, for the King of all Masters and seekers is coming.

This is all part of the Divine Plan. The Kingdom of God is a Revelation which is slowly unveiling Itself to those who are *prepared.*

The Chosen Ones 688
Christ-Consciousness 443
The Coming of Christ in the Heart 727
The Kingdom is at Hand 1453
On Love and Meditation 1140
The Threefold Way 1236

The Kingdom of God is *manifesting upon Earth now.* The Light from the Kingdom of God is lighting up ever more Human Souls who will come forth and declare: "The Kingdom of God is at hand." That is, it is coming. In fact, it has already arrived. The Heart of Humanity is slowly being prepared, slowly being opened to receive the Light of Love, Hope and Revelation. Give Us a hand!

How will the Kingdom of God, the Kingdom of Love, the Kingdom of the Heart, *materialize* on Earth, in this Physical World? You can help! You can *voluntarily* take upon yourself the responsibility of helping bring down the Kingdom of God onto this physical Earth-plane through an open Heart and the Power of Active Love in your life. For these are the essential characteristics of the Human Kingdom and the Kingdom of God.

First, however, you must be consciously linked to your Soul. This Conscious-Linking (Yoga) is the Spiritual Path (Deva-Mārga) which consists of *meditation and selfless Heart-Service.* This is the Shining Path (Jyotir-Mārga), the Path of Light.

Will you follow It?

I hope to *inspire* you to look at the larger view, to contemplate the wonderful possibilities for yourself and Humanity. I hope that you set your Heart to attain the great Vision that I have indicated in these pages.

Universal Service

Become Light-Workers for the Kingdom of God.

The Kingdom of God is everywhere, within the Heart of every human being.

Become energized by the Spirit.

All true Servers of Humanity must pass through the Fires of Purification

Material circumstances are not obstacles to the Spirit.

When you see a good deed which you can do, do it.

Activity is not contrary to Spiritual Life.

Silence and Passivity are essential.

Do not let an opportunity slip by to serve the Christ within you, who rules your Heart and is the Master of the Kingdom of God.

All true Servers of Humanity must pass through the Fires of Purification, of trouble and travail, of difficulties and struggles.

Ultimately, the Soul will prevail over the personality.

∞

In the past, the seekers thought only of themselves, of their personal Salvation and Liberation.

Then the emphasis became Service towards the Teacher or Master in self-forgetfulness.

Now you serve the Christ, who is within every Heart and is the Light of the World. This is Universal Service.

The World Priest 1619
The Active and Passive Way 1011
Tapas: Spiritual Purification 571
The Path of Purification 1337
The Universal Christ 440
Persevering to the End until Final Liberation 1101

CHAPTER 72

In Service to the Spiritual Hierarchy

The Function of the Spiritual Hierarchy

The Spiritual Hierarchy is a group of advanced human and angelic beings dedicated to the Service of all evolving life-forms upon this planet. The Spiritual Hierarchy is a group of *Servers*, working from the Invisible Worlds. Some have physical bodies, some do not.

The function of the Spiritual Hierarchy is to bring down the Will of God

The primary objective of the Hierarchy is to change Human Consciousness and quicken Human Evolution. The members of the Hierarchy work *selflessly* for the greater good of All. This greater good consists of Spiritual Realization and Spiritual Life in Union with the Divine for everyone in the Man-species. The goal is to lift Mankind out of material consciousness into Spiritual Consciousness and to cooperate with the Divine Plan for the evolution of our planet.

The function of the Spiritual Hierarchy is to bring down the Will of God (which begins on the Plane of Ādi, two planes above Nirvāṇa) and to slowly manifest It in the lower Kingdoms, plane after plane, realm after realm, age after age, cooperating with and guiding the evolutionary energies in all the worlds, until the Glorious Consummation of the Great Age when the Star of the Great King shall shine perfectly also on the Physical Plane, as it is shining perfectly now in Nirvāṇa.

The great Purpose of the Spiritual Hierarchy is the ultimate Perfection of the planet and of all Life within it and upon it.

Let Thy Will Be Done

The expression *The Kingdom of God* is used to represent several things:

- The invisible Spiritual Hierarchy.
- Specifically, the Nirvāṇic Plane.
- Generally, all the invisible planes.

In Reality, however, the *Kingdom of God* includes everything from Ādi downwards, including the Physical Plane. The flow of the great Revelation of the Kingdom of God presses downward from Ādi throughout the ages: down through the Nirvāṇic Planes, the Buddhic Planes, the Causal Worlds, the Mental and Astral Planes, finally manifesting on the Physical Plane, in this Physical World. Jesus was referring to this fact when He said:

Let Thy Will be done on Earth as it is in Heaven.

In Nirvāṇa the Will of God is perfectly expressed; therefore, in Nirvāṇa there is Perfection, *Beatitude*.

The Invisible Government 980
Saṅgha: the Spiritual Hierarchy 394
The Christ-Hierarchy and Śamballa 396
Brotherhoods of Light and Darkness 228
The Unfoldment of the Light 718
The Kingdom of God 123

Cosmic Spiritual Hierarchies

Solar-Systemic Spiritual Hierarchies

Planetary Spiritual Hierarchies

The Spiritual Hierarchy of our Planet Earth

As viewed from the perspective of the Man-species

	Positions	*Current Holder*			
Universal Power	**Kumāra** God-State	**Sanat Kumāra**	Plane of Ādi	*The Ninth Cosmic Expansion*	DIVINE EVOLUTIONS
Universal Wisdom-Consciousness	**Buddha** Lord of Wisdom	**Śakyamuni Buddha**	Plane of Ādi	*The Eighth Cosmic Expansion*	SUPERHUMAN EVOLUTION
Universal Love-Consciousness	**Bodhisattva** Lord of Compassion	**Maitreya** The Christ	Plane of Ādi; Monadic Plane	*The Seventh Cosmic Expansion*	SUPERHUMAN EVOLUTION
The Ascension of the Spirit	**Īśa** Great Master, Lord		Monadic Plane; Nirvāṇa	*The Sixth Cosmic Expansion*	SUPERHUMAN EVOLUTION
The Resurrection of the Spiritual Self	**Asekha** Master		Monadic Plane; Nirvāṇa	*The Fifth Cosmic Expansion*	SUPERHUMAN EVOLUTION
The Crucifixion of the Personal Self	**Arhat** Saint		Nirvāṇa	*The Fourth Cosmic Expansion*	HUMAN EVOLUTION
The Transfiguration on the Mount				*The Third Cosmic Expansion*	HUMAN EVOLUTION
The Baptism by Fire and the Holy Ghost				*The Second Cosmic Expansion*	HUMAN EVOLUTION
The Birth of the Christ within the Heart (the Christ Child)				*The First Cosmic Expansion*	HUMAN EVOLUTION

The hundreds of millions of human beings on this planet

Hierarchies of Life

The Buddha and the Christ

The Buddha and the Christ are Living Beings in the Here and Now

The words CHRIST (CHRISTOS, in Ancient Greek) and BUDDHA (Sanskrit) each represent a State of Being, of evolutionary attainment, as well as the Person who is currently fulfilling that role for the Spiritual Hierarchy of our planet.

CHRISTOS, in old Greek, means "the Anointed One" or one who has been anointed with the sacred oil of the Mysteries. (In those days they rubbed perfumed oil on important people as a mark of respect.) It is *not* the oil that is important, however, but the attainment of the Christ-State, the Christ-Consciousness!

BUDDHA, in Sanskrit, means "One who is Awake" or "the Awake One". Again, this does *not* mean someone who is awake on the Physical Plane in the physical body! It means One who is Awake on a very high plane of our Solar System, who is in a very high state of Consciousness. In fact, for One who is a Buddha, the Physical Plane "awake state" is a state of complete sleep!

MAITREYA, in Sanskrit, means "the Compassionate One". It was the Lord Christ, ĪŚA-MAITREYA, who overshadowed that Great Master who was called JOSHUA (Jesus).

The Buddha is the Embodiment of Wisdom (the Head), the Illumined Mind in the species of Man. The Buddha-Mind is the *Head* of the Spiritual Hierarchy of our planet.

The Christ is the Embodiment of Love (the Heart), the Awakened Compassionate Heart, the Power of Unifying Love. The Christ-Love is the *Heart* of the Spiritual Hierarchy of our planet.

Neither the Buddha nor the Christ (MAITREYA) is merely an historical figure we can "pray to". They are Living Beings in the Here and Now, who we can commune with and know directly, first hand, if we are but willing to undergo the necessary spiritual training.

The Triumph of the Christ we celebrate on the full moon of April (Easter).

The Triumph of the Buddha we celebrate on the full moon of May (Wesak festival).

To Worship the Divine Incarnations 1270

The Mystery of Jesus the Christ 664

Buddha Initiation Mantra

To Connect to the Lord Buddha

Meditate in the Third-Eye…

Ōṁ Muni Muni Mahāmuni Śākyamuniye Svāhā

Muni: an Enlightened One.
Mahā: great, omnipresent, everywhere.

Christ Initiation Mantra

To Connect to the Lord Christ

Meditate in the Heart…

Ōṁ Namo Maitreyāya Namo

Maitreya: the Compassionate One.
Namo: salutations.

How to Become a Buddha or a Christ

First you have to develop Buddhic Consciousness, that is, the ability to be *conscious* on the Buddhic Plane, the World of Oneness, Unity, Love, Compassion, Bliss, Joy and Beauty. To develop Buddhic Consciousness:

a. You must *enter your Heart* through devotion, prayer, chanting, and visualization of the Master or Deity-Form in your Heart.

b. You must *express Love* in the Three Worlds *practically.* That is, you must consciously practise Service, loving kindness, loving deeds, *without thought for yourself,* without any advantage, return or benefit for you. Your Service, or Love-expressed, must be truly self-less, ego-less.

c. You must also *meditate regularly,* using your Higher Mind, and study and expand your mind-knowledge about the Spiritual Life, about spiritual facts and principles.

Thus, Devotion in the Heart, Meditation in the Head, and Love expressed in selfless Service (without thought of reward for yourself) will lead you to Buddhic Consciousness. Having reached Buddhic Consciousness, the *Masters* and *Saints* of the Hierarchy *will help you* from the Inner Worlds in the great Transformation Processes into Christhood and Buddhahood.

Ōṁ Namo Maitreyāya Namo

Pure Devotion

Initiation Mantram

Meditate in the Heart…

Klīṁ Kṛṣṇāya Govindāya Gopījana Vallabhāya Svāhā

I draw myself near to the God-Self within me who is shining with Light,
The Devotees of God are in Love with Him,
To that Shining God I offer myself.

As you meditate on this Mantram you will attract the attention of the Christ

Klīṁ Kṛṣṇāya: I draw myself near to the God-Self within me.
Govindāya: who is shining with Light.
Gopījana: the Devotees of God.
Vallabhāya: are in Love with Him.
Svāhā: I offer myself.

This Mantram is to the Christ: the Christ-Self within Man (that is, within *you*) and the Christ of the Spiritual Hierarchy, the Lord Maitreya. As you meditate on this Mantram you will connect to the Buddhi Principle within you, the Christ-Consciousness, and you will also attract the attention of the Christ.

Devotion to Kṛṣṇa 449
The Universal Christ 440
The Cosmic Christ 662
Christ-Consciousness 443
The Solar and Human Heart 1592

1 In Humanity	2 In the Hierarchy	3 In the Solar System	4 In the Cosmos
The Second Aspect of the Truine Self	Lord Maitreya	The Heart of the Sun	The Cosmic Christ
The Buddhi	The Heart of the Spiritual Hierarchy	The Heart of the Solar Logos	The Heart of the Universe
The Buddhic Principle in the Heart Centre	The Planetary Word (Logos)	The Solar-Systemic Word (Logos)	The Cosmic Word (Logos)

The Mystery of the Christ

Jesus: the Fire of Love

YESHŪAH AL-HAYYĪM
The Living Jesus.

YESHŪAH (ancient Hebrew): God who Saves, the Saving Grace of God, the Liberator, the Fire of God.

AL-HAYYĪM: God the Living, the Living God.

The Great Master Jesus is a living Embodiment of the Fire of God

The Initiated Gnostics kept the Spiritual Knowledge regarding Christianity for three hundred years before they were completely destroyed by the Christian church (which simply became part of the Roman Empire). The Gnostics used this Hebrew Mantra, "The *Living* Jesus", for nearly three hundred years *after* the physical death of Jesus. Was the Great Master Jesus, the Lord, alive after His death?

The Great Master (Lord) Jesus has a special purpose, a special function in the Spiritual Hierarchy: that of embodying the Sixth Ray of Divine Energy, which is intense, fiery and absolute Devotion to Deity. He is a living Embodiment of the Fire of God, a Living, Eternal Fire which acts as a Purifying Furnace, a Saving Grace and the Fire of Love for the Mystics, those Souls who walk the Way of the Heart, in all religions, all over the world.

Jesus is Ever-Living.

The Jesus Mantra

To Connect to the Lord Jesus

YESHŪA EL-HAYYĪM
The Living Fire of God.

Meditate in the Heart Centre…

To Call upon Jesus 679
The Gnostic Teachings 1108
Names of the Great Master Jesus 661
Yeshua: the Secret Hebrew Name 1276
The Mystery of Jesus and Mary 665
The Jesus Mantra and the Sacred Heart Initiation 1356

Īśvara Maitreya

The Hierarchical Mantrams

To Connect to the Spiritual Hierarchy

1

Meditate in the Head…

1. I am a Point of Light in the Greater Light of the Mind of God.
2. I am a Point of Love in the Greater Love of the Heart of God.
3. I am a Point of Power in the Greater Power of the Will of God.
4. To Bless, to Heal and to Inspire the Children of Man, who are the Children of God.

These statements are to be focused in the Mind as acts of Realization. Or another way is to focus each statement as follows:

1. In the Head.
2. In the Heart.
3. In the Base Centre.
4. In the Throat Centre.

The Way of the Mind 1247

2

Meditate in the Heart…

May the Blessings of the Great Lord Maitreya rest upon you,
the Omnipresent Consciousness of the Christ.

Maitreya: friendly, compassionate, benevolent.
Īśvara Maitreya: the Lord Christ.

Maitreya is the World Teacher, the Teacher of Angels and Man, responsible for the *spiritual* development of the Angelic species and Mankind upon this planet. Maitreya looks after all religious development upon this planet through His agents, the Spiritual Teachers, Saints, Yogīs, Adepts and Mystics, in all religions (Christianity being but one of them).

The Universal Christ 440

3

Meditate in the Heart...

There is a Peace that passes all understanding;
it abides in the Hearts of those who live in the Eternal.

There is a Power that makes all things new;
it lives and moves in those who know the Self as One.

May that Peace brood over you, that Power uplift you,
until you stand where the One Initiator is invoked,
until you see His Star shine forth!

The highest Yoga is Eternal Oneness with the Monad

The Eternal is Ātman, the Spiritual Self. This is your true nature, the true Man, pure Beingness, *above* the body, emotional nature and mind structure. The objective of Yoga (union, re-integration) is to seek out this Self, Yourself, and to *realize* it in pure experience. A connecting point to the Ātman is the Heart.

The Self as One is the Monad, the Indivisible Unity of the Spirit. On the level of the Monad, all is One: Man, God, Cosmos, all One. Therefore, the highest Yoga (absorption) is Eternal Oneness with the Monad, the highest attainment for the Man-species on this planet for this Cosmic Cycle of Evolution.

The Star of the One Initiator shines above the head of the very advanced Yogī, the Ṛṣi (the Sage, the Adept), the Draṣṭuḥ (the Seer), the One who experiences Reality.

4

Do I do this, O Lord of Light and Life, in Thy Name and for Thee,
Lord of Lords, King of Kings, the Ancient of Days?

This Mantram is too sacred to be given an explanation here, revealing its purpose and who the *Lord of Light* is. All we can safely say here is that it is for very advanced people on the Path, and the Mantram must not be degenerated for popular use. It has a meaning for those who have attained Self-Realization, Union with God, and are on the Path of pure selfless Service towards all Life.

Postscript

If you read this book once in your lifetime, you will never be the same again. If you study it, you will accomplish great miracles in your Mind. And if you practise it, you shall walk with the gods.

O, Wanderer in the Darkness! This is my gift to you.

If you have known the Root, you have known the branches also

Generations may come and go, but Truth remains ever steadfast. What is Truth? It is the silent knowing of the Mind. It is the flowering of Knowledge into the sweetness of Enlightenment. After that, what is there to know? If you have known the Root, you have known the branches also.

This small planet of ours is but a fragment of the Divine Plan. Would you *know* the All, you would know that the Worlds are limitless.

Each sentient being knows only according to its mind. Some know a little, some know a lot, and some know hardly anything at all. In its infinite divisions the Mind is split into many factions, and yet the mind of a bee and the mind of a Man is the One Mind of the All.

My Teaching is for the few, those who can understand and *do*. If you are one of those, Salvation is yours.

I work for the Christ and in the Name of the Christ. The Work is twofold:

a. To bring out the New, the Here and Now, the New Energies, the new contact with the Truth.

b. To salvage the old Ways and traditions and *renew* them wherever possible.

A World Teacher is not somebody who just repeats an old tradition or the views of an old sect while travelling around the world. A true World Teacher teaches from the New, as the Spirit inspires *Now*, and is able to *tune-in* and *sympathize* with the Truth which was unveiled in *all* the true religions of the world, of all times.

Christ-Consciousness 443

Mind-Only 974
The One 1686
Tao: the Universal Mind 775
Perceptions of the One Mind 490
Inspiration by the Mind of Light 1113
The New and Eternal Way 516

This is a Book of God.
Here is the Self-Revelation of Divine Existence.
Here is the Law of the Mind, the Divine Manifestation.
All Knowledge is Omnipotent. All Knowledge is Divine.

I stand Witness to the Truth.
Peace be upon you.
Thus have I said.

The Shoreless Worlds are endless in Infinite Space.
No ordinary human mind can contain the All. All speculation is useless.
But all real Knowledge is a ladder upon which you may climb to the
Temple of Divine Wisdom.

The Temple of Wisdom stands at the Shores of endless Worlds.
Before you were born, the Mind knew it all. The Mind was before you
and shall be after you are gone. Give yourself to the Mind of Light,
let Its Radiance illumine your darkness.

Thus have I said,
And thus have I gone.

Understand that we are making Religion together: I who am speaking
and you who are listening. There is no Religion without a listener.
In this process is the miracle of Creation, the miracle of Mind Re-Creation.

I have come to speak to you of the Truth, the Boundless Life in God.
Truth has never had a beginning and Truth shall never have an end.
The Ocean of Truth is vaster than the Mind of Man, but Its currents
touch your mind. You cannot know Truth in its fullest manifestation,
but you can pick pebbles from its shore.

Thus have I said to you, O Learner,
And thus have I done.

This is the Seal of Truth, the ever unknowable Mind,
the ever unreachable Star, the Light of Truth,
the Song of Joy, the Haven of Liberation.

If you want to know, be silent and just listen to the Wise.

Thus have I said,
And thus have I done.

Imre Vallyon